A Patristic GREEK READER

Rodney A. Whitacre

B
Baker Academic
a division of Baker Publishing Group
Grand Rapids, Michigan

Published by Baker Academic
a division of Baker Publishing Group
P.O. Box 6287, Grand Rapids, MI 49516-6287
www.bakeracademic.com

Baker Academic edition published 2012
ISBN 978-0-8010-4801-2

Previously published in 2007 by Hendrickson Publishers

Printed in the United States of America

The Library of Congress has cataloged the original edition as follows:
A patristic Greek reader / [edited by] Rodney A. Whitacre.
p. cm.
Includes bibliographical references.
ISBN 978-1-59856-043-5 (alk. paper)
1. Christian literature, Early. 2. Christian literature, Early—Translations into English. I. Whitacre, Rodney A.
BR63.P38 2007
270.1—dc22 2007014984

I am grateful to Walter de Gruyter for permission to use Greek texts from Athanasios Kambylis, ed., *Symeon Neos Theologos, Hymen* (Supplementa Byzantina 3; Berlin: de Gruyter, 1976).

I am grateful to Professor Stuart George Hall for permission to use the Greek text from *Melito of Sardis: On Pascha and Fragments* (Oxford Early Christian Texts; Oxford: Clarendon Press, 1979).

I am grateful to the *Thesaurus Linguae Graecae*, University of California, Irvine, for permission to use their digital versions of Greek texts from Justin Martyr, Gregory of Nazianzus, John Chrysostom, and the *Apophthegmata Patrum*.

Cover Art: Saint Athanasius. Mosaic. Location: S. Marco, Venice, Italy.
The inscription on the scroll reads, according to John Ruskin's (19th century) reconstruction and translation, "As the Godhead is one, so also by God's gift is light."
Photo Credit: Scala/Art Resource, N.Y. Used with permission.

For Margaret

Table of Contents

Part II Translations of All Texts

Preface

I fell in love with ancient Greek when I was ten years old. In vacation Bible school that summer we learned about the travels of the Apostle Paul, and one of our exercises was to trace the Greek alphabet. It fascinated me. I can still picture the page.

When I began college at Whitman College, in Walla Walla, Washington, a couple of us asked one of our professors, Roy Hoover, to offer an informal course in ancient Greek. He graciously did so, but we did not make it very far, given the pressure of our regular coursework. After my sophomore year I transferred to Gordon College. I missed Whitman, but one of the great delights at Gordon was the chance to take a number of courses in Greek under the instruction of William G. MacDonald. I acknowledge a great debt to him for his instruction and example. This training prepared me to teach basic Greek at Gordon-Conwell while I was enrolled as a student. That experience was a great pleasure and privilege, and I am very thankful for the mentoring of my teaching that I received from David M. Scholer, and later from Andrew T. Lincoln. These two professors, along with J. Ramsey Michaels and Gordon D. Fee, helped me in many ways for which I am thankful, not least in the improvement of my knowledge of Greek.

While I was a student at Gordon-Conwell, I discovered the ancient church fathers and began my gradual, informal exploration of them. The Greek Fathers were of particular interest, so much so that I began my doctoral studies in Patristics. Though I ended up completing my research in New Testament, my active interest in the Greek Fathers never waned.

I have had this book in mind for a number of years. I shared my early ideas with some of the staff at Hendrickson, in particular, David Townsley, James Ernest, Phil Frank, and Patrick Alexander, who had taken courses in Greek from me and/or had taught Greek under my direction while I was Director of the Greek Language Program at Gordon-Conwell, after completing my doctoral studies. James was especially helpful as I honed the idea, and his doctoral studies in Patristics enabled him to offer a number of substantive suggestions.

I have also received much encouragement from my colleagues, the faculty, staff, and students at Trinity School for Ministry, Ambridge, Pennsylvania. I am particularly grateful to the students in my course, "The Greek Fathers in Their Own Words," since they served as beta-testers for the early drafts of some of this material. Mary Moody and Rosa Lee Richards offered particularly extensive feedback, which enabled me to improve my approach to the notes.

I am grateful for the help Shirley Decker-Lucke provided in overseeing the process of accepting the manuscript for publication by Hendrickson, and for Patrick LaCosse's care in copyediting a labor intensive project. I am especially thankful to Mark House for his editorial work, offering substantial help both with general issues and with particular details in the Greek.

I am very thankful for the love and support of my wife Margaret, my sons Seth and Chad, my daughter-in-law Jessica, and my granddaughters Leah and Miriam, each of whom has been an encouragement in this project and in so many other ways.

This book is written with deep thankfulness to God for the privilege of knowing this language and these writings (and even more so, of course, the Septuagint and the Greek New Testament), and for the chance to share this material with others. May it be for the glory of God and the advance of his kingdom.

Feast of the Transfiguration
August 6, 2005

O God, who on the mount didst reveal to chosen witnesses thine only-begotten Son wonderfully transfigured, in raiment white and glistening; Mercifully grant that we, being delivered from the disquietude of this world, may be permitted to behold the King in his beauty, who with thee, O Father, and thee, O Holy Ghost, liveth and reigneth, one God, world without end. Amen. (Book of Common Prayer)

Abbreviations

General and Grammatical Abbreviations

1	first person
2	second person
3	third person
abs.	absolute
acc.	accusative
act.	active
adj.	adjective, adjectival
adv.	adverb, adverbial
aor.	aorist
appos.	apposition
art.	article, articular
attend. circ.	attendant circumstance
attrib.	attributive
ca.	circa
cf.	compare
circ.	circumstantial
col.	column(s)
comp.	compound
compl.	complement
conj.	conjunction
d.	died
dat.	dative
depon.	deponent
dir.	direct
disc.	discourse
ed(s).	edition(s), editor(s)
e.g.	for example
epex.	epexegetical
fem.	feminine
fr.	from
fut.	future
gen.	genitive

imper.	impersonal
impf.	imperfect
impv.	imperative
indecl.	indeclinable
indef.	indefinite
indic.	indicative
indir.	indirect
inf(s).	infinitive(s)
intrans.	intransitive
liq.	liquid
masc.	masculine
mid.	middle
mod(s).	modifier(s), modifies, modifying
MS(s).	manuscript(s)
n.d.	no date
neg.	negative
neut.	neuter
nom.	nominative
obj(s).	object(s), objective
opt.	optative
pass.	passive
pf.	perfect
pl.	plural
plpf.	pluperfect
poss.	possessive
pred.	predicate
prep.	preposition
pres.	present
pron.	pronoun
ptc(s).	participle(s)
ref(s).	reference(s), refer(s), referring
rel.	relative
sg.	singular
subj(s).	subject(s), subject(ive)
subjun.	subjunctive
subst(s).	substantive(s), substantival(ly)
temp.	temporal
trans.	transitive
untransl.	untranslated
voc.	vocative
w.	with

Abbreviations for Primary Sources

1 Apol.	Justin, *First Apology*
1 Clem.	*1 Clement*

2 Apol.	Justin, *Second Apology*
C. Gent.	Athanasius, *Contra gentes (Against the Pagans)*
Dial.	Justin, *Dialogue with Trypho*
Did.	*Didache*
Diogn.	*Diognetus*
Disc.	Symeon the New Theologian, *Discourse*
Eph.	Ignatius, *To the Ephesians*
Hist. eccl.	Eusebius, *Historia ecclesiastica (Ecclesiastical History)*
Inc.	Athanasius, *De incarnatione (On the Incarnation)*
Magn.	Ignatius, *To the Magnesians*
Mart. Pol.	*Martyrdom of Polycarp*
Or.	Gregory of Nazianzus, *Orations*
Paed.	Clement of Alexandria, *Paedagogus (Christ the Educator)*
Pasch.	Melito, *On Pascha*
Phil.	Ignatius, *To the Philippians*
Phld.	Ignatius, *To the Philadelphians*
Rom.	Ignatius, *To the Romans*
Smyrn.	Ignatius, *To the Smyrnaeans*
Strom.	Clement of Alexandria, *Stromata (Miscellanies)*
Trall.	Ignatius, *To the Trallians*
Vit. Const.	Eusebius, *Vita Constantini (Life of Constantine)*

Abbreviations for Secondary Sources

ANF	*Ante-Nicene Fathers*, 10 vols.
BDAG	Danker, *A Greek-English Lexicon of the New Testament and Other Early Christian Literature*
BDF	Blass/Debrunner, *A Greek Grammar of the New Testament and Other Early Christian Literature*
Denn	Denniston, *The Greek Particles*
ESV	English Standard Version
LSI	Liddell/Scott, *An Intermediate Greek-English Lexicon*
LSJ	Liddell/Scott/Jones, *A Greek-English Lexicon*
LXX	Septuagint
NPNF[1]	*Nicene and Post-Nicene Fathers, Series 1*, 14 vols.
NPNF[2]	*Nicene and Post-Nicene Fathers, Series 2*, 14 vols.
Nunn	Nunn, *A Short Syntax*
PG	Migne, *Patrologiae cursus completus: Series graeca*, 162 vols.
PGL	Lampe, *A Patristic Greek Lexicon*
Smy	Smyth, *Greek Grammar*
TLG	*Thesaurus linguae graecae*
Wal	Wallace, *Greek Grammar Beyond the Basics*
Yng	Young, *Intermediate Greek Grammar*

Introduction

This book is like a bouquet of flowers. The writings of the early church Fathers can be thought of as a wonderful garden containing a wide variety of plants. For this book I have selected from this garden a few items that represent something of the insight, power, and beauty to be found in the Fathers.

I have been interested in the writings of the church Fathers for many years. Indeed, the first year and a half of my doctoral studies were in Patristics under the direction of Professor Geoffrey Lampe of Cambridge University. Although I switched to New Testament to complete my degree, I have remained interested in the Fathers and continue to live with them. So I am not a Patristics scholar, but merely a Christian in a family (the church) that continues to be addressed by these ancestors. This book represents, therefore, the offering of an amateur gardener, not the contribution of a botanist or a horticulturalist.

The Two Main Goals of This Reader

I have two main goals in this book, one general and one more specific. My general goal is to provide an introduction to the richness found in the writings of the Fathers. These ancient Christian teachers are among the primary guides to life in Christ, second only to the Holy Scriptures.[1] They help us understand the revelation of God in Christ and the new life that is now available in Christ by the Spirit.

I am offering these selections from faith and for faith, but there are obviously other ways to approach the Fathers. Some people are interested in Patristics not because the Fathers are members of one's family who are trusted guides, but rather from a more strictly historical concern. The study of the life and thought of the ancient church is indeed a fascinating and complex field of study, whether one shares the faith of the Fathers or not. I trust that this book will be of help to such readers. It should at least help increase their fluency in reading Greek, if they are near the outset of their studies.

My second, more specific goal is to help those who have studied ancient Greek to improve their familiarity with the language. In the past there have been helpful collections of texts in the original Greek (and Latin), which can still be obtained through used book

[1] I believe the liturgy is another primary guide, second to the Scriptures.

dealers.[2] None of these books, however, includes notes for reading the texts in Greek. The unique contribution of this reader is the inclusion of such notes.

In any language, to read a text in the original enables one both to follow the author's thought with more precision and nuance and to experience the beauty of expression that often goes beyond mere conveyance of ideas to touch the heart. Such clarity and inspiration are certainly benefits for those reading Greek, and such has been my experience with each of the passages offered here.

The Meaning of "Patristic"

Patristics is the study of the writers and writings of the ancient church. It is not synonymous with the study of church history, but rather focuses on one major part of the evidence used in the study of church history.

Those familiar with patristic studies may be surprised at some of the selections included in this reader, since sometimes the study of Patristics has been limited to the period between the New Testament and the Council of Chalcedon in 451. Most scholars today, however, extend the period to Gregory the Great (d. 604) in the West, and in the East either to John of Damascus (d. ca. 749), or even to the ninth century. Migne's great collection of texts published in the nineteenth century included Latin authors to the early thirteenth century, and Greek authors to the fall of Constantinople (1453).[3] I prefer Migne's larger corpus because otherwise much that is interesting and significant is left out. The transition to the Schoolmen in the West in the thirteenth century and the fall of the Byzantine Empire in the East mark much clearer turning points than the earlier dates sometimes proposed for delimiting patristic studies.

"Patristic" comes from the use of the word "father" (Greek πατήρ and Latin *pater*) to refer to those individuals in the community's past who were seen as authoritative and life-giving guides. The term was used in the Old Testament for the patriarchs (e.g., Exod 3:13, 15; Deut 1:8), as well as for the master-disciple relationship (e.g., 2 Kgs 2:12; Prov 1:8). In the New Testament, the patriarchs of Israel were seen as the fathers of all Christians, including Gentile Christians (Rom 4:16; 2 Pet 3:4, cf. also *1 Clem.* 4:8). Paul used father language of his own role of bringing people to life through the gospel, and his role as a guide whose teaching was authoritative and whose life was to be imitated (e.g., 1 Cor 4:14–21). This more extended sense continued in the church in the second and third centuries,[4] and

[2] For example, Henry Melvill Gwatkin, *Selections from Early Writers Illustrative of Church History to the Time of Constantine* (London: Macmillan, 1893); M. J. Rouët de Journel, S. J., *Enchiridion patristicum: loci ss. patrum, doctorum scriptorum ecclesiasticorum* (22nd ed.; Barcelona: Herder, 1962); M. J. Rouët de Journel, S. J. and J. Dutilleul, S. J., *Enchiridion asceticum: loci ss. patrum et scriptorum ecclesiasticorum ad ascesim spectantes* (5th ed.; Barcelona: Herder, 1958).

[3] J.-P. Migne, ed., *Patrologiae cursus completus: Series graeca* (162 vols.; Paris, 1857–1886); and *Patrologiae cursus completus: Series latina* (217 vols.; Paris, 1844–1864). More precisely, *PG* includes the Greek authors up to 1439.

[4] "For when any person has been taught from the mouth of another, he is termed the son of him who instructs him, and the latter [is called] his father" (Irenaeus, *Against Heresies* 4.41.2, *ANF*). "It is a good thing, I reckon, to leave to posterity good children. This is the case with children of our bodies. But words are the progeny of the soul. Hence we call those who have instructed us, fathers. . . . And every one who is instructed, is in respect of subjection the son of his instructor" (Clement of Alexandria, *Miscellanies* 1.1, *ANF*).

by the fourth century the use of the word "father" to speak of the teachers of the past who were spiritual parents and guides became common. Thus the term came to refer to earlier teachers of the church who were recognized by the church as sound in their doctrine and exemplary in their pattern of life.

While the term "patristic" derives from this background, it now has a wider use. Already in the nineteenth century, Migne included in his collection authors such as Origen, who were not accepted by the ancient church as spiritual parents and guides. Indeed, Migne's subtitle refers to "all Fathers, Doctors and Ecclesiastical Writers." This sense has prevailed, and the term has come to refer to the study of ecclesiastical writers to the seventh century in the West and the ninth century in the East.

The terms "patristics" and "church fathers" strike some today as chauvinistic. Recent scholarship has been attentive to the contribution of women during these centuries, but the writings of few women from this period have been preserved. Given the patriarchal character of the ancient church and the fact that Patristics is not the study of church history in general but of the writings and writers that remain, the terms "patristics" and "church fathers" continue to be appropriate.

An Approach to Reading the Fathers

While this book is not meant to be an introduction to the Fathers, a few brief observations may be of help to readers who are new to this material. Many people find the Fathers difficult to understand. Most of the patristic writings are addressed to particular situations, and some of this difficulty is due to ignorance of the historical and cultural settings of the Fathers. A good introductory book, such as that by Henry Chadwick[5] or Stuart G. Hall,[6] will provide much of the necessary initial orientation. Often the way the Fathers express themselves and develop their arguments, especially their use of Scripture, strikes modern readers as strange. For help with these issues, see the introductory books by Christopher Hall.[7] Fortunately, there are many resources available for those who wish to pursue these ancient writings, and many new books are being published every year.

Amidst the recent explosion of interest in the Fathers, there are several different approaches to the material. My own approach, which lies behind my selection of texts, is grounded in biblical theology.[8] The Scriptures witness to the revelation of God in Israel, in Jesus, and in the earliest church as it unfolded through redemptive history. One way of approaching this witness of Scripture is to see it as the inspired revelation of the *person* of God, the *plan* of God, and the *pattern* of life that is in keeping with God's character. These three themes—person, plan, and pattern—are at the heart of the biblical witness, that is, biblical theology. Amidst the diversity and historical development in the Scriptures, there

---

[5] Henry Chadwick, *The Early Church* (rev. ed.; The Pelican History of the Church, vol. 1; London: Penguin, 1993).

[6] Stuart G. Hall, *Doctrine and Practice in the Early Church* (Grand Rapids, Mich.: Eerdmans, 1991).

[7] Christopher A. Hall, *Reading Scripture with the Fathers* (Downers Grove, Ill.: InterVarsity, 1998) and *Learning Theology with the Church Fathers* (Downers Grove, Ill.: InterVarsity, 2002).

[8] My approach to biblical theology is similar to that found in T. Desmond Alexander and Brian S. Rosner, eds., *New Dictionary of Biblical Theology* (Downers Grove, Ill: InterVarsity, 2000).

is a coherent unity that can be seen under these three headings. The Scriptures are those writings that the church came to recognize during the early patristic period as both uniquely inspired and authoritative, providing the foundation and the criterion (or *canon*, from κανών, a straight bar, and hence a rule or standard) for faith and discipleship.

I approach the Fathers, whom I view as my ancestors, as a disciple and family member, focusing on the same three themes I find in biblical theology. The flower of life and truth revealed in Scripture continues to unfold as each of these themes is developed in the Fathers. A great deal of energy in the early church was spent in discussion of the person and character of God, that is, the mystery of the Trinity—both the unity of the Godhead and the characteristics of each of the divine persons. Included here is also the teaching about the two natures of Christ, both divine and human. The second general theme, the plan of God, is also discussed in many of the writings. They reflect profoundly on the salvation that has been accomplished through the death and resurrection of Jesus, they try to understand the relation between Israel and the church in God's work in history, and they develop further the church's understanding of the cosmic dimensions of God's plan, already touched on by Paul (e.g., 1 Cor 15:20–28; Eph 1:10). Many of the writings are also concerned with the third theme, God's pattern of life for the people of God. The forms which life in Christ should take, both on the personal and the corporate level, are frequently discussed. This theme includes the patterns of relationship within the body of Christ as well as with those outside the body. The nature of the sacraments and the institutional structures that are appropriate for the people of God also come under the corporate dimension of this third theme. On the level of the individual, we find teaching about love, prayer, asceticism, and holiness of life.

I am not suggesting that the Fathers simply speak with one voice on any of these matters. The Fathers at times argued with one another, and there is diversity and development throughout their writings. Some of the early Fathers used expressions that have come to be seen as unfortunate in the light of later controversies that helped fine-tune the church's emerging theological understanding. Indeed, throughout the life of the church down to the present day, the family has exercised discernment as it has sought to understand which thoughts and practices are actually a further unfolding of the flower of God's life and truth and which are not. Some developments are in keeping, as it were, with the genetic code of the plant, and some are not. In the patristic era it sometimes took quite a while to sort out particular issues, but amidst the conflict and diversity, the church discerned a "mind of the Fathers" that is in keeping with the "Scriptural mind," to use Florovsky's terms.[9]

Many today would dispute whether there ever was such a "mind of the Fathers," and certainly many of the teachings of the Fathers are questioned today by various groups. Even among those who approach the Fathers in the way I have described, there is disagree-

[9] Georges Florovsky, *Bible, Church, Tradition: An Eastern Orthodox View* (The Collected Works of Georges Florovsky, vol. 1; Belmont, Mass.: Nordland, 1972), ch. 1 and *passim*. Examples of works I have found helpful for this approach to understanding the Fathers include Louis Bouyer, *The Spirituality of the New Testament and the Fathers* (trans. Mary P. Ryan; History of Christian Spirituality; New York: Seabury Press, 1963), and Olivier Clément, *The Roots of Christian Mysticism: Text and Commentary* (trans. Theodore Berkeley and Jeremy Hummerstone; Hyde Park, N.Y.: New City Press, 1995). Bouyer's book on biblical theology, *The Meaning of Sacred Scripture* (trans. Mary Perkins Ryan; Liturgical Studies; Notre Dame, Ind.: University of Notre Dame, 1958), is also very suggestive.

ment in some areas, so I am not suggesting that everything is neat and tidy. Furthermore, the centuries since the patristic period have seen further developments of many of the themes they discussed and the introduction of new concerns. But the approach I have described seems to be consistent with what I find both in the biblical witnesses and in the Fathers themselves. So, while keeping in mind such developments, I seek the Fathers' guidance for understanding God's person, plan, and pattern, and I seek to encounter the God these ancestors of mine encountered.

The Selections from the Fathers

The selections included in this reader represent a variety of genres, including sermon, poem, treatise, letter, history, story, church order, apology, and martyr account. Some of the passages I have included have played a major role in the history of Christian doctrine, while others give glimpses into early views on issues such as leadership in the church, the sacraments, pastoral care, and prayer. Still other passages are historically relevant for understanding the developing relationship between church and empire. Despite this diversity of genre and content, I am able to offer, from a garden that covers many acres, only a very few flowers, and these in turn represent only a portion of the varieties available. I have arranged the selections roughly in chronological order. Because the dating of several selections is uncertain, such order is debatable at points.

Several of these writings are referred to by more than one title, which can cause confusion. Many have a Greek title, but most are usually referred to by a title in Latin. Several have English titles as well. *The SBL Handbook of Style* lists most of these writings, along with their Latin titles and English titles.[10] Guided by this list, I have used the English title wherever possible. At the first reference to a work, I include in parentheses its Latin title and its standard abbreviation, as given in *The SBL Handbook of Style.* For documents not listed in the *SBL Handbook,* I use an English translation of the title and note its common (usually Latin-based) abbreviation.

The Greek Notes

Those wishing to read the Greek New Testament have an abundance of resources available, but for help reading other Hellenistic Greek texts and the church Fathers, there is less to choose from. H. P. V. Nunn includes an appendix in his *A Short Syntax of New Testament Greek* that contains twenty-two pages of readings, mostly from the early Fathers.[11] He includes some very brief notes to help one read these texts. Clarence Hale includes a few brief notes along with extensive vocabulary help and a list of principal parts for a selection of readings drawn mostly from the Old Testament Pseudepigrapha and the New

[10] Patrick H. Alexander, John F. Kutsko, James D. Ernest, Shirley A. Decker-Lucke, and David L. Petersen, eds., *The SBL Handbook of Style For Ancient Near Eastern, Biblical, and Early Christian Studies* (Peabody, Mass.: Hendrickson, 1999), 81–82, 237–63.

[11] H. P. V. Nunn, *A Short Syntax of New Testament Greek* (5th ed.; Cambridge: Cambridge University Press, 1938).

Testament Apocrypha.[12] Allen Wikgren's *Hellenistic Greek Texts* contains some two hundred pages of Hellenistic Greek readings from a variety of sources.[13] He does not offer any helps, but does include a lexicon for the words used in the texts. Another good resource is Conybeare and Stock's *Grammar of Septuagint Greek,* which provides brief notes for two hundred pages of material from narrative portions of the Septuagint.[14]

I used most of these books as I was learning Greek, and I found them valuable, though I would have been helped by more extensive sets of notes. I then discovered that there are a number of books that provide more complete notes for reading various texts from the Classical period, such as Plato's *Apology.*[15] These guides are wonderful resources, and in the present book I seek to provide similar help for those interested in reading patristic texts.[16]

I am assuming a knowledge of basic Greek such as is represented by a one year course. Since first year courses differ somewhat in the material they cover, I offer different levels of help in the notes. For the easier texts I offer a great deal of help, even including some material that anyone who passed any first year Greek class should know. I hope some students who did not do all that well in Greek, or whose knowledge of Greek has faded, will be tempted to try some of these easier passages that offer more extensive help. For other passages, especially those that are more advanced, I assume a greater familiarity with the language, though still only on a basic level. For some points of grammar that recur frequently, such as the use of the definite article for a possessive pronoun, I often include a note, but sometimes, especially in the more advanced texts, I let the translation call attention to the point.

I have chosen passages that represent different styles of Greek and different degrees of difficulty. The *Didache,* for example, contains some of the easiest Greek to be found anywhere. I offer thorough notes for this text, especially in chapters 7–10, as an encouragement to those whose skills in Greek are weak. Other authors, such as Eusebius of Caesarea, are more challenging. I have indicated the level of difficulty at the beginning of each text and in Appendix C. My assessments of difficulty are derived from a comparison of the texts in relation to one another. Some students, of course, will find even the easier texts to be a challenge, while others may have little difficulty with any of the texts offered here.

I have tried to present the notes in a format that enables one to read the passages as rapidly as possible. While most courses only lead the student to sip a text like wine, there

---

[12] Clarence B. Hale, *Let's Read Greek: A Graded Reader* (Chicago: Moody, 1968).

[13] Allen Wikgren, with the collaboration of Ernest Cadman Colwell and Ralph Marcus, *Hellenistic Greek Texts* (Chicago: University of Chicago Press, 1947).

[14] F. C. Conybeare and St. George Stock, *Grammar of Septuagint Greek, With Selected Readings from the Septuagint According to the Text of Swete* (1905; repr., Peabody, Mass.: Hendrickson, 1988).

[15] For example, James J. Helm, *Plato Apology: Text, Grammatical Commentary, Vocabulary* (rev. ed.; Wauconda, Ill.: Bolchazy-Carducci, 1997).

[16] For a valuable set of very extensive notes on a single set of patristic texts see *St Gregory of Nazianzus: Poemata Arcana* (Oxford Theological Monographs; Clarendon Press, 1997), edited with a textual introduction by C. Moreschini, introduction, translation and commentary by D. A. Sykes, English translation of textual introduction by Leofranc Holford-Strevens. The Greek text with English translations of these eight poems is forty-six pages long, followed by 214 pages of notes and commentary.

is much to be gained from guzzling a text like beer. Accordingly, the Greek text and accompanying notes appear together on each page.

Vocabulary help is given in the notes for all the words in a passage that occur less than fifty times in the New Testament. (For words that occur more than fifty times in the New Testament, see Appendix A.) Vocabulary notes for words repeated within a chapter or section are given only at their first occurrence in that chapter or section, but are repeated at their first occurrence in subsequent chapters within the same work. For longer chapters, this means that vocabulary help for a particular word may be found several pages earlier. Nevertheless, every word used in a passage will be found either listed in the given chapter or in the list of words in Appendix A. The knowledge of certain basic principal parts, listed in Appendix B, is also assumed. Along with vocabulary help, I provide notes on difficult parsings, points of grammar, and idioms.

Where possible I cite standard lexicons and grammars for both New Testament Greek and Classical Greek. I cite the primary lexicon for Patristic Greek (*PGL*)[17] when the primary lexicons for Classical Greek (LSJ) and for the New Testament and other early Christian texts (BDAG) are inadequate. For the selections from the Apostolic Fathers, however, I usually cite only BDAG since these texts are included within the purview of this lexicon.

The notes are concise, making extensive use of abbreviations. Here is an example:

> **διὰ τό**–w. inf. for causal clause (Wal: 596; Smy: 2034; BDAG 2c: 226).

The number after a colon refers to a page number, except for the grammars by Smyth and BDF, which are cited by paragraph number. Thus, information on the use of διὰ τό plus an infinitive for a causal clause will be found on page 596 of Wallace's *Greek Grammar Beyond the Basics* and in paragraph 2034 of Smyth's *Greek Grammar*, as well as in section 2c of the Bauer-Danker lexicon's article on διά, found on page 226.

I provide very little commentary on the passages, since that is not the focus of these notes. But some brief comments have been included at times, as well as a few references to studies and translations. When I cite a resource not found in the list of abbreviations, I give the author's name and a page number. The Bibliography includes subsections for each author/text included in this reader, so a particular resource thus cited will be found in the appropriate subsection of the Bibliography.

I have retained most of the conventions adopted by each of the particular editions of the texts used here. For example, some editions capitalize θεός and others do not; some are strict in distinguishing a quotation from an allusion, while others include allusions in quotation marks. Some conventions, however, I have standardized, such as how to signal quoted material,[18] the use of iota subscript in certain words, and the use of the grave accent.[19]

For some texts included here there is no critical edition, while for others there are several such editions. In the Bibliography I list one or two of the main critical editions, where they exist. Any deeper study of these texts should rely on these critical editions where available.

---

17 See the Bibliography for details regarding these resources.

18 Boldface type seemed the clearest and least cluttered option.

19 *PG* retains the grave accent before commas. I have changed these to acute accents in keeping with current practice.

In the notes I indicate most of the differences between the edition provided and those listed in the Bibliography. Only rarely do these differences significantly effect the meaning of a passage, but this information may help when using English translations, since a given translation may be based on an edition other than the one used here. Since there are still other editions for some of these texts than those listed in the Bibliography, caution is needed when using translations.

Accordingly, I have provided my own translations. These translations are quite wooden, since they are primarily intended as an aid to those translating the Greek texts and as a check on work done.[20] Some of the published translations may convey well the meaning of the text, but the English translation may be so unlike the Greek that the student may have trouble using it to help make sense out of the material being translated. By contrast, my translations seek to adhere to the Greek structure as much as possible. Accordingly, I retain the generic masculine when necessary for this purpose,[21] and I make extensive use of brackets to help the reader see the exact relation between the Greek and the English. However, while the translations provided here are not meant to be polished, nor a model for translation, I trust that they are not so awkward that English readers find them unreadable.

The helps contained in this reader should provide all that is necessary to enable a student who has a sound knowledge of first year morphology to read these texts. For those who need additional help, I provide a review of basic morphology on the following web site: http://www.tesm.edu. There I also provide help for recognizing the structure of some of the complex Greek sentences included in this book, as well as a list of errata. Any errors in this book reported to me (rwhitacre@tesm.edu) will be posted.

Suggestions for Using This Reader

I advise those who have completed only one year of Greek study to begin with the easier texts (see Appendix C). The notes for *Didache* 7–10 are the most extensive, so this would be a good place to begin for those just getting started. Those with a more extensive knowledge of Greek can, of course, start anywhere, according to interest.

Before beginning to read a selection, you will probably find it helpful to read the brief description of the selection provided. As you work through a selection, I suggest you read by entire clauses and sentences, trying to pick up the sense as it comes to you in the Greek word order.[22] Some students may first have to hunt for the verb, subject, direct

[20] At times I provide an even more wooden translation in a note, when I think it might help make sense of the Greek, but would be too awkward for even a very literal translation.

[21] Indeed, as Bart Ehrman observes, in connection with his retention of the generic masculine in his own recent translation of the Apostolic Fathers, the "strong patriarchal biases of the texts . . . form part of their historical interest and significance" (*The Apostolic Fathers, Vol. 1* [LCL 24; Cambridge, Mass.: Harvard University Press, 2003], viii).

[22] For encouragement and direction in developing this skill, see the address given in 1887 by William Gardner Hale, *The Art of Reading Latin: How to Teach It* (Boston: Ginn, 1887), available at www.bu.edu/mahoa/hale_art.html. While this piece is about Latin, the concepts discussed are readily applicable to Greek even without a knowledge of Latin.

object, and indirect object before attempting to make sense out of whatever else is in the sentence. The important thing is that you take whatever initial steps are necessary to make sense out of the Greek. Once you have sorted out a sentence you should read back through it in Greek, trying to pick up the sense in the order in which it was written. This rereading will help increase your fluency. Likewise, after completing a whole selection you should reread it several times, trying to understand it in the order in which it was written.

Similarly, as you learn vocabulary, try to associate the Greek word with the thing/concept/action it is related to, rather than just with an English word. In this way you will begin to read and understand the Greek directly, as opposed to merely translating it.[23] Once you have sorted out a selection and have been able to understand it, you could consult some of the published English translations for ideas of how to translate it more effectively. Keep in mind, however, that there are several editions available for many of these passages, and that a particular translation may not be based on the same edition of the Greek text that I use here.

Suggestions for Further Reading in the Fathers

It is my hope that this reader will prepare you to go on and read further in the Greek Fathers in their own language. Many who do go on will choose to work through a passage that is especially significant to them, which they have come across in their reading of the Fathers in English. If you are new to the field, as you read introductory works such as those by Chadwick and Hall, watch for discussions of particular writings of the Fathers that sound interesting. For a more systematic approach, see the older work by H. B. Swete, *Patristic Study,* which provides an introduction to the study of Patristics and includes a suggested reading list of key texts.[24]

Ministers and others for whom the New Testament is their primary focus for Greek study may want to work through some or all of the Apostolic Fathers. These texts are an especially good choice since BDAG covers them, and there are several good translations and Greek texts readily available.[25] Some Bible software programs, such as BibleWorks (http://www.bibleworks.com/) and Logos Software (http://www.logos.com/), include the Greek text of the Apostolic Fathers, and an electronic edition of Kirsopp Lake's edition is available on the Web (http://www.ccel.org/ccel/lake/fathers2.html).

Finding the Greek text for a particular author can sometimes be difficult if you do not have access to a good library, though inter-library loan may help. Information about

---

[23] C. S. Lewis captures this idea wonderfully. "The very formula, '*Naus* means a ship,' is wrong. *Naus* and *ship* both mean a thing, they do not mean one another. Behind *Naus*, as behind *navis* or *naca*, we want to have a picture of a dark, slender mass with sail or oars, climbing the ridges, with no officious English word intruding." C. S. Lewis, *Surprised by Joy: The Shape of My Early Life* (New York: Harcourt, Brace & World, 1955), 141. Lewis's entire description of his instruction in Greek is inspiring, especially his experience of reading large portions of Greek under his second Greek teacher (pp. 140–41).

[24] Henry Barclay Swete, *Patristic Study* (Handbooks for the Clergy; London: Longmans, Green and Co., 1909), 142–179.

[25] See especially those by Ehrman and Holmes in the Bibliography.

published texts is available in the older work by Quasten,[26] as well as the more recent works of Moreschini,[27] Döpp,[28] Kannengiesser,[29] and Drobner,[30] among others.

The lexicons and grammars I have cited in the notes will be sufficient for your further reading, especially LSJ, *PGL*, and Smyth's *Grammar*. Both LSJ and Smyth are available on-line at the Perseus Web site (http://www.perseus.tufts.edu/), which also includes a helpful tool for parsing words.

Though expensive, the best resource for both texts and tools is the *Thesaurus Linguae Graecae* (*TLG*). This on-line resource contains the great majority of Greek texts from Homer through the fall of Constantinople (1453), and new texts are being added continually. The *TLG* texts can also be linked to the Perseus Web site's parsing and lexical features. Over twenty patristic texts are available to non-subscribers through the abridged/trial version, available through the *TLG* Web site (http://www.tlg.uci.edu/).

Clearly, the resources available both in published form and on the Web make it easier than ever to read the Fathers in their own language. May you find joy and edification as you gather flowers for your own bouquet from this very large garden.

---

26 Johannes Quasten, *Patrology* (3 vols.; Westminster, Md.: Newman, 1950–1953; repr. Allen, Tex.: Christian Classics, n.d.). Quasten's *Patrology* was brought to completion by a team of scholars in a fourth volume edited by Angelo di Berardino, covering Latin patristic literature from Nicea to Chalcedon.

27 Claudio Moreschini and Enrico Norelli, *Early Christian Greek and Latin Literature: A Literary History* (Peabody, Mass.: Hendrickson, 2005).

28 Siegmar Döpp and Wilhelm Geerlings, eds., *Dictionary of Early Christian Literature* (trans. Matthew O'Connell; New York: Crossroad Publishing, 2000).

29 Charles Kannengiesser, *Handbook of Patristic Exegesis: The Bible in Ancient Christianity* (2 vols.; The Bible in Ancient Christianity vols. 1–2; Leiden: Brill, 2004).

30 Hubertus R. Drobner, *Fathers of the Church: A Comprehensive Introduction* (trans. Siegfried S. Schatzmann; Peabody, Mass.: Hendrickson, 2007).

Greek Texts and Notes

The Didache

Introduction

None of the writings of the New Testament gives us a detailed description of the life and organization of the earliest church. We can piece together a general picture from the glimpses we have, but there is much that is unclear. In the *Didache* (*Did.*) we have a precious window into the life of the earliest church from the time of the apostles and just afterwards. We learn something of the shape and organization of the church as it continued to develop, and we get to listen in on the liturgical community at prayer. The early church's concern for discipleship also shines through, as we hear a strong challenge to holiness, which is passed on through an ancient form of exhortation known as the Two Ways tradition, as well as through the distinctively Christian sense of eschatological urgency.

The *Didache* takes the form of a small ancient manual for church leaders. It had dropped out of sight until 1873, when Archbishop Philotheos Bryennios of Nicomedia found a copy in a church in Istanbul. He published the text in 1883, and since then scholars have poured an enormous amount of energy into its investigation, with few results that find universal agreement. For scholars there is little that is simple about the *Didache* except its Greek style.

Much of the *Didache* appears to be very early, perhaps even from the middle of the first century. Most scholars believe that later material has been added, at times by simply patching texts together. According to most estimates, the final form we have probably comes from 70–150. It likely originated near Antioch in Syria, though Egypt and Palestine have also been suggested.

The document begins with moral instruction in a form known as the Two Ways tradition, setting out the way of life and the way of death. This form of teaching is found in the Old Testament (e.g., Deut 30:15–20) and was well known not only in Judaism but also in the Greco-Roman world. Following these moral guidelines are brief instructions for regulating the life of a congregation, including matters of baptism, fasting, the eucharist, itinerant prophets, and the local ministry of bishops and deacons. These instructions are quite simple compared to later developments. The final chapter consists of an eschatological warning about the end of the world, which includes material from Jesus' teaching as found in Matthew's Gospel.

The *Didache* was popular in the ancient church and was taken up in later church manuals. Some of the Fathers even quoted it as Scripture. In more recent times, however, its spiritual value has been less appreciated. Often it is seen as an example of Jewish-Christian legalism with little theological content. To some extent this assessment is fair, such as when the *Didache* interprets Jesus' command not to fast like the hypocrites (Matt 6:16–18) as referring to which days of the week to fast rather than to one's inner disposition (*Did.* 8.1). But moral instruction and the regulation of church life are common themes in the New Testament, since the gospel includes the fact that a new way of life is now available and is to be expressed in the lives of individuals and communities. However, in the New Testament, unlike the *Didache,* such instruction is mixed with teaching about God, which provides a context for understanding and appropriating this new life. Also, most of the New Testament is addressed to congregations, not just the leaders, as appears to be the case in the *Didache.*

Nevertheless, there are some wonderful theological resources in the *Didache.* The call to holiness found in the Two Ways passage and in the concluding eschatological warning is an important gospel theme. The instructions concerning baptism and the eucharist are particularly rich with implicit theology. Indeed, one of the eucharistic prayers (*Did.* 9) has been adapted as a popular hymn in some sections of the church today. How the Didachist understood these theological resources, however, is unclear because the document contains so little explicit theological reflection. Accordingly, some readers may join the Fathers in interpreting this text as expressing orthodox thought, while others may find in it all sorts of eccentric views. Thus, while the *Didache* is a text of great significance for understanding the history of the church, what exactly it tells us about the life and thought of the early church remains a matter of some debate.

Edition used:	J. B. Lightfoot, rev., tran. *The Apostolic Fathers.* Edited and completed by J. R. Harmer. 1891. Repr., Berkeley, Calif.: Apocryphile, 2004.
Level of difficulty:	Easy [1]

Didache 1–6 The Way of Life and the Way of Death

Διδαχὴ Κυρίου διὰ τῶν δώδεκα ἀποστόλων τοῖς ἔθνεσιν.

1.1 Ὁδοὶ δύο εἰσί, μία τῆς ζωῆς καὶ μία τοῦ θανάτου, διαφορὰ δὲ πολλὴ μεταξὺ τῶν δύο ὁδῶν. 1.2 Ἡ μὲν οὖν **ὁδὸς τῆς ζωῆς** ἐστὶν αὕτη· πρῶτον, **ἀγαπήσεις τὸν Θεὸν** τὸν ποιήσαντά σε· δεύτερον, **τὸν πλησίον σου ὡς σεαυτόν· πάντα δὲ ὅσα ἐὰν θελήσῃς μὴ γίνεσθαί σοι, καὶ σὺ ἄλλῳ μὴ ποίει.** 1.3 τούτων δὲ τῶν λόγων ἡ διδαχή ἐστιν αὕτη· **Εὐλογεῖτε τοὺς καταρωμένους ὑμῖν καὶ προσεύχεσθε** ὑπὲρ τῶν ἐχθρῶν ὑμῶν, νηστεύετε δὲ **ὑπὲρ τῶν διωκόντων ὑμᾶς. ποία γὰρ χάρις, ἐὰν ἀγαπᾶτε τοὺς ἀγαπῶντας ὑμᾶς; οὐχὶ καὶ τὰ ἔθνη τὸ αὐτὸ ποιοῦσιν; ὑμεῖς δὲ ἀγαπᾶτε τοὺς μισοῦντας ὑμᾶς** καὶ οὐχ ἕξετε ἐχθρόν. 1.4 ἀπέχου τῶν σαρκικῶν καὶ σωματικῶν ἐπιθυμιῶν. **ἐάν τις σοι δῷ ῥάπισμα εἰς τὴν δεξιὰν σιαγόνα,**

Διδαχή → ἡ διδαχή, *teaching.*

1.1 **διαφορά** → ἡ διαφορά, *difference.* • **διαφορὰ δὲ πολλή** — since there is no art., these words may form either a pred. or attrib. and thus can be rendered either "and the difference between the two ways is great" or "and there is a great difference between the two ways." • **μεταξύ** — *between.* • **δύο** — *two.*

1.2 **μὲν οὖν** — expresses continuation, *so, then* (BDAG, μέν 2e: 630). • **πρῶτον** → πρῶτος, η, ον, *first.* • **ποιήσαντα** — aor. act. ptc. masc. acc. sg. → ποιέω. • **δεύτερον** → δεύτερος, α, ον, *second.* • **πλησίον** → πλησίος, α, ον, *near;* here subst., *neighbor.* • **σεαυτόν** → σεαυτοῦ, *yourself;* the lexical form is gen. because the word is not used in the nom. • **ἐάν** — here signals a general or indef. clause w. πάντα ὅσα, *whatever, everything which.* • **γίνεσθαι** — the inf. for indir. disc., here giving the content of what one wants (Wal: 603; Smy: 2018). Usually in English an inf. cannot be used for indir. disc., but it can be so used in the case of verbs of wishing or wanting, *whatever you want not to happen* (or, *be done*) *to you.*

1.3 **λόγων** → λόγος — here, *matter, subject* (LSI AVII: 477; BDAG 1aε: 600). • **εὐλογεῖτε** — pres. act. impv. 2 pl. → εὐλογέω, *I bless.* The pres. impv. occurs frequently in this text. The pres. impv. is used for continued, repeated, or customary activity (Wal: 721–22). • **καταρωμένους** — pres. mid. (depon.) ptc. masc. acc. pl. → καταράομαι, *I curse,* w. acc. or dat. • **ἐχθρῶν** → ἐχθρός, ά, όν, *hated;* here subst., *enemy.* • **νηστεύετε** — pres. act. impv. 2 pl. → νηστεύω, *I fast.* • **διωκόντων** — pres. act. ptc. masc. gen. pl. → διώκω, *I persecute.* A ptc. w. an art. will almost always function as a noun or an adj. (Wal: 617–21). • **ποία** → ποῖος, α, ον, *what kind of?* • **χάρις** — here, *credit* (BDAG 2b: 1079). • **τὸ αὐτὸ ποιοῦσιν** — Ehrman's text has τοῦτο ἀγαπᾶτε. • **ἀγαπᾶτε** — Ehrman's text has φιλεῖτε. • **μισοῦντας** — pres. act. ptc. masc. acc. pl. → μισέω, *I hate.* • **οὐχ ἕξετε ἐχθρόν** — this fut. could be predictive, "you will not have an enemy," or imperatival, "you shall not have hatred" (Wal: 568–69).

1.4 **ἀπέχου** — pres. mid. impv. 2 sg. → ἀπέχω, *I receive in full;* mid., *keep away, abstain.* • **σαρκικῶν** → σαρκικός, ή, όν, *fleshly.* • **σωματικῶν** → σωματικός,

στρέψον αὐτῷ καὶ τὴν ἄλλην, καὶ ἔσῃ τέλειος· **ἐὰν ἀγγαρεύσῃ σέ τις μίλιον ἕν, ὕπαγε μετ' αὐτοῦ δύο· ἐὰν ἄρῃ τις τὸ ἱμάτιόν σου, δὸς αὐτῷ καὶ τὸν χιτῶνα· ἐὰν λάβῃ τις ἀπὸ σοῦ τὸ σόν, μὴ ἀπαίτει·** οὐδὲ γὰρ δύνασαι.
1.5 παντὶ τῷ αἰτοῦντί σε δίδου καὶ μὴ ἀπαίτει· πᾶσι γὰρ θέλει δίδοσθαι ὁ πατὴρ ἐκ τῶν ἰδίων χαρισμάτων. μακάριος ὁ διδοὺς κατὰ τὴν ἐντολήν· ἀθῷος γάρ ἐστιν. οὐαὶ τῷ λαμβάνοντι· εἰ μὲν γὰρ χρείαν ἔχων λαμβάνει τις, ἀθῷος ἔσται· ὁ δὲ μὴ χρείαν ἔχων δώσει δίκην, ἵνα τί ἔλαβε καὶ εἰς τί· ἐν συνοχῇ δὲ γενόμενος ἐξετασθήσεται περὶ ὧν ἔπραξε καὶ **οὐκ ἐξελεύσεται ἐκεῖθεν, μέχρις οὗ ἀποδῷ τὸν ἔσχατον κοδράντην.**
1.6 ἀλλὰ καὶ περὶ

ή, όν, *bodily.* • **ἐπιθυμιῶν** → ἡ ἐπιθυμία, *a desire, longing, craving.* • **δῷ** — aor. act. subjun. 3 sg. → δίδωμι. • **ῥάπισμα** → τὸ ῥάπισμα, *a blow, a slap.* • **σιαγόνα** — acc. sg. → ἡ σιαγών, *cheek.* • **στρέψον** — aor. act. impv. 2 sg. → στρέφω, *I turn.* • **ἔσῃ** — fut. act. indic. 2 sg. → εἰμί. • **τέλειος** → τέλειος, α, ον, *perfect, complete.* • **ἀγγαρεύσῃ** — aor. act. subjun. 3 sg. → ἀγγαρεύω, *I press into service, force, compel.* • **μίλιον** → τὸ μίλιον, *mile.* • **ἄρῃ** — aor. act. subjun. 3 sg. → αἴρω. • **δός** — aor. act. impv. 2 sg. → δίδωμι. • **χιτῶνα** — acc. sg. → ὁ χιτών, *tunic,* the garment worn next to the skin. The art. expresses possession, *your tunic* (Wal: 215; Smy: 1121). • **λάβῃ** — 2 aor. act. subjun. 3 sg. → λαμβάνω. • **σόν** → σός, ή, όν, *your.* • **ἀπαίτει** — pres. act. impv. 3 sg. → ἀπαιτέω, *I ask for, demand.* • **δύνασαι** — pres. mid. (depon.) indic. 2 sg. → δύναμαι. οὐδὲ γὰρ δύνασαι, *for neither are you able (to do so)* could mean such an action is not in keeping w. the way of life the author is describing, or it could reflect the social position of the audience: "Let yourself be robbed, because you cannot really defend yourself, no matter what!" (Niederwimmer: 79).

1.5 **αἰτοῦντι** — pres. act. ptc. masc. dat. sg. → αἰτέω. • **δίδου** — pres. act. impv. 2 sg. → δίδωμι. • **δίδοσθαι** — pres. pass. inf. → δίδωμι. Inf. for indir. disc. (Wal: 603; Smy: 2016). • **χαρισμάτων** — gen. pl. → τὸ χάρισμα, *gift.* • **διδούς** — pres. act. ptc. masc. nom. sg. → δίδωμι. • **ἀθῷος** → ἀθῷος, ον, *innocent, guiltless.* • **οὐαί** — *woe.* • **χρείαν** → ἡ χρεία, *a need.* • **χρείαν ἔχων . . . τις** — "someone having need." • **ἔσται** — fut. mid. (depon.) indic. 3 sg. → εἰμί. • **δίκην** → ἡ δίκη, *satisfaction, punishment.* • **δώσει δίκην** — δίδωμι δίκην usually means *I suffer punishment,* but in light of the following clause, here it seems to mean, *give satisfaction* in the sense, *give a satisfactory account.* • **ἵνα τί** — *why.* • **συνοχῇ** → ἡ συνοχή, *prison.* • **γενόμενος** — 2 aor. mid. (depon.) ptc. masc. nom. sg. → γίνομαι. Circ. ptc., temp.; here, *move, arrive* (BDAG 6: 198), *after having arrived (in prison).* • **ἐξετασθήσεται** — fut. pass. indic. 3 sg. → ἐξετάζω, *I question, examine.* • **ἔπραξε** — aor. act. indic. 3 sg. → πράσσω, *I do.* • **ἐξελεύσεται** — fut. mid. (depon.) indic. 3 sg. → ἐξέρχομαι. • **ἐκεῖθεν** — *from there.* • **μέχρις** → μέχρι, *until,* w. final ς (sometimes added before vowels). Also used, as here, w. οὗ for the same meaning: μέχρις οὗ, *until.* • **ἀποδῷ** — aor. act. subjun. 3 sg. → ἀποδίδωμι, *I pay back.* • **κοδράντην** — acc. sg. → ὁ κοδράντης, *quadrans,* the smallest Roman coin.

1.6 **ἀλλά** — BDAG (2: 45) says that ἀλλά here indicates a transition to something different or contrasted. There is indeed a shift at this point, in that the focus moves from the one asking for money to the one giving money. But δέ signals this shift, while ἀλλὰ καί is ascensive *not only this, but also* (cf. BDAG 3: 45): *But not only this, but also concerning this it has been said.* Since this translation is awkward in

τούτου δὲ εἴρηται· **Ἱδρωσάτω ἡ ἐλεημοσύνη σου εἰς τὰς χεῖράς σου, μέχρις ἂν γνῷς, τίνι δῷς.**

2.1 Δευτέρα δὲ ἐντολὴ τῆς διδαχῆς· 2.2 **Οὐ φονεύσεις, οὐ μοιχεύσεις,** οὐ παιδοφθορήσεις, οὐ πορνεύσεις, **οὐ κλέψεις,** οὐ μαγεύσεις, οὐ φαρμακεύσεις, οὐ φονεύσεις τέκνον ἐν φθορᾷ οὐδὲ γεννηθέντα ἀποκτενεῖς, **οὐκ ἐπιθυμήσεις τὰ τοῦ πλησίον.** 2.3 **οὐκ ἐπιορκήσεις, οὐ ψευδομαρτυρήσεις,** οὐ κακολογήσεις, οὐ μνησικακήσεις· 2.4 οὐκ ἔσῃ διγνώμων οὐδὲ δίγλωσσος· παγὶς γὰρ θανάτου ἡ διγλωσσία. 2.5 οὐκ ἔσται ὁ λόγος σου ψευδής, οὐ κενός, ἀλλὰ μεμεστωμένος πράξει. 2.6 οὐκ ἔσῃ πλεονέκτης οὐδὲ ἅρπαξ οὐδὲ ὑποκριτὴς οὐδὲ κακοήθης οὐδὲ ὑπερήφανος. οὐ λήψῃ βουλὴν πονηρὰν

English, I have omitted the first *but* in the translation. • **εἴρηται** — pf. pass. indic. 3 sg. → ἐρῶ (listed in lexicons under εἶπον), *I say, speak, it has been said.* • **ἱδρωσάτω** — aor. act. impv. 3 sg. → ἱδρόω, *I sweat, perspire.* • **ἐλεημοσύνη** → ἡ ἐλεημοσύνη, *alms.* • **μέχρις ἂν γνῷς** — indef. temp. clause, *until such time as you know.* • **τίνι δῷς** — indir. deliberative question, *to whom you are to give.*

2.1 **δευτέρα** → δεύτερος, α, ον, *second.* • **διδαχῆς** → ἡ διδαχή, *teaching.*

2.2 **φονεύσεις** → φονεύω, *I murder.* Fut. for impv. (Wal: 569) occurs frequently in this text. • **μοιχεύσεις** → μοιχεύω, *I commit adultery.* • **παιδοφθορήσεις** → παιδοφθορέω, *I commit sodomy, have same-sex sexual activity with boys* (BDAG: 750). • **πορνεύσεις** → πορνεύω, *I engage in illicit sex.* • **κλέψεις** → κλέπτω, *I steal.* • **μαγεύσεις** → μαγεύω, *I practice magic.* • **φαρμακεύσεις** → φαρμακεύω, *I make magic potions, practice magic.* • **φθορᾷ** → ἡ φθορά, *corruption; abortion.* • **γεννηθέντα** — aor. pass. ptc. neut. acc. pl. → γεννάω. The texts of Ehrman and Holmes have the sg. γεννηθέν. • **ἀποκτενεῖς** — liq. fut. act. indic. 2 sg. → ἀποκτείνω. • **ἐπιθυμήσεις** → ἐπιθυμέω, *I desire, long for.* • **πλησίον** — the neut. of πλησίος, α, ον; here subst., ὁ πλησίον, *neighbor* (BDAG: 830).

2.3 **ἐπιορκήσεις** → ἐπιορκέω, *I swear falsely, break one's oath.* • **ψευδομαρτυρήσεις** → ψευδομαρτυρέω, *I give false testimony.* • **κακολογήσεις** → κακολογέω, *I speak evil of, revile, insult.* • **μνησικακήσεις** → μνησικακέω, *I remember evil, bear a grudge.*

2.4 **ἔσῃ** — fut. mid. (depon.) indic. 2 sg. → εἰμί. • **διγνώμων** → διγνώμων, ον, *double-minded.* • **δίγλωσσος** → δίγλωσσος, ον, *double-tongued.* • **παγίς** → ἡ παγίς, *a trap, snare.* • **θανάτου** — attrib. gen. (Wal: 86; Smy: 1320); παγίς . . . θανάτου, *a deadly trap.* • **διγλωσσία** → ἡ διγλωσσία, *doubleness of speech, duplicity.*

2.5 **ἔσται** — fut. mid. (depon.) indic. 3 sg. → εἰμί. • **ψευδής** → ψευδής, ές, *false, lying.* • **κενός** → κενός, ή, όν, *empty.* • **μεμεστωμένος** — pf. pass. ptc. masc. nom. sg. → μεστόω, *I fill, fulfill.* • **πράξει** — dat. sg. → ἡ πρᾶξις, *an act, action, deed.* μεμεστωμένος πράξει — *filled with action* or *fulfilled in action.*

2.6 **πλεονέκτης** → ὁ πλεονέκτης, *a greedy person.* • **ἅρπαξ** → ὁ ἅρπαξ, *robber.* • **ὑποκριτής** → ὁ ὑποκριτής, *hypocrite.* • **κακοήθης** → κακοήθης, ες, *malicious, spiteful.* • **ὑπερήφανος** → ὑπερήφανος, ον, *arrogant.* • **λήψῃ** — fut. mid. (depon.) indic. 2 sg. → λαμβάνω, here, *devise* (cf. BDAG 9: 584 and the clearer discussion in the BDAG ref. following βουλήν below). • **βουλήν** → ἡ βουλή, *a plan* (cf. BDAG 2a: 181).

κατὰ τοῦ πλησίον σου. 2.7 **οὐ μισήσεις** πάντα ἄνθρωπον, **ἀλλὰ οὓς μὲν ἐλέγξεις,** περὶ δὲ ὧν προσεύξῃ, **οὓς δὲ ἀγαπήσεις** ὑπὲρ τὴν ψυχήν σου.

3.1 Τέκνον μου, φεῦγε ἀπὸ παντὸς πονηροῦ καὶ ἀπὸ παντὸς ὁμοίου αὐτοῦ. 3.2 Μὴ γίνου ὀργίλος· ὁδηγεῖ γὰρ ἡ ὀργὴ πρὸς τὸν φόνον· μηδὲ ζηλωτὴς μηδὲ ἐριστικὸς μηδὲ θυμικός· ἐκ γὰρ τούτων ἁπάντων φόνοι γεννῶνται. 3.3 τέκνον μου, μὴ γίνου ἐπιθυμητής· ὁδηγεῖ γὰρ ἡ ἐπιθυμία πρὸς τὴν πορνείαν· μηδὲ αἰσχρολόγος μηδὲ ὑψηλόφθαλμος· ἐκ γὰρ τούτων ἁπάντων μοιχεῖαι γεννῶνται. 3.4 τέκνον μου, **μὴ γίνου οἰωνοσκόπος·** ἐπειδὴ ὁδηγεῖ εἰς τὴν εἰδωλολατρίαν· μηδὲ ἐπαοιδὸς μηδὲ μαθηματικὸς μηδὲ περικαθαίρων μηδὲ θέλε αὐτὰ βλέπειν· ἐκ γὰρ τούτων ἁπάντων εἰδωλολατρία

2.7 **μισήσεις** → μισέω, *I hate.* • **ἐλέγξεις** — fut. act. indic. 2 sg. → ἐλέγχω, *I convict, correct, reprove.* • **οὓς μέν . . . οὓς δέ** — rel. pron. w. μέν . . . δέ, *some . . . others* (BDAG, μέν 1c: 630).

3.1 **φεῦγε** — pres. act. impv. 2 sg. → φεύγω, *I flee.* • **ὁμοίου** → ὅμοιος, α, ον, *like, resembling,* w. gen. of comparison (Wal: 110; Smy: 1069). ὁμοίου αὐτοῦ, *like it.*

3.2 **γίνου** — pres. mid. (depon.) impv. 2 sg. → γίνομαι. • **ὀργίλος** → ὀργίλος, η, ον, *inclined to anger, quick-tempered.* • **ὁδηγεῖ** → ὁδηγέω, *I lead.* • **ὀργή** → ἡ ὀργή, *anger.* • **φόνον** → ὁ φόνος, *a murder.* • **ζηλωτής** → ὁ ζηλωτής, *enthusiast, adherent; jealous person.* Pred. nom. w. μὴ γίνου. • **ἐριστικός** → ἐριστικός, ή, όν, *contentious, quarrelsome.* • **θυμικός** → θυμικός, ή, όν, *hot-tempered.* • **ἁπάντων** → ἅπας, ἅπασα, ἅπαν, intensive form of πᾶς, *all.*

3.3 **ἐπιθυμητής** → ὁ ἐπιθυμητής, *one who desires/lusts.* • **ἐπιθυμία** → ἡ ἐπιθυμία, *desire, lust.* • **πορνείαν** → ἡ πορνεία, *unchastity, fornication, sexual sin.* • **αἰσχρολόγος** → ὁ αἰσχρολόγος, *a foul-mouthed person.* In this context perhaps not shameful in general, but specifically due to sexual content. • **ὑψηλόφθαλμος** → ὑψηλόφθαλμος, ον, *lifting up the eyes.* The comp. w. ὑψηλός suggests arrogance/haughtiness (BDAG, ὑψηλός 2: 1044). The context suggests lustful/impure use of the eyes, so perhaps, *immodest eye.* Other translations include, "bold gazes" (Niederwimmer), "let your eyes roam" (Holmes), "lecherous" (Ehrman). • **μοιχεῖαι** → ἡ μοιχεία, *adultery.* The pl. of abstract nouns refer to "the single kinds, cases, occasions, manifestations of the idea expressed by the abstract substantive" (Smy: 1000); here, *acts of adultery.*

3.4 **οἰωνοσκόπος** → ὁ οἰωνοσκόπος, *soothsayer, augur.* "οἰωνός 'a bird of omen,' σκοπός 'watcher' . . . one who obtains omens fr. the behavior of birds" (BDAG, οἰωνοσκόπος: 701). • **ἐπειδή** — *because, since.* • **εἰδωλολατρίαν** → ἡ εἰδωλολατρία, *idolatry.* • **ἐπαοιδός** → ὁ ἐπαοιδός, *enchanter,* "one who uses charms or incantations to get what one desires" (BDAG: 359). • **μαθηματικός** → μαθηματικός, ά, όν, *fond of learning, mathematical, astronomical;* here subst., *astrologer.* "The study of mathematics was a core feature of ancient learning and was closely associated with the study of celestial phenomena. The latter emphasis in our lit. and in the sense *astrologer*" (BDAG: 609). • **περικαθαίρων** → περικαθαίρω, *purify completely;* here ptc., subst., "*one who performs purificatory rites* of propitiatory magic for gain, *magician*" (BDAG: 801). • **βλέπειν** — Ehrman's text adds μηδὲ ἀκούειν.

γεννᾶται. 3.5 τέκνον μου, μὴ γίνου ψεύστης, ἐπειδὴ ὁδηγεῖ τὸ ψεῦσμα εἰς τὴν κλοπήν· μηδὲ φιλάργυρος μηδὲ κενόδοξος· ἐκ γὰρ τούτων ἁπάντων κλοπαὶ γεννῶνται. 3.6 τέκνον μου, μὴ γίνου γόγγυσος· ἐπειδὴ ὁδηγεῖ εἰς τὴν βλασφημίαν· μηδὲ αὐθάδης μηδὲ πονηρόφρων· ἐκ γὰρ τούτων ἁπάντων βλασφημίαι γεννῶνται. 3.7 ἴσθι δὲ πραΰς· ἐπεὶ **οἱ πραεῖς κληρονομήσουσι τὴν γῆν.** 3.8 γίνου μακρόθυμος καὶ ἐλεήμων καὶ ἄκακος καὶ **ἡσύχιος** καὶ ἀγαθὸς **καὶ τρέμων τοὺς λόγους** διὰ παντός, οὓς ἤκουσας. 3.9 οὐχ ὑψώσεις σεαυτὸν οὐδὲ δώσεις τῇ ψυχῇ σου θράσος. οὐ κολληθήσεται ἡ ψυχή σου μετὰ ὑψηλῶν, ἀλλὰ μετὰ δικαίων καὶ ταπεινῶν ἀναστραφήσῃ. 3.10 τὰ συμβαίνοντά σοι ἐνεργήματα ὡς ἀγαθὰ προσδέξῃ, εἰδὼς ὅτι ἄτερ Θεοῦ οὐδὲν γίνεται.

3.5 **ψεύστης** → ὁ ψεύστης, *liar.* • **ψεῦσμα** → τὸ ψεῦσμα, *a lie, falsehood.* Words ending w. μα usually denote a result of an action, but see BDAG (1097) for the more active sense of this word in some contexts, *lying, untruthfulness, undependability.* • **κλοπήν** → ἡ κλοπή, *theft, stealing.* • **φιλάργυρος** → φιλάργυρος, ον, *fond of money, avaricious.* • **κενόδοξος** → κενόδοξος, ον, *conceited, boastful.*

3.6 **γόγγυσος** → γόγγυσος, ον, *complaining;* subst., *a grumbler.* • **βλασφημίαν** → ἡ βλασφημία, *reviling, disrespect, slander;* here probably ref. to denigration of God, *blasphemy.* • **αὐθάδης** → αὐθάδης, ες, *self-willed, stubborn, arrogant.* • **πονηρόφρων** → πονηρόφρων, ον, *evil-minded.*

3.7 **ἴσθι** — pres. act. impv. 2 sg. → εἰμί. • **πραΰς** → πραΰς, πραεῖα, πραΰ, *gentle, humble.* • **ἐπεί** — *since, for.* • **κληρονομήσουσι** → κληρονομέω, *I inherit.*

3.8 **μακρόθυμος** → μακρόθυμος, ον, *patient.* • **ἐλεήμων** → ἐλεήμων, ον, *merciful.* • **ἄκακος** → ἄκακος, ον, *innocent, guileless.* • **ἡσύχιος** → ἡσύχιος, ον, *quiet, tranquil.* • **τρέμων** — pres. act. ptc. masc. nom. sg. → τρέμω, *I tremble at, am in awe of.* • **διὰ παντός** — *always* (BDAG, διά A2a.: 224).

3.9 **ὑψώσεις** → ὑψόω, *I exalt.* • **σεαυτόν** → σεαυτοῦ,-τῆς,-τοῦ, reflexive pron., *yourself.* There are no nom. forms. • **δώσεις** — fut. act. indic. 2 sg. → δίδωμι, here, *I allow* (BDAG 13: 243). • **θράσος** → τὸ θράσος, *arrogance, shamelessness.* οὐδὲ δώσεις τῇ ψυχῇ σου θράσος, "nor shall you give arrogance to your soul," *nor shall you allow your soul/yourself to be arrogant.* • **κολληθήσεται** — fut. pass. indic. 3 sg. → κολλάω, *I join, associate with.* • **ὑψηλῶν** → ὑψηλός, ή, όν, *high, exalted, proud, haughty.* This is a good example of the qualitative sense of some anarthrous nouns, stressing the quality or traits of the class to which these people belong (Wal: 244). • **ταπεινῶν** → ταπεινός, ή, όν — *lowly, humble.* • **ἀναστραφήσῃ** — fut. pass. indic. 2 sg. → ἀναστρέφω, *turn upside down, turn back;* pass., *associate.*

3.10 **συμβαίνοντα** — pres. act. ptc. neut. acc. pl. → συμβαίνω, *happen.* • **ἐνεργήματα** — acc. pl. → τὸ ἐνέργημα, *activity, experience.* • **προσδέξῃ** — fut. pass. indic. 2 sg. → προσδέχομαι, *I receive, welcome.* • **εἰδώς** — pf. act. ptc. masc. nom. sg. → οἶδα. • **ἄτερ** — prep., *without, apart from.*

4.1 Τέκνον μου, **τοῦ λαλοῦντός σοι τὸν λόγον τοῦ Θεοῦ μνησθήσῃ** νυκτὸς καὶ ἡμέρας· τιμήσεις δὲ αὐτὸν ὡς Κύριον· ὅθεν γὰρ ἡ κυριότης λαλεῖται, ἐκεῖ Κύριός ἐστιν. 4.2 ἐκζητήσεις δὲ καθ' ἡμέραν τὰ πρόσωπα τῶν ἁγίων, ἵνα ἐπαναπαῇς τοῖς λόγοις αὐτῶν. 4.3 οὐ ποιήσεις σχίσμα, εἰρηνεύσεις δὲ μαχομένους. κρινεῖς δικαίως, οὐ λήψῃ πρόσωπον ἐλέγξαι ἐπὶ παραπτώμασιν. 4.4 οὐ διψυχήσεις, πότερον ἔσται ἢ οὔ. 4.5 **μὴ γίνου πρὸς μὲν τὸ λαβεῖν ἐκτείνων τὰς χεῖρας, πρὸς δὲ τὸ δοῦναι συσπῶν·** 4.6 ἐὰν ἔχῃς διὰ τῶν χειρῶν σου, δώσεις λύτρωσιν ἁμαρτιῶν σου. 4.7 οὐ διστάσεις δοῦναι

4.1 **λαλοῦντος** — pres. act. ptc. masc. gen. sg. → λαλέω. • **μνησθήσῃ** — fut. pass. indic. 2 sg. → μιμνήσκομαι, *I remember,* w. gen. • **τιμήσεις** — fut. act. indic. 2 sg. → τιμάω, *I honor.* • **ὅθεν** — *from where.* • **κυριότης** → ἡ κυριότης, *the Lord's nature.* ὅθεν γὰρ ἡ κυριότης λαλεῖται, ἐκεῖ κύριός ἐστιν — "for whence the Lord's nature is spoken, there is the Lord."

4.2 **ἐκζητήσεις** → ἐκζητέω, *I seek, seek out.* • **καθ' ἡμέραν** — *daily.* Distributive use of κατά (BDAG, κατά B2c: 512). • **τὰ πρόσωπα τῶν ἁγίων** — *faces,* in the sense of the personal presence of the saints w. whom one can be in relationship. • **ἐπαναπαῇς** — 2 aor. pass. subjun. 2 sg. → ἐπαναπαύομαι, *I rest, find rest/comfort/support.* In Hellenistic Greek the 2 aor. pass. at times replaced an intrans. act. or mid. (BDF: 76.2).

4.3 **ποιήσεις** → ποιέω, here, *I cause* (BDAG 2: 839). • **σχίσμα** → τό σχίσμα, *division.* • **εἰρηνεύσεις** → εἰρηνεύω, *I reconcile.* • **μαχομένους** — pres. mid. (depon.) ptc. masc. acc. pl. → μάχομαι, *I fight, quarrel, dispute.* • **δικαίως** — *righteously.* • **λήψῃ** — fut. mid. (depon.) indic. 2 sg. → λαμβάνω. λαμβάνω πρόσωπον, *I show partiality or favoritism* (BDAG, πρόσωπον 1bα: 888). • **ἐλέγξαι** — aor. act. inf. → ἐλέγχω, *I convict, correct, reprove.* Inf. for purpose or result (Wal: 590, 592; Smy: 2008, 2011). "You shall not show partiality that you may reprove (the guilty) for (their) offenses." • **παραπτώμασιν** — dat. pl. → τό παράπτωμα, *offense, wrongdoing, sin.*

4.4 **διψυχήσεις** → διψυχέω, *I am of two minds, am double-minded, am undecided, am changeable, doubt.* • **πότερον** → πότερος, α, ον, *whether,* often found in the fixed form πότερον (BDAG: 856). οὐ διψυχήσεις, πότερον ἔσται ἢ οὔ — *you shall not be double-minded whether it will be or not.* There is much debate about the specific ref. intended here by πότερον ἔσται ἢ οὔ (cf. Niederwimmer: 106–7 who thinks the context may suggest it ref. to a timid judge). Possibly it is merely a general expression to describe double-mindedness.

4.5 **πρός** — here, *regarding* (BDAG 3e: 875). • **λαβεῖν** — 2 aor. act. inf. → λαμβάνω. Here the inf. as a verbal noun (*receiving*) functions as the obj. of a prep. πρὸς τὸ λαβεῖν, *when it comes to receiving.* Wal: 589 appears to miss this usage, but cf. Smy. 2034b. • **ἐκτείνων** → ἐκτείνω, *I stretch out.* Subst. ptc. • **δοῦναι** — aor. act. inf. → δίδωμι. • **συσπῶν** → συσπάω, *draw together.* Another subst. ptc. The ref. could be either to clenching/closing one's hands or to pulling them back (cf. BDAG: 978), instead of giving.

4.6 **διὰ τῶν χειρῶν σου**, i.e., "through (working w.) your hands." • **δώσεις** — fut. act. indic. 2 sg. → δίδωμι. Ehrman's text has δὸς εἰς (δός — aor. act. impv. 2 sg.). • **λύτρωσιν** — acc. sg. → ἡ λύτρωσις, *a ransom,* here in the sense of *ransom-*

οὐδὲ διδοὺς γογγύσεις· γνώσῃ γὰρ τίς ἐστιν ὁ τοῦ μισθοῦ καλὸς ἀνταποδότης. 4.8 οὐκ ἀποστραφήσῃ τὸν ἐνδεόμενον, συγκοινωνήσεις δὲ πάντα τῷ ἀδελφῷ σου καὶ οὐκ ἐρεῖς **ἴδια εἶναι·** εἰ γὰρ ἐν τῷ ἀθανάτῳ κοινωνοί ἐστε, πόσῳ μᾶλλον ἐν τοῖς θνητοῖς; 4.9 οὐκ ἀρεῖς τὴν χεῖρά σου ἀπὸ τοῦ υἱοῦ σου ἢ ἀπὸ τῆς θυγατρός σου, ἀλλὰ ἀπὸ νεότητος διδάξεις τὸν φόβον τοῦ Θεοῦ. 4.10 οὐκ ἐπιτάξεις δούλῳ σου ἢ παιδίσκῃ, τοῖς ἐπὶ τὸν αὐτὸν Θεὸν ἐλπίζουσιν, ἐν πικρίᾳ σου, μήποτε οὐ μὴ φοβηθήσονται τὸν ἐπ' ἀμφοτέροις Θεόν· οὐ γὰρ ἔρχεται κατὰ πρόσωπον καλέσαι, ἀλλ' ἐφ' οὓς τὸ πνεῦμα ἡτοίμασεν. 4.11 ὑμεῖς δὲ οἱ δοῦλοι ὑποταγήσεσθε τοῖς κυρίοις ὑμῶν ὡς τύπῳ Θεοῦ ἐν αἰσχύνῃ καὶ φόβῳ. 4.12 μισήσεις πᾶσαν ὑπόκρισιν καὶ πᾶν ὃ

---

money (BDAG 2: 606). • **ἁμαρτιῶν** — gen. of ref. (Wal: 127), *with reference to your sins, for your sins.*

4.7 **διστάσεις** → διστάζω, *I doubt, waver, hesitate.* • **διδούς** — pres. act. ptc. masc. nom. sg. → δίδωμι. Circ. ptc., temp., *while giving, when you give.* • **γογγύσεις** → γογγύζω, *I grumble.* • **γνώσῃ** — fut. mid. (depon.) indic. 2 sg. → γίνωσκω, here, *I recognize* (BDAG 7: 200). • **μισθοῦ** → ὁ μισθός, *pay, reward.* • **ἀνταποδότης** → ὁ ἀνταποδότης, *recompenser, paymaster.*

4.8 **ἀποστραφήσῃ** — fut. mid. indic. 2 sg. → ἀποστρέφω, *I turn away;* mid., *reject, repudiate* (BDAG 3: 123). • **ἐνδεόμενον** — pres. mid. ptc. masc. acc. sg. → ἐνδέω, *I am in want, am needy.* Same meaning for all voices. • **συγκοινωνήσεις** → συγκοινωνέω, *I share.* • **ἐρεῖς** → ἐρῶ, used for the fut. of λέγω, since λέγω itself does not have a fut. form (BDAG, λέγω: 588; εἶπον: 286). • **εἶναι** → εἰμί. Inf. for indir. disc. (Wal: 603; Smy: 2016). • **ἀθανάτῳ** → ἀθάνατος, ον, *immortal.* • **κοινωνοί** → ὁ κοινωνός, *partner, sharer.* • **πόσῳ** → πόσος, η, ον, *how great, how much;* w. μᾶλλον, *how much more* (BDAG, πόσος 1: 855). • **θνητοῖς** → **θνητός**, ή, όν, *mortal.*

4.9 **ἀρεῖς** — liq. fut. act. indic. 2 sg. → αἴρω. *To take away the hand* is a metaphor for withdrawing from someone (BDAG, αἴρω 1a: 28), so the author is calling upon his readers/hearers to accept responsibility for their children. • **θυγατρός** — gen. sg. → ἡ θυγάτηρ, *daughter.* • **νεότητος** — gen. sg. → ἡ νεότης, *youth.* • **φόβον** → ὁ φόβος, *a fear.*

4.10 **ἐπιτάξεις** — fut. act. indic. 2 sg. → ἐπιτάσσω, *I order, command,* w. dat. • **παιδίσκῃ** → ἡ παιδίσκη, *female slave.* • **ἐλπίζουσιν** → ἐλπίζω, *I hope.* • **πικρίᾳ** → ἡ πικρία, *bitterness, harshness, anger.* ἐν πικρίᾳ σου mod. οὐκ ἐπιτάξεις. • **μήποτε** — *lest.* • **οὐ μή** — strong negation, *certainly not* (LSJ I: 577; BDAG, μή 4: 646). • **ἀμφοτέροις** → ἀμφότεροι, αι, α, *both.* τὸν ἐπ' ἀμφοτέροις Θεόν, *the God who is over you both.* • **κατὰ πρόσωπον** — *with partiality* (BDAG, πρόσωπον 1bβℸ: 888). • **ἡτοίμασεν** — aor. act. indic. 3 sg. → ἑτοιμάζω, *I prepare.* • **ἀλλ' ἐφ' οὓς τὸ πνεῦμα ἡτοίμασεν** — repeat the verb ἔρχεται.

4.11 **ὑποταγήσεσθε** — 2 fut. pass. indic. 2 pl. → ὑποτάσσω, *I subject, subordinate.* • **τύπῳ** → ὁ τύπος, *a type, pattern, model.* • **αἰσχύνῃ** → ἡ αἰσχύνη, *modesty, reverence.*

4.12 **μισήσεις** → μισέω, *I hate.* • **ὑπόκρισιν** — acc. sg. → ἡ ὑπόκρισις, *hypocrisy, pretense, outward show.* • **ἀρεστόν** → ἀρεστός, ή, όν, *pleasing.*

μὴ ἀρεστὸν τῷ Κυρίῳ. 4.13 οὐ μὴ ἐγκαταλίπῃς ἐντολὰς Κυρίου, φυλάξεις δὲ ἃ παρέλαβες, μήτε προστιθεὶς μήτε ἀφαιρῶν. 4.14 ἐν ἐκκλησίᾳ ἐξομολογήσῃ τὰ παραπτώματά σου, καὶ οὐ προσελεύσῃ ἐπὶ προσευχήν σου ἐν συνειδήσει πονηρᾷ. αὕτη ἐστὶν ἡ ὁδὸς τῆς ζωῆς.

5.1 Ἡ δὲ τοῦ θανάτου ὁδός ἐστιν αὕτη· πρῶτον πάντων πονηρά ἐστι καὶ κατάρας μεστή· φόνοι, μοιχεῖαι, ἐπιθυμίαι, πορνεῖαι, κλοπαί, εἰδωλολατρίαι, μαγεῖαι, φαρμακίαι, ἁρπαγαί, ψευδομαρτυρίαι, ὑποκρίσεις, διπλοκαρδία, δόλος, ὑπερηφανία, κακία, αὐθάδεια, πλεονεξία, αἰσχρολογία, ζηλοτυπία, θρασύτης, ὕψος, ἀλαζονεία· 5.2 διῶκται ἀγαθῶν, μισοῦντες ἀλήθειαν, ἀγαπῶντες ψεῦδος, οὐ γινώσκοντες μισθὸν δικαιοσύνης, οὐ **κολλώμενοι ἀγαθῷ** οὐδὲ κρίσει δικαίᾳ, ἀγρυπνοῦντες οὐκ εἰς τὸ ἀγαθόν, ἀλλ᾽ εἰς τὸ πονηρόν· ὧν μακρὰν πραΰτης καὶ ὑπομονή, μάταια ἀγαπῶντες,

---

4.13 **ἐγκαταλίπῃς** — 2 aor. act. subjun. 2 sg. → ἐγκαταλείπω, *I forsake, abandon, desert.* οὐ μή w. the aor. subjun. expresses emphatic negation (Wal: 468). • **ἐντολάς Κυρίου** — an example of a gen. mod. making an anarthrous word def., the so-called Apollonius' Corollary (Wal: 250). • **φυλάξεις** — fut. act. indic. 2 sg. → φυλάσσω, *I guard.* • **παρέλαβες** — 2 aor. act. indic. 2 sg. → παραλαμβάνω, *receive.* • **προστιθείς** — pres. act. ptc. masc. nom. sg. → προστίθημι, *add.* Circ. ptc., perhaps for the means by which they are to guard (Wal: 628). • **ἀφαιρῶν** — pres. act. ptc. masc. nom. sg. → ἀφαιρέω, *I take away, subtract.*

4.14 **ἐξομολογήσῃ** — fut. mid. indic. 2 sg. → ἐξομολογέω, *I promise; confess;* mid., *confess, admit.* • **παραπτώματα** — acc. pl. → τὸ παράπτωμα, *transgression, wrongdoing.* • **προσελεύσῃ** — fut. mid. (depon.) indic. 2 sg. → προσέρχομαι. • **προσευχήν** → ἡ προσευχή, *prayer.* • **συνειδήσει** — dat. sg. → ἡ συνείδησις, *conscience.*

5.1 **κατάρας** → ἡ κατάρα, *curse.* • **μεστή** → μεστός, ή, όν, *full,* w. gen. • **φόνοι** → ὁ φόνος, *a murder, killing.* • **μοιχεῖαι** → ἡ μοιχεία, *adultery.* • **ἐπιθυμίαι** → ἡ ἐπιθυμία, *a desire, craving, lust.* • **πορνεῖαι** → ἡ πορνεία, *unchastity, fornication, sexual sin.* • **κλοπαί** → ἡ κλοπή, *theft, stealing.* • **εἰδωλολατρίαι** → ἡ εἰδωλολατρία, *idolatry.* • **μαγεῖαι** → ἡ μαγεία, *magic.* • **φαρμακίαι** → ἡ φαρμακία (listed in lexicons under the alternate form φαρμακεία), *sorcery.* • **ἁρπαγαί** → ἡ ἁρπαγή, *robbery.* • **ψευδομαρτυρίαι** → ἡ ψευδομαρτυρία, *false witness/testimony.* • **ὑποκρίσεις** — nom. pl. → ἡ ὑπόκρισις, *hypocrisy, pretense, outward show.* • **διπλοκαρδία** → ἡ διπλοκαρδία, *double-heartedness, duplicity.* • **δόλος** → ὁ δόλος, *deceit.* • **ὑπερηφανία** → ἡ ὑπερηφανία, *arrogance, haughtiness.* • **κακία** → ἡ κακία, *wickedness.* • **αὐθάδεια** → ἡ αὐθάδεια, *proud willfulness, stubbornness.* • **πλεονεξία** → ἡ πλεονεξία, *greediness.* • **αἰσχρολογία** → ἡ αἰσχρολογία, *obscene talk.* • **ζηλοτυπία** → ἡ ζηλοτυπία, *jealousy.* • **θρασύτης** → ὁ θρασύτης, *arrogant boldness.* • **ὕψος** → τό ὕψος, *pride, arrogance.* • **ἀλαζονεία** → ἡ ἀλαζονεία, *pretension, arrogance.* After this word Ehrman's text adds ἀφοβία (*fearlessness; lack of reverence*).

5.2 **διῶκται** — nom. pl. → ὁ διώκτης, *persecutor.* • **μισοῦντες** → μισέω, *I hate.* • **ψεῦδος** → τὸ ψεῦδος, *lie, falsehood.* • **μισθόν** → ὁ μισθός, *pay, reward.* • **κολλώμενοι** → κολλάω, *I join, associate with, adhere to.* • **κρίσει** — dat. sg. → ἡ κρίσις, *judgment.* • **ἀγρυπνοῦντες** → ἀγρυπνέω, *I am alert.* • **μακράν** — a fixed form from μακρός, ά, όν used as an adv. or, as here, as a prep. w. gen., *far*

διώκοντες ἀνταπόδομα, οὐκ ἐλεοῦντες πτωχόν, οὐ πονοῦντες ἐπὶ καταπονουμένῳ, οὐ γινώσκοντες τὸν ποιήσαντα αὐτούς, φονεῖς τέκνων, φθορεῖς πλάσματος Θεοῦ, ἀποστρεφόμενοι τὸν ἐνδεόμενον, καταπονοῦντες τὸν θλιβόμενον, πλουσίων παράκλητοι, πενήτων ἄνομοι κριταί, πανθαμάρτητοι· ῥυσθείητε, τέκνα, ἀπὸ τούτων ἁπάντων.

6.1 Ὅρα μή τις σε πλανήσῃ ἀπὸ ταύτης τῆς ὁδοῦ τῆς διδαχῆς, ἐπεὶ
παρεκτὸς Θεοῦ σε διδάσκει. 6.2 εἰ μὲν γὰρ δύνασαι βαστάσαι ὅλον τὸν
ζυγὸν τοῦ Κυρίου, τέλειος ἔσῃ· εἰ δ' οὐ δύνασαι, ὃ δύνῃ, τοῦτο ποίει. 6.3
Περὶ δὲ τῆς βρώσεως, ὃ δύνασαι, βάστασον· ἀπὸ δὲ τοῦ εἰδωλοθύτου λίαν πρόσεχε· λατρεία γάρ ἐστιν θεῶν νεκρῶν.

---

away from. ὧν μακρὰν πραΰτης καὶ ὑπομονή, "far away from whom are gentleness and patience." Less woodenly: "from whom gentleness and patience are far away" (BDAG, μακράν 1b: 612). • **πραΰτης** → ἡ πραΰτης, *gentleness.* • **ὑπομονή** → ἡ ὑπομονή, *patience.* • **μάταια** → μάταιος, α, ον — *empty, useless;* here subst., *what is worthless, empty.* • **διώκοντες** → διώκω, *I pursue.* • **ἀνταπόδομα** → τὸ ἀνταπόδομα, *reward.* • **ἐλεοῦντες** → ἐλεέω, *I have compassion/mercy/pity.* • **πτωχόν** → πτωχός, ή, όν, *poor.* • **πονοῦντες** → πονέω, *I toil, undergo trouble.* • **καταπονουμένῳ** → καταπονέω, *I oppress.* πονοῦντες . . . καταπονουμένῳ, a wordplay which cannot be conveyed well in English. • **φονεῖς** — nom. pl. → ὁ φονεύς, *murderer.* • **φθορεῖς** — nom. pl. → ὁ φθορεύς, *corrupter, destroyer, seducer.* • **πλάσματος** — gen. sg. → τὸ πλάσμα, *that which is formed/molded, image, figure.* φθορεῖς πλάσματος θεοῦ, "corrupters/destroyers of that which is formed by God." πλάσματος: obj. gen.; θεοῦ: gen. of agency (Wal: 126). The ref. may be to abortion (cf. BDAG, πλάσμα: 823). • **ἀποστρεφόμενοι** → ἀποστρέφω, *I turn away;* mid., *turn away from, reject.* • **ἐνδεόμενον** → ἐνδέω, *I am in want, am needy.* Same meaning for all voices. • **θλιβόμενον** → θλίβω, *I afflict, oppress.* • **πλουσίων** → πλούσιος, α, ον, *rich.* • **παράκλητοι** → ὁ παράκλητος, *defender, advocate.* • **πενήτων** — gen. pl. → τὸ πενής, *poor, needy.* • **ἄνομοι** → ἄνομος, ον, *lawless.* • **κριταί** → ὁ κριτής, *a judge.* • **πανθαμάρτητοι** → πανθαμάρτητος, ον, *altogether/utterly sinful.* • **ῥυσθείητε** — aor. pass. opt. 2 pl. → ῥύομαι, *I rescue, deliver.* Opt. of wish, *may you be delivered* (Wal: 481; Smy: 1814). • **τούτων** — the ref. could be either to the sorts of people mentioned or to the sins. • **ἁπάντων** → ἅπας, ἅπασα, ἅπαν, *all,* intensive form of πᾶς.

6.1 **ὅρα** — pres. act. impv. 2 sg. → ὁράω. • **πλανήσῃ** — aor. act. subjun. 3 sg. → πλανάω, *I lead astray.* W. μή for prohibition (Wal: 723). • **διδαχῆς** → ἡ διδαχή, *teaching.* • **ἐπεί** — *for, since, because.* • **παρεκτός** — adv., *apart from, without.*

6.2 **βαστάσαι** — aor. act. inf. → βαστάζω, *I bear, carry.* • **ζυγόν** → ὁ ζυγός, *yoke.* • **τέλειος** → τέλειος, α, ον, *perfect, complete.* • **δύνασαι . . . δύνῃ** — δύναμαι has two forms for the pres. mid. (depon.) indic. 2 sg., both of which, interestingly, occur here together.

6.3 **βρώσεως** — gen. sg. → ἡ βρῶσις, *food.* • **βάστασον** — aor. act. impv. 2 sg. → βαστάζω. • **εἰδωλοθύτου** → εἰδωλόθυτος, ον, *food sacrificed to idols.* • **λίαν** — *very, very much.* • **πρόσεχε** — pres. act. impv. 2 sg. → προσέχω, *I am concerned about;* w. ἀπό, *beware of* (BDAG 1: 879). • **λατρεία** → ἡ λατρεία, *worship.*

Didache 7 Concerning Baptism

7.1 Περὶ δὲ τοῦ βαπτίσματος, οὕτω βαπτίσατε· ταῦτα πάντα προειπόντες βαπτίσατε **εἰς τὸ ὄνομα τοῦ Πατρὸς καὶ τοῦ Υἱοῦ καὶ τοῦ ἁγίου Πνεύματος** ἐν ὕδατι ζῶντι. 7.2 ἐὰν δὲ μὴ ἔχῃς ὕδωρ ζῶν, εἰς ἄλλο ὕδωρ βάπτισον· εἰ δ' οὐ δύνασαι ἐν ψυχρῷ, ἐν θερμῷ. 7.3 ἐὰν δὲ ἀμφότερα μὴ ἔχῃς, ἔκχεον εἰς τὴν κεφαλὴν τρὶς ὕδωρ εἰς ὄνομα Πατρὸς καὶ Υἱοῦ καὶ ἁγίου Πνεύματος. 7.4 πρὸ δὲ τοῦ βαπτίσματος προνηστευσάτω ὁ βαπτίζων καὶ ὁ βαπτιζόμενος καὶ εἴ τινες ἄλλοι δύνανται. κελεύεις δὲ νηστεῦσαι τὸν βαπτιζόμενον πρὸ μιᾶς ἢ δύο.

Didache 8 Concerning Fasting and Prayer

8.1 Αἱ δὲ νηστεῖαι ὑμῶν μὴ ἔστωσαν μετὰ τῶν ὑποκριτῶν· νηστεύουσι γὰρ δευτέρᾳ σαββάτων καὶ πέμπτῃ· ὑμεῖς δὲ νηστεύσατε τετράδα καὶ παρα-

---

7.1 **βαπτίσματος** — gen. sg. → τὸ βάπτισμα, *baptism.* • **οὕτω** — οὕτως. • **ταῦτα πάντα** — ref. to the material covered in the first six chapters. • **προειπόντες** — 2 aor. act. ptc. masc. nom. pl. → προλέγω, *I explain previously.* Circ. ptc., temp., "after having first explained . . ." • **ζῶντι** — pres. act. ptc. neut. dat. sg. → ζάω. Adj. ptc., mod. ὕδατι, ref. to, "spring water in contrast w. cistern water" (BDAG, ζάω 4: 426), *flowing water.*

7.2 **ἔχῃς** — The shift from pl. to sg. is perhaps a sign of a later redactor. • **ζῶν** — pres. act. ptc. neut. acc. sg. → ζάω, adj. ptc., mod. ὕδωρ • **βάπτισον** — aor. act. impv. 2 sg. → βαπτίζω. • **ψυχρῷ** — neut. dat. sg. → ψυχρός, ή, όν, *cool, cold,* neut. to agree w. implied ὕδωρ. • **θερμῷ** — neut. dat. sg. → θερμός, ή, όν, *warm,* neut. to agree w. implied ὕδωρ.

7.3 **ἀμφότερα** — neut. acc. pl. → ἀμφότεροι, αι, α, *both, either.* • **ἔκχεον** — aor. act. impv. 2 sg. → ἐκχέω, *I pour out.* This vb. uses 1 aor. endings w. no sigma. • **εἰς** (τὴν κεφαλήν) — *onto, on.* • **τρίς** — adv., *three times.*

7.4 **πρό** — *before,* w. gen. • **προνηστευσάτω** — aor. act. impv. 3 sg. → προνηστεύω, *I fast beforehand.* When there is more than one subj., a sg. verb may be used if the nearest, most important, or more emphatic subj. is sg. (Smy: 968, cf. Wal: 401). • **κελεύεις** — pres. act. indic. 2 sg. → κελεύω, *I command.* After the string of impv. this indic. is striking. This grammatical change could be a sign that sources have been joined together. Or perhaps the author is using an unsophisticated form, continuing to tell the leader what to do, but expressing it as though alongside as a coach. • **νηστεῦσαι** — aor. act. inf. → νηστεύω, *I fast.* Indir. disc., the content of the command (Wal: 603; Smy: 2016). • **μιᾶς** — fem. acc. sg. → εἷς, fem. to agree w. implied ἡμέρα. πρὸ μιᾶς ἢ δύο, *one or two days before.*

8.1 **νηστεῖαι** — nom. pl. → ἡ νηστεία, *a fast.* • **ἔστωσαν** — pres. act. impv. 3 pl. → εἰμί. • **ὑποκριτῶν** — gen. pl. → ὁ ὑποκριτής, *hypocrite.* • **νηστεύουσι** →

σκευήν. 8.2 μηδὲ προσεύχεσθε ὡς **οἱ ὑποκριταί,** ἀλλ' ὡς ἐκέλευσεν ὁ Κύριος ἐν τῷ εὐαγγελίῳ αὐτοῦ, **οὕτως προσεύχεσθε· Πάτερ ἡμῶν ὁ ἐν τῷ οὐρανῷ, ἁγιασθήτω τὸ ὄνομά σου, ἐλθέτω ἡ βασιλεία σου, γενηθήτω τὸ θέλημά σου ὡς ἐν οὐρανῷ καὶ ἐπὶ γῆς· τὸν ἄρτον ἡμῶν τὸν ἐπιούσιον δὸς ἡμῖν σήμερον, καὶ ἄφες ἡμῖν τὴν ὀφειλὴν ἡμῶν, ὡς καὶ ἡμεῖς ἀφίεμεν τοῖς ὀφειλέταις ἡμῶν, καὶ μὴ εἰσενέγκῃς ἡμᾶς εἰς πειρασμόν, ἀλλὰ ῥῦσαι ἡμᾶς ἀπὸ τοῦ πονηροῦ·** ὅτι σοῦ ἐστιν ἡ δύναμις καὶ ἡ δόξα εἰς τοὺς αἰῶνας. 8.3 τρὶς τῆς ἡμέρας οὕτω προσεύχεσθε.

νηστεύω, *I fast.* • **δευτέρᾳ** — fem. dat. sg. → δεύτερος, α, ον, *second,* fem. to agree w. implied ἡμέρα. • **σαββάτων** — gen. pl. → τὸ σαββάτον, *a week.* Both the sg. and pl. of this word are used for "a week." • **πέμπτῃ** — fem. dat. sg. → πέμπτος, η, ον, *fifth,* fem. to agree w. implied ἡμέρα. • **νηστεύσατε** — aor. act. impv. 2 pl. → νηστεύω. • **τετράδα** — acc. sg. → ἡ τετράς, *four, fourth day of the week, Wednesday.* • **παρασκευήν** — acc. sg. → ἡ παρασκευή — *preparation; sixth day of the week, Friday.* Normally the dat. of time is used for indicating when something takes place, as in the first part of this sentence (δευτέρᾳ and πέμπτῃ). The acc. usually is used for how long something goes on, but here the two acc., τετράδα and παρασκευήν, function like dat., telling when to fast rather than how long. This use of the acc. for when something happens occurs commonly w. the word ὥρα and occasionally, as here, w. other words (cf. BDF: 161.3).

8.2 **ἐκέλευσεν** — aor. act. indic. 3 sg. → κελεύω, *I command.* • **ἁγιασθήτω** — aor. pass. impv. 3 sg. → ἁγιάζω, *I sanctify, treat as holy, reverence.* • **ἐλθέτω** — 2 aor. act. impv. 3 sg. → ἔρχομαι. • **γενηθήτω** — 2 aor. pass. (depon.) impv. 3 sg. → γίνομαι. • **ἐπιούσιον** — masc. acc. sg. → ἐπιούσιος, ον, *of the Kingdom.* This word was apparently coined by those who first translated this prayer. It is usually translated "daily," but this meaning is unlikely since Greek has several ways to express "daily," and thus there was no need to create a word. Etymology yields such meanings as "necessary for existence," "for today," "for tomorrow," "for the future" (BDAG: 376–77). In the context of the Lord's Prayer the word seems to refer to that which is necessary for life in the Kingdom, which would include both material and spiritual resources. • **δός** — aor. act. impv. 2 sg. → δίδωμι. • **σήμερον** — adv., *today.* • **ἄφες** — aor. act. impv. 2 sg. → ἀφίημι. • **ὀφειλήν** — acc. sg. → ἡ ὀφειλή, *a debt.* • **ἀφίεμεν** — pres. act. indic. 1 sg. → ἀφίημι. The more regular form would be ἀφίομεν. This irregular form also occurs in some MSS. of the Lord's Prayer at Luke 11:4. • **ὀφειλέταις** — dat. pl. → ὁ ὀφειλέτης, *debtor.* • **εἰσενέγκῃς** — aor. act. subjun. 2 sg. → εἰσφέρω, *I bring* or *lead into.* • **πειρασμόν** — acc. sg. → ὁ πειρασμός, *temptation.* • **ῥῦσαι** — aor. mid. (depon.) impv. 2 sg. → ῥύομαι, *I rescue.* • **ἀπὸ τοῦ πονηροῦ** — often translated, "from evil," but the presence of the art., especially within a prep. phrase (Wal: 247), signifies, "*the* evil," or, in keeping w. the context and the general thought in the Gospels, *the evil one* (Wal: 233).

8.3 **τρίς** — adv., *three times.* τρὶς τῆς ἡμέρας, *three times a day.* τῆς ἡμέρας: gen. of time (Wal: 122; Smy: 1444). • **οὕτω** → οὕτως.

Didache 9–10 Concerning the Eucharist

9.1 Περὶ δὲ τῆς εὐχαριστίας, οὕτω εὐχαριστήσατε· 9.2 πρῶτον περὶ τοῦ
ποτηρίου· Εὐχαριστοῦμέν σοι, Πάτερ ἡμῶν, ὑπὲρ τῆς ἁγίας ἀμπέλου
Δαυεὶδ τοῦ παιδός σου, ἧς ἐγνώρισας ἡμῖν διὰ Ἰησοῦ τοῦ παιδός σου· σοὶ
ἡ δόξα εἰς τοὺς αἰῶνας. 9.3 περὶ δὲ τοῦ κλάσματος· Εὐχαριστοῦμέν σοι,
Πάτερ ἡμῶν, ὑπὲρ τῆς ζωῆς καὶ γνώσεως, ἧς ἐγνώρισας ἡμῖν διὰ Ἰησοῦ
τοῦ παιδός σου· σοὶ ἡ δόξα εἰς τοὺς αἰῶνας. 9.4 ὥσπερ ἦν τοῦτο τὸ κλάσμα
διεσκορπισμένον ἐπάνω τῶν ὀρέων καὶ συναχθὲν ἐγένετο ἕν, οὕτω συναχθήτω σου ἡ ἐκκλησία ἀπὸ τῶν περάτων τῆς γῆς εἰς τὴν σὴν βασιλείαν·
ὅτι σοῦ ἐστὶν ἡ δόξα καὶ ἡ δύναμις διὰ Ἰησοῦ Χριστοῦ εἰς τοὺς αἰῶνας. 9.5
μηδεὶς δὲ φαγέτω μηδὲ πιέτω ἀπὸ τῆς εὐχαριστίας ὑμῶν, ἀλλ' οἱ βαπτισθέντες εἰς ὄνομα Κυρίου. καὶ γὰρ περὶ τούτου εἴρηκεν ὁ Κύριος· **Μὴ δῶτε
τὸ ἅγιον τοῖς κυσί.**

10.1 Μετὰ δὲ τὸ ἐμπλησθῆναι οὕτως εὐχαριστήσατε· 10.2 Εὐχαριστοῦμέν
σοι, Πάτερ ἅγιε, ὑπὲρ τοῦ ἁγίου ὀνόματός σου, οὗ κατεσκήνωσας ἐν ταῖς

9.1 **εὐχαριστίας** — gen. sg. → ἡ εὐχαριστία, *thanksgiving, thanks, the Eucharist.* • **οὕτω** — οὕτως. • **εὐχαριστήσατε** — aor. act. impv. 2 pl. → εὐχαριστέω, *give thanks.*

9.2 **πρῶτον** — Here the acc. is used as an adverb, *first.* • **ποτηρίου** — gen. sg. → τὸ ποτήριον, *cup.* • **ἀμπέλου** — gen. sg. → ἡ ἄμπελος, *vine.* • **Δαυείδ** → ὁ Δαυείδ (indecl., listed in BDAG under the alternate spelling Δαυίδ), *David.* • **παιδός** — masc. gen. sg. → ὁ or ἡ παῖς, *child, servant.* • **ἐγνώρισας** — aor. act. indic. 2 sg. → γνωρίζω, *I make known, reveal.* • **ἡ δόξα** — here used in a pred., *to you be the glory.*

9.3 **κλάσματος** — gen. sg. → τὸ κλάσμα, *fragment, piece.* • **γνώσεως** — gen. sg. → ἡ γνῶσις, *knowledge.*

9.4 **ὥσπερ** — particle, *just as, as.* • **διεσκορπισμένον** — pf. pass. ptc. neut. nom. sg. → διασκορπίζω, *I scatter.* This verb forms the plpf. using a periphrastic construction: ἦν . . . διεσκορπισμένον, *had been scattered.* It is common in periphrastics for the form of εἰμί to be separated from the ptc. • **ἐπάνω** — adv., functioning as an improper prep., *over, upon.* • **συναχθέν** — aor. pass. ptc. neut. nom. sg. → συνάγω. Circ. ptc. temp., "(after) having been gathered (together) . . ." • **συναχθήτω** — aor. pass. impv. 3 sg. → συνάγω. • **περάτων** — gen. pl. → τὸ πέρας, *an end.* • **σήν** — fem. acc. sg. → σός, σή, σόν, *your.* • **εἰς τοὺς αἰῶνας** — *unto the ages,* is often translated *to eternity, eternally, in perpetuity* (BDAG, αἰών 1b: 32).

9.5 **φαγέτω** — 2 aor. act. impv. 3 sg. → ἐσθίω. • **πιέτω** — 2 aor. act. impv. 3 sg. → πίνω. • **βαπτισθέντες** — aor. pass. ptc. masc. nom. pl. → βαπτίζω. Attrib. ptc. as a subst.; here the subj. • **καί** — intensive use, *even, indeed, in fact.* • **εἴρηκεν** — pf. act. indic. 3 sg. → λέγω. • **δῶτε** — aor. act. impv. 2 pl. → δίδωμι. • **κυσί** — dat. pl. → ὁ κύων, *dog.*

10.1 **ἐμπλησθῆναι** — aor. pass. inf. → ἐμπίμπλημι, *I fill, satisfy.* Art. inf. w. μετά for temp. clause (Wal: 594), "after being filled/satisfied . . ." • **εὐχαριστήσατε** — aor. act. impv. 2 pl. → εὐχαριστέω, *I give thanks.*

καρδίαις ἡμῶν, καὶ ὑπὲρ τῆς γνώσεως καὶ πίστεως καὶ ἀθανασίας, ἧς ἐγνώρισας ἡμῖν διὰ Ἰησοῦ τοῦ παιδός σου· σοὶ ἡ δόξα εἰς τοὺς αἰῶνας. 10.3 σύ, δέσποτα παντοκράτορ, ἔκτισας τὰ πάντα ἕνεκεν τοῦ ὀνόματός σου, τροφήν τε καὶ ποτὸν ἔδωκας τοῖς ἀνθρώποις εἰς ἀπόλαυσιν ἵνα σοι εὐχαριστήσωσιν, ἡμῖν δὲ ἐχαρίσω πνευματικὴν τροφὴν καὶ ποτὸν καὶ ζωὴν αἰώνιον διὰ τοῦ παιδός σου. 10.4 πρὸ πάντων εὐχαριστοῦμέν σοι ὅτι δυνατὸς εἶ σύ· σοὶ ἡ δόξα εἰς τοὺς αἰῶνας. 10.5 μνήσθητι, Κύριε, τῆς ἐκκλησίας σου τοῦ ῥύσασθαι αὐτὴν ἀπὸ παντὸς πονηροῦ καὶ **τελειῶσαι** αὐτὴν **ἐν τῇ ἀγάπῃ** σου, καὶ **σύναξον** αὐτὴν **ἀπὸ τῶν τεσσάρων ἀνέμων,** τὴν ἁγιασθεῖσαν εἰς τὴν σὴν βασιλείαν, ἣν ἡτοίμασας αὐτῇ· ὅτι σοῦ ἐστιν ἡ δύναμις καὶ ἡ δόξα εἰς τοὺς αἰῶνας. 10.6 ἐλθέτω χάρις καὶ παρελθέτω ὁ κόσμος οὗτος. ὡσαννὰ τῷ Θεῷ Δαυείδ. εἴ τις ἅγιός ἐστιν, ἐρχέσθω· εἴ τις οὐκ ἐστί, μετανοείτω. **μαρὰν ἀθά.** ἀμήν. 10.7 τοῖς δὲ προφήταις ἐπιτρέπετε εὐχαριστεῖν ὅσα θέλουσιν.

10.2 **κατεσκήνωσας** — aor. act. indic. 2 sg. → κατασκηνόω, *I cause to dwell.* • **γνώσεως** — gen. sg. → ἡ γνῶσις, *knowledge.* • **ἀθανασίας** — gen. sg. → ἡ ἀθανασία, *immortality.* • **ἐγνώρισας** — aor. act. indic. 2 sg. → γνωρίζω, *I make known, reveal.* • **παιδός** — masc. gen. sg. → ὁ or ἡ παῖς, *child, servant.* • **ἡ δόξα** — here used predicatively, *to you be the glory.*

10.3 **δέσποτα** — voc. sg. → ὁ δεσπότης, *master.* • **παντοκράτορ** — voc. sg. → ὁ παντοκράτωρ, *almighty.* • **ἔκτισας** — aor. act. indic. 2 sg. → κτίζω, *I create.* • **τὰ πάντα** — *the universe, everything.* • **ἕνεκεν** — improper prep., *for the sake of, on account of.* • **τροφήν** → ἡ τροφή, *nourishment, food.* • **ποτόν** — acc. sg. → τὸ ποτόν, *drink.* • **ἔδωκας** — aor. act. indic. 2 sg. → δίδωμι. • **ἀπόλαυσιν** — acc. sg. → ἡ ἀπόλαυσις, *enjoyment.* • **ἐχαρίσω** — aor. mid. (depon.) indic. 2 sg. → χαρίζομαι, *I give freely, give graciously.* • **πνευματικήν** — fem. acc. sg. → πνευματικός, ή, όν, *spiritual.*

10.4 **πρό** — *above all,* w. gen. (BDAG 3: 864). • **δυνατός** — masc. nom. sg. → δυνατός, ή, όν, *powerful, mighty.* • **σύ** — This word is not included in Ehrman's text.

10.5 **μνήσθητι** — aor. pass. (depon.) impv. 2 sg. → μιμνήσκομαι, *I remember.* • **ῥύσασθαι** — aor. mid. (depon.) inf. → ῥύομαι, *I rescue.* Inf. for purpose or result (Wal: 590, 592; Smy: 2008, 2011). Τοῦ w. an inf. does not change the meaning of the inf. For a list of uses of the inf. which can include τοῦ, see Wal: 610. • **τελειῶσαι** — aor. act. inf. → τελειόω, *I complete, make perfect.* Inf. for purpose or result. • **σύναξον** — aor. act. impv. 2 sg. → συνάγω. This verb also uses a 2 aor. form (συνήγαγον), as in its uncompounded form. • **τεσσάρων** — masc. gen. pl. → τέσσαρες, τέσσαρα, *four.* • **ἀνέμων** — gen. pl. → ὁ ἄνεμος, *wind.* • **ἁγιασθεῖσαν** — aor. pass. ptc. fem. acc. sg. → ἁγιάζω, *I sanctify, consecrate.* Attrib. ptc., subst. in appos. to αὐτήν which ref. to ἡ ἐκκλησία. Ehrman's text does not have τὴν ἁγιασθεῖσαν. • **σήν** — fem. acc. sg. → σός, σή, σόν, *your.* • **ἡτοίμασας** — aor. act. indic. 2 sg. → ἑτοιμάζω, *I prepare.*

10.6 **ἐλθέτω** – 2 aor. act. impv. 3 sg. → ἔρχομαι. • **παρελθέτω** — 2 aor. act. impv. 3 sg. → παρέχομαι, *I pass by, pass away, come to an end, disappear.* • **ὡσαννά** — indecl., *hosanna.* • **Δαυείδ** → ὁ Δαυείδ (indecl., listed in BDAG under the alternate spelling Δαυίδ), *David.* • **ἐρχέσθω** — pres. mid. (depon.) impv. 3 sg. →

Didache 11–13 Concerning Teachers, Apostles, and Prophets

11.1 Ὃς ἂν οὖν ἐλθὼν διδάξῃ ὑμᾶς ταῦτα πάντα τὰ προειρημένα, δέξασθε αὐτόν· 11.2 ἐὰν δὲ αὐτὸς ὁ διδάσκων στραφεὶς διδάσκῃ ἄλλην διδαχὴν εἰς τὸ καταλῦσαι, μὴ αὐτοῦ ἀκούσητε· εἰς δὲ τὸ προσθεῖναι δικαιοσύνην καὶ γνῶσιν Κυρίου, δέξασθε αὐτὸν ὡς Κύριον. 11.3 Περὶ δὲ τῶν ἀποστόλων καὶ προφητῶν κατὰ τὸ δόγμα τοῦ εὐαγγελίου οὕτως ποιήσατε. 11.4 πᾶς δὲ ἀπόστολος ἐρχόμενος πρὸς ὑμᾶς δεχθήτω ὡς Κύριος· 11.5 οὐ μενεῖ δὲ εἰ μὴ ἡμέραν μίαν· ἐὰν δὲ ᾖ χρεία, καὶ τὴν ἄλλην· τρεῖς δὲ ἐὰν μείνῃ, ψευδοπροφήτης ἐστίν· 11.6 ἐξερχόμενος δὲ ὁ ἀπόστολος μηδὲν λαμβανέτω εἰ μὴ ἄρτον, ἕως οὗ αὐλισθῇ· ἐὰν δὲ ἀργύριον αἰτῇ, ψευδοπροφήτης ἐστί. 11.7 καὶ πάντα προφήτην λαλοῦντα ἐν πνεύματι οὐ πειράσετε οὐδὲ διακρι-

---

ἔρχομαι. • **μετανοείτω** — pres. act. impv. 3 sg. → μετανοέω, *I repent.* • **μαρὰν ἀθά** — indecl., *maranatha.* (See note in the translation.)

10.7 **ἐπιτρέπετε** — pres. act. impv. 2 pl. → ἐπιτρέπω, *I allow, permit,* w. dat. • **εὐχαριστεῖν** — pres. act. inf. → εὐχαριστέω, *I give thanks.* Inf. for indir. disc., the content of what is to be allowed (Wal: 603; Smy: 2016).

11.1 **ἐλθών** — 2 aor. act. ptc. masc. nom. sg. → ἔρχομαι. Attend. circ. • **διδάξῃ** — aor. act. subjun. 3 sg. → διδάσκω. • **προειρημένα** — pf. pass. ptc. neut. acc. pl. → προλέγω, *I speak/explain previously.* • **δέξασθε** — aor. mid. (depon.) impv. 2 pl. → δέχομαι.

11.2 **στραφείς** — 2 aor. pass. ptc. masc. nom. sg. → στρέφω, *I turn, change.* Attend. circ. • **διδαχήν** → ἡ διδαχή, *teaching.* • **ἀκούσητε** — aor. act. subjun. 2 pl. → ἀκούω. W. μή for prohibition (Wal: 723). • **καταλῦσαι** — aor. act. inf. → καταλύω, *I destroy.* Inf. as subst. The implied obj. is either the hearers or the true teaching, i.e., all that has been mentioned previously. • **προσθεῖναι** — aor. act. inf. → προστίθημι, *I add, increase.* Art. inf. w. εἰς for purpose clause (Wal: 590). The previous context provides the introductory clause, "But if someone teaches . . ." • **γνῶσιν** — acc. sg. → ἡ γνῶσις, *knowledge.* • **δέξασθε αὐτὸν ὡς κύριον** — cf. 4.1.

11.3 **δόγμα** → τὸ δόγμα, *rule, doctrine.* κατὰ τὸ δόγμα τοῦ εὐαγγελίου mod. οὕτως ποιήσατε.

11.4 **δεχθήτω** — aor. pass. impv. 3 sg. → δέχομαι.

11.5 **μενεῖ** — liq. fut. act. indic. 3 sg. → μένω. • **εἰ μή** — *except.* • **ᾖ** — pres. act. subjun. 3 sg. → εἰμί. • **χρεία** → ἡ χρεία, *a need.* • **τρεῖς** → τρεῖς, τρία, *three.* • **μείνῃ** — liq. aor. act. subjun. 3 sg. → μένω. • **ψευδοπροφήτης** → ὁ ψευδοπροφήτης, *false prophet.*

11.6 **λαμβανέτω** — pres. act. impv. 3 sg. → λαμβάνω. • **ἕως οὗ** — *until.* • **αὐλισθῇ** — aor. pass. subjun. 3 sg. → αὐλίζομαι, *I spend the night, find lodging for the night.* ἕως οὗ αὐλισθῇ, i.e., enough bread to get him to his next night's lodging. • **ἀργύριον** → τὸ ἀργύριον, *silver, money.*

νεῖτε· πᾶσα γὰρ ἁμαρτία ἀφεθήσεται, αὕτη δὲ ἡ ἁμαρτία οὐκ ἀφεθήσεται.
11.8 οὐ πᾶς δὲ ὁ λαλῶν ἐν πνεύματι προφήτης ἐστίν, ἀλλ' ἐὰν ἔχῃ τοὺς
τρόπους Κυρίου. Ἀπὸ οὖν τῶν τρόπων γνωσθήσεται ὁ ψευδοφροφήτης καὶ
ὁ προφήτης. 11.9 καὶ πᾶς προφήτης ὁρίζων τράπεζαν ἐν πνεύματι οὐ
φάγεται ἀπ' αὐτῆς· εἰ δὲ μήγε, ψευδοπροφήτης ἐστίν. 11.10 πᾶς δὲ προφήτης
διδάσκων τὴν ἀλήθειαν, εἰ ἃ διδάσκει οὐ ποιεῖ, ψευδοπροφήτης ἐστίν.
11.11 πᾶς δὲ προφήτης δεδοκιμασμένος ἀληθινὸς ποιῶν εἰς μυστήριον
κοσμικὸν ἐκκλησίας, μὴ διδάσκων δὲ ποιεῖν ὅσα αὐτὸς ποιεῖ, οὐ κριθήσεται ἐφ' ὑμῶν· μετὰ Θεοῦ γὰρ ἔχει τὴν κρίσιν· ὡσαύτως γὰρ ἐποίησαν καὶ
οἱ ἀρχαῖοι προφῆται. 11.12 ὃς δ' ἂν εἴπῃ ἐν πνεύματι· Δός μοι ἀργύρια ἢ
ἕτερά τινα, οὐκ ἀκούσεσθε αὐτοῦ· ἐὰν δὲ περὶ ἄλλων ὑστερούντων εἴπῃ
δοῦναι, μηδεὶς αὐτὸν κρινέτω.

11.7 **πειράσετε** — fut. act. indic. 2 pl. → πειράζω, *I test.* • **διακρινεῖτε** — liq. fut. act. indic. 2 pl. → διακρίνω, *I evaluate, judge.* • **ἀφεθήσεται** — fut. pass. indic. 3 sg. → ἀφίημι.

11.8 **τρόπους** → ὁ τρόπος, *way, manner.* • **γνωσθήσεται** — fut. pass. indic. 3 sg. → γινώσκω, here, *I recognize* (BDAG 7: 200). A comp. subj. can take a sg. verb (Wal: 401; Smy: 968).

11.9 **ὁρίζων** → ὁρίζω, *I determine, order.* • **τράπεζαν** → ἡ τράπεζα, *table, meal, food.* • **φάγεται** — fut. mid. (depon.) indic. 3 sg. → ἐσθίω. • **εἰ δὲ μήγε** — *otherwise.*

11.11 **δεδοκιμασμένος** — pf. pass. ptc. masc. nom. sg. → δοκιμάζω, *I examine; I prove; I approve.* • **ἀληθινός** → ἀληθινός, ή, όν, *true, genuine, authentic, real.* • **ποιῶν** — perhaps circ. ptc., conditional, though, as often w. a circ. ptc., more than one option is viable. • **μυστήριον** → τὸ μυστήριον, *mystery;* here, *transcendent/ultimate reality, secret* (BDAG 2c: 662). • **κοσμικόν** → κοσμικός, ή, όν, *earthly.* εἰς μυστήριον κοσμικὸν ἐκκλησίας could be taken in at least two ways, according to different uses of εἰς. On the one hand, εἰς may signify a point of reference (BDAG, εἰς 5: 291), and the text could refer to the prophet doing something in accord with the earthly mystery of the church (cf. BDAG, μυστήριον 2c: 662), that is, to symbolize the transcendent reality of the church. On the other hand, εἰς could refer to a goal (BDAG, εἰς 4: 290), and the text would mean that the prophet is doing something for the sake of the earthy mystery of the church, that is, to actualize in some way the transcendent reality of the church. The ideas of both reference and goal fit the examples of the Old Testament prophets mentioned in the text. See further the note in the translation. • **διδάσκων** — perhaps continuing the conditional. • **κριθήσεται** — fut. pass. indic. 3 sg. → κρίνω. • **κρίσιν** — acc. sg. → ἡ κρίσις, *judgment,* art. for poss. pron. (Wal: 215; Smy: 1121). • **ὡσαύτως** — *similarly, likewise.* • **ἀρχαῖοι** → ἀρχαῖος, α, ον, *ancient.*

11.12 **εἴπῃ** — 2 aor. act. subjun. 3 sg. → λέγω. • **δός** — aor. act. impv. 2 sg. → δίδωμι. • **ἀκούσεσθε** — ἀκούω sometimes has a depon. fut., as here (BDAG: 37; Smy: 805–6). • **ὑστερούντων** — pres. act. ptc. masc. gen. pl. → ὑστερέω, *I lack, am needy.* • **δοῦναι** — aor. act. inf. → δίδωμι. Inf. for indir. disc. (Wal: 603; Smy: 2016).

12.1 Πᾶς δὲ ὁ **ἐρχόμενος ἐν ὀνόματι Κυρίου** δεχθήτω· ἔπειτα δὲ δοκιμάσαντες αὐτὸν γνώσεσθε. σύνεσιν γὰρ ἕξετε δεξιὰν καὶ ἀριστεράν. 12.2 εἰ μὲν παρόδιός ἐστιν ὁ ἐρχόμενος, βοηθεῖτε αὐτῷ ὅσον δύνασθε· οὐ μενεῖ δὲ πρὸς ὑμᾶς εἰ μὴ δύο ἢ τρεῖς ἡμέρας, ἐὰν ᾖ ἀνάγκη. 12.3 εἰ δὲ θέλει πρὸς ὑμᾶς καθῆσθαι, τεχνίτης ὤν, ἐργαζέσθω καὶ φαγέτω. 12.4 εἰ δὲ οὐκ ἔχει τέχνην, κατὰ τὴν σύνεσιν ὑμῶν προνοήσατε, πῶς μὴ ἀργὸς μεθ' ὑμῶν ζήσεται Χριστιανός. 12.5 εἰ δ' οὐ θέλει οὕτω ποιεῖν, χριστέμπορός ἐστιν· προσέχετε ἀπὸ τῶν τοιούτων.

13.1 Πᾶς δὲ προφήτης ἀληθινὸς θέλων καθῆσθαι πρὸς ὑμᾶς **ἄξιός ἐστιν τῆς τροφῆς αὐτοῦ.** 13.2 ὡσαύτως διδάσκαλος ἀληθινός **ἐστιν ἄξιος** καὶ

12.1 **δεχθήτω** aor. pass. impv. 3 sg. → δέχομαι. • **ἔπειτα** — *then.* • **δοκιμάσαντες** → δοκιμάζω, *I examine; I prove; I approve.* • **γνώσεσθε** — fut. mid. (depon.) indic. 2 pl. → γινώσκω. W. αὐτόν as dir. obj. • **σύνεσιν** — acc. sg. → ἡ σύνεσις, *understanding.* σύνεσιν γὰρ ἕξετε could be taken as a parenthetical remark (Niederwimmer 183, note 8), as in Holmes, where the words are set off by dashes. Ehrman has ἔχετε, which would fit well as a parenthetical remark, though he does not punctuate it as such. See next note. • **ἀριστεράν** → ἀριστερός, ά, όν, *left* (as opposed to right). If σύνεσιν γὰρ ἕξετε/ἔχετε is parenthetical, then δεξιὰν καὶ ἀριστεράν could be objects of γνώσεσθε. But as the text is punctuated in Lightfoot and Ehrman, these adj. mod. σύνεσιν, "right and left understanding." Either way, the idiom means to distinguish between what is true and false, as the description of the ignorance of the Ninevites in Jonah 4:11 (LXX) suggests, οἵτινες οὐκ ἔγνωσαν δεχιὰν αὐτῶν ἢ ἀριστερὰν αὐτῶν (cf. BDAG, ἀριστερός: 131). In the translation I have followed Ehrman's punctuation, placing a comma after γνώσεσθε instead of a period, as in Lightfoot.

12.2 **παρόδιος** → παρόδιος, ον, *traveling by/through.* • **βοηθεῖτε** — pres. act. impv. 2 pl. → βοηθέω, *I help, aid.* • **εἰ μή** — *except.* • **τρεῖς** → τρεῖς, τρία, *three.* δύο ἢ τρεῖς ἡμέρας, *for two or three days.* Acc. of extent of time (Wal: 201; Smy: 1582). • **ᾖ** — pres. act. subjun. 3 sg. → εἰμί. • **ἀνάγκη** → ἡ ἀνάγκη, *necessity.* "If there be necessity," less woodenly, *if it is necessary.*

12.3 **καθῆσθαι** — pres. mid. (depon.) inf. → κάθημαι, *I live, settle.* • **τεχνίτης** → ὁ τεχνίτης, *skilled laborer.* • **ὤν** — pres. act. ptc. masc. nom. sg. → εἰμί. Circ. ptc. for a conditional. • **ἐργαζέσθω** — pres. mid. (depon.) impv. 3 sg. → ἐργάζομαι, *I work.* • **φαγέτω** — 2 aor. act. impv. 3 sg. → ἐσθίω.

12.4 **τέχνην** → ἡ τέχνη, *craft, skill, trade.* • **προνοήσατε** — aor. act. impv. 2 pl. → προνοέω, *I take thought (for).* • **ἀργός** → ἀργός, ή, όν, *unemployed, idle.* • **Χριστιανός** → ὁ Χριστιανός, *Christian.* In appos. to the subj.

12.5 **οὕτω** — οὕτως. • **χριστέμπορος** → ὁ χριστέμπορος, *Christmonger, one who trades on Christ,* i.e., "one who carries on a cheap trade in (the teachings of) Christ" (BDAG: 1090). • **προσέχετε** — pres. act. impv. 2 pl. → προσέχω, *I am concerned about;* w. ἀπό, *beware of.*

13.1 **ἀληθινός** → ἀληθινός, ή, όν, *true, genuine, authentic, real.* • **καθῆσθαι** — pres. mid. (depon.) inf. → κάθημαι, *I live, settle.* • **ἄξιος** → ἄξιος, α, ον, *worthy.* • **τροφῆς** → ἡ τροφή, *nourishment, food.*

αὐτός, ὥσπερ ὁ **ἐργάτης, τῆς τροφῆς αὐτοῦ.** 13.3 πᾶσαν οὖν ἀπαρχὴν γεννημάτων ληνοῦ καὶ ἅλωνος, βοῶν τε καὶ προβάτων λαβὼν δώσεις τὴν ἀπαρχὴν τοῖς προφήταις· αὐτοὶ γάρ εἰσιν οἱ ἀρχιερεῖς ὑμῶν. 13.4 ἐὰν δὲ μὴ ἔχητε προφήτην, δότε τοῖς πτωχοῖς. 13.5 ἐὰν σιτίαν ποιῇς, τὴν ἀπαρχὴν λαβὼν δὸς κατὰ τὴν ἐντολήν. 13.6 ὡσαύτως κεράμιον οἴνου ἢ ἐλαίου ἀνοίξας τὴν ἀπαρχὴν λαβὼν δὸς τοῖς προφήταις· 13.7 ἀργυρίου δὲ καὶ ἱματισμοῦ καὶ παντὸς κτήματος λαβὼν τὴν ἀπαρχήν, ὡς ἄν σοι δόξῃ, δὸς κατὰ τὴν ἐντολήν.

Didache 14 Concerning the Lord's Day

14.1 Κατὰ κυριακὴν δὲ Κυρίου συναχθέντες κλάσατε ἄρτον καὶ εὐχαριστήσατε προεξομολογησάμενοι τὰ παραπτώματα ὑμῶν, ὅπως καθαρὰ ἡ θυσία ὑμῶν ᾖ. 14.2 πᾶς δὲ ἔχων τὴν ἀμφιβολίαν μετὰ τοῦ ἑταίρου αὐτοῦ

13.2 **ὡσαύτως** — *similarly, likewise.* • **ὥσπερ** — *just as.* • **ἐργάτης** → ὁ ἐργάτης, *worker.*

13.3 **ἀπαρχήν** → ἡ ἀπαρχή, *firstfruit.* • **γεννημάτων** — gen. pl. → τὸ γέννημα, *that which is produced.* • **ληνοῦ** → ἡ ληνός, *wine-press.* • **ἅλωνος** → ἡ ἅλων, *threshing floor.* • **βοῶν** → ὁ or ἡ βοῦς, masc., *ox;* fem., *cow;* pl., *cattle.* • **προβάτων** — gen. pl. → τὸ πρόβατον, *sheep.* • **λαβών** — 2 aor. act. ptc. masc. nom. sg. → λαμβάνω. • **δώσεις** — fut. act. indic. 2 sg. → δίδωμι. • **ἀρχιερεῖς** — nom. pl. → ὁ ἀρχιερεύς, *high priest.*

13.4 **δότε** — aor. act. impv. 2 pl. → δίδωμι. • **πτωχοῖς** → πτωχός, ή, όν, *poor.*

13.5 **σιτίαν** → ἡ σιτία, *dough, bread.* σιτίαν ποιῇς, either "prepare dough" or "make bread." • **λαβών** — This is a good example of an attend. circ. ptc. taking on the mood of the main verb, here an impv. The next two verses contain further examples w. these same verbs.

13.6 **κεράμιον** → τὸ κεράμιον, *earthenware vessel, jar.* • **οἴνου** → ὁ οἶνος, *wine.* • **ἐλαίου** → τὸ ἔλαιον, *olive oil.* • **ἀνοίξας** — aor. act. ptc. masc. nom. sg. → ἀνοίγω, *I open.* Circ. ptc., temp. or conditional.

13.7 **ἀργυρίου** → τὸ ἀργύριον, *silver, money.* This gen. and the ones following modify τὴν ἀπαρχήν. • **ἱματισμοῦ** → ὁ ἱματισμός, *clothing.* • **κτήματος** — gen. sg. → τὸ κτῆμα, *possession.* • **δόξῃ** — aor. act. subjun. 3 sg. → δοκέω, *I think, consider.*

14.1 **κυριακήν** → κυριακός, ή, όν, *the Lord's;* here fem., *the Lord's day* (ἡ ἡμέρα), i.e., Sunday. κατὰ κυριακὴν δὲ κυρίου, "and on each Lord's day of the Lord." Distributive use of κατά (BDAG, κατά B2c: 512), *and on each of the Lord's own days.* • **συναχθέντες** — aor. pass. ptc. masc. nom. pl. → συνάγω, *I gather together.* • **κλάσατε** — aor. act. impv. 2 pl. → κλάω, *I break.* • **εὐχαριστήσατε** — aor. act. impv. 2 pl. → εὐχαριστέω, *I give thanks.* • **προεξομολογησάμενοι** — aor. mid. (depon.) ptc. masc. nom. pl. → προεξομολογέομαι, *I confess beforehand.* • **παραπτώματα** — acc. pl. → τὸ παράπτωμα, *offense, sin.* • **καθαρά** → καθαρός, ά, όν, *pure.* • **θυσία** → ἡ θυσία, *a sacrifice.* • **ᾖ** — pres. act. subjun. 3 sg. → εἰμί.

μὴ συνελθέτω ὑμῖν, ἕως οὗ διαλλαγῶσιν, ἵνα μὴ κοινωθῇ ἡ θυσία ὑμῶν. 14.3 αὕτη γάρ ἐστιν ἡ ῥηθεῖσα ὑπὸ Κυρίου· **Ἐν παντὶ τόπῳ καὶ χρόνῳ προσφέρειν μοι θυσίαν καθαράν· ὅτι βασιλεὺς μέγας εἰμί, λέγει Κύριος, καὶ τὸ ὄνομά μου θαυμαστὸν ἐν τοῖς ἔθνεσι.**

Didache 15 Some Gospel Admonitions

15.1 Χειροτονήσατε οὖν ἑαυτοῖς ἐπισκόπους καὶ διακόνους ἀξίους τοῦ Κυρίου, ἄνδρας πραεῖς καὶ ἀφιλαργύρους καὶ ἀληθεῖς καὶ δεδοκιμασμένους· ὑμῖν γὰρ λειτουργοῦσι καὶ αὐτοὶ τὴν λειτουργίαν τῶν προφητῶν καὶ διδασκάλων. 15.2 μὴ οὖν ὑπερίδητε αὐτούς· αὐτοὶ γάρ εἰσιν οἱ τετιμημένοι ὑμῶν μετὰ τῶν προφητῶν καὶ διδασκάλων. 15.3 Ἐλέγχετε δὲ ἀλλήλους μὴ ἐν ὀργῇ, ἀλλ᾿ ἐν εἰρήνῃ, ὡς ἔχετε ἐν τῷ εὐαγγελίῳ· καὶ παντὶ ἀστοχοῦντι κατὰ τοῦ ἑτέρου μηδεὶς λαλείτω μηδὲ παρ᾿ ὑμῶν ἀκουέτω, ἕως

14.2 **πᾶς . . . μή** — In such constructions English idiom negates the subj. rather than the verb, "no one . . . is to join." • **ἀμφιβολίαν** → ἡ ἀμφιβολία, *quarrel.* • **ἑταίρου** → ὁ ἑταῖρος, *companion.* • **συνελθέτω** — 2 aor. act. impv. 3 sg. → συνέρχομαι, *I join, come together with,* w. dat. • **ἕως οὗ** — *until.* • **διαλλαγῶσιν** — aor. act. subjun. 3 pl. → διαλλάσσω, *reconcile,* w. dat. Listed in BDAG as a depon. (διαλλάσσομαι), but act. in the aor. (διηλλάγην). • **κοινωθῇ** — aor. pass. subjun. 3 sg. → κοινόω, *make common/unclean, defile.*

14.3 **ῥηθεῖσα** — aor. pass. ptc. fem. nom. sg. → λέγω, *that which was spoken;* fem. in agreement w. θυσία. • **προσφέρειν** → προσφέρω, *I bring, offer, present.* Inf. for impv. (Smy: 2013). • **θαυμαστόν** → θαυμαστός, ή, όν, *wonderful, marvelous.* Pred. nom.

15.1 **χειροτονήσατε** — aor. act. impv. 2 pl. → χειροτονέω, *I choose for an office or task, appoint, install.* • **ἐπισκόπους** → ὁ ἐπίσκοπος, *bishop.* • **διακόνους** → ὁ διάκονος, *deacon.* • **ἀξίους** → ἄξιος, α, ον, *worthy.* • **πραεῖς** — masc. acc. pl. → πραΰς, πρεῖα, πραΰ, *gentle, humble.* • **ἀφιλαργύρους** → ἀφιλάργυρος, ον, *not loving money.* • **ἀληθεῖς** — masc. acc. pl. → ἀληθής, ές, *true.* • **δεδοκιμασμένους** — pf. pass. ptc. masc. acc. pl. → δοκιμάζω, *I examine; prove, approve.* • **λειτουργοῦσι** → λειτουργέω, *I minister, serve, perform a ministry/service,* esp. ritual and cultic service. • **λειτουργίαν** → ἡ λειτουργία, *ministry, service,* esp. ritual and cultic service. Cognate acc. (Wal: 189; Smy: 1563).

15.2 **ὑπερίδητε** — 2 aor. act. subjun. 2 pl. → ὑπεροράω, *I disdain, despise, overlook, disregard.* Prohibitive subjun., the equivalent of an impv. (Smy: 1800). • **τετιμημένοι** — pf. pass. ptc. masc. nom. pl. → τιμάω, *I honor.* οἱ τετιμημένοι ὑμῶν, *your honored ones.*

15.3 **ἐλέγχετε** → ἐλέγχω, *I convict, correct, reprove.* • **ὀργῇ** → ἡ ὀργή, *anger, wrath.* • **ἀστοχοῦντι** — pres. act. ptc. masc. dat. sg. → ἀστοχέω, *I miss, fail;* w. κατά, *wrong someone.* • **ἕως οὗ** — *until.* • **μετανοήσῃ** — aor. act. subjun. 3 sg. → μετανοέω, *repent.*

οὗ μετανοήσῃ. 15.4 τὰς δὲ εὐχὰς ὑμῶν καὶ τὰς ἐλεημοσύνας καὶ πάσας τὰς πράξεις οὕτως ποιήσατε, ὡς ἔχετε ἐν τῷ εὐαγγελίῳ τοῦ Κυρίου ἡμῶν.

Didache 16 Live in the Light of the Lord's Coming

16.1 **Γρηγορεῖτε** ὑπὲρ τῆς ζωῆς ὑμῶν· **οἱ λύχνοι ὑμῶν μὴ σβεσθήτωσαν, καὶ αἱ ὀσφύες ὑμῶν μὴ ἐκλυέσθωσαν, ἀλλὰ γίνεσθε ἕτοιμοι· οὐ γὰρ οἴδατε τὴν ὥραν, ἐν ᾗ ὁ Κύριος ἡμῶν ἔρχεται.** 16.2 πυκνῶς δὲ συναχθήσεσθε ζητοῦντες τὰ ἀνήκοντα ταῖς ψυχαῖς ὑμῶν. οὐ γὰρ ὠφελήσει ὑμᾶς ὁ πᾶς χρόνος τῆς πίστεως ὑμῶν, ἐὰν μὴ ἐν τῷ ἐσχάτῳ καιρῷ τελειωθῆτε.
16.3 ἐν γὰρ ταῖς ἐσχάταις ἡμέραις πληθυνθήσονται **οἱ ψευδοπροφῆται** καὶ οἱ φθορεῖς, καὶ στραφήσονται τὰ πρόβατα εἰς λύκους, καὶ ἡ ἀγάπη στραφήσεται εἰς μῖσος· 16.4 αὐξανούσης γὰρ τῆς ἀνομίας **μισήσουσιν ἀλλήλους καὶ διώξουσιν καὶ παραδώσουσι. καὶ τότε φανήσεται** ὁ κοσμοπλανὴς ὡς υἱὸς Θεοῦ καὶ **ποιήσει σημεῖα καὶ τέρατα** καὶ ἡ γῆ παραδοθήσεται εἰς

15.4 **εὐχάς** → ἡ εὐχή, *prayer.* • **ἐλεημοσύνας** → ἡ ἐλεημοσύνη, *alms, act of mercy.* • **πράξεις** — acc. pl. → ἡ πρᾶξις, *act, action, deed.*

16.1 **γρηγορεῖτε** → γρηγορέω, *I watch.* This verse contains two pres. impv. and two aor. impv., which provide good examples of the nuances of these tenses. A pres. impv. views an action as on-going. Here they are positive commands, "keep watching . . . be constantly prepared." An aor. impv. views the action as a whole and can include an ingressive idea, if the context warrants it (Wal: 717), as here, "do not let you lamps become quenched . . . do not let your loins become weakened." • **λύχνοι** → ὁ λύχνος, *lamp.* • **σβεσθήτωσαν** — aor. pass. impv. 3 pl. → σβέννυμι, *I quench, put out.* • **ὀσφύες** — nom. pl. → ἡ ὀσφῦς, *loins.* • **ἐκλυέσθωσαν** — pres. pass. impv. 3 p. → ἐκλύω, *I become weary/weak, give out.* • **ἕτοιμοι** → ἕτοιμος, η, ον, *ready.*

16.2 **πυκνῶς** — *frequently, often.* • **συναχθήσεσθε** — fut. pass. indic. 2 pl. → συνάγω, *I gather together.* • **ἀνήκοντα** — pres. act. ptc. neut. acc. pl. → ἀνήκω, *I refer, relate, belong.* • **ὠφελήσει** → ὠφελέω, *I aid, help.* • **ἐὰν μή** — *unless.* • **τελειωθῆτε** — aor. pass. subjun. 2 pl. → τελειόω, *I make perfect.*

16.3 **πληθυνθήσονται** — fut. pass. indic. 3 pl. → πληθύνω, *I increase, grow, multiply;* pass., *be multiplied, grow, increase.* • **ψευδοπροφῆται** → ὁ ψευδοπροφήτης, *false prophet.* • **φθορεῖς** — nom. pl. → ὁ φθορεύς, *seducer, corrupter.* • **στραφήσονται** — fut. pass. indic. 3 pl. → στρέφω, *I turn, change.* • **πρόβατα** → τὸ πρόβατον, *sheep.* • **λύκους** → ὁ λύκος, *wolf.* • **μῖσος** → τὸ μῖσος, *hatred, hate.*

16.4 **αὐξανούσης** — pres. act. ptc. fem. gen. sg. → αὐξάνω, *I grow, increase.* Gen. abs. • **ἀνομίας** → ἡ ἀνομία, *lawlessness.* Subj. of gen. abs. • **μισήσουσιν** → μισέω, *I hate.* • **διώξουσιν** → διώκω, *I persecute.* • **παραδώσουσι** — fut. act. indic. 3 pl. → παραδίδωμι, here, *I betray.* • **φανήσεται** — fut. pass. indic. 3 sg. → φαίνω, *I shine;* pass., *appear.* • **κοσμοπλανής** → ὁ κοσμοπλανής, *deceiver of the world.* • **τέρατα** — acc. pl. → τὸ τέρας, *wonder, omen, portent.* • **ἀθέμιτα** — neut. acc. pl. → ἀθέμιτος, ον, *forbidden, wanton, disgusting.* • **οὐδέποτε** — *never.*

χεῖρας αὐτοῦ, καὶ ποιήσει ἀθέμιτα, ἃ οὐδέποτε γέγονεν ἐξ αἰῶνος. 16.5 τότε ἥξει ἡ κτίσις τῶν ἀνθρώπων εἰς τὴν πύρωσιν τῆς δοκιμασίας, καὶ σκανδαλισθήσονται πολλοὶ καὶ ἀπολοῦνται, **οἱ δὲ ὑπομείναντες** ἐν τῇ πίστει αὐτῶν **σωθήσονται** ὑπ' αὐτοῦ τοῦ καταθέματος. 16.6 **καὶ τότε φανήσεται τὰ σημεῖα** τῆς ἀληθείας· πρῶτον σημεῖον ἐκπετάσεως ἐν οὐρανῷ, εἶτα σημεῖον φωνῆς σάλπιγγος, καὶ τὸ τρίτον ἀνάστασις νεκρῶν· 16.7 οὐ πάντων δέ, ἀλλ' ὡς ἐρρέθη· **Ἥξει ὁ Κύριος καὶ πάντες οἱ ἅγιοι μετ' αὐτοῦ.** 16.8 **τότε ὄψεται** ὁ κόσμος τὸν Κύριον **ἐρχόμενον ἐπάνω τῶν νεφελῶν τοῦ οὐρανοῦ.**

• **αἰῶνος** — here, *the past, earliest times.* ἐξ αἰῶνος, *since the beginning* (BDAG, αἰών 1a: 32).

16.5 **ἥξει** → ἥκω, *I have come, am present, come.* • **κτίσις** → ἡ κτίσις, *creation.* ἡ κτίσις τῶν ἀνθρώπων, "the creation of humans," i.e., the part of creation consisting of humanity. Gen. of explanation/appos. (Wal: 95; Smy: 1322). • **πύρωσιν** — acc. sg. → ἡ πύρωσις, *burning.* • **δοκιμασίας** → ἡ δοκιμασία, *testing, examination.* Perhaps an attributed gen. (Wal: 89), *the fiery test* (BDAG, πύρωσις 2: 900). • **σκανδαλισθήσονται** — fut. pass. indic. 3 pl. → σκανδαλίζω, *I cause to sin;* pass., *am led into sin, fall away.* • **ἀπολοῦνται** — fut. mid. indic. 3 pl. ἀπολῶ is an alternate liq. form of fut. → ἀπόλλυμι. • **ὑπομείναντες** — liq. aor. act. ptc. masc. nom. pl. → ὑπομένω, *I endure.* • **καταθέματος** — gen. sg. → τὸ κατάθεμα, *accursed thing.* ὑπ' αὐτοῦ τοῦ καταθέματος, *by him, the one accursed,* or *by the accursed one himself.*

16.6 **ἐκπετάσεως** — gen. sg. → ἡ ἐκπέτασις, *opening.* σημεῖον ἐκπετάσεως, "a sign which consists of an opening." Gen. of explanation/appos. (Wal: 95; Smy: 1322). • **εἶτα** — *then, next* (not to be confused w. εἴτε, *if, whether*). • **σάλπιγγος** — gen. sg. → ἡ σάλπιγξ, *trumpet.* • **ἀνάστασις** → ἡ ἀνάστασις, *resurrection.*

16.7 **ἐρρέθη** — aor. pass. indic. 3 sg. → λέγω.

16.8 **ὄψεται** — fut. mid. (depon.) 3 sg. → ὁράω. • **ἐπάνω** — *upon.* • **νεφελῶν** → ἡ νεφέλη, *cloud.*

Clement of Rome

1 Clement

Introduction

First Clement is a letter written late in the first century from the church in Rome to the church in Corinth to address a division that had taken place at Corinth. The saints in Corinth were as refractory at the end of the first century as they had been in the middle of the century, when Paul had to address several letters to them. The contrast Paul drew between arrogance and jealousy over against Christ-like humility and love is further emphasized and developed in profound ways in this lengthy letter.

Though it does not mention an author by name, later church fathers held that this letter was written in the name of the church at Rome by Clement, the third bishop of Rome, during the reign of the Emperor Domitian (81–96; Irenaeus, *Against Heresies* 3.3.3; Eusebius, *Hist. eccl.* 3.15–16; 4.23.11). While the text itself does not contradict this information, the description of leadership in the church (*1 Clem.* 40–44) describes a form of the office of bishop that many scholars believe would not have developed until the next decade or two—that of the bishop as the single chief person in authority.

The letter describes a situation in which some of the Corinthian Christians had rebelled against the leaders of the church (*1 Clem.* 3.3; 44.3, 6; 47.6), resulting in the rejection of these leaders and the fragmentation of the church. Paul had addressed problems of divisiveness in his two letters to Corinth and had faced the rejection of his own leadership by some in that church. Clement reminds them of their earlier factionalism over leaders (47.1–3) and takes them to task for rebelling against those whom the apostles had appointed (42–44).

Clement begins by praising the Corinthians for the exemplary form of Christian community they had modeled (*1 Clem.* 1–2), until jealousy had arisen to destroy their unity and harmony (3). Much of the long letter that follows is a contrast between jealousy and disharmony on the one hand, and love, humility, unity and order on the other. To make his point Clement includes extensive references to the Old Testament, as well as to Christian writings that would become part of the New Testament. He refers to forty-two different characters from the Old Testament to illustrate either the virtue of humility and obedience or the vice of jealousy and rebellion, and he cites texts from fifteen different books of the Old Testament. In one passage he quotes extensively from Isaiah 53 and Psalm 22 as he depicts Christ as the ultimate example of humility and obedience (16), echoing Paul's own lesson to the Corinthians regarding Christ, that "though he was rich, yet for your sake he became poor" (2 Cor 8:9, ESV). Along with these writings of the church, Clement also appeals to the order that is seen in nature, noting how each part fulfills its assigned role (19–20). In the church

God has likewise assigned different roles for clergy and laity, and each should fulfill their assigned role, especially with regard to worship (40–41). The divisions at Corinth are thus revealed to be against God's will as it is known from several sources.

Clement believes that God is speaking through him, and thus the Corinthians would be guilty of great sin if they were to disobey (*1 Clem.* 59.1). Clement has felt obligated to write (1.1), but it is unclear whether this is because some at Corinth have appealed to him, or whether he felt a responsibility to help a community in trouble (perhaps on the analogy of the spiritual person helping the one who has transgressed, Gal 6:1), or because he believes he has a responsibility due to his position of authority. Because *1 Clement* shows the church at Rome at a very early date correcting another church, it has played an important role in the later claims of universal jurisdiction and the primacy of the bishop of Rome. This evidence, however, can be read in more than one way, since *1 Clement* makes no reference to a bishop in Rome, let alone his primacy and universal jurisdiction, and the correction offered is limited to admonition and advice.

The selections included here are only a few of the many rich passages found in *1 Clement*. The first text selected, chapters 5–6, is of great historical importance, since it is the earliest reference we have to the martyrdom of Peter and Paul. The second selection, chapters 47–50, contains an example of Clement's appeal to the Corinthians for unity and illustrates some aspects of his use of the Old Testament and material that would become part of the New Testament. In the middle of this second selection is a beautiful description of love, echoing 1 Corinthians 13.

Edition used:	J. B. Lightfoot, rev., tran. *The Apostolic Fathers.* Edited and completed by J. R. Harmer. 1891. Repr., Berkeley, Calif.: Apocryphile, 2004.
Level of difficulty:	Easy [1–2]
Note:	Lightfoot uses square brackets to indicate doubtful readings.

1 Clement 5–6 The Deaths of Peter and Paul

5.1 Ἀλλ᾽ ἵνα τῶν ἀρχαίων ὑποδειγμάτων παυσώμεθα, ἔλθωμεν ἐπὶ τοὺς
ἔγγιστα γενομένους ἀθλητάς· λάβωμεν τῆς γενεᾶς ἡμῶν τὰ γενναῖα ὑπο-
δείγματα. 5.2 Διὰ ζῆλον καὶ φθόνον οἱ μέγιστοι καὶ δικαιότατοι στῦλοι
ἐδιώχθησαν καὶ ἕως θανάτου ἤθλησαν. 5.3 Λάβωμεν πρὸ ὀφθαλμῶν ἡμῶν
τοὺς ἀγαθοὺς ἀποστόλους· 5.4 Πέτρον, ὃς διὰ ζῆλον ἄδικον οὐχ ἕνα οὐδὲ
δύο ἀλλὰ πλείονας ὑπήνεγκεν πόνους, καὶ οὕτω μαρτυρήσας ἐπορεύθη εἰς
τὸν ὀφειλόμενον τόπον τῆς δόξης. 5.5 Διὰ ζῆλον καὶ ἔριν Παῦλος ὑπομονῆς βραβεῖον ὑπέδειξεν, 5.6 ἑπτάκις δεσμὰ φορέσας, φυγαδευθείς, λιθασθείς, κῆρυξ γενόμενος ἔν τε τῇ ἀνατολῇ καὶ ἐν τῇ δύσει, τὸ γενναῖον τῆς
πίστεως αὐτοῦ κλέος ἔλαβεν, 5.7 δικαιοσύνην διδάξας ὅλον τὸν κόσμον

5.1 **ἀρχαίων** → ἀρχαῖος, α, ον, *ancient, old.* • **ὑποδειγμάτων** → τὸ ὑπόδειγμα, *example.* • **παυσώμεθα** — aor. mid. subjun. → παύω, *I stop;* mid., *stop (oneself), cease,* w. gen. Here w. ἵνα for a purpose clause. • **ἔλθωμεν** — 2 aor. act. subjun. → ἔρχομαι. Hortatory subjun. (Wal: 464; Smy: 1797). • **ἔγγιστα** — adv., *a very short time ago, quite recently,* superlative of the adv. ἐγγύς (BDAG, ἐγγύς 2b: 271). • **γενομένους** — attrib. ptc. w. τούς, *those who were/became.* • **ἀθλητάς** → ὁ ἀθλητής, *athlete.* • **λάβωμεν** — 2 aor. act. subjun. → λαμβάνω. Hortatory subjun. • **γενεᾶς** → ἡ γενεά, *generation.* • **γενναῖα** → γενναῖος, α, ον, *noble, illustrious.*

5.2 **ζῆλον** → ὁ ζῆλος, *jealousy.* • **φθόνον** → ὁ φρόνος, *envy.* • **μέγιστοι** → μέγιστος, η, ον, *greatest, supreme,* superlative of μέγας, μεγάλη, μέγα. • **δικαιότατοι** → δικαιότατος, η, ον, *most righteous,* superlative of δίκαιος, α, ον. • **στῦλοι** → ὁ στῦλος, *pillar.* Cf. Gal 2:9; Rev 3:12. • **ἐδιώχθησαν** → διώκω, *I persecute.* • **ἤθλησαν** → ἀθλέω, *I compete, contend.*

5.3 **λάβωμεν** → λαμβάνω, here w. πρό, *set.* • **πρό** — prep., *before.*

5.4 **Πέτρον** → ὁ Πέτρος, *Peter.* • **ἄδικον** → ἄδικος, ον, *unjust.* • **ὑπήνεγκεν** — aor. act. indic. 3 sg. → ὑποφέρω, *I submit to, endure.* • **πόνους** → ὁ πόνος, *affliction.* • **οὕτω** → οὕτως. • **μαρτυρήσας** → μαρτυρέω, *I bear witness.* Circ. ptc. • **ὀφειλόμενον** → ὀφείλω, *I owe;* here, *which he deserved* (BDAG 2aα: 743).

5.5 **ἔριν** → ἡ ἔρις, *strife.* • **Παῦλος** → ὁ Παῦλος, *Paul.* • **ὑπομονῆς** → ἡ ὑπομονή, *patience, endurance.* • **βραβεῖον** → τὸ βραβεῖον, *a prize.* • **ὑπέδειξεν** — aor. act. indic. → ὑποδείκνυμι, *I point out; show, set forth.* Holmes's text puts this word in brackets, while Ehrman's text has ἔδειξεν (aor. → δείκνυμι, *show*).

5.6 **ἑπτάκις** — adv., *seven times.* • **δεσμά** — irregular pl. → ὁ δεσμός, *chain.* • **φορέσας** — aor. act. ptc. → φορέω, *I bear constantly/regularly, wear frequently.* • **φυγαδευθείς** — aor. pass. ptc. → φυγαδεύω, *I banish from a country, send into exile.* • **λιθασθείς** — aor. pass. ptc. → λιθάζω, *I stone.* • **κῆρυξ** → ὁ κῆρυξ, *herald.* • **ἔν** — prep. ἐν, accented due to the following enclitic. • **ἀνατολῇ** → ἡ ἀνατολή, *east.* • **δύσει** → ἡ δύσις, *west.* • **γενναῖον** — here mod. κλέος. • **κλέος** → τὸ κλέος, *fame, glory.* τῆς πίστεως αὐτοῦ κλέος, *renown for his faith* (BDAG, γενναῖος: 193).

καὶ ἐπὶ τὸ τέρμα τῆς δύσεως ἐλθών· καὶ μαρτυρήσας ἐπὶ τῶν ἡγουμένων, οὕτως ἀπηλλάγη τοῦ κόσμου καὶ εἰς τὸν ἅγιον τόπον ἐπορεύθη, ὑπομονῆς γενόμενος μέγιστος ὑπογραμμός.

6.1 Τούτοις τοῖς ἀνδράσιν ὁσίως πολιτευσαμένοις συνηθροίσθη πολὺ πλῆθος ἐκλεκτῶν, οἵτινες πολλαῖς αἰκίαις καὶ βασάνοις, διὰ ζῆλος παθόντες, ὑπόδειγμα κάλλιστον ἐγένοντο ἐν ἡμῖν. 6.2 Διὰ ζῆλος διωχθεῖσαι γυναῖκες, Δαναΐδες καὶ Δίρκαι, αἰκίσματα δεινὰ καὶ ἀνόσια παθοῦσαι, ἐπὶ τὸν τῆς πίστεως βέβαιον δρόμον κατήντησαν καὶ ἔλαβον γέρας γενναῖον αἱ ἀσθενεῖς τῷ σώματι. 6.3 ζῆλος ἀπηλλοτρίωσεν γαμετὰς ἀνδρῶν καὶ ἠλλοίωσεν τὸ ῥηθὲν ὑπὸ τοῦ πατρὸς ἡμῶν Ἀδάμ, **Τοῦτο νῦν ὀστοῦν ἐκ**

5.7 **διδάξας** — aor. act. ptc. → δίδασκω. W. double acc. of person and thing (Wal: 181; Smy: 1620). • **τέρμα** → τὸ τέρμα, *end, limit, boundary.* • **ἐλθών** — aor. act. ptc. → ἔρχομαι. • **ἡγουμένων** — pres. mid. (depon.) ptc. → ἡγέομαι, *I lead.* Attrib. ptc. for "leaders/rulers." • **ἀπηλλάγη** — 2 aor. pass. indic. 3 sg. → ἀπαλλάσσω, *I set free; leave, depart,* w. gen. • **ἐπορεύθη** — Ehrman's text has ἀνελήμφθη (aor. pass. → ἀναλαμβάνω, *I take up*). • **ὑπομονῆς** → ἡ ὑπομονή, *patient endurance.* Mod. ὑπογραμμός. • **ὑπογραμμός** → ὁ ὑπογραμμός, *example.*

6.1 **ὁσίως** — adv., *devoutly, in a holy manner.* • **πολιτευσαμένοις** → πολιτεύω, *I live, lead one's life;* mid. w. act. sense. • **συνηθροίσθη** → συναθροίζω, *I gather; unite with, am joined to;* pass. w. act. sense. • **πολύ** → πολύς, πολλή, πολύ, here, *great.* • **πλῆθος** → τὸ πλῆθος, *multitude.* • **ἐκλεκτῶν** → ἐκλεκτός, ή, όν, *chosen, elect.* • **οἵτινες** → ὅστις. • **αἰκίαις** → ἡ αἰκία, *injurious treatment, torture.* Perhaps dat. of instrument (BDAG, πάσχω 3aβ: 785). Ehrman's text has acc., πολλὰς αἰκίας καὶ βασάνους. • **βασάνοις** → ἡ βάσανος, *inquiry by torture, torture, torment.* • **ζῆλος** → ὁ ζῆλος, *jealousy.* This noun is also found, as here, as a neut. (BDAG: 427). • **παθόντες** — 2 aor. act. ptc. → πάσχω, *I suffer.* • **ὑπόδειγμα** → τὸ ὑπόδειγμα, *example.* • **κάλλιστον** → κάλλιστος, η, ον, *most beautiful, exquisite,* superlative of καλός.

6.2 **διωχθεῖσαι** — aor. pass. ptc. → διώκω, *I persecute.* Circ. ptc., either temp. or attend. circ. • **Δαναΐδες** → αἱ Δαναΐδες, *the Danaids.* • **Δίρκαι** → ἡ Δίρκη, *Dirce.* Both nom. are in appos. to γυναῖκες. • **αἰκίσματα** → τὸ αἴκισμα, *mistreatment, torment.* • **δεινά** → δεινός, η, ον, *terrible.* • **ἀνόσια** → ἀνόσιος, ον, *unholy.* • **παθοῦσαι** — 2 aor. act. ptc. → πάσχω. Either a second circ. ptc. or an attrib. ptc. mod. (and explaining) Δαναΐδες καὶ Δίρκαι, *"Danaids and Dirces" who suffered terrible and unholy torments.* • **βέβαιον** → βέβαιος, α, ον, *reliable, steadfast;* here perhaps as an adv. (Wal: 200; Smy: 1606), "*steadfastly finish the course of faith*" (BDAG 2: 172) or "*they securely reached the goal in the race of faith*" (BDAG, δρόμος 1: 261). • **δρόμον** → ὁ δρόμος, *course, race.* • **κατήντησαν** → καταντάω, *I arrive, reach, attain.* • **ἔλαβον** — 2 aor. act. indic. → λαμβάνω. • **γέρας** → τὸ γέρας, *a prize, reward.* • **γενναῖον** → γενναῖος, α, ον, *noble, illustrious* • **ἀσθενεῖς** → ἀσθενής, ές, *weak.*

6.3 **ἀπηλλοτρίωσεν** → ἀπαλλοτριόω, *estrange, alienate.* • **γαμετάς** → ἡ γαμετή, *wife.* • **ἀνδρῶν** — gen. of separation (Wal: 107; Smy: 1392), *from husbands.* • **ἠλλοίωσεν** → ἀλλοιόω, *I change.* • **ῥηθέν** — aor. pass. ptc. neut. acc. sg. →

τῶν ὀστέων μου καὶ σὰρξ ἐκ τῆς σαρκός μου. 6.4 ζῆλος καὶ ἔρις πόλεις μεγάλας κατέστρεψεν καὶ ἔθνη μεγάλα ἐξερίζωσεν.

1 Clement 47–50 Love

47.1 Ἀναλάβετε τὴν ἐπιστολὴν τοῦ μακαρίου Παύλου τοῦ ἀποστόλου.
47.2 τί πρῶτον ὑμῖν ἐν ἀρχῇ τοῦ εὐαγγελίου ἔγραψεν; 47.3 ἐπ' ἀληθείας
πνευματικῶς ἐπέστειλεν ὑμῖν περὶ αὐτοῦ τε καὶ Κηφᾶ τε καὶ Ἀπολλώ, διὰ
τὸ καὶ τότε προσκλίσεις ὑμᾶς πεποιῆσθαι· 47.4 ἀλλ' ἡ πρόσκλισις ἐκείνη
ἧττονα ἁμαρτίαν ὑμῖν προσήνεγκεν· προσεκλίθητε γὰρ ἀποστόλοις μεμαρτυρημένοις καὶ ἀνδρὶ δεδοκιμασμένῳ παρ' αὐτοῖς. 47.5 νυνὶ δὲ κατανοήσατε
τίνες ὑμᾶς διέστρεψαν καὶ τὸ σεμνὸν τῆς περιβοήτου φιλαδελφίας ὑμῶν

εἶπον (λέγω). • **Ἀδάμ** → ὁ Ἀδάμ, *Adam*. Cf. Gen 2:23. • **ὀστοῦν** → τὸ ὀστοῦν (listed in lexicons under its alternate uncontracted form ὀστέον), *bone*.

6.4 **ἔρις** → ἡ ἔρις, *strife*. • **κατέστρεψεν** → καταστρέφω, *I upset, overturn; destroy, ruin*. Sg. verb w. a comp. subj. (Wal: 401, Smy: 968). • **ἐξερίζωσεν** → ἐκριζόω, *I uproot*.

47.1 **ἀναλάβετε** — aor. → ἀναλαμβάνω, *I take up*. • **ἐπιστολήν** → ἡ ἐπιστολή, *letter*.

47.2 **πρῶτον** — neut. sg. for adv., *first, earlier, before, to begin with* (BDAG 1aβ: 893). • **ἔγραψεν** — aor. → γράφω.

47.3 **ἐπ' ἀληθείας** — *in accordance with the truth, truly, in truth and reality* (LSI I3: 34; BDAG, ἀλήθεια 3: 43). • **πνευματικῶς** — *spiritually, in a spiritual way/manner; full of the* (divine) *Spirit* (BDAG 2: 837). • **ἐπέστειλεν** — aor. → ἐπιστέλλω, *I send a letter*. • **αὐτοῦ** — Ehrman's text has ἑαυτοῦ. • **Κηφᾶ** — gen. → ὁ Κηφᾶς, *Cephas*, i.e., Peter. • **Ἀπολλώ** — gen. → ὁ Ἀπολλῶς, *Apollos*. • **διὰ τό** — w. inf. for cause (Wal: 596). • **καί** — ascensive use, *even*. • **προσκλίσεις** — acc. pl. → ἡ πρόσκλισις, *inclination; partisan strife* (BDAG: 881). • **πεποιῆσθαι** — In the mid. ποιέω means to *I make/do something for myself* or *of myself* (BDAG 7a: 841). The meaning "make" can be rendered *you had split into factions* (Holmes), while "do" can yield *you were . . . engaged in partisanship* (Ehrman).

47.4 **ἧττονα** — fem. acc. sg. → ἥττων, ον (also appears as ἥσσων, ον), *lesser*. Holmes's text has the neut. acc. sg. ἧττον, but translates it as an adj. mod. ἁμαρτίαν, "less sin." • **προσήνεγκεν** — aor. → προσφέρω, *I bring to/upon*. • **προσεκλίθητε** — aor. pass → προσκλίνω, *I incline towards; split into factions over, am partisan towards*, w. dat. • **μεμαρτυρημένοις** — pf. ptc., in pass., *I approved, of good reputation* (BDAG 2b: 618). The ref. is to Peter and Paul (1 Cor 1:12). • **δεδοκιμασμένῳ** — pf. ptc. → δοκιμάζω, *I prove by testing, approve*. The ref. is to Apollos (1 Cor 1:12).

47.5 **νυνί** — *now*. • **κατανοήσατε** — aor. impv. → κατανοέω, *I notice, consider, think about*. • **τίνες** — "*who?* in the sense, *what sort of person?*" (BDAG 1aב: 1007). • **διέστρεψαν** — aor. → διαστρέφω, *I turn about, deform, pervert, mislead*. • **σεμνόν** → σεμνός, ή, όν, *worthy of respect*; here subst., *respect*. • **περιβοήτου** — περιβόητος, ον, *much talked about, famous*. • **φιλαδελφίας** → ἡ φιλαδελφία, *love of brother*. • **ἐμείωσαν** — aor. → μειόω, *I diminish*.

ἐμείωσαν. 47.6 αἰσχρά, ἀγαπητοί, καὶ λίαν αἰσχρά, καὶ ἀνάξια τῆς ἐν Χριστῷ ἀγωγῆς, ἀκούεσθαι τὴν βεβαιοτάτην καὶ ἀρχαίαν Κορινθίων ἐκκλησίαν δι᾽ ἓν ἢ δύο πρόσωπα στασιάζειν πρὸς τοὺς πρεσβυτέρους. 47.7 καὶ αὕτη ἡ ἀκοὴ οὐ μόνον εἰς ἡμᾶς ἐχώρησεν ἀλλὰ καὶ εἰς τοὺς ἑτεροκλινεῖς ὑπάρχοντας ἀφ᾽ ἡμῶν, ὥστε καὶ βλασφημίας ἐπιφέρεσθαι τῷ ὀνόματι Κυρίου διὰ τὴν ὑμετέραν ἀφροσύνην, ἑαυτοῖς δὲ κίνδυνον ἐπεξεργάζεσθαι.

48.1 Ἐξάρωμεν οὖν τοῦτο ἐν τάχει καὶ προσπέσωμεν τῷ δεσπότῃ καὶ κλαύσωμεν ἱκετεύοντες αὐτόν, ὅπως ἵλεως γενόμενος ἐπικαταλλαγῇ ἡμῖν καὶ ἐπὶ τὴν σεμνὴν τῆς φιλαδελφίας ἡμῶν ἁγνὴν ἀγωγὴν ἀποκαταστήσῃ ἡμᾶς. 48.2 πύλη γὰρ δικαιοσύνης ἀνεῳγυῖα εἰς ζωὴν αὕτη, καθὼς γέγραπται· **Ἀνοίξατέ μοι πύλας δικαιοσύνης· ἵνα εἰσελθὼν ἐν αὐταῖς ἐξομολο-**

47.6 **αἰσχρά** → αἰσχρός, ά, όν, *shameful.* • **καί** — emphatic use, *indeed.* • **λίαν** — *very, exceedingly.* • **ἀνάξια** → ἀνάξιος, ον, *unworthy,* w. gen. • **ἀγωγῆς** → ἡ ἀγωγή, *way of life, conduct.* • **ἀκούεσθαι** — the subj. of the sentence, the core of which is, lit., "to be heard is shameful." English usually uses a preparatory "it" for this use of the inf. (Nunn: 24), "it is shameful that . . ." • **βεβαιοτάτην** → βεβαιότατης, superlative of βέβαιος, α, ον, *firm, reliable, abiding;* here, *well-established, dependable* (BDAG 2: 172). • **ἀρχαίαν** → ἀρχαῖος, α, ον, *ancient.* • **Κορινθίων** → ὁ Κορίνθιος, *Corinthian.* • **ἐκκλησίαν** — the subj. of the content clause after ἀκούεσθαι. The acc. is used due to the inf., στασιάζειν, for indir. disc. • **πρόσωπα** — here, *person* (BDAG 2: 888). • **στασιάζειν** → στασιάζω, *I rebel.* Inf. for indir. disc. (Wal: 603; Smy: 2016). • **πρός** — here, *against* (LSI CI4: 684; BDAG 3d: 874).

47.7 **ἀκοή** — *report.* • **ἐχώρησεν** — aor. → χωρέω, *I am spread abroad, reach.* • **ἑτεροκλινεῖς** — masc. acc. pl. → ἑτεροκλινής, ές, *leaning;* here, *having other allegiance* (BDAG: 399). "Those who are leaning from us" may be taken as *those who stand opposed to us* (Ehrman) or *those who differ from us* (Holmes). • **βλασφημίας** — acc. pl. → ἡ βλασφημία, *blasphemy.* The subj. of ἐπιφέρεσθαι in this result clause. • **ἐπιφέρεσθαι** → ἐπιφέρω, *I bring/lay upon.* • **ὑμετέραν** → ὑμέτερος, α, ον, *your.* • **ἀφροσύνην** → ἡ ἀφροσύνη, *foolishness, senselessness.* • **κίνδυνον** → ὁ κίνδυνος, *danger.* • **ἐπεξεργάζεσθαι** → ἐπεξεργάζομαι, *I produce in addition, cause besides.*

48.1 **ἐξάρωμεν** — aor. subjun. → ἐξαίρω, *I lift up/off, remove,* hortatory. • **τάχει** — dat. → τὸ τάχος, *speed.* ἐν τάχει, *quickly* (BDAG, τάχος 1: 992). • **προσπέσωμεν** — aor. subjun. → προσπίπτω, *I fall down before.* Hortatory, w. dat. • **δεσπότῃ** → ὁ δεσπότης, *master.* • **κλαύσωμεν** — aor. subjun. → κλαίω, *I weep,* hortatory. • **ἱκετεύοντες** — pres. ptc. → ἱκετεύω, *I approach as a suppliant, beseech, pray.* • **ἵλεως** → ἵλεως, ων, *gracious.* • **ἐπικαταλλαγῇ** — aor. pass. subjun. → ἐπικαταλλάσσομαι, *I am reconciled to someone.* • **σεμνήν** → σεμνός, ή, όν, *venerable, respectable, honorable.* • **φιλαδελφίας** → ἡ φιλαδελφία, *love of brother.* • **ἁγνήν** → ἁγνός, ή, όν, *pure.* • **ἀγωγήν** → ἡ ἀγωγή, *way of life, conduct.* • **ἀποκαταστήσῃ** — aor. subjun. → ἀποκαθίστημι, *I restore.*

48.2 **πύλη** — *gate.* • **ἀνεῳγυῖα** — pf. act. ptc. → ἀνοίγω (a byform of ἀνοίγνυμι), *I open.* • **ἀνοίξατε** — aor. impv. → ἀνοίγω. Cf. Ps 118:19–20 (LXX, 117:19–20). • **εἰσελθών** — 2 aor. ptc. → εἰσέρχομαι. • **ἐξομολογήσωμαι** — aor. mid.

γήσωμαι τῷ Κυρίῳ. 48.3 **Αὕτη ἡ πύλη τοῦ Κυρίου, δίκαιοι εἰσελεύσονται ἐν αὐτῇ.** 48.4 Πολλῶν οὖν πυλῶν ἀνεῳγυιῶν, ἡ ἐν δικαιοσύνῃ αὕτη ἐστὶν ἡ ἐν Χριστῷ, ἐν ᾗ μακάριοι πάντες οἱ εἰσελθόντες καὶ κατευθύνοντες τὴν πορείαν αὐτῶν ἐν ὁσιότητι καὶ δικαιοσύνῃ, ἀταράχως πάντα ἐπιτελοῦντες. 48.5 ἤτω τις πιστός, ἤτω δυνατὸς γνῶσιν ἐξειπεῖν, ἤτω σοφὸς ἐν διακρίσει λόγων, ἤτω γοργὸς ἐν ἔργοις, ἤτω ἁγνός. 48.6 τοσούτῳ γὰρ μᾶλλον ταπεινοφρονεῖν ὀφείλει, ὅσῳ δοκεῖ μᾶλλον μείζων εἶναι, καὶ ζητεῖν τὸ κοινωφελὲς πᾶσιν καὶ μὴ τὸ ἑαυτοῦ.

49.1 Ὁ ἔχων ἀγάπην ἐν Χριστῷ ποιησάτω τὰ τοῦ Χριστοῦ παραγγέλματα. 49.2 τὸν δεσμὸν τῆς ἀγάπης τοῦ Θεοῦ τίς δύναται ἐξηγήσασθαι; 49.3 τὸ μεγαλεῖον τῆς καλλονῆς αὐτοῦ τίς ἀρκετὸς ἐξειπεῖν; 49.4 τὸ ὕψος εἰς ὃ

(depon.) subjun. → ἐξομολογέομαι, *I acknowledge, praise.* Ehrman's text has the fut. ἐξομολογήσομαι and omits the ἵνα.

48.4 **ἀνεῳγυιῶν** — concessive ptc., *although having opened.* Gen. abs. • **ἡ ἐν δικαιοσύνῃ** — pred. nom. of ἐστίν. • **ἡ ἐν Χριστῷ** — in appos. to ἡ ἐν δικαιοσύνῃ. • **κατευθύνοντες** → κατευθύνω, *I make/keep straight, direct.* • **πορείαν** → ἡ πορεία, *journey, path.* • **ὁσιότητι** → ἡ ὁσιότης, *holiness, piety.* • **ἀταράχως** — *without confusion/disturbance.* • **ἐπιτελοῦντες** → ἐπιτελέω, *I complete, accomplish.*

48.5 **ἤτω** — pres. act. impv. 3 sg. → εἰμί. • **πιστός** → πιστός, ή, όν, *faithful.* • **δυνατός** → δυνατός, ή, όν, *able, capable.* • **γνῶσιν** — acc. sg. → ἡ γνῶσις, *knowledge.* • **ἐξειπεῖν** — 2 aor. inf. → ἐξεῖπον (used for the aor. of ἐξαγορεύω, see LSJ or BDAG), *I speak forth, declare, expound.* • **σοφός** → σοφός, ή, όν, *wise.* • **διακρίσει** — dat. sg. → ἡ διάκρισις, *distinguishing; interpretation.* Cf. 1 Cor 14:29. • **γοργός** → γοργός, ή, όν, *vigorous, strenuous.* Instead of ἤτω γοργὸς ἐν ἔργοις, ἤτω ἁγνός, Ehrman's text has ἤτω ἁγνὸς ἐν ἔργοις.

48.6 **τοσούτῳ** → τοσοῦτος, τοσαύτη, τοσοῦτον, *so much.* Used with the comparative μᾶλλον, and correlative with ὅσος, *by so much more . . . the more.* "For by as much more ought he to be humble, the more he seems to be great," that is, as much as a person appears to be great, all the more he ought to be humble. Cf. Smy: 2468–77; BDAG 5: 1012. • **ταπεινοφρονεῖν** → ταπεινοφρονέω, *I am humble.* • **ὀφείλει** → ὀφείλω, *I ought.* • **δοκεῖ** → δοκέω, *I think, seem, appear to be, am reputed to be.* • **μείζων** → μείζων, ον, comparative of μέγας, *greater, more.* • **κοινωφελές** → κοινωφελής, ές, *generally useful, of common use;* here, *seek the common good of all* (BDAG: 554).

49.1 **ποιησάτω** — aor. impv. → ποιέω. • **παραγγέλματα** → τὸ παράγγελμα, *instruction, precept.*

49.2 **δεσμόν** → ὁ δεσμός, *bond.* • **ἐξηγήσασθαι** — aor. inf. → ἐξηγέομαι, *I explain.*

49.3 **μεγαλεῖον** → μεγαλεῖος, α, ον, *magnificent, splendid;* here subst., *magnificence.* • **καλλονῆς** → ἡ καλλονή, *beauty.* • **ἀρκετός** → ἀρκετός, ή, όν, *sufficient, adequate.* • **ἐξειπεῖν** — 2 aor. inf. → ἐξεῖπον, *I speak forth, declare, expound.* See note at 48.5.

49.4 **ὕψος** → τὸ ὕψος, *height.* • **ἀνάγει** → ἀνάγω, *I lead up.* • **ἀνεκδιήγητον** → ἀνεκδιήγητος, ον, *indescribable, ineffable.* Cf. 2 Cor 9:15.

ἀνάγει ἡ ἀγάπη ἀνεκδιήγητόν ἐστιν. 49.5 ἀγάπη κολλᾷ ἡμᾶς τῷ Θεῷ· **ἀγάπη καλύπτει πλῆθος ἁμαρτιῶν·** ἀγάπη πάντα ἀνέχεται, πάντα μακροθυμεῖ· οὐδὲν βάναυσον ἐν ἀγάπῃ, οὐδὲν ὑπερήφανον· ἀγάπη σχίσμα οὐκ ἔχει, ἀγάπη οὐ στασιάζει, ἀγάπη πάντα ποιεῖ ἐν ὁμονοίᾳ· ἐν τῇ ἀγάπῃ ἐτελειώθησαν πάντες οἱ ἐκλεκτοὶ τοῦ Θεοῦ· δίχα ἀγάπης οὐδὲν εὐάρεστόν ἐστιν τῷ Θεῷ. 49.6 ἐν ἀγάπῃ προσελάβετο ἡμᾶς ὁ δεσπότης· διὰ τὴν ἀγάπην, ἣν ἔσχεν πρὸς ἡμᾶς, τὸ αἷμα αὐτοῦ ἔδωκεν ὑπὲρ ἡμῶν Ἰησοῦς Χριστὸς ὁ Κύριος ἡμῶν ἐν θελήματι Θεοῦ, καὶ τὴν σάρκα ὑπὲρ τῆς σαρκὸς ἡμῶν καὶ τὴν ψυχὴν ὑπὲρ τῶν ψυχῶν ἡμῶν.

50.1 Ὁρᾶτε, ἀγαπητοί, πῶς μέγα καὶ θαυμαστόν ἐστιν ἡ ἀγάπη, καὶ τῆς τελειότητος αὐτῆς οὐκ ἐστὶν ἐξήγησις· 50.2 τίς ἱκανὸς ἐν αὐτῇ εὑρεθῆναι, εἰ μὴ οὓς ἂν καταξιώσῃ ὁ Θεός; δεώμεθα οὖν καὶ αἰτώμεθα ἀπὸ τοῦ ἐλέους αὐτοῦ, ἵνα ἐν ἀγάπῃ εὑρεθῶμεν δίχα προσκλίσεως ἀνθρωπίνης ἄμωμοι. 50.3 Αἱ γενεαὶ πᾶσαι ἀπὸ Ἀδὰμ ἕως τῆσδε [τῆς] ἡμέρας παρῆλθον, ἀλλ' οἱ ἐν ἀγάπῃ τελειωθέντες κατὰ τὴν τοῦ Θεοῦ χάριν ἔχουσιν χῶρον εὐσεβῶν·

49.5 **κολλᾷ** → κολλάω, *I glue, bind closely, unite.* • **καλύπτει** → καλύπτω, *I cover.* Cf. 1 Pet 4:8. • **πλῆθος** → τὸ πλῆθος, *great number, multitude.* • **ἀνέχεται** → ἀνέχω, *I endure.* • **μακροθυμεῖ** → μακροθυμέω, *I am patient.* W. πάντα as acc. of respect (Wal: 203; Smy: 1600), *in all things, about everything.* • **βάναυσον** → βάναυσος, ον, *vulgar, coarse.* • **ὑπερήφανον** → ὑπερήφανος, ον, *haughty, arrogant.* • **σχίσμα** → τὸ σχίσμα, *schism.* • **ἔχει** — here, *cause* (BDAG 8: 422). • **στασιάζει** → στασιάζω, *I revolt, rebel.* • **ὁμονοίᾳ** → ἡ ὁμόνοια, *oneness of mind or thought, harmony.* • **ἐτελειώθησαν** — aor. pass. → τελειόω, *I make perfect/complete.* • **ἐκλεκτοί** → ἐκλεκτός, ή, όν, *chosen, elect.* • **δίχα** — *apart from, without,* w. gen. • **εὐάρεστον** → εὐάρεστος, ον, *well-pleasing.*

49.6 **προσελάβετο** — 2 aor. mid. → προσλαμβάνω, mid., *I receive.* • **δεσπότης** → ὁ δεσπότης, *master.* • **ἔσχεν** — aor. → ἔχω. • **τὴν σάρκα . . . τὴν ψυχήν** — good examples of the use of the art. for a poss. (Wal: 215; Smy: 1121).

50.1 **θαυμαστόν** → θαυμαστός, ή, όν, *marvelous, amazing.* • **τελειότητος** → ἡ τελειότης, *completeness, perfection.* • **ἐξήγησις** → ἡ ἐξήγησις, *description, interpretation.*

50.2 **ἱκανός** → ἱκανός, ή, όν, *adequate, fit, qualified.* • **εὑρεθῆναι** — aor. pass. inf. → εὑρίσκω. • **εἰ μή** — *except.* • **καταξιώσῃ** — aor. subjun. act. → καταξιόω, *I consider worthy.* • **δεώμεθα** → δέομαι, *I plead, implore.* Hortatory subjun. • **ἐλέους** → τὸ ἔλεος, *mercy.* • **δίχα** — *apart from, without.* • **προσκλίσεως** → ἡ πρόσκλισις, *inclination; partisan strife* (BDAG: 881). • **ἀνθρωπίνης** → ἀνθρώπινος, ή, όν, *human.* • **ἄμωμοι** → ἄμωμος, ον, *blameless.*

50.3 **γενεαί** → ἡ γενεά, *generation.* • **Ἀδάμ** → ὁ Ἀδάμ, indecl., *Adam.* • **τῆσδε** — fem. gen. sg. → ὅδε, ἥδε, τόδε, *this.* • **[τῆς]** — Ehrman's text does not have this word, while Holmes's text retains it without brackets. • **παρῆλθον** — aor. → παρέρχομαι, *I pass away.* • **τελειωθέντες** — aor. pass. ptc. → τελειόω, *I make complete/perfect.* • **κατά** — here, *because of, on the basis of* (BDAG B5aδ: 512, cf. LSJ BV: 403). • **χῶρον** → ὁ χῶρος, *place.* • **εὐσεβῶν** → εὐσεβής, ές, *pious,*

οἳ φανερωθήσονται ἐν τῇ ἐπισκοπῇ τῆς βασιλείας τοῦ Θεοῦ. 50.4 γέγραπται γάρ· **Εἰσέλθετε εἰς τὰ ταμεῖα μικρὸν ὅσον ὅσον, ἕως οὗ παρέλθῃ ἡ ὀργὴ καὶ ὁ θυμός μου, καὶ μνησθήσομαι ἡμέρας ἀγαθῆς καὶ ἀναστήσω ὑμᾶς ἐκ τῶν θηκῶν ὑμῶν.** 50.5 Μακάριοι ἦμεν, ἀγαπητοί, εἰ τὰ προστάγματα τοῦ Θεοῦ ἐποιοῦμεν ἐν ὁμονοίᾳ ἀγάπης, εἰς τὸ ἀφεθῆναι ἡμῖν δι' ἀγάπης τὰς ἁμαρτίας. 50.6 γέγραπται γάρ· **Μακάριοι ὧν ἀφέθησαν αἱ ἀνομίαι καὶ ὧν ἐπεκαλύφθησαν αἱ ἁμαρτίαι· μακάριος ἀνὴρ οὗ οὐ μὴ λογίσηται Κύριος ἁμαρτίαν, οὐδέ ἐστιν ἐν τῷ στόματι αὐτοῦ δόλος.** 50.7 Οὗτος ὁ μακαρισμὸς ἐγένετο ἐπὶ τοὺς ἐκλελεγμένους ὑπὸ τοῦ Θεοῦ διὰ Ἰησοῦ Χριστοῦ τοῦ Κυρίου ἡμῶν, ᾧ ἡ δόξα εἰς τοὺς αἰῶνας τῶν αἰώνων. ἀμήν.

---

reverent, godly. With/among the godly. Gen. of association (Wal: 128). • **φανερωθήσονται** → φανερόω, *I make manifest, reveal.* • **ἐπισκοπῇ** → ἡ ἐπισκοπή, *visitation.* • **Θεοῦ** — The texts of Holmes and Ehrman have Χριστοῦ.

50.4 **εἰσέλθετε** → εἰσέρχομαι. • **ταμεῖα** → τὸ ταμεῖον, *inner room* • **μικρόν** → μικρός, ά, όν, *small, short.* μικρὸν ὅσον ὅσον, *for a very little while* (BDAG 1b: 729). Acc. of extent of time (Wal: 201; Smy: 1582). Cf. Isa 26:20; Heb 10:37. • **ἕως οὗ** — *until.* • **ὀργή** → ἡ ὀργή, *wrath, anger.* • **θυμός** → ὁ θυμός, *wrath, anger.* • **μνησθήσομαι** → μιμνήσκομαι, *I remember,* w. gen. • **θηκῶν** → ἡ θήκη, *grave.* Cf. Ezek 37:12.

50.5 **ἦμεν** — The texts of Ehrman and Holmes have ἐσμεν. • **προστάγματα** → τὸ πρόσταγμα, *commandment.* • **ὁμονοίᾳ** → ἡ ὁμόνοια, *oneness of mind or thought, harmony.* • **ἀφεθῆναι** — aor. pass. inf. → ἀφίημι. W. εἰς τό for a purpose or result clause. • **τὰς ἁμαρτίας** — subj. of inf.; def. art. for poss., *our sins* (Wal: 215; Smy: 1121).

50.6 **ἀνομίαι** → ἡ ἀνομία, *lawlessness, sin.* • **ἐπεκαλύφθησαν** → ἐπικαλύπτω, *I cover over.* • **λογίσηται** → λογίζομαι, *I reckon, count, take into account.* Subjun. with οὐ μή for emphatic negation (Wal: 468; BDAG, μή 4: 646). • **δόλος** → ὁ δόλος, *deceit.* Cf. Ps 32:1–2 (LXX, 31:1–2); Rom 4:7–8.

50.7 **μακαρισμός** → ὁ μακαρισμός, *blessing.* • **ἐκλελεγμένους** → ἐκλέγομαι, *I choose.*

Ignatius of Antioch

To the Romans

Introduction

Ignatius, bishop of Antioch (in Syria), was intense! The seven letters we have from him reflect this intensity, which is not surprising since they were written as he was traveling to Rome to face execution for being a Christian. These letters are historically significant since they are among our few witnesses to the life and thought of the church immediately after most, if not all, of the New Testament had been written. But they are also of great spiritual significance for their reflection of the way in which martyrdom manifests the cruciformity that is at the heart of discipleship according to the New Testament.

According to Eusebius (*Hist. eccl.* 3.34–36), Ignatius was arrested in Antioch and taken to Rome for execution sometime in the middle of the reign of the Emperor Trajan (98–117). On his way to Rome, he wrote to five churches who were encouraging him, and he wrote ahead to the church in Rome to prepare for his arrival. He also wrote a seventh letter to Polycarp, the bishop of Smyrna.

In these letters Ignatius thanks the believers for their love and encourages them to be steadfast in their faith. He tells them to resist false teachings and, in particular, the notion that Christians should retain the customs of Judaism, thereby denying that Jesus fulfilled the Jewish law. They should also beware of the tenets of Docetism, which denied that Jesus was fully human. Part of the believers' safeguard against such false teaching is their unity with their leaders through the three-fold ministry of the bishop, the priest, and the deacon. Ignatius states strongly that the bishop is the central authority. Believers are to do nothing without the bishop (e.g., *To the Smyrneans* [*Smyrn.*] 8), for the bishop represents God the Father (e.g., *To the Magnesians* [*Magn.*] 6–7).

In addition, Ignatius speaks of God's providential care and the outworking of his plan of redemption in history (e.g., *To the Ephesians* [*Eph.*] 18.2). Jesus is the fulfillment of God's purposes and the key to interpreting the Jewish Scriptures (*To the Philadelphians* [*Phld.*] 8.2). Indeed, the Old Testament prophets were Jesus' disciples in the Spirit as they awaited him as their teacher (*Magn.* 9.2). At several points Ignatius uses creedal language to describe Jesus, emphasizing his descent from the line of David and his birth, death, and resurrection (*Magn.* 11.1; *To the Trallians* [*Trall.*] 9.1–2; *Smyrn.* 1.1–2). Such strong statements about Jesus' humanity are matched by equally strong statements of his deity, as Ignatius frequently speaks of Jesus as God (e.g., *To the Romans* [*Rom.*], introduction; 3.3).

Ignatius encourages his fellow Christians to be true to Christ and to live in keeping with the other-worldly life of God that has broken into this world. The Pauline themes of being in Christ and of Christ as indwelling believers are foundational for Ignatius's view of the Christian life. Christians are those who "carry God" (*Eph.* 9.2), which is the meaning of Ignatius's own nickname, Theophoros. In the eucharist they share in the very flesh of Christ (*Smyrn.* 7.1), which he describes as the medicine of immortality (*Eph.* 20.2). He repeatedly encourages true discipleship, as when he says, "Do not talk about Jesus Christ and at the same time long for the world" (*Rom.* 7.1). The spiritual realm dominates his vision as he calls believers to take up their cross and follow their Lord.

To the Romans contains Ignatius's most developed discussion of martyrdom, as he tells the Christians in Rome not to try to prevent his martyrdom. He is not a masochist seeking suffering for its own sake. Rather, Ignatius wants to be done with the life of this old world and live the new life of God in fellowship with Christ. He is eager to go through the death of a martyr precisely because he does so in imitation of Christ and as a witness to the true life that is in Christ, in contrast to this world.

These brief letters are rich in their reflection on God, the church, and discipleship. The language Ignatius uses is passionate and full of striking expressions and imagery. Like Ignatius himself, his letters are a stimulating and challenging witness to believers today.

Edition used: J. B. Lightfoot, rev., tran. *The Apostolic Fathers.* Edited and completed by J. R. Harmer. 1891. Repr., Berkeley, Calif.: Apocryphile, 2004.

Level of difficulty: Easy [1–2]

Note: Lightfoot uses square brackets to indicate doubtful readings.

To the Romans Salutation I Greet the Church in Rome

Ρωμαίοις Ἰγνάτιος

Ἰγνάτιος, ὁ καὶ Θεοφόρος, τῇ ἠλεημένῃ ἐν μεγαλειότητι πατρὸς ὑψίστου καὶ Ἰησοῦ Χριστοῦ, τοῦ μόνου υἱοῦ αὐτοῦ, ἐκκλησίᾳ ἠγαπημένῃ καὶ πεφωτισμένῃ ἐν θελήματι τοῦ θελήσαντος τὰ πάντα ἅ ἔστιν, κατὰ πίστιν καὶ ἀγάπην Ἰησοῦ Χριστοῦ τοῦ Θεοῦ ἡμῶν, ἥτις καὶ προκάθηται ἐν τόπῳ χωρίου Ῥωμαίων, ἀξιόθεος, ἀξιοπρεπής, ἀξιομακάριστος, ἀξιέπαινος, ἀξιοεπίτευκτος, ἀξίαγνος, καὶ προκαθημένη τῆς ἀγάπης, χριστόνομος, πατρώνυμος· ἣν καὶ ἀσπάζομαι ἐν ὀνόματι Ἰησοῦ Χριστοῦ υἱοῦ πατρός· κατὰ σάρκα καὶ πνεῦμα ἡνωμένοις πάσῃ ἐντολῇ αὐτοῦ, πεπληρωμένοις χάριτος Θεοῦ ἀδιακρίτως καὶ ἀποδιϋλισμένοις ἀπὸ παντὸς ἀλλοτρίου χρώματος, πλεῖστα ἐν Ἰησοῦ Χριστῷ τῷ Θεῷ ἡμῶν ἀμώμως χαίρειν.

Salutation

Ἰγνάτιος → ὁ Ἰγνάτιος, *Ignatius.* • **Θεοφόρος** → ὁ Θεοφόρος, *Theophorus,* Ignatius's surname meaning *god-bearing,* from θεοφόρος, ον. ὁ καὶ Θεοφόρος, *also called Theophorus.* • **ἠλεημένῃ** → ἐλεέω, *I show mercy.* τῇ stretches forward to ἐκκλησίᾳ. • **μεγαλειότητι** → ἡ μεγαλειότης, *majesty.* • **ὑψίστου** → ὕψιστος, η, ον, *highest, the Most High.* • **Ἰησοῦ Χριστοῦ** — As often in the NT, it is uncertain whether the gen. is obj. or subj., i.e., whether the ref. is to faith and love towards Jesus Christ or to Jesus' own faith and love. • **πεφωτισμένῃ** → φωτίζω, *I enlighten.* • **ἥτις** — ref. to the church. • **προκάθηται** → προκάθημαι, *I preside (over), lead,* w. gen. if trans. • **χωρίου** → τὸ χωρίον, *place, environs.* • **Ῥωμαίων** → Ῥωμαῖος, α, ον, *Roman.* • **ἀξιόθεος** → ἀξιόθεος, ον, *worthy of God.* Beginning a string of two-termination adjs. that use the-ος form for both masc. and, as here, the fem. • **ἀξιοπρεπής** → ἀξιοπρεπής, ές, *worthy of honor.* • **ἀξιομακάριστος** → ἀξιομακάριστος, ον, *worthy of blessing.* • **ἀξιέπαινος** → ἀξιέπαινος, ον, *worthy of praise.* • **ἀξιοεπίτευκτος** → ἀξιοεπίτευκτος, ον, *worthy of success.* • **ἀξίαγνος** → ἀξιόαγνος, ον, *worthy of sanctification* (Lightfoot uses an uncommon spelling). • **χριστόνομος** → χριστόνομος, ον, *keeping the law of Christ.* • **πατρώνυμος** → πατρώνυμος, ον, *named after the Father, bearing the name of the Father.* • **κατά** — here, *with respect to, in relation to* (BDAG B6: 513). • **ἡνωμένοις** → ἑνόω, *I unite.* The focus has been on the community as a whole and the shift to a pl. now focuses on the individuals within the community. • **ἀδιακρίτως** → ἀδιακρίτως, *without wavering.* • **ἀποδιϋλισμένοις** → ἀποδιϋλίζω, *I strain, filter.* • **ἀλλοτρίου** → ἀλλότριος, α, ον, *strange, alien.* • **χρώματος** → χρῶμα, ατος, τό, *color.* Here "alien color" is used as an image of an impurity in the Roman Christians' faith (cf. BDAG 1: 1093). • **πλεῖστα** → πλεῖστος, η, ον, *most,* superlative of πολύς, ή, ύ. The formula πλεῖστα χαίρειν is a standard greeting (BDAG, πολύς 3bα: 850), *heartiest greetings.* • **ἀμώμως** → ἀμώμως, *blamelessly, without blame.* • **χαίρειν** → χαίρω, *I rejoice.* The inf. used for *greetings* (Wal: 608).

To the Romans 1–2 Do Not Try to Prevent My Martyrdom

1.1 Ἐπεὶ εὐξάμενος Θεῷ ἐπέτυχον ἰδεῖν ὑμῶν τὰ ἀξιόθεα πρόσωπα, ὡς καὶ πλέον ἢ ᾐτούμην λαβεῖν· δεδεμένος γὰρ ἐν Χριστῷ Ἰησοῦ ἐλπίζω ὑμᾶς ἀσπάσασθαι, ἐάνπερ θέλημα ᾖ τοῦ ἀξιωθῆναί με εἰς τέλος εἶναι· 1.2 ἡ μὲν γὰρ ἀρχὴ εὐοικονόμητός ἐστιν, ἐὰν πέρατος ἐπιτύχω εἰς τὸ τὸν κλῆρόν μου ἀνεμποδίστως ἀπολαβεῖν. φοβοῦμαι γὰρ τὴν ὑμῶν ἀγάπην, μὴ αὐτή με ἀδικήσῃ· ὑμῖν γὰρ εὐχερές ἐστιν, ὃ θέλετε ποιῆσαι, ἐμοὶ δὲ δύσκολόν ἐστιν τοῦ Θεοῦ ἐπιτυχεῖν, ἐάνπερ ὑμεῖς μὴ φείσησθέ μου.

2.1 Οὐ γὰρ θέλω ὑμᾶς ἀνθρωπαρεσκῆσαι ἀλλὰ Θεῷ ἀρέσαι, ὥσπερ καὶ ἀρέσκετε. οὔτε γὰρ ἐγώ ποτε ἕξω καιρὸν τοιοῦτον Θεοῦ ἐπιτυχεῖν· οὔτε ὑμεῖς, ἐὰν σιωπήσητε, κρείττονι ἔργῳ ἔχετε ἐπιγραφῆναι. ἐὰν γὰρ σιωπήσητε ἀπ' ἐμοῦ, ἐγὼ λόγος Θεοῦ· ἐὰν δὲ ἐρασθῆτε τῆς σαρκός μου, πάλιν

1.1 **ἐπεί** — *since, because.* • **εὐξάμενος** → εὔχομαι, *I pray.* • **ἐπέτυχον** → ἐπιτυγχάνω, *I obtain, attain, reach,* w. gen. or acc. • **ἰδεῖν** — dir. obj. of ἐπέτυχον, *the sight, the seeing,* or *obtained (my desire) to see.* • **ἀξιόθεα** → ἀξιόθεος, ον, *worthy of God.* • **ὡς** — here the equivalent of ὥστε w. inf. for result (LSI, ὡς BIII: 908; BDAG 4: 1105). • **πλέον** — an alternative form of πλείων. • **ἤ** — Ehrman's text omits ἤ, while Holmes's text retains it in angle brackets. Without ἤ the ὡς would be *as,* and the meaning would be "as I have been asking to receive yet more." • **ᾐτούμην** — impf. mid. indic. → αἰτέω. • **δεδεμένος** → δέω, *I bind.* Here the ref. is to his being bound in chains as a prisoner for the sake of Christ. Ignatius's thought jumps at this point, signaled in the translation by a dash. • **ἐλπίζω** → ἐλπίζω, *I hope.* • **ἀσπάσασθαι** → ἀσπάζομαι, *I greet.* • **ἐάνπερ** — *if only, if indeed.* • **ἀξιωθῆναι** → ἀξιόω, *I consider worthy.* Inf. for the content of the θέλημα, *if indeed it be (God's) will that I be considered worthy.* • **τέλος** → τὸ τέλος, *end.* εἰς τέλος εἶναι, either *to reach the end/goal* or *to be (faithful) to the end.*

1.2 **εὐοικονόμητος** → εὐοικονόμητος, ον, *well-ordered.* • **πέρατος** → τὸ πέρας, *end, limit, boundary; completion, conclusion.* Instead of ἐὰν πέρατος Ehrman's text has ἐάνπερ χάριτος. • **εἰς** — w. art. inf. for purpose (Wal: 590). • **κλῆρον** → ὁ κλῆρος, *lot, portion, share.* • **ἀνεμποδίστως** → ἀνεμποδίστως, *unhindered.* • **ἀπολαβεῖν** → ἀπολαμβάνω, *I receive.* εἰς τό w. inf. for a purpose or result clause (Wal: 611). • **αὐτή** — intensive, *that your love itself/precisely your love not wrong me.* • **ἀδικήσῃ** → ἀδικέω, *I do wrong.* • **εὐχερές** → εὐχερής, ές, *easily inclined, easy.* • **δύσκολον** → δύσκολος, ον, *difficult.* • **ἐπιτυχεῖν** — 2 aor. act. inf. → ἐπιτυγχάνω. • **φείσησθε** — aor. mid. (depon.) subjun. → φείδομαι, *I spare,* w. gen.

2.1 **ἀνθρωπαρεσκῆσαι** → ἀνθρωπαρεσκέω, *I please people, am a people-pleaser.* • **ἀρέσαι** — aor. act. inf. → ἀρέσκω, *I please.* • **ὥσπερ** — *as in fact, as indeed.* • **ποτέ** — *ever.,* w. neg., *never* (BDAG 1: 856). • **ἐπιτυχεῖν** — 2 aor. act. inf. → ἐπιτυγχάνω, *I obtain, attain,* w. gen. or acc. See note in the translation of 1.2. • **σιωπήσητε** → σιωπάω, *I keep silent,* i.e., do not prevent my martyrdom. • **κρείττονι** → κρείττων, ον, *better, higher.* • **ἔχετε** — w. inf., *can* (Smy: 2000a), ἔχετε ἐπιγραφῆναι, *can you be recorded.* • **ἐπιγραφῆναι** → ἐπιγράφω, *I write in/on, record.* • **σιωπήσητε ἀπ' ἐμοῦ** — *are silent and leave me alone* (BDAG,

ἔσομαι φωνή. 2.2 πλέον [δὲ] μοι μὴ παράσχησθε τοῦ σπονδισθῆναι Θεῷ, ὡς ἔτι θυσιαστήριον ἕτοιμόν ἐστιν· ἵνα ἐν ἀγάπῃ χορὸς γενόμενοι ᾄσητε τῷ πατρὶ ἐν Ἰησοῦ Χριστῷ, ὅτι τὸν ἐπίσκοπον Συρίας κατηξίωσεν ὁ Θεὸς εὑρεθῆναι εἰς δύσιν, ἀπὸ ἀνατολῆς μεταπεμψάμενος. καλὸν τὸ δῦναι ἀπὸ κόσμου πρὸς Θεόν, ἵνα εἰς αὐτὸν ἀνατείλω.

To the Romans 3 Pray for Me that I May Be a True Christian

3.1 Οὐδέποτε ἐβασκάνατε οὐδενί· ἄλλους ἐδιδάξατε. ἐγὼ δὲ θέλω ἵνα κἀκεῖνα βέβαια ᾖ ἃ μαθητεύοντες ἐντέλλεσθε. 3.2 μόνον μοι δύναμιν αἰτεῖσθε ἔσωθέν τε καὶ ἔξωθεν, ἵνα μὴ μόνον λέγω ἀλλὰ καὶ θέλω· ἵνα μὴ μόνον λέγωμαι Χριστιανός, ἀλλὰ καὶ εὑρεθῶ. ἐὰν γὰρ εὑρεθῶ, καὶ λέγεσθαι δύναμαι, καὶ τότε πιστὸς εἶναι, ὅταν κόσμῳ μὴ φαίνωμαι. 3.3 οὐδὲν φαινόμενον καλόν. ὁ γὰρ Θεὸς ἡμῶν Ἰησοῦς Χριστός, ἐν πατρὶ ὤν, μᾶλλον φαίνεται. οὐ πεισμονῆς τὸ ἔργον ἀλλὰ μεγέθους ἐστὶν ὁ χριστιανισμός, ὅταν μισῆται ὑπὸ κόσμου.

σιωπάω 1: 925). • **ἐρασθῆτε** → ἐράω, *I desire, have a longing for, feel fervently about,* w. gen.; depon. in aor. (LSI: 311).

2.2 **[δέ]** — The texts of Ehrman and Holmes do not have brackets. • **παράσχησθε** — 2 aor. mid. subjun. → παρέχω, *I grant.* πλέον μοι μὴ παράσχησθε, *grant me nothing more than.* • **σπονδισθῆναι** → σπονδίζω, *I pour out (as an offering).* • **ὡς** — here, *while* (LSI V2: 908; BDAG 8b: 1105). • **θυσιαστήριον** → τὸ θυσιαστήριον, *altar.* • **ἕτοιμον** → ἕτοιμος, η, ον, *ready.* • **χορός** → ὁ χορός, *chorus, choir.* • **ᾄσητε** → ᾄδω, *I sing.* • **ἐπίσκοπον** → ὁ ἐπίσκοπος, *bishop.* • **Συρίας** → ἡ Συρία, *Syria.* • **κατηξίωσεν** → καταξιόω, *I consider worthy.* • **δύσιν** → ἡ δύσις, *setting, West.* • **ἀνατολῆς** → ἡ ἀνατολή, *rising, East.* • **μεταπεμψάμενος** → μεταπέμπω, *I send for, summon.* εἰς δύσιν ἀπὸ ἀνατολῆς μεταπεμψάμενος, *at the setting* (of the sun) *having summoned him from the rising* (of the sun). The mid. voice adds that God summoned him for his own purposes, an indir. mid. (Wal: 419; Smy: 1719). • **δῦναι** — aor. act. inf. → δύνω, *I go down, set.* καλὸν τὸ δῦναι, *it is good to set.* • **ἀνατείλω** — aor. act. subjun. → ἀνατέλλω, *I rise.*

3.1 **οὐδέποτε** — *never.* • **ἐβασκάνατε** → βασκαίνω, *I envy.* • **κἀκεῖνα** → κἀκεῖνος, η, ο, *and that one/thing, this one, that one,* from crasis of καὶ ἐκεῖνος. • **βέβαια** → βέβαιος, α, ον, *firm, established;* here, *consistent.* • **μαθητεύοντες** → μαθητεύω, *I teach, instruct disciples.* • **ἐντέλλεσθε** → ἐντέλλω, *I command.*

3.2 **αἰτεῖσθε** → αἰτέω, here, *I pray* (BDAG 2: 30). • **ἔσωθεν** → ἔσωθεν, *inside, inward.* • **ἔξωθεν** → ἔξωθεν, *outside, outward.* • **Χριστιανός** → Χριστιανός, ὁ, *Christian.* • **εὑρεθῶ** — i.e., "be found to be a Christian." • **πιστός** → πιστός, ή, όν, *faithful.* • **φαίνωμαι** → φαίνω, *I appear, am/become visible;* pass. w. act. intrans. sense.

3.3 **οὐδέν** — subj., modified by the attrib. ptc. • **καλόν** — pred. compl. • **μᾶλλον** — here, *to a greater degree than before, now more than ever* (BDAG 1: 613). • **πεισμονῆς**

To the Romans 4–5 May I Attain to God through the Wild Beasts

4.1 Ἐγὼ γράφω πάσαις ταῖς ἐκκλησίαις, καὶ ἐντέλλομαι πᾶσιν ὅτι [ἐγὼ] ἑκὼν ὑπὲρ Θεοῦ ἀποθνήσκω, ἐάνπερ ὑμεῖς μὴ κωλύσητε. παρακαλῶ ὑμᾶς, μὴ εὔνοια ἄκαιρος γένησθέ μοι. ἄφετέ με θηρίων εἶναι, δι' ὧν [ἔν-]εστιν Θεοῦ ἐπιτυχεῖν. σῖτός εἰμι Θεοῦ, καὶ δι' ὀδόντων θηρίων ἀλήθομαι, ἵνα καθαρὸς ἄρτος εὑρεθῶ [τοῦ Χριστοῦ]. 4.2 μᾶλλον κολακεύσατε τὰ θηρία, ἵνα μοι τάφος γένωνται, καὶ μηθὲν καταλίπωσιν τῶν τοῦ σώματός μου, ἵνα μὴ κοιμηθεὶς βαρύς τινι γένωμαι. τότε ἔσομαι μαθητὴς ἀληθῶς Ἰησοῦ Χριστοῦ, ὅτε οὐδὲ τὸ σῶμά μου ὁ κόσμος ὄψεται. λιτανεύσατε τὸν Κύριον ὑπὲρ ἐμοῦ, ἵνα διὰ τῶν ὀργάνων τούτων Θεῷ θυσία εὑρεθῶ. 4.3 οὐχ ὡς Πέτρος καὶ Παῦλος διατάσσομαι ὑμῖν· ἐκεῖνοι ἀπόστολοι, ἐγὼ κατάκριτος·

→ ἡ πεισμονή, *persuasion.* • **μεγέθους** → τὸ μέγεθος, *greatness.* • **χριστιανισμός** → ὁ χριστιανισμός, *Christianity.* • **μισῆται** → μισέω, *I hate.*

4.1 **ἐντέλλομαι** → ἐντέλλω, *I order, command;* mid. depon. BDAG suggests here, *say emphatically* (BDAG: 339), but the lexicons give no other examples of this use. So it seems ὅτι gives the reason for the command, rather than its content. The content has already been expressed clearly in the context and is repeated in what follows. • **[ἐγώ]** — The texts of Ehrman and Holmes do not have brackets. • **ἑκών** → ἑκών, οῦσα, όν, *willing(ly), glad(ly).* • **ἐάνπερ** → ἐάνπερ — *if indeed.* • **κωλύσητε** → κωλύω, *I hinder, prevent.* • **παρακαλῶ** → παρακαλέω, *I request, implore, entreat.* • **εὔνοια** → ἡ εὔνοια, *favor, kindness.* • **ἄκαιρος** → ἄκαιρος, ον, *unseasonable, untimely.* • **θηρίων** → τὸ θηρίον, *animal, beast, wild beasts;* here, of "*wild animals* in a controlled setting, namely of fighting w. animals in an arena" (BDAG 1aγ: 456). Gen. of possession. The texts of Holmes and Ehrman add βοράν (→ ἡ βορά, *food*), "permit me to be food for wild beasts." • **ἔνεστιν** → ἔνειμι — imper. verb w. dat. and inf., *one may/can.* Here the dat. must be supplied, *I can attain God.* The texts of Ehrman and Holmes do not have brackets. • **ἐπιτυχεῖν** — 2 aor. act. inf. → ἐπιτυγχάνω, *I obtain, attain,* w. gen. or acc. See note in the translation of 1.2. • **σῖτος** → ὁ σῖτος, *wheat, grain.* • **ὀδόντων** → ὁ ὀδούς, *tooth.* • **ἀλήθομαι** → ἀλήθω, *I grind.* • **καθαρός** → καθαρός, ά, όν, *pure.* • **[τοῦ Χριστοῦ]** — Holmes's text omits these words, while Ehrman's text has them without the brackets.

4.2 **μᾶλλον** — i.e., rather than hinder my martyrdom. • **κολακεύσατε** → κολακεύω, *I entice.* • **τάφος** → ὁ τάφος, *grave, tomb.* • **μηθέν** → μηθέν — a later form of μηδείς, μηδεμία, μηδέν. μηθέν . . . τῶν τοῦ σώματός μου. The idea is something like "nothing of the bits of my body," i.e., absolutely nothing left of any part of my body. • **καταλίπωσιν** → καταλείπω, *I leave.* • **μή** — mod. γένωμαι. • **κοιμηθείς** → κοιμάω, *I sleep, fall asleep;* pass. w. act. sense. • **βαρύς** → βαρύς, εῖα, ύ, *heavy (burden);* subst., *burden.* • **ἀληθῶς** → ἀληθῶς, *truly.* • **λιτανεύσατε** → λιτανεύω, *I pray to, petition.* • **Κύριον** — Ehrman's text has Χριστόν instead. • **ὀργάνων** → τὸ ὄργανον, *tool, instrument.* • **Θεῷ** — The texts of Holmes and Ehrman have θεοῦ instead. • **θυσία** → ἡ θυσία, *sacrifice.* Pred. nom. w. a pass. trans. verb (Wal: 40).

ἐκεῖνοι ἐλεύθεροι, ἐγὼ δὲ μέχρι νῦν δοῦλος. ἀλλ' ἐὰν πάθω, ἀπελεύθερος Ἰησοῦ Χριστοῦ, καὶ ἀναστήσομαι ἐν αὐτῷ ἐλεύθερος. νῦν μανθάνω δεδεμένος μηδὲν ἐπιθυμεῖν.

5.1 Ἀπὸ Συρίας μέχρι Ῥώμης θηριομαχῶ, διὰ γῆς καὶ θαλάσσης, νυκτὸς καὶ ἡμέρας, ἐνδεδεμένος δέκα λεοπάρδοις, ὅ ἐστιν στρατιωτικὸν τάγμα, οἳ καὶ εὐεργετούμενοι χείρους γίνονται. ἐν δὲ τοῖς ἀδικήμασιν αὐτῶν μᾶλλον μαθητεύομαι· **ἀλλ' οὐ παρὰ τοῦτο δεδικαίωμαι.** 5.2 ὀναίμην τῶν θηρίων τῶν ἐμοὶ ἡτοιμασμένων, ἃ καὶ εὔχομαι σύντομά μοι εὑρεθῆναι· ἃ καὶ κολακεύσω συντόμως με καταφαγεῖν, οὐχ ὥσπερ τινῶν δειλαινόμενα οὐχ ἥψαντο· κἂν αὐτὰ δὲ ἑκόντα μὴ θέλῃ, ἐγὼ προσβιάσομαι. 5.3 συγγνώμην μοι ἔχετε· τί μοι συμφέρει ἐγὼ γινώσκω· νῦν ἄρχομαι μαθητὴς εἶναι· μηθέν με ζηλώσαι τῶν ὁρατῶν καὶ τῶν ἀοράτων, ἵνα Ἰησοῦ Χριστοῦ ἐπιτύχω.

4.3 **διατάσσομαι** → διατάσσω, *I order;* also act. sense in mid., w. dat. • **κατάκριτος** → κατάκριτος, ον, *condemned.* • **ἐλεύθεροι** → ἐλεύθερος, α, ον, *free.* • **μέχρι** — *until;* here w. νῦν, *right up to now.* • **πάθω** — 2 aor. act. subjun. → πάσχω, *I suffer.* • **ἀπελεύθερος** → ὁ ἀπελεύθερος, *freedman.* • **νῦν** — here, *in the meantime* (BDAG 2a: 681). • **μανθάνω** → μανθάνω, *I learn.* • **δεδεμένος** → δέω, *I bind.* • **ἐπιθυμεῖν** → ἐπιθυμέω, *I desire.*

5.1 **Συρίας** → Συρία, ἡ, *Syria.* • **μέχρι** — *until, as far as.* • **Ῥώμης** → ἡ Ῥώμη, *Rome.* • **θηριομαχῶ** → θηριομαχέω, *I fight with wild beasts.* • **ἐνδεδεμένος** → ἐνδέω, *I bind in/on/to.* • **δέκα** — *ten,* indecl. • **λεοπάρδοις** → ὁ λεόπαρδος, *leopard.* • **στρατιωτικόν** → στρατιωτικός, ή, όν, *of soldiers.* • **τάγμα** → τὸ τάγμα, *division, group;* as a military term for a "body of troops in various numbers" (BDAG 1a: 987), *detachment.* • **εὐεργετούμενοι** → εὐεργετέω, *I do good, benefit, treat well.* • **χείρους** → χείρων, ον, *worse.* • **ἀδικήμασιν** → τὸ ἀδίκημα, *mistreatment.* • **μαθητεύομαι** → μαθητεύω, *I teach, instruct disciples; am/become a disciple.* • **παρά** — here, *because of* (BDAG C5: 758). • **δεδικαίωμαι** → δικαιόω, *I justify, vindicate.*

5.2 **ὀναίμην** — aor. mid. opt. 1 sg. → ὀνίνημι, *I have benefit/profit of, enjoy.* W. gen. of the person or thing that is the source of the joy/profit. "May I have the pleasure/benefit of." • **θηρίων** → τὸ θηρίον, *animal, beast.* See note in the translation of 4.1. • **ἡτοιμασμένων** → ἑτοιμάζω, *I prepare.* • **ἃ** — Not in Ehrman's text. • **εὔχομαι** → εὔχομαι, *I pray.* • **σύντομά** → σύντομος, ον, *short, close at hand, ready.* • **εὑρεθῆναι** — w. ref. to the beasts, *that they be found.* Inf. for indir. disc. (Wal: 603; Smy: 2016). • **κολακεύσω** → κολακεύω, *I flatter; entice.* • **συντόμως** → συντόμως, *promptly.* • **καταφαγεῖν** → κατεσθίω, *I devour.* • **ὥσπερ** — *as in fact, as indeed.* • **δειλαινόμενα** → δειλαίνω, *I am cowardly, fearful.* • **ἥψαντο** → ἅπτω, *I kindle;* mid., *touch.* Gnomic aor. (Wal: 562; Smy: 1931). • **κἂν** — *even if,* crasis of καί and ἐάν. • **ἑκόντα** → ἑκών, ἑκοῦσα, ἑκόν, *willingly.* • **θέλῃ** — pres. act. subjun. → θέλω, in the sg. w. the neut. pl. subj. αὐτά. • **προσβιάσομαι** → προσβιάζομαι, *I compel, use force.*

5.3 **συγγνώμην** → ἡ συγγνώμη, *concession, pardon,* w. ἔχω; *I pardon, am indulgent to,* w. dat. • **συμφέρει** → συμφέρω, *I help, am profitable/useful.* • **μηθέν** — a later form of μηδείς, μηδεμία, μηδέν. • **ζηλώσαι** — aor. act. opt. 3 sg. → ζηλόω,

πῦρ καὶ σταυρὸς θηρίων τε συστάσεις, [ἀνατομαί, διαιρέσεις], σκορπισμοὶ ὀστέων, συγκοπαὶ μελῶν, ἀλεσμοὶ ὅλου τοῦ σώματος, κακαὶ κολάσεις τοῦ διαβόλου ἐπ' ἐμὲ ἐρχέσθωσαν· μόνον ἵνα Ἰησοῦ Χριστοῦ ἐπιτύχω.

To the Romans 6–8 I No Longer Desire the World, Only Christ

6.1 Οὐδέν μοι ὠφελήσει τὰ πέρατα τοῦ κόσμου, οὐδὲ αἱ βασιλεῖαι τοῦ αἰῶνος τούτου· καλόν μοι ἀποθανεῖν διὰ Ἰησοῦν Χριστὸν, ἢ βασιλεύειν τῶν περάτων τῆς γῆς. ἐκεῖνον ζητῶ, τὸν ὑπὲρ ἡμῶν ἀποθανόντα· ἐκεῖνον θέλω, τὸν [δι' ἡμᾶς] ἀναστάντα. ὁ τοκετός μοι ἐπίκειται. 6.2 σύγγνωτέ μοι, ἀδελφοί· μὴ ἐμποδίσητέ μοι ζῆσαι, μὴ θελήσητέ με ἀποθανεῖν. τὸν τοῦ Θεοῦ θέλοντα εἶναι κόσμῳ μὴ χαρίσησθε, μηδὲ ὕλῃ κολακεύσητε. ἄφετέ με καθαρὸν φῶς λαβεῖν· ἐκεῖ παραγενόμενος ἄνθρωπος ἔσομαι. 6.3

I strive, desire, make much of, court someone's favor, am envious towards; here, *May nothing among things visible and invisible envy me,* though perhaps Ignatius means nothing should desire him, i.e., like the Roman Christians would do if they hindered his martyrdom. • **ὁρατῶν** → ὁρατός, ή, όν, *visible.* Partitive gen. (Wal: 84; Smy: 1306). • **ἀοράτων** → ἀόρατος, ον, *invisible.* Partitive gen. (Wal: 84; Smy: 1306). • **ἐπιτύχω** — 2 aor. act. subjun. → ἐπιτυγχάνω, *I obtain, attain,* w. gen. or acc. See note on 1.2 in the translation. • **σταυρός** → ὁ σταυρός, *a cross.* • **συστάσεις** → ἡ σύστασις, *an encounter.* • **ἀνατομαί** → ἡ ἀνατομή, *cutting up, mutilation.* The texts of Ehrman and Holmes do not have brackets. • **διαιρέσεις** → ἡ διαίρεσις, *division, tearing apart.* • **σκορπισμοί** → ὁ σκορπισμός, *scattering.* • **ὀστέων** → τὸ ὀστέον, *bone.* • **συγκοπαί** → ἡ συγκοπή, *cutting to pieces, mangling.* Ehrman's text has συγκοπή. • **μελῶν** → τὸ μέλος, *limb, part.* • **ἀλεσμοί** → ὁ ἀλεσμός, *grinding.* • **κολάσεις** → ἡ κόλασις, *punishment, torture.* • **διαβόλου** → διάβολος, ον, *slanderous;* subst., *slanderer, adversary, the devil.*

6.1 **οὐδέν** — here, *in no way, not at all* (BDAG 2bγ: 735). • **ὠφελήσει** → ὠφελέω, *I profit, help, am of use to.* • **πέρατα** → τὸ πέρας, *end, limit.* • **οὐδὲ αἱ βασιλεῖαι** — Supply ὠφελήσει μοι. • **καλόν** — often used with ἤ or other constructions to mean "it is better" (BDAG 2dγ: 505). • **διά** — Ehrman's text has εἰς. • **βασιλεύειν** → βασιλεύω, *I reign.* • **[δι' ἡμᾶς]** — The texts of Ehrman and Holmes do not have brackets. • **ἀναστάντα** — aor. act. ptc. → ἀνίστημι. • **τοκετός** → ὁ τοκετός, *childbearing, giving birth.* • **ἐπίκειται** → ἐπίκειμαι, *I lie/am upon.*

6.2 **σύγγνωτε** — aor. act. impv. → συγγινώσκω, *I agree, have the same opinion/purpose/wish,* here perhaps, *understand my position* (BDAG: 950). • **ἐμποδίσητε** → ἐμποδίζω, *I hinder.* • **ζῆσαι** — aor. act. inf. → ζάω, here, "hinder" in English requires, *living.* • **τὸν τοῦ θεοῦ θέλοντα εἶναι** — attrib. ptc., *one who wants to be God's.* • **χαρίσησθε** → χαρίζομαι, *I give (graciously).* • **ὕλῃ** → ἡ ὕλη, *matter, material, stuff.* • **κολακεύσητε** → κολακεύω, *I flatter; entice.* Holmes's text has this word in angle brackets, while Ehrman's text has ἐξαπατήσητε (→ ἐξαπατάω, *I deceive, cheat*), with no brackets. • **καθαρόν** → καθαρός, ά, όν, *pure, clean.* • **παραγενόμενος** → παραγίνομαι, *I arrive, am present.*

ἐπιτρέψατέ μοι μιμητὴν εἶναι τοῦ πάθους τοῦ Θεοῦ μου. εἴ τις αὐτὸν ἐν ἑαυτῷ ἔχει, νοησάτω ὃ θέλω καὶ συμπαθείτω μοι εἰδὼς τὰ συνέχοντά με.

7.1 Ὁ ἄρχων τοῦ αἰῶνος τούτου διαρπάσαι με βούλεται καὶ τὴν εἰς Θεόν μου γνώμην διαφθεῖραι. μηδεὶς οὖν τῶν παρόντων ὑμῶν βοηθείτω αὐτῷ· μᾶλλον ἐμοὶ γίνεσθε, τουτέστιν τοῦ Θεοῦ. μὴ λαλεῖτε Ἰησοῦν Χριστὸν κόσμον δὲ ἐπιθυμεῖτε. 7.2 βασκανία ἐν ὑμῖν μὴ κατοικείτω· μηδ᾽ ἂν ἐγὼ παρὼν παρακαλῶ ὑμᾶς, πείσθητέ μοι, τούτοις δὲ μᾶλλον πιστεύσατε, οἷς γράφω ὑμῖν. ζῶν [γὰρ] γράφω ὑμῖν, ἐρῶν τοῦ ἀποθανεῖν· ὁ ἐμὸς ἔρως ἐσταύρωται, καὶ οὐκ ἔστιν ἐν ἐμοὶ πῦρ φιλόϋλον, ὕδωρ δὲ ζῶν καὶ λαλοῦν ἐν ἐμοί, ἔσωθέν μοι λέγον· Δεῦρο πρὸς τὸν πατέρα. 7.3 οὐχ ἥδομαι τροφῇ φθορᾶς οὐδὲ ἡδοναῖς τοῦ βίου τούτου· ἄρτον Θεοῦ θέλω, ὅ ἐστιν σὰρξ τοῦ Χριστοῦ τοῦ ἐκ σπέρματος Δαυείδ, καὶ πόμα θέλω τὸ αἷμα αὐτοῦ, ὅ ἐστιν ἀγάπη ἄφθαρτος.

6.3 **ἐπιτρέψατε** → ἐπιτρέπω, *I allow, permit.* • **μιμητήν** → ὁ μιμητής, *imitator.* • **πάθους** → τὸ πάθος, *suffering.* • **νοησάτω** → νοέω, *I perceive, understand.* • **συμπαθείτω** → συμπαθέω, *I sympathize with.* • **συνέχοντα** → συνέχω, *I distress, urge on, impel, direct, control.*

7.1 **ἄρχων** → ὁ ἄρχων, *ruler.* • **διαρπάσαι** → διαρπάζω, *I plunder thoroughly, rob, snatch, take captive.* • **βούλεται** → βούλομαι, *I will, wish, desire.* • **εἰς** — here, *with reference to, regarding* (BDAG 5: 291). • **γνώμην** → ἡ γνώμη, *purpose, intention, mind.* • **διαφθεῖραι** → διαφθείρω, *I spoil, destroy, ruin, corrupt.* • **παρόντων** — pres. act. ptc. → πάρειμι, *I am present.* τῶν παρόντων ὑμῶν: *among you who are present.* Partitive gen. (Wal: 84; Smy: 1306). • **βοηθείτω** → βοηθέω, *I help.* • **τουτέστιν** — crasis of τοῦτ᾽ ἔστιν, *this/that means, that is to say, that is.* • **δέ** — here, "a marker with an additive relation, with possible suggestion of contrast, *at the same time*" (BDAG 3: 213). • **ἐπιθυμεῖτε** → ἐπιθυμέω, *I desire, long for.*

7.2 **βασκανία** → ἡ βασκανία, *envy.* • **κατοικείτω** → κατοικέω, *I live, dwell.* • **ἄν** — here for ἐάν (LSI: 51; BDAG II: 57). • **παρών** — pres. act. ptc. → πάρειμι. • **πείσθητέ μοι** — dir. disc. of his exhortation, "Be persuaded by me," or "Obey me" (cf. BDAG, πείθω 3: 792). • **πιστεύσατε** — Ehrman's text has πείσθητε. • **[γάρ]** — The texts of Ehrman and Holmes do not have brackets. • **ἐρῶν** → ἐράω, *I desire, yearn, long for, love.* • **ἔρως** → ἔρως, ωτος, ὁ, *desire, ardor, fondness, love.* • **ἐσταύρωται** — pf. pass. indic. → σταυράω, *I crucify.* Cf. Gal 5:24; 6:14. • **φιλόϋλον** → φιλόϋλος, ον, *loving material things.* • **καὶ λαλοῦν** — Lightfoot marks these words as being corrupt in the MSS. Holmes's text retains them unmarked, and Ehrman's text has them with no textual note at all. • **ἔσωθεν** → ἔσωθεν, *inside, from within.* • **δεῦρο** — adv., *over here, come here, come!*

7.3 **ἥδομαι** → ἥδομαι, *I delight in, take pleasure in.* • **τροφῇ** → ἡ τροφή, *food.* • **φθορᾶς** → ἡ φθορά, *corruption, dissolution, deterioration.* • **ἡδοναῖς** → ἡ ἡδονή, *pleasure, delight, enjoyment.* • **βίου** → ὁ βίος, *life.* • **τοῦ Χριστοῦ** — Ehrman's text does not have τοῦ. • **σπέρματος** → τὸ σπέρμα, *seed.* • **Δαυείδ** → ὁ Δαυείδ (indecl., listed in BDAG under the alternate spelling Δαυίδ), *David.* • **πόμα** → τὸ πόμα, *drink.* • **τὸ αἷμα αὐτοῦ** — in appos. to πόμα. • **ἄφθαρτος** → ἄφθαρτος, ον, *incorruptible, imperishable.*

8.1 Οὐκέτι θέλω κατὰ ἀνθρώπους ζῆν· τοῦτο δὲ ἔσται, ἐὰν ὑμεῖς θελήσητε. θελήσατε, ἵνα καὶ ὑμεῖς θεληθῆτε. 8.2 δι᾽ ὀλίγων γραμμάτων αἰτοῦμαι ὑμᾶς· πιστεύσατέ μοι. Ἰησοῦς δὲ Χριστὸς ὑμῖν ταῦτα φανερώσει, ὅτι ἀληθῶς λέγω· τὸ ἀψευδὲς στόμα, ἐν ᾧ ὁ πατὴρ ἐλάλησεν [ἀληθῶς]. 8.3 αἰτήσασθε περὶ ἐμοῦ, ἵνα ἐπιτύχω [ἐν πνεύματι ἁγίῳ]. οὐ κατὰ σάρκα ὑμῖν ἔγραψα, ἀλλὰ κατὰ γνώμην Θεοῦ. ἐὰν πάθω, ἠθελήσατε· ἐὰν ἀποδοκιμασθῶ, ἐμισήσατε.

To the Romans 9–10 My Concluding Greetings and Requests

9.1 Μνημονεύετε ἐν τῇ προσευχῇ ὑμῶν τῆς ἐν Συρίᾳ ἐκκλησίας, ἥτις ἀντὶ ἐμοῦ ποιμένι τῷ Θεῷ χρῆται· μόνος αὐτὴν Ἰησοῦς Χριστὸς ἐπισκοπήσει καὶ ἡ ὑμῶν ἀγάπη. 9.2 ἐγὼ δὲ αἰσχύνομαι ἐξ αὐτῶν λέγεσθαι· οὐδὲ γὰρ ἄξιός εἰμι, ὢν ἔσχατος αὐτῶν καὶ ἔκτρωμα· ἀλλ᾽ ἠλέημαί τις εἶναι, ἐὰν

8.1 **οὐκέτι** — *no longer.* • **ἔσται** → εἰμί. Here εἰμί has the unusual meaning, *I occur, happen, take place* (BDAG 6: 285).

8.2 **ὀλίγων** → ὀλίγος, η, ον, *few.* • **γραμμάτων** → γράμμα, ατος, τό, *letter.* • **φανερώσει** → φανερόω, *I reveal, make known.* • **ὅτι** — This could be in appos. to ταῦτα, "Jesus Christ will reveal these things to you, namely, that I am speaking truly," but perhaps more likely causal, Christ will confirm the truth of what Ignatius has been saying. • **ἀληθῶς** → ἀληθῶς — *truly.* • **ἀψευδές** → ἀψευδής, ές, *without lie or deceit; truthful, trustworthy.* τὸ ἀψευδὲς στόμα could be in appos. to the subj. of λέγω (i.e., Ignatius), but the substance is more appropriate to Christ, especially the aor. ἐλάλησεν, so it should be taken in appos. to Ἰησοῦς . . . Χριστός. • **[ἀληθῶς]** — Holmes's text retains this word w. no brackets. Ehrman's text has the words in reverse order, ἀληθῶς ἐλάλησεν.

8.3 **αἰτήσασθε** → αἰτέω, here, *I pray* (BDAG 2: 30). • **ἐπιτύχω** — 2 aor. act. subjun. → ἐπιτυγχάνω, *I obtain, attain,* w. gen. or acc. See the note on 1.2 in the translation. • **[ἐν πνεύματι ἁγίῳ]** — The texts of Ehrman and Holmes do not have these words. • **γνώμην** → γνώμη, ἡ, *purpose, intention, mind.* • **πάθω** — 2 aor. act. subjun. → πάσχω, *I suffer.* • **ἠθελήσατε** — θέλω is augmented in keeping w. its earlier form ἐθέλω. • **ἀποδοκιμασθῶ** → ἀποδοκιμάζω, *I reject.* • **ἐμισήσατε** → μισέω, *I hate.* ἐὰν ἀποδοκιμασθῶ, ἐμισήσατε, "if I am rejected [i.e., his martyrdom is hindered], you hated (me) [through the hindering of his martyrdom]."

9.1 **μνημονεύετε** → μνημονεύω, *I remember.* • **προσευχῇ** → ἡ προσευχή, *prayer.* • **Συρίᾳ** → ἡ Συρία, *Syria.* • **ἀντί** — *instead of, in place of.* • **ποιμένι** → ὁ ποιμήν, *a shepherd.* • **χρῆται** → χράομαι, *I use, have dealings with;* here, *resorts to,* w. double dat. of person and compl. (BDAG 1a: 1088). ἥτις ἀντὶ ἐμοῦ ποιμένι τῷ θεῷ χρῆται, *which resorts to God as shepherd instead of me,* ref. to his absence from them as he is taken to Rome. • **ἐπισκοπήσει** → ἐπισκοπέω, *I oversee, am a bishop.*

9.2 **αἰσχύνομαι** → αἰσχύνω, mid. and pass. w. act. sense, *I am ashamed.* • **ἐξ** — for a partitive gen. (BDAG 4: 297; BDF: 164), *one of them;* obj. of inf. • **λέγεσθαι** —

Θεοῦ ἐπιτύχω. 9.3 ἀσπάζεται ὑμᾶς τὸ ἐμὸν πνεῦμα καὶ ἡ ἀγάπη τῶν ἐκκλησιῶν τῶν δεξαμένων με εἰς ὄνομα Ἰησοῦ Χριστοῦ, οὐχ ὡς παροδεύοντα· καὶ γὰρ αἱ μὴ προσήκουσαί μοι τῇ ὁδῷ τῇ κατὰ σάρκα κατὰ πόλιν με προῆγον.

10.1 Γράφω δὲ ὑμῖν ταῦτα ἀπὸ Σμύρνης δι' Ἐφεσίων τῶν ἀξιομακαρίστων. ἔστιν δὲ καὶ ἅμα ἐμοὶ σὺν ἄλλοις πολλοῖς καὶ Κρόκος, τὸ ποθητόν [μοι] ὄνομα. 10.2 περὶ τῶν προελθόντων με ἀπὸ Συρίας εἰς Ῥώμην εἰς δόξαν [τοῦ] Θεοῦ πιστεύω ὑμᾶς ἐπεγνωκέναι. οἷς καὶ δηλώσατε ἐγγύς με ὄντα· πάντες γάρ εἰσιν ἄξιοι [τοῦ] Θεοῦ καὶ ὑμῶν· οὓς πρέπον ὑμῖν ἐστιν κατὰ πάντα ἀναπαῦσαι. 10.3 ἔγραψα δὲ ὑμῖν ταῦτα τῇ πρὸ ἐννέα καλανδῶν Σεπτεμβρίων. ἔρρωσθε εἰς τέλος ἐν ὑπομονῇ Ἰησοῦ Χριστοῦ.

---

here, *I call.* • **ἄξιος** → ἄξιος, α, ον, *worthy.* • **ἔκτρωμα** → τὸ ἔκτρωμα, *untimely birth,* "a birth that violates the normal period of gestation (whether induced as abortion, or natural premature birth or miscarriage . . . or birth beyond term)" (BDAG: 311). Cf. 1 Cor 15:8. • **ἠλέημαι** → ἐλεέω, *I show mercy.* Cf. 1 Tim 1:16. • **τις εἶναι** — *to be someone.* Inf. for purpose or result (Wal: 590, 592; Smy: 2008, 2011). • **ἐπιτύχω** — 2 aor. act. subjun. → ἐπιτυγχάνω, *I obtain, attain,* w. gen. or acc. See note on 1.2 in the translation.

9.3 **ἀσπάζεται** → ἀσπάζομαι, *I greet.* • **παροδεύοντα** → παροδεύω, *I pass by.* Attrib. part. • **προσήκουσαι** → προσήκω, *I come to, approach, am near,* w. dat. αἱ μὴ προσήκουσαί μοι, the fem. form ref. to the churches, *churches that were not near me.* • **κατὰ πόλιν** — *city by city, from city to city.* Distributive use of κατά (BDAG B1d: 512). • **προῆγον** → προάγω, *I go before.*

10.1 **Σμύρνης** → ἡ Σμύρνα, *Smyrna.* • **Ἐφεσίων** → Ἐφέσιος, α, ον, *Ephesian.* • **ἀξιομακαρίστων** → ἀξιομακάριστος, ον, *most worthy of blessing.* • **ἅμα** — *together with.* • **Κρόκος** → ὁ Κρόκος, *Crocus.* • **ποθητόν** → ποθητός, ή, όν, *dearly beloved.* • **[μοι]** — The texts of Holmes and Ehrman do not have brackets.

10.2 **προελθόντων** → προέρχομαι, *I go before, precede.* • **Συρίας** → ἡ Συρία, *Syria.* • **Ῥώμην** → ἡ Ῥώμη, *Rome.* • **[τοῦ]** — Holmes's text omits the brackets; Ehrman's text omits the word. • **ἐπεγνωκέναι** — pf. act. inf. → ἐπιγινώσκω, *I know, have information, learn.* Inf. for indir. disc. (Wal: 603; Smy: 2016), the content of what he believes. • **δηλώσατε** → δηλόω, *I reveal, explain, make clear.* • **ἐγγύς** — *near.* • **ὄντα** → εἰμι — ptc. for indir. disc. (Wal: 645; Smy: 2106–15). ἐγγύς με ὄντα is the content of what they are to explain, *that I am near.* • **ἄξιοι** → ἄξιος, α, ον, *worthy.* • **πρέπον** → πρέπω, *I am fitting,* πρέπον ἐστιν, *it is fitting/proper/right.* • **κατὰ πάντα** — *in every way.* • **ἀναπαῦσαι** → ἀναπαύω, *I cause to rest, refresh.*

10.3 **ἔγραψα** → γράφω. Epistolary aor. (Wal: 562; Smy: 1942), *I am writing.* • **πρό** — *before.* • **ἐννέα** — indecl., *nine.* • **καλανδῶν** → αἱ καλάνδαι, *the calends,* "the first day of the month in the Roman calendar" (BDAG: 502). • **Σεπτεμβρίων** → ὁ Σεπτέμβριος, *September.* τῇ πρὸ ἐννέα καλανδῶν Σεπτεμβρίων. The art. is fem. since ἡμέρα is understood: *on the ninth day before the calends of September,* i.e., August 24th. • **ἔρρωσθε** — pf. pass. impv. → ῥώννυμι, *I strengthen.* ἔρρωσθε is a common conclusion to a letter so it could be translated *farewell* or *goodbye,* though Ignatius's addition suggests it is not a mere stock expression for him. • **τέλος** → τὸ τέλος, *end.* • **ὑπομονῇ** → ἡ ὑπομονή, *patient endurance.*

The Epistle to Diognetus

Introduction

It has been said that the *Epistle to Diognetus* (*Diogn.*) "deserves to rank among the most brilliant and beautiful works of Christian Greek literature."[1] This brief letter is an attractive attempt to commend Christianity during the second century, when the church was facing increasing opposition from Gentiles. How should Christians commend the faith to those with no background in the biblical worldview? The question is increasingly relevant today, which makes this little document of more than just historical interest, despite numerous differences between the modern context and that of the second century.

Christians have been involved in conflict from the very beginning. The New Testament records conflict between Jesus and the Jewish leadership, and this is followed by growing conflict between Christians and many of the Jews, including both leaders and non-leaders. As Christianity grew in the second century, the conflict with many within Judaism continued and conflict with Gentiles became much more significant. The Gentiles considered Christians to be atheists since they did not accept the Greco-Roman deities. They also saw Christianity as a recent, upstart development, which was a mark against it in the eyes of many. Furthermore, Gentiles often misunderstood the actual teaching and practice of the Christians. They thought the familial relations within the church sounded incestuous and they also confused the eucharist with cannibalism. The intellectuals looked down on the literary quality of the Scriptures, and some of the satirists of the day considered Christians in general as gullible simpletons.

In the second century, from around the year 130 on, several Christians with the necessary intellectual gifts and training responded to these charges and misunderstandings. They are known as the Apologists since they sought to offer an *apology* for Christianity, that is, an explanation and defense of Christianity over against both Judaism and Greco-Roman thought and religion. The *Epistle to Diognetus* is one such writing.

Unfortunately, we know very little about this brief document. We know neither who wrote it, when it was written, the exact circumstances it reflects, nor the identity of Diognetus, to whom it is addressed. There has been much speculation about each of these

[1] Johannes Quasten, *Patrology* (3 vols.; Westminster, Md.: Newman, 1950-1953; repr. Allen, Tex.: Christian Classics, n.d.), 1:251. Quasten's *Patrology* was brought to completion by a team of scholars in a fourth volume edited by Angelo di Berardino, covering Latin patristic literature from Nicea to Chalcedon.

topics, but the only point that is widely accepted is that the work should be dated somewhere in the second century. The author, who writes with a good style, was probably a well-educated Gentile.

Only one manuscript of the *Epistle to Diognetus* is known. That manuscript was discovered in 1436 but was destroyed in a fire in Strasbourg in 1870 during the Franco-German War. Fortunately, it had been copied several times, though the copies do not always agree. The original manuscript itself was in imperfect condition, with gaps in the text. Furthermore, it appears that in its present form two documents have been combined, since the final two chapters of the *Epistle to Diognetus* seem to be from a sermon, unlike the apology found in the first ten chapters.

The *Epistle to Diognetus* is addressed to a person who wants to learn about the Christian view of God and the Christian lifestyle, and also how Christianity differs from the beliefs of both the Greeks and the Jews (*Diogn.* 1). The author begins by criticizing the idolatry of the Greeks (2), then the foolishness of Jewish sacrifices, Sabbath laws, and ritual regulations (3–4). He next turns to a glowing description of Christianity (5–6) and the divine revelation that came through the Son of God (7–8). He continues with an explanation of why God waited to send the Son (9), and then concludes with an appeal to Diognetus to come to a knowledge of the Father and to imitate him, thereby experiencing true happiness (10).

The author appeals to nature and the coming of the Son as revelation of the kindness of the Father and a call to a counter-cultural life. While Christians are separate from the society, they are also vital to it, like the soul to the body (6). Thus, the *Epistle to Diognetus* contains an attractive presentation of the person of God in a form accessible to one unfamiliar with the biblical story. In addition, its vision of the Christian community is both beautiful and challenging.

Edition used: J. B. Lightfoot, rev., tran. *The Apostolic Fathers.* Edited and completed by J. R. Harmer. 1891. Repr., Berkeley, Calif.: Apocryphile, 2004.

Level of difficulty: Intermediate [2–3]

Note: Lightfoot uses square brackets to indicate doubtful readings.

The Epistle to Diognetus 5–7 Christians in the World

5.1 Χριστιανοὶ γὰρ οὔτε γῇ οὔτε φωνῇ οὔτε ἔσθεσι διακεκριμένοι τῶν λοιπῶν εἰσὶν ἀνθρώπων. 5.2 οὔτε γάρ που πόλεις ἰδίας κατοικοῦσιν οὔτε διαλέκτῳ τινὶ παρηλλαγμένῃ χρῶνται οὔτε βίον παράσημον ἀσκοῦσιν. 5.3 οὐ μὴν ἐπινοίᾳ τινὶ καὶ φροντίδι πολυπραγμόνων ἀνθρώπων μάθημα τοιοῦτ' αὐτοῖς ἐστὶν εὑρημένον, οὐδὲ δόγματος ἀνθρωπίνου προεστᾶσιν ὥσπερ ἔνιοι. 5.4 κατοικοῦντες δὲ πόλεις Ἑλληνίδας τε καὶ βαρβάρους ὡς ἕκαστος ἐκληρώθη, καὶ τοῖς ἐγχωρίοις ἔθεσιν ἀκολουθοῦντες ἔν τε ἐσθῆτι καὶ διαίτῃ καὶ τῷ λοιπῷ βίῳ, θαυμαστὴν καὶ ὁμολογουμένως παράδοξον ἐνδείκνυνται τὴν κατάστασιν τῆς ἑαυτῶν πολιτείας. 5.5 πατρίδας οἰκοῦσιν

5.1 **Χριστιανοί** → ὁ Χριστιανός, *Christian.* • **φωνῇ** → ἡ φωνή, here, *language.* • **ἔσθεσι** — dat. pl. BDAG gives ἡ ἐσθής, *clothing,* but the normal form of the dat. pl. for this form would be ἐσθῆσιν (a form found 116 times in the literature covered by *TLG*). The ε in the stem would fit the pattern τὸ ἔσθος, *clothing,* a rare word in classical writers, but fairly common in later ecclesiastical writers. The more common ἐσθής is also found in 5.4. Some MSS. have a different word here, ἔθεσι (→ τὸ ἔθος, *custom*), used below, 5.4. • **διακεκριμένοι** — pf. pass. ptc. → διακρίνω, *I separate, distinguish;* pass., *am differentiated from,* w. gen. Periphrastic.

5.2 **που** — *somewhere,* enclitic adv. after a neg., *nowhere.* • **κατοικοῦσιν** → κατοικέω, *I live, dwell.* • **διαλέκτῳ** → ἡ διάλεκτος, *dialect, language.* • **παρηλλαγμένῃ** — pf. pass. ptc. → παραλλάσσω, *I change, deviate;* in the pf. pass. ptc., *strange, extraordinary, peculiar* (BDAG: 768). • **χρῶνται** → χράομαι, *I use, employ.* • **βίον** → ὁ βίος, *life.* • **παράσημον** → παράσημος, ον, *peculiar, odd.* • **ἀσκοῦσιν** → ἀσκέω, *I practice, engage in.*

5.3 **μήν** — particle, *indeed.* οὐ μήν with the following οὐδέ, *not of course . . . nor.* • **ἐπινοίᾳ** → ἡ ἐπίνοια, *thought, intention.* • **φροντίδι** → ἡ φροντίς, *reflection, thought.* • **πολυπραγμόνων** → πολυπράγμων, ον, *inquisitive; meddlesome.* • **μάθημα** → τὸ μάθημα, *lesson learned, knowledge.* Holmes's text has angle brackets around this word, indicating doubt about the reading. • **τοιοῦτ'** → τοιοῦτος. The texts of Holmes and Ehrman have τοῦτ'. • **εὑρημένον** — pf. pass. ptc. → εὑρίσκω, periphrastic. • **δόγματος** → τὸ δόγμα, *doctrine.* • **ἀνθρωπίνου** → ἀνθρώπινος, η, ον, *human.* • **προεστᾶσιν** — pf. act. indic. 3 pl. → προΐστημι, *I care for,* w. gen. • **ὥσπερ** — *as.* • **ἔνιοι** → ἔνιοι, αι, α, *some.*

5.4 **δέ** — after a neg., *rather* (BDAG 4c: 213). • **Ἑλληνίδας** → ἡ Ἑλληνίς, *Greek woman.* Often used, as here, as an adj., *Greek.* • **βαρβάρους** → βάρβαρος, ον, *non-Greek, foreign.* • **ἐκληρώθη** → κληρόω, *I appoint by lot;* pass., *one's lot is cast.* • **καί** — Holmes's text has angle brackets around this word. • **ἐγχωρίοις** → ἐγχώριος, ον, *local.* • **ἔθεσιν** → τὸ ἔθος, *custom.* • **ἐσθῆτι** → ἡ ἐσθής, *clothing,* • **διαίτῃ** → ἡ δίαιτα, *food, diet.* • **θαυμαστήν** → θαυμαστός, ή, όν, *amazing, marvelous.* • **ὁμολογουμένως** — *undeniably.* • **παράδοξον** → παράδοξος, ον, *strange, remarkable.* • **ἐνδείκνυνται** → ἐνδείκνυμι, *I show, demonstrate.* • **κατάστασιν** → ἡ κατάστασις, *character.* • **πολιτείας** → ἡ πολιτεία, *citizenship, a*

ἰδίας, ἀλλ' ὡς πάροικοι· μετέχουσι πάντων ὡς πολῖται, καὶ πανθ' ὑπομένουσιν ὡς ξένοι· πᾶσα ξένη πατρίς ἐστιν αὐτῶν, καὶ πᾶσα πατρὶς ξένη.
5.6 γαμοῦσιν ὡς πάντες, τεκνογονοῦσιν· ἀλλ' οὐ ῥίπτουσι τὰ γεννώμενα.
5.7 τράπεζαν κοινὴν παρατίθενται, ἀλλ' οὐ κοίτην. 5.8 ἐν σαρκὶ τυγχάνουσιν, ἀλλ' οὐ κατὰ σάρκα ζῶσιν. 5.9 ἐπὶ γῆς διατρίβουσιν, ἀλλ' ἐν
οὐρανῷ πολιτεύονται. 5.10 πείθονται τοῖς ὡρισμένοις νόμοις, καὶ τοῖς ἰδίοις
βίοις νικῶσι τοὺς νόμους. 5.11 ἀγαπῶσι πάντας, καὶ ὑπὸ πάντων διώκονται. 5.12 ἀγνοοῦνται, καὶ κατακρίνονται· θανατοῦνται, καὶ ζωοποιοῦνται. 5.13 πτωχεύουσι, καὶ πλουτίζουσι πολλούς· πάντων ὑστεροῦνται, καὶ
ἐν πᾶσι περισσεύουσιν. 5.14 ἀτιμοῦνται, καὶ ἐν ταῖς ἀτιμίαις δοξάζονται·

---

body of citizens. The word ref. to their homeland and its customs, which Christians maintain now as resident aliens (see 5.5).

5.5 **πατρίδας** → ἡ πατρίς, *fatherland, homeland, native country.* • **οἰκοῦσιν** → οἰκέω, *I live, dwell.* • **πάροικοι** → πάροικος, ον, *alien, strange.* • **μετέχουσι** → μετέχω, *I share, participate.* • **πολῖται** → ὁ πολίτης, *citizen.* • **καί** — here introducing something surprising or unexpected, *and yet* (BDAG 1bη: 495). • **πάνθ'** → πᾶς, simple elision of πάντα, w. the τ aspirated because of the rough breathing on the following word. • **ὑπομένουσιν** → ὑπομένω, *I endure.* • **ξένοι** → ξένος, η, ον, *strange, foreign.*

5.6 **γαμοῦσιν** → γαμέω, *I marry.* • **τεκνογονοῦσιν** → τεκνογονέω, *I bear/beget/have children.* • **ῥίπτουσι** → ῥίπτω, *I throw; expose* (of newborns, see BDAG 1: 906). • **τὰ γεννώμενα** — neut. like τέκνον, "the children that are born," *offspring.* The art. is poss. (Wal: 215; Smy: 1121).

5.7 **τράπεζαν** → ἡ τράπεζα, *table; meal, food.* • **κοινήν** → κοινός, ή, όν, *common.* Holmes's text has brackets around this word. • **παρατίθενται** → παρατίθημι, *I set before;* "Mid., of hospitality *set, spread*" (BDAG 1: 772). • **κοίτην** → ἡ κοίτη, *bed; marriage-bed; "they furnish a common table, but not a bed (for sex)"* (BDAG 1b: 554).

5.8 **τυγχάνουσιν** → τυγχάνω, *I happen to be, I find myself.*

5.9 **διατρίβουσιν** → διατρίβω, *I spend time, stay, remain.* • **πολιτεύονται** → πολιτεύω, *I am a citizen, live as a citizen, have my citizenship/home.* The mid. is often used as a depon.

5.10 **ὡρισμένοις** → ὁρίζω, *I determine, fix, set.* • **νικῶσι** → νικάω, *I conquer; surpass, outdo.*

5.11 **διώκονται** → διώκω, *I pursue, persecute.*

5.12 **ἀγνοοῦνται** → ἀγνέω, *I do not know, am ignorant of.* • **κατακρίνονται** → κατακρίνω, *I condemn, pronounce a sentence against.* • **θανατοῦνται** → θανατόω, *I put to death.* • **ζωοποιοῦνται** → ζωοποιέω, *I make alive, bring to life.*

5.13 **πτωχεύουσι** → πτωχεύω, *I am (extremely) poor.* • **πλουτίζουσι** → πλουτίζω, *I make rich.* • **ὑστεροῦνται** → ὑστερέω, *I lack, am in need.* • **περισσεύουσιν** → περισσεύω, *I abound.*

5.14 **ἀτιμοῦνται** → ἀτιμόω, *I dishonor, disgrace.* • **ἀτιμίαις** → ἡ ἀτιμία, *dishonor, disgrace.* Art. for possession (Wal: 215; Smy: 1121). • **βλασφημοῦνται** → βλασφημέω, *I slander.* • **δικαιοῦνται** → δικαιόω, *I vindicate.*

βλασφημοῦνται, καὶ δικαιοῦνται. 5.15 λοιδοροῦνται καὶ εὐλογοῦσιν· ὑβρίζονται, καὶ τιμῶσιν. 5.16 ἀγαθοποιοῦντες ὡς κακοὶ κολάζονται· κολαζόμενοι χαίρουσιν ὡς ζωοποιούμενοι. 5.17 ὑπὸ Ἰουδαίων ὡς ἀλλόφυλοι πολεμοῦνται καὶ ὑπὸ Ἑλλήνων διώκονται, καὶ τὴν αἰτίαν τῆς ἔχθρας εἰπεῖν οἱ μισοῦντες οὐκ ἔχουσιν.

6.1 Ἁπλῶς δ' εἰπεῖν, ὅπερ ἐστὶν ἐν σώματι ψυχή, τοῦτ' εἰσὶν ἐν κόσμῳ Χριστιανοί. 6.2 ἔσπαρται κατὰ πάντων τῶν τοῦ σώματος μελῶν ἡ ψυχή, καὶ Χριστιανοὶ κατὰ τὰς τοῦ κόσμου πόλεις. 6.3 οἰκεῖ μὲν ἐν τῷ σώματι ψυχή, οὐκ ἔστι δὲ ἐκ τοῦ σώματος· καὶ Χριστιανοὶ ἐν κόσμῳ οἰκοῦσιν, οὐκ εἰσὶ δὲ ἐκ τοῦ κόσμου. 6.4 ἀόρατος ἡ ψυχὴ ἐν ὁρατῷ φρουρεῖται τῷ σώματι· καὶ Χριστιανοὶ γινώσκονται μὲν ὄντες ἐν τῷ κοσμῷ, ἀόρατος δὲ αὐτῶν ἡ θεοσέβεια μένει. 6.5 μισεῖ τὴν ψυχὴν ἡ σὰρξ καὶ πολεμεῖ μηδὲν ἀδικουμένη, διότι ταῖς ἡδοναῖς κωλύεται χρῆσθαι· μισεῖ καὶ Χριστιανοὺς ὁ κόσμος μηδὲν ἀδικούμενος, ὅτι ταῖς ἡδοναῖς ἀντιτάσσονται. 6.6 ἡ ψυχὴ τὴν μισοῦσαν ἀγαπᾷ σάρκα καὶ τὰ μέλη· καὶ Χριστιανοὶ τοὺς μισοῦντας

5.15 **λοιδοροῦνται** → λοιδορόω, *I revile, abuse.* • **εὐλογοῦσιν** → εὐλογέω, *I bless.* • **ὑβρίζονται** → ὑβρίζω, *I insult, mistreat.* • **τιμῶσιν** → τιμάω, *I honor.*

5.16 **ἀγαθοποιοῦντες** → ἀγαθοποιέω, *I do good.* Circ. ptc., concessive. • **κολάζονται** → κολάζω, *I punish, penalize.*

5.17 **ἀλλόφυλοι** → ἀλλόφυλος, ον, *alien, foreign.* • **πολεμοῦνται** → πολεμέω, *I wage war against, am hostile.* • **Ἑλλήνων** → ὁ Ἕλλην, *Greek.* • **αἰτίαν** → ἡ αἰτία, *reason, cause;* w. gen., *reason for/cause of.* • **ἔχθρας** → ἡ ἔχθρα, *hostility, enmity.* Art. for poss. (Wal: 215; Smy: 1121). • **μισοῦντες** → μισέω, *I hate.* • **ἔχουσιν** — ἔχω w. inf., *I can, am able* (BDAG 5: 421).

6.1 **ἁπλῶς** — *simply.* ἁπλῶς δ' εἰπεῖν, *to put it simply, in a word.* • **ὅπερ** → ὅσπερ, ἥπερ, ὅπερ (listed in BDAG under ὅς, 1jε: 727), *what/which indeed/in fact.* • **Χριστιανοί** → ὁ Χριστιανός, *Christian.*

6.2 **ἔσπαρται** — pf. pass. indic. 3 pl. → σπείρω, *I sow; scatter, spread, disperse.* • **κατά** — here, *through, throughout* (BDAG B1a: 511). • **μελῶν** → τὸ μέλος, *member.*

6.3 **οἰκεῖ** → οἰκέω, *I dwell, live.*

6.4 **ἀόρατος** → ἀόρατος, ον, *invisible.* W. implicit ὤν, "while being invisible," "although being invisible." • **ὁρατῷ** → ὁρατός, ή, όν, *visible.* • **φρουρεῖται** → φρουρέω, *I confine.* • **ὄντες** → εἰμί. Circ. ptc., perhaps causal. Holmes's text has μὲν ὄντες • **θεοσέβεια** → ἡ θεοσέβεια, *piety, worship; religion* (cf. *PGL* II: 635). Note BDAG's definition, "reverence for God or set of beliefs and practices relating to interest in God" (BDAG: 452).

6.5 **μισεῖ** → μισέω, *I hate.* • **πολεμεῖ** → πολεμέω, *I wage war against, am hostile.* • **ἀδικουμένη** → ἀδικέω, *I do wrong, mistreat.* Circ. ptc., concessive. • **διότι** — *because.* • **ἡδοναῖς** → ἡ ἡδονή, *pleasure.* • **κωλύεται** → κωλύω, *I prevent/forbid from doing,* w. inf. • **χρῆσθαι** → χράομαι, *I make use of, indulge,* w. dat. • **ἀντιτάσσονται** → ἀντιτάσσω, *I oppose;* mid., *set oneself against.*

6.6 **τὰ μέλη** — perhaps a poss. art. (Wal: 215; Smy: 1121).

ἀγαπῶσιν. 6.7 ἐγκέκλεισται μὲν ἡ ψυχὴ τῷ σώματι, συνέχει δὲ αὐτὴ τὸ σῶμα· καὶ Χριστιανοὶ κατέχονται μὲν ὡς ἐν φρουρᾷ τῷ κόσμῳ, αὐτοὶ δὲ συνέχουσι τὸν κόσμον. 6.8 ἀθάνατος ἡ ψυχὴ ἐν θνητῷ σκηνώματι κατοικεῖ· καὶ Χριστιανοὶ παροικοῦσιν ἐν φθαρτοῖς, τὴν ἐν οὐρανοῖς ἀφθαρσίαν προσδεχόμενοι. 6.9 κακουργουμένη σιτίοις καὶ ποτοῖς ἡ ψυχὴ βελτιοῦται· καὶ Χριστιανοὶ κολαζόμενοι καθ' ἡμέραν πλεονάζουσι μᾶλλον. 6.10 εἰς τοσαύτην αὐτοὺς τάξιν ἔθετο ὁ Θεός, ἣν οὐ θεμιτὸν αὐτοῖς παραιτήσασθαι.

7.1 Οὐ γὰρ ἐπίγειον, ὡς ἔφην, εὕρημα τοῦτ' αὐτοῖς παρεδόθη, οὐδὲ θνητὴν ἐπίνοιαν φυλάσσειν οὕτως ἀξιοῦσιν ἐπιμελῶς, οὐδὲ ἀνθρωπίνων οἰκονομίαν μυστηρίων πεπίστευνται. 7.2 ἀλλ' αὐτὸς ἀληθῶς ὁ παντοκράτωρ καὶ παντοκτίστης καὶ ἀόρατος Θεός, αὐτὸς ἀπ' οὐρανῶν τὴν ἀλήθειαν καὶ τὸν λόγον τὸν ἅγιον καὶ ἀπερινόητον ἀνθρώποις ἐνίδρυσε καὶ ἐγκατεστήριξε ταῖς καρδίαις αὐτῶν, οὐ καθάπερ ἄν τις εἰκάσειεν ἄνθρωπος, ὑπηρέτην

6.7 **ἐγκέκλεισται** → ἐγκλείω, *I lock up, shut up, enclose.* • **συνέχει** → συνέχω, *I hold together, sustain.* • **κατέχονται** → κατέχω, *I detain, confine.* • **φρουρᾷ** → ἡ φρουρά, *prison.*

6.8 **ἀθάνατος** → ἀθάνατος, ον, *immortal.* W. implicit ὢν, as in 6.4. • **θνητῷ** → θνητός, ή, όν, *mortal.* • **σκηνώματι** → τὸ σκήνωμα, *dwelling, habitation.* • **κατοικεῖ** → κατοικέω, *I dwell, live.* • **παροικοῦσιν** → παροικέω, *I live as a stranger.* • **φθαρτοῖς** → φθαρτός, ή, όν, *perishable.* • **ἀφθαρσίαν** → ἡ ἀφθαρσία, *immortality, incorruptibility, that which is imperishable.* • **προσδεχόμενοι** → προσδέχομαι, *I wait for.*

6.9 **κακουργουμένη** → κακουργέω, *I treat badly.* Perhaps temp. • **σιτίοις** → τὸ σιτίον, *food.* Dat. of ref. (Wal: 144; Smy: 1496). • **ποτοῖς** → τὸ ποτόν, *drink.* Dat. of ref. (Wal: 144; Smy: 1496). • **βελτιοῦται** → βελτιόω, *I improve, become better.* • **κολαζόμενοι** → κολάζω, *I punish, penalize.* • **καθ' ἡμέραν** — *daily, every day* (BDAG, ἡμέρα 2c: 437). • **πλεονάζουσι** → πλεονάζω, *I increase.*

6.10 **τοσαύτην** → τοσοῦτος, τοσαύτη, τοσοῦτον, *so great.* • **τάξιν** → ἡ τάξις, *a position.* • **ἔθετο** — aor. → τίθημι. • **θεμιτόν** → θεμιτός, ή, όν, *allowed, right.* οὐ θεμιτόν, *it is not right,* w. inf. • **παραιτήσασθαι** → παραιτέομαι, *I decline, refuse, avoid, reject.* Epex. inf. (Wal: 607).

7.1 **ἐπίγειον** → ἐπίγειος, ον, *earthly.* • **ἔφην** → φημί. • **εὕρημα** → τὸ εὕρημα, *discovery, invention.* Attrib. w. τοῦτ'. • **παρεδόθη** → παραδίδωμι. • **θνητήν** → θνητός, ή, όν, *mortal.* • **ἐπίνοιαν** → ἡ ἐπίνοια, *idea, thought.* • **φυλάσσειν** → φυλάσσω, *I guard.* • **ἀξιοῦσιν** → ἀξιόω, *I consider worthy/deserving,* w. inf. • **ἐπιμελῶς** — *carefully, diligently.* • **ἀνθρωπίνων** → ἀνθρώπινος, η, ον, *human.* • **οἰκονομίαν** → ἡ οἰκονομία, *administration, oversight.* See 1 Cor 9:17; Eph 3:2–3. • **μυστηρίων** → τὸ μυστήριον, *mystery.*

7.2 **ἀληθῶς** — *truly, in reality.* • **παντοκράτωρ** → ὁ παντοκράτωρ, *the Almighty.* • **παντοκτίστης** → ὁ παντοκτίστης, *the Creator of the universe* • **ἀόρατος** → ἀόρατος, ον, *invisible.* • **ἀπερινόητον** → ἀπερινόητος, ον, *incomprehensible.* • **ἐνίδρυσε** → ἐνιδρύω, *I place/establish in.* • **ἐγκατεστήριξε** → ἐγκαταστηρίζω, *I establish, fix firmly in.* • **καθάπερ** — *as, just as.* • **εἰκάσειεν** — aor. act.

τινὰ πέμψας ἢ ἄγγελον ἢ ἄρχοντα ἤ τινα τῶν διεπόντων τὰ ἐπίγεια ἤ τινα τῶν πεπιστευμένων τὰς ἐν οὐρανοῖς διοικήσεις, ἀλλ' αὐτὸν τὸν τεχνίτην καὶ δημιουργὸν τῶν ὅλων, ᾧ τοὺς οὐρανοὺς ἔκτισεν, ᾧ τὴν θάλασσαν ἰδίοις ὅροις ἐνέκλεισεν, οὗ τὰ μυστήρια πιστῶς πάντα φυλάσσει τὰ στοιχεῖα, παρ' οὗ τὰ μέτρα τῶν τῆς ἡμέρας δρόμων [ἥλιος] εἴληφε φυλάσσειν, ᾧ πειθαρχεῖ σελήνη νυκτὶ φαίνειν κελεύοντι, ᾧ πειθαρχεῖ τὰ ἄστρα τῷ τῆς σελήνης ἀκολουθοῦντα δρόμῳ, ᾧ πάντα διατέτακται καὶ διώρισται καὶ ὑποτέτακται, οὐρανοὶ καὶ τὰ ἐν οὐρανοῖς, γῆ καὶ τὰ ἐν τῇ γῇ, θάλασσα καὶ τὰ ἐν τῇ θαλάσσῃ, πῦρ, ἀήρ, ἄβυσσος, τὰ ἐν ὕψεσι, τὰ ἐν βάθεσι, τὰ ἐν τῷ μεταξύ· τοῦτον πρὸς αὐτοὺς ἀπέστειλεν. 7.3 ἆρά γε, ὡς ἀνθρώπων ἄν τις λογίσαιτο, ἐπὶ τυραννίδι καὶ φόβῳ καὶ καταπλήξει; 7.4 οὐμενοῦν· ἀλλ' ἐν ἐπιεικείᾳ [καὶ] πραΰτητι ὡς βασιλεὺς πέμπων υἱὸν βασιλέα ἔπεμψεν, ὡς

---

opt. 3 sg. → εἰκάζω, *I suppose, imagine, guess.* • **ἄνθρωπος** — The texts of Ehrman and Holmes have ἀνθρώποις, an indir. obj. w. πέμψας. • **ὑπηρέτην** → ὁ ὑπηρέτης, *helper, assistant.* • **ἄρχοντα** → ὁ ἄρχων, *ruler.* • **διεπόντων** → διέπω, *I administer, manage.* Partitive gen. (Wal: 84; Smy: 1306). • **ἐπίγεια** → ἐπίγειος, ον, *earthly.* • **διοικήσεις** → ἡ διοίκησις, *administration, management.* • **τεχνίτην** → ὁ τεχνίτης, *artisan, designer.* • **δημιουργόν** → ὁ δημιουργός, *builder, maker, creator.* • **ἔκτισεν** → κτίζω, *I create.* • **ὅροις** → ὁ ὅρος, *boundary, limit.* • **ἐνέκλεισεν** → ἐγκλείω, *I lock up, shut up, enclose.* • **μυστήρια** → τὸ μυστήριον, *mystery.* • **πιστῶς** — *faithfully.* • **πάντα** — mod. τὰ στοιχεῖα. • **φυλάσσει** → φυλάσσω, *I guard; keep, observe.* • **στοιχεῖα** → τὸ στοιχεῖον, *elements,* i.e., the "substances underlying the natural world, the basic *elements* fr. which everything in the world is made and of which it is composed" (BDAG 1a: 946). See 8.2 below. • **μέτρα** → τὸ μέτρον, *measure.* • **δρόμων** → ὁ δρόμος, *course.* • **ἥλιος** → ὁ ἥλιος, *sun.* • **πειθαρχεῖ** → πειθαρχέω, *I obey.* • **σελήνη** → ἡ σελήνη, *moon.* • **νυκτί** — dat. of time when (Wal: 155; Smy: 1539). • **φαίνειν** → φαίνω, *I shine.* Indir. disc., the content of the command (Wal: 603; Smy: 2016). • **κελεύοντι** → κελεύω, *I order, command.* Dat. since the subj. of the circ. ptc. is ᾧ, *when/as he commands.* • **ἄστρα** → ὁ ἀστήρ, *star.* • **διατέτακται** → διατάσσω, *I set in order.* • **διώρισται** — pf. → διορίζω, *I set limits to, distinguish by establishing boundaries, delimit.* • **ὑποτέτακται** → ὑποτάσσω, *I subject, put into subjection.* • **ἀήρ** → ὁ ἀήρ, *air.* • **ἄβυσσος** → ἡ ἄβυσσος, *depth, abyss,* i.e., here, "immensely deep space" in contrast with sky and earth (BDAG 1: 2). See Gen 1:2. • **ὕψεσι** → τὸ ὕψος, *height.* • **βάθεσι** → τὸ βάθος, *depth.* • **μεταξύ** — here as adv., *between, in the middle.*

7.3 **ἆρά γε** — *well, then.* • **λογίσαιτο** — aor. opt. → λογίζομαι, *I think, suppose, consider.* Potential opt. (Smy: 1824), *as some human* (lit., *one among human beings*) *might think/suppose,* emphasizing that this is how a human would take things into account, as opposed to God's way. • **ἐπὶ τυραννίδι** — supply "he sent him" or "it was" from the context. • **ἐπί** — here, *for* (BDAG 11: 366). • **τυραννίδι** → ἡ τυραννίς, *tyranny, despotic rule.* • **φόβῳ** → ὁ φόβος, *a fear.* • **καταπλήξει** → ἡ κατάπληξις, *terror.*

7.4 **οὐμενοῦν** (listed in LSI under οὐ μὲν οὖν) — *not at all, certainly not, by no means* (BDAG: 736). • **ἐπιεικείᾳ** → ἡ ἐπιείκεια, *gentleness.* • **πραΰτητι** →

Θεὸν ἔπεμψεν, ὡς [ἄνθρωπον] πρὸς ἀνθρώπους ἔπεμψεν, ὡς σῴζων ἔπεμψεν, ὡς πείθων, οὐ βιαζόμενος· βία γὰρ οὐ πρόσεστι τῷ Θεῷ. 7.5 ἔπεμψεν ὡς καλῶν, οὐ διώκων· ἔπεμψεν ὡς ἀγαπῶν, οὐ κρίνων. 7.6 πέμψει γὰρ αὐτὸν κρίνοντα, καὶ τίς αὐτοῦ τὴν παρουσίαν ὑποστήσεται; . . . [The MS has a section missing at this point.] 7.7 [Οὐχ ὁρᾷς] παραβαλλομένους θηρίοις, ἵνα ἀρνήσωνται τὸν Κύριον, καὶ μὴ νικωμένους; 7.8 οὐχ ὁρᾷς ὅσῳ πλείονες κολάζονται, τοσούτῳ πλεονάζοντας ἄλλους; 7.9 ταῦτα ἀνθρώπου οὐ δοκεῖ τὰ ἔργα, ταῦτα δύναμίς ἐστι Θεοῦ· ταῦτα τῆς παρουσίας αὐτοῦ δείγματα.

ἡ πραΰτης, *humility, courtesy.* • **ὡς πρὸς ἀνθρώπους** — all modern editions emend the text by the addition of ἄνθρωπον: ὡς ἄνθρωπον πρὸς ἀνθρώπους. • **βιαζόμενος** → βιάζω, *I dominate, compel, use force;* often, as here, as a depon. mid. • **βία** → ἡ βία, *force, violence.* • **πρόσεστι** → πρόσειμι, *I belong to, am an attribute of,* w. dat.

7.5 **διώκων** → διώκω, *I pursue, persecute.*

7.6 **παρουσίαν** → ἡ παρουσία, *presence, coming.* • **ὑποστήσεται** → ὑφίστημι, *I resist, face, endure.* An allusion to Mal 3:2.

7.7 **οὐχ ὁρᾷς** — editors, beginning with Stephanus in 1592, have supplied these words on the basis of the context (7.6) to introduce the text that follows a gap in the MS. • **παραβαλλομένους** → παραβάλλω, *I throw to.* Attrib. ptc. • **θηρίοις** → τὸ θηρίον, *animal, beast.* • **ἀρνήσωνται** → ἀρνέομαι, *I deny.* • **νικωμένους** → νικάω, *I conquer, overcome.*

7.8 **ὅσῳ** — see note below on τοσούτῳ. • **πλείονες** → πλείων, here as subst., *the larger part, the majority* (BDAG, πολύς 1bβ: 848; 2bβ: 849). • **κολάζονται** → κολάζω, *I punish.* • **τοσούτῳ** → τοσοῦτος, τοσαύτη, τοσοῦτον, *so great.* ὅσῳ . . . τοσούτῳ are correlative, *the more . . . the more.* • **πλεονάζοντας** → πλεονάζω, *I increase.*

7.9 **δοκεῖ** → δοκέω, *I seem, appear to be.* • **δείγματα** → τὸ δεῖγμα, *proof.* Pred. nom.

The Martyrdom of Polycarp

Introduction

"For eighty-six years I have been his servant, and he did me no wrong. And how am I able to blaspheme my king who saved me?" So said Polycarp when he was encouraged to swear by the Emperor, and so save himself from martyrdom. The *Martyrdom of Polycarp* (*Mart. Pol.*) is one of the earliest and most gripping of the martyr accounts from the early church. The story is told with simplicity, but great dramatic effect. The saintliness of Polycarp and his love and peace in facing his martyrdom paint a very moving picture. Throughout the history of the church, Polycarp's martyrdom has strengthened believers to take courage and be faithful.

The *Martyrdom of Polycarp* is the oldest account of a Christian martyr we have apart from the martyrdom of Stephen in Acts 7. The text says the martyrdom took place on February 23 at 2 p.m., but the year is not given (*Mart. Pol.* 21). The traditional date for Polycarp's death is February 23, 155, though some scholars suggest February 22, 156, as the actual date. Eusebius, however, places his death a decade later, in 166 or 167, during the widespread persecution of Christians under Marcus Aurelius, who ruled from 161 to 180 (Eusebius, *Hist. eccl.* 4.14.10–15.1). The account was written by an eyewitness and therefore was probably written not long after Polycarp's death, either 155–160 or 170–180.

Polycarp was a major link between the apostles and the later leaders of the church. Irenaeus, one of the main leaders in the latter half of the second century, says he sat in Polycarp's house and heard him recount the teachings of the apostle John and others who had seen the Lord (*Hist. eccl.* 5.20). Irenaeus says that Polycarp

> was not only instructed by apostles, and conversed with many who had seen Christ, but was also, by apostles in Asia, appointed bishop of the Church in Smyrna, whom I also saw in my early youth, for he tarried [on earth] a very long time, and, when a very old man, gloriously and most nobly suffering martyrdom, departed this life, having always taught the things which he had learned from the apostles, and which the Church has handed down, and which alone are true (Irenaeus, *Against Heresies* 3.3.4, *ANF*).

Along with the *Martyrdom of Polycarp* and Irenaeus's testimony, we also have a letter Ignatius of Antioch wrote to Polycarp while Ignatius was on his way to his own martyrdom, as well as a letter Polycarp himself wrote to the Christians in Philadelphia. The Philadelphians had requested copies of Ignatius's letters and also wanted to receive instruction from Polycarp regarding righteousness. As he spells out the way of discipleship, Polycarp describes righteousness in very practical terms, quoting several times from the Old Testament and extensively from documents later included in the New Testament.

The *Martyrdom of Polycarp* testifies that Polycarp actually lived in his life what he taught in his letter to the Philadelphians. We see Polycarp as a saintly old man who had served the Lord Jesus throughout his long life (*Mart. Pol.* 9.3). The believers revered him (13.2), and even the ones sent to arrest him bore witness to his godliness (7.3).

The document begins with a statement that the events leading up to his death took place so that the Lord might show "a martyrdom in keeping with the gospel" (*Mart. Pol.* 1.1; cf. 19.1). An explicit example follows immediately, "For he waited to be betrayed, as also did the Lord" (1.2). At least a dozen such parallels are described,[1] showing Polycarp's martyrdom as an imitation of Christ's.

The *Martyrdom of Polycarp* gives a clear picture of the non-Christians' view of Christians as atheists (*Mart. Pol.* 3.2; 9.2), since Christians denied the Greco-Roman deities. Likewise, the central issue between the Christians and the government is very clearly focused, for to confess Caesar as Lord (8.2) is to blaspheme Christ (9.3).

Polycarp, according to this account, is gentle and humble, but also firm and fearless. He becomes an example to imitate, and his bones are collected to celebrate the "birthday of his martyrdom" (*Mart. Pol.* 18.3). The honor and veneration shown to the martyrs, however, is clearly distinguished from the worship due to Christ (17). The point is also made that while the martyrs are greatly to be honored, one should not seek martyrdom by handing oneself over to the authorities (4).

The *Martyrdom of Polycarp* begins by referring to a local persecution that has arisen, which has resulted in several martyrdoms. The authorities specifically target Polycarp and begin a search for him. The believers prevail upon Polycarp to hide, but he is soon found because he is betrayed by members of his own household (*Mart. Pol.* 6.2). When the authorities come upon him, he responds, "God's will be done" (7.1), another of the parallels with Jesus (Luke 22:42). He requests permission to pray and is allowed to do so, continuing in prayer for two hours. The selection included here picks up the story just after this prayer.

Edition used:	J. B. Lightfoot, rev., tran. *The Apostolic Fathers.* Edited and completed by J. R. Harmer. 1891. Repr., Berkeley, Calif.: Apocryphile, 2004.
Level of difficulty:	Easy [1–2]

[1] Cf. Clayton N. Jefford, Kenneth J. Harder, and Louis D. Amezaga Jr., *Reading the Apostolic Fathers: An Introduction* (Peabody, Mass.: Hendrickson, 1996), 94–95.

The Martyrdom of Polycarp 8–18 Polycarp's Arrest, Trial, and Martyrdom

8.1 Ἐπεὶ δέ ποτε κατέπαυσεν τὴν προσευχήν, μνημονεύσας ἁπάντων καὶ τῶν πώποτε συμβεβληκότων αὐτῷ, μικρῶν τε καὶ μεγάλων, ἐνδόξων τε καὶ ἀδόξων, καὶ πάσης τῆς κατὰ τὴν οἰκουμένην καθολικῆς ἐκκλησίας, τῆς ὥρας ἐλθούσης τοῦ ἐξιέναι, ὄνῳ καθίσαντες αὐτὸν ἤγαγον εἰς τὴν πόλιν, ὄντος σαββάτου μεγάλου. 8.2 καὶ ὑπήντα αὐτῷ ὁ εἰρήναρχος Ἡρῴδης καὶ ὁ πατὴρ αὐτοῦ Νικήτης, οἳ καὶ μεταθέντες αὐτὸν ἐπὶ τὴν καροῦχαν ἔπειθον παρακαθεζόμενοι καὶ λέγοντες· Τί γὰρ κακόν ἐστιν εἰπεῖν, Κύριος Καῖσαρ, καὶ ἐπιθῦσαι, καὶ τὰ τούτοις ἀκόλουθα, καὶ διασῴζεσθαι; ὁ δὲ τὰ μὲν πρῶτα οὐκ ἀπεκρίνατο αὐτοῖς, ἐπιμενόντων δὲ αὐτῶν ἔφη· Οὐ μέλλω ποιεῖν ὃ συμβουλεύετέ μοι. 8.3 οἱ δέ, ἀποτυχόντες τοῦ πεῖσαι αὐτόν, δεινὰ

8.1 **ἐπεί** — *when, since, because.* • **ποτέ** — *at last* (BDAG 1: 856). • **κατέπαυσεν** → καταπαύω, *I stop, bring to an end, finish.* • **προσευχήν** → ἡ προσευχή, *prayer.* A good example of the poss. art. (Wal: 215; Smy: 1121). • **μνημονεύσας** → μνημονεύω, *I remember.* • **ἁπάντων** → ἅπας, ασα, αν, *all, everyone.* • **πώποτε** — adv., *ever.* • **συμβεβληκότων** — pf. act. ptc. → συμβάλλω, *I meet, come into contact with.* • **μικρῶν** → μικρός, ά, όν, *small.* • **ἐνδόξων** → ἔνδοξος, ον, *honored, distinguished.* • **ἀδόξων** → ἄδοξος, ον, *without reputation, obscure.* • **κατά** — here, *throughout* (BDAG B1a: 511). • **οἰκουμένην** → ἡ οἰκουμένη, *world, inhabited earth.* • **καθολικῆς** → καθολικός, ή, όν, *general, universal.* • **ἐλθούσης** — 2 aor. act. ptc. → ἔρχομαι. Gen. abs. • **ἐξιέναι** — pres. inf. → ἔξειμι, *I go out, go away, depart.* • **ὄνῳ** → ὁ and ἡ ὄνος, *donkey.* • **καθίσαντες** → καθίζω, *I seat, set.* Circ. ptc., either temp. or attend. circ. • **ὄντος** — pres. ptc. → εἰμί. Gen. abs.

8.2 **ὑπήντα** — impf. act. indic. 3 sg. → ὑπαντάω, *I go to meet, meet,* w. dat. A sg. verb is often used w. a comp. subj. (Wal: 401; Smy: 968). • **εἰρήναρχος** → ὁ εἰρήναρχος, *chief of police.* • **Ἡρῴδης** → ὁ Ἡρῴδης, *Herod.* • **Νικήτης** → ὁ Νικήτης, *Nicetes.* • **μεταθέντες** — aor. pass. ptc. → μετατίθημι, *I transfer;* pass., *have someone transferred.* • **καροῦχαν** → ἡ καροῦχα, *carriage.* • **ἔπειθον** → πείθω — a good example of the conative impf. (Wal: 550; Smy: 1895). • **παρακαθεζόμενοι** → παρακαθέζομαι, *I sit beside.* • **γάρ** — "oft. in questions, where the English idiom leaves the word untransl. add *then, pray,* or prefixes *what!* or *why!* to the question" (BDAG 1f: 189). • **κακόν** → κακός, here, *wrong, harm* (BDAG 3: 501). • **Καῖσαρ** → ὁ Καῖσαρ, *Caesar.* • **ἐπιθῦσαι** → ἐπιθύω, *I offer a sacrifice.* • **ἀκόλουθα** → ἀκόλουθος, ον, *following.* τὰ τούτοις ἀκόλουθα, *and so forth* (BDAG: 37). This expression seems to be part of Herod's and Nicetes's question. Lightfoot, however, takes it as the author's comment, which is possible though perhaps somewhat less likely due to the position of the following inf. • **διασῴζεσθαι** → διασῴζω, *I save, rescue.* Note the mid. • **ὁ δέ** — art. used as a pron., *but he.* This is common in narrative (BDAG 1c: 686). • **πρῶτα** → πρῶτος, τὰ πρῶτα, *at first* (BDAG 1a: 893). • **ἐπιμενόντων** → ἐπιμένω, *I continue, persist in.* Gen. abs., causal. • **ἔφη** — 2 aor. act. indic. → φημί. • **συμβουλεύετε** → συμβουλεύω, *I advise.*

ῥήματα ἔλεγον καὶ μετὰ σπουδῆς καθῄρουν αὐτόν, ὡς κατιόντα ἀπὸ τῆς καρούχας ἀποσῦραι τὸ ἀντικνήμιον. καὶ μὴ ἐπιστραφείς, ὡς οὐδὲν πεπονθώς, προθύμως μετὰ σπουδῆς ἐπορεύετο, ἀγόμενος εἰς τὸ στάδιον, θορύβου τηλικούτου ὄντος ἐν τῷ σταδίῳ ὡς μηδὲ ἀκουσθῆναί τινα δύνασθαι.

9.1 Τῷ δὲ Πολυκάρπῳ εἰσιόντι εἰς τὸ στάδιον φωνὴ ἐξ οὐρανοῦ ἐγένετο· Ἴσχυε, Πολύκαρπε καὶ ἀνδρίζου. καὶ τὸν μὲν εἰπόντα οὐδεὶς εἶδεν, τὴν δὲ φωνὴν τῶν ἡμετέρων οἱ παρόντες ἤκουσαν. καὶ λοιπὸν προσαχθέντος αὐτοῦ, θόρυβος ἦν μέγας ἀκουσάντων ὅτι Πολύκαρπος συνείληπται. 9.2 προσαχθέντα οὖν αὐτὸν ἀνηρώτα ὁ ἀνθύπατος, εἰ αὐτὸς εἴη· τοῦ δὲ ὁμολογοῦντος, ἔπειθεν ἀρνεῖσθαι λέγων, Αἰδέσθητί σου τὴν ἡλικίαν, καὶ ἕτερα τούτοις ἀκόλουθα, ὡς ἔθος αὐτοῖς λέγειν· Ὄμοσον τὴν Καίσαρος τύχην, μετανόησον, εἶπον, Αἶρε τοὺς ἀθέους. ὁ δὲ Πολύκαρπος ἐμβριθεῖ τῷ

8.3 **ἀποτυχόντες** — 2 aor. act. ptc. → ἀποτυγχάνω, *I fail.* • **πεῖσαι** — aor. act. inf. → πείθω. • **δεινά** → δεινός, ή, όν, *terrible, fearful.* • **ἔλεγον** → λέγω — perhaps an ingressive/inchoative impf. (Wal: 544; Smy: 1900). • **σπουδῆς** → ἡ σπουδή, *haste, speed.* • **καθῄρουν** — impf. act. indic. → καθαιρέω, *I take down, bring down, put down.* • **ὡς** — w. inf. for result (BDAG 4: 1105), *so that he scraped his shin.* A second instance of this use of ὡς comes at the end of section 8.3. • **κατιόντα** — pres. act. ptc. → κάτειμι, *I come down, get down.* • **ἀποσῦραι** — aor. act. inf. → ἀποσύρω, *I tear, scrape.* • **ἀντικνήμιον** → τὸ ἀντικνήμιον, *shin.* • **ἐπιστραφείς** → ἐπιστρέφω, *I turn.* • **πεπονθώς** — 2 pf. act. ptc. masc. nom. sg. → πάσχω, *I suffer.* • **προθύμως** — adv., *eagerly.* • **στάδιον** → τὸ στάδιον, *arena, stadium.* • **θορύβου** → ὁ θόρυβος, *noise, clamor.* Subj. of gen. abs. • **τηλικούτου** → τηλικοῦτος, αύτη, οῦτο, *so great, very great.*

9.1 **Πολυκάρπῳ** → ὁ Πολύκαρπος, *Polycarp.* • **εἰσιόντι** — pres. act. ptc. → εἴσειμι, *I enter.* Dat. ptc. for time (Smy: 1498) *when/as he entered.* • **στάδιον** → τὸ στάδιον, *arena, stadium.* • **ἴσχυε** → ἰσχύω, *I am strong.* • **ἀνδρίζου** → ἀνδρίζομαι, *I act like a man, am courageous.* • **ἡμετέρων** → ἡμέτερος, α, ον, *our;* here, *our people.* Partitive gen. (Wal: 84; Smy: 1306). • **παρόντες** — pres. act. ptc. → πάρειμι, *I am present.* • **προσαχθέντος** → προσάγω, *I bring forward.* Gen. abs. • **θόρυβος** → ὁ θόρυβος, *noise, clamor.* • **συνείληπται** — 2 pf. pass. indic. → συλλαμβάνω, *I seize, grasp, apprehend, arrest.*

9.2 **προσαχθέντα** → προσάγω. Mod. αὐτόν, "him having been brought forward," *after he was brought forward.* • **ἀνηρώτα** — impf. act. indic. → ἀνερωτάω, *I ask.* • **ἀνθύπατος** → ὁ ἀνθύπατος, *proconsul.* • **εἴη** — pres. opt. 3 sg. → εἰμί. Opt. for indir. question (Wal: 483; Smy: 2599). The texts of Ehrman and Holmes include the pred. nom. Πολύκαρπος, *whether he were Polycarp.* • **ὁμολογοῦντος** → ὁμολογέω, *I confess.* Gen. abs. The subj. is the art. in τοῦ δέ, the art. serving as a pron. (BDAG 1c: 686). • **ἔπειθεν** → πείθω. A good example of the conative impf. (Wal: 550; Smy: 1895). • **ἀρνεῖσθαι** → ἀρνέομαι, *I deny.* • **αἰδέσθητι** — aor. pass. impv. 2 sg. → αἰδέομαι, *I respect;* here, *have regard for.* • **ἡλικίαν** → ἡ ἡλικία, *age.* • **ἀκόλουθα** → ἀκόλουθος, ον, *following.* καὶ ἕτερα τούτοις ἀκόλουθα, *and other such things* (BDAG: 37). • **ὡς** — Ehrman's text has ὧν. • **ἔθος** → τὸ ἔθος, *habit, custom.* Supply, "it is." • **ὄμοσον** — aor. act. impv. → ὀμνύω, *I swear.* W. acc. for that by which one swears. • **Καίσαρος** → ὁ Καῖσαρ,

προσώπῳ εἰς πάντα τὸν ὄχλον τὸν ἐν τῷ σταδίῳ ἀνόμων ἐθνῶν ἐμβλέψας καὶ ἐπισείσας αὐτοῖς τὴν χεῖρα, στενάξας τε καὶ ἀναβλέψας εἰς τὸν οὐρανόν, εἶπεν· Αἶρε τοὺς ἀθέους. 9.3 ἐγκειμένου δὲ τοῦ ἀνθυπάτου καὶ λέγοντος· Ὄμοσον, καὶ ἀπολύω σε· λοιδόρησον τὸν Χριστόν· ἔφη ὁ Πολύκαρπος· Ὀγδοήκοντα καὶ ἓξ ἔτη [ἔχω] δουλεύω[ν] αὐτῷ καὶ οὐδέν με ἠδίκησεν· καὶ πῶς δύναμαι βλασφημῆσαι τὸν βασιλέα μου, τὸν σώσαντά με;

10.1 Ἐπιμένοντος δὲ πάλιν αὐτοῦ καὶ λέγοντος, Ὄμοσον τὴν Καίσαρος τύχην, ἀπεκρίνατο· Εἰ κενοδοξεῖς ἵνα ὀμόσω τὴν Καίσαρος τύχην, ὡς σὺ λέγεις, προσποιεῖ δὲ ἀγνοεῖν με τίς εἰμι, μετὰ παρρησίας ἄκουε· Χριστιανός εἰμι. εἰ δὲ θέλεις τὸν τοῦ χριστιανισμοῦ μαθεῖν λόγον, δὸς ἡμέραν καὶ ἄκουσον. 10.2 ἔφη ὁ ἀνθύπατος· Πεῖσον τὸν δῆμον. ὁ δὲ Πολύκαρπος

Caesar. • **τύχην** → ἡ τύχη, *fortune.* A ref. to the guardian spirit. Acc. of oaths (Wal: 204; Smy: 1596). • **μετανόησον** → μετανοέω, *I repent.* • **ἀθέους** → ἄθεος, ον, *without God;* subst., *atheist.* • **ἐμβριθεῖ** → ἐμβριθής, ές, *dignified, serious.* • **ἀνόμων** → ἄνομος, ον, *lawless.* • **ἐθνῶν** → τὸ ἔθνος, here, *unbeliever* (BDAG 2a: 276). • **ἐμβλέψας** → ἐμβλέπω, *I look at, gaze upon.* Circ. ptc., either temp. or attend. circ. • **ἐπισείσας** — aor. act. ptc. → ἐπισείω, *I shake at/against.* Circ. ptc., either temp. or attend. circ. Since this word is used of a "threatening gesture" (BDAG 1: 378), w. χείρ the English idiom would be, "shake one's fist." • **στενάξας** — aor. act. ptc. → στενάζω, *I sigh, groan.* Circ. ptc., either temp. or attend. circ. • **ἀναβλέψας** → ἀναβλέπω, *I look up.* Circ. ptc., either temp. or attend. circ.

9.3 **ἐγκειμένου** → ἔγκειμαι, *I insist, warn urgently.* Gen. abs. • **ἀπολύω** → ἀπολύω, *I release, set free.* A futuristic pres. (Smy: 1879), which "typically adds the connotations of immediacy and certainty" (Wal: 535). • **λοιδόρησον** → λοιδορέω, *I revile, abuse.* • **ἔφη** — 2 aor. act. indic. → φημί. • **ὀγδοήκοντα** → ὀγδοήκοντα, indecl., *eighty.* • **ἕξ** → ἕξ, indecl., *six.* • **ἔτη** → τὸ ἔτος, *year.* Acc. for extent of time (Wal: 201; Smy: 1582) • **ἔχω** — here, *be (in a certain way),* describing a state or condition (BDAG 10b: 422). Woodenly: "for 86 years I am in the condition of serving him," *for 86 years I have been his servant.* Holmes's text has ἔχω δουλεύων without brackets; Ehrman's text does not have the material in brackets, but simply has δουλεύω. • **δουλεύων** → δουλεύω, *I serve,* w. dat. • **ἠδίκησεν** → ἀδικέω, *I do wrong.* • **βλασφημῆσαι** → βλασφημέω, *I blaspheme, slander, revile.*

10.1 **ἐπιμένοντος** → ἐπιμένω, *I continue, persist in.* Gen. abs. • **ὄμοσον** — aor. act. impv. → ὀμνύω, *I swear.* • **Καίσαρος** → ὁ Καῖσαρ, *Caesar.* • **τύχην** → ἡ τύχη, *fortune.* A ref. to the guardian spirit. • **κενοδοξεῖς** → κενοδοξέω, *I vainly imagine.* • **προσποιεῖ** — pres. mid. indic. 2 sg. → προσποιέω, *I pretend.* Normally the form would be προσποιῇ; for this unusual form see BDF: 27. • **ἀγνοεῖν** → ἀγνοέω, *I am ignorant.* ἀγνοεῖν με τίς εἰμι. Very woodenly: "to be ignorant of me, (namely) who I am." • **παρρησίας** → ἡ παρρησία, *openness, frankness, plainness.* μετὰ παρρησίας, *plainly* (BDAG, παρρησία 1: 781). • **Χριστιανός** → ὁ Χριστιανός, *Christian.* • **χριστιανισμοῦ** → ὁ χριστιανισμός, *Christianity, the Christian Way* • **μαθεῖν** — 2 aor. act. inf. → μανθάνω, *I learn.* • **λόγον** — here, *message.* • **δός** — aor. act. impv. 2 sg. → δίδωμι.

10.2 **ἔφη** — 2 aor. act. indic. → φημί. • **ἀνθύπατος** → ὁ ἀνθύπατος, *proconsul.* • **πεῖσον** — aor. act. impv. → πείθω. • **δῆμον** → ὁ δῆμος, *people, crowd.*

εἶπεν· Σὲ μὲν κἂν λόγου ἠξίωσα· δεδιδάγμεθα γὰρ ἀρχαῖς καὶ ἐξουσίαις ὑπὸ Θεοῦ τεταγμέναις τιμὴν κατὰ τὸ προσῆκον τὴν μὴ βλάπτουσαν ἡμᾶς, ἀπονέμειν· ἐκείνους δὲ οὐκ ἀξίους ἡγοῦμαι τοῦ ἀπολογεῖσθαι αὐτοῖς.

11.1 Ὁ δὲ ἀνθύπατος εἶπεν· Θηρία ἔχω, τούτοις σε παραβαλῶ, ἐὰν μὴ μετανοήσῃς. ὁ δὲ εἶπεν· Κάλει· ἀμετάθετος γὰρ ἡμῖν ἡ ἀπὸ τῶν κρειττόνων ἐπὶ τὰ χείρω μετάνοια· καλὸν δὲ μετατίθεσθαι ἀπὸ τῶν χαλεπῶν ἐπὶ τὰ δίκαια. 11.2 ὁ δὲ πάλιν πρὸς αὐτόν· Πυρί σε ποιήσω δαπανηθῆναι· εἰ τῶν θηρίων καταφρονεῖς, ἐὰν μὴ μετανοήσῃς. ὁ δὲ Πολύκαρπος· Πῦρ ἀπειλεῖς τὸ πρὸς ὥραν καιόμενον καὶ μετ᾽ ὀλίγον σβεννύμενον· ἀγνοεῖς γὰρ τὸ τῆς μελλούσης κρίσεως καὶ αἰωνίου κολάσεως τοῖς ἀσεβέσι τηρούμενον πῦρ. ἀλλὰ τί βραδύνεις; φέρε ὃ βούλει.

• **Πολύκαρπος** → ὁ Πολύκαρπος, *Polycarp.* • **κἂν** — crasis of καί and ἐάν, here, *at least* (BDAG 3: 507). Ehrman's text has καί. • **ἠξίωσα** — pf. act. indic. → ἀξιόω, *I consider worthy.* Ehrman's text has ἠξίωκα. • **δεδιδάγμεθα** — pf. pass. indic. → διδάσκω. The content of the teaching is provided by the inf. ἀπονέμειν. • **τεταγμέναις** — pf. pass. ptc. → τάσσω, *I arrange, put in place.* Adj. ptc., mod. ἀρχαις καὶ ἐξουσίαις. • **τιμήν** → ἡ τιμή, *honor.* • **προσῆκον** — pres. act. ptc. → προσήκω, *I am fitting.* κατὰ τὸ προσῆκον, *as is fitting* (BDAG 2: 880). • **βλάπτουσαν** — pres. act. ptc. → βλάπτω, *I harm, injure.* Adj. ptc., mod. τιμήν. "Honor that does not harm us" would not include the sacrifices to the emperor that the officials were demanding. • **ἀπονέμειν** → ἀπονέμω, *assign, show, pay, accord.* • **ἀξίους** → ἄξιος, α, ον, *worthy.* • **ἡγοῦμαι** → ἡγέομαι, *I think, consider, regard.* • **ἀπολογεῖσθαι** → ἀπολογέομαι, *I defend oneself.* Epex. inf., mod. ἀξίους (Wal: 607; Smy: 2006).

11.1 **ἀνθύπατος** → ὁ ἀνθύπατος, *proconsul.* • **θηρία** → τὸ θηρίον, *beast,* "oft. of *wild animals* in a controlled setting, namely of fighting w. animals in an arena" (BDAG 1aγ: 456). • **παραβαλῶ** → παραβάλλω, *I throw to.* • **ἐὰν μή** — *unless.* • **μετανοήσῃς** → μετανοέω, *I repent.* • **ὁ δέ** — art. used as a pron., *and/but he.* Common in narrative (BDAG 1c: 686). • **κάλει** → καλέω, *I call.* • **ἀμετάθετος** → ἀμετάθετος, ον, *impossible.* Pred. nom. Note the wordplay w. μετάνοια (BDAG 2: 53). • **κρειττόνων** → κρείττων, ον, *better.* • **χείρω** — neut. acc. pl. → χείρων, ον, *worse.* • **μετάνοια** → ἡ μετάνοια, *repentance.* Subj. w. verb "to be" elided. • **μετατίθεσθαι** → μετατίθημι, *I change.* This inf. is the subj. ("to change . . . is good/noble"), but such constructions are usually translated, *it is good to change* (BDAG 2dγ: 505). • **χαλεπῶν** → χαλεπός, ή, όν, *hard, difficult; evil.* • **δίκαια** → δίκαιος, α, ον, *right, righteous, upright.*

11.2 **ποιήσω** → ποιέω. Here w. acc. and inf., *I cause* (BDAG 2h: 840). Ehrman's text has ποῖω. • **δαπανηθῆναι** → δαπανάω, *I spend; wear out, destroy;* w. "fire," *consume.* • **εἰ** — here, *since* (BDAG 3: 278), though cf. Wal: 690. • **καταφρονεῖς** → καταφρονέω, *I look down on, scorn, despise.* • **Πολύκαρπος** → ὁ Πολύκαρπος, *Polycarp.* Ehrman's text adds εἶπεν. • **ἀπειλεῖς** → ἀπειλέω, *I threaten, warn.* • **ὥραν** → ὥρα, here, *a short while* (BDAG 2b: 1102). • **καιόμενον** → καίω, *I burn.* The pass. can have an act. sense (BDAG 1a: 499). • **ὀλίγον** → ὀλίγος, η, ον, *few; short.* • **σβεννύμενον** → σβέννυμι, *I quench, put out, extinguish.* • **ἀγνοεῖς** → ἀγνοέω, *I am ignorant, do not know.* • **τὸ τῆς** — τὸ goes w. πῦρ at the end of the sentence, w. the intervening material mod. τὸ πῦρ. • **κρίσεως** → ἡ κρίσις, *judgment.*

12.1 Ταῦτα δὲ καὶ ἕτερα πλείονα λέγων, θάρσους καὶ χαρᾶς ἐνεπίμπλατο, καὶ τὸ πρόσωπον αὐτοῦ χάριτος ἐπληροῦτο, ὥστε οὐ μόνον μὴ συμπεσεῖν ταραχθέντα ὑπὸ τῶν λεγομένων πρὸς αὐτόν, ἀλλὰ τοὐναντίον τὸν ἀνθύπατον ἐκστῆναι, πέμψαι τε τὸν ἑαυτοῦ κήρυκα, ἐν μέσῳ τῷ σταδίῳ κηρῦξαι τρίς· Πολύκαρπος ὡμολόγησεν ἑαυτὸν Χριστιανὸν εἶναι. 12.2 τούτου λεχθέντος ὑπὸ τοῦ κήρυκος, ἅπαν τὸ πλῆθος ἐθνῶν τε καὶ Ἰουδαίων τῶν τὴν Σμύρναν κατοικούντων ἀκατασχέτῳ θυμῷ καὶ μεγάλῃ φωνῇ ἐπεβόα· Οὗτός ἐστιν ὁ τῆς Ἀσίας διδάσκαλος, ὁ πατὴρ τῶν Χριστιανῶν, ὁ τῶν ἡμετέρων θεῶν καθαιρέτης, ὁ πολλοὺς διδάσκων μὴ θύειν μηδὲ προσκυνεῖν. ταῦτα λέγοντες ἐπεβόων καὶ ἠρώτων τὸν Ἀσιάρχην Φίλιππον, ἵνα ἐπαφῇ τῷ Πολυκάρπῳ λέοντα. ὁ δὲ ἔφη μὴ εἶναι ἐξὸν αὐτῷ, ἐπειδὴ πεπληρώκει τὰ

• **κολάσεως** → ἡ κόλασις, *punishment.* • **ἀσεβέσι** → ἀσεβής, ές, *ungodly.* • **βραδύνεις** → βραδύνω, *I hesitate, delay.* • **βούλει** → βούλομαι, *I will, wish, want, desire.*

12.1 **θάρσους** → τὸ θάρσος, *courage.* • **ἐνεπίμπλατο** — impf. pass. indic. → ἐμπιμπλάω (alternate form of ἐμπίμπλημι), *I fill,* w. gen. • **ἐπληροῦτο** — impf. pass. indic. → πληρόω. • **συμπεσεῖν** — 2 aor. act. inf. → συμπίπτω, *I collapse.* • **ταραχθέντα** — aor. pass. ptc. → ταράσσω, *I shake.* • **τοὐναντίον** → ἐναντίος, α, ον, *opposite.* τὸ ἐναντίον combines to form τοὐναντίον, *on the contrary, on the other hand* (BDAG 2: 330; LSI IIc: 258). • **ἀνθύπατον** → ὁ ἀνθύπατος, *proconsul.* • **ἐκστῆναι** — aor. act. inf. → ἐξίστημι, *I confuse, amaze, astound.* The inf. continues the ὥστε clause. • **πέμψαι** — aor. act. inf. → πέμπω. Inf. of result w. ἐκστῆναι. The proconsul was astounded, w. the result that he sent. • **κήρυκα** → ὁ κῆρυξ, *herald.* • **σταδίῳ** → τὸ στάδιον, *arena, stadium.* Ehrman's text has τοῦ σταδίου. • **κηρῦξαι** — aor. act. inf. → κηρύσσω, *I announce, proclaim.* • **τρίς** — adv., *three times.* • **Πολύκαρπος** → ὁ Πολύκαρπος, *Polycarp.* • **ὡμολόγησεν** → ὁμολογέω, *I confess.* The inf. εἶναι supplies the content of the confession. • **Χριστιανόν** → ὁ Χριστιανός, *Christian.*

12.2 **λεχθέντος** — aor. pass. ptc. → λέγω. Gen. abs. An unusual form since λέγω occurs mostly only in the pres. and impf. (cf. BDAG: 588). • **ἅπαν** → ἅπας, ασα, αν, *whole, all.* • **πλῆθος** → τὸ πλῆθος, *crowd.* • **Ἰουδαίων** → Ἰουδαῖος, α, ον, *Judean, Jew.* • **Σμύρναν** → ἡ Σμύρνα, *Smyrna.* • **κατοικούντων** → κατοικέω, *I live, dwell, reside.* • **ἀκατασχέτῳ** → ἀκατάσχετος, ον, *uncontrollable.* • **θυμῷ** → ὁ θυμός, *rage, anger.* • **μεγάλῃ** → μέγας, here, *loud.* • **ἐπεβόα** → ἐπιβοάω, *I cry out loudly.* • **Ἀσίας** → ἡ Ἀσία , *Asia.* Ehrman's text has ἀσεβείας (→ ἀσεβεία, *impiety*). • **ἡμετέρων** → ἡμέτερος, α, ον, *our.* • **καθαιρέτης** → ὁ καθαιρέτης, *destroyer.* • **θύειν** → θύω, *I sacrifice.* • **προσκυνεῖν** → προσκυνέω, *I worship.* Ehrman's text adds τοῖς θεοῖς. • **Ἀσιάρχην** → ὁ Ἀσιάρχης, *Asiarch.* • **Φίλιππον** → ὁ Φίλιππος, *Philip.* • **ἵνα** — for dir. obj., *that* (Wal: 475). • **ἐπαφῇ** — aor. act. subjun. 3 sg. → ἐπαφίημι, *I let loose upon.* • **λέοντα** → ὁ λέων, *lion.* • **ὁ δέ** — art. used as a pron., *but he.* This is common in narrative (BDAG 1c: 686). • **ἔφη** — 2 aor. act. indic. → φημί. • **ἐξόν** — pres. act. ptc. → ἔξειμι. This verb is only used impersonally, usually in the form ἔξεστιν, which is the lexical form, *it is right/authorized/permitted/proper.* The ptc. is used w. a copula as an equivalent for ἔξεστιν (see BDAG 1d: 348). Here the copula is an inf., εἶναι, for indir. disc. (Wal: 603; Smy: 2016). ἔξεστιν and ἐξόν usually have an inf. for that which is permitted,

κυνηγέσια. 12.3 τότε ἔδοξεν αὐτοῖς ὁμοθυμαδὸν ἐπιβοῆσαι, ὥστε τὸν Πολύκαρπον ζῶντα κατακαῦσαι. ἔδει γὰρ τὸ τῆς φανερωθείσης ἐπὶ τοῦ προσκεφαλαίου ὀπτασίας πληρωθῆναι, ὅτε ἰδὼν αὐτὸ καιόμενον προσευχόμενος εἶπεν ἐπιστραφεὶς τοῖς σὺν αὐτῷ πιστοῖς προφητικῶς· Δεῖ με ζῶντα καῆναι.

13.1 Ταῦτα οὖν μετὰ τοσούτου τάχους ἐγένετο, θᾶττον ἢ ἐλέγετο, τῶν ὄχλων παραχρῆμα συναγόντων ἔκ τε τῶν ἐργαστηρίων καὶ βαλανείων ξύλα καὶ φρύγανα, μάλιστα Ἰουδαίων προθύμως, ὡς ἔθος αὐτοῖς, εἰς ταῦτα ὑπουργούντων. 13.2 ὅτε δὲ ἡ πυρκαϊὰ ἡτοιμάσθη, ἀποθέμενος ἑαυτῷ πάντα τὰ ἱμάτια καὶ λύσας τὴν ζώνην, ἐπειρᾶτο καὶ ὑπολύειν ἑαυτόν, μὴ πρότερον τοῦτο ποιῶν διὰ τὸ ἀεὶ ἕκαστον τῶν πιστῶν σπουδάζειν ὅστις

---

but here the inf. must be supplied from the context, *permitted (to do so).* • **ἐπειδή** — *since.* • **πεπληρώκει** — pf. → πληρόω. If Philip is the subj. then it is saying, *since he had completed/finished the animal hunts,* meaning he had brought them to a close. If that were the sense, there are other words that would have expressed it better. Here the subj. is probably τὰ κυνηγέσια, and πληρόω has a less common intrans. use, *since the animal hunts had been completed/had finished* (BDAG 5: 829). • **κυνηγέσια** → τὸ κυνηγέσιον, *animal hunt.*

12.3 **ἔδοξεν** → δοκέω, *seem;* here used impersonally, *it seems best, decide, resolve,* w. inf. (BDAG 2bβ: 255). • **ὁμοθυμαδόν** — adv., *with one mind/purpose/impulse; together.* • **ζῶντα** — pres. act. ptc. → ζάω. • **κατακαῦσαι** — aor. act. inf. → κατακαίω, *I burn up, consume by fire.* The subj. must be supplied from the context, simply, *he,* ref. to Philip. • **ἔδει** — impf. → δεῖ. • **τό** — The art. packages the subj. Woodenly: "the matter of the vision . . ." • **φανερωθείσης** → φανερόω, *I reveal.* • **ἐπί** — here, *concerning, about* (BDAG 8: 365). • **προσκεφαλαίου** → τὸ προσκεφάλαιον, *pillow.* • **ὀπτασίας** → ἡ ὀπτασία, *vision.* This vision is recounted in *Mart. Pol.* 5. • **ἰδών** — 2 aor. act. ptc. → εἶδον. • **καιόμενον** → καίω, *I burn (up).* • **ἐπιστραφείς** → ἐπιστρέφω, *I turn.* • **πιστοῖς** → πιστός, ή, όν, *faithful.* • **προφητικῶς** — adv., *prophetically.* • **καῆναι** — 2 aor. pass. inf. → καίω.

13.1 **τοσούτου** → τοσοῦτος, αύτη, οῦτον, *so much, such.* • **τάχους** → τὸ τάχος, *speed.* • **θᾶττον** — adv., *more quickly, faster* (BDAG, ταχέως: 992). • **ἢ ἐλέγετο** — "Than it was being told," seems like an epistolary sense (Smy: 1942b), i.e., that it is being told by the author in this account. • **παραχρῆμα** — adv., *at once, immediately.* • **συναγόντων** — 2 aor. act. ptc. → συνάγω, *I gather, collect.* Gen. abs. • **ἐργαστηρίων** → τὸ ἐργαστήριον, *workshop.* • **βαλανείων** → τὸ βαλανεῖον, *bathhouse.* • **ξύλα** → τὸ ξύλον, *wood.* • **φρύγανα** → τὸ φρύγανον, *shrub, brush, brushwood.* • **μάλιστα** — *especially, particularly,* superlative of the adv. μάλα. • **Ἰουδαίων** → Ἰουδαῖος, α, ον, *Judean, Jew.* Subj. of gen. abs. • **προθύμως** — adv., *willingly, eagerly, freely.* • **ἔθος** → τὸ ἔθος, *habit, custom.* • **ὑπουργούντων** → ὑπουργέω, *I help, assist.* Gen. abs.

13.2 **πυρκαϊά** → ἡ πυρκαϊά, *funeral pyre.* • **ἡτοιμάσθη** → ἑτοιμάζω, *I prepare.* • **ἀποθέμενος** — aor. mid. ptc. → ἀποτίθημι, *I take off.* • **λύσας** → λύω, *I loose, untie.* • **ζώνην** → ἡ ζώνη, *belt.* • **ἐπειρᾶτο** → πειράω, *I try;* mid. w. act. sense (BDAG: 793). • **ὑπολύειν** → ὑπολύω, *I untie, take off one's sandals/shoes.* • **πρότερον** → πρότερος, α, ον, *earlier;* here neut. sg. for adv., *formerly, previously.*

τάχιον τοῦ χρωτὸς αὐτοῦ ἅψηται· [ἐν] παντὶ γὰρ ἀγαθῆς ἕνεκεν πολιτείας καὶ πρὸ τῆς πολιᾶς ἐκεκόσμητο. 13.3 εὐθέως οὖν αὐτῷ περιετίθετο τὰ πρὸς τὴν πυρὰν ἡρμοσμένα ὄργανα. μελλόντων δὲ αὐτῶν καὶ προσηλοῦν εἶπεν· Ἄφετέ με οὕτως· ὁ γὰρ δοὺς ὑπομεῖναι τὸ πῦρ δώσει καὶ χωρὶς τῆς ὑμετέρας ἐκ τῶν ἥλων ἀσφαλείας ἄσκυλτον ἐπιμεῖναι τῇ πυρᾷ.

14.1 Οἱ δὲ οὐ καθήλωσαν μέν, προσέδησαν δὲ αὐτόν. ὁ δὲ ὀπίσω τὰς χεῖρας ποιήσας καὶ προσδεθείς, ὥσπερ κριὸς ἐπίσημος ἐκ μεγάλου ποιμνίου εἰς προσφοράν, ὁλοκαύτωμα δεκτὸν τῷ Θεῷ ἡτοιμασμένον, ἀναβλέψας εἰς τὸν οὐρανὸν εἶπεν· Κύριε ὁ Θεὸς ὁ παντοκράτωρ, ὁ τοῦ ἀγαπητοῦ καὶ εὐλογητοῦ παιδός σου Ἰησοῦ Χριστοῦ πατήρ, δι᾽ οὗ τὴν περὶ σοῦ ἐπίγνωσιν εἰλήφαμεν, ὁ Θεὸς [ὁ] ἀγγέλων καὶ δυνάμεων καὶ πάσης κτίσεως

• **ποιῶν** → ποιέω. Here perhaps concessive circ. ptc. • **ἀεί** — adv., *always.* • **πιστῶν** → πιστός, ή, όν, *faithful.* • **σπουδάζειν** → σπουδάζω, *I am eager, hasten.* Art. inf. w. διά for causal clause (Wal: 596). • **τάχιον** — adv., *more quickly, faster,* comparative of ταχέως. • **χρωτός** → ὁ χρώς, *skin.* • **ἅψηται** — aor. mid. subjun. → ἅπτω; mid., *touch.* • **[ἐν] παντί** — *in every way* (BDAG 2bβ: 783). Mod. ἐκεκόσμητο. Ehrman's text does not have ἐν. • **ἀγαθῆς** — before this word Ehrman's text includes καλῷ, which would go w. παντί, "with every good thing." • **ἕνεκεν** — (listed in lexicons under the alternate form ἕνεκα), *because of.* Here it is between a noun and its adj. mod., *because of a good way of life.* • **πολιτείας** → ἡ πολιτεία, *way of life, conduct.* • **πρό** — *before.* • **πολιᾶς** → ἡ πολιά, *old age.* Ehrman's text has μαρτυρίας (→ μαρτυρία, *martyrdom*) instead. • **ἐκεκόσμητο** — plpf. pass. indic. → κοσμέω, *I adorn, make beautiful/attractive.*

13.3 **εὐθέως** — adv., *at once, immediately.* • **περιετίθετο** → περιτίθημι, *I put/place around.* • **ἡρμοσμένα** — pf. pass. ptc. → ἁρμόζω, *I make ready, prepare.* • **ὄργανα** → τὸ ὄργανον, *tool, instrument.* "Since the pyre itself has taken shape out of wood that was gathered (13.2), the ὄρ. must refer to the incendiary material placed around Polycarp (αὐτῷ περιετίθετο) and designed to produce an intense flame" (BDAG: 720). • **μελλόντων** → μέλλω. Gen. abs. • **προσηλοῦν** — pres. act. inf. → προσηλόω, *I nail (fast/securely)* • **ἄφετε** — aor. act. impv. → ἀφίημι. • **δούς** — aor. act. ptc. masc. nom. sg. → δίδωμι. • **ὑπομεῖναι** — aor. act. inf. → ὑπομένω, *I remain; endure.* • **χωρίς** — adv., *without.* • **ὑμετέρας** → ὑμέτερος, α, ον, *your.* • **ἥλων** → ὁ ἧλος, *nail.* • **ἀσφαλείας** → ἡ ἀσφαλεία, *security.* • **ἄσκυλτον** → ἄσκυλτος, ον, *unmoved, without moving.* • **ἐπιμεῖναι** → ἐπιμένω, *I remain, stay.*

14.1 **οἱ δέ** — art. used as a pron., *and they.* This construction is common in narrative (BDAG 1c: 686). • **καθήλωσαν** → καθηλόω, *I nail (on).* • **προσέδησαν** → προσδέω, *I tie, bind.* • **ὀπίσω** — adv., *behind.* • **ποιήσας** → ποιέω, "making/causing (his hands behind)," *putting (his hands behind him).* • **ὥσπερ** — *as, just as, like.* • **κριός** → ὁ κριός, *ram, male sheep.* • **ἐπίσημος** → ἐπίσημος, ον, *splendid, outstanding.* • **ποιμνίου** → τὸ ποίμνιον, *flock.* • **προσφοράν** → ἡ προσφωρά, *sacrifice, offering.* • **ὁλοκαύτωμα** → τὸ ὁλοκαύτωμα, *whole burnt offering.* • **δεκτόν** → δεκτός, ή, όν, *acceptable.* • **ἡτοιμασμένον** → ἑτοιμάζω, *I prepare.* • **ἀναβλέψας** → ἀναβλέπω, *I look up.* • **παντοκράτωρ** → ὁ παντοκράτωρ, *Almighty.* • **ἀγαπητοῦ** → ἀγαπητός, ή, όν, *beloved.* • **εὐλογητοῦ** → εὐλογητός, ή, όν, *blessed.* • **παιδός** → ὁ παῖς, *son, child; servant.* • **ἐπίγνωσιν** → ἡ ἐπίγνωσις,

παντός τε τοῦ γένους τῶν δικαίων οἳ ζῶσιν ἐνώπιόν σου· 14.2 εὐλογῶ σε, ὅτι κατηξίωσάς με τῆς ἡμέρας καὶ ὥρας ταύτης, τοῦ λαβεῖν με μέρος ἐν ἀριθμῷ τῶν μαρτύρων, ἐν τῷ ποτηρίῳ τοῦ Χριστοῦ [σου] **εἰς ἀνάστασιν ζωῆς** αἰωνίου ψυχῆς τε καὶ σώματος ἐν ἀφθαρσίᾳ πνεύματος ἁγίου· ἐν οἷς προσδεχθείην ἐνώπιόν σου σήμερον ἐν θυσίᾳ πίονι καὶ προσδεκτῇ, καθὼς προητοίμασας καὶ προεφανέρωσας καὶ ἐπλήρωσας, ὁ ἀψευδὴς καὶ ἀληθινὸς Θεός. 14.3 διὰ τοῦτο καὶ περὶ πάντων σε αἰνῶ, σὲ εὐλογῶ, σὲ δοξάζω διὰ τοῦ αἰωνίου καὶ ἐπουρανίου ἀρχιερέως Ἰησοῦ Χριστοῦ, ἀγαπητοῦ σου παιδός, δι᾽ οὗ σοι σὺν αὐτῷ καὶ πνεύματι ἁγίῳ [ἡ] δόξα καὶ νῦν [καὶ ἀεὶ] καὶ εἰς τοὺς μέλλοντας αἰῶνας. ἀμήν.

15.1 Ἀναπέμψαντος δὲ αὐτοῦ τὸ ἀμὴν καὶ πληρώσαντος τὴν εὐχήν, οἱ τοῦ πυρὸς ἄνθρωποι ἐξῆψαν τὸ πῦρ. μεγάλης δὲ ἐκλαμψάσης φλογός, θαῦμα εἴδομεν, οἷς ἰδεῖν ἐδόθη· οἳ καὶ ἐτηρήθημεν εἰς τὸ ἀναγγεῖλαι τοῖς λοιποῖς τὰ γενόμενα. 15.2 τὸ γὰρ πῦρ καμάρας εἶδος ποιῆσαν, ὥσπερ ὀθόνη πλοίου

---

knowledge. • **εἰλήφαμεν** → λαμβάνω. • **[ὁ]** — This word is not in the texts of either Holmes or Ehrman. • **κτίσεως** → ἡ κτίσις, *creation.* Ehrman's text adds τῆς before κτίσεως. • **γένους** → τὸ γένος, *family, race.* • **δικαίων** → δίκαιος, α, ον, *righteous, just.* • **ἐνώπιον** — *before.*

14.2 **εὐλογῶ** → εὐλογέω, *I bless.* • **κατηξίωσας** → καταξιόω, *I consider worthy.* Ehrman's text has ἠξίωσας (→ ἀξιόω, *I consider worthy*). • **λαβεῖν** → λαμβάνω. Inf. for purpose or result (Wal: 590, 592; Smy: 2008, 2011, cf. 2025, 2030, 2032e). • **μέρος** → τὸ μέρος, *part; share.* • **ἀριθμῷ** → ὁ ἀριθμός, *number.* • **μαρτύρων** → ὁ μάρτυς, *martyr.* • **ποτηρίῳ** → τὸ ποτήριον, *cup.* • **[σου]** — Ehrman's text does not have brackets. • **ἀνάστασιν** → ἡ ἀνάστασις, *resurrection.* • **ἀφθαρσίᾳ** → ἡ ἀφθαρσία, *immortality.* • **προσδεχθείην** — aor. pass. opt. 1 sg. → προσδέχομαι, *I receive.* Opt. of wish, *may I be received* (Wal: 481; Smy: 1814). • **σήμερον** — adv., *today.* • **θυσίᾳ** → ἡ θυσία, *sacrifice, offering.* • **πίονι** → ὁ and ἡ πίων, *fat.* • **προσδεκτῇ** → προσδεκτός, ή, όν, *acceptable.* • **προητοίμασας** → προετοιμάζω, *I prepare beforehand.* • **προεφανέρωσας** → προφανερόω, *I reveal beforehand.* • **ἀψευδής** → ἀψευδής, ές, *free of deceit, truthful, trustworthy.* • **ἀληθινός** → ἀληθινός, ή, όν, *true, trustworthy.* ὁ ἀψευδὴς καὶ ἀληθινὸς θεός is in appos. to the subj., "you."

14.3 **αἰνῶ** → αἰνέω, *I praise.* • **δοξάζω** → δοξάζω, *I praise, honor, extol, glorify.* • **ἐπουρανίου** → ἐπουράνιος, ον, *heavenly.* • **ἀρχιερέως** → ὁ ἀρχιερεύς, *high priest.* • **ἀεί** — adv., *ever, always.* The texts of Holmes and Ehrman do not have the bracketed words, so they read, δόξα καὶ νῦν καὶ εἰς . . . • **μέλλοντας** → μέλλω. The ptc. can have the meaning, *future, to come* (BDAG 3: 628).

15.1 **ἀναπέμψαντος** → ἀναπέμπω, *send up.* Gen. abs. • **εὐχήν** → ἡ εὐχή, *prayer.* • **πυρός** — οἱ τοῦ πυρὸς ἄνθρωποι, "men of the fire," *the men in charge of the fire.* • **ἐξῆψαν** → ἐξάπτω, *I light, kindle.* • **ἐκλαμψάσης** → ἐκλάμπω, *I shine out; blaze up.* Gen. abs. • **φλογός** → ἡ φλόξ, *a flame.* Subj. of gen. abs. • **θαῦμα** → τὸ θαῦμα, *a wonder.* • **ἰδεῖν** → εἶδον (ὁράω). • **ἐδόθη** → δίδωμι. • **ἀναγγεῖλαι** — aor. act. inf. → ἀναγγέλλω, *I report.* W. εἰς τό for purpose (Wal: 590).

ὑπὸ πνεύματος πληρουμένη, κύκλῳ περιετείχισεν τὸ σῶμα τοῦ μάρτυρος· καὶ ἦν μέσον, οὐχ ὡς σὰρξ καιομένη, ἀλλ᾽ ὡς [ἄρτος ὀπτώμενος, ἢ ὡς] χρυσὸς καὶ ἄργυρος ἐν καμίνῳ πυρούμενος. καὶ γὰρ εὐωδίας τοσαύτης ἀντελαβόμεθα, ὡς λιβανωτοῦ πνέοντος ἢ ἄλλου τινὸς τῶν τιμίων ἀρωμάτων.

16.1 Πέρας οὖν ἰδόντες οἱ ἄνομοι μὴ δυνάμενον αὐτοῦ τὸ σῶμα ὑπὸ τοῦ πυρὸς δαπανηθῆναι, ἐκέλευσαν προσελθόντα αὐτῷ κομφέκτορα παραβῦσαι ξιφίδιον. καὶ τοῦτο ποιήσαντος, ἐξῆλθεν [περιστερὰ καὶ] πλῆθος αἵματος, ὥστε κατασβέσαι τὸ πῦρ καὶ θαυμάσαι πάντα τὸν ὄχλον, εἰ τοσαύτη τις διαφορὰ μεταξὺ τῶν τε ἀπίστων καὶ τῶν ἐκλεκτῶν· 16.2 ὧν εἷς καὶ οὗτος γεγόνει ὁ θαυμασιώτατος [Πολύκαρπος], ἐν τοῖς καθ᾽ ἡμᾶς χρόνοις διδάσκαλος ἀποστολικὸς καὶ προφητικὸς γενόμενος, ἐπίσκοπος

15.2 **καμάρας** → ἡ καμάρα, *arch, vault, vaulted room.* • **εἶδος** → τὸ εἶδος, *form, shape.* • **ποιῆσαν** — aor. act. ptc. neut. nom. sg. → ποιέω. • **ὥσπερ** — *as, just as, like.* • **ὀθόνη** → ἡ ὀθόνη, *sheet; (ship's) sail.* • **πνεύματος** → τὸ πνεῦμα, here, *wind.* • **κύκλῳ** — adv. *around.* This dat. of κύκλος (*ring, circle*) became fixed as an adv. • **περιετείχισεν** → περιτειχίζω, *I surround with a wall, surround.* • **μάρτυρος** → ὁ μάρτυς, *martyr.* • **καιομένη** → καίω, *I burn.* The fem. indicates it mod. σάρξ. • **ὀπτώμενος** → ὀπτάω, *I bake.* The texts of neither Holmes nor Ehrman have brackets. • **χρυσός** → ὁ χρυσός, *gold.* • **ἄργυρος** → ὁ ἄργυρος, *silver.* • **καμίνῳ** → ἡ κάμινος, *oven, furnace.* • **πυρούμενος** → πυρόω, *I burn.* • **εὐωδίας** → ἡ εὐωδία, *aroma, fragrance.* • **τοσαύτης** → τοσοῦτος, αύτη, οῦτον, *so great, so strong.* • **ἀντελαβόμεθα** → ἀντιλαμβάνω, in mid., *I lay hold of; perceive, notice,* w. gen. • **λιβανωτοῦ** → ὁ λιβανωτός, *incense.* • **πνέοντος** → πνέω, *I blow, breathe, send forth an odor.* • **τιμίων** → τίμιος, α, ον, *costly, precious.* • **ἀρωμάτων** → τὸ ἄρωμα, *fragrant spice, perfume.*

16.1 **πέρας** — adv., *finally, in conclusion, furthermore.* • **οὖν** — The texts of Ehrman and Holmes have instead γοῦν, *at any rate, anyway; hence, then, so* (formed from γε and οὖν). • **ἰδόντες** → εἶδον. • **ἄνομοι** → ἄνομος, ον, *lawless.* • **δαπανηθῆναι** → δαπανάω, *I spend; wear out, destroy.* • **ἐκέλευσαν** → κελεύω, *I command, order.* • **προσελθόντα** → προσέρχομα. Attend. circ., w. the inf. παραβῦσαι. • **κομφέκτορα** → ὁ κομφέκτωρ, *executioner.* • **παραβῦσαι** → παραβύω, *I plunge into.* Inf. for indir. disc. (Wal: 603; Smy: 2016), the content of what they ordered. • **ξιφίδιον** → τὸ ξιφίδιον, *short sword, dagger.* • **ἐξῆλθεν** → ἐξέρχομαι. • **περιστερά** → ἡ περιστερά, *dove.* Holmes's text omits the words in brackets; Ehrman's text has the words, but without the brackets. • **πλῆθος** → τὸ πλῆθος, *number, amount; large amount.* • **κατασβέσαι** — aor. act. inf. → κατασβέννυμι, *I put out, quench.* Supply a subj. • **θαυμάσαι** — aor. act. inf. → θαυμάζω, *I marvel, am astonished.* Continuing the ὥστε clause. • **εἰ** — here introduces an indir. question, *that* (BDAG 2: 277). • **τοσαύτη** → τοσοῦτος, αύτη, οῦτον, *so great, so strong.* • **διαφορά** → ἡ διάφορα, *difference.* • **μεταξύ** — adv., *between.* • **ἀπίστων** → ἄπιστος, ον, *unbelieving.* • **ἐκλεκτῶν** → ἐκλεκτός, ή, όν, *chosen, elect.*

16.2 **θαυμασιώτατος** → θαυμασιώτατος, η, ον, *most remarkable/wonderful/admirable.* Superlative of θαυμάσιος, α, ον. • **Πολύκαρπος** → ὁ Πολύκαρπος, *Polycarp.*

τῆς ἐν Σμύρνῃ ἁγίας ἐκκλησίας· πᾶν γὰρ ῥῆμα, ὃ ἀφῆκεν ἐκ τοῦ στόματος αὐτοῦ, ἐτελειώθη καὶ τελειωθήσεται.

17.1 Ὁ δὲ ἀντίζηλος καὶ βάσκανος καὶ πονηρός, ὁ ἀντικείμενος τῷ γένει τῶν δικαίων, ἰδὼν τό τε μέγεθος αὐτοῦ τῆς μαρτυρίας καὶ τὴν ἀπ' ἀρχῆς ἀνεπίληπτον πολιτείαν, ἐστεφανωμένον τε τὸν τῆς ἀφθαρσίας στέφανον καὶ βραβεῖον ἀναντίρρητον ἀπενηνεγμένον, ἐπετήδευσεν ὡς μηδὲ τὸ σωμάτιον αὐτοῦ ὑφ' ἡμῶν ληφθῆναι, καίπερ πολλῶν ἐπιθυμούντων τοῦτο ποιῆσαι καὶ κοινωνῆσαι τῷ ἁγίῳ αὐτοῦ σαρκίῳ. 17.2 ὑπέβαλεν γοῦν Νικήτην τὸν τοῦ Ἡρῴδου πατέρα, ἀδελφὸν δὲ Ἄλκης, ἐντυχεῖν τῷ ἄρχοντι ὥστε μὴ δοῦναι αὐτοῦ τὸ σῶμα, μή, φησίν, ἀφέντες τὸν ἐσταυρωμένον, τοῦτον ἄρξωνται σέβεσθαι· καὶ ταῦτα [εἶπον] ὑποβαλλόντων καὶ ἐνι-

---

The texts of Ehrman and Holmes have no brackets. • **καθ' ἡμᾶς** — here κατά serves as a poss., *our* (BDAG 7b: 513). • **ἀποστολικός** → ἀποστολικός, ή, όν, *apostolic.* • **προφητικός** → προφητικός, ή, όν, *prophetic.* • **ἐπίσκοπος** → ὁ ἐπίσκοπος, *overseer, bishop.* Ehrman's text adds τε after this word. • **Σμύρνῃ** → ἡ Σμύρνα, *Smyrna.* • **ἁγίας** — Ehrman's text has instead καθολικῆς (→ καθολικός, ή, όν, *general, universal*). • **ἀφῆκεν** → ἀφίημι. • **ἐτελειώθη** → τελειόω, *I complete, accomplish, fulfill.* Ehrman's text has καί before this word.

17.1 **ἀντίζηλος** → ὁ ἀντίζηλος, *jealous one, adversary.* • **βάσκανος** → ὁ βάσκανος, *envious one.* • **ἀντικείμενος** → ἀντίκειμαι, *I oppose,* w. dat. ὁ ἀντικείμενος, *the opponent, enemy, adversary.* • **γένει** → τὸ γένος, *family, race.* • **δικαίων** → δίκαιος, α, ον, *righteous, just.* • **ἰδών** → εἶδον. • **μέγεθος** → τὸ μέγεθος, *greatness.* • **μαρτυρίας** → ἡ μαρτυρία, *witness, martyrdom.* • **ἀνεπίληπτον** → ἀνεπίλη(μ)πτος, ον, *irreproachable.* • **πολιτείαν** → ἡ πολιτεία, *way of life, conduct.* • **ἐστεφανωμένον** → στεφανόω, *I crown.* • **ἀφθαρσίας** → ἡ ἀφθαρσία, *immortality.* • **στέφανον** → ὁ στέφανος, *crown.* Cognate acc. (Wal: 189; Smy: 1563). • **βραβεῖον** → τὸ βραβεῖον, *prize, award.* • **ἀναντίρρητον** → ἀναντίρρητος, ον, *undeniable, not to be contradicted, incontestable.* • **ἀπενηνεγμένον** — pf. mid. ptc. → ἀποφέρω, *I take away;* mid., *carry off, win.* • **ἐπετήδευσεν** → ἐπιτηδεύω, *I take care.* • **ὡς** — here w. inf. for purpose, *that* (BDAG 9b: 1106). • **σωμάτιον** → τὸ σωμάτιον, *little body, poor body,* diminutive of σῶμα. • **ληφθῆναι** → λαμβάνω. • **καίπερ** — *although.* • **ἐπιθυμούντων** → ἐπιθυμέω, *I desire.* Gen. abs. • **κοινωνῆσαι** → κοινωνέω, *I share, have a share.* • **σαρκίῳ** → τὸ σαρκίον, *a piece of flesh.*

17.2 **ὑπέβαλεν** → ὑποβάλλω, *I suggest, whisper, instigate (secretly), incite.* • **γοῦν** — *at any rate, anyway; hence, then, so,* formed from γε and οὖν. • **Νικήτην** → ὁ Νικήτης, *Nicetes.* • **Ἡρῴδου** → ὁ Ἡρῴδης, *Herod.* • **Ἄλκης** → ἡ Ἄλκη, *Alce.* • **ἐντυχεῖν** — 2 aor. act. inf. → ἐντυγχάνω, *I appeal.* • **ἄρχοντι** → ὁ ἄρχων, *ruler, official.* • **δοῦναι** → δίδωμι. • **ἀφέντες** → ἀφίημι. • **ἐσταυρωμένον** → σταυρόω, *I crucify.* • **τοῦτον** — dir. obj. of σέβεσθαι. • **ἄρξωνται** → ἄρχω. • **σέβεσθαι** → σέβω, *I worship.* Both act. and mid. are used w. this meaning. • **[εἶπον]** — Neither Holmes nor Ehrman has brackets. • **ἐνισχυόντων** → ἐνισχύω, *I strengthen, urge insistently* (BDAG 2: 337). Gen. abs., along w. ὑποβαλλόντων, perhaps causal. • **Ἰουδαίων** → Ἰουδαῖος, α, ον, *Judean, Jew.* Subj.

swuËmtym τῶν Ἰουδαίων, οἳ καὶ ἐτήρησαν, μελλόντων ἡμῶν ἐκ τοῦ πυρὸς αὐτὸν λαμβάνειν, ἀγνοοῦντες ὅτι οὔτε τὸν Χριστόν ποτε καταλιπεῖν δυνησόμεθα, τὸν ὑπὲρ τῆς τοῦ παντὸς κόσμου τῶν σωζομένων σωτηρίας παθόντα, ἄμωμον ὑπὲρ ἁμαρτωλῶν, οὔτε ἕτερόν τινα σέβεσθαι. 17.3 τοῦτον μὲν γὰρ υἱὸν ὄντα τοῦ Θεοῦ προσκυνοῦμεν, τοὺς δὲ μάρτυρας ὡς μαθητὰς καὶ μιμητὰς τοῦ Κυρίου ἀγαπῶμεν ἀξίως ἕνεκεν εὐνοίας ἀνυπερβλήτου τῆς εἰς τὸν ἴδιον βασιλέα καὶ διδάσκαλον· ὧν γένοιτο καὶ ἡμᾶς συγκοινωνούς τε καὶ συμμαθητὰς γενέσθαι.

18.1 Ἰδὼν οὖν ὁ κεντυρίων τὴν τῶν Ἰουδαίων γενομένην φιλονεικίαν, θεὶς αὐτὸν ἐν μέσῳ, ὡς ἔθος αὐτοῖς, ἔκαυσεν. 18.2 οὕτως τε ἡμεῖς ὕστερον ἀνελόμενοι τὰ τιμιώτερα λίθων πολυτελῶν καὶ δοκιμώτερα ὑπὲρ χρυσίον

---

of gen. abs. • **ἐτήρησαν** → τηρέω, here w. the sense, *I keep watch over, guard.* • **μελλόντων** → μέλλω. Gen. abs., w. λαμβάνειν, *when we were about to take.* • **ἀγνοοῦντες** → ἀγνοέω, *I do not know, I am ignorant.* • **ποτε** — particle, *at some time or other;* w. a neg., *not ever, never.* • **καταλιπεῖν** — 2 aor. act. inf. → καταλείπω, *I leave, abandon.* • **σωτηρίας** → ἡ σωτηρία, *salvation.* • **παθόντα** — 2 aor. act. ptc. → πάσχω, *I suffer.* Attrib. ptc. w. τόν, mod. Χριστόν. • **ἄμωμον** → ἄμωμος, ον, *unblemished, blameless.* • **ἁμαρτωλῶν** → ἁμαρτωλός, όν, *sinful;* subst., *sinner.*

17.3 **ὄντα** → εἰμί. • **μάρτυρας** → ὁ μάρτυς, *martyr.* • **μιμητάς** → ὁ μιμητής, *imitator.* • **ἀξίως** — adv., *worthily, suitably, in a suitable manner.* • **ἕνεκεν** — (listed in lexicons under ἕνεκα), *because of, on account of,* w. gen. Ehrman's text has ἕνεκα. • **εὐνοίας** → ἡ εὔνοια, *affection.* • **ἀνυπερβλήτου** → ἀνυπέρβλητος, ον, *unsurpassable, unexcelled.* • **γένοιτο** — 2 aor. mid. (depon.) opt. 3 sg. → γίνομαι. Opt. of wish, *may it be* (Wal: 481; Smy: 1814). • **ἡμᾶς** — subj. of γενέσθαι. • **συγκοινωνούς** → ὁ συγκοινωνός, *participant, partner.* Pred. nom. w. γενέσθαι. Ehrman's text has κοινωνούς (→ κοινωνός, *partner*). • **συμμαθητάς** → ὁ συμμαθητής, *fellow-disciple.* Pred. nom. w. γενέσθαι. • **γενέσθαι** → γίνομαι (listed in LSI under γίγνομαι). Inf. for indir. disc., the content of what is wished. Very woodenly: "whose partners and fellow-disciples may it be that we also become."

18.1 **ἰδών** → εἶδον. • **κεντυρίων** → ὁ κεντυρίων, *centurion.* • **Ἰουδαίων** → Ἰουδαῖος, α, ον, *Judean, Jew.* Gen. of agency (Wal: 126). • **φιλονεικίαν** → ἡ φιλονεικία, *contentiousness.* • **θείς** → τίθημι. Attend. circ. • **ἔθος** → τὸ ἔθος, *habit, custom.* Supply a verb. "As it is a custom for them," *as is their custom.* • **ἔκαυσεν** — aor. act. indic. → καίω, *I burn.*

18.2 **ὕστερον** → ὕστερος, α, ον, *the second;* neut. for adv., *later, thereafter.* • **ἀνελόμενοι** — 2 aor. mid. ptc. → ἀναιρέω, *I take away.* • **τά** — goes w. ὀστᾶ, w. the intervening material as mods. • **τιμιώτερα** → τιμιώτερος, α, ον, *more/very costly/precious,* comparative of τίμιος, α, ον. • **λίθων** → ὁ λίθος, *stone.* • **πολυτελῶν** → πολυτελής, ές, *very expensive/costly.* • **δοκιμώτερα** → δοκιμώτερος, α, ον, *more precious,* comparative of δόκιμος, ον. • **ὑπέρ** — w. comparatives, *than*

ὀστᾶ αὐτοῦ, ἀπεθέμεθα ὅπου καὶ ἀκόλουθον ἦν. 18.3 ἔνθα ὡς δυνατὸν ἡμῖν συναγομένοις ἐν ἀγαλλιάσει καὶ χαρᾷ παρέξει ὁ Κύριος ἐπιτελεῖν τὴν τοῦ μαρτυρίου αὐτοῦ ἡμέραν γενέθλιον εἴς τε τὴν τῶν προηθληκότων μνήμην καὶ τῶν μελλόντων ἄσκησίν τε καὶ ἑτοιμασίαν.

(BDAG B: 1031). • **χρυσίον** → τὸ χρυσίον, *gold.* • **ὀστᾶ** → τὸ ὀστοῦν (listed in lexicons under the uncontracted form ὀστέον), *bone.* • **ἀπεθέμεθα** → ἀποτίθημι, *I put away, deposit* (BDAG 3: 124). • **ἀκόλουθον** → ἀκόλουθος, ον, *following; suitable* (BDAG: 37).

18.3 **ἔνθα** — adv., *there.* • **δυνατόν** → δυνατός, ή, όν, *able.* ὡς δυνατὸν ἡμῖν, "as it is possible for us," *as we are able.* The dat. anticipates παρέξει, which takes a dat. • **συναγομένοις** → συνάγω, *I gather together.* Dat. in agreement w. ἡμῖν. Note the mid. • **ἀγαλλιάσει** → ἡ ἀγαλλίασις, *exultation.* • **παρέξει** — fut. act. indic. → παρέχω, *I grant,* w. dat. and inf. • **ἐπιτελεῖν** → ἐπιτελέω, *I complete, accomplish, perform;* here, *celebrate* (BDAG 2: 383). • **μαρτυρίου** → τὸ μαρτύριον, *testimony; martyrdom.* • **γενέθλιον** → γενέθλιος, ον, *pertaining to one's birth;* w. ἡμέρα, *birthday.* Ch. 21 says the martyrdom took place at 2 p.m. on February 23rd. • **προηθληκότων** — pf. act. ptc. → προαθλέω, *I compete in former times.* • **μνήμην** → ἡ μνήμη, *recollection, memory.* • **μελλόντων** — here attrib. ptc., *those to come in the future* (BDAG 3: 628). Mod. ἄσκησίν τε καὶ ἑτοιμασίαν. • **ἄσκησιν** → ἡ ἄσκησις, *practice, training.* Continues the εἰς phrase, as signaled by τε . . . καί. • **ἑτοιμασίαν** → ἡ ἑτοιμασία, *preparation.* Also part of the εἰς phrase, as signaled by the second τε . . . καί.

Introduction

Paul's engagement with the philosophers in Athens, recounted in Acts 17:16–34, is often deemed to have been a failure since only two converts are mentioned. Furthermore, when Paul later writes to the Corinthians, he mentions that not many of them were wise according to worldly standards (1 Cor 1:26), and he draws a strong contrast between the wisdom of this world and the gospel, declaring that he "decided to know nothing among you except Jesus Christ and him crucified" (1 Cor 2:2, ESV). It may seem as if he decided, after his experience in Athens, not to engage the philosophers again and to reject that whole approach to commending the gospel. Such a wholesale rejection, however, is not Paul's point, and his approach at Athens has much to commend it.[1] While not many of the "wise" became Christians, some did, as 1 Cor 1:26 implies. What would it have been like for a philosopher to convert to Christ? In Justyn Martyr we have an example of such a convert, who found in Christ the truth that is only partially glimpsed in the philosophies of Greece. Paul's engagement in Acts 17 is developed much more extensively by Justin and the other Apologists.

Justin was born in Flavia Neapolis, Palestine (modern Nablus), early in the second century, and was brought up in a pagan home. Nothing is known about his youth except his mention of his search, probably in Ephesus, for truth among the philosophies, including the Stoics, Peripatetics, Pythagoreans, and the Platonists. While in his Platonist phase, he one day met an old man who showed him the weakness of Platonism, especially in its view of the soul, and told him of the Old Testament prophets, who "were witnesses to the truth which is above all demonstration" and who "glorified the Creator, the God and Father of all things, and proclaimed his Son, the Christ sent by him" (*Dialogue with Trypho* [*Dial.*] 7, *ANF*). This conversation had a dramatic effect on Justin: "Straightway a flame was kindled in my soul, and a love of the prophets and of those men who are friends of Christ possessed me. When I turned his words over in my mind I found that this philosophy alone is safe and profitable. So for this reason I am a philosopher" (*Dial.* 8, *ANF*).

After his conversion, therefore, Justin continued as a philosopher, even wearing the distinctive philosopher's garment. He remained in Ephesus for some time and then moved to Rome, though little is known about the details of his activities. Eusebius mentions a number

[1] On Paul's engagement with the philosophers in Acts and its relation to Paul's approach in 1 Corinthians, see Bruce Winter, "Introducing the Athenians to God: Paul's failed apologetic in Acts 17?," *Themelios* 31 (2005): 38–59.

of works written by Justin (Eusebius, *Hist. eccl.* 4.18.1–6), of which only three survive. The *First Apology* (*1 Apol.*) is addressed to the emperor, Antonius Pius (ruled 138–161), complaining about the irrational and unfair condemnation of Christianity by many Romans based on false information. He argues that Christians are neither atheistic nor immoral, noting points of contact with pagan philosophy but showing that Christianity has a superior view of God and a superior way of life. In particular, Justin develops the Stoic idea of the *logos spermatikos,* that is, that God's Logos (Word) is spread throughout the world. The presence of this Logos accounts for the elements of truth found among the pagans (e.g., *2 Apol.* 8), but Justin stresses that this Logos actually became manifest in the Old Testament theophanies and then "took shape, and became man, and was called Jesus Christ" (*1 Apol.* 5, *ANF*). A large section of the *First Apology* consists of proofs for Christ's divinity from prophecy. Such argumentation from the Old Testament also plays a major role in his *Dialogue with Trypho,* as one would expect since Trypho was a Jew. In his *Second Apology* he develops further his notion of the *logos spermatikos,* clarifying his case in the light of the recent martyrdom of several Christians and the criticisms of Crescens, a Cynic philosopher.

Unlike some other early Christian writers such as Tatian and Tertullian, Justin has a very positive view of Greek philosophy, especially Platonism, but he is also very clear about the superiority of Christ and Christianity (e.g., *2 Apol.* 10, 13). His thought is based on the revelatory Scriptures, as the account of his conversion cited above might lead one to expect. So, while he draws connections between the philosophies and Christianity where he can, he also points out the differences quite clearly. He is one of the first Christian thinkers to attempt such an engagement with Greco-Roman philosophy. Not surprisingly, then, his thought is not always well developed. Indeed, at one point his Platonic background influences him to argue for God's transcendence in such a way that his writing could later be used to support the position of Arius in the fourth century, who argued that the Son is not God in the fullest sense. Nevertheless, Justin's thought is not merely Platonism expressed in Christian terms. Rather, in Justin we see "not so much a hellenization of Christianity as the Christianizing of Hellenism."[2]

In the selections included here from the *First Apology,* Justin describes the Christian practice of baptism and the eucharist. Actually, *1 Apol.* 65 seems to describe the eucharist as celebrated at baptism, while *1 Apol.* 67 refers to the regular Sunday worship. These descriptions are part of his attempt to correct misperceptions about Christianity, since there were scandalous rumors about what Christians did when they gathered, including even a charge of cannibalism. In the process of correcting such misperceptions among the opponents of Christianity, Justin has given us one of the most extensive descriptions we now have of worship in these early centuries of the church's life.

Edition used: E.J. Goodspeed. *Die ältesten Apologeten.* Göttingen: Vandenhoeck & Ruprecht, 1915.

Level of difficulty: Advanced [3–5]

[2] Louis Bouyer, *The Spirituality of the New Testament and the Fathers* (trans. Mary P. Ryan; vol. 1 of *A History of Christian Spirituality*; New York: Seabury Press, 1963), 219. See also Jean Daniélou, *Gospel Message and Hellenistic Culture* (vol. 2 of *A History of Early Christian Doctrine Before the Council of Nicaea*; ed., trans., and postscript John Austin Baker; Philadelphia: Westminster, 1973).

First Apology 61 Baptism

61.1 Ὃν τρόπον δὲ καὶ ἀνεθήκαμεν ἑαυτοὺς τῷ θεῷ καινοποιηθέντες διὰ τοῦ Χριστοῦ, ἐξηγησόμεθα, ὅπως μὴ τοῦτο παραλιπόντες δόξωμεν πονηρεύειν τι ἐν τῇ ἐξηγήσει. 61.2 ὅσοι ἂν πεισθῶσι καὶ πιστεύωσιν ἀληθῆ ταῦτα τὰ ὑφ' ἡμῶν διδασκόμενα καὶ λεγόμενα εἶναι, καὶ βιοῦν οὕτως δύνασθαι ὑπισχνῶνται, εὔχεσθαί τε καὶ αἰτεῖν νηστεύοντες παρὰ τοῦ θεοῦ τῶν προημαρτημένων ἄφεσιν διδάσκονται, ἡμῶν συνευχομένων καὶ συννηστευόντων αὐτοῖς. 61.3 ἔπειτα ἄγονται ὑφ' ἡμῶν ἔνθα ὕδωρ ἐστί, καὶ τρόπον ἀναγεννήσεως, ὃν καὶ ἡμεῖς αὐτοὶ ἀνεγεννήθημεν, ἀναγεννῶνται· **ἐπ' ὀνόματος** γὰρ **τοῦ πατρὸς** τῶν ὅλων καὶ δεσπότου θεοῦ **καὶ τοῦ σωτῆρος ἡμῶν** Ἰησοῦ Χριστοῦ **καὶ πνεύματος ἁγίου** τὸ ἐν τῷ ὕδατι τότε λουτρὸν

61.1 **τρόπον** → ὁ τρόπος, *way, manner.* ὃν τρόπον, *in the way in which, (just) as* (BDAG 1: 1017) • **ἀνεθήκαμεν** → ἀνατίθημι, *I dedicate.* • **καινοποιηθέντες** → καινοποιέω, *I make new.* • **ἐξηγησόμεθα** → ἐξηγέομαι, *I recount, relate, tell.* • **ὅπως μή** — *lest, so that . . . not.* • **παραλιπόντες** — 2 aor. act. ptc. → παραλείπω, *I pass over, leave untold, omit.* Circ. ptc. for conditional. • **δόξωμεν** → δοκέω, *I seem.* • **πονηρεύειν** → πονηρεύομαι, *I act wickedly, do wrong.* This verb is normally depon. The act. here is an anomaly (*PGL*: 1120). • **ἐξηγήσει** → ἡ ἐξήγησις, *description, explanation.* The art. is probably poss. (Wal: 215; Smy: 1121).

61.2 **ὅσοι** — w. ἄν and subjun. for a general expression, *all those who* (BDAG 2: 729). • **πεισθῶσι** — aor. pass. subjun. → πείθω. • **ἀληθῆ** → ἀληθής, ές, *true.* • **εἶναι** — inf. for indir. disc. (Wal: 603; Smy: 2016), here the content of πεισθῶσι καὶ πιστεύωσιν, w. ταῦτα as the subj. and ἀληθῆ the pred. compl. • **βιοῦν** → βιόω, *I live.* Compl. inf. w. δύνασθαι. • **ὑπισχνῶνται** → ὑπισχνέομαι, *I promise, take upon oneself, undertake to do.* Subjun. since it continues to build the complex subj. ὅσοι ἄν. • **εὔχεσθαι** → εὔχομαι, *I pray.* Obj. of διδάσκονται, as also αἰτεῖν. • **νηστεύοντες** → νηστεύω, *I fast.* • **παρὰ τοῦ θεοῦ** — mod. αἰτεῖν. • **προημαρτημένων** → προαμαρτάνω, *I sin before/previously.* • **ἄφεσιν** → ἡ ἄφεσις, *letting go, dismissal, release; pardon.* • **συνευχομένων** → συνεύχομαι, *I pray with.* Gen. abs. • **συννηστευόντων** → συννηστεύω, *I fast with.* Gen. abs.

61.3 **ἔπειτα** — adv., *then.* • **ἔνθα** — rel., *where.* • **τρόπον** — acc. of manner (Smy: 1608; Wal: 200), *in the way/manner.* • **ἀναγεννήσεως** → ἀναγέννησις, *regeneration* (*PGL*: 97–98). • **ἀνεγεννήθημεν** → ἀναγεννάω, *I regenerate, cause to be born again.* • **ἐπ'** — here, *in.* This section could contain what is said over the candidates before they are then (τότε) washed. But since there is no signal in the text for this meaning, more likely the section simply mod. λουτρὸν ποιοῦνται, w. the idea that first they are led and then they wash. • **τοῦ πατρὸς τῶν ὅλων καὶ δεσπότου** — can be taken in appos. to θεοῦ. • **τῶν ὅλων** — *the universe, everything* (LSI II1: 553; BDAG 3: 704). • **δεσπότου** → ὁ δεσπότης, *master.* • **σωτῆρος** → ὁ σωτήρ, *Savior.* • **λουτρόν** → τὸ λουτρόν, *bath, washing.* • **ποιοῦνται** — in the mid., "I make/do something for/of myself" often combines with a noun for a periphrasis for a simple verb (LSI AII4: 651; BDAG 7: 841), so here w. τὸ . . . λουτρόν, *they wash.*

ποιοῦνται. 61.4 καὶ γὰρ ὁ Χριστὸς εἶπεν· **Ἂν μὴ ἀναγεννηθῆτε, οὐ μὴ εἰσέλθητε εἰς τὴν βασιλείαν τῶν οὐρανῶν.** 61.5 ὅτι δὲ καὶ ἀδύνατον εἰς τὰς μήτρας τῶν τεκουσῶν τοὺς ἅπαξ γενομένους ἐμβῆναι, φανερὸν πᾶσίν ἐστι. 61.6 καὶ διὰ Ἠσαΐου τοῦ προφήτου, ὡς προεγράψαμεν, εἴρηται, τίνα τρόπον φεύξονται τὰς ἁμαρτίας οἱ ἁμαρτήσαντες καὶ μετανοοῦντες. 61.7 ἐλέχθη δὲ οὕτως·

> **Λούσασθε, καθαροὶ γένεσθε, ἀφέλετε τὰς πονηρίας ἀπὸ τῶν ψυχῶν ὑμῶν, μάθετε καλὸν ποιεῖν, κρίνατε ὀρφανῷ καὶ δικαιώσατε χήραν, καὶ δεῦτε καὶ διαλεχθῶμεν, λέγει κύριος· καὶ ἐὰν ὦσιν αἱ ἁμαρτίαι ὑμῶν ὡς φοινικοῦν, ὡσεὶ ἔριον λευκανῶ, καὶ ἐὰν ὦσιν ὡς κόκκινον, ὡς χιόνα λευκανῶ.** 61.8 **ἐὰν δὲ μὴ εἰσακούσητέ μου, μάχαιρα ὑμᾶς κατέδεται· τὸ γὰρ στόμα κυρίου ἐλάλησε ταῦτα.**

61.9 καὶ λόγον δὲ εἰς τοῦτο παρὰ τῶν ἀποστόλων ἐμάθομεν τοῦτον. 61.10 ἐπειδὴ τὴν πρώτην γένεσιν ἡμῶν ἀγνοοῦντες κατ' ἀνάγκην γεγεννήμεθα ἐξ

61.4 **ἄν** — here equals ἐάν (LSI: 51; BDAG II: 57). Cf. John 3:5. • **οὐ μή** — emphatic negation (BDAG, μή 4: 646; cf. LSI, οὐ μή I: 577).

61.5 **ἀδύνατον** → ἀδύνατος, ον, *unable.* W. or without ἐστίν the adj. can mean, *it is impossible* (LSI II: 14; BDAG 2a: 22). • **μήτρας** → ἡ μήτρα, *womb.* • **τεκουσῶν** — 2 aor. act. ptc. fem. gen. pl. → τίκτω, *I give birth to, bear.* • **ἅπαξ** — adv., *once, once for all.* • **γενομένους** → γίνομαι, here, *I am born.* Acc. subj. of the inf. • **ἐμβῆναι** — aor. act. inf. → ἐμβαίνω, *I enter.* • **φανερόν** → φανερός, ά, όν, *manifest, evident.*

61.6 **Ἠσαΐου** → ὁ Ἠσαΐας, *Isaiah.* • **προεγράψαμεν** → προγράφω, *I write before/ earlier/above.* The ref. is to *1 Apol.* 44. • **τίνα τρόπον** — "what way," *how.* • **φεύξονται** — fut. mid. (depon.) indic. → φεύγω, *I flee, escape.* • **ἁμαρτήσαντες** — aor. act. ptc. → ἁμαρτάνω, *I sin.* • **μετανοοῦντες** → μετανοέω, *I repent.*

61.7 **ἐλέχθη** — aor. pass. indic. → λέγω. • **λούσασθε** → λούω, *I wash.* • **καθαροί** → καθαρός, ά, όν, *clean, pure.* • **ἀφέλετε** — 2 aor. act. impv. → ἀφαιρέω, *I remove.* • **πονηρίας** → ἡ πονηρία, *sinfulness, wickedness.* • **μάθετε** — 2 aor. act. impv. → μανθάνω, *I learn.* • **κρίνατε** → κρίνω, here, *I see to it that justice is done,* w. dat. (BDAG 6: 569). • **ὀρφανῷ** → ὀρφανός, ή, όν, *orphan.* • **δικαιώσατε** → δικαιόω, *I do justice, show justice.* • **χήραν** → ἡ χήρα, *widow.* • **δεῦτε** — adv, *come!* • **διαλεχθῶμεν** — aor. pass. subjun. (depon.) → διαλέγω, *I discuss, argue.* • **φοινικοῦν** → φοινικοῦς, ῆ, οῦν (listed in LSI under its uncontracted form φοινίκεος), *purple-red, purple, crimson.* • **ὡσεί** — *as, like.* • **ἔριον** → τὸ ἔριον, *white wool.* • **λευκανῶ** — fut. indic. act. → λευκαίνω, *I make white.* • **κόκκινον** → κόκκινος, η, ον, *red, scarlet.* • **χιόνα** → ἡ χιών, *snow.*

61.8 **εἰσακούσητέ** → εἰσακούω, *I hear; obey,* w. gen. • **μάχαιρα** → ἡ μάχαιρα, *sword.* • **κατέδεται** — fut. mid. (depon.) indic. → κατεσθίω, *I devour.*

61.9 **λόγον** — here, *reason, ground* (LSI BI3: 477; BDAG 2c: 601). Pendent acc. (Wal: 198). • **τοῦτον** — i.e., that which follows.

61.10 **ἐπειδή** — *since, when.* • **γένεσιν** → ἡ γένεσις, *birth.* Acc. of time (Wal: 201; Smy: 1582). • **ἀγνοοῦντες** → ἀγνοέω, *I am ignorant.* Attend. circ. • **ἀνάγκην** →

ὑγρᾶς σπορᾶς κατὰ μῖξιν τὴν τῶν γονέων πρὸς ἀλλήλους καὶ ἐν ἔθεσι φαύλοις καὶ πονηραῖς ἀνατροφαῖς γεγόναμεν, ὅπως μὴ ἀνάγκης τέκνα μηδὲ ἀγνοίας μένωμεν ἀλλὰ προαιρέσεως καὶ ἐπιστήμης, ἀφέσεώς τε ἁμαρτιῶν ὑπὲρ ὧν προημάρτομεν τύχωμεν, ἐν τῷ ὕδατι ἐπονομάζεται τῷ ἑλομένῳ ἀναγεννηθῆναι καὶ μετανοήσαντι ἐπὶ τοῖς ἡμαρτημένοις τὸ τοῦ πατρὸς τῶν ὅλων καὶ δεσπότου θεοῦ ὄνομα, αὐτὸ τοῦτο μόνον ἐπιλέγοντος τοῦ τὸν λουσόμενον ἄγοντος ἐπὶ τὸ λουτρόν. 61.11 ὄνομα γὰρ τῷ ἀρρήτῳ θεῷ οὐδεὶς ἔχει εἰπεῖν· εἰ δέ τις τολμήσειεν εἶναι λέγειν, μέμηνε τὴν ἄσωτον μανίαν. 61.12 καλεῖται δὲ τοῦτο τὸ λουτρὸν φωτισμός, ὡς φωτιζομένων τὴν διάνοιαν τῶν ταῦτα μανθανόντων. 61.13 καὶ ἐπ' ὀνόματος δὲ Ἰησοῦ Χριστοῦ, τοῦ σταυρωθέντος ἐπὶ Ποντίου Πιλάτου, καὶ ἐπ' ὀνόματος πνεύματος ἁγίου, ὃ διὰ τῶν προφητῶν προεκήρυξε τὰ κατὰ τὸν Ἰησοῦν πάντα, ὁ φωτιζόμενος λούεται.

ἡ ἀνάγκη, *force, necessity, compulsion.* κατ' ἀνάγκην, *by force* (LSI: 53). Mod. γεγεννήμεθα. • **γεγεννήμεθα** → γεννάω, *I beget, bear; bring forth.* • **ὑγρᾶς** → ὑγρός, ά, όν, *wet, moist.* • **σπορᾶς** → ἡ σπορά, *sowing; seed.* • **μῖξιν** → ἡ μῖξις, *mixing, mingling; sexual intercourse.* • **γονέων** → ὁ γονεύς, *parent.* • **ἔθεσι** → τὸ ἔθος, *custom, habit.* • **φαύλοις** → φαῦλος, η, ον, *base, low-grade.* • **πονηραῖς** → πονηρός, ά, όν, *wicked, bad.* • **ἀνατροφαῖς** → ἡ ἀνατροφή, *education, up-bringing.* • **γεγόναμεν** → γίνομαι (γίγνομαι in LSI), here w. ἐν, *I am engaged in* (LSI II3b: 165, cf. BDAG 5c: 198). • **ἀγνοίας** → ἡ ἄγνοια, *ignorance.* • **προαιρέσεως** → ἡ προαίρεσις, *choice, purpose.* • **ἐπιστήμης** → ἡ ἐπιστήμη, *knowledge, understanding.* • **ὑπέρ** — here, *concerning* (LSI AIII: 833; BDAG 3: 1031). • **τύχωμεν** — 2 aor. act. subjun. → τυγχάνω, *I get; have,* w. gen. • **ἐπονομάζεται** → ἐπονομάζω, *I pronounce a name over.* • **ἑλομένῳ** — 2 aor. mid. ptc. → αἱρέω, *I take;* mid., *choose.* • **ἡμαρτημένοις** — pf. pass. ptc. → ἁμαρτάνω, ἐπὶ τοῖς ἡμαρτημένοις, *of the sins (having been) committed.* • **τοῦτο** — i.e., τοῦτο ὄνομα. • **ἐπιλέγοντος** → ἐπιλέγω, *I recite over, say over* (*PGL* 2: 526). Gen. abs. • **ἄγοντος** → ἄγω, subj. of gen. abs.

61.11 **ὄνομα** — often takes a dat. for the one possessing the name (Wal: 150; Smy: 1478; BDAG 1a: 711). • **ἀρρήτῳ** → ἄρρητος, η, ον, *unspoken, not to be spoken, unable to be spoken, ineffable.* • **ἔχει** — here w. inf., *I am able, can* (LSI AIII1: 341; BDAG 5: 421). • **τολμήσειεν** — aor. act. opt. 3 sg. → τολμάω, *I dare to do something.* • **εἶναι** — inf. for indir. disc. w. λέγειν, "dare to say that it is (possible to speak the name of the ineffable God)." • **μέμηνε** — pf. act. indic. 3 sg. → μαίνομαι, *I am mad; rave.* The pf. has a pres. sense (LSI: 484). • **ἄσωτον** → ἄσωτος, ον, *abandoned, hopeless.* • **μανίαν** → ἡ μανία, *madness, frenzy.* Cognate acc. (Wal: 189; Smy: 1563), *rave with a madness.*

61.12 **φωτισμός** → ὁ φωτισμός, *illumination.* • **ὡς** — here, *since, because* (LSI BIV: 908; BDAG 3aβ: 1105). • **φωτιζομένων** → φωτίζω, *I illuminate,* gen. abs. • **διάνοιαν** → ἡ διάνοια, *mind.* Acc. of ref. (Wal: 203; Smy: 1600). • **μανθανόντων** → μανθάνω, *I learn.* Subj. of gen. abs.

61.13 **σταυρωθέντος** → στευρόω, *I crucify.* • **ἐπί** — here, *under, in the time of* (LSI AII: 286; BDAG 18a: 367). • **Ποντίου** → ὁ Πόντιος, *Pontius.* • **Πιλάτου** → ὁ Πιλᾶτος, *Pilate.* • **προεκήρυξε** → προκηρύσσω, *I proclaim in advance* (*PGL*: 1153).

First Apology 65–67 Eucharist and Sunday Worship

65.1 Ἡμεῖς δὲ μετὰ τὸ οὕτως λοῦσαι τὸν πεπεισμένον καὶ συγκατατεθειμένον ἐπὶ τοὺς λεγομένους ἀδελφοὺς ἄγομεν, ἔνθα συνηγμένοι εἰσί, κοινὰς εὐχὰς ποιησόμενοι ὑπέρ τε ἑαυτῶν καὶ τοῦ φωτισθέντος καὶ ἄλλων πανταχοῦ πάντων εὐτόνως, ὅπως καταξιωθῶμεν τὰ ἀληθῆ μαθόντες καὶ δι' ἔργων ἀγαθοὶ πολιτευταὶ καὶ φύλακες τῶν ἐντεταλμένων εὑρεθῆναι, ὅπως τὴν αἰώνιον σωτηρίαν σωθῶμεν. 65.2 ἀλλήλους φιλήματι ἀσπαζόμεθα παυσάμενοι τῶν εὐχῶν. 65.3 ἔπειτα προσφέρεται τῷ προεστῶτι τῶν ἀδελφῶν ἄρτος καὶ ποτήριον ὕδατος καὶ κράματος, καὶ οὗτος λαβὼν αἶνον καὶ δόξαν τῷ πατρὶ τῶν ὅλων διὰ τοῦ ὀνόματος τοῦ υἱοῦ καὶ τοῦ πνεύματος τοῦ ἁγίου ἀναπέμπει καὶ εὐχαριστίαν ὑπὲρ τοῦ κατηξιῶσθαι τούτων παρ' αὐτοῦ ἐπὶ πολὺ ποιεῖται· οὗ συντελέσαντος τὰς εὐχὰς καὶ τὴν

65.1 **λοῦσαι** → λούω, *I wash.* μετὰ τό w. inf. for temp. clause, *after.* • **συγκατατεθειμένον** — aor. pass. ptc. → συγκατατίθημι, *I agree, consent.* • **ἀδελφούς** — dir. obj. of λεγομένους. Supply an obj. for ἄγομεν. • **ἔνθα** — rel., *where.* • **συνηγμένοι** — pf. pass. ptc. → σύναγω. • **κοινάς** → κοινός, ή, όν, *common.* • **εὐχάς** → ἡ εὐχή, *prayer.* • **ποιησόμενοι** — in the mid., "I make/do something for/of myself" often combines with a noun for a periphrasis for a simple verb (LSI AII4: 651; BDAG 7: 841). The fut. ptc. usually denotes purpose, esp. w. verbs meaning "come," "go," or "send" (Smy: 2065), here, *in order to pray common prayers.* • **φωτισθέντος** → φωτίζω, *I illuminate.* • **πανταχοῦ** — adv., *everywhere.* • **εὐτόνως** — adv., *energetically, vigorously.* • **καταξιωθῶμεν** → καταξιόω, *I consider to be worthy.* • **ἀληθῆ** → ἀληθής, ές, *true.* • **μαθόντες** — 2 aor. act. ptc. → μανθάνω, *I learn.* • **πολιτευταί** → ὁ πολιτευτής, *statesman; one who behaves; devotee, follower of the Christian life* (*PGL*: 1114). This word is distinct from the more common πολίτης, "citizen" (cf. LSI, LSJ, and *PGL*). • **φύλακες** → ὁ φύλαξ, *guardian, keeper.* • **ἐντεταλμένων** — pf. pass. ptc. → ἐντέλλω, *I command.* • **εὑρεθῆναι** — i.e., "found to be." • **σωτηρίαν** → ἡ σωτηρία, *salvation.* Cognate acc. (Wal: 189; Smy: 1563), *with an eternal salvation.*

65.2 **φιλήματι** → τὸ φίλημα, *kiss.* • **ἀσπαζόμεθα** → ἀσπάζομαι, *I greet.* • **παυσάμενοι** → παύω, *I cause to stop;* mid., *cease, finish,* w. gen.

65.3 **ἔπειτα** — adv., *then.* • **προσφέρεται** → προσφέρω, *I bring.* • **προεστῶτι** — pf. act. ptc. masc. dat. sg. → προΐστημι, *I set/stand before/over.* The pf. ptc. is commonly used for the noun, *leader.* • **ποτήριον** → τὸ ποτήριον, *cup.* • **κράματος** → τὸ κρᾶμα, *mixed wine.* • **αἶνον** → ὁ αἶνος, *praise.* Dir. obj. (w. δόξαν) of ἀναπέμπει. • **τῶν ὅλων** — *the universe, everything* (LSI III: 553; BDAG 3: 704). • **ἀναπέμπει** → ἀναπέμπω, *I send up.* • **εὐχαριστίαν** → ἡ εὐχαριστία, *thanksgiving.* W. mid. of ποιέω as a periphrasis for "give thanks" (cf. note on 65.1). • **κατηξιῶσθαι** — obj. of the prep., "for the being considered worthy by him of these things." • **ἐπὶ πολύ** — *for a long time* (LSI IV3b: 659; BDAG 2aב: 849). • **οὗ** — rel. pron. for οὗτος (LSI A: 572), normally only in the nom., but here the subj. of a gen. abs., *after he has finished.* • **συντελέσαντος** → συντελέω, *I bring to an end, complete, finish.* Gen. abs. • **εὐχάς** → ἡ εὐχή, *prayer.* • **παρών** — pres. ptc. → πάρειμι, *I am present.* • **ἐπευφημεῖ** → ἐπευφημέω, *I shout assent.*

εὐχαριστίαν πᾶς ὁ παρὼν λαὸς ἐπευφημεῖ λέγων· Ἀμήν. 65.4 τὸ δὲ Ἀμὴν τῇ Ἑβραΐδι φωνῇ τὸ Γένοιτο σημαίνει. 65.5 εὐχαριστήσαντος δὲ τοῦ προεστῶτος καὶ ἐπευφημήσαντος παντὸς τοῦ λαοῦ οἱ καλούμενοι παρ' ἡμῖν διάκονοι διδόασιν ἑκάστῳ τῶν παρόντων μεταλαβεῖν ἀπὸ τοῦ εὐχαριστηθέντος ἄρτου καὶ οἴνου καὶ ὕδατος καὶ τοῖς οὐ παροῦσιν ἀποφέρουσι.

66.1 Καὶ ἡ τροφὴ αὕτη καλεῖται παρ' ἡμῖν εὐχαριστία, ἧς οὐδενὶ ἄλλῳ μετασχεῖν ἐξόν ἐστιν ἢ τῷ πιστεύοντι ἀληθῆ εἶναι τὰ δεδιδαγμένα ὑφ' ἡμῶν, καὶ λουσαμένῳ τὸ ὑπὲρ ἀφέσεως ἁμαρτιῶν καὶ εἰς ἀναγέννησιν λουτρόν, καὶ οὕτως βιοῦντι ὡς ὁ Χριστὸς παρέδωκεν. 66.2 οὐ γὰρ ὡς κοινὸν ἄρτον οὐδὲ κοινὸν πόμα ταῦτα λαμβάνομεν· ἀλλ' ὃν τρόπον διὰ λόγου θεοῦ σαρκοποιηθεὶς Ἰησοῦς Χριστὸς ὁ σωτὴρ ἡμῶν καὶ σάρκα καὶ αἷμα ὑπὲρ σωτηρίας ἡμῶν ἔσχεν, οὕτως καὶ τὴν δι' εὐχῆς λόγου τοῦ παρ' αὐτοῦ εὐχαριστηθεῖσαν τροφήν, ἐξ ἧς αἷμα καὶ σάρκες κατὰ μεταβολὴν τρέφονται ἡμῶν, ἐκείνου τοῦ σαρκοποιηθέντος Ἰησοῦ καὶ σάρκα καὶ αἷμα

65.4 **Ἑβραΐδι** → ἡ Ἑβραΐς, *Hebrew.* • **φωνῇ** → φωνή, here, *language.* • **γένοιτο** — 2 aor. mid. (depon.) opt. 3 sg. → γίνομαι, *may it be.* • **σημαίνει** → σημαίνω, *I mean, signify.*

65.5 **εὐχαριστήσαντος** → εὐχαριστέω, *I give thanks.* Gen. abs. • **ἐπευφημήσαντος** — gen. abs. • **διάκονοι** → ὁ διάκονος, *deacon.* • **μεταλαβεῖν** — 2 aor. act. inf. → μεταλαμβάνω, *I have/get a share, partake of.* δίδωμι w. an inf. of a verb for eating or drinking is common (LSJ 4: 422). Cf. Luke 8:55; Rev 16:6. • **ἀποφέρουσι** → ἀποφέρω, *I take/carry away.* Supply the obj.

66.1 **τροφή** → ἡ τροφή, *food.* • **εὐχαριστία** → ἡ εὐχαριστία, *thanksgiving; Eucharist.* • **μετασχεῖν** → μετέχω, *I share in.* • **ἐξόν** — ptc. → ἔξεστι, *it is allowed,* imper. verb w. inf. and dat. • **ἀληθῆ** → ἀληθής, ές, *true.* • **δεδιδαγμένα** — pf. pass. ptc. → διδάσκω. • **λουσαμένῳ** → λούω, *I wash.* A permissive/causative mid. (Wal: 425; Smy: 1725), *allowed himself to be baptized.* • **ἀφέσεως** → ἡ ἄφεσις, *letting go, dismissal, release; pardon.* • **ἀναγέννησιν** → ἡ ἀναγέννησις, *regeneration.* • **λουτρόν** → τὸ λουτρόν, *bath, washing.* Cognate acc. (Wal: 189; Smy: 1563). • **βιοῦντι** → βιόω, *I live.* • **παρέδωκεν** → παραδίδωμι, *I deliver, pass on, teach.*

66.2 **κοινόν** → κοινός, ή, όν, *common, ordinary.* • **πόμα** → τὸ πόμα (listed in LSI under the more common form τὸ πῶμα), *a drink.* • **τρόπον** → ὁ τρόπος, *way, manner,* ὃν τρόπον, "which way," i.e., *the way in which; in the same way as,* picked up below by οὕτως καί. • **σαρκοποιηθείς** → σαρκοποιέω, *I become/am made flesh.* • **σωτήρ** → ὁ σωτήρ, *Savior.* • **σωτηρίας** → ἡ σωτηρία, *salvation.* • **εὐχῆς** → ἡ εὐχή, *prayer.* δι' εὐχῆς λόγου τοῦ παρ' αὐτοῦ mod. εὐχαριστηθεῖσαν, for which thanks has been given through a word of prayer *which is from him.* • **εὐχαριστηθεῖσαν** — aor. pass. ptc. → εὐχαριστέω, *I give thanks.* Mod. τροφήν, *the food for which we have given thanks.* • **τροφήν** — the subj. of εἶναι below. • **ἐξ ἧς** — ref. to τροφήν. • **κατά** — here, *in accordance with, because of, as a result of* (BDAG 5aδ: 512). • **μεταβολήν** → ἡ μεταβολή, *change.* • **τρέφονται** → τρέφω, *I maintain, support; nourish.* • **ἡμῶν** — mod. αἷμα καὶ σάρκες. Placed here perhaps for the rhetorical effect of being followed by ἐκείνου. • **ἐκείνου . . . Ἰησοῦ** — mod. καὶ σάρκα καὶ αἷμα. • **καὶ σάρκα**

ἐδιδάχθημεν εἶναι. 66.3 οἱ γὰρ ἀπόστολοι ἐν τοῖς γενομένοις ὑπ' αὐτῶν ἀπομνημονεύμασιν, ἃ καλεῖται εὐαγγέλια, οὕτως παρέδωκαν ἐντετάλθαι αὐτοῖς· **τὸν Ἰησοῦν λαβόντα ἄρτον εὐχαριστήσαντα εἰπεῖν· Τοῦτο ποιεῖτε εἰς τὴν ἀνάμνησίν μου, τοῦτ' ἔστι τὸ σῶμά μου· καὶ τὸ ποτήριον ὁμοίως λαβόντα καὶ εὐχαριστήσαντα εἰπεῖν· Τοῦτό ἐστι τὸ αἷμά μου·** καὶ μόνοις αὐτοῖς μεταδοῦναι. 66.4 ὅπερ καὶ ἐν τοῖς τοῦ Μίθρα μυστηρίοις παρέδωκαν γίνεσθαι μιμησάμενοι οἱ πονηροὶ δαίμονες· ὅτι γὰρ ἄρτος καὶ ποτήριον ὕδατος τίθεται ἐν ταῖς τοῦ μυουμένου τελεταῖς μετ' ἐπιλόγων τινῶν, ἢ ἐπίστασθε ἢ μαθεῖν δύνασθε.

67.1 Ἡμεῖς δὲ μετὰ ταῦτα λοιπὸν ἀεὶ τούτων ἀλλήλους ἀναμιμνήσκομεν· καὶ οἱ ἔχοντες τοῖς λειπομένοις πᾶσιν ἐπικουροῦμεν, καὶ σύνεσμεν ἀλλήλοις ἀεί. 67.2 ἐπὶ πᾶσί τε οἷς προσφερόμεθα εὐλογοῦμεν τὸν ποιητὴν τῶν

καὶ αἷμα — pred. compl. of εἶναι. • **εἶναι** — inf. for indir. disc., the content of that which we have been taught: "we have been taught that the food is the flesh and blood."

66.3 **γενομένοις** → γίνομαι (listed in LSI under γίγνομαι), here, *I produce* (LSI I2: 164; BDAG 2: 197). • **ἀπομνημονεύμασιν** → τὸ ἀπομνημόνευμα, *memoir.* • **εὐαγγέλια** → τὸ εὐαγγέλιον, *gospel.* • **ἐντετάλθαι** — pf. pass. inf. → ἐντέλλω, *I command.* Inf. for indir. disc. (Wal: 603; Smy: 2016), i.e., the content of what the apostles passed on (παρέδωκαν), *they thus passed on that which had been commanded them.* "Had" is used instead of "have" due to English sequence of tenses. • **εἰπεῖν** — Both instances of this inf. are indir. disc. in parallel with ἐντετάλθαι. Jesus' statements are part of what they passed on. • **ἀνάμνησίν** → ἡ ἀνάμνησις, *remembrance, recollection.* • **ποτήριον** → τὸ ποτήριον, *cup.* • **ὁμοίως** — adv., *similarly, likewise, in the same way.* • **μεταδοῦναι** — aor. act. inf. → μεταδίδωμι, *I impart, share.* This inf. gives the final part of what Justin says the apostles passed on, namely, that Jesus shared the bread and cup only with the apostles.

66.4 **ὅπερ** → ὅσπερ, ἥπερ, ὅπερ, *the very thing which; which.* • **Μίθρα** → ὁ Μίθρας, *Mithras.* • **μυστηρίοις** → τὸ μυστήριον, *mystery.* • **γίνεσθαι** — inf. for the content of παρέδωκαν, as above. The evil demons passed on that such things should take place. • **μιμησάμενοι** → μιμέομαι, *I imitate.* • **δαίμονες** → ὁ δαίμων, *demon.* • **τίθεται** — A comp. subj. usually has a pl. verb, but the use of a sg. verb, as here, is not uncommon (Wal: 401; Smy: 968). Often this construction emphasizes one of the subjs., but that is unlikely here. • **μυουμένου** → μυέω, *I initiate into the mysteries;* pass., *I am initiated.* • **τελεταῖς** → ἡ τελετή, *initiation;* pl., *mystic rites at initiation.* • **ἐπιλόγων** → ἐπίλογος, *incantation* (*PGL*: 527). • **ἐπίστασθε** — pres. mid. (depon.) indic. → ἐπίσταμαι, *I know.* • **μαθεῖν** → μανθάνω, *I learn.*

67.1 **λοιπόν** — here, *finally.* Justin is moving to the final section of his description of Christian worship. • **ἀεί** — adv., *always.* • **ἀναμιμνήσκομεν** → ἀναμιμνησκω, *I remind,* w. gen. or double acc. • **λειπομένοις** → λείπω, *I leave;* mid. and pass., *I lack, am in want.* • **ἐπικουροῦμεν** → ἐπικουρέω, *I aid, help.* • **σύνεσμεν** → σύνειμι, *I am with.*

πάντων διὰ τοῦ υἱοῦ αὐτοῦ Ἰησοῦ Χριστοῦ καὶ διὰ πνεύματος τοῦ ἁγίου.
67.3 καὶ τῇ τοῦ ἡλίου λεγομένῃ ἡμέρᾳ πάντων κατὰ πόλεις ἢ ἀγροὺς μενόντων ἐπὶ τὸ αὐτὸ συνέλευσις γίνεται, καὶ τὰ ἀπομνημονεύματα τῶν ἀποστόλων ἢ τὰ συγγράμματα τῶν προφητῶν ἀναγινώσκεται, μέχρις ἐγχωρεῖ.
67.4 εἶτα παυσαμένου τοῦ ἀναγινώσκοντος ὁ προεστὼς διὰ λόγου τὴν νουθεσίαν καὶ πρόκλησιν τῆς τῶν καλῶν τούτων μιμήσεως ποιεῖται. 67.5
ἔπειτα ἀνιστάμεθα κοινῇ πάντες καὶ εὐχὰς πέμπομεν· καί, ὡς προέφημεν, παυσαμένων ἡμῶν τῆς εὐχῆς ἄρτος προσφέρεται καὶ οἶνος καὶ ὕδωρ, καὶ ὁ προεστὼς εὐχὰς ὁμοίως καὶ εὐχαριστίας, ὅση δύναμις αὐτῷ, ἀναπέμπει, καὶ ὁ λαὸς ἐπευφημεῖ λέγων τὸ Ἀμήν, καὶ ἡ διάδοσις καὶ ἡ μετάληψις ἀπὸ

67.2 **οἷς** — attraction of the rel. (Wal: 338; Smy: 2522). • **προσφερόμεθα** → προσφέρω, *I bring to, offer, give;* mid. can mean, *take to oneself as food or drink; set out food or drink* (LSI C: 699; *PGL* J: 1183). • **εὐλογοῦμεν** → εὐλογέω, *I bless.* • **ποιητήν** → ὁ ποιητής, *maker.*

67.3 **ἡλίου** → ὁ ἥλιος, *sun.* • **κατά** — here, *in, among, throughout.* • **ἀγρούς** → ὁ ἀγρός, *field; country.* • **μενόντων** — here, *I live, dwell.* πάντων . . . μενόντων mod. συνέλευσις. • **ἐπὶ τὸ αὐτό** — *together* (BDAG, αὐτός 3b: 153). • **συνέλευσις** → ἡ συνέλευσις, *meeting, a coming together.* • **ἀπομνημονεύματα** → τὸ ἀπομνημόνευμα, *memoir.* See 66.3 above. • **συγγράμματα** → τὸ σύγγραμμα, *writing.* • **ἀναγινώσκεται** → ἀναγινώσκω (listed in lexicons under the alternate form ἀναγιγνώσκω), *I read.* • **μέχρις** — (listed in lexicons under the alternate form μέχρι), *as far as; until.* • **ἐγχωρεῖ** → ἐγχωρέω, *I give room; allow, permit.* μέχρις ἐγχωρεῖ, *as long as time permits.*

67.4 **εἶτα** — adv., *then.* • **παυσαμένου** → παύω, *I cause to stop;* mid., *cease, stop.* Gen. abs. • **προεστώς** — pf. act. ptc. masc. nom. sg. → προΐστημι, *I set/stand before/over.* The pf. ptc. is commonly used for the noun, *leader.* • **λόγου** — here perhaps, *discourse, message* (LSI III: 477; BDAG 1aβ: 599). • **νουθεσίαν** → ἡ νουθεσία, *admonition, instruction.* • **πρόκλησιν** → ἡ πρόκλησις, *challenge.* • **μιμήσεως** → ἡ μίμησις, *imitation.* Obj. gen., which cannot be retained in English. Cf. next note. • **ποιεῖται** — in the mid., "I make/do something for/of myself" often combines with a noun for a periphrasis for a simple verb (LSI AII4: 651; BDAG 7: 841), so here, "through a word the leader makes an admonition and challenge of the imitation of these good things," *the leader admonishes and challenges us in a message to imitate these good things.*

67.5 **ἔπειτα** — adv., *then.* • **κοινῇ** → κοινός, ή, όν, *common.* κοινῇ is used as an adv., *in concert, together.* • **εὐχάς** → ἡ εὐχή, *prayer.* • **προέφημεν** — 2 aor. indic. act. → πρόφημι, *I say before.* • **παυσαμένων** — gen. abs. • **προσφέρεται** — another sg. verb w. a comp. subj. See note on 66.4. • **ὁμοίως** — adv., *similarly, likewise, in the same way.* • **εὐχαριστίας** → ἡ εὐχαριστία, *thanksgiving.* • **δύναμις** — here, *ability.* • **αὐτῷ** — dat. of possession (Wal: 149; Smy: 1476). ὅση δύναμις αὐτῷ, "as much ability as is his," *according to his ability.* • **ἀναπέμπει** → ἀναπέμπω, *I send up.* • **λαός** → ὁ λαός, *people.* • **ἐπευφημεῖ** → ἐπευφημέω, *I shout assent.* • **διάδοσις** → ἡ διάδοσις, *distribution.* • **μετάληψις** → ἡ μετάληψις, *participation.* • **ἀπό** — here partitive (LSI I4: 94). The translation varies w. English

τῶν εὐχαριστηθέντων ἑκάστῳ γίνεται, καὶ τοῖς οὐ παροῦσι διὰ τῶν διακόνων πέμπεται. 67.6 οἱ εὐποροῦντες δὲ καὶ βουλόμενοι κατὰ προαίρεσιν ἕκαστος τὴν ἑαυτοῦ ὃ βούλεται δίδωσι, καὶ τὸ συλλεγόμενον παρὰ τῷ προεστῶτι ἀποτίθεται, καὶ αὐτὸς ἐπικουρεῖ ὀρφανοῖς τε καὶ χήραις, καὶ τοῖς διὰ *νόσον* ἢ δι᾽ ἄλλην αἰτίαν λειπομένοις, καὶ τοῖς ἐν δεσμοῖς οὖσι, καὶ τοῖς παρεπιδήμοις οὖσι ξένοις, καὶ ἁπλῶς πᾶσι τοῖς ἐν χρείᾳ οὖσι κηδεμὼν γίνεται. 67.7 τὴν δὲ τοῦ ἡλίου ἡμέραν κοινῇ πάντες τὴν συνέλευσιν ποιούμεθα, ἐπειδὴ πρώτη ἐστὶν ἡμέρα, ἐν ᾗ ὁ θεὸς τὸ σκότος καὶ τὴν ὕλην τρέψας κόσμον ἐποίησε, καὶ Ἰησοῦς Χριστὸς ὁ ἡμέτερος σωτὴρ τῇ αὐτῇ ἡμέρᾳ ἐκ νεκρῶν ἀνέστη· τῇ γὰρ πρὸ τῆς κρονικῆς ἐσταύρωσαν αὐτόν, καὶ τῇ μετὰ τὴν κρονικήν, ἥτις ἐστὶν ἡλίου ἡμέρα, φανεὶς τοῖς ἀποστόλοις αὐτοῦ καὶ μαθηταῖς ἐδίδαξε ταῦτα, ἅπερ εἰς ἐπίσκεψιν καὶ ὑμῖν ἀνεδώκαμεν.

---

idiom, e.g., "distribution of," "participation in." • **εὐχαριστηθέντων** → εὐχαριστέω, *I give thanks.* • **γίνεται** — another sg. verb w. a comp. subj. See note on 66.4. • **παροῦσι** — pres. ptc. masc. dat. pl. → πάρειμι, *I am present.* • **διακόνων** → ὁ διάκονος, *deacon.*

67.6 **εὐποροῦντες** → εὐπορέω, *I prosper, thrive, am well off.* • **βουλόμενοι** → βούλομαι, *I will, wish, want to, am willing.* • **προαίρεσιν** → ἡ προαίρεσις, *choice.* • **τὴν ἑαυτοῦ** — mod. προαίρεσιν. • **συλλεγόμενον** → συλλέγω, *I collect.* • **ἀποτίθεται** → ἀποτίθημι, *I put aside.* • **ὀρφανοῖς** → ὀρφανός, ή, όν, *orphan.* • **χήραις** → ἡ χήρα, *widow.* • **νόσον** → ἡ νόσος, *sickness.* • **αἰτίαν** → ἡ αἰτία, *cause, reason.* • **δεσμοῖς** → ὁ δεσμός, *bond, fetter.* • **παρεπιδήμοις** → παρεπίδημος, ον, *sojourning, residing temporarily.* • **ξένοις** → ξένος, η, ον, *strange.* • **ἁπλῶς** — adv., *simply, in a word.* • **χρείᾳ** → ἡ χρεία, *a need.* • **κηδεμών** → ὁ κηδεμών, *protector, guardian.*

67.7 **ποιούμεθα** — in the mid., "I make/do something for/of myself" often combines with a noun for a periphrasis for a simple verb (LSI AII4: 651; BDAG 7: 841), so here w. συνέλευσιν, *we gather.* • **ἐπειδή** — *because, since.* • **σκότος** → τὸ σκότος, *darkness.* • **ὕλην** → ἡ ὕλη, *material, matter, stuff.* • **τρέψας** → τρέπω, *I turn, change, alter.* • **ἡμέτερος** → ἡμέτερος, α, ον, *our.* • **σωτήρ** → ὁ σωτήρ, *Savior.* • **πρό** — *before,* w. gen. • **κρονικῆς** → κρονικός, ή, όν, *of Saturn.* τῇ [ἡμέρᾳ] . . . πρὸ τῆς κρονικῆς, "on the day before that of Saturn/Saturn's." • **ἐσταύρωσαν** → σταυρόω, *I crucify.* • **φανείς** — aor. pass. ptc. masc. nom. sg. → φαίνω, *I appear.* Attend. circ. • **ἅπερ** → ὅσπερ, ἥπερ, ὅπερ, *the very thing which; which.* • **ἐπίσκεψιν** → ἡ ἐπίσκεψις, *inspection, consideration, investigation.* • **ἀνεδώκαμεν** → ἀναδίδωμι, *I hold up and give, offer, submit.* Aor. for pf. (Smy: 1940).

Melito of Sardis

On Pascha

Introduction

Jesus and the writers of the New Testament make extensive use of typology in their interpretation of the Old Testament. That is, they see the Scriptures as an organic whole that bears witness to Christ through the people, events, and institutions of the Old Testament, which provide patterns ("types") that are repeated in the life of Jesus and his church. Such interpretation is pervasive among the Fathers and is nowhere better illustrated than in *On Pascha* (*Pasch.*) by Melito of Sardis. Indeed, in this work he not only provides a moving example of typology, but even includes a discussion of it. *On Pascha* is thus important for its use of Scripture, as well as being a very powerful retelling of the Exodus from Egypt.

Melito was the bishop of Sardis, a major city in Asia Minor (modern Turkey), during the second half of the second century. We are dependent on Eusebius for most of our information about him (Eusebius, *Hist. eccl.* 4.26.1–14; 5.24.5; 5.28.5). Melito was active on at least two major fronts, addressing issues between the church and the empire, as well as issues within the church. On the first front, Eusebius quotes from a letter from Melito to Emperor Marcus Aurelius, complaining about the unjust treatment of Christians by Roman authorities (*Hist. eccl.* 4.26.5–10). In Melito's letter we have our earliest example of the argument made by Christian apologists that the peace Rome has enjoyed since the reign of Augustus is due to the coming of Christ and the presence of Christians in the empire.

One of the points of discussion on the second front, dealing with issues within the church, concerned the contents of the canon of Scripture. Eusebius quotes a letter of Melito to one Onesimus (whose identity is now unknown), who had often requested information from Melito regarding the number of books in the Old Testament and their order. Melito replies, "when I came to the east and reached the place where these things were preached and done, and learnt accurately the books of the Old Testament, I set down the facts and sent them to you" (Loeb). Melito then lists the books found today in the Protestant canon, with the exception of Esther, which is omitted, and the Wisdom of Solomon, which is included (*Hist. eccl.* 4.26.12–14). This passage is the earliest known use of the term "Old Testament" (παλαιὰ διαθήκη) for the Jewish scriptures.

Melito also played a role in the Quartodeciman Controversy, which arose in the second century regarding the proper date for the celebration of *Pascha*, that is, Easter (cf. *Hist. eccl.* 5.23–25). Some Christians, including Melito, believed that Christian Pascha should be celebrated on the same day as the Jewish Passover, which in different years would fall on different days of the week. Other Christians believed Pascha should always be on a Sunday, specifically, the Sunday after the Jewish Passover. Thus the one side emphasized typological connections in salvation history, and the other emphasized associations of Sunday with the resurrection. The controversy was not settled until the Council of Nicea (325), when Sunday was set as the proper day for Easter.

Eusebius lists a large number of writings by Melito (*Hist. eccl.* 4.26). Until a manuscript of *On Pascha* (*Pasch.*) was discovered in 1932, we had only fragments of this writing. *On Pascha* is a sermon that represents Melito's position in the Quartodeciman Controversy, for in it he develops extensively the typology between the account of the Passover in Exodus 12 and the redemption that Christ has accomplished. He refers to both the Exodus Passover and the redemptive work of Christ as *mysteries* (μυστήρια), defined in this context by Quasten as "actions having a supernatural effect beyond their historical setting."[1] Indeed, the redemptive work at the Exodus itself, and throughout the Old Testament, was the work of the one who became incarnate in Jesus (*Pasch.* 81–86). Such interconnections in salvation history are the grounds for typology, and Melito includes in this sermon not only an extensive example of typology, but also a valuable discussion of it (sections 35–45). This discussion shows the care Melito takes in his interpretation. He is also very careful in his use of language, for he crafts the sermon according to rhetorical conventions of the day.[2] When this document came to light, it surprised scholars since many had thought Christians did not make use of such rhetoric before the fourth century. The sermon is full of powerful imagery and striking expressions.

Along with the profound reflection on the saving work of Christ, Melito expresses repeatedly the divinity of Christ, while also affirming the humanity of Christ and the reality of the incarnation (e.g., *Pasch.*, sections 70–71). In addition, he includes a strong condemnation of the Jews for rejecting their Messiah (sections 72–99). Here we find the earliest known example of the charge of deicide against the Jews in Melito's statement that "God has been murdered" (ὁ θεὸς πεφόνευται, section 96). To some extent, this anti-Jewish polemic may reflect Melito's need to draw a sharp contrast between Christianity and Judaism because his Quartodecimian stance looked like a Judaizing tendency to some Christians.[3]

The sermon is 105 sections long, of which the first forty-five have been included here. Sections 1–34 work out a typology of Exodus 12, followed in sections 35–45 with a discussion of typology in general.

Edition used:	Stuart George Hall, ed. and tran. *Melito of Sardis: On Pascha and Fragments.* Oxford Early Christian Texts. Oxford: Clarendon Press, 1979.
Level of difficulty:	Intermediate [1–4]

---

[1] Quasten, *Patrology,* 1:243.

[2] Stewart-Sykes has a helpful overview of Melito's use of rhetoric in his introduction to Melito of Sardis, *On Pascha, With the Fragments of Melito and Other Material Related to the Quartodecimans* (trans. and annotated by Alistair Stewart-Sykes; Popular Patristics Series; Crestwood, N.Y.: St. Vladimir's Seminary Press, 2001), 14–17.

[3] See Stewart-Sykes' discussion in Melito of Sardis, *On Pascha,* 25–27, and Lynn H. Cohick, *The Peri Pascha Attributed to Melito of Sardis: Setting, Purpose, and Sources* (Brown Judaic Studies 327; Providence, R.I.: Brown University Press, 2000), 52–87.

Note 1: Since this text is divided by sections rather than chapters, the frequency of the Greek help differs from the other selections. Here I repeat help for words that have not occurred in the previous two sections. So you should find help for any given word either in the section you are reading, or in one of the two previous sections, or in the list in Appendix A.

Note 2: Hall's text uses square brackets to indicate, "words or letters which do not appear in Greek manuscripts but probably stood in them before damage to the codices." He uses angle brackets to indicate, "words or letters omitted by the Greek witnesses and restored by conjecture or from the versions" (Hall: xlvii).

On Pascha 1–45 The Mystery of the Pascha

Μελιτῶνος Περὶ Πάσχα

1 Ἡ μὲν γραφὴ τῆς ἑβραϊκῆς Ἐξόδου ἀνέγνωσται
καὶ τὰ ῥήματα τοῦ μυστηρίου διασεσάφηται,
πῶς τὸ πρόβατον θύεται
καὶ πῶς ὁ λαὸς σῴζεται
<καὶ πῶς ὁ Φαραὼ διὰ τοῦ μυστηρίου μαστίζεται>.
2 τοίνυν ξύνετε, ὦ ἀγαπητοί,
ὅπως ἐστὶν καινὸν καὶ παλαιόν,
ἀΐδιον καὶ πρόσκαιρον,
φθαρτὸν καὶ ἄφθαρτον,
θνητὸν καὶ ἀθάνατον τὸ τοῦ πάσχα μυστήριον·
3 παλαιὸν μὲν κατὰ τὸν νόμον,
καινὸν δὲ [κατὰ τὸν] λόγον·
πρόσκαιρον κατὰ τὸν [τύπον],
ἀΐδιον διὰ τὴν χάριν·
φθαρτ[ὸν διὰ τὴν] τοῦ προβάτου σφαγήν,
ἄφθαρτον [διὰ τὴν] τοῦ κυρίου ζωήν·

Title

Μελιτῶνος → ὁ Μελίτων, *Melito.* • **Πάσχα** → τὸ πάσχα, indecl., *Pascha.* This word is a transliteration of the Hebrew/Aramaic for "Passover." Christians used it to refer to the Passover festival, the Passover meal (Seder), the Passover lamb, and for the Christian celebration of what later is referred to as Holy Week and Easter. These uses are all interrelated so it is best simply to transliterate the term.

Section 1

ἑβραϊκῆς → ἑβραϊκός, η, ον, *Hebrew.* • **Ἐξόδου** → ἡ ἔξοδος, *exit; Exodus.* Gen. of content (Wal: 92; Smy: 1323), specifically, communicative content (Yng: 27). • **ἀνέγνωσται** — pf. pass. indic. → ἀναγινώσκω (listed in lexicons under ἀναγιγνώσκω), *I read.* • **ῥήματα** — here, *events* (BDAG 2: 905). • **μυστηρίου** → τὸ μυστήριον, *mystery.* • **διασεσάφηται** → διασαφέω, *I make very clear.* • **πρόβατον** → τὸ πρόβατον, *sheep.* • **θύεται** → θύω, *I sacrifice.* • **Φαραώ** → ὁ Φαραώ, indecl., *Pharaoh.* Perler's text does not have the material in brackets. • **μαστίζεται** → μαστίζω, *I strike with a whip, scourge.*

Section 2

τοίνυν — *therefore.* • **ξύνετε** — pres. act. impv. → συνίημι, *I understand.* • **ὦ** — In Classical Greek ὦ w. voc. is "a mere address" (LSI 2: 904), but in Hellenistic Greek ὦ signals emphasis and/or emotion (Wal: 67–70; BDF: 146). • **ἀγαπητοί** → ἀγαπητός, ή, όν, *beloved.* • **ὅπως** — Perler's text has οὕτως. • **καινόν** → καινός, ή, όν, *new.* • **παλαιόν** → παλαιός, ά, όν, *old.* • **ἀΐδιον** → ἀΐδιος, ον, *eternal.* • **πρόσκαιρον** → πρόσκαιρος, ον, *temporary.* • **φθαρτόν** → φθαρτός, ή, όν, *perishable.* • **ἄφθαρτον** → ἄφθαρτος, ον, *imperishable.* • **θνητόν** → θνητός, ή, όν, *mortal.* • **ἀθάνατον** → ἀθάνατος, ον, *immortal.* • **μυστήριον** — subj.

θνητὸν διὰ τὴν [εἰς γῆν] ταφήν,
ἀθάνατον δ[ιὰ τ]ὴν ἐκ [νεκρῶν] ἀνάστασιν.
4 παλαιὸς [μὲν ὁ νόμος,]
[καινὸς δὲ ὁ] λόγος·
πρόσκαιρο[ς ὁ τύπος,]
[ἀΐδιος δὲ ἡ χάρις·]
[φ]θα[ρτὸν τὸ πρόβατον,]
[ἄφθαρτος ὁ κύριος·]
[μὴ συντριβεὶς ὡς ἀμνός,]
[ἀνασταθεὶς δὲ ὡς θεός.]
[εἰ καὶ γὰρ ὡς πρόβατον εἰς σφαγὴν ἤχθη,]
[ἀλλ' οὐκ ἦν πρόβατον·]
[εἰ καὶ ὡς ἀμνὸς ἄφωνος,]
[ἀλ]λ' οὐδὲ ἀμνὸς ἦν.
ὁ μὲν γὰρ τύπος [ἐγένετο,]
[ἡ δὲ] ἀλήθεια ηὑρίσκετο.
5 ἀντὶ γὰρ τοῦ [ἀμνοῦ υἱὸ]ς ἐγένετο
καὶ ἀντὶ τοῦ προβάτου ἄν[θρωπ]ος,
[ἐ]ν δὲ τῷ ἀνθρώπῳ Χριστὸς ὃς κεχώρηκεν [τὰ] πάντα.
6 ἡ γοῦν τοῦ προβάτου σφαγὴ
καὶ ἡ τοῦ αἵματος πομπὴ
καὶ ἡ τοῦ νόμου γραφὴ εἰς Χριστὸν Ἰησοῦν κεχώρηκεν,

Section 3

κατά — here, *concerning, regarding, with respect to* (LSI IV2: 403; BDAG 6: 513). • **τύπον** → ὁ τύπος, *type.* • **σφαγήν** → ἡ σφαγή, *slaughter.* • **ταφήν** → ἡ ταφή, *burial.* • **ἀνάστασιν** → ἡ ἀνάστασις, *resurrection.*

Section 4

πρόβατον → τὸ πρόβατον, *sheep.* • **συντριβείς** → συντρίβω, *I crush, break.* Cf. John 19:36; Exod 12:46; Num 9:12; Ps 34:20. Perler's text has σφαγείς (2 aor. pass. ptc. → σφάζω, *I slaughter*), "having been slaughtered as a lamb." • **ἀμνός** → ὁ and ἡ ἀμνός, *lamb.* • **ἀνασταθείς** → ἀνίστημι. Perler's text has the act. form ἀναστάς. • **εἰ καί** — *although* (BDAG, εἰ 6e: 278). Perler's text does not have εἰ, only καί, both here and two lines below. • **ἤχθη** → ἄγω. • **ἄφωνος** → ἄφωνος, ον, *voiceless, speechless, silent.* • **ἐγένετο** — here perhaps, *I am present, I am there, exist* (BDAG 8: 199). • **ἀλήθεια** → ἡ ἀλήθεια, here, *reality* (LSI 2: 34; BDAG 3: 42). • **ηὑρίσκετο** — impf. → εὑρίσκω. The pass. can mean *be present* (*PGL:* 574), but here the context may suggest *appear,* on the analogy of the pass. w. a neg. for *disappear* (BDAG 1a: 411): the reality "was becoming able to be found."

Section 5

ἀντί — *instead of.* • **υἱός** — Perler's text has θεός. • **κεχώρηκεν** → χωρέω, *I hold, contain; go forth, reach.* Intensive pf. (Wal: 574; Smy: 1946–7). Here the verb is trans., *hold, contain.* Contrast section 6 below.

Section 6

γοῦν — *therefore, hence, then, at any rate.* • **σφαγή** → ἡ σφαγή, *slaughter.* • **αἵματος** — Perler's text has πάσχα (→ τὸ πάσχα, indecl., *Pascha, the Passover*).

δι' ὃν τὰ πάντα ἐν τῷ πρεσβυτέρῳ νόμῳ ἐγένετο,
μᾶλλον δὲ ἐν τῷ νέῳ λόγῳ.
7 καὶ γὰρ ὁ νόμος λόγος ἐγένετο,
καὶ ὁ παλαιὸς καινός,
συνεξελθὼν ἐκ Σιὼν καὶ Ἰερουσαλήμ,
καὶ ἡ ἐντολὴ χάρις,
καὶ ὁ τύπος ἀλήθεια,
καὶ ὁ ἀμνὸς υἱός,
καὶ τὸ πρόβατον ἄνθρωπος,
καὶ ὁ ἄνθρωπος θεός.
8 ὡς γὰρ υἱὸς τεχθείς,
καὶ ὡς ἀμνὸς ἀχθείς,
καὶ ὡς πρόβατον σφαγείς,
καὶ ὡς ἄνθρωπος ταφείς,
ἀνέστη ἐκ νεκρῶν ὡς θεὸς φύσει θεὸς ὢν καὶ ἄνθρωπος.
9 ὅς ἐστιν τὰ πάντα·
καθ' ὃ κρίνει νόμος,
καθ' ὃ διδάσκει λόγος,
καθ' ὃ σῴζει χάρις,
καθ' ὃ γεννᾷ πατήρ,

• **πομπή** → ἡ πομπή, *display, show* (*PGL* 3: 1120). W. the reading πάσχα, πομπή would probably have its common meaning, *solemn procession.* • **κεχώρηκεν** → χωρέω, *I hold, contain; go forth, reach.* Here the verb is intrans., *go forth, reach,* also indicated by εἰς. Contrast section 5 above. • **πρεσβυτέρῳ** → πρεσβύτερος, α, ον, *older, old.* • **μᾶλλον** — μᾶλλον δέ usually means, *rather,* but this sense is contrary to the thought throughout the passage, so here μᾶλλον probably means, *still more* (LSI II2: 485), indicating the superiority of the new to the old without suggesting that the old was without value. • **νέῳ** → νέος, α, ον, *new.*

Section 7

ὁ νόμος λόγος ἐγένετο — perhaps echoing John 1:14, ὁ λόγος σὰρξ ἐγένετο. • **παλαιός** → παλαιός, ά, όν, *old.* • **καινός** → καινός, ή, όν, *new.* • **συνεξελθών** → συνεξέρχομαι, *I come/go out with/together.* • **Σιών** → ἡ Σιών, indecl., *Mt. Zion.* • **Ἰερουσαλήμ** → ἡ Ἰερουσαλήμ, indecl (listed in BDAG under the alternate form Ἱεροσόλυμα), *Jerusalem.* • **τύπος** → ὁ τύπος, *type.* • **ἀλήθεια** → ἡ ἀλήθεια, here and below, *reality* (LSI 2: 34; BDAG 3: 42). • **ἀμνός** → ὁ and ἡ ἀμνός, *lamb.* • **πρόβατον** → τὸ πρόβατον, *sheep.*

Section 8

τεχθείς — aor. pass. ptc. → τίκτω, *I am born.* • **ἀχθείς** → ἄγω. • **σφαγείς** — 2 aor. pass. ptc. → σφάζω, *I slaughter.* • **ταφείς** — 2 aor. pass. ptc. → θάπτω, *I bury.* • **ἀνέστη** → ἀνίστημι. • **φύσει** → ἡ φύσις, *nature.*

Section 9

καθ' ὃ — here, *because of* (BDAG B5aδ: 512). καθ' ὃ κρίνει νόμος, "(He is) law, because of which he judges." That is, he does these things because of who he is, as the first line of this section indicates. • **γεννᾷ** → γεννάω, *I beget.* • **πάσχει** → πάσχω, *I suffer.*

καθ' ὃ γεννᾶται υἱός,
καθ' ὃ πάσχει πρόβατον,
καθ' ὃ θάπτεται ἄνθρωπος,
καθ' ὃ ἀνίσταται θεός.
10 οὗτός ἐστιν Ἰησοῦς ὁ Χριστός,
ᾧ ἡ δόξα εἰς τοὺς αἰῶνας τῶν αἰώνων. ἀμήν.
11 Τοῦτό ἐστιν τὸ τοῦ πάσχα μυστήριον
καθὼς ἐν τῷ νόμῳ γέγραπται,
ὡς μικρῷ πρόσθεν ἀνέγνωσται·
διηγήσομαι δὲ τὰ ῥήματα τῆς γραφῆς,
πῶς ὁ θεὸς ἐντέταλται Μωυσεῖ ἐν Αἰγύπτῳ,
ὁπότε βούλεται τὸν μὲν Φαραὼ δῆσαι ὑπὸ μάστιγα,
τὸν δὲ Ἰσραὴλ λῦσαι ἀπὸ μάστιγος διὰ χειρὸς Μωυσέως.
12 Ἰδοὺ γάρ, φησίν, λήμψῃ ἄσπιλον ἀμνὸν καὶ ἄμωμον,
καὶ πρὸς ἑσπέραν σφάξεις αὐτὸν μετὰ τῶν υἱῶν Ἰσραήλ,
καὶ νύκτωρ ἔδεσθε αὐτὸ μετὰ σπουδῆς·
ὀστοῦν οὐ συντρίψεις αὐτοῦ.
13 οὕτως, φησίν, ποιήσεις.
ἐν μιᾷ νυκτὶ ἔδεσθε αὐτὸ κατὰ πατριὰς καὶ δήμους,

Section 11

πάσχα → τὸ πάσχα, indecl., *Pascha, the Passover.* • **μυστήριον** → τὸ μυστήριον, *mystery.* • **μικρῷ** → μικρός, ά, όν, *small, little.* μικρῷ (χρονῷ), *a short time.* Dat. of time (Wal: 155; Smy: 1539). • **πρόσθεν** — adv., *before, earlier.* • **ἀνέγνωσται** — pf. pass. indic. → ἀναγινώσκω (listed in lexicons under ἀναγιγνώσκω), *I read.* • **διηγήσομαι** → διηγέομαι, *I set out in detail, describe in full, tell.* • **ῥήματα** — here, *events* (BDAG 2: 905). • **ἐντέταλται** → ἐντέλλω, *I command,* mostly in the mid. Perler's text has ἐντέλλεται. • **Μωυσεῖ** → ὁ Μωυσῆς (listed in BDAG under the alternate form Μωϋσῆς), *Moses.* • **Αἰγύπτῳ** → ἡ Αἴγυπτος, *Egypt.* • **ὁπότε** — adv., *when.* Perler's text has ὁπόταν, *whenever.* • **βούλεται** → βούλομαι, *I wish, want, desire.* • **Φαραώ** → ὁ Φαραώ, indecl., *Pharaoh.* • **δῆσαι** — aor. act. inf. → δέω, *I bind.* • **μάστιγα** → ἡ μάστιξ, *a whip, scourge, lash; plague.* One of many wordplays in *On Pascha*, the first μάστιξ is the extended meaning, "plague," and in the next line the ref. is literal, *whip.* • **λῦσαι** — aor. act. inf. → λύω, *I loosen, set free; do away with, destroy.*

Section 12

λήμψῃ → λαμβάνω. • **ἄσπιλον** → ἄσπιλος, ον, *without spot.* • **ἀμνόν** → ὁ and ἡ ἀμνός, *lamb.* • **ἄμωμον** → ἄμωμος, ον, *without blemish.* • **ἑσπέραν** → ἡ ἑσπέρα, *evening.* For πρὸς ἑσπέραν Perler's text has ἑσπέρας. Gen. of time (Wal: 122; Smy: 1444). • **σφάξεις** → σφάζω, *I slaughter.* • **νύκτωρ** — adv., *at/by night.* • **ἔδεσθε** — fut. mid. (depon.) indic. → ἐσθίω. Note the alternation between sg. and pl. in these sections. • **σπουδῆς** → ἡ σπουδή, *haste, speed.* • **ὀστοῦν** → τὸ ὀστοῦν (listed in lexicons under the alternate uncontracted form ὀστέον), *bone.* • **συντρίψεις** → συντρίβω, *I shatter, smash, break.*

Section 13

αὐτό — Perler's text has αὐτόν. • **κατά** — here, *by.* Distributive use (LSI BII: 403; BDAG B1d: 512). • **πατριάς** → ἡ πατρία, *family, clan.* • **δήμους** → ὁ δῆμος,

περιεζωσμένοι τὰς ὀσφύας ὑμῶν
καὶ αἱ ῥάβδοι ἐν ταῖς χερσὶν ὑμῶν.
ἔστιν γὰρ τοῦτο πάσχα κυρίου,
μνημόσυνον αἰώνιον τοῖς υἱοῖς Ἰσραήλ.
14 λαβόντες δὲ τὸ τοῦ προβάτου αἷμα
χρίσατε τὰ πρόθυρα τῶν οἰκιῶν ὑμῶν,
τιθέντες ἐπὶ τοὺς σταθμοὺς τῆς εἰσόδου
τὸ σημεῖον τοῦ αἵματος εἰς δυσωπίαν τοῦ ἀγγέλου.
ἰδοὺ γάρ, πατάσσω Αἴγυπτον
καὶ ἐν μιᾷ νυκτὶ ἀτεκνωθήσεται ἀπὸ κτήνους ἕως ἀνθρώπου.
15 τότε Μωυσῆς σφάξας τὸ πρόβατον
[καὶ] νύκτωρ διατελέσας τὸ μυστήριον μετὰ τῶν υἱῶν Ἰσραὴλ
ἐσφράγισεν τὰς τῶν οἰκιῶν θύρας
εἰς φρουρὰν τοῦ λαοῦ καὶ εἰς δυσωπίαν τοῦ ἀγγέλου.
16 Ὁπότε δὲ τὸ πρόβατον σφάζεται
καὶ τὸ πάσχα βιβρώσκεται
καὶ τὸ μυστήριον τελεῖται
καὶ ὁ λαὸς εὐφραίνεται
καὶ ὁ Ἰσραὴλ σφραγίζεται,
τότε ἀφίκετο ὁ ἄγγελος πατάσσειν Αἴγυπτον,

---

township, community, company, band. This may refer to the provision for small families to join together for the meal (Exod 12:4). • **περιεζωσμένοι** — pf. pass. ptc. → περιζώννυμαι, *I gird (around oneself).* • **ὀσφύας** → ἡ ὀσφύς, *loin.* • **ῥάβδοι** → ἡ ῥάβδος, *rod, staff.* Art. for possession (Wal: 215; Smy: 1121), which occurs a number of times in *On Pascha.* • **μνημόσυνον** → τὸ μνημόσυνον, *remembrance, memorial.*

Section 14

λαβόντες → λαμβάνω. • **προβάτου** → τὸ πρόβατον, *sheep.* • **χρίσατε** → χρίω, *I anoint, rub, smear.* • **πρόθυρα** → τὸ πρόθυρον, *front door, porch, forecourt.* • **οἰκιῶν** → τὸ οἰκίον, *house.* • **τιθέντες** → τίθημι. • **σταθμούς** → ὁ σταθμός, *doorpost.* • **εἰσόδου** → ἡ εἴσοδος, *entrance.* • **δυσωπίαν** → ἡ δυσωπία, *shame; discomfiture; persuasion* (*PGL*: 394). • **πατάσσω** → πατάσσω, *I strike.* Perler's text has the fut., πατάξω. • **Αἴγυπτον** → ἡ Αἴγυπτος, *Egypt.* • **ἀτεκνωθήσεται** → ἀτεκνόω, *I make childless.* • **κτήνους** → τὸ κτῆνος, *beast,* pl., *flocks and herds.*

Section 15

Μωυσῆς → ὁ Μωυσῆς (listed in BDAG under the alternate form Μωϋσῆς), *Moses.* • **σφάξας** — aor. act. ptc. → σφάζω, *I slaughter.* • **νύκτωρ** — adv., *at/by night.* • **διατελέσας** — aor. act. ptc. → διατελέω, *I bring to an end, accomplish.* • **μυστήριον** → τὸ μυστήριον, *mystery.* • **ἐσφράγισεν** → σφραγίζω, *I seal.* • **θύρας** → ἡ θύρα, *door.* • **φρουράν** → ἡ φρουρά, *watch, guard.* • **λαοῦ** — here, *for the people.* Obj. gen.

Section 16

ὁπότε — *when.* • **πάσχα** → τὸ πάσχα, indecl., *Pascha, the Passover.* • **βιβρώσκεται** → βιβρώσκω, *I eat.* • **τελεῖται** → τελέω, *I complete.* • **εὐφραίνεται** → εὐφραίνω, *I gladden;* pass. w. act. sense, *I enjoy myself, am happy, rejoice, celebrate.* • **ἀφίκετο** — impf. pass. indic. → ἀφίκω, *I arrive, come to, reach; extend.* ἀφίκω is

τὴν ἀμύητον τοῦ μυστηρίου,
τὴν ἄμοιρον τοῦ πάσχα,
τὴν ἀσφράγιστον τοῦ αἵματος,
τὴν ἀφρούρητον τοῦ πνεύματος,
τὴν ἐχθράν,
τὴν ἄπιστον·
(17) ἐν μιᾷ νυκτὶ πατάξας ἠτέκνωσεν.
17 περιελθὼν γὰρ τὸν Ἰσραὴλ ὁ ἄγγελος
καὶ ἰδὼν ἐσφραγισμένον τῷ τοῦ προβάτου αἵματι,
ἦλθεν ἐπ' Αἴγυπτον,
καὶ τὸν σκληροτράχηλον Φαραὼ διὰ πένθους ἐδάμασεν,
ἐνδύσας αὐτὸν οὐ στολὴν φαιὰν
οὐδὲ πέπλον περιεσχισμένον,
ἀλλ' ὅλην Αἴγυπτον περιεσχισμένην
πενθοῦσαν ἐπὶ τοῖς πρωτοτόκοις αὐτῆς.
18 ὅλη γὰρ Αἴγυπτος γενηθεῖσα ἐν πόνοις καὶ πληγαῖς,
ἐν δάκρυσιν καὶ κοπετοῖς,
ἀφίκετο πρὸς τὸν Φαραὼ ὅλη πενθήρης
οὐ μόνον τῷ σχήματι ἀλλὰ καὶ τῇ ψυχῇ,

---

a variant of the much more common verb ἀφικνέομαι, *arrive* (LSJ: 290). If the form here is not used as a depon., then the point may be not just that the angel arrived, but that he "was being extended," i.e., sent by God. A form of ἀφικνέομαι occurs in section 18 below. • **ἀμύητον** → ἀμύητος, ον, *uninitiated.* Fem. since the ref. is to ἡ Αἴγυπτος, beginning a string of acc. mod. of Αἴγυπτον. • **ἄμοιρον** → ἄμοιρος, ον, *without a part/share in.* • **ἀσφράγιστον** → ἀσφράγιστος, ον, *not sealed.* • **αἵματος** — gen. of means (Wal: 125). • **ἀφρούρητον** → ἀφρούρητος, ον, *unguarded.* • **πνεύματος** — gen. of agency (Wal: 126). • **ἐχθράν** → ἐχθρός, ά, όν, *hated; hostile.* • **ἄπιστον** → ἄπιστος, ον, *faithless, not to be trusted, unbelieving.*

Section 17

περιελθών — 2 aor. act. ptc. → περιέρχομαι, *I go around.* • **ἰδών** → εἶδον. • **ἐσφραγισμένον** — ptc. for indic. disc. (Wal: 645; Smy: 2106–15). • **προβάτου** → τὸ πρόβατον, *sheep.* • **Αἴγυπτον** → ἡ Αἴγυπτος, *Egypt.* • **σκληροτράχηλον** → σκληροτράχηλος, ον, *stiff-necked.* • **Φαραώ** → ὁ Φαραώ, indecl., *Pharaoh.* • **πένθους** → τὸ πένθος, *grief.* • **ἐδάμασεν** → δαμάζω, *I overpower, subdue, conquer.* • **ἐνδύσας** → ἐνδύω, *I put on, clothe.* W. double acc. of person and thing (Wal: 181), referred to by Smyth (1620) as internal and external object. Here describing mourning dress. • **στόλην** → ἡ στολή, *garment.* • **φαιάν** → φαιός, ά, όν, *gray.* • **πέπλον** → ὁ πέπλος, *a robe.* • **περιεσχισμένον** → περισχίζω, *I split, slit and tear off;* here, *torn.* • **πενθοῦσαν** → πενθέω, *I mourn, bewail, lament.* • **πρωτοτόκοις** → πρωτότοκος, ον, *firstborn.*

Section 18

γενηθεῖσα — 2 aor. pass. ptc. → γίνομαι. • **πόνοις** → ὁ πόνος, *distress, pain.* • **πληγαῖς** → ἡ πληγή, *blow, stroke; wound.* • **δάκρυσιν** → τὸ δάκρυ, *a tear.* • **κοπετοῖς** → ὁ κοπετός, *mourning, lamentation.* • **ἀφίκετο** — aor. mid. (depon.) indic. 3 sg. → ἀφικνέομαι, *I arrive, come to.* • **πενθήρης** → πενθήρης, ές, *lamenting, mourning.* In appos. to the subj. ὅλη Αἴγυπτος. • **σχήματι** → τὸ σχῆμα,

περιεσχισμένη οὐ μόνον τὰς στολὰς τῆς περιβολῆς
ἀλλὰ καὶ τοὺς μαστοὺς τῆς τρυφῆς.
19 ἦν δὲ καινὸν θέαμα ἰδεῖν,
ἔνθα κοπτομένους ἔνθα κωκύοντας,
καὶ μέσον Φαραὼ πενθήρη
ἐπὶ σάκκῳ καὶ σποδῷ καθήμενον,
περιβεβλημένον τὸ ψηλαφητὸν σκότος ὡς ἱμάτιον πενθικόν,
περιεζωσμένον ὅλ[ην] Αἴγυπτον ὡς κιθῶνα πένθους.
20 ἦν γὰρ περικειμένη Αἴγυπτος τὸν Φαραὼ
ὡς περιβολὴ κωκυτοῦ.
τοιοῦτος ὑφάνθη κιθὼν τῷ τυραννικῷ σώματι·
τοιαύτην ἐνέδυσεν στολὴν τὸν σκληρὸν Φαραὼ
ὁ τῆς δικαιοσύνης ἄγγελος·
πένθος πικρὸν καὶ σκότος ψηλαφητόν,
καὶ ἀτεκνίαν καινὴν ἐπὶ τῶν πρωτοτόκων αὐτῆς.
21 ἦν γὰρ ταχινὸς καὶ ἀκόρεστος ὁ τῶν πρωτοτόκων θάνατος,
(21) ἦν [δὲ] καινὸν τρόπαιον ἰδεῖν

---

form, shape, appearance. • **στολάς** → ἡ στολή. Acc. of ref. (Wal: 203; Smy: 1600). • **περιβολῆς** → ἡ περιβολή, *covering.* Attrib. gen. (Wal: 86), also called gen. of quality (Smy: 1320). • **μαστούς** → ὁ μαστός, *breast.* • **τρυφῆς** → ἡ τρυφή, *softness, delicacy.* Attrib. gen. (Wal: 86), also called gen. of quality (Smy: 1320).

Section 19

καινόν → καινός, ή, όν, *new;* here, *strange, remarkable, unknown* (BDAG 2: 497). • **θέαμα** → τὸ θέαμα, *sight, spectacle.* • **ἰδεῖν** → εἶδον. • **ἔνθα** — adv., *there.* ἔνθα (καὶ) ἔνθα, *here (and) there* (LSI I1: 262). • **κοπτομένους** → κόπτω, *I strike, beat.* Note the mid. • **κωκύοντας** → κωκύω, *I shriek, wail.* • **σάκκῳ** → ὁ σάκκος, *sackcloth.* • **σποδῷ** → ἡ σποδός, *ashes.* • **περιβεβλημένον** → περιβάλλω, *I throw around.* • **ψηλαφητόν** → ψηλαφητός, ή, όν, *that can be felt, palpable.* • **σκότος** → ὁ σκότος, *darkness.* • **πενθικόν** → πενθικός, ή, όν, *of/for mourning.* • **περιεζωσμένον** — pf. pass. ptc. → περιζώννυμαι, *I gird (around oneself), gird/clothe oneself with,* w. acc. • **κιθῶνα** → ὁ κιθών, *garment worn next to the skin, tunic,* an alternate form of χιτών.

Section 20

περικειμένη → περίκειμαι, *I lie around.* • **Αἴγυπτος** → ἡ Αἴγυπτος, *Egypt.* • **Φαραώ** → ὁ Φαραώ, indecl., *Pharaoh.* • **κωκυτοῦ** → ὁ κωκυτός, *shrieking, wailing.* Attrib. gen. (Wal: 86), also called gen. of quality (Smy: 1320). • **ὑφάνθη** → ὑφαίνω, *I weave.* • **τυραννικῷ** → τυραννικός, ή, όν, *of/for a tyrant, tyrannical.* • **ἐνεδύσεν** → ἐνδύω, *I put on, clothe.* W. double acc. of person and thing (Wal: 181), referred to by Smyth (1620) as internal and external object. • **σκληρόν** → σκληρός, ά, όν, *hard, harsh.* • **πένθος** → τὸ πένθος, *grief.* • **πικρόν** → πικρός, ά, όν, *sharp, bitter.* • **ἀτεκνίαν** → ἡ ἀτεκνία, *childlessness.* • **καινήν** — Perler's text has Καὶ ἦν, having ended the sentence at ἀτεκνίαν: "And it [childlessness] was upon her firstborn . . ." • **πρωτοτόκων** → πρωτότοκος, ον, *firstborn.*

Section 21

ταχινός → ταχινός, ή, όν, *quick, fast, swift.* • **ἀκόρεστος** → ἀκόρεστος, ον, *insatiable.* • **τρόπαιον** → τὸ τρόπαιον, *trophy, monument, memorial.* • **ἰδεῖν** →

ἐπὶ τῶν πιπτόντων νεκρῶν ἐν μιᾷ ῥοπῇ.
καὶ ἐγένετο τοῦ θανάτου τροφὴ
ἡ τῶν κειμένων τροπή.
22 καινὴν δὲ συμφορὰν ἐὰν ἀκούσητε θαυμάσετε·
τάδε γὰρ περιέσχεν τοὺς Αἰγυπτίους,
νὺξ μακρὰ
καὶ σκότος ψηλαφητὸν
καὶ θάνατος ψηλαφῶν
καὶ ἄγγελος ἐκθλίβων
καὶ ᾅδης καταπίνων τοὺς πρωτοτόκους αὐτῶν.
23 τὸ δὲ καινότερον καὶ φοβερώτερον ἀκοῦσαι ἔχετε·
ἐν τῷ ψηλαφητῷ σκότει ὁ ἀψηλάφητος θάνατος ἐκρύβετο,
καὶ τὸ μὲν σκότος ἐψηλάφων οἱ δυστυχεῖς Αἰγύπτιοι,
ὁ δὲ θάνατος ἐξεραυνῶν ἐψηλάφα τοὺς πρωτοτόκους τῶν Αἰγυπτίων
τοῦ ἀγγέλου κελεύοντος.
24 εἴ τις οὖν ἐψηλάφα τὸ σκότος
ὑπὸ τοῦ θανάτου ἐξήγετο.
καί τις πρωτότοκος χειρὶ σκοτεινὸν σῶμα ἐναγκαλισάμενος
τῇ ψυχῇ ἐκδειματωθεὶς οἰκτρὸν καὶ φοβερὸν ἀνεβόησεν·

εἶδον. Perhaps epex. (Wal: 607; Smy: 2006). • **ῥοπῇ** → ἡ ῥοπή, *critical moment, turning point.* • **τροφή** → ἡ τροφή, *food.* • **κειμένων** → κεῖμαι, *I lie, lie down, recline.* • **τροπή** → ἡ τροπή, *turn, turning, rout (of an enemy).*

Section 22

καινήν → καινός, ή, όν, *new;* here, *strange, remarkable, unknown* (BDAG 2: 497). • **συμφοράν** → ἡ συμφορά, *event; misfortune.* • **θαυμάσετε** → θαυμάζω, *I wonder, marvel, am astonished, am amazed at.* • **τάδε** → ὅδε, ἥδε, τόδε, *this.* • **περιέσχεν** — 2 aor. act. indic. → περιέχω, *I encompass, surround.* • **Αἰγυπτίους** → Αἰγύπτιος, α, ον, *Egyptian.* • **μακρά** → μακρός, ά, όν, *long.* • **σκότος** → ὁ σκότος, *darkness.* • **ψηλαφητόν** → ψηλαφητός, ή, όν, *that can be felt, palpable.* • **ψηλαφῶν** → ψηλαφάω, *I feel/grope about; touch, handle.* • **ἐκθλίβων** → ἐκθλίβω, *I squeeze much/greatly/hard; distress greatly.* • **ᾅδης** → ὁ ᾅδης, *Hades.* • **καταπίνων** → καταπίνω, *I gulp down.*

Section 23

καινότερον → καινότερος, α, ον, *newer, unprecedented.* • **φοβερώτερον** → φοβερώτερος, α, ον, *more dreadful.* • **ἀψηλάφητος** → ἀψηλάφητος, ον, *untouched, untouchable.* • **ἐκρύβετο** — 2 aor. mid. indic. → κρύπτω, *I hide.* Note the mid. • **ἐψηλάφων** — impf. act. indic. → ψηλαφάω. • **δυστυχεῖς** → δυστυχής, ές, *unlucky, unfortunate.* • **ἐξεραυνῶν** → ἐξεραυνάω, *I search out.* • **πρωτοτόκους** → πρωτότοκος, ον, *firstborn.* • **κελεύοντος** → κελεύω, *I order, command.* Gen. abs.

Section 24

ὑπό — Perler's text has ὑπέρ. • **ἐξήγετο** → ἐξάγω, *I lead out/away.* • **σκοτεινόν** → σκοτεινός, ή, όν, *dark.* • **ἐναγκαλισάμενος** → ἐναγκαλίζομαι, *I take in one's arms;* here w. χειρί, *clasp.* • **ἐκδειματωθείς** → ἐκδειματόω, *I greatly frighten.* Attend. circ. This rare word occurs also in Wis 17:6. There are a number of similarities between Melito's description of the terrors at the Exodus and that found in Wis

Τίνα κρατεῖ ἡ δεξιά μου;
τίνα τρέμει ἡ ψυχή μου;
τίς μοι σκοτεινὸς περικέχυται ὅλῳ τῷ σώματι;
εἰ μὲν πατήρ, βοήθησον·
εἰ δὲ μήτηρ, συμπάθησον·
εἰ δὲ ἀδελφός, προσλάλησον·
εἰ δὲ φίλος, συστάθητι·
εἰ δὲ ἐχθρός, ἀπαλλάγηθι, ὅτι πρωτότοκος ἐγώ.
25 πρὸ δὲ τοῦ σιωπῆσαι τὸν πρωτότοκον,
ἡ μακρὰ σιωπὴ κατέσχεν αὐτὸν προσειποῦσα·
Πρωτότοκος ἐμὸς εἶ·
ἐγώ σοι πέπρωμαι ἡ τοῦ θανάτου σιωπή.
26 ἕτερος δέ τις πρωτότοκος νοήσας τὴν τῶν πρωτοτόκων ἅλωσιν
ἑαυτὸν ἀπαρνεῖτο ἵνα μὴ θάνῃ πικρῶς·
Οὔκ εἰμι πρωτότοκος,
τριτῷ γεγέννημαι καρπῷ.
ὁ δὲ ψευσθῆναι μὴ δυνάμενος τοῦ πρωτοτόκου προσήπτετο,
πρηνὴς δὲ ἔπιπτεν σιγῶν.

17.1—18:19. • **οἰκτρόν** → οἰκτρός, ά, όν, *pitiable;* neut. sg. for adv., *piteously, miserably.* • **φοβερόν** → φοβερός, ά, όν, *fearful;* neut. sg. for adv., *fearfully, terribly.* • **ἀνεβόησεν** → ἀναβοάω, *I cry out.* • **κρατεῖ** → κρατέω, *I lay hold of, seize.* • **δεξιά** → δεξιός, ά, όν, *right hand/side.* ἡ δεξιά, *right hand* (ἡ χείρ is understood). • **τρέμει** → τρέμω, *I tremble;* w. acc., *tremble at, fear.* • **περικέχυται** — pf. pass. indic. → περιχέω, *I pour around;* pass., *embrace.* • **βοήθησον** → βοηθέω, *I help.* For these verbs supply the dir. obj., "me." • **συμπάθησον** → συμπαθέω, *I sympathize.* • **προσλάλησον** → προσλαλέω, *I talk to/with.* • **φίλος** → φίλος, η, ον, *loved, dear;* subst., *friend.* • **συστάθητι** → συνίστημι; pass., *I stand with/by.* Perler's text has εὐστάθησον (aor. act. impv. → εὐσταθέω, *I am steady, stable; calm*). • **ἐχθρός** → ἐχθρός, ά, όν, *hated;* subst., *enemy.* • **ἀπαλλάγηθι** — aor. pass. impv. → ἀπαλλάσσω, *I set free;* pass., *depart.*

Section 25

πρό — *before.* • **σιωπῆσαι** → σιωπάω, *I am silent.* Inf. w. prep. πρό for a temp. clause, w. subj. in the acc. • **μακρά** → μακρός, ά, όν, *long.* • **σιωπή** → ἡ σιωπή, *silence.* • **κατέσχεν** — 2 aor. act. indic. → κατέχω, *I hold fast.* • **προσειποῦσα** → προσεῖπον, *I speak to.* • **πέπρωμαι** — pf. pass. indic. → πόρω, *I furnish;* pf., *am fated, am destined.* Here, *I am destined for you; I am your destiny* (cf. Hall; Stewart-Sykes).

Section 26

πρωτότοκος → πρωτότοκος, ον, *firstborn.* • **νοήσας** → νοέω, *I perceive, observe, notice.* • **ἅλωσιν** → ἡ ἅλωσις, *capture.* • **ἀπαρνεῖτο** — impf. mid. (depon.) indic. → ἀπαρνέομαι, *I deny utterly, deny.* Ingressive (Wal: 544; Smy: 1900). • **θάνῃ** — 2 aor. act. subjun. → θνήσκω, *I die.* • **πικρῶς** — adv., *bitterly.* • **τρίτῳ** → τρίτος, η, ον, *third.* • **καρπῷ** → ὁ καρπός, here, *offspring* (LSJ 3: 879; BDAG 1aβ: 510), probably a form of dat. of location (Wal: 153–7; Smy: 1530–43). τρίτῳ καρπῷ, "at third fruit/offspring," refers to the place in the order of births, *at third (place in the order of) offspring.* • **ψευσθῆναι** → ψεύδω, *I deceive.* • **προσήπτετο** → προσάπτω, *I fasten to;* mid., *lay hold of,* w. gen. • **πρηνής** → πρηνής, ές,

ὑπὸ δὲ μιὰν ῥοπὴν ὁ πρωτότοκος καρπὸς τῶν Αἰγυπτίων ἀπώλετο·
ὁ πρωτόσπορος,
ὁ πρωτότοκος,
ὁ ποθητός,
ὁ περίψυκτος ἠδαφίσθη χαμαί·
οὐχ ὁ τῶν ἀνθρώπων μόνον,
ἀλλὰ καὶ τῶν ἀλόγων ζῴων.

27 μύκημα δὲ ἐν τοῖς πεδίοις τῆς γῆς ἠκούετο
ἀποδυρομένων κτηνῶν ἐπὶ τῶν τροφίμων αὐτῶν·
καὶ γὰρ δάμαλις ὑπόμοσχος
καὶ ἵππος ὑπόπωλος
καὶ τὰ λοιπὰ κτήνη λοχευόμενα καὶ σπαργῶντα
πικρὸν καὶ ἐλεεινὸν ἀπωδύροντο ἐπὶ τῶν πρωτοτόκων καρπῶν.

28 οἰμωγὴ δέ τις καὶ κοπετὸς ἐπὶ τῇ τῶν ἀνθρώπων ἀπωλείᾳ ἐγένετο,
ἐπὶ τῇ τῶν πρωτοτόκων νεκρῶν.
ὅλη γὰρ ἐπώζεσεν Αἴγυπτος ἐπὶ τῶν ἀτάφων σωμάτων.

---

face downwards. • **σιγῶν** → σιγάω, *I am silent/still.* Attend. circ. • **ὑπό** — here, *at.* • **ῥοπήν** → ἡ ῥοπή, *critical moment, turning point.* • **Αἰγυπτίων** → Αἰγύπτιος, α, ον, *Egyptian.* • **ἀπώλετο** — 2 aor. mid. indic. → ἀπόλλυμι, *I destroy;* mid., *perish, am ruined.* • **πρωτόσπορος** → πρωτόσπορος, ον, *first-sown, first-begotten, first-born.* • **ποθητός** → ποθητός, ή, όν, *longed-for, desired.* • **περίψυκτος** → περίψυκτος, ον, *fondled, dandled; beloved.* Perler's text has περιψηκτός, a word not in the lexicons. Since the word is probably related to περιψάω, "wipe around, wipe clean" (cf. Perler: 149), the context suggests the ref. would be to a newborn who has been wiped clean. Perler himself, however, translates it "le choyé," "the pampered one," which is in keeping with περίψυκτος. • **ἠδαφίσθη** → ἐδαφίζω, *I dash to the ground.* • **χαμαί** — adv., *on the ground.* • **ἀλόγων** → ἄλογος, ον, *speechless, irrational, brute (beasts).* • **ζῴων** → ζῳός, ή, όν, *alive, living.* The entry in LSJ does not have an iota subscript because classical authors did not include it.

Section 27

μύκημα → τὸ μύκημα, *lowing, bellowing, roaring.* • **πεδίοις** → τὸ πεδίον, *plain* (flat open country). • **ἀποδυρομένων** → ἀποδύρομαι, *I lament bitterly.* Gen. abs. • **κτηνῶν** → τὸ κτῆνος, *beast,* pl., *flocks and herds.* • **τροφίμων** → τρόφιμος, ον, *nourishing;* subst., *nurslings.* • **δάμαλις** → ἡ δάμαλις, *heifer, young cow.* • **ὑπόμοσχος** → ὑπόμοσχος, ον, *with a nursing calf under* her (*PGL*: 1452). • **ἵππος** → ὁ and ἡ ἵππος, *horse, mare.* • **ὑπόπωλος** → ὑπόπωλος, ον, *with a foal under her.* • **λοχευόμενα** → λοχεύω, *I bring to birth, bear children.* The act. can be used of the midwife while the mid. has an act. meaning, but is used of the mother (LSI: 479). • **σπαργῶντα** → σπαργάω, *I am full to bursting.* The context suggests the picture is of nursing animals full of milk. • **πικρόν** → πικρός, ά, όν, *sharp, bitter,* neut. sg. for adv. • **ἐλεεινόν** → ἐλεεινός, ή, όν, *pitiable, piteous,* neut. sg. for adv.

Section 28

οἰμωγή → ἡ οἰμωγή, *loud wailing, lamentation.* • **τις** — Not in Perler's text. • **κοπετός** → ὁ κοπετός, *mourning, lamentation.* • **ἀπωλείᾳ** → ἡ ἀπώλεια, *destruction.* • **ἐπὶ τῇ τῶν πρωτοτόκων νεκρῶν** — the art. τῇ ref. again to ἀπωλείᾳ. • **ἐπώζεσεν** → ἐπόζω, *I become stinking.* • **Αἴγυπτος** → ἡ Αἴγυπτος, *Egypt.* • **ἐπί** — here,

29 ἦν δὲ θεάσασθαι φοβερὸν θέαμα
τῶν Αἰγυπτίων μητέρας λυσικόμους,
πατέρας λυσίφρονας,
δεινὸν ἀνακωκύοντας τῇ αἰγυπτιακῇ φωνῇ·
Δυστυχεῖς ἠτεκνώμεθα ὑπὸ μίαν ῥοπὴν ἀπὸ τοῦ πρωτοτόκου καρποῦ.
ἦσαν δὲ ἐπὶ μασθῶν κοπτόμενοι,
χερσὶν τύπτοντες κροτήματα ἐπὶ τῆς τῶν νεκρῶν ὀρχήσεως.
30 Τοιαύτη συμφορὰ περιέσχεν Αἴγυπτον,
ἄφνω δὲ ἠτέκνωσεν αὐτήν.
ἦν δὲ ὁ Ἰσραὴλ φρουρούμενος ὑπὸ τῆς τοῦ προβάτου σφαγῆς,
καί γε συνεφωτίζετο ὑπὸ τοῦ χυθέντος αἵματος,
καὶ τεῖχος ηὑρίσκετο τοῦ λαοῦ ὁ τοῦ προβάτου θάνατος.

---

in the presence of (LSJ A5: 286; BDAG 2a: 363). Perler's text has ἀπό. • **ἀτάφων** → ἄταφος, ον, *unburied.*

Section 29

θεάσασθαι → θεάομαι, *I look on, gaze at, behold.* Mod. φοβερόν. • **φοβερόν** → φοβερός, ά, όν, *fearful.* • **θέαμα** → τὸ θέαμα, *sight, spectacle.* • **Αἰγυπτίων** → Αἰγύπτιος, α, ον, *Egyptian.* Partitive gen. (Wal: 84; Smy: 1306). • **λυσικόμους** → λυσίκομος, η, ον, *with unbound hair* (*PGL*: 814); "with hair undone" (cf. Hall; Stewart-Sykes). • **λυσίφρονας** → λυσίφρων, ον, *distracted* (*PGL*: 815). Since the word family around φρονέω concerns the mind, here (matching λυσικόμους), "with minds undone" (cf. Hall; Stewart-Sykes). • **δεινόν** → δεινός, ή, όν, *fearful, terrible, dread;* neut. acc. for adv., *terribly, dreadfully.* • **ἀνακωκύοντας** → ἀνακωκύω, *I wail aloud.* • **Αἰγυπτιακῇ** → Αἰγυπτιακός, ή, όν, *of/for Egyptians.* • **φωνῇ** → ἡ φωνή, here, *language.* • **δυστυχεῖς** → δυστυχής, ές, *unlucky, unfortunate.* • **ἠτεκνώμεθα** → ἀτεκνόω, *I make childless.* • **ὑπό** — here, *at* (LSJ CIII2: 1875). • **ῥοπήν** → ἡ ῥοπή, *critical moment, turning point.* • **ἀπό** — here w. a verb denoting separation (BDAG 1b: 105). • **πρωτοτόκου** → πρωτότοκος, ον, *firstborn.* • **καρποῦ** → ὁ καρπός, here, *offspring* (LSJ 3: 879; BDAG 1aβ: 510). • **μασθῶν** → ὁ μασθός, *breast,* a late form of μαστός. Perler's text has μαστῶν. • **κοπτόμενοι** → κόπτω, *I strike, beat.* Note the mid. • **τύπτοντες** → τύπτω, *I beat, strike.* • **κροτήματα** → τὸ κρότημα, *work wrought by a hammer; (musical) instrument.* The ref. here is to some form of percussive musical instrument. The lexicons do not note this meaning, but *TLG* provides examples, such as Gregory of Nazianzus, *Carmina moralia* (*PG* 37, col. 656, line 8), and *Carmina de se ipso* (*PG* 37, col. 1438, line 22). • **ὀρχήσεως** → ἡ ὄρχησις, *dancing, dance.*

Section 30

συμφορά → ἡ συμφορά, *event; misfortune.* • **περιέσχεν** — 2 aor. act. indic. → περιέχω, *I encompass, surround.* • **ἄφνω** — adv., *suddenly.* • **φρουρούμενος** → φρουρέω, *I guard.* • **προβάτου** → τὸ πρόβατον, *sheep.* • **σφαγῆς** → ἡ σφαγή, *slaughter.* • **γε** — *at least, even, indeed* (BDAG: 190). • **συνεφωτίζετο** → συμφωτίζομαι, *I give light together;* pass., *am illumined together. PGL*: 1293 interprets this as a ref. to baptism, *be baptized together.* • **χυθέντος** — aor. pass. ptc. → χέω, *I pour, shed.* Either a noun, "the shedding of blood," or an adj., "the shed blood." • **τεῖχος** → τὸ τεῖχος, *wall.* Pred. nom. w. εὑρίσκω in the pass. (Wal: 40). • **λαοῦ** — here, *for the people.*

31 ὦ μυστηρίου καινοῦ καὶ ἀνεκδιηγήτου·
ἡ τοῦ προβάτου σφαγὴ ηὑρίσκετο τοῦ Ἰσραὴλ σωτηρία,
καὶ ὁ τοῦ προβάτου θάνατος ζωὴ τοῦ λαοῦ ἐγένετο,
καὶ τὸ αἷμα ἐδυσώπησεν τὸν ἄγγελον.
32 λέγε μοι, ὦ ἄγγελε, τί ἐδυσωπήθης;
τὴν τοῦ προβάτου σφαγὴν ἢ τὴν τοῦ κυρίου ζωήν;
τὸν τοῦ προβάτου θάνατον ἢ τὸν τοῦ κυρίου τύπον;
τὸ τοῦ προβάτου αἷμα ἢ τὸ τοῦ κυρίου πνεῦμα;
33 δῆλος εἶ δυσωπηθεὶς
ἰδὼν τὸ τοῦ κυρίου μυστήριον ἐν τῷ προβάτῳ γινόμενον,
τὴν τοῦ κυρίου ζωὴν ἐν τῇ τοῦ προβάτου σφαγῇ,
τὸν τοῦ κυρίου τύπον ἐν τῷ τοῦ προβάτου θανάτῳ,
διὰ τοῦτο οὐκ ἐπάταξας τὸν Ἰσραήλ
ἀλλὰ μόνην Αἴγυπτον ἠτέκνωσας.
34 Τί τοῦτο τὸ καινὸν μυστήριον,
Αἴγυπτον μὲν παταχθῆναι εἰς ἀπώλειαν,
τὸν δὲ Ἰσραὴλ φυλαχθῆναι εἰς σωτηρίαν;
ἀκούσατε τὴν δύναμιν τοῦ μυστηρίου.
35 οὐδέν ἐστιν, ἀγαπητοί, τὸ λεγόμενον καὶ γινόμενον

Section 31

μυστηρίου → τὸ μυστήριον, *mystery.* • **καινοῦ** → καινός, ή, όν, *new;* here, *strange, remarkable, unknown* (BDAG 2: 497). • **ἀνεκδιηγήτου** → ἀνεκδιήγητος, ον, *ineffable, indescribable.* • **σωτηρία** → ἡ σωτηρία, *salvation.* Pred. nom. w. εὑρίσκω in the pass. (Wal: 40). • **ἐδυσώπησεν** → δυσωπέω, *I put to shame; persuade, win over* (*PGL*: 394).

Section 32

τύπον → ὁ τύπος, *type.*

Section 33

δῆλος → δῆλος, η, ον, *clear, evident;* w. εἰμί and a ptc., "it is clear that" (LSI II: 182; BDAG: 222). • **ἰδών** — aor. act. ptc. → εἶδον. Circ. ptc., causal. • **προβάτῳ** → τὸ πρόβατον, *sheep.* • **γινόμενον** — ptc. for indir. disc., the content of the seeing (Wal: 165; Smy: 2110). • **σφαγῇ** → ἡ σφαγή, *slaughter.* • **ἐπάταξας** — aor. act. indic. → πατάσσω, *I strike.* • **Αἴγυπτον** → ἡ Αἴγυπτος, *Egypt.* • **ἠτέκνωσας** → ἀτεκνόω, *I make childless.*

Section 34

Τί — here in pred. position. • **καινόν** → καινός, ή, όν, *new;* here, *strange, remarkable, unknown* (BDAG 2: 497). • **μυστήριον** → τὸ μυστήριον, *mystery.* • **παταχθῆναι** — aor. pass. inf. → πατάσσω. Inf. in appos. to μυστήριον for the content of the mystery. • **ἀπώλειαν** → ἡ ἀπώλεια, *destruction.* • **φυλαχθῆναι** — aor. pass. inf. → φυλάσσω, *I guard.* Another inf. in appos. to μυστήριον. • **σωτηρίαν** → ἡ σωτηρία, *salvation.* • **δύναμιν** — here, *force* in the sense of *meaning* (LSI III: 213 and the note in Stewart-Sykes: 45).

Section 35

ἀγαπητοί → ἀγαπητός, ή, όν, *beloved.* • **τὸ λεγόμενον καὶ γινόμενον** — These ptcs. could be the subj. ("What is said and done is nothing," Hall: 17), but the

δίχα παραβολῆς καὶ προκεντήματος.
πάντα ὅσα ἐὰν γίνεται καὶ λέγεται παραβολῆς τυγχάνει,
τὸ μὲν λεγόμενον παραβολῆς,
τὸ δὲ γινόμενον προτυπώσεως·
ἵνα ὡς ἂν τὸ γινόμενον διὰ τῆς προτυπώσεως δείκνυται,
οὕτως καὶ τὸ λαλούμενον διὰ τῆς παραβολῆς φωτισθῇ.
36 τοῦτο δὴ γίνεται ἐπὶ προκατασκευῆς·
ἔργον οὐκ ἀνίσταται,
διὰ δὲ τὸ μέλλον διὰ τῆς τυπικῆς εἰκόνος ὁρᾶσθαι·
διὰ τοῦτο τοῦ μέλλοντος γίνεται προκέντημα
ἢ ἐκ κηροῦ ἢ ἐκ πηλοῦ ἢ ἐκ ξύλου,
ἵνα τὸ μέλλον ἀνίστασθαι
ὑψηλότερον ἐν μεγέθει
καὶ ἰσχυρότερον ἐν δυνάμει

---

passage is making the opposite point, the importance of what is seen and done. So these ptcs. mod. οὐδέν, "There is nothing which is spoken and produced." The point is how common it is to use a preliminary sketch or model. • **δίχα** — *apart from, without,* w. gen. • **παραβολῆς** → ἡ παραβολή, here, *comparison, illustration, analogy* (LSI 2: 594; BDAG 2: 759). • **προκεντήματος** → τὸ προκέντημα, *a thing traced out beforehand, preliminary design/pattern.* • **ἐάν** — here functions like ἄν (LSI II: 219; BDAG 3: 268). • **τυγχάνει** → τυγχάνω, *I hit, meet with; obtain, get* (LSI AII2: 823), w. gen. • **τό . . . προτυπώσεως** — This very compact statement can be understood in several ways. Among other possibilities, the gen. could be source (Wal: 109; Smy: 1410) or means (Wal: 125), "that which is spoken is from/ by an analogy," or, as in my translation, the gen. can be the obj. of an elided repetition of τυγχάνει. • **προτυπώσεως** → ἡ προτύπωσις, *prefiguration, prototype.* • **δείκνυται** → δείκνυμι, *I display, point out, explain.* • **φωτισθῇ** → φωτίζω, *I enlighten, illuminate; instruct, teach.*

Section 36

τοῦτο δὴ γίνεται — Instead of these words Perler's text has Εἰ μή. • **δή** — *indeed.* • **ἐπί** — here perhaps, *during* (LSI AII1: 286; BDAG 18a: 367). • **προκατασκευῆς** → ἡ προκατασκευή, *a preparation.* • **ἔργον** — here in the sense of the finished work, in contrast to the prototype. • **ἀνίσταται** → ἀνίστημι, here, *I build* (LSI I2: 73), though this translation does not capture the word's connotations when Melito later uses it for the building/raising up of the church (sections 41–43). • **διὰ δέ** — Perler's text has Ἢ οὐ. • **μέλλον** — attrib. ptc., obj. of prep. • **τυπικῆς** → τυπικός, ή, όν, *conforming to type, typal.* • **εἰκόνος** → ἡ εἰκών, *image.* • **ὁρᾶσθαι** — Perler's text has ὁρᾶται. • **κηροῦ** → ὁ κηρός, *wax.* • **πηλοῦ** → ὁ and ἡ πηλός, *clay.* • **ξύλου** → τὸ ξύλον, *wood.* • **ὑψηλότερον** → ὑψηλότερος, α, ον, *higher, taller,* comparative of ὑψηλός. • **μεγέθει** → τὸ μέγεθος, *greatness, size, height.* • **ἰσχυρότερον** → ἰσχυρότερος, α, ον, *stronger,* comparative of ἰσχυρός. • **σχήματι** → τὸ σχῆμα, *form, shape, appearance.* • **πλούσιον** → πλούσιος, α, ον, *rich.* • **κατασκευῇ** → ἡ κατασκευή, *preparation, construction; art, craftsmanship* (*PGL*: 718). • **μικροῦ** → μικρός, ά, όν, *small, little.* • **φθαρτοῦ** → φθαρτός, ή, όν, *perishable.* • **ὁραθῇ** → ὁράω — the subjun. of the ἵνα clause that began five lines earlier.

καὶ καλὸν ἐν σχήματι
καὶ πλούσιον ἐν τῇ κατασκευῇ
διὰ μικροῦ καὶ φθαρτοῦ προκεντήματος ὁραθῇ.
37 ὁπόταν δὲ ἀναστῇ πρὸς ὃ ὁ τύπος,
τό ποτε τοῦ μέλλοντος τὴν εἰκόνα φέρον,
τοῦτ᾽ ὡς ἄχρηστον γινόμενον λύεται,
παραχωρῆσαν τῷ φύσει ἀληθεῖ τὴν περὶ αὐτοῦ εἰκόνα.
γίνεται δὲ τό ποτε τίμιον ἄτιμον
τοῦ φύσει τιμίου φανερωθέντος.
38 ἑκάστῳ γὰρ ἴδιος καιρός·
ἴδιος χρόνος τοῦ τύπου,
ἴδιος χρόνος τῆς ὕλης
ἴδιος χρόνος τῆς ἀληθείας.
ποιεῖς τὸν τύπον·
τοῦτον ποθεῖς
ὅτι τοῦ μέλλοντος ἐν αὐτῷ τὴν εἰκόνα βλέπεις.
προκομίζεις τὴν ὕλην τῷ τύπῳ·
ταύτην ποθεῖς
διὰ τὸ μέλλον ἐν αὐτῇ ἀνίστασθαι.
ἀπαρτίζεις τὸ ἔργον·
τοῦτο μόνον ποθεῖς,
τοῦτο μόνον φιλεῖς,
ἐν αὐτῷ μόνῳ τὸν τύπον καὶ τὴν ὕλην καὶ τὴν ἀλήθειαν βλέπων.

Section 37

ὁπόταν — adv., *when.* • **ἀναστῇ** → ἀνίστημι. The subj. is not expressed, but the neut. ὅ that follows shows it is, "that thing," • **πρός** — here, *with regard/reference to* (LSI CIII1: 684; BDAG 3e: 875). Supply a verb for ὁ τύπος. • **τύπος** → ὁ τύπος, *type.* • **τό . . . γινόμενον** — The sense indicates that this material describes ὁ τύπος. The gender should therefore be masc. not neut., but the ὅ may have produced this irregularity, which continues through this sentence. • **ποτε** → **ποτέ**, *at some time, once, at one time.* • **ὡς** — here, *since* (LSI BIV: 908). • **ἄχρηστον** → ἄχρηστος, ον, *useless.* • **λύεται** → λύω, *I loosen, set free; do away with, destroy.* • **παραχωρῆσαν** — aor. act. ptc. neut. nom. sg. → παραχωρέω, *I yield.* • **φύσει** → ἡ φύσις, *nature.* • **ἀληθεῖ** → ἀληθής, ές, *true, real.* • **τίμιον** → τίμιος, α, ον, *valued, valuable, precious.* • **ἄτιμον** → ἄτιμος, ον, *not valued, without value, worthless.* • **φανερωθέντος** → φανερόω, *I make manifest, reveal.* Gen. abs., causal.

Section 38

ὕλης → ἡ ὕλη, *matter, material, stuff.* • **ἴδιος χρόνος τοῦ τύπου** — Perler's text has τοῦ τύπου ἴδιος χρόνος. • **ἴδιος χρόνος τῆς ὕλης** — Perler's text has τῆς ὕλης ἴδιος χρόνος. • **ἴδιος χρόνος τῆς ἀληθείας. ποιεῖς τὸν τύπον** — Perler's text has τῆς ἀληθείας ποιεῖς τὸν τύπον. • **ἀληθείας** → ἡ ἀλήθεια, here, *reality* (LSI 2: 34; BDAG 3: 42). • **ποθεῖς** → ποθέω, *long for, desire.* • **προκομίζεις** → προκομίζω, *I bring forward, produce.* • **ταύτην** — Perler's text has τοῦτον. • **ἀνίστασθαι** — supplementary inf. • **ἀπαρτίζεις** → ἀπαρτίζω, *I complete.* • **φιλεῖς** → φιλέω, *I love, feel affection for.* • **βλέπων** — circ. ptc., reason.

39 Ὡς γοῦν ἐν τοῖς φθαρτοῖς παραδείγμασιν,
οὕτως δὴ καὶ ἐν τοῖς ἀφθάρτοις·
ὡς ἐν τοῖς ἐπιγείοις,
οὕτω δὴ καὶ ἐν τοῖς ἐπουρανίοις.
καὶ γὰρ ἡ τοῦ κυρίου σωτηρία καὶ ἀλήθεια ἐν τῷ λαῷ προετυπώθη,
καὶ τὰ τοῦ εὐαγγελίου δόγματα ὑπὸ τοῦ νόμου προεκηρύχθη.
40 ἐγένετο οὖν ὁ λαὸς τύπος προκεντήματος
καὶ ὁ νόμος γραφὴ παραβολῆς·
τὸ δὲ εὐαγγέλιον διήγημα νόμου καὶ πλήρωμα,
ἡ δὲ ἐκκλησία ἀποδοχεῖον τῆς ἀληθείας.
41 ἦν οὖν ὁ τύπος τίμιος πρὸ τῆς ἀληθείας
καὶ ἦν ἡ παραβολὴ θαυμαστὴ πρὸ τῆς ἑρμηνείας·
τοῦτ᾽ ἔστιν ὁ λαὸς ἦν τίμιος πρὸ τοῦ τὴν ἐκκλησίαν ἀνασταθῆναι,
καὶ ὁ νόμος θαυμαστὸς πρὸ τοῦ τὸ εὐαγγέλιον φωτισθῆναι.
42 ὁπότε δὲ ἡ ἐκκλησία ἀνέστη
καὶ τὸ εὐαγγέλιον προέστη,
ὁ τύπος ἐκενώθη παραδοὺς τῇ ἀληθείᾳ τὴν δύναμιν,
καὶ ὁ νόμος ἐπληρώθη παραδοὺς τῷ εὐαγγελίῳ τὴν δύναμιν.

Section 39

γοῦν — *therefore, hence, then, at any rate.* • **φθαρτοῖς** → φθαρτός, ή, όν, *perishable.* • **παραδείγμασιν** → τὸ παράδειγμα, *pattern, model.* • **δή** — *indeed.* • **ἀφθάρτοις** → ἄφθαρτος, ον, *imperishable.* • **ἐπιγείοις** → ἐπίγειος, ον, *earthly.* • **οὕτω** — οὕτως. Perler's text has οὕτως. • **ἐπουρανίοις** → ἐπουράνιος, ον, *heavenly.* • **σωτηρία** → ἡ σωτηρία, *salvation.* • **προετυπώθη** → προτυπόω, *I mold beforehand, prefigure.* Comp. subj. w. a sg. verb (Wal: 401; Smy: 968). • **δόγματα** → τὸ δόγμα, *a decree.* • **προεκηρύχθη** → προκηρύσσω, *I proclaim in advance* (*PGL*: 1153).

Section 40

τύπος → ὁ τύπος, *type.* • **προκεντήματος** → τὸ προκέντημα, *a thing traced out beforehand, design, pattern.* Perhaps gen. of destination/purpose (Wal: 100). • **παραβολῆς** → ἡ παραβολή, here, *comparison, illustration, analogy* (LSI 2: 594; BDAG 2: 759), perhaps gen. of destination/purpose. • **διήγημα** → τὸ διήγημα, *tale, discourse, statement.* • **πλήρωμα** → τὸ πλήρωμα, *fullness, filling up, completing, completion.* • **ἀποδοχεῖον** → τὸ ἀποδοχεῖον, *storehouse.*

Section 41

τίμιος → τίμιος, α, ον, *valued, valuable, precious.* • **πρό** — *before.* • **ἀληθείας** → ἡ ἀλήθεια, here, *reality* (LSI 2: 34; BDAG 3: 42). • **θαυμαστή** → θαυμαστός, ή, όν, *wondrous, wonderful, marvelous.* • **ἑρμηνείας** → ἡ ἑρμηνεία, *interpretation, explanation.* • **ἀνασταθῆναι** → ἀνίστημι. Inf. w. πρὸ τοῦ for a temp. clause (Wal: 596). Here the translation *build* can still be used (cf. sections 36–38), though this translation does not capture the word's connotations here for the raising up of the church. • **φωτισθῆναι** → φωτίζω, *I enlighten, illuminate, bring to light; instruct, teach.* Inf. w. πρὸ τοῦ for a temp. clause (Wal: 596).

Section 42

ὁπότε — *when.* • **ἀνέστη** → ἀνίστημι. • **προέστη** → πρόειμι, *I go forward/forth,* formed from εἶμι, *I go,* not εἰμί, *I am.* • **ἐκενώθη** → κενόω, *I empty.* • **παραδούς**

43 ὃν τρόπον ὁ τύπος κενοῦται τῷ φύσει ἀληθεῖ τὴν εἰκόνα παραδούς,
καὶ ἡ παραβολὴ πληροῦται ὑπὸ τῆς ἑρμηνείας φωτισθεῖσα,
οὕτως δὴ καὶ ὁ νόμος ἐπληρώθη τοῦ εὐαγγελίου φωτισθέντος,
καὶ ὁ λαὸς ἐκενώθη τῆς ἐκκλησίας ἀνασταθείσης·
καὶ ὁ τύπος ἐλύθη τοῦ κυρίου φανερωθέντος,
καὶ σήμερον γέγονεν τά ποτε τίμια ἄτιμα
τῶν φύσει τιμίων φανερωθέντων.
44 Ἦν γάρ ποτε τίμιος ἡ τοῦ προβάτου σφαγή,
νῦν δὲ ἄτιμος διὰ τὴν τοῦ κυρίου ζωήν·
τίμιος ὁ τοῦ προβάτου θάνατος,
νῦν δὲ ἄτιμος διὰ τὴν τοῦ κυρίου σωτηρίαν·
τίμιον τὸ τοῦ προβάτου αἷμα,
νῦν δὲ ἄτιμον διὰ τὸ τοῦ κυρίου πνεῦμα·
τίμιος ὁ ἄφωνος ἀμνός,
νῦν δὲ ἄτιμος διὰ τὸν ἄμωμον υἱόν·
τίμιος ὁ κάτω ναός,
νῦν δὲ ἄτιμος διὰ τὸν ἄνω Χριστόν.
45 ἦν τίμιος ἡ κάτω Ἰερουσαλήμ,
νῦν δὲ ἄτιμος διὰ τὴν ἄνω Ἰερουσαλήμ·

— aor. act. ptc. → παραδίδωμι, *I hand over, transmit, pass on.* • **δύναμιν** — here, *force* in the sense of *meaning* (LSI III: 213 and the note in Stewart-Sykes: 45). • **ἐπληρώθη** → πληρόω, *I fill full, fulfill.*

Section 43

τρόπον → ὁ τρόπος, *way.* ὃν τρόπον, *the manner in which, (just) as* (BDAG 1: 1017), picked up by οὕτως below. • **τύπος** → ὁ τύπος, *type.* • **φύσει** → ἡ φύσις, *nature.* • **ἀληθεῖ** → ἀληθής, ές, *true, real.* • **εἰκόνα** → ἡ εἰκών, *image.* • **παραβολή** → ἡ παραβολή, here, *comparison, illustration, analogy* (LSI 2: 594; BDAG 2: 759). • **πληροῦται ὑπό** — Perler's text has κενοῦται διά. • **ἑρμηνείας** → ἡ ἑρμηνεία, *interpretation, explanation.* • **φωτισθεῖσα** — aor. pass. ptc. → φωτίζω. • **δή** — *indeed.* • **φωτισθέντος** — gen. abs., temp. • **ἀνασταθείσης** — aor. pass. ptc. → ἀνίστημι. Gen. abs., temp. • **ἐλύθη** → λύω, *I loosen, set free; do away with, destroy.* • **φανερωθέντος** → φανερόω, *I make manifest, reveal.* Gen. abs., temp. • **σήμερον** — adv., *today.* • **ποτε** → ποτέ, *at some time, once, at one time.* • **ἄτιμα** → ἄτιμος, ον, *not valued, without value, worthless.* • **φανερωθέντων** — gen. abs., causal.

Section 44

τίμιος → τίμιος, α, ον, *valued, valuable, precious.* • **προβάτου** → τὸ πρόβατον, *sheep.* • **σφαγή** → ἡ σφαγή, *slaughter.* • **σωτηρίαν** → ἡ σωτηρία, *salvation.* • **ἄφωνος** → ἄφωνος, ον, *voiceless, speechless, silent.* • **ἀμνός** → ὁ and ἡ ἀμνός, *lamb.* • **ἄμωμον** → ἄμωμος, ον, *without blame, unblemished.* • **κάτω** — adv., *below.* • **ναός** → ὁ ναός, *temple.* • **ἄνω** — adv., *above.*

Section 45

Ἰερουσαλήμ → ἡ Ἰερουσαλήμ, indecl. (listed in BDAG under the alternate form Ἱεροσόλυμα), *Jerusalem.* • **στενή** → στενός, ή, όν, *narrow.* • **κληρονομία** →

ἦν τίμιος ἡ στενὴ κληρονομία,
    νῦν δὲ ἄτιμος διὰ τὴν πλατεῖαν χάριν.
οὐ γὰρ ἐφ' ἑνὶ τόπῳ οὐδὲ ἐν βραχεῖ σχοινίσματι
    ἡ τοῦ θεοῦ δόξα καθίδρυται,
ἀλλ' ἐπὶ πάντα τὰ πέρατα τῆς οἰκουμένης
    ἐκκέχυται ἡ χάρις αὐτοῦ,
καὶ ἐνταῦθα κατεσκήνωκεν ὁ παντοκράτωρ θεὸς
    διὰ Χριστοῦ Ἰησοῦ·
    ᾧ ἡ δόξα εἰς τοὺς αἰῶνας. ἀμήν.

ἡ κληρονομία, *inheritance.* • **πλατεῖαν** → πλατύς, εῖα, ύ, *broad.* • **βραχεῖ** → βραχύς, εῖα, ύ, *small, little.* • **σχοινίσματι** → τὸ σχοίνισμα, *piece of land.* • **καθίδρυται** → καθιδρύω, *I settle.* • **πέρατα** → τὸ πέρας, *end, boundary.* • **οἰκουμένης** → ἡ οἰκουμένη, *inhabited world.* • **ἐκκέχυται** — pf. pass. indic. → ἐκχέω, *I pour out.* • **ἐνταῦθα** — *here, there.* • **κατεσκήνωκεν** → κατασκηνόω, *I settle.* • **παντοκράτωρ** → ὁ παντοκράτωρ, *almighty.*

Clement of Alexandria

Miscellanies

Introduction

How do Christians understand the truth claims made by various philosophical views in their cultural setting? Some Christians totally reject teachings from schools of thought in the culture, while others find elements of truth to be affirmed. Clement of Alexandria (ca. 150–215), a convert to Christianity from philosophy, was among the latter. As one of the most learned Christians of his day, he engaged the philosophies he had earlier embraced in ways that brought out both their similarities and differences with the Christian faith.

Clement has not left an account of his conversion, nor much about his life in general, but he does mention traveling extensively to seek out Christian teachers. After travels in Greece, southern Italy, Syria, and Palestine, he finally settled in Alexandria to remain under the best teacher he had found (*Miscellanies* [*Stromata,* or *Stromateis; Strom.*] 1.11). According to Eusebius (*Ecclesiastical History* [*Hist. eccl.*] 6.6.1; 6.13.2) that teacher was Pantaenus, the one whom Clement eventually succeeded as the head of the Christian catechetical school in Alexandria. One of Clement's students was Origen, who became the greatest Christian teacher of his day. Clement served in this post until around 202, when persecution caused him to leave Egypt and flee to Cappadocia (in central Turkey today), and then to Jerusalem, where he remained until his death.

Eusebius mentions a number of writings by Clement (*Hist. eccl.* 6.13), many of which do not survive. Several of his writings that are available represent a new stage in Christian writing. Most Christian writings in the second century had been *apologies,* that is, defenses of Christianity against Jewish and Greco-Roman attacks, including counter-attacks. Clement certainly critiques Greco-Roman views and argues against the view that Christianity is unreasonable. He also, like his contemporary Irenaeus, speaks against Gnosticism; but in addition to these apologetic themes, he seeks to provide instruction for Christians in a more positive form. Earlier teachers had done so orally, but now Clement attempts to provide such instruction in written form, a practice he found it necessary to defend (cf. *Strom.* 1.1).

In one such writing, *Christ the Educator* (*Paedagogus; Paed.*), Clement gives instructions to those who have become Christians. He begins by discussing the nature of Christian instruction and identifying the Educator of Christians as, "the holy God Jesus, the Word, who is the guide of all humanity" (*Paed.* 1.7, *ANF*). He then shows both the primacy of love and the role that fear plays, followed by a description of the lifestyle of one who is instructed by the Word and in communion with God. The keynote of this lifestyle is neither legalism nor a harsh asceticism, but the discipline that characterizes a heart guided by the Word and set free from false attachments. Clement concludes with a prayer and a beautiful hymn to the Educator, Christ the Savior.

At the end of *Christ the Educator,* Clement says that those who have received the training he has offered are ready to go on and be taught by the Logos himself (*Paed.* 3.12). In *Miscellanies* Clement offers this more developed teaching to the mature Christian, whom he calls "the true gnostic."[1] *Miscellanies* is not a systematic exposition, but rather, following a common genre of the day, a miscellaneous collection of material. Clement discusses such topics as the relation between philosophy and Christian truth, the role of faith and fear in the Christian life, marriage, martyrdom, the role of symbolism in the knowledge of God, the role of philosophy and revelation in the preparation of a true gnostic, and a description of some of the characteristics of the true gnostic, that is, the Christian who is one with God through knowledge and love.

Because some Christians whom Clement addresses find the teachings of heretical Gnostics appealing, he affirms the elements in Gnosticism that are congruent with Christianity, but also shows the difference between the two. Clement must also address, however, another set of Christians who mistrust all intellectual effort to understand and promote the faith. For these people Clement critiques the philosophies, but also argues for the important role such study plays, contending that there are elements of truth in the Greek philosophies. With this balanced approach, Clement is "at once breaking up old systems and creating a new synthesis."[2]

The first two selections included here illustrate Clement's emphasis on the positive role of philosophy, as well as his belief that the fullness of truth is available only in Christ. Clement has an extensive knowledge of the ancient philosophers, quoting some 360 passages from their writings. But for him clearly the Scriptures are primary, alluding to the Old Testament writings some 1500 times and to the New Testament some 2,000 times.[3] This concern of Clement for the Scriptures and his appreciation of the importance of salvation history are illustrated in the final three selections.

Edition used:	*Strom.* 1.5: *PG* 8, col. 717, 720
	Strom. 1.20: *PG* 8, col. 817
	Strom. 6.13: *PG* 9, col. 328
	Strom. 6.15: *PG* 9, col. 348, 349
	Strom. 7.16: *PG* 9, col. 532, 533
Level of difficulty:	Upper intermediate to advanced [3–5]

[1] See the selection from *Miscellanies* 7.16 for an example of Clement's use of the term "gnostic" to refer to a mature Christian.

[2] E. F. Osborn, *The Philosophy of Clement of Alexandria* (Cambridge: Cambridge University Press, 1957), 13.

[3] Quasten, *Patrology,* 2:6.

Miscellanies 1.5 Philosophy Was a Form of Preparation for the Gospel

Ἦν μὲν οὖν πρὸ τῆς τοῦ Κυρίου παρουσίας εἰς δικαιοσύνην Ἕλλησιν ἀναγκαία φιλοσοφία· νυνὶ δὲ χρησίμη πρὸς θεοσέβειαν γίνεται, προπαιδεία τις οὖσα τοῖς τὴν πίστιν δι' ἀποδείξεως καρπουμένοις· ὅτι **ὁ πούς σου,** φησίν, **οὐ μὴ προσκόψῃ,** ἐπὶ τὴν πρόνοιαν τὰ καλὰ ἀναφέροντος, ἐάν τε Ἑλληνικὰ ᾖ, ἐάν τε ἡμέτερα. Πάντων μὲν γὰρ αἴτιος τῶν καλῶν ὁ Θεός· ἀλλὰ τῶν μέν, κατὰ προηγούμενον, ὡς τῆς τε Διαθήκης τῆς Παλαιᾶς, καὶ τῆς Νέας, τῶν δὲ κατ' ἐπακολούθημα, ὡς τῆς φιλοσοφίας. Τάχα δὲ καὶ προηγουμένως τοῖς Ἕλλησιν ἐδόθη τότε, πρὶν ἢ τὸν Κύριον καλέσαι καὶ τοὺς Ἕλληνας· **ἐπαιδαγώγει** γὰρ καὶ αὐτὴ τὸ Ἑλληνικόν, ὡς **ὁ νόμος** τοὺς Ἑβραίους, **εἰς Χριστόν.** Προπαρασκευάζει τοίνυν ἡ φιλοσοφία, προοδοποιοῦσα τὸν ὑπὸ Χριστοῦ τελειούμενον. **Αὐτίκα τὴν σοφίαν,** ὁ Σολομών, **περιχαράκωσον,** φησίν, **καὶ ὑπερυψώσει σε· στεφάνῳ δὲ τρυφῆς ὑπερασπίσει σε·**

1.5 **πρό** — *before,* w. gen. • **παρουσίας** → ἡ παρουσία, *coming, advent.* • **Ἕλλησιν** → ὁ Ἕλλην, *Greek.* Acc. of respect (Smy: 1600; Wal: 203 discusses this usage only w. verbs, not adj.). • **ἀναγκαία** → ἀναγκαῖος, α, ον, *necessary, essential.* • **φιλοσοφία** → ἡ φιλοσοφία, *philosophy.* • **νυνί** — emphatic form of νῦν. • **χρησίμη** → χρήσιμος, η, ον, *useful, beneficial.* • **θεοσέβειαν** → ἡ θεοσέβεια, *piety, godliness, reverence towards God.* • **προπαιδεία** → ἡ προπαιδεία, *preparatory teaching/training/education.* • **ἀποδείξεως** → ἡ ἀπόδειξις, *exposition, display, proof/proving, demonstration.* • **καρπουμένοις** → καρπόω, *I bear fruit;* mid., *get fruit for oneself, derive profit from.* • **προσκόψῃ** → προσκόπτω, *I stumble.* • **πρόνοιαν** → ἡ πρόνοια, *divine providence.* • **ἀναφέροντος** → ἀναφέρω, *I carry up; ascribe.* Gen. abs. • **ἐάν τε . . . ἐάν τε** — *whether . . . or whether* (BDAG 1cδ: 268). • **Ἑλληνικά** → Ἑλληνικός, ή, όν, *Greek.* • **ἡμέτερα** → ἡμέτερος, α, ον, *our,* i.e., Christian. • **αἴτιος** → αἴτιος, α, ον, *a cause.* Pred. nom. • **τῶν μέν . . . τῶν δέ** — here, *some . . . but others.* • **κατά** — here as periphrasis for an adv. (LSJ BVIII: 403; BDAG B5bβ: 513). • **προηγούμενον** → προηγέομαι, *I go first.* The ptc. here means, *primary* (*PGL* 7: 1148). God is the direct cause. • **διαθήκης** → ἡ διαθήκη, *testament.* • **παλαιᾶς** → παλαιός, ά, όν, *old.* • **νέας** → νέος, α, ον, *new.* • **ἐπακολούθημα** → τὸ ἐπακολούθημα, *consequence.* God is the indirect/secondary cause. • **τάχα** — *perhaps.* • **προηγουμένως** — adv., *primarily, directly.* • **τότε** — adv., here, *formerly, in an earlier time.* • **πρὶν ἤ** — conj., *before,* w. acc. and inf. (BDAG aβ: 863). • **καλέσαι** — aor. act. inf. → καλέω. • **ἐπαιδαγώγει** → παιδαγωγέω, *I act as a paidagogus* (cf. Gal 3:24), *train, educate.* Perhaps the sense here is, *conduct, escort,* since this was the main duty of the παιδαγωγός, rather than teaching itself (BDAG: 748). Impf. may suggest, "used to." • **Ἑβραίους** → ὁ Ἑβραῖος, *a Hebrew.* • **προπαρασκευάζει** → προπαρασκευάζω, *I prepare beforehand.* • **τοίνυν** — *therefore.* • **προοδοποιοῦσα** → προοδοποιέω, *I prepare the way before.* • **τελειούμενον** → τελειόω, *I complete, bring to its goal/end, make perfect.* • **αὐτίκα** — adv., *now; for example* (LSJ: 279). • **Σολομών** → ὁ Σολομών, *Solomon.* • **περιχαράκωσον** → περιχαρακόω, *I surround with a*

ἐπεὶ καὶ σύ, τῷ θριγκῷ ὑπεροχυρώσας αὐτὴν διὰ φιλοσοφίας καὶ πολυτελείας ὀρθῆς, ἀνεπίβατον τοῖς σοφισταῖς τηρήσεις. Μία μὲν οὖν ἡ τῆς ἀληθείας ὁδός· ἀλλ' εἰς αὐτήν, καθάπερ εἰς ἀένναον ποταμόν, ἐκρέουσι τὰ ῥεῖθρα ἄλλα ἄλλοθεν. Ἐνθέως οὖν ἄρα εἴρηται· **Ἄκουε, υἱέ μου, καὶ δέξαι ἐμοὺς λόγους,** φησίν, **ἵνα σοι γένωνται πολλαὶ ὁδοὶ βίου· ὁδοὺς γὰρ σοφίας διδάσκω σε, ὅπως μὴ ἐκλίπωσίν σε αἱ πηγαί,** αἱ τῆς αὐτῆς ἐκβλύζουσαι γῆς. Οὐ δὴ μόνον ἑνός τινος δικαίου ὁδοὺς πλείονας σωτηρίους κατέλεξεν· ἐπιφέρει δὲ ἄλλας πολλῶν πολλὰς δικαίων ὁδούς, μηνύων ὧδέ πως· **Αἱ δὲ ὁδοὶ τῶν δικαίων ὁμοίως φωτὶ λάμπουσιν.** Εἶεν δ' ἂν καὶ αἱ ἐντολαὶ καὶ αἱ προπαιδεῖαι, ὁδοὶ καὶ ἀφορμαὶ τοῦ βίου.

Miscellanies 1.20 While Philosophy Was an Aid towards the Truth, the Fullness of the Truth Is in Christ

Αὐτοτελὴς μὲν οὖν καὶ ἀπροσδεὴς ἡ κατὰ τὸν Σωτῆρα διδασκαλία, **δύναμις οὖσα καὶ σοφία τοῦ θεοῦ·** προσιοῦσα δὲ φιλοσοφία ἡ Ἑλληνική, οὐ

---

stockade. • **ὑπερυψώσει** → ὑπερυψόω, *I exalt greatly.* • **στεφάνῳ** → ὁ στέφανος, *a crown.* • **τρυφῆς** → ἡ τρυφή, *luxury, splendor; enjoyment, delight.* • **ὑπερασπίσει** → ὑπερασπίζω, *I protect.* • **ἐπεί** — conj., *when, after; since, for.* • **θριγκῷ** → ὁ θριγκός, *wall.* This image is developed further in *Strom.* 1.20. • **ὑπεροχυρώσας** → ὑπεροχυρόω, *I make exceedingly firm* (*PGL*: 1441). • **πολυτελείας** → ἡ πολυτέλεια, *extravagance, richness; cost, expense* (*PGL*: 1119). • **ὀρθῆς** → ὀρθός, ή, όν, *right.* • **ἀνεπίβατον** → ἀνεπίβατος, ον, *inaccessible.* • **σοφισταῖς** → ὁ σοφιστής, *sophist.* • **τηρήσεις** — Früchtel's text has τηρήσαις (aor. act. opt. 2 sg. → τηρέω). Opt. for fut. (Smy: 2404). • **καθάπερ** — *just as.* • **ἀένναον** → ἀένναος, a corrupt form of ἀέναος, ον, *ever-flowing.* Früchtel's text has the more proper form ἀέναον. • **ποταμόν** → ὁ ποταμός, *river.* • **ἐκρέουσι** → ἐκρέω, *I flow out/forth.* • **τὰ ῥεῖθρα** → τὸ ῥεῖθρον, *river, stream.* • **ἄλλοθεν** — adv., *from another/different place.* • **ἐνθέως** — adv., *by inspiration* (*PGL*: 475). • **ἄρα** — particle, *so, then.* • **δέξαι** — aor. mid. (depon.) impv. 2 sg. → δέχομαι. • **γένωνται** — here γίνομαι has the sense, *I belong to,* w. dat. (BDAG 9b: 199). Or σοι could be a dat. of possession (Wal: 149; Smy: 1476), "that yours may be." • **βίου** → ὁ βίος, *life.* • **ἐκλίπωσίν** — 2 aor. → ἐκλείπω, *I leave, fail, abandon.* • **πηγαί** → ἡ πηγή, *stream, fountain, spring.* • **ἐκβλύζουσαι** — pres. act. ptc. → ἐκβλύζω, *I gush out.* Attrib. ptc., mod. αἱ πηγαί. • **δή** — *surely, indeed.* • **σωτηρίους** → σωτήριος, ον, *saving, delivering.* • **κατέλεξεν** — aor. act. indic. → καταλέγω, *I recount, reckon, tally.* • **ἐπιφέρει** → ἐπιφέρω, *I add.* • **ἄλλας πολλῶν πολλὰς δικαίων ὁδούς** — The acc. dir. obj. and the gen. mod. are mixed together, "many other paths of many righteous persons." • **μηνύων** → μηνύω, *I reveal; declare, indicate.* • **ὧδέ πως** — *somehow so/thus* (LSI: 714). • **ὁμοίως** — adv., *like.* • **λάμπουσιν** → λάμπω, *I shine.* • **εἶεν** — pres. act. opt. 3 pl. → εἰμί, *I would be.* Potential opt. (Smy: 1824). • **ἀφορμαί** → ἡ ἀφορμή, *starting point; occasion; resource.* ὁδοὶ καὶ ἀφορμαὶ • τοῦ βίου forms the pred. compl.

1.20 **αὐτοτελής** → αὐτοτελής, ές, *complete in itself.* Pred. nom. • **ἀπροσδεής** → ἀπροσδεής, ές, *without need of more/addition.* Pred. nom. • **Σωτῆρα** → ὁ σωτήρ,

δυνατωτέραν ποιεῖ τὴν ἀλήθειαν, ἀλλ᾽ ἀδύνατον παρέχουσα τὴν κατ᾽ αὐτῆς σοφιστικὴν ἐπιχείρησιν, καὶ διακρουομένη τὰς δολερὰς κατὰ τῆς ἀληθείας ἐπιβουλάς, **φραγμὸς** οἰκεῖος εἴρηται καὶ θριγκὸς εἶναι **τοῦ ἀμπελῶνος.** Καὶ ἡ μέν, ὡς ἄρτος, ἀναγκαία πρὸς τὸ ζῆν, ἡ κατὰ τὴν πίστιν ἀλήθεια· ἡ προπαιδεία δὲ προσοψήματι ἔοικεν καὶ τραγήματι, **Δείπνου δὲ λήγοντος, γλυκὺ τρωγάλιον,** κατὰ τὸν Θηβαῖον Πίνδαρον.

Miscellanies 6.13 The Covenant of Salvation Is One throughout Time

Μία μὲν γὰρ τῷ ὄντι διαθήκη ἡ σωτήριος, ἀπὸ καταβολῆς κόσμου εἰς ἡμᾶς διήκουσα, κατὰ διαφόρους γενεάς τε καὶ χρόνους, διάφορος εἶναι τὴν δόσιν ὑποληφθεῖσα. Ἀκόλουθον γὰρ εἶναι μίαν ἀμετάθετον σωτηρίας

Savior. • **διδασκαλία** → ἡ διδασκαλία, *teaching.* • **δύναμις** — Cf. 1 Cor 1:24. • **προσιοῦσα** — pres. act. ptc. → πρόσειμι, *I go to;* here, *add* (LSJ 5: 1508). This verb is a comp. of πρός and εἶμι (*I go*), not εἰμί (*I am*). • **φιλοσοφία** → ἡ φιλοσοφία, *philosophy.* • **Ἑλληνική** → Ἑλληνικός, ή, όν, *Greek.* • **δυνατωτέραν** → δυνατώτερος, α, ον, *more powerful,* comparative of δυνατός, ή, όν. • **ἀδύνατον** → ἀδύνατος, ον, *powerless.* The compl. in a double acc. of obj. and compl. • **παρέχουσα** → παρέχω, *I cause.* • **σοφιστικήν** → σοφιστικός, ή, όν, *of a sophist, sophistic.* • **ἐπιχείρησιν** → ἡ ἐπιχείρησις, *attack.* • **διακρουομένη** → διακρούω; mid., *I drive from oneself, get rid of.* • **δολεράς** → δολερός, ά, όν, *deceitful, deceptive, treacherous.* • **ἐπιβουλάς** → ἡ ἐπιβουλή, *a plan against, plot.* • **φραγμός** → ὁ φραγμός, *fence, hedge.* • **οἰκεῖος** → οἰκεῖος, α, ον, *proper.* Früchtel's text has the related adv. οἰκείως. • **θριγκός** → ὁ θριγκός, *wall.* • **ἀμπελῶνος** → ὁ ἀμπελών, *vineyard.* • **ἀναγκαία** → ἀναγκαῖος, α, ον, *necessary, indispensable.* Subst., subj. • **ζῆν** — pres. act. inf. → ζάω. • **πίστιν** → πίστις, here a technical term, *the Faith,* "as equivalent of Christian religion" (*PGL*: 1086). • **ἀλήθεια** — pred. nom. • **προπαιδεία** → ἡ προπαιδεία, *preparatory teaching/training/education.* • **προσοψήματι** → τὸ προσόψημα, *anything eaten with or besides the regular meal* (LSJ: 1522), *a side-dish.* • **ἔοικεν** → ἔοικα, *I am like,* w. dat. Pf. w. pres. sense. • **τραγήματι** → τὸ τράγημα, *that which is eaten for eating's sake, dessert.* • **δείπνου** → τὸ δεῖπνον, *dinner.* Subj. of gen. abs. • **λήγοντος** → λήγω, *I come to an end.* • **γλυκύ** → γλυκύς, εῖα, ύ, *sweet, delightful.* • **τρωγάλιον** → τὸ τρωγάλιον, *dessert.* • **Θηβαῖον** → Θηβαῖος, α, ον, *Theban.* • **Πίνδαρον** → ὁ Πίνδαριος, *Pindar.*

6.13 **μία** — pred. nom. • **τῷ ὄντι** — *in reality, in fact.* • **διαθήκη** → ἡ διαθήκη, *covenant.* Subj. in pred. position. • **σωτήριος** → σωτήριος, ον, *saving.* • **καταβολῆς** → ἡ καταβολή, *foundation.* • **διήκουσα** → διήκω, *I extend, reach.* • **κατά** — here the distributive use (LSI BII: 403; BDAG B2c: 512), *by, in.* • **διαφόρους** → διάφορος, ον, *different.* • **γενεάς** → ἡ γενεά, *generation.* • **εἶναι** — obj. of ὑποληφθεῖσα. • **δόσιν** → ἡ δόσις, *gift.* Acc. of respect (Wal: 203; Smy: 1600). • **ὑποληφθεῖσα** — aor. pass. ptc. → ὑπολαμβάνω, *I accept, apprehend.* Concessive ptc., "although apprehended to be," *although thought of as.* • **ἀκόλουθον** → ἀκόλουθος, ον, *following; fitting, suitable* (*PGL* 1: 63), w. epex. inf. (Wal: 607;

δόσιν, παρ' ἑνὸς Θεοῦ, δι' ἑνὸς Κυρίου πολυτρόπως ὠφελοῦσαν· δι' ἣν αἰτίαν **τὸ μεσότοιχον** αἴρεται τὸ διορίζον τοῦ Ἰουδαίου τὸν Ἕλληνα εἰς περιούσιον λαόν. Καὶ οὕτως ἄμφω εἰς τὴν ἑνότητα τῆς πίστεως καταντῶσιν· καὶ ἡ ἐξ ἀμφοῖν ἐκλογὴ μία.

Miscellanies 6.15 The Rule of the Truth Is the Harmony of the Old and New Testaments in Christ

Ψεῦσται τοίνυν τῷ ὄντι οὐχ οἱ συμπεριφερόμενοι δι' οἰκονομίαν σωτηρίας, οὐδ' οἱ περί τινα τῶν ἐν μέρει σφαλλόμενοι, ἀλλ' οἱ εἰς τὰ κυριώτατα παραπίπτοντες, καὶ ἀθετοῦντες μὲν τὸν Κύριον, τὸ ὅσον ἐπ' αὐτοῖς, ἀποστεροῦντες δὲ τοῦ Κυρίου τὴν ἀληθῆ διδασκαλίαν· οἱ μὴ κατ' ἀξίαν τοῦ Θεοῦ καὶ τοῦ Κυρίου τὰς Γραφὰς λέγοντές τε καὶ παραδιδόντες· παραθήκη γὰρ ἀποδιδομένη Θεῷ ἡ κατὰ τὴν τοῦ Κυρίου διδασκαλίαν διὰ τῶν

Smy: 2006); here, *for it is fitting that there is.* • **ἀμετάθετον** → ἀμετάθετος, ον, *unalterable, unchangeable.* • **σωτηρίας** → ἡ σωτηρία, *salvation.* • **πολυτρόπως** — adv., *in many ways.* • **ὠφελοῦσαν** → ὠφελέω, *I help, benefit.* Perhaps a concessive ptc. • **αἰτίαν** → ἡ αἰτία, *reason, cause.* • **μεσότοιχον** → τὸ μεσότοιχον, *dividing wall.* • **διορίζον** → διορίζω, *I separate.* • **Ἰουδαίου** → ὁ Ἰουδαῖος, *Jew.* Gen. of separation (Wal: 107; Smy: 1392). • **Ἕλληνα** → ὁ Ἕλλην, *Greek.* • **εἰς** — here for purpose or result (LSI V: 231; BDAG 4e,f: 290), *that.* • **περιούσιον** → περιούσιος, ον, *chosen, special.* Cf. Exod 19:5; Titus 2:14. • **ἄμφω** — *both* (LSJ: 96). • **ἑνότητα** → ἡ ἑνότης, *unity.* Cf. Eph 4:13. • **καταντῶσιν** → καταντάω, *I arrive at, attain, reach.* • **ἀμφοῖν** — gen. sg. → ἄμφω. • **ἐκλογή** → ἡ ἐκλογή, *choice, selection, election.*

6.15 **ψεῦσται** → ἡ ψεύστης, *liar.* • **τοίνυν** — *therefore, so, accordingly.* • **τῷ ὄντι** — *in reality, in fact.* • **συμπεριφερόμενοι** → συμπεριφέρω, *I show indulgence, make allowances* (*PGL* 4: 1287). • **οἰκονομίαν** → ἡ οἰκονομία, *order, plan* (BDAG 2: 697). • **σωτηρίας** → ἡ σωτηρία, *salvation.* • **μέρει** → τὸ μέρος, *part;* here perhaps w. the idea of small parts (LSJ IV: 1105). • περί τινα τῶν ἐν μέρει, *concerning some of the particular parts.* • **σφαλλόμενοι** → *I trip up;* pass., *I err, am mistaken.* • **κυριώτατα** → κυριώτατος, η, ον, superlative of κύριος, α, ον. When used of things κύριος means, *authoritative, decisive.* The superlative means, *important, principle* (LSJ II1: 1013). • **παραπίπτοντες** → παραπίπτω, *I go astray* (*PGL* 1: 1023). • **ἀθετοῦντες** → ἀθετέω, *I set aside, deny, reject.* • **τὸ ὅσον ἐπ' αὐτοῖς** — The art. and neut. acc. may form an adv. expression (Wal: 293), w. ἐπί here meaning *in dependence on, in the power of:* "as much as is in their power," *as much as they can.* Or the art. may substantize ὅσον as an acc. of ref., w. ἐπί here meaning, *against:* "they deny the Lord with regard to as much as he is against them," i.e., in whatever matters they disagree with the Lord they stick with their own views and thereby deny him. • **ἀποστεροῦντες** → ἀποστερέω, *I rob; detach/ withdraw from.* • **ἀληθῆ** → ἀληθής, ές, *true.* • **διδασκαλίαν** → ἡ διδασκαλία, *teaching.* • **κατά** — here as periphrasis for an adv. (LSI BVIII: 403; BDAG B5bβ: 513). • **ἀξίαν** → ἄξιος, α, ον, *worthy.* • **παραθήκη** → ἡ παραθήκη, *a deposit.* Pred. nom. Cf. 1 Tim 6:20; 2 Tim 1:14. • **ἀποδιδομένη** → ἀποδίδωμι, *I*

ἀποστόλων αὐτοῦ, τῆς θεοσεβοῦς παραδόσεως σύνεσίς τε καὶ συνάσκησις· **Ὃ δὲ ἀκούετε εἰς τὸ οὖς,** ἐπικεκρυμμένως δηλονότι καὶ ἐν μυστηρίῳ· (τὰ τοιαῦτα γὰρ εἰς τὸ οὖς λέγεσθαι ἀλληγορεῖται·) **ἐπὶ τῶν δωμάτων,** φησί, **κηρύξατε·** μεγαλοφρόνως τε ἐκδεξάμενοι καὶ ὑψηγόρως παραδιδόντες, καὶ κατὰ τὸν τῆς ἀληθείας κανόνα, διασαφοῦντες τὰς Γραφάς· οὔτε γὰρ ἡ προφητεία, οὔτε ὁ Σωτὴρ αὐτός, ἁπλῶς οὕτως ὡς τοῖς ἐπιτυχοῦσιν εὐάλωτα εἶναι, τὰ θεῖα μυστήρια ἀπεφθέγξατο, ἀλλ' ἐν παραβολαῖς διελέξατο. Λέγουσιν γοῦν οἱ ἀπόστολοι περὶ τοῦ Κυρίου, ὅτι **πάντα ἐν παραβολαῖς ἐλάλησε, καὶ οὐδὲν ἄνευ παραβολῆς ἐλάλει αὐτοῖς.** Εἰ δὲ **πάντα δι' αὐτοῦ ἐγένετο, καὶ χωρὶς αὐτοῦ ἐγένετο οὐδὲ ἕν,** καὶ ἡ προφητεία ἄρα καὶ ὁ νόμος δι' αὐτοῦ τε ἐγένετο, καὶ ἐν παραβολαῖς ἐλαλήθησαν δι' αὐτοῦ· πλὴν **Ἅπαντα ὀρθὰ ἐνώπιον τῶν συνιέντων,** φησὶν ἡ Γραφή· τουτέστι τῶν ὅσοι ὑπ' αὐτοῦ σαφηνισθεῖσαν τῶν Γραφῶν ἐξήγησιν κατὰ τὸν ἐκκλησιαστικὸν κανόνα ἐκδεχόμενοι διασῴζουσι. Κανὼν δὲ ἐκκλησιαστικὸς ἡ συνῳδία καὶ ἡ συμφωνία νόμου τε καὶ προφητῶν τῇ κατὰ τὴν τοῦ Κυρίου παρουσίαν παραδιδομένῃ διαθήκῃ.

---

render, give back, return. Attrib. ptc., mod. παραθήκη. • **ἡ κατά . . .** — the art. is w. σύνεσις, forming a complex subj. • **θεοσεβοῦς** → θεοσεβής, ές, *God-fearing, devout.* • **παραδόσεως** → ἡ παράδοσις, *tradition.* Obj. gen., mod. διδασκαλίαν. • **σύνεσις** → ἡ σύνεσις, *insight, understanding.* Subj., along w. συνάσκησις. • **συνάσκησις** → ἡ συνάσκησις, *training.* • **οὖς** → τὸ οὖς, *ear.* • **ἐπικεκρυμμένως** — adv., *mysteriously, in a hidden manner.* • **δηλονότι** — *that is to say, namely,* from δῆλόν [ἐστιν] ὅτι. • **μυστηρίῳ** → τὸ μυστήριον, *mystery.* • **ἀλληγορεῖται** → ἀλληγορέω, *I say allegorically* (*PGL* 3: 74). • **δωμάτων** → τὸ δῶμα, *house; housetop.* • **κηρύξατε** → κηρύσσω, *I proclaim.* • **μεγαλοφρόνως** — adv., *with high thoughts, high-mindedly* (LSJ, φρονέω II2b: 1956). • **ἐκδεξάμενοι** → ἐκδέχομαι, *I receive.* • **ὑψηγόρως** — adv., *in lofty language.* (*PGL*: 1467). • **παραδιδόντες** → παραδίδωμι, *I hand over, pass on, deliver.* • **κανόνα** → ὁ κανών, *rule, canon.* (*PGL*: 701–2). • **διασαφοῦντες** → διασαφέω, *I explain very clearly, interpret clearly.* • **προφητεία** → ἡ προφητεία, *prophecy.* • **σωτήρ** → ὁ σωτήρ, *Savior.* • **ἁπλῶς** — adv., *simply, plainly, openly.* • **ὡς** — w. inf. for result, *so that* (LSI BIII: 908; BDAG 4: 1105). • **ἐπιτυχοῦσιν** — 2 aor. act. ptc. → ἐπιτυγχάνω, *meet with;* abs., *the first person one meets, any chance person.* Attrib. ptc. • **εὐάλωτα** → εὐάλωτος, ον, *easy to be taken/caught,* neut. pl. anticipating τὰ μυστήρια. • **θεῖα** → θεῖος, α, ον, *divine.* • **ἀπεφθέγξατο** → ἀποφθέγγομαι, *I speak one's opinion plainly, utter an apophthegm* (ἀπόφθεγμα, *a terse pointed saying*). • **διελέξατο** → διαλέγω, mid., *I discourse, inform, instruct.* • **γοῦν** — particle, *at least then, at any rate.* From γε οὖν, often introducing evidence for a point just made. • **ἄνευ** — prep., *without.* • **χωρίς** — prep., *without.* • **ἄρα** — particle, *then, therefore.* • **πλήν** — *but.* • **ἅπαντα** → ἅπας, ἅπασα, ἅπαν, *everyone, everything.* Subj. of pred. clause. • **ὀρθά** → ὀρθός, ή, όν, *straight, right, correct, true.* • **συνιέντων** → συνίημι, *I understand.* • **τουτέστι** — *that is to say,* from τοῦτ' ἔστι. • **τῶν ὅσοι** — The gen. art. makes the clause that follows a mod. of τῶν συνιέντων. ὅσοι is the subj. of διασῴζουσι. • **σαφηνισθεῖσαν** → σαφηνίζω, *I make clear, explain.* Attrib. ptc., mod. ἐξήγησιν. • **ἐξήγησιν** → ἡ ἐξήγησις, *interpretation, explanation.* Dir. obj. of διασῴζουσι. • **ἐκκλησιαστικόν** → ἐκκλησιαστικός, ή, όν, *of/for the church, ecclesiastical.* • **ἐκδεχόμενοι** — attend.

Miscellanies 7.16 Scripture Interprets Scripture, in Contrast to the Abuse of Scripture by the False Teachers

Ἔχομεν γὰρ τὴν ἀρχὴν τῆς διδασκαλίας τὸν Κύριον, διά τε τῶν προφητῶν, διά τε τοῦ Εὐαγγελίου, καὶ διὰ τῶν μακαρίων ἀποστόλων, **πολυτρόπως καὶ πολυμερῶς** ἐξ ἀρχῆς εἰς τέλος ἡγούμενον τῆς γνώσεως. Τὴν ἀρχὴν δ᾽ εἴ τις ἕτερον δεῖσθαι ὑπολάβοι, οὐκέτ᾽ ἂν ὄντως ἀρχὴ φυλαχθείη. Ὁ μὲν οὖν ἐξ ἑαυτοῦ πιστὸς τῇ κυριακῇ Γραφῇ τε καὶ φωνῇ ἀξιόπιστος εἰκότως ἂν διὰ τοῦ Κυρίου πρὸς τὴν τῶν ἀνθρώπων εὐεργεσίαν ἐνεργουμένη. Ἀμέλει πρὸς τὴν τῶν πραγμάτων εὕρεσιν, αὐτῇ χρώμεθα κριτηρίῳ· τὸ κρινόμενον δὲ πᾶν ἔτι ἄπιστον πρὶν κριθῆναι· ὥστ᾽ οὐδ᾽ ἀρχὴ τὸ κρίσεως δεόμενον. Εἰκότως τοίνυν πίστει περιβαλόντες ἀναπόδεικτον τὴν ἀρχήν, ἐκ περιουσίας καὶ τὰς ἀποδείξεις παρ᾽ αὐτῆς τῆς ἀρχῆς περὶ τῆς ἀρχῆς λαβόντες,

---

circ. • **διασῴζουσι** → διασῴζω, *I preserve, maintain.* • **συνῳδία** → ἡ συνῳδία, *concord.* • **συμφωνία** → ἡ συμφωνία, *harmony.* • **παρουσίαν** → ἡ παρουσία, *presence, arrival.* • **διαθήκη** → ἡ διαθήκη, *covenant.*

7.16 **ἀρχήν** — here, *source* (LSJ 1: 252). In appos. to τὸν Κύριον. • **διδασκαλίας** → ἡ διδασκαλία, *teaching.* • **μακαρίων** → μακάριος, α, ον, *blessed.* • **πολυτρόπως** — adv., *in many/various ways.* • **πολυμερῶς** — adv., *in many/various parts.* • **τέλος** → τὸ τέλος, *end.* • **ἡγούμενον** → ἡγέομαι, *I lead; introduce,* w. gen. (*PGL* 2: 601). Attrib. ptc., mod. κύριον. • **γνώσεως** → ἡ γνῶσις, *knowledge.* • **τὴν ἀρχήν** — pendant acc. (Wal: 198), emphasizing the topic just introduced. • **ἕτερον** — acc. subj. of inf. Other editions have the gen. ἑτέρου. • **δεῖσθαι** — pres. mid. (depon.) inf. → δέομαι, *I am in need of,* w. gen. Inf. for indir. disc. w. ὑπολάβοι (Wal: 603; Smy: 2016). • **ὑπολάβοι** — 2 aor. act. opt. 3 sg. → ὑπολαμβάνω, *I suppose, assume.* • **οὐκέτ᾽** → οὐκέτι, *no longer.* • **ὄντως** — adv., *truly, really.* • **φυλαχθείη** — aor. pass. opt. 3 sg. → φυλάσσω, *I preserve, maintain.* • **πιστός** → πιστός, η, ον, *faithful, believing.* • **κυριακῇ** → κυριακός, ή, όν, *of/for the Lord.* Mod. both γραφῇ and φωνῇ. • **ἀξιόπιστος** → ἀξιόπιστος, ον, *trustworthy.* • **εἰκότως** — adv., *rightly, suitably, fairly, as is reasonable.* Früchtel's text has ὡς between εἰκότως and ἄν, ὡς ἂν . . . ἐνεργουμένη, "as that which would be effective." • **εὐεργεσίαν** → ἡ εὐεργεσία, *benefit.* • **ἐνεργουμένη** → ἐνεργέω, *I work, act, am effective.* Attrib. ptc., mod. τῇ κυριακῇ Γραφῇ τε καὶ φωνῇ. • **ἀμέλει** — adv., *by all means, of course, certainly.* • **πραγμάτων** → τὸ πρᾶγμα, *thing.* • **εὕρεσιν** → ἡ εὕρεσις, *discovery.* • **χρώμεθα** → χράομαι, *I use;* w. double dat., *use as* (LSJ, χράω(B) CIII3: 2002). • **κριτηρίῳ** → τὸ κριτήριον, *means for judging, criterion, standard.* • **ἄπιστον** → ἄπιστος, η, ον, *not trusted, not believed,* pred. nom. • **πρίν** — *before,* w. inf. • **κριθῆναι** — aor. pass. inf. → κρίνω. • **ὥστ᾽** — ὥστε. • **ἀρχή** — here, *first principle* (LSJ 2: 252). Pred. nom. • **κρίσεως** → ἡ κρίσις, *judging, judgment.* • **δεόμενον** → δέω, *I bind;* mid., *am in need of.* • **τοίνυν** — *therefore.* • **περιβαλόντες** → περιβάλλω, *I throw around; encompass, embrace.* Circ. ptc., perhaps for means. Früchtel's text has περιλαβόντες (→ περιλαμβάνω, *embrace, encom- pass).* • **ἀναπόδεικτον** → ἀναπόδεικτος, ον, *indemonstrable.* • **περιουσίας** → ἡ περιουσία, *abundance.* ἐκ περιουσίας, *out of the abundance of their store* (LSJ II: 1381). • **ἀποδείξεις** →

φωνῇ Κυρίου παιδευόμεθα πρὸς τὴν ἐπίγνωσιν τῆς ἀληθείας. Οὐ γὰρ ἁπλῶς ἀποφαινομένοις ἀνθρώποις προσέχοιμεν, οἷς καὶ ἀνταποφαίνεσθαι ἐπίσης ἔξεστιν. Εἰ δ' οὐκ ἀρκεῖ μόνον ἁπλῶς εἰπεῖν τὸ δόξαν, ἀλλὰ πιστώσασθαι δεῖ τὸ λεχθέν, οὐ τὴν ἐξ ἀνθρώπων ἀναμένομεν μαρτυρίαν, ἀλλὰ τῇ τοῦ Κυρίου φωνῇ πιστούμεθα τὸ ζητούμενον· ἣ πασῶν ἀποδείξεων ἐχεγγυωτέρα, μᾶλλον δὲ ἣ μόνη ἀπόδειξις οὖσα τυγχάνει· καθ' ἣν ἐπιστήμην οἱ μὲν ἀπογευσάμενοι μόνον τῶν Γραφῶν πιστοί, οἱ δὲ καὶ προσωτέρω χωρήσαντες ἀκριβεῖς γνώμονες τῆς ἀληθείας ὑπάρχουσιν, οἱ γνωστικοί· ἐπεὶ κἀν τοῖς κατὰ τὸν βίον ἔχουσί τι πλέον οἱ τεχνῖται τῶν ἰδιωτῶν, καὶ παρὰ τὰς κοινὰς ἐννοίας ἐκτυποῦσι τὸ βέλτιον. Οὕτως οὖν καὶ ἡμεῖς, ἀπ' αὐτῶν περὶ αὐτῶν τῶν Γραφῶν τελείως ἀποδεικνύντες, ἐκ πίστεως πειθόμεθα ἀποδεικτικῶς. Κἂν τολμήσωσι προφητικαῖς χρήσασθαι Γραφαῖς καὶ οἱ τὰς αἱρέσεις μετιόντες, πρῶτον μὲν οὐ πάσαις, ἔπειτα οὐ

ἡ ἀπόδειξις, *demonstration, proof.* • **παιδευόμεθα** → παιδεύω, *I train, teach.* • **πρός** — here, *with reference to, regarding* (LSI CIII1: 684; BDAG 3e: 875). • **ἐπίγνωσιν** → ἡ ἐπίγνωσις, *knowledge.* • **ἁπλῶς** — adv., *simply.* • **ἀποφαινομένοις** → ἀποφαίνω, *I make known;* mid., *give/express an opinion.* • **προσέχοιμεν** — pres. act. opt. 1 pl. → προσέχω, *I give heed to, follow,* w. dat. • **ἀνταποφαίνεσθαι** → ἀνταποφαίνω, *I show on the other hand;* mid., *hold a contrary opinion* (*PGL* 2: 150). • **ἐπίσης** — for ἐπ' ἴσης, *equally* (ἴσης → ἴσος, η, ον, *equal*). • **ἔξεστιν** — imper. verb, 3 sg. → ἔξειμι, *it is right; it is possible,* w. inf. • **ἀρκεῖ** → ἀρκέω, *I am enough/sufficient/adequate.* • **δόξαν** → ἡ δόξα, here (and below), *opinion.* • **πιστώσασθαι** → πιστόω, *I make trustworthy;* mid., *confirm, prove.* • **λεχθέν** — aor. pass. ptc. → λέγω. • **ἀναμένομεν** → ἀναμένω, *I wait for.* • **μαρτυρίαν** → ἡ μαρτυρία, *testimony, witness.* • **ζητούμενον** → ζητέω, here, *I investigate.* • **ἐχεγγυωτέρα** → ἐχεγγυώτερος, α, ον, *more trustworthy,* comparative of ἐχέγγυος, ον, w. a gen. of comparison. • **τυγχάνει** → τυγχάνω, *I hit upon, happen.* W. the ptc. of εἰμί the combination equals εἰμί. • **κατά** — here, *with respect to, in relation to, pertaining to, regarding* (LSI IV2: 403; BDAG B6: 513). • **ἐπιστήμην** → ἡ ἐπιστήμη, *knowledge.* • **ἀπογευσάμενοι** → ἀπογεύω, *I give a taste of;* mid., *take a taste of.* • **προσωτέρω** — *further,* comparative of πρόσω. • **χωρήσαντες** → χωρέω, *I go forward, advance.* • **ἀκριβεῖς** → ἀκριβής, ές, *exact, precise.* • **γνώμονες** → ὁ γνώμων, *interpreter.* • **γνωστικοί** → γνωστικός, ή, όν, *of/for knowing, one who possesses true knowledge.* Clement uses the subst. as a technical term for the *perfect/mature Christian.* See *PGL* IIA: 320 for a survey of Clement's use. • **ἐπεί** — *when, since.* • **κἀν** — crasis for καὶ ἐν. Cf. the more common, κἄν, *even if,* which occurs below. • **βίον** → ὁ βίος, *life.* • **ἔχουσι** — here indic., not ptc. • **πλέον** — alternate neut. → πλείων. • **τεχνῖται** → ἡ τεχνίτης, *artisan, skilled worker.* • **ἰδιωτῶν** → ὁ ἰδιώτης, *an individual, an ordinary person.* Gen. of comparison (Wal: 110; Smy: 1069). • **παρά** — here, *beyond* (LSI C8: 593; BDAG 3: 757). • **κοινάς** → κοινός, ή, όν, *common.* • **ἐννοίας** → ἡ ἔννοια, *thought.* • **ἐκτυποῦσι** → ἐκτυπόω, *work in relief, model.* • **βέλτιον** → βελτίων, ον, *better,* comparative of ἀγαθός. • **τελείως** — adv., *fully, perfectly, completely.* • **ἀποδεικνύντες** → ἀποδείκνυμι, *I point out, show; proclaim; prove, demonstrate.* Circ. ptc., perhaps for means. • **πειθόμεθα** → πείθω; mid., *I am persuaded, believe; obey* • **ἀποδεικτικῶς** — adv., *with/by demonstration.* • **κἂν** — *even if.* • **τολμήσωσι** → τολμάω, *I dare.* • **προφητικαῖς** → προφητικός, ή, όν, *prophetic.* • **αἱρέσεις** → ἡ αἵρεσις,

τελείαις, οὐδὲ ὡς τὸ σῶμα καὶ τὸ ὕφος τῆς προφητείας ὑπαγορεύει· ἀλλ' ἐκλεγόμενοι τὰ ἀμφιβόλως εἰρημένα, εἰς τὰς ἰδίας μετάγουσι δόξας, ὀλίγας σποράδην ἀπανθιζόμενοι φωνάς· οὐ τὸ σημαινόμενον ἀπ' αὐτῶν σκοποῦντες, ἀλλ' αὐτῇ ψιλῇ ἀποχρώμενοι τῇ λέξει. Σχεδὸν γὰρ ἐν πᾶσιν οἷς προσφέρονται ῥητοῖς, εὕροις ἂν αὐτοὺς ὡς τοῖς ὀνόμασι μόνοις προσανέχουσι, τὰ σημαινόμενα ὑπαλλάττοντες· οὔθ' ὡς λέγονται γινώσκοντες, οὔθ' ὡς ἔχειν πεφύκασι χρώμενοι αἷς καὶ δὴ κομίζουσιν ἐκλογαῖς. Ἡ ἀλήθεια δὲ οὐκ ἐν τῷ μετατιθέναι τὰ σημαινόμενα εὑρίσκεται· (οὕτω μὲν γὰρ ἀνατρέψουσι πᾶσαν ἀληθῆ διδασκαλίαν·) ἀλλ' ἐν τῷ διασκέψασθαι τί τῷ Κυρίῳ καὶ τῷ παντοκράτορι Θεῷ τελείως οἰκεῖόν τε καὶ πρέπον, κἂν τῷ βεβαιοῦν ἕκαστον τῶν ἀποδεικνυμένων κατὰ τὰς Γραφὰς ἐξ αὐτῶν πάλιν τῶν ὁμοίων Γραφῶν.

---

way/system of thought; heresy; heretic (*PGL*: 51). • **μετιόντες** → μέτειμι, *I am among.* • **πρῶτον** — here acc. for adv., *first.* • **πάσαις** — dat. because it continues from χρήσασθαι, which takes a dat. • **ἔπειτα** — *then.* • **τελείαις** → τέλειος, α, ον, *complete.* • **ὕφος** → τὸ ὕφος, *web.* • **προφητείας** → ἡ προφητεία, *prophecy.* • **ὑπαγορεύει** → ὑπαγορεύω, *I suggest; prescribe* (*PGL* 3: 1432). • **ἐκλεγόμενοι** → ἐκλέγομαι, *I choose, select.* • **ἀμφιβόλως** — adv., *ambiguously.* • **εἰρημένα** — pf. pass. ptc. → λέγω. • **μετάγουσι** → μετάγω, *I move, remove; transfer* (*PGL* 2b: 851). • **ὀλίγας** → ὀλίγος, η, ον, *few.* • **σποράδην** — adv, *here and there.* • **ἀπανθιζόμενοι** → ἀπανθίζω, *I pluck flowers.* • **φωνάς** → φωνή, here, *phrase.* • **σημαινόμενον** → σημαίνω, *I show by a sign.* The pf. pass. ptc. means *meaning* (*PGL* 3: 1231). • **σκοποῦντες** → σκοπέω, *I look at, consider, examine.* • **ψιλῇ** → ψιλός, ή, όν, *bare.* • **ἀποχρώμενοι** → ἀποχράω, *I suffice;* pass., *am contented with.* • **λέξει** → ἡ λέξις, *saying.* • **σχεδόν** — adv., *close; nearly, almost.* • **προσφέρονται** → προσφέρω, *I bring, present, use.* • **ῥητοῖς** → ῥητός, ή, όν, *stated;* neut. used as subst., *passage, text* (*PGL* 3: 1217). • **εὕροις** — 2 aor. act. opt. 2 sg. → εὑρίσκω. Potential opt. (Smy: 1824), w. an understood protasis (cf. LSI III2: 51; LSJ IIIc: 96). • **αὐτούς** — dir. obj. of προσανέχουσι. • **ὀνόμασι** — here, *expression* (LSI V: 560). • **προσανέχουσι** → προσανέχω, *I attend to* (LSJ III: 1502), usually w. dat., but occasionally, as here, w. acc. (αὐτούς). • **ὑπαλλάττοντες** → ὑπαλλάττω (listed in LSI under the alternate form ὑπαλλάσσω), *I alter* (LSJ 2: 1852). • **οὔθ'** → οὔτε. • **λέγονται** — Here the mid. has the sense, *I claim/assert for myself.* • **πεφύκασι** → φύω, *I bring forth.* The pf. has the pres. sense of *I am* so and so *by nature,* and w. inf., *I am by nature disposed to do* so and so (LSI II2: 877); so here w. ἔχειν, "as they are by nature disposed to have," *in keeping with their true nature.* • **καὶ δή** — particles, *what is more* (LSI, δή II5: 181), or, better here, *actually* (Denn: 250–53). • **κομίζουσιν** → κομίζω, *I bring in/up.* • **ἐκλογαῖς** → ἡ ἐκλογή, *extract, passage.* Dir. obj. of χρώμενοι. • **μετατιθέναι** → μετατίθημι, *I change.* The first of a series of infs. as dir. obj. of εὑρίσκεται. • **ἀνατρέψουσι** → ἀνατρέπω, *I overturn, ruin.* • **ἀληθῆ** → ἀληθής, ές, *true.* • **διασκέψασθαι** → διασκοπέω, *I examine,* depon. in the aor. • **παντοκράτορι** → ὁ παντοκράτωρ, *the Almighty.* • **οἰκεῖον** → οἰκεῖος, α, ον, *belonging to, conformable to the nature of,* w. dat. • **πρέπον** → πρέπω — the neut. ptc. often means *that which is fitting/proper/appropriate,* w. dat. • **βεβαιοῦν** → βεβαιόω, *I make firm/sure, establish.* • **πάλιν** — here, *in turn.* • **ὁμοίων** → ὅμοιος, α, ον, *like, similar.*

Eusebius
Ecclesiastical History and Life of Constantine

Introduction

A foundational conviction of the biblical faith is that God is working out a sovereign plan that moves from creation to new creation, by way of redemption. Christianity is primarily about deeds in history that represent the in-breaking of the kingdom of God and the furtherance of God's plan to unite all things in Christ. Accordingly, history matters a great deal, and when we come to Eusebius, we come to the most important historian in the ancient church after Luke and his Acts of the Apostles.

Eusebius (ca. 260—ca. 339) was a student under Pamphilus in Caesarea (in Palestine), a cosmopolitan city and center of learning at the time. Pamphilus had studied in Caesarea under Origen, the greatest Christian scholar of his day. Eusebius himself continued the scholarly tradition, becoming, "well versed in Scripture, pagan and Christian history, ancient literature, philosophy, geography, technical chronology, exegesis, philology and paleography."[1]

While Eusebius wrote on many subjects in a variety of genres, he is best known as the father of church history. His work *Ecclesiastical History* (*Historia ecclesiastica; Hist. eccl.*) was the first history of the church, and it remains one of the most valuable resources available for the history of the early church. In its ten books he covers the period from the beginning of the church to the year 324, when Constantine became sole ruler of the empire. Eusebius does not try to cover everything that took place during these years, but rather writes with an apologetic concern. In his introduction he lists some of the topics he will cover, including information on the church's bishops, teachers, and authors, discussion of heretics, God's punishment of the Jews for rejecting the Messiah, details regarding persecutions against the Christians, and accounts of the martyrs (*Hist. eccl.* 1.1.1–3). Eusebius continues the salvation-historical perspective found in the Bible, seeing God's hand at work in the triumph of the church over the empire that had been persecuting the church. He points out that the beginning of the Roman Empire coincided with the coming of Christ (*Hist. eccl.* 1.2.23), and he maintains that the conversion of the emperor and the acceptance of Christianity as the state-sanctioned religion signals the victory of Christianity and demonstrates the superiority of Christianity over all other religions.

---

[1] Quasten, *Patrology*, 3:311.

In his *Ecclesiastical History* Eusebius includes extensive quotations from both Christian and non-Christian sources. Many of these works no longer exist, so these excerpts are particularly valuable. Accordingly, while scholars question the reliability of some of Eusebius' information, they also acknowledge a great debt to him. He also accumulated such quotations in some of his more specifically apologetic works, including the *Preparation for the Gospel* and the *Demonstration of the Gospel*. These works illustrate a further aspect of his salvation-historical perspective, for he argues that God was at work in pagan as well as Jewish spheres in preparation for the advent of the Word.

Eusebius was not a secluded scholar, but as the bishop of Caesarea (consecrated in about 313), he was actively engaged in the controversies of his day. One of the greatest of the controversies was over the nature of Christ. Arius, a priest from Alexandria, was teaching that Christ was a creature, a teaching that had been condemned at the Council of Nicea (325). Eusebius took a mediating position on the subject. While he accepted the decision of the Council, he was not satisfied with it since he thought it led to Sabellianism, that is, the view that the Son is not a divine person but merely a mode of the Father's being. Because of Eusebius' concerns over Nicea and his lack of support for Athanasius, one of Nicaea's great defenders, later generations saw him as heretical or at least theologically suspect.

The selections included here are brief examples of his content and style. In the excerpt from the *Ecclesiastical History*, he contrasts the humble style of the New Testament writers with their spiritual insight and power, continuing a theme found in the biblical writers themselves (e.g., 1 Cor 2:4) and helping cultured readers not be scandalized by the character of the writings. The second selection, from the *Life of Constantine* (*Vita Constantini; Vit. Const.*), depicts the Emperor Constantine as a pious person being guided by God. Eusebius notes Constantine's decision to follow his father in embracing the one supreme God, in contrast to the other emperors who had called upon multiple gods and goddesses (*Vit. Const.* 13–18). Constantine had based this decision on the success his father had enjoyed, again in contrast to the experience of the other emperors (*Vit. Const.* 27). The excerpt included here picks up the story by recounting Constantine's famous vision of the cross. This passage's description of the conversion of the emperor and its linking of the cross with military might mark one of the most significant turning points in Christian history. In this passage we also see Eusebius' personal acquaintance with and appreciation of the emperor. This work is not meant to be straightforward history, but rather a *panegyric*, that is, a formal and elaborate expression of praise.

Editions used:	*Ecclesiastical History* 3.24.1–4: *PG* 20, col. 264–5 *Life of Constantine* 1.28–29: *PG* 20, col. 944
Level of difficulty:	*Ecclesiastical History:* Advanced [3–5] *Life of Constantine:* Advanced [3–5]

Note: the section numbers for *Ecclesiastical History* follow the Loeb edition of Kirsopp Lake.

Ecclesiastical History 3.24.1–5 On the Style of the Gospels

1 Φέρε δὲ καὶ τοῦδε τοῦ ἀποστόλου τὰς ἀναντιρρήτους ὑποσημηνώμεθα γραφάς. 2 Καὶ δὴ τὸ κατ' αὐτὸν Εὐαγγέλιον ταῖς ὑπὸ τὸν οὐρανὸν διεγνωσμένον Ἐκκλησίαις, πρῶτον ἀνωμολογήσθω. Ὅτι γε μὴν εὐλόγως πρὸς τῶν ἀρχαίων ἐν τετάρτῃ μοίρᾳ τῶν ἄλλων τριῶν κατείλεκται, ταύτῃ ἂν γένοιτο δῆλον. 3 Οἱ θεσπέσιοι καὶ ὡς ἀληθῶς θεοπρεπεῖς, φημὶ δὲ τοῦ Χριστοῦ τοὺς ἀποστόλους, τὸν βίον ἄκρως κεκαθαρμένοι, καὶ ἀρετῇ πάσῃ τὰς ψυχὰς κεκοσμημένοι, τὴν δὲ γλῶτταν ἰδιωτεύοντες, τῇ γε μὴν πρὸς τοῦ Σωτῆρος αὐτοῖς δεδωρημένῃ θείᾳ καὶ παραδοξοποιῷ δυνάμει θαρσοῦντες, τὸ μὲν ἐν περινοίᾳ καὶ τέχνῃ λόγων τὰ τοῦ διδασκάλου μαθήματα πρεσβεύειν, οὔτε

Ecclesiastical History

3.24.1 **φέρε** → φέρω. This impv. can be used, as here, as an adv., *come, now, well* (LSI IX: 858). • **τοῦδε** → ὅδε, ἥδε, τόδε, *this.* • **τοῦ ἀποστόλου** — ref. to John. • **ἀναντιρρήτους** → ἀναντίρρητος, ον, *undeniable, undisputed.* • **ὑποσημηνώμεθα** — aor. mid. subjun. → ὑποσημαίνω, *I indicate, intimate.* Hortatory subjun. Lake and Bardy's text has ἐπισημηνώμεθα (→ ἐπισημαίνω, *I set a mark upon;* mid., *indicate*).

3.24.2 **δή** — *indeed.* καὶ δή can mean, *above all* (LSI II5: 181). • **διεγνωσμένον** — pf. pass. ptc. → διαγιγνώσκω, *I discern, distinguish.* This Gospel has been diagnosed (cf. ἡ διάγνωσις, from the same word family as διαγιγνώσκω) as authoritative, so, perhaps here, *ratified, recognized.* • **πρῶτον** → πρῶτος, here neut. acc. for adv. • **ἀνωμολογήσθω** — pf. pass. impv. → ἀνομολογέομαι, *I agree upon; admit, acknowledge.* • **ὅτι** — here providing the subj. of γένοιτο. • **γε μὴν** — *nevertheless* (LSJ, γε I5: 340). • **εὐλόγως** — adv., *with good reason, reasonably.* • **πρός** — here, *according to, in accordance with* (LSI CIII5: 684; BDAG 3eδ: 875). • **ἀρχαίων** → ἀρχαῖος, α, ον, *ancient.* • **τετάρτῃ** → τέταρτος, η, ον, *fourth.* • **μοίρᾳ** → ἡ μοῖρα, *part, division, place.* • **τριῶν** → οἱ and αἱ τρεῖς, *three.* Gen. of ref. (Wal: 127). • **κατείλεκται** — pf. pass. indic. → καταλέγω, *I enlist, list* (cf. *PGL*: 710). • **ταύτῃ** — fem. probably for implicit τῇ ὁδῷ, *in this way.* • **γένοιτο** — 2 aor. opt. → γίνομαι. • **δῆλον** → δῆλος, η, ον, *clear, evident.*

3.24.3 **θεσπέσιοι** → θεσπέσιος, α, ον, *divinely sounding; divine, holy* (*PGL* 2: 646). • **ἀληθῶς** — adv., *truly, in reality.* ὡς augments the adv., *in very truth, most truly* (LSI, ὡς AIII: 908). • **θεοπρεπεῖς** → θεοπρεπής, ές, *worthy of God.* • **ἀποστόλους** — acc. of ref. (Wal: 203 ; Smy: 1600). • **βίον** → ὁ βίος, *life.* W. art. for possession (Wal: 215; Smy: 1121). • **ἄκρως** — adv., *utterly, completely.* • **κεκαθαρμένοι** — pf. pass. ptc. → καθαίρω, *I make clean, purify.* • **ἀρετῇ** → ἡ ἀρετή, *virtue, excellence.* • **κεκοσμημένοι** → κοσμέω, *I adorn.* • **γλῶτταν** → ἡ γλῶττα, an alternate form of γλῶσσα., here, *speech.* • **ἰδιωτεύοντες** → ἰδιωτεύω, *I am unskilled.* • **γε μήν** — *nevertheless* (LSJ, γε I5: 340). • **πρός** — w. gen., *from.* • **σωτῆρος** → ὁ σωτήρ, *Savior.* • **δεδωρημένῃ** → δωρέω, *I give.* • **θείᾳ** → θεῖος, α, ον, *divine.* • **παραδοξοποιῷ** → παραδοξοποιός, α, ον, *wonderworking* (*PGL* 1: 1014). • **θαρσοῦντες** → θαρσέω, *I have confidence in,* w. dat. or acc.

ᾔδεσαν οὔτε ἐνεχείρουν· τῇ δὲ τοῦ θείου Πνεύματος τοῦ συνεργοῦντος αὐτοῖς ἀποδείξει, καὶ τῇ δι' αὐτῶν συντελουμένῃ θαυματουργῷ τοῦ Χριστοῦ δυνάμει μόνῃ χρώμενοι, τῆς τῶν οὐρανῶν βασιλείας τὴν γνῶσιν ἐπὶ πᾶσαν κατήγγελλον τὴν οἰκουμένην, σπουδῆς τῆς περὶ τὸ λογογραφεῖν μικρὰν ποιούμενοι φροντίδα. 4 Καὶ τοῦτ' ἔπραττον, ἅτε μείζονι καὶ ὑπὲρ ἄνθρωπον ἐξυπηρετούμενοι διακονίᾳ. Ὁ γοῦν Παῦλος πάντων ἐν παρασκευῇ λόγων δυνατώτατος, νοήμασί τε ἱκανώτατος γεγονώς, οὐ πλέον τῶν βραχυτάτων Ἐπιστολῶν γραφῇ παραδέδωκεν, καίτοι μυρία γε καὶ ἀπόρρητα λέγειν ἔχων, ἅτε τῶν μέχρις οὐρανοῦ τρίτου θεωρημάτων ἐπιψαύσας, ἐπ' αὐτόν τε τὸν θεοπρεπῆ παράδεισον ἀναρπασθείς, καὶ τῶν ἐκεῖσε ῥημάτων

• **τό** — w. the inf. πρεσβεύειν as the dir. obj. of ᾔδεσαν and ἐνεχείρουν. • **περινοίᾳ** → ἡ περινοία, *over-wiseness, subtlety.* Lake and Bardy's text has πειθοῖ (dat. sg. → ἡ πειθώ, *persuasiveness*). Cf. 1 Cor 2:4 and BDAG: 791 on πειθός. • **τέχνῃ** → ἡ τέχνη, *art, skill.* • **λόγων** — attributed gen. (Wal: 89), *with subtle and artistic words.* • **μαθήματα** → τὸ μάθημα, *lesson.* • **πρεσβεύειν** → πρεσβεύω, *I represent* (LSJ III: 1462). • **ᾔδεσαν** — plpf. act. indic. 3 pl. → οἶδα, w. inf., *I know how* (LSI, εἴδω B2: 227; BDAG, οἶδα 3: 694). • **ἐνεχείρουν** → ἐγχειρέω, *I attempt.* • **συνεργοῦντος** → συνεργέω, *I work together with.* • **ἀποδείξει** → ἡ ἀπόδειξις, *proof.* τῇ . . . ἀποδείξει καὶ τῇ . . . δυνάμει. Dir. obj. of χρώμενοι. • **συντελουμένῃ** → συντελέω, *I complete, accomplish, carry out.* • **θαυματουργῷ** → θαυματουργός, η, ον, *miracle-working* (*PGL*: 614). • **χρώμενοι** → χράομαι, *I use,* w. dat. • **γνῶσιν** → ἡ γνῶσις, *knowledge.* • **κατήγγελλον** → καταγγέλλω, *I announce, declare, proclaim.* • **οἰκουμένην** → ἡ οἰκουμένη, *the inhabited world.* • **σπουδῆς** → ἡ σπουδή, *zeal, exertion, trouble, attention.* Dir. obj. of ποιούμενοι φροντίδα. • **λογογραφεῖν** → λογογραφέω, *I write speeches/ prose/books.* This prep. phrase is an adj. mod. of σπουδῆς as signaled by τῆς. In the next sentence a prep. phrase (ὑπὲρ ἄνθρωπον) serves this function without an art. • **μικράν** → μικρός, α, ον, *little.* • **ποιούμενοι** — here combining w. a noun as a periphrasis for a simple verbal idea (LSI A4: 651; BDAG 7a: 841). ποιούμενοι φροντίδα, *care.* Verbs of caring take a gen. for their dir. obj. (Smy: 1356; Wal: 131). • **φροντίδα** → ἡ φροντίς, *thought, care, attention.*

3.24.4 **τοῦτ'** → τοῦτο. • **ἔπραττον** → πράττω (listed in lexicons under the alternate form πράσσω), *I achieve; do.* • **ἅτε** — adv., *inasmuch as, seeing that.* • **μείζονι** → μείζων, ον, *greater,* comparative of μέγας. • **ἐξυπηρετούμενοι** → ἐξυπηρετέω, *I assist;* mid., *serve, obey* (*PGL* 2a: 503). • **διακονίᾳ** → ἡ διακονία, *service, ministry.* • **γοῦν** — *at any rate, at all events, certainly, indeed.* • **Παῦλος** → ὁ Παῦλος, *Paul.* • **παρασκευῇ** → ἡ παρασκευή, *preparation.* • **δυνατώτατος** → δυνατώτατος, η, ον, *strongest, most able,* superlative of δυνατός. Pred. nom. w. γεγονώς. • **νοήμασιν** → τὸ νόημα, *thought; understanding.* • **ἱκανώτατος** → ἱκανώτατος, η, ον, *most competent,* superlative of ἱκανός. Pred. nom. w. γεγονώς. • **γεγονώς** — pf. act. ptc. → γίνομαι. • **πλέον** → πλέων, ον — an alternate form of πλείων. • **βραχυτάτων** → βραχύτατος, η, ον, *briefest, shortest, smallest,* superlative of βραχύς. • **ἐπιστολῶν** → ἡ ἐπιστολή, *letter.* • **παραδέδωκεν** → παραδίδωμι, *I pass on, hand down, transmit.* • **καίτοι** — *although.* • **μυρία** → μυρίος, α, ον, *numberless, countless.* • **γε** — *indeed, in fact, at least.* • **ἀπόρρητα** → ἀπόρρητος, ον, *ineffable.* • **μέχρις** — *even to, as far as.* • **τρίτου** → τρίτος, η, ον, *third.* • **θεωρημάτων** → το θεώρημα, *vision, sight.* • **ἐπιψαύσας** →

ἀρρήτων ἀξιωθεὶς ἐπακοῦσαι. 5 Οὐκ ἄπειροι μὲν οὖν ὑπῆρχον τῶν αὐτῶν καὶ οἱ λοιποὶ τοῦ Σωτῆρος ἡμῶν φοιτηταί, δώδεκα μὲν ἀπόστολοι, ἑβδομήκοντα δὲ μαθηταί, ἄλλοι τε ἐπὶ τούτοις μυρίοι. Ὅμως δ' οὖν ἐξ ἁπάντων τῶν τοῦ Κυρίου μαθητῶν, ὑπομνήματα Ματθαῖος ἡμῖν καὶ Ἰωάννης μόνοι καταλελοίπασιν· οὓς καὶ ἐπάναγκες ἐπὶ τὴν γραφὴν ἐλθεῖν κατέχει λόγος.

Life of Constantine 1.28–29 Constantine's Vision of the Cross

28 Ἀνεκαλεῖτο δῆτα ἐν εὐχαῖς τοῦτον ἀντιβολῶν καὶ ποτνιώμενος, φῆναι αὐτῷ ἑαυτὸν ὅστις εἴη, καὶ τὴν ἑαυτοῦ δεξιὰν τοῖς προκειμένοις ἐπορέξαι.

ἐπιψαύω, *I touch (lightly); attain,* w. gen. • **θεοπρεπῆ** → θεοπρεπής, ές, *worthy of God.* • **παράδεισον** → ὁ παράδεισος, *paradise.* • **ἀναρπασθείς** — aor. pass. ptc. → ἀναρπάζω, *I snatch up, carry away.* Attend. circ. • **ἐκεῖσε** — adv., *to that place; there.* • **ἀρρήτων** → ἄρρητος, η, ον, *not to be spoken.* • **ἀξιωθείς** → ἀξιόω, *I consider worthy.* Attend. circ. • **ἐπακοῦσαι** — aor. act. inf. → ἐπακούω, *I listen, hear,* w. gen.

3.24.5 **ἄπειροι** → ἄπειρος, ον, *without experience, unacquainted with.* • **μὲν οὖν** — *now, now then, now indeed* (cf. BDAG, μέν 1aα: 629; οὖν 2d: 737). • **ὑπῆρχον** → ὑπάρχω. • **σωτῆρος** → ὁ σωτήρ, *Savior.* • **φοιτηταί** → ὁ φοιτητής, *pupil, student, disciple.* • **δώδεκα μέν** — here μέν "does not emphasize a contrast, but separates one thought from another in a series, so that they may be easily distinguished" (BDAG 1c: 630). • **ἑβδομήκοντα** → οἱ and αἱ and τὰ ἑβδομήκοντα, *seventy.* • **ἐπί** — here, *in addition* (LSJ BI5: 287; BDAG 7: 365). • **μυρίοι** → μυρίος, α, ον, *numberless, countless.* • **ὅμως** — *nevertheless,* not to be confused with ὁμῶς, *equally.* • **οὖν** — here, *but, however, yet* (BDAG 4: 737). • **ἁπάντων** → ἅπας, ἅπασα, ἅπαν, *all.* • **μαθητῶν** — Bardy and Lake's text has διατριβῶν → ἡ διατριβή, *discourse* (LSJ 2b: 416), "records of all the Lord's discourses." • **ὑπομνήματα** → τὸ ὑπόμνημα, *remembrance, memoranda, notes; record, account* (cf. *PGL*: 1451). • **Ματθαῖος** → ὁ Ματθαῖος (listed in BDAG under the alternate form Μαθθαῖος), *Matthew.* • **Ἰωάννης** → ὁ Ἰωάννης, *John.* • **καταλελοίπασιν** — pf. act. indic. → καταλείπω, *I leave behind.* • **οὕς** — subj. of inf. • **ἐπάναγκες** → ἐπανάγκης, only used in the neut., *it is necessary;* as an adv., *by compulsion.* • **ἐλθεῖν** → ἔρχομαι. • **κατέχει** → κατέχω, *I hold fast; I am current,* of rumors and reports (*PGL* B1b: 731); κατέχει λόγος, *word has it.*

Life of Constantine

1.28 **ἀνεκαλεῖτο** → ἀνακαλέω, *I call again and again, invoke, appeal to.* • **δῆτα** — *certainly.* • **εὐχαῖς** → ἡ εὐχή, *prayer.* • **ἀντιβολῶν** → ἀντιβολέω, *I entreat.* • **ποτνιώμενος** → ποτνιάομαι, *I cry aloud.* • **φῆναι** — aor. act. inf. → φαίνω, *I reveal.* Inf. for indir. disc., the content of the entreaties (Wal: 603; Smy: 2016). • **εἴη** — pres. act. opt. 3 sg. → εἰμί. • **προκειμένοις** → πρόκειμαι, *I set before, lie before.* Dat. of ref. (Wal: 144; Smy: 1496). • **ἐπορέξαι** → ἐπορέγω, *I hold/stretch out to.* A second inf. for the content of the entreaties. • **εὐχομένῳ** → εὔχομαι,

Εὐχομένῳ δὲ ταῦτα καὶ λιπαρῶς ἱκετεύοντι τῷ βασιλεῖ, θεοσημία τις ἐπιφαίνεται παραδοξοτάτη· ἣν τάχα μὲν ἄλλου λέγοντος, οὐ ῥᾴδιον ἦν ἀποδέξασθαι, αὐτοῦ δὲ τοῦ νικητοῦ βασιλέως, τοῖς τὴν γραφὴν διηγουμένοις ἡμῖν μακροῖς ὕστερον χρόνοις, ὅτε ἠξιώθημεν τῆς αὐτοῦ γνώσεώς τε καὶ ὁμιλίας, ἐξαγγείλαντος, ὅρκοις τε πιστωσαμένου τὸν λόγον, τίς ἂν ἀμφιβάλοι μὴ οὐχὶ πιστεῦσαι τῷ διηγήματι; μάλισθ' ὅτε καὶ ὁ μετὰ ταῦτα χρόνος ἀληθῆ τῷ λόγῳ παρέσχε τὴν μαρτυρίαν. Ἀμφὶ μεσημβρινὰς ἡλίου ὥρας, ἤδη τῆς ἡμέρας ἀποκλινούσης, αὐτοῖς ὀφθαλμοῖς ἰδεῖν ἔφη ἐν αὐτῷ οὐρανῷ ὑπερκείμενον τοῦ ἡλίου σταυροῦ τρόπαιον, ἐκ φωτὸς συνιστάμενον, γραφήν τε αὐτῷ συνῆφθαι, λέγουσαν· τούτῳ νίκα. Θάμβος δ' ἐπὶ τῷ

I pray. Dat. ptc. for time (Smy: 1498). • **λιπαρῶς** — adv., *earnestly* (*PGL*: 803). • **ἱκετεύοντι** → ἱκετεύω, *I supplicate, beseech.* Dat. ptc. for time (Smy: 1498). • **τῷ βασιλεῖ** → ὁ βασιλεύς. Subj. of the dat. ptc. for time (Smy: 1498). • **θεοσημία** → ἡ θεοσημία (listed in LSJ under the alternate form θεοσημεία), *sign from God.* • **ἐπιφαίνεται** → ἐπιφαίνω, *I show forth;* pass., *come suddenly into view, appear.* • **παραδοξοτάτη** → παραδοξότατος, η, ον, *most incredible,* superlative of παράδοξος. • **τάχα** — *perhaps.* • **ἄλλου** — subj. of gen. abs. • **λέγοντος** — gen. abs., conditional. • **ῥᾴδιον** → ῥᾴδιος, α, ον, *easy.* • **ἀποδέξασθαι** → ἀποδέχομαι, *I accept.* Epex. inf. w. ῥᾴδιον (Wal: 607; Smy: 2006). • **νικητοῦ** → ὁ νικητής, *conqueror.* • **βασιλέως** — subj. of gen. abs. w. the ptcs. ἐξαγγείλαντος and πιστωσαμένου. • **διηγουμένοις** → διηγέομαι, *I set out in detail, describe in full.* • **μακροῖς** → μακρός, ά, όν, *long* • **ὕστερον** → ὕστερος, α, ον, *long, later;* here neut. acc. for adv., *later.* • **χρόνοις** — dat. of time (Wal: 155; Smy: 1539), mod. διηγουμένοις. • **ἠξιώθημεν** → ἀξιόω, *I consider worthy.* • **γνώσεως** → ἡ γνῶσις, *knowledge, acquaintance.* • **ὁμιλίας** → ἡ ὁμιλία, *being together, company.* • **ἐξαγγείλαντος** — aor. act. ptc. → ἐξαγγέλλω, *I report.* Gen. abs., causal. • **ὅρκοις** → ὁ ὅρκος, *oath.* • **πιστωσαμένου** → πιστόω, *I make trustworthy;* mid., *confirm, guarantee.* Continues the gen. abs. • **λόγον** — here, *matter, subject* (LSI AVII: 477; BDAG 1aβ: 599). • **ἀμφιβάλοι** — 2 aor. act. opt. 3 sg. → ἀμφιβάλλω, *I doubt; dispute,* w. inf. • **μὴ ουχί** — This combination of neg. is common w. verbs w. a neg. meaning. In questions that expect a neg. answer this double neg. has, "virtually an affirmative sense" (Smy: 2742; cf. LSI, μὴ οὐ II: 510). • **διηγήματι** → τὸ διήγημα, *tale, narrative, account.* • **μάλισθ'** → μάλιστα, *especially,* superlative of μάλα. • **ἀληθῆ** → ἀληθής, ές, *true.* • **παρέσχε** — 2 aor. act. indic. → παρέχω, *I show.* Here w. double acc. of obj. and compl. (Wal: 182; Smy: 1613). • **μαρτυρίαν** → ἡ μαρτυρία, *testimony.* • **ἀμφί** — *about,* w. gen. • **μεσημβρινάς** → μεσημβρινός, ή, όν, *noontime, noon.* • **ἡλίου** → ὁ ἥλιος, *sun; day.* • **ὥρας** → ἡ ὥρα, here, *a part of the day, the time of day* (LSI II: 906). ἡλίου ὥρας could be, *the time of day.* But perhaps the point of this appos. to μεσημβρινάς is the contrast between the sun and the brighter vision he is describing, so, simply, *the sun's hour.* • **ἀποκλινούσης** → ἀποκλίνω, *decline.* Gen. abs. • **ἰδεῖν** → εἶδον. Indir. disc. The context indicates a pl. subj., in particular the ref. to the army and, probably, αὐτοῖς ὀφθαλμοῖς. • **ἔφη** — aor. act. indic. → φημί. • **ὑπερκείμενον** → ὑπέρκειμαι, *I lie above, am situated/placed above,* w. gen. • **σταυροῦ** → ὁ σταυρός, *cross.* • **τρόπαιον** → τὸ τρόπαιον, *trophy.* • **συνιστάμενον** — aor. mid. ptc. → συνίστημι, mid., *I consist of,* w. gen. (BDAG B2: 973). • **γραφήν** → ἡ γραφή, here, *inscription.* • **συνῆφθαι** — aor. pass. inf.

θεάματι κρατῆσαι αὐτόν τε καὶ τὸ στρατιωτικὸν ἅπαν, ὃ δὴ στελλομένῳ ποι πορείαν συνείπετό τε καὶ θεωρὸν ἐγίνετο τοῦ θαύματος.

29 Καὶ δὴ διαπορεῖν πρὸς ἑαυτὸν ἔλεγε, τί ποτε εἴη τὸ φάσμα. Ἐνθυμουμένῳ δ' αὐτῷ καὶ ἐπὶ πολὺ λογιζομένῳ νὺξ ἐπῄει καταλαβοῦσα· ἐνταῦθα δὴ ὑπνοῦντι αὐτῷ, τὸν Χριστὸν τοῦ Θεοῦ σὺν τῷ φανέντι κατ' οὐρανὸν σημείῳ ὀφθῆναί τε καὶ παρακελεύσασθαι, μίμημα ποιησάμενον τοῦ κατ' οὐρανὸν ὀφθέντος σημείου, τούτῳ πρὸς τὰς τῶν πολεμίων συμβολὰς ἀλεξήματι χρῆσθαι.

→ συνάπτω, *I fasten, attach* (*PGL* IA1: 1305). Subst. inf. • **νίκα** → νικάω, *I conquer.* • **θάμβος** → τὸ θάμβος, *astonishment, amazement.* • **θεάματι** → τὸ θέαμα, *sight.* • **κρατῆσαι** — aor. act. opt. 3 sg. → κρατέω, *I conquer, seize.* Potential opt. (Smy: 1821). • **στρατιωτικόν** → στρατιωτικός, ή, όν, *of/for soldiers;* subst. in pl., *army.* • **ἅπαν** → ἅπας, ἅπασα, ἅπαν, *all.* • **δή** — *indeed, in fact.* • **στελλομένῳ** → στέλλω, *I dispatch (on an expedition); send.* Dat. ptc. for time (Smy: 1498). • **ποι** — adv., *to somewhere, to some place.* • **πορείαν** → ἡ πορεία, *journey.* • **συνείπετο** — aor. mid. indic. → συνεῖπον, *I confirm, help to tell.* • **θεωρόν** → ὁ θεωρός, *spectator;* here in the sense, *eyewitness.* • **θαύματος** → τὸ θαῦμα, *wonder, marvel, miracle.* Obj. gen.

1.29 **δή** — *indeed, in fact.* • **διαπορεῖν** → διαπορέω, *I am at a loss, am greatly perplexed.* Inf. for indir. disc. (Wal: 603; Smy: 2016). • **τί ποτε** — *whatever.* • **εἴη** — pres. act. opt. 3 sg. → εἰμί. • **φάσμα** → τὸ φάσμα, *apparition.* • **ἐνθυμουμένῳ** → ἐνθυμέομαι, *I think much/deeply.* Dat. ptc. for time (Smy: 1498). • **αὐτῷ** — subj. of the ptc. (Smy: 1498). • **ἐπὶ πολύ** — *for a long time* (BDAG, πολύς 2aβב: 849). • **λογιζομένῳ** → λογίζομαι, *I consider, ponder.* • **ἐπῄει** — impf. act. indic. 3 sg. → ἔπειμι, *I come upon.* • **καταλαβοῦσα** → καταλαμβανω, *I catch, overtake.* Attend. circ. • **ἐνταῦθα** — *then.* Winkelmann's text has the alternate form ἔνθα here. • **ὑπνοῦντι** → ὑπνόω, *I sleep.* Dat. ptc. for time (Smy: 1498). • **αὐτῷ** — subj. of the ptc. (Smy: 1498). • **τὸν Χριστόν** — subj. of inf. ὀφθῆναί τε καὶ παρακελεύσασθαι. • **φανέντι** — 2 aor. pass. ptc. → φαίνω, *I make appear;* pass., *appear.* • **ὀφθῆναι** — aor. pass. inf. → ὁράω. The pass. can have the sense of allowing oneself to be seen, hence, *I appear* (LSI V: 565; BDAG A1d: 719). This inf. and παρακελεύσασθαι appear to be similar to the use of the inf. in exclamations (Smy: 2015). • **παρακελεύσασθαι** → παρακελεύομαι, *I order, command.* • **μίμημα** → τὸ μίμημα, *a copy.* • **ποιησάμενον** → ποιέω, the mid. suggests ποιέω here combines w. the noun as a periphrasis for a simple verbal idea (LSI A4: 651; BDAG 7a: 841), *I copy.* Attend. circ. w. χρῆσθαι. • **κατ'** — here, *in* (BDAG B1a: 511). • **πρός** — *in reference to* (LSI CIII1: 684; BDAG 3eβ: 875), so here, *in.* • **τὰς τῶν** — perhaps examples of the art. for a poss. (Wal: 215; Smy: 1121). • **πολεμίων** → πολέμιος, α, ον, *of the enemy;* subst., *enemy.* • **συμβολάς** → ἡ συμβολή, *a coming together; encounter, engagement, battle.* • **ἀλεξήματι** → τὸ ἀλέξημα, *defense, remedy, guard, protection.* • **χρῆσθαι** → χράομαι, *I use;* w. double dat., *use* x *as* y (BDAG 2a: 1088). Indir. disc., the content of what was commanded.

Athanasius

On the Incarnation

Introduction

One of the deepest mysteries of the Christian faith is the incarnation, and one of the most important discussions of this mystery in the history of the church is Athanasius's *On the Incarnation* (*De incarnatione; Inc.*). C. S. Lewis said, "When I first opened his *De Incarnatione* I soon discovered by a very simple test that I was reading a masterpiece," since, "only a master mind could, in the fourth century, have written so deeply on such a subject with such classical simplicity."[1]

Athanasius (ca. 298/9–373) lived through one of the most significant turning points in the history of the church, as the church moved from being a persecuted sect to being the favored religion of the empire. It was also a time of great controversy in the church over several issues, especially the nature of Christ. Arius, a priest in Alexandria, had gained a large following for his teaching that Christ was not co-eternal with the Father and therefore not fully God. This teaching was condemned at the Council of Nicea in 325, which Athanasius attended as a deacon assisting his bishop, Alexander of Alexandria. Three years later, in 328, Athanasius himself was consecrated bishop of Alexandria at the age of twenty-nine. Throughout his forty-five-year tenure, he was engaged in controversy, especially with the Arians. The decision at Nicea did not settle the matter, and Arius's teaching spread throughout the empire. With the government involved in the theological controversies, the conflict had a political side, and Athanasius was sent into exile for his opposition to Arianism five times during his years as bishop.

Despite the chaos of his life, Athanasius was able to write extensively, and indeed, many of his works were written to instruct his diocese while in exile. His writings are not abstract treatises, but rather address the issues facing the church of his time. The selections included here are from *On the Incarnation*, which most scholars believe is one of his earlier pieces since he does not directly address Arian teaching in it. It is often dated 318, but may have been written a bit later, 328–335, that is, between his consecration as bishop and his first exile.

On the Incarnation is actually the second part of a two-volume work, along with the first volume, *Against the Pagans* (*Contra gentes; C. Gent.*). In these books Athanasius sets

---

[1] C. S. Lewis, Introduction to *St. Athanasius* On the Incarnation. *The Treatise De Incarnatione Verbi Dei, by Athanasius* (rev. ed.; trans. and ed. by A Religious of C. S. M. V.; London: Mowbray, 1953), 9.

out to defend "the faith which is in keeping with our Savior Christ" against the charge that it is "irrational" (ἄλογος, *C. Gent.* 1, cf. *Inc.* 1). He begins *Against the Pagans* by arguing against various pagan views, while defending the Christian beliefs that God is one, that the entire creation was created good, that Christ, the Word/Logos of God, created and sustains all things, giving order and unity to all, and that humanity has sinned and fallen into illusion. In choosing to depart from the Logos, in whose image they were made, humans have embraced corruption and impermanence. Restoration can only come through a return to the Logos, in whom alone is life and permanence.

Athanasius begins *On the Incarnation* by reviewing what he said in *Against the Pagans* regarding creation, mankind's place in it, and the fall (*Inc.* 2–7). He next describes the incarnation and its purpose of overcoming the condition caused by the fall (8–10). In particular, through a renewal of the image of God in humankind, the incarnation overcame humanities' loss of the knowledge of God (11–19). Next, Athanasius turns to the death and resurrection of the incarnate Logos, showing that Christ thereby overcame humankind's debt and death (20–31). Having established his main points, Athanasius combats both Jewish (33–40) and pagan (41–55) errors. He concludes by pointing the reader to the Scriptures for further teaching on the matters he has discussed (56), and cautions that one must have the right disposition and manner of life in order to understand the Scriptures properly (57).

The selections included here represent key chapters from all but one of the sections of *On the Incarnation* as just outlined. The argument requires careful thought, but repays the effort.[2] Athanasius helps us think through key foundational truths of the Christian revelation, including, in particular, what it means that God is both utterly transcendent and yet near, what it means that the Word became flesh and died and rose again within the history of this fallen world, and what it means that we are created in the image of God and are offered restoration to the very life of God.

Edition used: Archibald Robertson. *St. Athanasius, On the Incarnation: The Greek Text Edited for the Use of Students.* 4th ed. London: David Nutt, 1910.

Level of difficulty: Intermediate to advanced [3–5]

Note: Robertson uses angle brackets <> to denote readings adopted without manuscript authority.

[2] Along with the studies listed in the Bibliography, the notes in Robertson's translation in *NPNF*[2] are helpful for following Athanasius's thought.

On the Incarnation 3 Creation and Fall

3.1 Ταῦτα μὲν οὗτοι μυθολογοῦσιν· ἡ δὲ ἔνθεος διδασκαλία καὶ ἡ κατὰ Χριστὸν πίστις τὴν μὲν τούτων ματαιολογίαν ὡς ἀθεότητα διαβάλλει. Οὔτε γὰρ αὐτομάτως, διὰ τὸ μὴ ἀπρονόητα εἶναι, οὔτε ἐκ προϋποκειμένης ὕλης, διὰ τὸ μὴ ἀσθενῆ εἶναι τὸν Θεόν· ἀλλ' ἐξ οὐκ ὄντων καὶ μηδαμῆ μηδαμῶς ὑπάρχοντα τὰ ὅλα εἰς τὸ εἶναι πεποιηκέναι τὸν Θεὸν διὰ τοῦ Λόγου οἶδεν, ᾗ φησὶ διὰ μὲν Μωϋσέως· **Ἐν ἀρχῇ ἐποίησεν ὁ Θεὸς τὸν οὐρανὸν καὶ τὴν γῆν·** διὰ δὲ τῆς ὠφελιμωτάτης βίβλου τοῦ Ποιμένος· **πρῶτον πάντων πίστευσον, ὅτι εἷς ἐστιν ὁ Θεός, ὁ τὰ πάντα κτίσας καὶ καταρτίσας, καὶ ποιήσας ἐκ τοῦ μὴ ὄντος εἰς τὸ εἶναι.** 3.2 Ὅπερ καὶ ὁ Παῦλος σημαίνων φησί· **Πίστει νοοῦμεν κατηρτίσθαι τοὺς αἰῶνας ῥήματι Θεοῦ, εἰς τὸ μὴ ἐκ φαινομένων τὰ βλεπόμενα γεγονέναι.** 3.3 Ὁ

3.1 **μυθολογοῦσιν** → μυθολογέω, *I tell myths/legends/stories.* • **ἔνθεος** → ἔνθεος, ον, *divinely inspired.* • **διδασκαλία** → ἡ διδασκαλία, *teaching.* • **μέν** — emphasizes ματαιολογίαν, highlighting the contrast with ἡ διδασκαλία καὶ ἡ πίστις. • **ματαιολογίαν** → ἡ ματαιολογία, *vain/foolish talk.* • **ἀθεότητα** → ἡ ἀθεότης, *godlessness* (*PGL* 2: 44). • **διαβάλλει** → διαβάλλω, *I accuse, reprove.* • **αὐτομάτως** — adv., *by itself, of its own accord.* • **διὰ τό** — w. inf. for causal clause (Wal: 596; Smy: 2034; BDAG 2c: 226). • **ἀπρονόητα** → ἀπρονόητος, ον, *without forethought.* οὔτε γὰρ αὐτομάτως, διὰ τὸ μὴ ἀπρονόητα εἶναι. Athanasius now presents the divinely inspired teaching to which he has just referred. He begins with a series of descriptions of God's act of creation before giving this main thought later in the sentence. The main verb in this sentence is οἶδεν, and the subj. must be supplied from the previous sentence: "For it [the teaching/faith] knows that God has brought the universe into existence not of its own accord, because there was not a lack of forethought . . . ," i.e., since there was forethought on God's part it did not happen spontaneously. • **προϋποκειμένης** → προϋπόκειμαι, *I am pre-existent.* • **ὕλης** → ἡ ὕλη, *matter, material, stuff.* • **ἀσθενῆ** → ἀσθενής, ές, *weak.* • **ὄντων** — subst., "things which do not exist." • **μηδαμῆ** — adv., *not at all.* • **μηδαμῶς** — adv., *in no way, not at all.* Combined w. μηδαμῆ these two adv. are euphonic and extremely emphatic. They modify ὑπάρχοντα. • **τὰ ὅλα** — *the universe.* Dir. obj. of πεποιηκέναι. • **τὸ εἶναι** — here used as a noun, "being/existence." • **πεποιηκέναι** — inf. for indir. disc., the content of what is known (Wal: 603; Smy: 2016). • **τὸν Θεόν** — subj. of the inf. πεποιηκέναι. • **ᾗ** — fem. dat. sg. of ὅς, here used as an adv. of manner, *as* (LSJ AbII: 1260). • **μέν** — signals the beginning of a series of quotes. • **Μωϋσέως** → ὁ Μωϋσῆς, *Moses.* Cf. Gen 1:1. • **ὠφελιμωτάτης** → ὠφελιμώτατος, η, ον, *most useful.* • **βίβλου** → ἡ βίβλος, *book.* • **Ποιμένος** → ἡ ποιμήν, *shepherd.* • **κτίσας** → κτίζω, *I create.* • **καταρτίσας** → καταρτίζω, *I prepare, make, create.* • **ποιήσας . . . εἰς τὸ εἶναι** — *brought into existence* (LSI, ποιέω II: 651; BDAG 2: 839).

3.2 **ὅπερ** → ὅσπερ, ἥπερ, ὅπερ, *which indeed.* • **Παῦλος** → ὁ Παῦλος, *Paul.* • **σημαίνων** → σημαίνω, *I point out, indicate.* Attend. circ. • **νοοῦμεν** → νοέω, *I understand.* • **κατηρτίσθαι** — pf. pass. inf. → καταρτίζω. Inf. for indir. disc.

Θεὸς γὰρ ἀγαθός ἐστι, μᾶλλον δὲ πηγὴ τῆς ἀγαθότητος ὑπάρχει· ἀγαθῷ δὲ περὶ οὐδενὸς ἂν γένοιτο φθόνος· ὅθεν οὐδενὶ τοῦ εἶναι φθονήσας, ἐξ οὐκ ὄντων τὰ πάντα πεποίηκε διὰ τοῦ ἰδίου Λόγου τοῦ Κυρίου ἡμῶν Ἰησοῦ Χριστοῦ· ἐν οἷς <πρὸ> πάντων τῶν ἐπὶ γῆς τὸ ἀνθρώπων γένος ἐλεήσας, καὶ θεωρήσας ὡς οὐχ ἱκανὸν εἴη κατὰ τὸν τῆς ἰδίας γενέσεως λόγον διαμένειν ἀεί, πλέον τι χαριζόμενος αὐτοῖς, οὐχ ἁπλῶς, ὥσπερ πάντα τὰ ἐπὶ γῆς ἄλογα ζῷα, ἔκτισε τοὺς ἀνθρώπους· ἀλλὰ κατὰ τὴν ἑαυτοῦ εἰκόνα ἐποίησεν αὐτούς, μεταδοὺς αὐτοῖς καὶ τῆς τοῦ ἰδίου Λόγου δυνάμεως, ἵνα ὥσπερ σκιάς τινας ἔχοντες τοῦ Λόγου καὶ γενόμενοι λογικοὶ διαμένειν ἐν μακαριότητι δυνηθῶσι, ζῶντες τὸν ἀληθινὸν καὶ ὄντως τῶν ἁγίων ἐν παραδείσῳ βίον. 3.4 Εἰδὼς δὲ πάλιν τὴν ἀνθρώπων εἰς ἀμφότερα νεύειν δυναμένην προαίρεσιν, προλαβὼν ἠσφαλίσατο νόμῳ καὶ τόπῳ τὴν δοθεῖσαν αὐτοῖς χάριν. εἰς τὸν ἑαυτοῦ γὰρ παράδεισον αὐτοὺς εἰσαγαγών, ἔδωκεν αὐτοῖς νόμον· ἵνα εἰ μὲν φυλάξοιεν τὴν χάριν, καὶ μένοιεν καλοί,

---

(Wal: 603; Smy: 2016). • **εἰς τὸ μὴ . . . γεγονέναι** — expressing result (Wal: 592). • **φαινομένων** → φαίνω, *I appear, am/become visible.* • **τὰ βλεπόμενα** — subj. of inf.

3.3 **πηγή** → ἡ πηγή, *well, fount.* Here definite, *the fount.* A def. pred. nom. that precedes an equative verb is usually anarthrous (Wal: 256–62). • **ἀγαθότητος** → ἡ ἀγαθότητος, *goodness.* • **γένοιτο** — 2 aor. mid. (depon.) opt. Potential opt., "there would be" (Smy: 1824). • **φθόνος** → ὁ φθόνος, *envy, jealousy.* • **ὅθεν** — *therefore.* • **φθονήσας** → φθονέω, *envy, I am jealous, begrudge.* • **ἐν οἷς πρὸ πάντων τῶν ἐπὶ γῆς**, "among which [things he had created] above all upon earth." • **πρό** — *before, above.* Kannengiesser's text includes πρό and Thomson omits it, though his translation includes the idea through the word "special": "of all those on earth he had special pity for the human race." • **γένος** → τὸ γένος, *race.* • **ἐλεήσας** → ἐλεέω, *I have/show mercy.* Attend. circ. • **ὡς** — here, *that,* introducing indir. disc. (LSI BI: 908; BDAG 5: 1105). • **ἱκανόν** → ἱκανός, ή, όν, *sufficient, adequate; able.* • **εἴη** — pres. act. opt. Potential opt., "would be." • **γενέσεως** → ἡ γένεσις, *origin.* • **λόγον** — here, *condition, limitation* (*PGL* Ii: 808). • **διαμένειν** → διαμένω, *I continue, remain.* Epex. inf. w. ἱκανόν (Wal: 607; Smy: 2006). • **ἀεί** — *always, forever.* • **πλέον τι** — *something more.* • **χαριζόμενος** → χαρίζομαι, *I give graciously.* Attend. circ. • **ἁπλῶς** — adv., *merely, only, simply.* • **ὥσπερ** — *as, like; as it were.* • **ἄλογα** → ἄλογος, ον, *irrational.* • **ζῷα** → τὸ ζῷον, *animal.* • **εἰκόνα** → ἡ εἰκών, *image.* • **μεταδούς** → μεταδίδωμι, *I give, share,* w. gen. • **σκιάς** → ἡ σκιά, *shadow, reflection.* • **λογικοί** → λογικός, ή, όν, *rational.* • **μακαριότητι** → ἡ μακαριότης, *blessedness.* • **ἀληθινόν** → ἀληθινός, ή, όν, *true.* • **ὄντως** — *really;* perhaps used here as an adj., *real* (LSJ: 1234): *the true and real life of the holy ones in Paradise.* The ref. is to angels. • **παραδείσῳ** → ὁ παράδεισος, *paradise.* • **βίον** → ὁ βίος, *life.*

3.4 **εἰδώς** — pf. act. ptc. → οἶδα. • **πάλιν** — here, *furthermore* (BDAG 3: 752). • **ἀμφότερα** → ἀμφότεροι, αι, α, *both, either.* εἰς ἀμφότερα, *towards either side.* • **νεύειν** → νεύω, *I incline towards.* • **προαίρεσιν** → ἡ προαίρεσις, *faculty of free choice.* • **προλαβών** → προλαμβάνω, *I do something beforehand, anticipate.* • **ἠσφαλίσατο** → ἀσφαλίζω, *I secure,* used mostly in the mid. • **δοθεῖσαν** — aor. pass. ptc. → δίδωμι. • **εἰσαγαγών** → εἰσάγω, *I lead/bring into.* • **φυλάξοιεν** — fut.

ἔχωσι τὴν ἐν παραδείσῳ ἄλυπον καὶ ἀνώδυνον καὶ ἀμέριμνον ζωήν, πρὸς τῷ καὶ τῆς ἐν οὐρανοῖς ἀφθαρσίας αὐτοὺς τὴν ἐπαγγελίαν ἔχειν· εἰ δὲ παραβαῖεν καὶ στραφέντες γένοιντο φαῦλοι, γινώσκοιεν ἑαυτοὺς τὴν ἐν θανάτῳ κατὰ φύσιν φθορὰν ὑπομένειν, καὶ μηκέτι μὲν ἐν παραδείσῳ ζῆν, ἔξω δὲ τούτου λοιπὸν ἀποθνήσκοντας μένειν ἐν τῷ θανάτῳ καὶ ἐν τῇ φθορᾷ. 3.5 Τοῦτο δὲ καὶ ἡ θεία γραφὴ προσημαίνει λέγουσα ἐκ προσώπου τοῦ Θεοῦ· **ἀπὸ παντὸς ξύλου τοῦ ἐν τῷ παραδείσῳ βρώσει φαγῇ· ἀπὸ δὲ τοῦ ξύλου τοῦ γινώσκειν καλὸν καὶ πονηρὸν οὐ φάγεσθε ἀπ' αὐτοῦ· ᾗ δ' ἂν ἡμέρᾳ φάγησθε, θανάτῳ ἀποθανεῖσθε.** τὸ δὲ θανάτῳ ἀποθανεῖσθε, τί ἂν ἄλλο εἴη ἢ τὸ μὴ μόνον ἀποθνήσκειν, ἀλλὰ καὶ ἐν τῇ τοῦ θανάτου φθορᾷ διαμένειν;

On the Incarnation 8–9 The Purpose of the Incarnation

8.1 Τούτου δὴ ἕνεκεν ὁ ἀσώματος καὶ ἄφθαρτος καὶ ἄϋλος τοῦ Θεοῦ Λόγος παραγίνεται εἰς τὴν ἡμετέραν χώραν, οὔτι γε μακρὰν ὢν πρότερον. οὐδὲν

---

act. opt. 3 pl. → φυλάσσω, *I watch, guard, keep.* The texts of Thomson and Kannengiesser have an aor. act. opt. here, φυλάξαιεν. • **μένοιεν** — pres. act. opt. 3 pl. → μένω. • **καλοί** — pred. adj. with the subj. where one might expect an acc. dir. obj. (Wal: 40, note 11). • **ἄλυπον** → ἄλυπος, ον, *free from sorrow/grief.* • **ἀνώδυνον** → ἀνώδυνος, ον, *free from pain.* • **ἀμέριμνον** → ἀμέριμνος, ον, *free from care.* • **πρὸς τῷ** with inf., *in addition to* (Smy: 2033b). • **ἀφθαρσίας** → ἡ ἀφθαρσία, *incorruptibility, immortality.* • **αὐτούς** — subj. of the inf., "in addition to them having." • **παραβαῖεν** — aor. act. opt. 3 pl. → παραβαίνω, *I transgress.* • **στραφέντες** → στρέφω, *turn.* Pass., *I turn around, twist, am perverted.* • **γένοιντο** — 2 aor. mid. (depon.) opt. 3 pl. → γίνομαι. • **φαῦλοι** → φαῦλος, η, ον, *bad, evil.* • **γινώσκοιεν** — pres. act. opt. 3 pl. → γίνωσκω. • **ἑαυτούς** — subj. of the inf. • **φύσιν** → ἡ φύσις, *nature.* • **φθοράν** → ἡ φθορά, *corruption, decay.* • **ὑπομένειν** → ὑπομένω, *I endure, suffer.* Inf. for indir. disc., w. γινώσκοιεν. • **μηκέτι** — *no longer.* • **ζῆν, . . . μένειν** — both infs. continue the indir. disc. • **ἔξω** — *outside of,* w. gen. • **λοιπόν** — adv., neut. → λοιπός, ή, όν, *from now on*

3.5 **θεία** → θεῖος, α, ον, *holy, sacred.* • **προσημαίνει** → προσημαίνω, *I announce, proclaim.* • **προσώπου** — here, *presence* (BDAG 1b: 887). • **ξύλου** → τὸ ξύλον, *tree.* • **βρώσει** → ἡ βρῶσις, *eating.* A cognate dat. (Wal: 168), here cognate to the verb in meaning not in form. It is used in the LXX to convey the sense of the cognate inf. in the Hebrew of Gen 2:16, since there is no cognate use of the inf. in Greek. Both the cognate inf. and cognate dat. emphasize the verb, "you shall/may indeed eat." • **καλὸν καὶ πονηρόν** — dir. obj. of γινώσκειν, "from the tree of knowing good and evil." • **φάγεσθε** — Thomson's text has φάγησθε. • **φάγησθε** — subjun. due to the indef. rel. clause. • **θανάτῳ** — another example of the cognate dat. (see note above on βρώσει). • **τὸ δέ** — introduces a quote. • **εἴη** — pres. act. opt. → εἰμί.

8.1 **δή** — particle, here marking a summation, *then.* • **ἕνεκεν** — (listed in lexicons under its alternate form ἕνεκα), *on account of, because of.* This prep. often follows

γὰρ αὐτοῦ κενὸν ὑπολέλειπται τῆς κτίσεως μέρος· πάντα δὲ διὰ πάντων πεπλήρωκεν αὐτὸς συνὼν τῷ ἑαυτοῦ Πατρί. ἀλλὰ παραγίνεται συγκαταβαίνων τῇ εἰς ἡμᾶς αὐτοῦ φιλανθρωπίᾳ καὶ ἐπιφανείᾳ. 8.2 Καὶ ἰδὼν τὸ λογικὸν ἀπολλύμενον γένος, καὶ τὸν θάνατον κατ' αὐτῶν βασιλεύοντα τῇ φθορᾷ· ὁρῶν δὲ καὶ τὴν ἀπειλὴν τῆς παραβάσεως διακρατοῦσαν τὴν καθ' ἡμῶν φθοράν· καὶ ὅτι ἄτοπον ἦν πρὸ τοῦ πληρωθῆναι τὸν νόμον λυθῆναι· ὁρῶν δὲ καὶ τὸ ἀπρεπὲς ἐν τῷ συμβεβηκότι, ὅτι ὧν αὐτὸς ἦν δημιουργός, ταῦτα παρηφανίζετο· ὁρῶν δὲ καὶ τὴν τῶν ἀνθρώπων ὑπερβάλλουσαν κακίαν, ὅτι κατ' ὀλίγον καὶ ἀφόρητον αὐτὴν ηὔξησαν καθ' ἑαυτῶν· ὁρῶν δὲ καὶ τὸ ὑπεύθυνον πάντων τῶν ἀνθρώπων πρὸς τὸν θάνατον· ἐλεήσας τὸ γένος ἡμῶν, καὶ τὴν ἀσθένειαν ἡμῶν οἰκτειρήσας, καὶ τῇ φθορᾷ ἡμῶν

---

its obj., here, τούτου, *for this reason* (BDAG 1: 334). • **ἀσώματος** → ἀσώματος, ον, *incorporeal, without a body.* • **ἄφθαρτος** → ἄφθαρτος, ον, *incorruptible.* • **ἄϋλος** → ἄϋλος, ον, *immaterial.* • **παραγίνεται** → παραγίνομαι, *I come.* • **ἡμετέραν** → ἡμέτερος, α, ον, *our.* • **χώραν** → ἡ χωρά, *place, region, realm, position, ground.* • **οὔτι** — neut. acc. sg. → οὔτις. Here used as an adv., *by no means, not at all.* • **γε** — particle adding emphasis, *indeed, at least* (often not able to be translated into English). • **μακράν** — adv., *far.* • **πρότερον** — neut. acc. sg. → πρότερος, α, ον. Here used as an adv., *before, formerly.* • **οὐδέν** — goes w. μέρος. • **αὐτοῦ** — goes w. κενόν. • **κενόν** → κενός, η, ον, *empty.* • **ὑπολέλειπται** → ὑπολείπω, *I leave something behind.* Pass., *am left (remaining).* • **κτίσεως** → ἡ κτίσις, *creation.* Mod. μέρος. • **μέρος** → τό μέρος, *part.* • **συνών** → σύνειμι, *I am with.* • **συγκαταβαίνων** → συγκαταβαίνω, *I come down with, condescend.* Here the senses of "descend" and "condescend" may combine (*PGL* 3b: 1267). • **φιλανθρωπίᾳ** → ἡ φιλανθρωπία, *love for mankind, benevolence.* • **ἐπιφανείᾳ** → ἡ ἐπιφάνεια, *appearance, manifestation.* • **τῇ εἰς ἡμᾶς αὐτοῦ φιλανθρωπίᾳ καὶ ἐπιφανείᾳ,** one art. binding the two nouns together, "in his benevolence and manifestation unto us."

8.2 **ἰδών** — the first in a long series of circ. ptcs. dependent on λαμβάνει near the end of 8.2. • **λογικόν** → λογικός, ή, όν, *rational, endowed with reason.* • **γένος** → τὸ γένος, *race.* • **κατ'** → κατά, here, *against* (LSI AII4: 402; BDAG 2: 511). • **βασιλεύοντα** → βασιλεύω, *I reign.* • **φθορᾷ** → ἡ φθορά, *corruption.* • **ἀπειλήν** → ἡ ἀπειλή, *threat, threat of punishment.* • **παραβάσεως** → ἡ παράβασις, *transgression.* • **διακρατοῦσαν** → διακρατέω, *I hold fast, maintain.* • **ἄτοπον** → ἄτοπος, ον, *out of place, absurd, disgusting.* • **πρό** — *before.* • **νόμον** — acc. subj. of both infs. Woodenly: "the law being destroyed before it was fulfilled was absurd." • **λυθῆναι** → λύω, *I loose, loosen, unravel, dissolve, abolish, break down, destroy.* • **ἀπρεπές** → ἀπρεπής, ές, *unfitting, improper.* • **συμβεβηκότι** → συμβαίνω, *I happen.* Simple obj. of the prep., "in what had happened." • **δημιουργός** → ὁ δημιουργός, *maker.* • **ταῦτα** — picks up the rel. clause ὧν. • **παρηφανίζετο** → παραφανίζω, *I make to disappear, do away with.* • **ὑπερβάλλουσαν** → ὑπερβάλλω, *I surpass, exceed.* • **κακίαν** → ἡ κακία, *evil, wickedness.* • **ὀλίγον** → ὀλίγος, η, ον, *few, little.* κατ' ὀλίγον, *little by little, gradually.* • **ἀφόρητον** → ἀφόρητος, ον, *unbearable, intolerable;* here as an adv., *intolerably, to an intolerable degree.* • **ηὔξησαν** → αὐξάνω, *I make grow, increase.* • **ὑπεύθυνον** → ὑπεύθυνος, ον, *liable to;* here with the art., *the liability.* • **ἐλεήσας** → ἐλεέω, *I have mercy.* • **ἀσθένειαν** → ἀσθένεια, *weakness, disease.* • **οἰκτειρήσας** → οἰκτείρω, *I have com-*

συγκαταβάς, καὶ τὴν τοῦ θανάτου κράτησιν οὐκ ἐνεγκών, ἵνα μὴ τὸ γενόμενον ἀπόληται καὶ εἰς ἀργὸν τοῦ Πατρὸς τὸ εἰς ἀνθρώπους ἔργον αὐτοῦ γένηται, λαμβάνει ἑαυτῷ σῶμα, καὶ τοῦτο οὐκ ἀλλότριον τοῦ ἡμετέρου. 8.3 Οὐ γὰρ ἁπλῶς ἠθέλησεν ἐν σώματι γενέσθαι, οὐδὲ μόνον ἤθελε φανῆναι· ἐδύνατο γάρ, εἰ μόνον ἤθελε φανῆναι, καὶ δι᾽ ἑτέρου κρείττονος τὴν θεοφάνειαν αὐτοῦ ποιήσασθαι· ἀλλὰ λαμβάνει τὸ ἡμέτερον, καὶ τοῦτο οὐχ ἁπλῶς, ἀλλ᾽ ἐξ ἀχράντου καὶ ἀμιάντου ἀνδρὸς ἀπείρου παρθένου, καθαρὸν καὶ ὄντως ἀμιγὲς τῆς ἀνδρῶν συνουσίας. αὐτὸς γὰρ δυνατὸς ὢν καὶ δημιουργὸς τῶν ὅλων, ἐν τῇ Παρθένῳ κατασκευάζει ἑαυτῷ ναὸν τὸ σῶμα, καὶ ἰδιοποιεῖται τοῦτο ὥσπερ ὄργανον, ἐν αὐτῷ γνωριζόμενος καὶ ἐνοικῶν. 8.4 Καὶ οὕτως ἀπὸ τῶν ἡμετέρων τὸ ὅμοιον λαβών, διὰ τὸ πάντας ὑπευθύνους εἶναι τῇ τοῦ θανάτου φθορᾷ, ἀντὶ πάντων αὐτὸ θανάτῳ παραδιδούς, προσῆγε τῷ Πατρί, καὶ τοῦτο φιλανθρώπως ποιῶν, ἵνα ὡς μὲν πάντων ἀποθανόντων ἐν αὐτῷ λυθῇ ὁ

---

passion upon. • **συγκαταβάς** — aor. act. ptc. → συγκαταβαίνω. • **κράτησιν** → ἡ κράτησις, *might, power.* • **ἐνεγκών** — 2 aor. act. ptc. → φέρω, *I bear;* here, *put up with, endure.* For οὐ instead of μή w. a ptc. see Smy: 2728; BDF: 430. The texts of Kannengiesser and Thomson have the later alternate aor. act. ptc. ἐνέγκας. • **ἵνα μή** — *lest.* • **τὸ γενόμενον** — here either, "the creature," or, more generally, "that which had come into being." • **ἀργόν** → ἀργός, όν, *not working, left undone, yielding no return.* εἰς ἀργόν is the pred. nom., "without effect." • **τοῦ Πατρός** — mod. ἔργον. • **αὐτοῦ** — mod. Πατρός. • **λαμβάνει** — historic pres. (Wal: 526; Smy: 1883). • **ἀλλότριον** → ἀλλότριος, α, ον, *another's, foreign, strange, alien.*

8.3 **ἁπλῶς** — adv., *merely, only, simply.* • **φανῆναι** — aor. pass. inf. → φαίνω, *I show;* pass., *appear.* • **κρείττονος** → κρείττων, ον, *stronger, better.* • **θεοφάνειαν** → ἡ θεοφάνεια, *divine manifestation.* • **ποιήσασθαι** — compl. of ἐδύνατο; mid., *I bring about, cause, effect.* • **ἀχράντου** → ἄχραντος, ον, *undefiled, immaculate.* • **ἀμιάντου** → ἀμίαντος, ον, *undefiled, pure.* • **ἀνδρός** — mod. ἀπείρου. • **ἀπείρου** → ἄπειρος, ον, *without experience, ignorant.* • **παρθένου** → ἡ παρθένος, *virgin.* • **καθαρόν** → καθαρός, ά, όν, *pure, clean.* • **ὄντως** — adv., *really, actually.* • **ἀμιγές** → ἀμιγής, ές, *unmixed, pure, virgin.* • **συνουσίας** → ἡ συνουσία, *association, sexual intercourse.* • **δυνατός** → δυνατός, ή, όν, *mighty, powerful.* • **κατασκευάζει** → κατασκευάζω, *I prepare.* • **ναόν** → ὁ ναός, *temple, inner shrine.* In appos. to τὸ σῶμα. • **σῶμα** — dir. obj. of κατασκευάζει. • **ἰδιοποιεῖται** → ἰδιοποιέω, *I appropriate to oneself.* • **ὥσπερ** — *as, like, as it were.* • **ὄργανον** → τὸ ὄργανον, *instrument, tool.* • **γνωριζόμενος** → γνωρίζω, *I make known;* pass., "become known." • **ἐνοικῶν** → ἐνοικέω, *I dwell, indwell.*

8.4 **ὅμοιον** → ὅμοιος, α, ον, *like.* Ref. to Christ's body. • **διὰ τό** — w. εἶναι for a causal clause whose subj. is πάντας. • **ὑπευθύνους** → ὑπεύθυνος, ον, w. dat., *subject to.* Pred. nom. w. εἶναι. • **ἀντί** — prep., *instead of, for, in behalf of.* • **αὐτό** — neut. since the ref. is Christ's body. • **παραδιδούς** → παραδίδωμι, *I hand over, surrender.* • **προσῆγε** → προσάγω, *I offer, bring to.* • **φιλανθρώπως** — adv., *in lovingkindness towards mankind.* • **ποιῶν** — attend. circ. • **ὡς** — Here perhaps used in a way similar to its use to emphasize adverbs and superlatives (LSI AIII: 908), though in this case with μέν . . . δέ, calling attention to the two reasons for the incarnation that are being described, *for one thing . . . for another thing.* • **μέν**

κατὰ τῆς φθορᾶς τῶν ἀνθρώπων νόμος (ἅτε δὴ πληρωθείσης τῆς ἐξουσίας ἐν τῷ κυριακῷ σώματι, καὶ μηκέτι χώραν ἔχοντος κατὰ τῶν ὁμοίων ἀνθρώπων)· ὡς δὲ εἰς φθορὰν ἀναστρέψαντας τοὺς ἀνθρώπους πάλιν εἰς τὴν ἀφθαρσίαν ἐπιστρέψῃ, καὶ ζωοποιήσῃ τούτους ἀπὸ τοῦ θανάτου, τῇ τοῦ σώματος ἰδιοποιήσει, καὶ τῇ τῆς ἀναστάσεως χάριτι, τὸν θάνατον ἀπ' αὐτῶν ὡς καλάμην ἀπὸ πυρὸς ἐξαφανίζων.

9.1 Συνιδὼν γὰρ ὁ Λόγος ὅτι ἄλλως οὐκ ἂν λυθείη τῶν ἀνθρώπων ἡ φθορά, εἰ μὴ διὰ τοῦ πάντως ἀποθανεῖν, οὐχ οἷόν τε δὲ ἦν τὸν Λόγον ἀποθανεῖν ἀθάνατον ὄντα καὶ τοῦ Πατρὸς Υἱόν, τούτου ἕνεκεν τὸ δυνάμενον ἀποθανεῖν ἑαυτῷ λαμβάνει σῶμα, ἵνα τοῦτο τοῦ ἐπὶ πάντων Λόγου μεταλαβὸν ἀντὶ πάντων ἱκανὸν γένηται τῷ θανάτῳ, καὶ διὰ τὸν ἐνοικήσαντα Λόγον, ἄφθαρτον διαμείνῃ, καὶ λοιπὸν ἀπὸ πάντων ἡ φθορὰ παύσηται τῇ τῆς ἀναστάσεως χάριτι. ὅθεν ὡς ἱερεῖον καὶ θῦμα παντὸς ἐλεύθερον σπίλου, ὃ

— introduces a series (LSJ AII2: 1102), here the first reason for the incarnation. Cf. δέ below. • **ἀποθανόντων** — gen. abs., causal. • **ἐν αὐτῷ** — mod. ἀποθανόντων. • **κατά** — here, *concerning, regarding* (LSI A5: 402). • **ἅτε** — neut. acc. pl. → ὅστε, here as an adv. with δή, *just as, inasmuch as, seeing that.* • **πληρωθείσης** — here, *I am finished, am at an end, bring to an end* (BDAG 5: 829). Gen. abs. • **ἐξουσίας** — subj. of the gen. abs. • **κυριακῷ** → κυριακός, ή, όν, *belonging to the Lord, the Lord's.* • **μηκέτι** — adv., *no longer.* • **ἔχοντος** — continues the gen. abs. χώραν ἔχω, *have place, apply* (*PGL* 2: 1536). • **δέ** — picks up the μέν above, giving the second reason for the incarnation. • **ἀναστρέψαντας** → ἀναστρέφω, *I turn back.* • **πάλιν** — mod. ἐπιστρέψῃ. • **ἀφθαρσίαν** → ἡ ἀφθαρσία, *incorruption.* • **ἐπιστρέψῃ** → ἐπιστέφω, *I turn.* Continuing the purpose clause introduced by ἵνα. • **ζωοποιήσῃ** → ζωοποιέω, *I make alive.* • **ἰδιοποιήσει** → ἡ ἰδιοποίησις, *appropriation to oneself* (*PGL* 1: 664). • **ἀναστάσεως** → ἡ ἀνάστασις, *resurrection.* • **καλάμην** → ἡ καλάμη, *straw.* • **ἐξαφανίζων** → ἐξαφανίζω, *I do away with, obliterate, remove.*

9.1 **συνιδών** → συνεῖδον (συνοράω), *I see clearly, understand.* • **ἄλλως** — adv., *otherwise, in another way, in any other way.* • **λυθείη** — aor. pass. opt. → λύω, *I loose, undo, put an end to, destroy;* "would not be loosed/undone/destroyed." • **φθορά** → ἡ φθορά, *corruption.* • **εἰ μή** — *if not, except.* • **πάντως** — adv., *in all ways, wholly;* as a mark of emphasis, *certainly, obviously, of course.* • **οἷον** → οἷος, α, ον, *such as;* here as an adv. adding emphasis and perhaps astonishment, *certainly, obviously, of course.* • **τε** — here this particle is simply joined to οἷον with no special force. • **λόγον** — acc. of ref. • **ἀποθανεῖν** — compl. w. ἦν, "But/Now there was certainly not dying with reference to the Word," i.e., "Now there was certainly no question of the Word dying." • **ἀθάνατον** → ἀθάνατος, ον, *immortal.* Pred. nom. w. ὄντα. • **ἕνεκεν** — *on account of, because of.* This prep. often follows its obj. • **δυνάμενον** — attrib., mod. σῶμα. • **τοῦτο** — subj. of γένηται. • **μεταλαβόν** — 2 aor. act. ptc. → μεταλαμβάνω, *I partake of, participate in,* w. gen. • **ἀντί** — prep., *instead of, for.* • **ἱκανόν** → ἱκανός, ή, όν, *sufficient, able, capable, qualified.* Pred. nom. • **ἐνοικήσαντα** → ἐνοικέω, *I dwell, indwell.* • **ἄφθαρτον** → ἄφθαρτος, ον, *incorruptible.* • **διαμείνῃ** → διαμένω, *I remain, continue.* Subjun. w. ἵνα above. • **λοιπόν** — here as an adj., "from now on." • **παύσηται** → παύω, *I stop;* mid., *cease, come to an end.* Subjun. w. ἵνα

αὐτὸς ἑαυτῷ ἔλαβε σῶμα προσάγων εἰς θάνατον, ἀπὸ πάντων εὐθὺς τῶν ὁμοίων ἠφάνιζε τὸν θάνατον τῇ προσφορᾷ τοῦ καταλλήλου. 9.2 Ὑπὲρ πάντας γὰρ ὢν ὁ Λόγος τοῦ Θεοῦ εἰκότως τὸν ἑαυτοῦ ναὸν καὶ τὸ σωματικὸν ὄργανον προσάγων ἀντίψυχον ὑπὲρ πάντων, ἐπλήρου τὸ ὀφειλόμενον ἐν τῷ θανάτῳ· καὶ <οὕτως συνὼν> διὰ τοῦ ὁμοίου τοῖς πᾶσιν ὁ ἄφθαρτος τοῦ Θεοῦ Υἱὸς, εἰκότως τοὺς πάντας ἐνέδυσεν ἀφθαρσίαν ἐν τῇ περὶ τῆς ἀναστάσεως ἐπαγγελίᾳ. καὶ αὐτὴ γὰρ ἡ ἐν τῷ θανάτῳ φθορὰ κατὰ τῶν ἀνθρώπων οὐκέτι χώραν ἔχει διὰ τὸν ἐνοικήσαντα Λόγον ἐν τούτοις διὰ τοῦ ἑνὸς σώματος. 9.3 Καὶ ὥσπερ μεγάλου βασιλέως εἰσελθόντος εἴς τινα πόλιν μεγάλην, καὶ οἰκήσαντος εἰς μίαν τῶν ἐν αὐτῇ οἰκιῶν, πάντως ἡ τοιαύτη πόλις τιμῆς πολλῆς καταξιοῦται, καὶ οὐκέτι τις ἐχθρὸς αὐτὴν οὔτε λῃστὴς ἐπιβαίνων καταστρέφει, πάσης δὲ μᾶλλον ἐπιμελείας ἀξιοῦται διὰ τὸν εἰς μίαν αὐτῆς οἰκίαν οἰκήσαντα βασιλέα· οὕτως καὶ ἐπὶ τοῦ πάντων Βασιλέως γέγονεν. 9.4 Ἐλθόντος γὰρ αὐτοῦ ἐπὶ τὴν ἡμετέραν χώραν, καὶ οἰκήσαντος εἰς ἓν τῶν ὁμοίων σῶμα, λοιπὸν πᾶσα ἡ κατὰ τῶν

---

above. • **ἀναστάσεως** → ἡ ἀνάστασις, *resurrection.* • **ὅθεν** — *hence, therefore.* • **ἱερεῖον** → τὸ ἱερεῖον, *sacrifice.* • **θῦμα** → τὸ θῦμα, *sacrifice, offering.* • **παντός** — mod. σπίλου. • **ἐλεύθερον** → ἐλεύθερος, α, ον, *free.* • **σπίλου** → ὁ σπῖλος, *stain.* • **προσάγων** → προσάγω, *I offer, bring to.* Attend. circ. • **ὁμοίων** → ὅμοιος, α, ον, *like.* • **ἠφάνιζε** → ἀφανίζω, *I destroy, abolish, put away.* • **προσφορᾷ** → ἡ προσφορά, *offering.* • **καταλλήλου** → καταλλήλος, ον, *correspondent, appropriate.* • **τῇ προσφορᾷ τοῦ καταλλήλου,** "by the offering of that which corresponds/is equivalent."

9.2 **εἰκότως** — adv., *naturally, reasonably.* • **ναόν** → ὁ ναός, *temple, inner shrine.* ναόν . . . ὄργανον. Both dir. objs. of προσάγων. • **σωματικόν** → σωματικός, ή, όν, *bodily.* • **ὄργανον** → τὸ ὄργανον, *instrument, tool.* Poss. art. (Wal: 215; Smy: 1121). • **προσάγων** → προσάγω, *I offer, bring to.* Means or cause. • **ἀντίψυχον** → ἀντίψυχος, ον, *as life for life;* subst., *a substitute.* Here, as the obj. compl. w. ναὸν . . . ὄργανον, *to be a substitute, as a substitute.* • **ὀφειλόμενον** → ὀφείλω, *I owe.* • **συνών** — pres. act. ptc. → σύνειμι, *I am joined with, am united with.* Perhaps causal. For οὕτως συνών the texts of Thomson and Kannengiesser have ὡς συνὼν δέ. • **ἐνέδυσεν** → ἐνδύω, *I put on, clothe someone with/in something,* w. double acc. • **ἀφθαρσίαν** → ἡ ἀφθαρσία, *incorruption.* • **οὐκέτι** — *no longer.* • **χώραν** → ἡ χώρα, *place, region, position, ground.* χώραν ἔχω, *have place, apply* (*PGL* 2: 1536). • **ἐν τούτοις** — context suggests *in them* rather than *among them.*

9.3 **ὥσπερ** — *as, like, as it were.* • **εἰσελθόντος** — gen. abs. Attend. circ. • **οἰκήσαντος** → οἰκέω, *I dwell.* Continuing the gen. abs. • **οἰκιῶν** → τὸ οἰκίον, *house.* • **τιμῆς** → ἡ τιμή, *honor.* • **καταξιοῦται** → καταξιόω, *I consider worthy,* w. gen. • **ἐχθρός** → ἐχθρός, ά, όν, *hostile;* subst., *enemy.* • **αὐτήν** — dir. obj. of καταστρέφει. • **λῃστής** → ὁ λῃτής, *robber.* • **ἐπιβαίνων** → ἐπιβαίνω, *I come upon, attack.* Attend. circ. • **καταστρέφει** → καταστρέφω, *I upset, overturn.* • **ἐπιμελείας** → ἡ ἐπιμέλεια, *care, attention.* • **ἀξιοῦται** → ἀξιόω, *I consider worthy.* • **ἐπί** — here, *in the case of* (LSJ AI2f: 621)

9.4 **ἐλθόντος** — gen. abs. Attend. circ. • **ἡμετέραν** → ἡμέτερος, α, ον, *our.* • **οἰκήσαντος** — continuing the gen. abs. • **ὁμοίων** — partitive gen. (Wal: 84; Smy:

ἀνθρώπων παρὰ τῶν ἐχθρῶν ἐπιβουλὴ πέπαυται, καὶ ἡ τοῦ θανάτου ἠφάνισται φθορὰ ἡ πάλαι κατ' αὐτῶν ἰσχύουσα. παραπωλώλει γὰρ ἂν τὸ τῶν ἀνθρώπων γένος, εἰ μὴ ὁ πάντων Δεσπότης καὶ Σωτὴρ τοῦ Θεοῦ Υἱὸς παρεγεγόνει πρὸς τὸ τοῦ θανάτου τέλος.

On the Incarnation 13 The Renewal of the Image of God

13.1 Οὕτω τοίνυν ἀλογωθέντων τῶν ἀνθρώπων, καὶ οὕτως τῆς δαιμονικῆς πλάνης ἐπισκιαζούσης τὰ πανταχοῦ, καὶ κρυπτούσης τὴν περὶ τοῦ ἀληθινοῦ Θεοῦ γνῶσιν, τί τὸν Θεὸν ἔδει ποιεῖν; σιωπῆσαι τὸ τηλικοῦτον, καὶ ἀφεῖναι τοὺς ἀνθρώπους ὑπὸ δαιμόνων πλανᾶσθαι, καὶ μὴ γινώσκειν αὐτοὺς τὸν Θεόν; 13.2 Καὶ τίς ἡ χρεία τοῦ καὶ ἐξ ἀρχῆς κατ' εἰκόνα Θεοῦ γενέσθαι τὸν ἄνθρωπον; ἔδει γὰρ αὐτὸν ἁπλῶς ὡς ἄλογον γενέσθαι, ἢ γενόμενον λογικὸν τὴν τῶν ἀλόγων ζωὴν βιοῦν. 13.3 Τίς δὲ ὅλως ἦν χρεία

1306). • **ἐπιβουλή** → ἡ ἐπιβουλή, *plan, plot.* • **πέπαυται** → παύω, *I stop, bring to an end.* • **ἠφάνισται** — pf. pass. indic. → ἀφανίζω. • **πάλαι** — adv., *formerly.* • **ἰσχύουσα** → ἰσχύω, *I am strong/mighty/powerful.* Attrib. ptc., mod. φθορά. • **παραπωλώλει** — plpf. act. indic. → παραπόλλυμι, *I destroy, perish.* • **γένος** → τὸ γένος, *race.* • **Δεσπότης** → ὁ δεσπότης, *master.* • **Σωτήρ** → ὁ Σωτήρ, *Savior.* For two nouns w. one art. see Wal: 270–90. • **παρεγεγόνει** — plpf. act. indic. → παραγίνομαι, *I come, arrive.* • **τέλος** → τὸ τέλος, *end.* πρὸς τὸ τοῦ θανάτου τέλος, "for the end of death," i.e., *to put an end to death.*

13.1 **οὕτω** → οὕτως. Here mod. the first gen. abs. • **τοίνυν** — *therefore, accordingly.* • **ἀλογωθέντων** → ἀλογέω, *I am out of my senses, am devoid of reason.* Gen. abs., perhaps temp. Elsewhere Athanasius ascribes this condition to the beasts (*Contra gentes* 19). Cf. *PGL*, ἀλογία 2: 78. • **δαιμονικῆς** → δαιμονικός, ή, όν, *demonic.* • **πλάνης** → ἡ πλάνη, *going astray, error.* Subj. of the second gen. abs. • **ἐπισκιαζούσης** → ἐπισκιάζω, *I throw a shadow on, overshadow.* A second gen. abs. • **πανταχοῦ** — adv., *everywhere.* τὰ πανταχοῦ, *every place.* • **κρυπτούσης** → κρύπτω, *I hide.* Another in the series of gen. abs. • **ἀληθινοῦ** → ἀληθινός, ή, όν, *true, real.* • **γνῶσιν** → ἡ γνῶσις, *knowledge.* • **ἔδει** — impf. → δεῖ (→ δέω), *it is necessary/fitting, one must/should.* An imper. verb expressing obligation or necessity, w. inf. • **σιωπῆσαι** → σιωπάω, *I am silent, keep silence.* From the context supply, "Was he supposed . . . " • **τηλικοῦτον** → τηλικοῦτος, -αύτη, -οῦτον, *so great.* Acc. of respect (Smy: 1600; Wal: 203). • **ἀφεῖναι** — aor. act. inf. → ἀφίημι. • **δαιμόνων** → ὁ and ἡ δαίμων, *evil spirit, demon.* • **πλανᾶσθαι** → πλανάω, *I lead astray, deceive.* Supplementary inf. w. ἀφεῖναι. • **αὐτούς** — subj. of γινώσκειν.

13.2 **χρεία** → ἡ χρεία, *a use, need,* w. gen. In pred. position w. τίς. • **τοῦ** — goes w. γενέσθαι. Most of this sentence is a subst. mod. χρεία. For the gen. articular inf. see Smy: 2032; Wal: 234. • **καί** — emphatic, *in fact, then.* • **εἰκόνα** → ἡ εἰκών, *image.* • **γενέσθαι** — epex. inf. (Wal: 607; Smy: 2006). • **ἄνθρωπον** — subj. of the inf. • **ἔδει** — cf. 13.1. Here, *it was necessary, he should.* • **ἁπλῶς** — adv., *simply.* • **ἄλογον** → ἄλογος, ον, *without reason.* • **λογικόν** → λογικός, ή, όν, *rational.* • **βιοῦν** — pres. act. inf. → βιόω, *I live.* The texts of Thomson and Kannengiesser have μή before βιοῦν, which makes more sense in the context.

ἐννοίας αὐτὸν λαβεῖν περὶ Θεοῦ ἐξ ἀρχῆς; εἰ γὰρ οὐδὲ νῦν ἄξιός ἐστι λαβεῖν, ἔδει μηδὲ κατὰ τὴν ἀρχὴν αὐτῷ δοθῆναι. 13.4 Τί δὲ καὶ ὄφελος τῷ πεποιηκότι Θεῷ, ἢ ποία δόξα αὐτῷ ἂν εἴη, εἰ οἱ ὑπὸ αὐτοῦ γενόμενοι ἄνθρωποι οὐ προσκυνοῦσιν αὐτῷ, ἀλλ' ἑτέρους εἶναι τοὺς πεποιηκότας αὐτοὺς νομίζουσιν; εὑρίσκεται γὰρ ὁ Θεὸς ἑτέροις καὶ οὐχ ἑαυτῷ τούτους δημιουργήσας. 13.5 Εἶτα βασιλεὺς μὲν ἄνθρωπος ὢν τὰς ὑπὸ αὐτοῦ κτισθείσας χώρας οὐκ ἀφίησιν ἐκδότους ἑτέροις δουλεύειν, οὐδὲ πρὸς ἄλλους καταφεύγειν· ἀλλὰ γράμμασιν αὐτοὺς ὑπομιμνήσκει, πολλάκις δὲ καὶ διὰ φίλων αὐτοῖς ἐπιστέλλει, εἰ δὲ καὶ χρεία γένηται, αὐτὸς παραγίνεται, τῇ παρουσίᾳ λοιπὸν αὐτοὺς δυσωπῶν· μόνον ἵνα μὴ ἑτέροις δουλεύσωσι, καὶ ἀργὸν αὐτοῦ τὸ ἔργον γένηται. 13.6 Οὐ πολλῷ πλέον ὁ Θεὸς τῶν ἑαυτοῦ κτισμάτων φείσεται πρὸς τὸ μὴ πλανηθῆναι ἀπ' αὐτοῦ, καὶ τοῖς οὐκ οὖσι δουλεύειν; μάλιστα ὅτι ἡ τοιαύτη πλάνη ἀπωλείας αὐτοῖς αἰτία καὶ ἀφανισμοῦ γίνεται, οὐκ ἔδει δὲ τὰ ἅπαξ κοινωνήσαντα τῆς τοῦ Θεοῦ

13.3 **ὅλως** — adv., *wholly, at all.* • **ἐννοίας** — acc. pl., obj. of the inf. → ἡ ἐννοία, *thought, notion, conception, idea.* • **αὐτόν** — subj. of the inf. • **λαβεῖν** — mod. χρεία as in 13.2, though now without the art.; epex. inf. (Wal: 607; Smy: 2006). • **οὐδέ . . . μηδέ** — *not . . . neither.* • **ἄξιος** → ἄξιος, α, ον, *worthy, fit.* • **ἔδει μηδέ** — *neither should it.* • **δοθῆναι** → δίδωμι.

13.4 **ὄφελος** → *help, profit, advantage,* w. dat. • **ποία** → ποῖος, α, ον, *of what sort? what kind of?* • **εἴη** — pres. act. opt. 3 sg. → εἰμί. • **ἑτέρους** — subj. of the inf. • **εἶναι** — inf. for indir. disc., the content of νομίζουσιν (Wal: 603; Smy: 2006). • **νομίζουσιν** → νομίζω, *I think.* • **εὑρίσκεται** — here pass., *for God is found.* Often w. ptc. (BDAG 1cα: 411). • **δημιουργήσας** → δημιουργέω, *I make, fabricate.* Of God, *create* (*PGL* 3: 341).

13.5 **εἶτα** — adv., *furthermore.* • **κτισθείσας** — aor. pass. ptc. fem. acc. pl. → κτίζω, *I found, build, colonize.* The word also means *create,* as later in this chapter. • **χώρας** → ἡ χώρα, *region, country.* • **ἀφίησιν** — pres. act. indic. 3 sg. → ἀφίημι. Here w. double acc. of obj. and compl. • **ἐκδότους** → ἔκδοτος, ον, *given up, delivered over, surrendered.* • **δουλεύειν** → δουλεύω, *I serve, am subject to,* w. dat. Mod. ἐκδότους. • **καταφεύγειν** → καταφεύγω, *I flee, take refuge.* • **γράμμασιν** → τὸ γράμμα, *letter.* • **ὑπομιμνήσκει** → ὑπομιμνήσκω, *I remind.* • **πολλάκις** — adv., *often.* • **καί** — emphatic, *in fact, indeed,* so also in the next clause. • **φίλων** → φίλος, η, ον, *loved, dear;* subst., *friend.* • **ἐπιστέλλει** → ἐπιστέλλω, *I send.* • **παραγίνεται** → παραγίνομαι, *I come.* • **παρουσίᾳ** → ἡ παρουσία, *presence, arrival.* • **λοιπόν** — could mean *finally,* but here perhaps, *further, besides,* i.e., in addition to the shame they should feel at his having sent friends. See further on 13.9. • **δυσωπῶν** → δυσωπέω, *I put to shame.* • **ἀργόν** → ἀργός, ή, όν, *yielding no return, useless, worthless, without effect.*

13.6 **πολλῷ πλέον** — *much more, much rather* (LSJ, πολύς III2a: 1443; BDAG, πολύς 2bβ: 849). • **κτισμάτων** → τὸ κτίσμα, *creature.* • **φείσεται** — fut. → φείδομαι, *I spare,* w. gen. • **πρὸς τό** — w. inf. for purpose clause. • **μάλιστα** — *especially.* • **ἀπωλείας** → ἡ ἀπώλεια, *destruction, annihilation, ruin.* • **αἰτία** → ἡ αἰτία, *cause, reason.* • **ἀφανισμοῦ** → ὁ ἀφανισμός, *destruction, extermination.* • **ἅπαξ** — adv., *once, once for all.* • **κοινωνήσαντα** → κοινωνέω, *I share, have a share.*

εἰκόνος ἀπολέσθαι. 13.7 Τί οὖν ἔδει ποιεῖν τὸν Θεόν; ἢ τί ἔδει γενέσθαι, ἀλλ' ἢ τὸ κατ' εἰκόνα πάλιν ἀνανεῶσαι, ἵνα δι' αὐτοῦ πάλιν αὐτὸν γνῶναι δυνηθῶσιν οἱ ἄνθρωποι; τοῦτο δὲ πῶς ἂν ἐγεγόνει, εἰ μὴ αὐτῆς τῆς τοῦ Θεοῦ εἰκόνος παραγενομένης τοῦ Σωτῆρος ἡμῶν Ἰησοῦ Χριστοῦ; δι' ἀνθρώπων μὲν γὰρ οὐκ ἦν δυνατόν, ἐπεὶ καὶ αὐτοὶ κατ' εἰκόνα γεγόνασιν· ἀλλ' οὐδὲ δι' ἀγγέλων· οὐδὲ γὰρ οὐδὲ αὐτοί εἰσιν εἰκόνες. ὅθεν ὁ τοῦ Θεοῦ Λόγος δι' ἑαυτοῦ παρεγένετο, ἵν' ὡς εἰκὼν ὢν τοῦ Πατρὸς τὸν κατ' εἰκόνα ἄνθρωπον ἀνακτίσαι δυνηθῇ. 13.8 Ἄλλως δὲ πάλιν οὐκ ἂν ἐγεγόνει, εἰ μὴ ὁ θάνατος ἦν καὶ ἡ φθορὰ ἐξαφανισθεῖσα. 13.9 Ὅθεν εἰκότως ἔλαβε σῶμα θνητόν, ἵνα καὶ ὁ θάνατος ἐν αὐτῷ λοιπὸν ἐξαφανισθῆναι δυνηθῇ, καὶ οἱ κατ' εἰκόνα πάλιν ἀνακαινισθῶσιν ἄνθρωποι. οὐκοῦν ἑτέρου πρὸς ταύτην τὴν χρείαν οὐκ ἦν, εἰ μὴ τῆς εἰκόνος τοῦ Πατρός.

On the Incarnation 20 The Effects of the Cross

20.1 Τὴν μὲν οὖν αἰτίαν τῆς σωματικῆς ἐπιφανείας αὐτοῦ, ὡς οἷόν τε ἦν, ἐκ μέρους, καὶ ὡς ἡμεῖς ἠδυνήθημεν νοῆσαι, προείπομεν, ὅτι οὐκ ἄλλου ἦν τὸ φθαρτὸν εἰς ἀφθαρσίαν μεταβαλεῖν, εἰ μὴ αὐτοῦ τοῦ Σωτῆρος, τοῦ καὶ

13.7 **ἀλλ' ἤ** — *except* (LSI I2: 37; BDAG 1a: 44). • **ἀνανεῶσαι** — aor. act. inf. → ἀνανεόομαι, *I renew.* • **γνῶναι** — aor. act. inf. → γίνωσκω. • **ἐγεγόνει** — plpf. act. indic. 3 sg. → γίνομαι. • **εἰ μή** — *except.* • **τῆς . . . παραγενομένης** — subst. ptc. Gen. of means (Wal: 125), *by the coming/presence.* • **Σωτῆρος** → ὁ σωτήρ, *Savior.* In appos. to τοῦ εἰκόνος. • **δυνατόν** → δυνατός, ή, όν, *possible.* • **ἐπεί** — *since.* The point is their creaturehood; they are not themselves the Image. • **οὐδέ** — οὐδέ repeated for emphasis. • **ὅθεν** — *whence, from which fact.* • **δι' ἑαυτοῦ** — "through himself," i.e., *in his own person.* διά for manner/way. • **ὡς** — w. ptc. for cause or reason (LSI BIV: 908; BDAG 3aβ: 1105). • **ἀνακτίσαι** — aor. act. inf. → ἀνακτίζω, *I recreate, create anew.*

13.8 **ἄλλως** — adv., *in another way.* • **φθορά** → ἡ φθορά, *decay, corruption.* • **ἐξαφανισθεῖσα** — aor. pass. ptc. → ἐξαφανίζω, *I destroy utterly.* Periphrastic, sg. verb w. a comp. subj. (Wal: 401; Smy: 968).

13.9 **εἰκότως** — *suitably, reasonably.* • **θνητόν** → θνητός, ή, όν, *mortal, liable to death.* • **λοιπόν** → λοιπός, here probably, *for the future, from then on.* • **ἀνακαινισθῶσιν** — aor. pass. subjun. → ἀνακαινίζω, *I renew.* • **οὐκοῦν** — adv., *then, therefore, accordingly.* • **ἑτέρου** — a partitive gen. (also called gen. of the divided whole) serving as the subj. (Smy: 928b, 1318, cf. 1306), "some other," *someone else.*

20.1 **αἰτίαν** → ἡ αἰτία, *cause, reason.* • **σωματικῆς** → σωματικός, ή, όν, *bodily, corporeal.* • **ἐπιφανείας** → ἡ ἐπιφάνεια, *manifestation.* • **οἷον** → οἷος, α, ον, *such as.* οἷόν τε ἐστί, *it is possible* (LSJ III3: 1209). • **μέρους** → τὸ μέρος, *part.* • **ἠδυνήθημεν** → δύναμαι. This verb uses η for its augment (Smy: 430). • **νοῆσαι** → νοέω, *I think, think out, understand.* • **προείπομεν** → προεῖπον, *I tell/state before/above.* • **οὐκ ἄλλου ἦν** — "it was not of another," *it did not belong to someone else.* • **φθαρτόν** → φθαρτός, ή, όν, *perishable, corruptible.* • **ἀφθαρσίαν** →

τὴν ἀρχὴν ἐξ οὐκ ὄντων πεποιηκότος τὰ ὅλα· καὶ οὐκ ἄλλου ἦν, τὸ κατ' εἰκόνα πάλιν ἀνακτίσαι τοῖς ἀνθρώποις, εἰ μὴ τῆς Εἰκόνος τοῦ Πατρός· καὶ οὐκ ἄλλου ἦν τὸ θνητὸν ἀθάνατον παραστῆσαι, εἰ μὴ τῆς Αὐτοζωῆς οὔσης τοῦ Κυρίου ἡμῶν Ἰησοῦ Χριστοῦ· καὶ οὐκ ἄλλου ἦν περὶ Πατρὸς διδάξαι, καὶ τὴν εἰδώλων καθαιρῆσαι θρησκείαν, εἰ μὴ τοῦ τὰ πάντα διακοσμοῦντος Λόγου, καὶ μόνου τοῦ Πατρὸς ὄντος Υἱοῦ μονογενοῦς ἀληθινοῦ. 20.2 Ἐπειδὴ δὲ καὶ τὸ ὀφειλόμενον παρὰ πάντων ἔδει λοιπὸν ἀποδοθῆναι· ὠφείλετο γὰρ πάντας, ὡς προεῖπον, ἀποθανεῖν, δι' ὃ μάλιστα καὶ ἐπεδήμησε· τούτου ἕνεκεν μετὰ τὰς περὶ θεότητος αὐτοῦ ἐκ τῶν ἔργων ἀποδείξεις, ἤδη λοιπὸν καὶ ὑπὲρ πάντων τὴν θυσίαν ἀνέφερεν, ἀντὶ πάντων τὸν ἑαυτοῦ ναὸν εἰς θάνατον παραδιδούς, ἵνα τοὺς μὲν πάντας ἀνυπευθύνους καὶ ἐλευθέρους τῆς ἀρχαίας παραβάσεως ποιήσῃ· δείξῃ δὲ ἑαυτὸν

ἡ ἀφθαρσία, *incorruption.* • **μεταβαλεῖν** → μεταβάλλω, *I turn, change, alter.* The inf. is the subj. Very woodenly: "To change corruption to incorruption was not anyone else's." It did not belong to anyone else to do this, and, as the following context suggests, it was impossible for anyone else to do it. • **Σωτῆρος** → ὁ σωτήρ, *Savior.* In appos. to ἄλλου. • **ἀρχήν** → ἀρχή — acc. of time. The acc. of time is used when the activity covers the entire period of time indicated (Wal: 210; Smy: 1583), so here, properly, "for the duration of the beginning," *throughout the beginning.* • **πεποιηκότος** — art. ptc. continues the appos. to ἄλλου. • **εἰκόνα** → ἡ εἰκών, *image.* • **ἀνακτίσαι** — aor. act. inf. → ἀνακτίζω, *I recreate, create anew.* Inf. for subj. • **θνητόν** → θνητός, ή, όν, *mortal.* • **ἀθάνατον** → ἀθάνατος, ον, *immortal.* Pred. nom., like a double acc. of obj. and compl. • **παραστῆσαι** — aor. act. ptc. → παρίστημι, *I make, render* (BDAG 1c: 778). Inf. for subj. The texts of Kannengiesser and Thomson have ἀναστῆσαι — aor. act. ptc. → ἀνίστημι. • **Αὐτοζωῆς** → ἡ αὐτοζωή, *absolute life, life in itself* (*PGL*: 269; LSJ supplement, p. 60 and cf. the related adj. αὐτόζῳος, ον in LSJ: 280). • **εἰδώλων** → τὸ εἴδωλον, *idol.* • **καθαιρῆσαι** → καθαιρέω, *I bring down, destroy.* • **θρησκείαν** → ἡ θρησκεία, *worship.* • **διακοσμοῦντος** → διακοσμέω, *I regulate, set in order.* • **μονογενοῦς** → μονογενής, ές, *one and only, unique; only-begotten* (BDAG: 658). • **ἀληθινοῦ** → ἀληθινός, ή, όν, *true.*

20.2 **ἐπειδή** — *since.* • **ὀφειλόμενον** → ὀφείλω, *I owe, ought.* • **ἔδει** — cf. 13.1; here, *it was necessary, he should.* • **λοιπόν** — adv., neut. of λοιπός, ή, όν, *further, finally;* here, *still* (so Thomson and cf. BDF: 451.6, citing Matt 26:45; Mark 14:41). • **ἀποδοθῆναι** — aor. pass. inf. → ἀποδίδωμι, *I repay.* • **ὠφείλετο** — impf. → ὀφείλω. • **πάντας** — subj. of inf. Some editions have πάντως (adv., *altogether, completely; certainly, obviously, of course*). • **ἀποθανεῖν** — 2 aor. act. inf. → ἀποθνήσκω, subj. of ὠφείλετο. For such constructions English uses a preparatory "it," "it is/was . . ." (Nunn: 24). • **μάλιστα** — adv., *precisely, especially.* • **ἐπεδήμησε** → ἐπιδημέω, *I come to reside in a place, dwell among/with, appear. PGL* (520–21) notes that each of these meanings is associated with the incarnation in various patristic writings. • **ἕνεκεν** — (listed in lexicons under the alternate form ἕνεκα) *on account of, because of.* This prep. often follows its obj., here τούτου. • **θεότητος** → ἡ θεότης, *divinity.* • **ἀποδείξεις** → ἡ ἀπόδειξις, *proof.* • **ἤδη λοιπόν** — *now finally, now at last.* • **θυσίαν** → ἡ θυσία, *sacrifice.* • **ἀνέφερεν** → ἀναφέρω, *I offer up.* • **ἀντί** — *on behalf of.* • **ναόν** → ὁ ναός, *temple.* • **παραδιδούς** — pres. act. ptc. masc. nom. sg. → παραδίδωμι, *I give up, give over.*

καὶ θανάτου κρείττονα, ἀπαρχὴν τῆς τῶν ὅλων ἀναστάσεως τὸ ἴδιον σῶμα ἄφθαρτον ἐπιδεικνύμενος. 20.3 Καὶ μήτοι θαυμάσῃς εἰ πολλάκις τὰ αὐτὰ περὶ τῶν αὐτῶν λέγομεν. ἐπειδὴ γὰρ περὶ τῆς εὐδοκίας τοῦ Θεοῦ λαλοῦμεν, διὰ τοῦτο τὸν αὐτὸν νοῦν διὰ πλειόνων ἑρμηνεύομεν, μὴ ἄρα τι παραλιμπάνειν δόξωμεν, καὶ ἔγκλημα γένηται ὡς ἐνδεῶς εἰρηκόσι· καὶ γὰρ βέλτιον ταὐτολογίας μέμψιν ὑποστῆναι, ἢ παραλεῖψαί τι τῶν ὀφειλόντων γραφῆναι. 20.4 Τὸ μὲν οὖν σῶμα, ὡς καὶ αὐτὸ κοινὴν ἔχον τοῖς πᾶσι τὴν οὐσίαν· σῶμα γὰρ ἦν ἀνθρώπινον· εἰ καὶ καινοτέρῳ θαύματι συνέστη ἐκ παρθένου μόνης, ὅμως θνητὸν ὂν κατὰ ἀκολουθίαν τῶν ὁμοίων καὶ ἀπέθνῃσκε· τῇ δὲ τοῦ Λόγου εἰς αὐτὸ ἐπιβάσει, οὐκέτι κατὰ τὴν ἰδίαν φύσιν

• **ἀνυπευθύνους** → ἀνυπεύθυνος, ον, *not liable to give account, not accountable.* • **ἐλευθέρους** → ἐλεύθερος, α, ον, *free.* • **ἀρχαίας** → ἀρχαῖος, α, ον, *ancient.* • **παραβάσεως** → ἡ παράβασις, *transgression.* • **ποιήσῃ** — here w. double acc. of obj. (πάντας) and compl. (τοὺς ἀνυπευθύνους καὶ ἐλευθέρους, Smy: 1613; Wal: 182). • **δείξῃ** — aor. act. subjun. 3 sg. → δείκνυμι, *I show.* Continuing the ἵνα clause. • **κρείττονα** → κρείττων, ον (listed in LSJ under the alternate form κρείσσων), *better.* • **ἀπαρχὴν** → ἡ ἀπαρχή, *first fruit.* • **ἀναστάσεως** → ἡ ἀνάστασις, *resurrection.* • **ἄφθαρτον** → ἄφθαρτος, ον, *incorruptible.* Pred. compl. w. σῶμα. • **ἐπιδεικνύμενος** → ἐπιδείκνυμι, *I display, show.* W. double acc. of obj. and compl.

20.3 **μήτοι** — stronger form of μή. • **θαυμάσῃς** → θαυμάζω, *I am surprised.* • **πολλάκις** — adv., *often, frequently.* • **εὐδοκίας** → ἡ εὐδοκία, *favor, good will, good pleasure* (BDAG: 404; *PGL*: 562). • **διὰ τοῦτο** — *therefore.* • **νοῦν** — acc. → ὁ νοῦς, *mind; meaning; thought, idea.* • **πλειόνων** → πλείων. διὰ πλειόνων, *in many ways.* • **ἑρμηνεύομεν** → ἑρμηνεύω, *I explain, interpret.* • **ἄρα** — *so, then; perhaps* (LSJ B6: 232). • **παραλιμπάνειν** → παραλιμπάνω, *I leave out, pass over.* • **δόξωμεν** — aor. act. subjun. → δοκέω, *I seem;* w. μή, *lest we seem.* • **ἔγκλημα** → τὸ ἔγκλημα, *charge, accusation, complaint.* • **ἐνδεῶς** — adv., *insufficiently.* • **εἰρηκόσι** — pf. act. ptc. masc. dat. pl. → ἐρῶ (λέγω). Dat. because the verb related to ἔγκλημα, ἐγκαλέω, takes a dat. for the one against whom a charge is brought (Smy: 1502), "and there be a charge as against those who have spoken insufficiently." • **βέλτιον** → βελτίων, ον, *better.* Pred. position w. the inf. Woodenly: "to submit to . . . is better." • **ταὐτολογίας** → ἡ ταὐτολογία, *repetition.* • **μέμψιν** → ἡ μέμψις, *blame.* • **ὑποστῆναι** — aor. act. inf. → ὑφίστημι, *I consent to, submit to.* • **παραλεῖψαι** → παραλείπω, *I leave out, neglect.* • **ὀφειλόντων** — partitive gen. (Wal: 84; Smy: 1306). • **γραφῆναι** — aor. pass. inf. → γράφω.

20.4 **τὸ . . . σῶμα** — poss. art. (Wal: 215; Smy: 1121). • **μέν** — signals the first topic, the humanity and mortality of Christ's body. • **ὡς** — here, *since* (LSJ BIV: 908). • **κοινὴν** → κοινός, ή, όν, *common.* Mod. οὐσίαν. • **ἔχον** — pres. act. ptc. → ἔχω. • **οὐσίαν** → ἡ οὐσία, *being, existence, nature.* • **ἀνθρώπινον** → ἀνθρώπινος, η, ον, *human.* • **καινοτέρῳ** → καινότερος, α, ον, *newer, unprecedented.* • **θαύματι** → τὸ θαῦμα, *miracle, wonder.* • **συνέστη** — aor. act. indic. 3 sg. → συνίστημι, *I set together;* here, *form* (*PGL* B2c: 1332). • **παρθένου** → ἡ παρθένος, *virgin.* • **ὅμως** — conj., *nevertheless,* not to be confused with with the adv. ὁμῶς, *equally.* • **ὂν** — attend. circ. ptc. w. ἀπέθνῃσκε, "it was mortal and died." • **ἀκολουθίαν** → ἡ ἀκολουθία, *following upon.* κατὰ ἀκολουθίαν, *in conformity with* (LSJ III: 52). • **ὁμοίων** → ὅμοιος, α, ον, *like,* used several times in

ἐφθείρετο· ἀλλὰ διὰ τὸν ἐνοικήσαντα τοῦ Θεοῦ Λόγον, ἐκτὸς ἐγίνετο φθορᾶς. 20.5 Καὶ συνέβαινεν ἀμφότερα ἐν ταὐτῷ γενέσθαι παραδόξως· ὅτι τε ὁ πάντων θάνατος ἐν τῷ Κυριακῷ σώματι ἐπληροῦτο, καὶ ὁ θάνατος καὶ ἡ φθορὰ διὰ τὸν συνόντα Λόγον ἐξηφανίζετο. θανάτου γὰρ ἦν χρεία, καὶ θάνατον ὑπὲρ πάντων ἔδει γενέσθαι, ἵνα τὸ παρὰ πάντων ὀφειλόμενον γένηται. 20.6 Ὅθεν, ὡς προεῖπον, ὁ Λόγος, ἐπεὶ οὐχ οἷόν τε ἦν αὐτὸν ἀποθανεῖν· ἀθάνατος γὰρ ἦν· ἔλαβεν ἑαυτῷ σῶμα τὸ δυνάμενον ἀποθανεῖν, ἵνα ὡς ἴδιον ἀντὶ πάντων αὐτὸ προσενέγκῃ, καὶ ὡς αὐτὸς ὑπὲρ πάντων πάσχων, διὰ τὴν πρὸς αὐτὸ ἐπίβασιν, **καταργήσῃ τὸν τὸ κράτος ἔχοντα τοῦ θανάτου, τουτέστι τὸν διάβολον· καὶ ἀπαλλάξῃ τούτους, ὅσοι φόβῳ θανάτου διὰ παντὸς τοῦ ζῆν ἔνοχοι ἦσαν δουλείας.**

On the Incarnation 44 The Necessity of the Incarnation

44.1 Ἀλλ' ἴσως συγκαταθήσονται μὲν τούτοις αἰσχυνόμενοι, θελήσουσι δὲ λέγειν, ὅτι ἔδει τὸν Θεόν, παιδεῦσαι καὶ σῶσαι θέλοντα τοὺς ἀνθρώπους,

---

Athanasius for Christ's human nature in relation to human nature in general (cf. *PGL* B: 954). • **δέ** — introduces the contrasting second topic. • **ἐπιβάσει** — *means of approach, access, entrance* (*PGL* 1: 517). • **οὐκέτι** — adv., *no longer.* • **φύσιν** → ἡ φύσις, *nature.* • **ἐφθείρετο** → φθείρω, *I ruin, destroy, corrupt.* • **ἐνοικήσαντα** → ἐνοικέω, *I dwell in.* • **ἐκτός** — adv., *outside, free from.* • **φθορᾶς** → ἡ φθορά, *corruption, ruin, decay, destruction.*

20.5 **συνέβαινεν** → συμβαίνω, *I happen.* Imper. use w. inf. *it happened, it came to pass* (LSI III: 758; BDAG 2: 956). • **ἀμφότερα** → ἀμφότερος, α, ον, *both.* Since the ref. of "both" comes later, it is smoother to translate, *two things.* • **ταὐτῷ** — from τῷ αὐτῷ, *the same* (LSJ III: 283). ἐν ταὐτῷ, *at the same time.* • **παραδόξως** — *unexpectedly, miraculously* (*PGL* 3: 1014). • **κυριακῷ** → κυριακός, ή, όν, *of the Lord, the Lord's.* • **συνόντα** → σύνειμι, *I am with, am joined/united with.* • **ἐξηφανίζετο** → ἐξαφανίζω, *I destroy utterly.* • **χρεία** → ἡ χρεία, *need, necessity,* w. gen. • **ἔδει** — impf. → δεῖ (→ δέω), *it is necessary/fitting, one must/should.* An imper. verb expressing obligation or necessity, w. inf.; here, *it was necessary that there be a death.*

20.6 **ὅθεν** — adv., *whence, from which fact.* • **ἐπεί** — *since, because.* • **προσενέγκῃ** — aor. act. subjun. → προσφέρω, *I offer.* • **πάσχων** → πάσχω, *I suffer.* • **καταργήσῃ** → καταργέω, *I make of no effect, abolish.* Continuing the ἵνα clause. • **κράτος** → τὸ κράτος, *power, might.* • **τουτέστιν** — crasis for τοῦτ' ἔστιν, *that is to say* (BDAG, εἰμί 2cα: 284). • **διάβολον** → διάβολος, ον, *slanderous;* subst., *adversary, devil.* • **ἀπαλλάξῃ** — aor. act. subjun. → ἀπαλλάσσω, *I free, release.* Continuing the ἵνα clause. • **φόβῳ** → ὁ φόβος, *fear.* • **ζῆν** — pres. act. inf. → ζάω. Since the inf. is used instead of the simple noun, this expression perhaps has the nuance *through all their lifetime, all their life long.* • **ἔνοχοι** → ἔνοχος, ον, *subject to,* w. gen. • **δουλείας** → ἡ δουλεία, *slavery.*

44.1 **ἴσως** — adv., *equally, perhaps.* • **συγκαταθήσονται** → συγκατατίθημι; mid., *I agree with,* w. dat. • **αἰσχυνόμενοι** → αἰσχύνω, *I dishonor;* pass., *I am ashamed.*

νεύματι μόνον ποιῆσαι, καὶ μὴ σώματος ἅψασθαι τὸν τούτου Λόγον, ὥσπερ οὖν καὶ πάλαι πεποίηκεν, ὅτε ἐκ τοῦ μὴ ὄντος αὐτὰ συνίστη. 44.2 Πρὸς δὲ ταύτην αὐτῶν τὴν ἀντίθεσιν εἰκότως ἂν λεχθείη ταῦτα, ὅτι πάλαι μὲν οὐδενὸς οὐδαμοῦ ὑπάρχοντος, νεύματος γέγονε χρεία καὶ βουλήσεως μόνης εἰς τὴν τοῦ παντὸς δημιουργίαν. ὅτε δὲ γέγονεν ὁ ἄνθρωπος, καὶ χρεία ἀπήτησεν οὐ τὰ μὴ ὄντα ἀλλὰ τὰ γενόμενα θεραπεῦσαι, ἀκόλουθον ἦν ἐν τοῖς ἤδη γενομένοις τὸν ἰατρὸν καὶ Σωτῆρα παραγενέσθαι, ἵνα καὶ τὰ ὄντα θεραπεύσῃ. γέγονε δὲ ἄνθρωπος διὰ τοῦτο, καὶ ἀνθρωπείῳ ὀργάνῳ κέχρηται τῷ σώματι. 44.3 Ἐπεὶ εἰ μὴ τοῦτον γενέσθαι ἔδει τὸν τρόπον, πῶς ἔδει τὸν Λόγον, ὀργάνῳ θέλοντα χρήσασθαι, παραγενέσθαι; ἢ πόθεν ἔδει τοῦτο λαβεῖν αὐτόν, εἰ μὴ ἐκ τῶν ἤδη γενομένων καὶ χρῃζόντων τῆς αὐτοῦ θειότητος διὰ τοῦ ὁμοίου; οὐδὲ γὰρ τὰ οὐκ ὄντα ἔχρῃζε σωτηρίας, ἵνα καὶ προστάξει μόνον ἀρκεσθῇ, ἀλλ' ὁ ἤδη γενόμενος ἄνθρωπος ἐφθείρετο καὶ παραπώλλυτο. ὅθεν εἰκότως ἀνθρωπίνῳ κέχρηται καλῶς ὀργάνῳ, καὶ εἰς

Attend. circ. • **θελήσουσι** — fut. act. indic. → θέλω. • **ἔδει** — cf. 13.1. Here, *it was necessary, he/it should.* The inf. is ποιῆσαι, w. the circ. ptc. θέλοντα coming between ἔδει and the inf. • **παιδεῦσαι** → παιδεύω, *I teach, educate.* Compl. inf. w. θέλοντα. • **νεύματι** → τὸ νεῦμα, *a nod, sign.* • **ἅψασθαι** → ἅπτω, *fasten;* mid., *lay hold of, touch,* w. gen. This inf. is also w. ἔδει. • **ὥσπερ** — adv., *as, just as.* • **πάλαι** — adv., *long ago.* • **συνίστη** — impf. act. indic. 3 sg. → συνίστημι, *I set together;* here, *frame, constitute* (*PGL* B2a: 1332).

44.2 **ἀντίθεσιν** → ἡ ἀντίθεσις, *opposition, objection.* • **εἰκότως** — adv., *fairly, reasonably.* • **λεχθείη** — aor. pass. opt. 3 sg. → λέγω. Potential opt. (Smy: 1824), *could be said.* • **οὐδενός** → οὐδείς — subj. of gen. abs. • **οὐδαμοῦ** → **οὐδαμός, ἡ, όν,** *not even one, no one,* appos. to οὐδενός. The texts of Kannengiesser and Thomson have οὐδαμῇ (adv., *in no way, not at all*). • **ὑπάρχοντος** — gen. abs., temp. • **χρεία** → ἡ χρεία, *need, necessity.* • **βουλήσεως** → ἡ βούλησις, *a willing, one's will.* • **δημιουργίαν** → ἡ δημιουργία, *making, creating.* • **ἀπήτησεν** — aor. → ἀπαιτέω, *I demand.* • **θεραπεῦσαι** → θεραπεύω, *I heal.* • **ἀκόλουθον** → ἀκόλουθος, ον, *following.* ἀκόλουθον ἦν, "it was following," *it followed.* • **ἰατρόν** → ὁ ἰατρός, *healer, physician.* Subj. of the inf. along w. Σωτῆρα. • **Σωτῆρα** → ὁ σωτήρ, *Savior.* • **παραγενέσθαι** → παραγίνομαι, *I come to, arrive.* Epex. inf. (Wal: 607; Smy: 2006), mod. ἀκόλουθον. • **διὰ τοῦτο** — *therefore, for this reason, because of this.* • **ἀνθρωπείῳ** → ἀνθρώπειος, α, ον, *human.* • **ὀργάνῳ** → τὸ ὄργανον, *instrument.* • **κέχρηται** — pf. mid. (depon.) indic. 3 sg. → χράομαι, *I use,* w. dat. • **τῷ σώματι** — poss. art. (Wal: 215; Smy: 1121).

44.3 **ἐπεί** — *since, for, for otherwise* (BDAG 2: 360). • **τοῦτον** — goes w. τὸν τρόπον to form the obj. w. the imper. verb ἔδει. • **τρόπον** → ὁ τρόπος, *way, manner.* • **θέλοντα** — circ. ptc., perhaps causal. • **χρήσασθαι** — supplementary inf. w. θέλοντα. • **παραγενέσθαι** — the inf. w. ἔδει. • **πόθεν** — adv., *from where, whence.* • **αὐτόν** — subj. of the imper. verb ἔδει. • **χρῃζόντων** → χρῄζω, *I need,* w. gen. • **θειότητος** → ἡ θειότης, *divine nature, divinity.* • **ὁμοίου** → ὅμοιος, α, ον, *like;* here, subst., *one like (them).* • **σωτηρίας** → ἡ σωτηρία, *salvation.* • **προστάξει** → ἡ πρόσταξις, *a command.* The ref. is to the creation. • **ἀρκεσθῇ** → ἀρκέω, *I am enough, am sufficient;* pass., *am satisfied with,* w. dat. • **ἐφθείρετο** → φθείρω, *I destroy, ruin.* • **παραπώλλυτο** — impf. pass. indic. 3 sg. → παρα-

πάντα ἑαυτὸν ἥπλωσεν ὁ Λόγος. 44.4 Ἔπειτα καὶ τοῦτο ἰστέον, ὅτι ἡ γενομένη φθορὰ οὐκ ἔξωθεν ἦν τοῦ σώματος, ἀλλ' αὐτῷ προσεγεγόνει, καὶ ἀνάγκη ἦν ἀντὶ τῆς φθορᾶς ζωὴν αὐτῷ προσπλακῆναι, ἵνα ὥσπερ ἐν τῷ σώματι γέγονεν ὁ θάνατος, οὕτως ἐν αὐτῷ γένηται καὶ ἡ ζωή. 44.5 Εἰ μὲν οὖν ἔξωθεν ἦν ὁ θάνατος τοῦ σώματος· ἔξωθεν ἔδει καὶ τὴν ζωὴν αὐτοῦ γεγονέναι. εἰ δὲ ἐν τῷ σώματι συνεπλάκη ὁ θάνατος, καὶ ὡς συνὼν αὐτῷ κατεκράτει τούτου· ἀνάγκη καὶ τὴν ζωὴν συμπλακῆναι τῷ σώματι, ἵνα ἀντενδυθὲν τὸ σῶμα τὴν ζωήν, ἀποβάλῃ τὴν φθοράν. ἄλλως τε εἰ καὶ ἐγεγόνει ἔξω τοῦ σώματος ὁ Λόγος, καὶ μὴ ἐν αὐτῷ, ὁ μὲν θάνατος ἡττᾶτο ὑπ' αὐτοῦ φυσικώτατα, ἅτε δὴ μὴ ἰσχύοντος τοῦ θανάτου κατὰ τῆς ζωῆς, οὐδὲν ἧττον δὲ ἔμενεν ἐν τῷ σώματι ἡ προσγενομένη φθορά. 44.6 Διὰ τοῦτο εἰκότως ἐνεδύσατο σῶμα ὁ Σωτήρ, ἵνα συμπλακέντος τοῦ σώματος τῇ ζωῇ, μηκέτι ὡς θνητὸν ἀπομείνῃ ἐν τῷ θανάτῳ· ἀλλ' ὡς ἐνδυσάμενον τὴν ἀθανασίαν, λοιπὸν ἀναστὰν ἀθάνατον διαμείνῃ. ἅπαξ γὰρ ἐνδυσάμενον φθορὰν οὐκ ἂν ἀνέστη, εἰ μὴ ἐνεδύσατο τὴν ζωήν· καὶ πάλιν θάνατος καθ'

πόλλυμι, *I destroy, perish.* • **ὅθεν** — adv., *from which, for which reason.* • **ἀνθρωπίνῳ** → ἀνθρώπινος, η, ον, *human.* • **καλῶς** — adv., *well, rightly.* • **ἥπλωσεν** → ἁπλόω, *I stretch out, extend;* here, *reveal* (*PGL* B2: 188).

44.4 **ἔπειτα** — adv., *then.* • **ἰστέον** — *one must see.* • **φθορά** → ἡ φθορά, *corruption.* • **ἔξωθεν** — *outside,* w. gen. • **προσεγεγόνει** — plpf. act. indic. 3 sg. → προσγίνομαι, *I attach oneself to.* • **ἀνάγκη** → ἡ ἀνάγκη, *necessity.* • **ἀντί** — prep., *instead of.* • **ζωήν** — subj. of inf. • **προσπλακῆναι** — aor. pass. inf. → προσπλέκω, *I connect with;* pass., *cling to;* here, *attach* (*PGL* 6: 1181). Epex. inf. w. ἀνάγκη (Wal: 607; Smy: 2006). • **ὥσπερ** — adv., *just as.*

44.5 **συνεπλάκη** — aor. pass. indic. 3 sg. → συμπλέκω, *I plait together, entangle; am joined* (*PGL* B3b: 1288), w. dat. • **ὡς** — here, *since* (LSI BIV: 908). • **συνών** → σύνειμι, *I am with, am joined with.* • **κατεκράτει** → κατακρατέω, *I prevail over, dominate.* • **συμπλακῆναι** — aor. pass. inf. → συμπλέκω. Epex. inf. w. ἀνάγκη (Wal: 607; Smy: 2006). • **ἀντενδυθέν** — aor. pass. ptc. → ἀντενδύομαι, *I put on instead.* • **ἀποβάλῃ** → ἀποβάλλω, *I throw off.* • **ἄλλως** — adv., *otherwise.* • **ἔξω** — adv., *outside,* w. gen. • **ἡττᾶτο** — impf. pass. indic. 3 sg. → ἡττάομαι (listed in LSI under its alternate form ἡσσάομαι), *I am less than another;* pass., *am defeated.* • **φυσικώτατα** → φυσικώτατος, η, ον, *most natural,* superlative of φυσικός, ή, όν. • **ἅτε** — adv., *inasmuch as, seeing that.* • **δή** — particle, *indeed, certainly, surely.* • **ἰσχύοντος** → ἰσχύω, *I prevail, am strong/mighty/powerful.* Gen. abs. • **ἧττον** → ἥττων, ον, *less.* οὐδὲν ἧττον, *nonetheless.*

44.6 **ἐνεδύσατο** → ἐνδύω, *I put on, dress someone;* mid., *put on (oneself).* • **συμπλακέντος** — aor. pass. ptc. → συμπλέκω. Gen. abs. • **μηκέτι** — adv., *no longer.* • **θνητόν** → θνητός, ή, όν, *mortal.* • **ἀπομείνῃ** → ἀπομένω, *I remain behind, stay* (*PGL* 1: 202). • **ἀθανασίαν** → ἡ ἀθανασία, *immortality.* • **ἀναστάν** — aor. act. ptc. neut. nom. sg. → ἀνίστημι. Attend. circ. w. διαμείνῃ, "(the body) might rise and remain." • **ἀθάνατον** → ἀθάνατος, ον, *immortal.* Dir. obj. of διαμείνῃ. • **διαμείνῃ** — aor. act. subjun. 3 sg. → διαμένω, *I remain.* • **ἅπαξ** — adv., *once.* • **ἀνέστη** — aor. act. indic. 3 sg. → ἀνίστημι. • **εἰ μή** — *unless.* • **πάλιν** — here,

ἑαυτὸν οὐκ ἂν φανείη, εἰ μὴ ἐν τῷ σώματι· διὰ τοῦτο ἐνεδύσατο σῶμα, ἵνα τὸν θάνατον ἐν τῷ σώματι εὑρὼν ἀπαλείψῃ. πῶς γὰρ ἂν ὅλως ὁ Κύριος ἐδείχθη ζωή, εἰ μὴ τὸ θνητὸν ἐζωοποίησε; 44.7 Καὶ ὥσπερ τῆς καλάμης ὑπὸ πυρὸς φύσει φθειρομένης, εἰ κωλύει τις τὸ πῦρ ἀπὸ τῆς καλάμης· οὐ καίεται μὲν ἡ καλάμη, μένει δὲ ὅλως πάλιν καλάμη ἡ καλάμη ὑποπτεύουσα τὴν τοῦ πυρὸς ἀπειλήν· φύσει γάρ ἐστιν ἀναλωτικόν ἐστιν αὐτῆς τὸ πῦρ· εἰ δέ τις ἐνδιδύσκοι τὴν καλάμην ἀμιάντῳ πολλῷ, ὃ δὴ λέγεται ἀντιπαθὲς εἶναι τοῦ πυρός, οὐκ ἔτι τὸ πῦρ φοβεῖται ἡ καλάμη, ἔχουσα τὴν ἀσφάλειαν ἐκ τοῦ ἐνδύματος τοῦ ἀκαύστου· 44.8 τὸν αὐτὸν δὴ τρόπον καὶ ἐπὶ τοῦ σώματος καὶ ἐπὶ τοῦ θανάτου ἄν τις εἴποι· ὅτι εἰ προστάξει μόνον κωλυθεὶς ἦν ὁ θάνατος ὑπ' αὐτοῦ, οὐδὲν ἧττον πάλιν ἦν θνητὸν καὶ φθαρτὸν κατὰ τὸν τῶν σωμάτων λόγον. ἀλλ' ἵνα μὴ τοῦτο γένηται, ἐνεδύσατο τὸν ἀσώματον τοῦ Θεοῦ Λόγον· καὶ οὕτως οὐκ ἔτι τὸν θάνατον οὐδὲ τὴν φθορὰν φοβεῖται, ἔχον ἔνδυμα τὴν ζωήν, καὶ ἐν αὐτῷ ἀφανιζομένης τῆς φθορᾶς.

---

also, again, furthermore (BDAG 3: 752). • **καθ' ἑαυτόν** — *in keeping with itself,* i.e., in keeping w. its nature. • **φανείη** — aor. pass. opt. 3 sg. → φαίνω, *I appear.* Potential opt. (Smy: 1824), "could/would not appear." • **ἀπαλείψῃ** — aor. act. subjun. 3 sg. → ἀπαλείφω, *I wipe off; wipe out, destroy* (*PGL* 3: 172). • **ὅλως** — adv., *actually, in fact* (cf. BDAG 2: 704). • **ἐδείχθη** — aor. pass. indic. 3 sg. → δείκνυμι, *I show.* • **ζωή** — here a pred., "be shown to be life," a construction that occurs with verbs that in the act. can take a double acc. of obj. and compl. • **ἐζωοποίησε** → ζωοποιέω, *I make alive.*

44.7 **καλάμης** → ἡ καλάμη, *straw, stubble.* Subj. of gen. abs. • **φύσει** → ἡ φύσις, *nature.* Dat. of manner, *naturally.* • **φθειρομένης** → φθείρω, *I destroy.* Gen. abs. • **κωλύει** → κωλύω, *I hinder, prevent, keep back/away.* • **καίεται** → καίομαι, *I ignite, burn.* • **πάλιν** — here, *in turn. But in turn, the straw remains, in fact, straw.* • **καλάμη** — when μένω means to continue in a certain state it takes an obj. in the nom., like the pred. compl. of an equative verb (Wal: 40, note 11). • **ὑποπτεύουσα** → ὑποπτεύω, *I suspect, am suspicious, look at something suspiciously/ apprehensively.* • **ἀπειλήν** → ἡ ἀπειλή, *a threat.* • **ἀναλωτικόν** → ἀναλωτικός, ή, όν, *consuming.* ἀναλωτικόν ἐστιν αὐτῆς, "is consuming of it," *consumes it.* • **ἐνδιδύσκοι** — pres. act. opt. 3 sg. → ἐνδιδύσκω, *I cover, put on.* • **ἀμιάντῳ** → τὸ ἀμίαντον, *asbestos* (LSJ 2: 83; *PGL*: 89). • **ἀντιπαθές** → ἀντιπαθής, ές, *a remedy.* • **ἀσφάλειαν** → ἡ ἀσφάλεια, *security, assurance, safety.* • **ἐνδύματος** → τὸ ἔνδυμα, *covering, clothing.* • **ἀκαύστου** → ἄκαυστος, ον, *incombustible.*

44.8 **τρόπον** → τρόπος — acc. of manner (Wal: 200; Smy: 1608). • **ἐπί** — here, *with regard to, concerning* (BDAG 8: 365). • **εἴποι** — 2 aor. act. opt. 3 sg. → εἶπον (λέγω). Potential opt. (Smy: 1824). • **κωλυθείς** — a rare aor. periphrastic, *had been kept away.* • **φθαρτόν** → φραρτός, ή, όν, *corruptible.* • **λόγον** → λόγος, here, *essential disposition,* i.e. a, "formative and regulative law of being" (*PGL* B5b: 808). • **ἀσώματον** → ἀσώματος, ον, *bodiless, incorporeal.* • **ἔχον** — pres. act. ptc. → ἔχω. • **ἔνδυμα** — pred. acc. w. τὴν ζωήν, "life to be a covering," *life as a covering.* • **ἀφανιζομένης** → ἀφανίζω, *I destroy utterly.* Gen. abs.

On the Incarnation 54 The Immeasurable Greatness of What the Incarnate Christ Achieved

54.1 Ὥσπερ οὖν εἴ τις ἀόρατον ὄντα τῇ φύσει τὸν Θεὸν καὶ μηδόλως ὁρώμενον ἐθέλοι ὁρᾶν, ἐκ τῶν ἔργων αὐτὸν καταλαμβάνει καὶ γινώσκει· οὕτως ὁ μὴ ὁρῶν τῇ διανοίᾳ τὸν Χριστόν, κἂν ἐκ τῶν ἔργων τοῦ σώματος καταμανθανέτω τοῦτον, καὶ δοκιμαζέτω εἰ ἀνθρώπινά ἐστιν ἢ Θεοῦ. 54.2 Καὶ ἐὰν μὲν ἀνθρώπινα ᾖ, χλευαζέτω· εἰ δὲ μὴ ἀνθρώπινά ἐστιν ἀλλὰ Θεοῦ γινώσκεται, μὴ γελάτω τὰ ἀχλεύαστα· ἀλλὰ μᾶλλον θαυμαζέτω, ὅτι διὰ τοιούτου πράγματος εὐτελοῦς, τὰ θεῖα ἡμῖν πεφανέρωται, καὶ διὰ τοῦ θανάτου ἡ ἀθανασία εἰς πάντας ἔφθασε, καὶ διὰ τῆς ἐνανθρωπήσεως τοῦ Λόγου ἡ τῶν πάντων ἐγνώσθη πρόνοια, καὶ ὁ ταύτης χορηγὸς καὶ δημιουργὸς αὐτὸς ὁ τοῦ Θεοῦ Λόγος. 54.3 Αὐτὸς γὰρ ἐνηνθρώπησεν, ἵνα ἡμεῖς θεοποιηθῶμεν· καὶ αὐτὸς ἐφανέρωσεν ἑαυτὸν διὰ σώματος, ἵνα ἡμεῖς τοῦ ἀοράτου Πατρὸς ἔννοιαν λάβωμεν· καὶ αὐτὸς ὑπέμεινε τὴν παρ' ἀνθρώπων ὕβριν, ἵνα ἡμεῖς ἀφθαρσίαν κληρονομήσωμεν. ἐβλάπτετο μὲν γὰρ αὐτὸς οὐδέν, ἀπαθὴς καὶ ἄφθαρτος καὶ Αὐτολόγος ὢν καὶ Θεός· τοὺς

54.1 **ὥσπερ** — *just as* • **ἀόρατον** → ἀόρατος, ον, *unseen, invisible.* • **φύσει** → ἡ φύσις, *nature.* Dat. of manner, *naturally, by nature.* • **μηδόλως** — adv., from μηδ' ὅλως, *not at all,* • **ἐθέλοι** — pres. act. opt. 3 sg. → ἐθέλω (older form of θέλω, cf. BDAG: 447). Opt. of wish (Smy: 1814). • **ὁρᾶν** — pres. act. inf. → ὁράω. • **καταλαμβάνει** → καταλαμβάνω, *I grasp, understand.* • **διανοίᾳ** → ἡ διάνοια, *understanding, thought, mind.* • **κἂν** — particle, *even if, even though; at least* (LSJ: 399; BDAG 3: 507), from crasis of καὶ ἐάν. • **καταμανθανέτω** → καταμανθάνω, *learn thoroughly/well, understand, discover.* • **δοκιμαζέτω** → δοκιμάζω, *I test.* • **ἀνθρώπινα** → ἀνθρώπινος, η, ον, *human.* • **ἐστιν** — The verb is sg., but since the implied subj. is the neut. pl. ἔργα, translate "they are."

54.2 **χλευαζέτω** → χλευάζω, *I mock, scoff.* • **γινώσκεται** → γίνωσκω; pass., *I judge, determine.* • **γελάτω** → γελάω, *I laugh.* • **ἀχλεύαστα** → ἀχλεύαστος, η, ον, *not to be mocked.* • **θαυμαζέτω** → θαυμάζω, *I marvel, wonder, am in awe.* • **πράγματος** → τὸ πράγμα, *deed, thing, event;* here, *means.* • **εὐτελοῦς** → εὐτελής, ές, *easily paid for; simple, lowly* (*PGL*: 577). • **θεῖα** → θεῖος, α, ον, *divine.* • **πεφανέρωται** → φανερόω, *I manifest, disclose, reveal.* • **ἀθανασία** → ἡ ἀθανασία, *immortality.* • **ἔφθασε** — aor. act. indic. → φθάνω, *I reach.* • **ἐνανθρωπήσεως** → ἡ ἐνανθρώπησις, *incarnation* (*PGL*: 463). • **πρόνοια** → ἡ πρόνοια, *forethought; divine providence, providential care.* Cf. *PGL* B: 1158–59 for passages related to this theme. • **χορηγός** → ὁ χορηγός, *one who supplies the costs; bestower, provider.* • **δημιουργός** → ὁ δημιουργός, *craftsworker, builder, maker, creator.*

54.3 **ἐνηνθρώπησεν** → ἐνανθρωπέω, *I become human, become incarnate.* • **θεοποιηθῶμεν** → θεοποιέω, *I deify, become god.* Cf. *PGL* C: 631 for passages related to this theme of theosis. • **ἔννοιαν** → ἡ ἔννοια, *thought, idea, concept.* • **ὑπέμεινε** → ὑπομένω, *I submit to; endure.* • **ὕβριν** → ἡ ὕβρις, *insolence, arrogance; shame, insult, mistreatment.* • **κληρονομήσωμεν** → κληρονομέω, *I inherit.* • **ἐβλάπτετο** → βλάπτω, *I harm, injure.* • **ἀπαθής** → ἀπαθής, ές, *impassible,* i.e., "being

δὲ πάσχοντας ἀνθρώπους, δι' οὓς καὶ ταῦτα ὑπέμεινεν, ἐν τῇ ἑαυτοῦ ἀπαθείᾳ ἐτήρει καὶ διέσῳζε. 54.4 Καὶ ὅλως τὰ κατορθώματα τοῦ Σωτῆρος τὰ διὰ τῆς ἐνανθρωπήσεως αὐτοῦ γενόμενα, τοιαῦτα καὶ τοσαῦτά ἐστιν, ἃ εἰ διηγήσασθαί τις ἐθελήσειεν, ἔοικεν τοῖς ἀφορῶσιν εἰς τὸ πέλαγος τῆς θαλάσσης, καὶ θέλουσιν ἀριθμεῖν τὰ κύματα ταύτης. ὡς γὰρ οὐ δύναται τοῖς ὀφθαλμοῖς περιλαβεῖν τὰ ὅλα κύματα, τῶν ἐπερχομένων παριόντων τὴν αἴσθησιν τοῦ πειράζοντος· οὕτω καὶ τῷ βουλομένῳ πάντα τὰ ἐν σώματι τοῦ Χριστοῦ κατορθώματα περιλαβεῖν, ἀδύνατον τὰ ὅλα κἂν τῷ λογισμῷ δέξασθαι, πλειόνων ὄντων τῶν παριόντων αὐτοῦ τὴν ἐνθύμησιν, ὧν αὐτὸς νομίζει περιειληφέναι. 54.5 Κάλλιον οὖν μὴ πρὸς τὰ ὅλα ἀφορῶντα λέγειν, ὧν οὐδὲ μέρος ἐξειπεῖν τις δύναται, ἀλλ' ἔτι ἑνὸς μνημο-

---

free not only from pain and emotion but also from any other form of passivity" (*PGL* B: 171). • **ἄφθαρτος** → ἄφθαρτος, ον, *incorruptible.* • **Αὐτολόγος** → ὁ αὐτολόγος, *very Word* (*PGL*: 271). • **πάσχοντας** → πάσχω, *suffer.* • **ἀπαθείᾳ** → ἡ ἀπαθεία, *impassibility.* • **ἐτήρει** → τηρέω, *I keep, maintain.* • **διέσῳζε** → διασῴζω, *I save, rescue.*

54.4 **ὅλως** — adv., *in short, in a word.* • **κατορθώματα** → τὸ κατόρθωμα, *success, virtuous action, achievement.* • **Σωτῆρος** → ὁ σωτήρ, *Savior.* • **τοσαῦτα** → τοσοῦτος,-αύτη,-οῦτον, *so many.* • **διηγήσασθαι** → διηγέομαι, *I tell, relate, describe.* • **ἐθελήσειεν** — aor. act. opt. 3 sg. → θέλω. • **ἔοικεν** → ἔοικα, *I am like.* This pf. verb has a pres. sense w. dat. • **ἀφορῶσιν** — pres. act. ptc. masc. dat. pl. → ἀφοράω, *I look at, have in view.* • **πέλαγος** → τὸ πέλαγος, *sea.* This word often suggests the vastness of the sea and can be used metaphorically for "vast amount." It is sometimes, as here, combined w. another word for sea (LSI: 617). τὸ πέλαγος τῆς θαλάσσης, *the vast expanse of the sea.* • **ἀριθμεῖν** → ἀριθμέω, *I count, number.* • **κύματα** → τὸ κῦμα, *wave.* • **περιλαβεῖν** → περιλαμβάνω, *I encompass, get hold of, take in, comprehend.* • **ἐπερχομένων** → ἐπέρχομαι, *I come on/upon.* Subj. of gen. abs. • **παριόντων** — pres. act. ptc. → πάρειμι, *I pass by, surpass.* Gen. abs., causal. There are two words w. the lexical form πάρειμι, one from εἰμί and the other, as here, from εἶμι, "I go." • **αἴσθησιν** → ἡ αἴσθησις, *perception.* • **πειράζοντος** → πειράζω, *I try, attempt.* Mod. αἴσθησιν. • **οὕτω** — alternate form of οὕτως. • **βουλομένῳ** → βούλομαι, *I want.* • **ἀδύνατον** → ἀδύνατος, ον, *unable, impossible;* pred., "it is impossible." • **λογισμῷ** → ὁ λογισμός, *counting, calculation; reason, reckoning.* The context immediately following suggests *counting* is in mind here. • **δέξασθαι** → δέχομαι. • **πλειόνων** — pred. compl. • **ὄντων** — gen. abs. • **τῶν παριόντων** — subj. of gen. abs. • **ἐνθύμησιν** → ἡ ἐνθύμησις, *consideration, thought, reflection, idea.* • **ὧν** — gen. of comparison w. πλειόνων. • **νομίζει** → νομίζω, *I think.* • **περιειληφέναι** — pf. act. inf. → περιλαμβάνω.

54.5

κάλλιον → καλλίων, ον, *better.* The acc. used as the comparative of καλῶς, the adv. of καλός, ή, όν. Here it is in pred. position with the inf., *it is better.* • **τὰ ὅλα** — *everything; the whole.* • **ἀφορῶντα** — perhaps attend. circ. w. λέγειν, "to have in view to speak," *aim at speaking* (so Robertson's translation). • **λέγειν** — the subj. Woodenly: "to not speak is better." λέγω πρός, *speak in reference to/regarding* (LSJ III1: 1034). • **μέρος** → τὸ μέρος, *part.* • **ἐξειπεῖν** → ἐξεῖπον, *I tell out, de-*

νεῦσαι καὶ σοὶ καταλιπεῖν τὰ ὅλα θαυμάζειν. πάντα γὰρ ἐπίσης ἔχει τὸ θαῦμα, καὶ ὅποι δ' ἂν τις ἀποβλέψῃ, ἐκεῖθεν τοῦ Λόγου τὴν θειότητα βλέπων ὑπερεκπλήττεται.

On the Incarnation 57 Prerequisites for Understanding the Things of God

57.1 Ἀλλὰ πρὸς τὴν ἐκ τῶν γραφῶν ἔρευναν καὶ γνῶσιν ἀληθῆ, χρεία βίου καλοῦ καὶ ψυχῆς καθαρᾶς καὶ τῆς κατὰ Χριστὸν ἀρετῆς, ἵνα δι' αὐτῆς ὁδεύσας ὁ νοῦς, τυχεῖν ὧν ὀρέγεται καὶ καταλαβεῖν δυνηθῇ, καθ' ὅσον ἐφικτόν ἐστι τῇ ἀνθρώπων φύσει περὶ τοῦ Θεοῦ Λόγου μανθάνειν. 57.2 Ἄνευ γὰρ καθαρᾶς διανοίας, καὶ τῆς πρὸς τοὺς ἁγίους τοῦ βίου μιμήσεως, οὐκ ἄν τις καταλαβεῖν δυνηθείη τοὺς τῶν ἁγίων λόγους. 57.3 Ὥσπερ γὰρ εἴ τις ἐθελήσειεν ἰδεῖν τὸ τοῦ ἡλίου φῶς, πάντως τὸν ὀφθαλμὸν ἀποσμήχει καὶ λαμπρύνει, σχεδὸν ὅμοιον τῷ ποθουμένῳ ἑαυτὸν διακαθαίρων, ἵνα οὕτως φῶς γενόμενος ὁ ὀφθαλμὸς τὸ τοῦ ἡλίου φῶς ἴδῃ, ἢ ὡς εἴ τις

---

clare. • **μνημονεῦσαι** → μνημονεύω, *I call to mind, remember, mention.* • **καταλιπεῖν** → καταλείπω, *I leave.* • **θαυμάζειν** → θαυμάζω, *I wonder, marvel.* • **ἐπίσης** — *equally, alike,* from ἐπ' ἴσης (ἴσος, η, ον, *equal, like*). • **θαῦμα** → τὸ θαῦμα, *a wonder, marvel.* • **ὅποι** — adv., *to which place;* w. ἄν and subjun., *wherever.* • **ἀποβλέψῃ** → ἀποβλέπω, *I look at carefully.* • **ἐκεῖθεν** — adv., *from that place, from there.* • **θειότητα** → ἡ θειότης, *divine nature, divinity.* • **ὑπερεκπλήττεται** → ὑπερεκπλήττω (listed in LSJ under the alternate from ὑπερεκπλήσσω), *I astonish beyond measure;* pass. *am exceedingly amazed.*

57.1 **ἔρευναν** → ἔρευνα, *search, inquiry.* • **γνῶσιν** → ἡ γνῶσις, *knowledge.* • **ἀληθῆ** → ἀληθής, ές, *true.* • **χρεία** → ἡ χρεία, *need, necessity,* w. gen. Here it provides the pred. of the sentence, *there is need,* or *it is necessary.* • **βίου** → ὁ βίος, *life.* • **καθαρᾶς** → καθαρός, ά, όν, *clean, pure.* • **ἀρετῆς** → ἡ ἀρετή, *virtue, excellence.* • **ὁδεύσας** → ὁδεύω, *travel, journey.* • **νοῦς** → ὁ νοῦς, *mind.* • **τυχεῖν** → τυγχάνω, *I hit, reach, gain, attain,* w. gen. • **ὀρέγεται** → ὀρέγω, in the mid., *I reach after, aim at,* w. gen. • **καταλαβεῖν** → καταλαμβάνω, *I grasp, understand.* • **καθ' ὅσον** → καθ' ὅσον, *to the degree that.* • **ἐφικτόν** → ἐφικτός, ή, όν, *easy to reach, accessible.* • **φύσει** → ἡ φύσις, *nature.* • **μανθάνειν** → μανθάνω, *I learn.* Mod. ἐφικτόν.

57.2 **ἄνευ** — *without, apart from,* w. gen. • **διανοίας** → ἡ διάνοια, *mind, thought.* • **πρός** — here, *in accordance with* (BDAG 3eδ: 875). • **μιμήσεως** → ἡ μίμησις, *imitation, copying.* • **δυνηθείη** — aor. opt. pass. 3 sg. → δύναμαι.

57.3 **ὥσπερ** — *as, like, as it were.* • **ἐθελήσειεν** — aor. act. opt. 3 sg. → ἐθέλω, a form of θέλω, occurring again later in this section. • **ἡλίου** → ὁ ἥλιος, *sun.* • **πάντως** — adv., *in all ways, wholly, certainly, obviously, of course.* • **ἀποσμήχει** → ἀποσμήχω, *I wipe off, wipe clean.* • **λαμπρύνει** → λαμπρύνω, *I make bright/brilliant.* • **σχεδόν** — adv., *near, nearly.* • **ὅμοιον** — adv., *like,* neut. of ὅμοιος, α, ον, w. dat. • **ποθουμένῳ** → ποθέω, *I desire, long for, yearn after.* Mod. ὅμοιον.

θελήσειεν ἰδεῖν πόλιν ἢ χώραν, πάντως ἐπὶ τὸν τόπον ἀφικνεῖται τῆς θέας ἕνεκεν· οὕτως ὁ θέλων τῶν θεολόγων τὴν διάνοιαν καταλαβεῖν, προαπονίψαι καὶ προαποπλῦναι τῷ βίῳ τὴν ψυχὴν ὀφείλει, καὶ πρὸς αὐτοὺς τοὺς ἁγίους ἀφικέσθαι τῇ ὁμοιότητι τῶν πράξεων αὐτῶν, ἵνα σὺν αὐτοῖς τῇ ἀγωγῇ τῆς συζήσεως γενόμενος, τὰ καὶ αὐτοῖς ἀποκαλυφθέντα παρὰ Θεοῦ κατανοήσῃ, καὶ λοιπὸν ὡς ἐκείνοις συναφθεὶς ἐκφύγῃ μὲν τὸν τῶν ἁμαρτωλῶν κίνδυνον καὶ τὸ τούτων πῦρ ἐν τῇ ἡμέρᾳ τῆς κρίσεως, ἀπολάβῃ δὲ τὰ τοῖς ἁγίοις ἀποκείμενα ἐν τῇ τῶν οὐρανῶν βασιλείᾳ, **ἃ ὀφθαλμὸς οὐκ εἶδεν, οὐδὲ οὖς ἤκουσεν, οὐδὲ ἐπὶ καρδίαν ἀνθρώπων ἀνέβη, ὅσα ἡτοίμασται τοῖς** κατ' ἀρετὴν βιοῦσι, καὶ ἀγαπῶσι τὸν Θεὸν καὶ Πατέρα, ἐν Χριστῷ Ἰησοῦ τῷ Κυρίῳ ἡμῶν, δι' οὗ καὶ μεθ' οὗ αὐτῷ τῷ Πατρὶ σὺν αὐτῷ τῷ Υἱῷ ἐν ἁγίῳ Πνεύματι, τιμὴ καὶ κράτος καὶ δόξα εἰς τοὺς αἰῶνας τῶν αἰώνων. Ἀμήν.

• **διακαθαίρων** → διακαθαίρω, *I cleanse or purge thoroughly.* • **θελήσειεν** — aor. act. opt. 3 sg. → θέλω. • **χώραν** → ἡ χώρα, *place, region, position, ground.* • **ἀφικνεῖται** → ἀφικνέομαι, *I arrive, reach, come to.* • **θέας** → ἡ θέα, *view, sight.* • **ἕνεκεν** (listed in lexicons under the alternate form ἕνεκα) — *on account of, because of, for the sake of.* This prep. often follows its obj. • **θεολόγων** → ὁ θεολόγος, *one who speaks of God, theologian.* • **προαπονίψαι** → προαπονίπτω, *I wash first, cleanse first.* • **προαποπλῦναι** → προαποπλύνω, *I wash first, cleanse first.* • **τῷ βίῳ** — dat. of means (Wal: 162; Smy: 1506). • **ὀφείλει** → ὀφείλω, *I owe, ought, must.* • **ὁμοιότητι** → ἡ ὁμοιότης, *likeness.* • **πράξεων** → ἡ πρᾶξις, *deed, action.* • **ἀγωγῇ** → ἡ ἀγωγή, *conduct, manner of life.* τῇ ἀγωγῇ τῆς συζήσεως, *in the conduct of a common life.* • **συζήσεως** → ἡ σύζησις, *living together, living in communion with.* • **ἀποκαλυφθέντα** → ἀποκαλύπτω, *I reveal.* • **κατανοήσῃ** → κατανοέω, *I understand.* • **ὡς** — here, *since* (LSI BIV: 908). • **συναφθείς** → συνάπτω, *I join together, unite.* • **ἐκφύγῃ** → ἐκφεύγω, *I flee away, escape.* Continues the ἵνα clause. • **ἁμαρτωλῶν** → ἁμαρτωλός, ον, *sinful;* subst., *sinner.* • **κίνδυνον** → ὁ κίνδυνος, *danger.* • **κρίσεως** → ἡ κρίσις, *judgment.* • **ἀπολάβῃ** → ἀπολαμβάνω, *receive.* Continues the ἵνα clause. • **ἀποκείμενα** → ἀπόκειμαι, *I lay up in store.* • **οὐρανῶν** → ὁ οὐρανός, often in the pl. following the Heb., which uses the dual. • **εἶδεν** — begins a series of aor. which here function somewhat like the pf. (Smy: 1940). • **οὖς** → τὸ οὖς, *ear.* • **ἀνέβη** → ἀναβαίνω, *I go up, arise.* • **ἡτοίμασται** → ἑτοιμάζω, *I prepare.* • **βιοῦσι** → βιόω, *I live.* • **τιμή** → ἡ τιμή, *an honor.* • **κράτος** → τὸ κράτος, *might, power.*

Gregory of Nazianzus

Orations

Introduction

The doctrines of the deity of Christ and the Holy Spirit were sources of great controversy in the early church, as they remain today for some. Gregory of Nazianzus (ca. 329–390) was one of the main theologians who helped clarify and establish the church's teaching on these crucial issues. His orations, which have made a major contribution to the history of Christian thought, earned Gregory the title "the Theologian" (which he shared with John the Apostle). For many in the ancient church, *theologian* was not an academic title for one who had learned about God, but rather a title of respect for one who knew God and who conveyed genuine insight regarding the mystery of God. In the famous saying of Evagrius of Pontus (346–399), "If you are a theologian, you will pray truly. And if you pray truly, you are a theologian"—εἰ θεολόγος εἶ, προσεύξῃ ἀληθῶς. Καὶ εἰ ἀληθῶς προσεύχῃ, θεολόγος εἶ (*Chapters on Prayer* 60).

Gregory of Nazianzus (ca. 329–390) was raised in a Christian home in Cappadocia (modern central Turkey) and had the benefit of an extensive education, including studies in Athens. He was so accomplished in rhetoric that his orations were later used as models for students to follow. He had a quiet disposition and preferred to live in private, pursue his studies, and follow an ascetical lifestyle. But the times would not allow him to remain secluded. Gregory's father, the bishop of Nazianzus, needed his son's help and in 361 ordained him, quite against Gregory's own will, to the priesthood. Gregory fled to a monastic setting.

Before long he repented and returned to take up his pastoral duties, preaching his first sermon at the Easter liturgy in 362. Since the people were angry with him because of his flight, Gregory defended his action in his second oration, in which he explained that he had fled because of the difficulties and weighty responsibilities of pastoral care. This oration became the seminal work in the ancient church on the office of the priesthood, and influenced both John Chrysostom's *Priesthood* and Gregory the Great's *Pastoral Rule*.

For a decade Gregory helped his father in Nazianzus, but then Gregory's friend, Basil of Caesarea, tricked him into becoming a bishop in an attempt to get him to help in Caesarea. Gregory, however, fled from what he considered a betrayal. Although he later returned, he never took up the post Basil had given him. Rather, he continued to help his father until his father died in 374, at which time Gregory refused to take his father's place as bishop. Gregory's mother died shortly thereafter, and he felt free to retire to a monastery for several years.

In 379 Gregory accepted the request of a small congregation in Constantinople, the capital of the Eastern Empire, to become their pastor. Since all the church buildings in the city were held by the Arians, who denied Christ's divinity, Gregory consecrated a house that he had been given, and the small church grew significantly under his ministry. A year later, near the end of 380, Theodosius I became Emperor of the Eastern Empire. Sympathetic to Gregory's Nicene orthodoxy, Theodosius appointed him the bishop of Constantinople. At a general council in 381, Gregory's position was confirmed. Nevertheless, he remained in office only a few weeks, after bishops from Egypt and Macedonia objected to his episcopacy on canonical grounds, and after Gregory had failed to handle well a schism that came as part of his new responsibilities. Gregory then returned to Nazianzus for several years, and in 384 withdrew to his family estate for the remainder of his life to devote himself to prayer and poetry.

Of Gregory's writings we have 249 letters, over 17,000 verses of poetry, and 44 authentic *Orations* (*Or.*; *Or.* 35 is not considered authentic). Over half of the orations (*Or.* 20–45) come from the years 379–381 when Gregory served in Constantinople. Of special importance are *Orations* 27–31, known as the Five Theological Orations. In these less homiletical orations, he combats views, prevalent in his day, which denied the deity of both Christ and the Holy Spirit.

Among the selections included here are portions from the first and last of the orations that we have, both of which are Easter sermons. I have also included several selections from Gregory's second oration regarding pastoral ministry. The other selections offer a brief glimpse of two of the Five Theological Orations, illustrating elements of Gregory's style, thought, and use of Scripture.

Editions used: *Oration* 1.3–5; 2.3, 21–22, 35–36: *PG* 35, cols. 397, 400, 409, 429, 432, 441, 444
Oration 29.20; 31:26: Arthur James Mason. *The Five Theological Orations of Gregory of Nazianzus.* Cambridge Patristic Texts. Cambridge: Cambridge University Press, 1899.
Oration 45.28–29: *PG* 36, cols. 661, 664

Levels of difficulty: *Oration* 1.3–5; Easy [1]
Oration 2.3, 21–22, 35–36: Advanced [4–5]
Oration 29.20: Easy [1]
Oration 31:26: Intermediate [3]
Oration 45.28–29: Easy to intermediate [1–3]

Oration 1.3–5 The Christian's Experience of Pascha and a Call to Christlikeness

1.3 Χθὲς ὁ ἀμνὸς ἐσφάζετο, καὶ ἐχρίοντο αἱ φλιαί, καὶ ἐθρήνησεν Αἴγυπτος τὰ πρωτότοκα, καὶ ἡμᾶς παρῆλθεν ὁ ὀλοθρεύων, καὶ ἡ σφραγὶς φοβερὰ καὶ αἰδέσιμος, καὶ τῷ τιμίῳ αἵματι ἐτειχίσθημεν· σήμερον καθαρῶς ἐφύγομεν Αἴγυπτον, καὶ Φαραὼ τὸν πικρὸν δεσπότην, καὶ τοὺς βαρεῖς ἐπιστάτας, καὶ τοῦ πηλοῦ καὶ τῆς πλινθείας ἠλευθερώθημεν· καὶ οὐδεὶς ὁ κωλύσων ἡμᾶς ἑορτάζειν Κυρίῳ τῷ Θεῷ ἡμῶν ἑορτὴν τὴν ἐξόδιον, καὶ ἑορτάζειν, **οὐκ ἐν ζύμῃ παλαιᾷ κακίας καὶ πονηρίας, ἀλλ' ἐν ἀζύμοις εἰλικρινείας καὶ ἀληθείας,** μηδὲν ἐπιφερομένους Αἰγυπτιακοῦ καὶ ἀθέου φυράματος.

1.4 Χθὲς συνεσταυρούμην Χριστῷ, σήμερον συνδοξάζομαι· χθὲς συνενεκρούμην, συζωοποιοῦμαι σήμερον· χθὲς συνεθαπτόμην, σήμερον συνεγείρομαι. Ἀλλὰ καρποφορήσωμεν τῷ ὑπὲρ ἡμῶν παθόντι καὶ ἀναστάντι.

1.3 **χθές** — adv., *yesterday.* • **ἀμνός** → ὁ ἄμνος, *lamb.* • **ἐσφάζετο** → σφάζω, *I slaughter.* • **ἐχρίοντο** → χρίω, *I anoint.* • **φλιαί** → ἡ φλιά, *doorpost.* • **ἐθρήνησεν** → θρηνέω, *I sing a dirge, wail.* • **Αἴγυπτος** → ἡ Αἴγυπτος, *Egypt.* • **πρωτότοκα** → πρωτοτόκος, ον, *firstborn.* Acc. of respect (Wal: 203; Smy: 1600). Art. may be poss. (Wal: 215; Smy: 1121). • **παρῆλθεν** → παρέρχομαι, *I pass, pass by, pass over.* • **ὀλοθρεύων** → ὀλοθρεύω, *I destroy.* • **σφραγίς** → ἡ σφραγίς, *seal.* • **φοβερά** → φοβερός, ά, όν, *fearful, dreadful.* Pred. position. • **αἰδέσιμος** → αἰδέσιμος, ον, *venerable, causing respect, awe-inspiring.* • **τιμίῳ** → τίμιος, α, ον, *precious.* • **ἐτειχίσθημεν** → τειχίζω, *I build a wall;* pass., *am walled in, fenced with walls.* • **σήμερον** — adv., *today.* • **καθαρῶς** — adv., *cleanly, clearly.* • **ἐφύγομεν** → φεύγω, *I flee.* • **Φαραώ** → ὁ Φαραώ, indecl., *Pharaoh.* • **πικρόν** → πικρός, ά, όν, *sharp, bitter.* • **δεσπότην** → ὁ δεσπότης, *despot, absolute ruler.* • **βαρεῖς** → βαρύς, εῖα, ύ, *heavy, oppressive.* • **ἐπιστάτας** → ὁ ἐπιστάτης, *commander.* • **πηλοῦ** → ὁ πηλός, *mud.* • **πλινθείας** → ἡ πλινθεία, *brick-making.* • **ἠλευθερώθημεν** → ἐλευθερόω, *I set free, liberate,* w. gen. • **κωλύσων** → κωλύω, *I hinder, prevent* one *from doing,* w. acc. and inf. Attrib. ptc. in pred. position w. οὐδείς. This construction in English uses, "There is . . ." (Nunn: 24). • **ἑορτάζειν** → ἑορτάζω, *I keep/celebrate a feast/festival.* • **ἑορτήν** → ἡ ἑορτή, *feast, festival.* • **ἐξόδιον** → ἐξόδιος, ον, *belonging to an exit/departure, the exodus.* • **ζύμῃ** → ζύμη, *leaven.* • **παλαιᾷ** → παλαιός, ά, όν, *old.* • **κακίας** → ἡ κακία, *depravity, vice.* • **πονηρίας** → ἡ πονηρία, *wickedness, baseness.* • **ἀζύμοις** → ἄζυμος, ον, *unfermented;* subst., *unleavened bread.* • **εἰλικρινείας** → ἡ εἰλικρίνεια, *sincerity.* • **ἐπιφερομένους** → ἐπιφέρω, *I bring.* Acc. pl. in agreement w. ἡμᾶς. • **Αἰγυπτιακοῦ** → Αἰγυπτιακός, ή, όν, *of/for Egyptians, Egyptian.* • **ἀθέου** → ἄθεος, ον, *godless, ungodly.* • **φυράματος** → τὸ φύραμα, *dough.*

1.4 **χθές** — adv., *yesterday.* • **συνεσταυρούμην** → συσταυρόω, *I crucify with.* • **σήμερον** — adv., *today.* • **συνδοξάζομαι** → συνδοξάζω, *I glorify with.* Supply the dir. obj. *him* for this series of verbs. • **συνενεκρούμην** → συννεκρόω, *I put to death with.* • **συζωοποιοῦμαι** → συωοποιέω, *I make alive with.* • **συνεθαπτόμην**

Χρυσόν με ἴσως οἴεσθε λέγειν, ἢ ἄργυρον, ἢ ὑφάσματα, ἢ λίθους τῶν διαφανῶν καὶ τιμίων, γῆς ῥέουσαν ὕλην, καὶ κάτω μένουσαν, ἧς ἀεὶ τὸ πλεῖον ἔχουσιν οἱ κακοὶ καὶ δοῦλοι τῶν κάτω καὶ τοῦ κοσμοκράτορος. Καρποφορήσωμεν ἡμᾶς αὐτούς, τὸ τιμιώτατον Θεῷ κτῆμα καὶ οἰκειότατον· ἀποδῶμεν τῇ εἰκόνι τὸ κατ' εἰκόνα, γνωρίσωμεν ἡμῶν τὸ ἀξίωμα, τιμήσωμεν τὸ ἀρχέτυπον, γνῶμεν τοῦ μυστηρίου τὴν δύναμιν, καὶ ὑπὲρ τίνος Χριστὸς ἀπέθανε.

1.5 Γενώμεθα ὡς Χριστός, ἐπεὶ καὶ Χριστὸς ὡς ἡμεῖς· γενώμεθα θεοὶ δι' αὐτόν, ἐπειδὴ κἀκεῖνος δι' ἡμᾶς ἄνθρωπος. Προσέλαβε τὸ χεῖρον, ἵνα δῷ τὸ βέλτιον· ἐπτώχευσεν, ἵν' ἡμεῖς τῇ ἐκείνου πτωχείᾳ πλουτήσωμεν· δούλου μορφὴν ἔλαβεν, ἵνα τὴν ἐλευθερίαν ἡμεῖς ἀπολάβωμεν· κατῆλθεν, ἵν' ὑψωθῶμεν· ἐπειράσθη, ἵνα νικήσωμεν· ἠτιμάσθη, ἵνα δοξάσῃ· ἀπέθανεν,

---

→ συνθάπτω, *I bury with.* • **συνεγείρομαι** → συνεγείρω, *I raise/rise with.* • **καρποφορήσωμεν** → καρποφορέω, *I bear fruit; offer* (*PGL* 3: 704). • **παθόντι** — 2 aor. act. ptc. masc. dat. sg. → πάσχω, *I suffer.* • **ἀναστάντι** — aor. act. ptc. masc. dat. sg. → ἀνίστημι, *I rise, raise.* • **χρυσόν** → ὁ χρυσός, *gold.* • **με** — subj. of inf. • **ἴσως** — adv., *perhaps, probably.* • **οἴεσθε** → οἴομαι, *I think, suppose.* • **λέγειν** — inf. for indir. disc. w. οἴεσθε (Wal: 603; Smy: 2016). • **ἄργυρον** → τὸ ἀργύριον, *silver.* • **ὑφάσματα** → τὸ ὕφασμα, *woven robe.* • **λίθους** → ὁ λίθος, *a stone.* • **διαφανῶν** → διαφανής, ές, *transparent.* Attrib. gen. (Wal: 86; Smy: 1320). • **τιμίων** → τίμιος, α, ον, *costly.* Attrib. gen. (Wal: 86; Smy: 1320). • **γῆς** — attrib. gen. (Wal: 86; Smy: 1320). • **ῥέουσαν** → ῥέω, *I flow; perish.* • **ὕλην** → ἡ ὕλη, *wood; material, matter, stuff.* • **κάτω** — adv., *below.* • **ἀεί** — adv., *always.* • **πλεῖον** — here, as subst. (acc. dir. obj.), *the greater/larger part* (BDAG, πολύς, 2bβ: 849). • **οἱ κακοὶ καὶ δοῦλοι** — the sg. art. w. two substs. indicates the ref. is to one group (Wal: 270). • **κάτω** — adv., *below;* subst. *this world (below)* (BDAG 1: 535). • **κοσμοκράτορος** → ὁ κοσμοκράτωρ, *world-ruler.* The sg. suggests the ref. is to Satan (cf. John 12:31), not evil spirits in general (cf. Eph 6:12). • **τιμιώτατον** → τιμιώτατος, η, ον, *most precious.* • **κτῆμα** → τὸ κτῆμα, *possession.* • **οἰκειότατον** → οἰκειότατος, η, ον, *most fitting/proper.* • **ἀποδῶμεν** → ἀποδίδωμι, *I give back, render.* • **εἰκόνι** → ἡ εἰκών, *image.* • **γνωρίσωμεν** → γνωρίζω, *I make known, know; acknowledge* (*PGL* B3: 318). • **ἀξίωμα** → τὸ ἀξίωμα, *honor, dignity, value.* • **τιμήσωμεν** → τιμάω, *I honor.* • **ἀρχέτυπον** → τὸ ἀρχέτυπον, *archetype* (*PGL* 5c: 233). • **γνῶμεν** — aor. act. subjun. 1 pl. → γινώσκω. • **μυστηρίου** → τὸ μυστήριον, *mystery.* • **καί** — perhaps ascensive, *even.* • **ἀπέθανε** — 2 aor. act. indic. 3 sg. → ἀποθνήσκω.

1.5 **ἐπεί** — *since, because.* • **ἐπειδή** — *since, because.* • **δι'** — here, *for the sake of* (LSI BIII2: 184; BDAG B2a: 225). • **κἀκεῖνος** → καί and ἐκεῖνος. • **ἄνθρωπος** — Supply a verb from the context. • **προσέλαβε** → προσλαμβάνω, *I take, partake of.* • **χεῖρον** → χείρων, ον, *worse.* • **δῷ** — aor. act. subjun. → δίδωμι. • **βέλτιον** → βελτίων, ον, *better.* • **ἐπτώχευσεν** → πτωχεύω, *I am a beggar, am poor.* • **πτωχείᾳ** → ἡ πτωχεία, *poverty.* • **πλουτήσωμεν** → πλουτέω, *I am rich.* • **μορφήν** → ἡ μορφή, *a form.* • **ἐλευθερίαν** → ἡ ἐλευθερία, *freedom, liberty.* • **ἀπολάβωμεν** → ἀπολαμβάνω, *I receive.* • **κατῆλθεν** → κατέρχομαι, *I come down.* • **ὑψωθῶμεν** → ὑψόω, *I lift up, raise high.* • **ἐπειράσθη** → πειράζω, *I tempt.* • **νικήσωμεν** → νικάω, *I conquer.* • **ἠτιμάσθη** → ἀτιμάζω, *I dishonor, shame.*

ἵνα σώσῃ· ἀνῆλθεν, ἵν' ἑλκύσῃ πρὸς ἑαυτὸν κάτω κειμένους ἐν τῷ τῆς ἁμαρτίας πτώματι. Πάντα διδότω τις, πάντα καρποφορείτω τῷ δόντι ἑαυτὸν λυτρὸν ὑπὲρ ἡμῶν καὶ ἀντάλλαγμα· δώσει δὲ οὐδὲν τοιοῦτον οἷον ἑαυτὸν τοῦ μυστηρίου συνιέντα, καὶ δι' ἐκεῖνον πάντα ὅσα ἐκεῖνος δι' ἡμᾶς γενόμενον.

Oration 2.3 The Key Prerequisite for Pastors and Their Role in the Body of Christ

2.3 Ἐγὼ γὰρ ἔπαθον τοῦτο, ὦ ἄνδρες, οὔτε ὡς ἀπαίδευτος καὶ ἀσύνετος, ἀλλὰ μᾶλλον, ἵνα καὶ μικρόν τι καυχήσωμαι, οὔτε ὡς ὑπερόπτης τῶν θείων νόμων καὶ διατάξεων. Ὅτι καθάπερ ἐν σώματι τὸ μέν τι ἄρχον ἐστὶ καὶ οἷον προκαθεζόμενον, τὸ δὲ ἀρχόμενον καὶ ἀγόμενον· οὕτω κἀν ταῖς Ἐκκλησίαις διέταξεν ὁ Θεὸς ἰσότητος νόμῳ τῆς ἐχούσης τὸ κατ' ἀξίαν, ἣ καὶ προνοίας, ἣ τὰ πάντα συνέδησε, τοὺς μὲν ποιμαίνεσθαί τε καὶ

• **δοξάσῃ** → δοξάζω, *I praise, honor.* • **ἀπέθανεν** — 2 aor. act. indic. → ἀποθνήσκω, *I die.* • **ἀνῆλθεν** → ἀνέρχομαι, *I go up, come up, ascend.* • **ἑλκύσῃ** — aor. act. subjun. → ἕλκω, *I draw.* • **κάτω** — adv., *below.* • **κειμένους** → κεῖμαι, *I lie.* • **πτώματι** → τὸ πτῶμα, *a fall; a fallen body, a corpse.* • **καρποφορείτω** → καρποφορέω, *I bear fruit; offer* (*PGL* 3: 704). • **δόντι** — aor. act. ptc. → δίδωμι. W. double acc. of obj. and compl. (Wal: 182; Smy: 1613). • **λυτρόν** → τὸ λύτρον, *a ransom.* • **ἀντάλλαγμα** → τὸ ἀντάλλαγμα, *an exchange.* • **οἷον** → οἷος, α, ον, *such as, like.* οὐδὲν τοιοῦτον οἷον ἑαυτόν, "nothing of such a kind such as oneself." The expression οὐδὲν οἷον, "nothing like" (LSI, οἷος II5: 549), has been intensified by the addition of τοιοῦτον, *nothing like oneself.* • **μυστηρίου** → τὸ μυστήριον, *mystery.* • **συνιέντα** — pres. act. ptc. → συνίημι, *I understand.* In agreement w. ἑαυτόν; usually w. acc., but can take gen. for dir. obj., as here (LSJ II3: 1718). • **γενόμενον** — also in agreement w. ἑαυτόν, returning to the thought at the beginning of 1.5.

2.3 **ἔπαθον** — 2 aor. act. indic. 1 sg. → πάσχω, *I experience, suffer.* The verb ref. to being acted upon, usually in a neg. sense (BDAG: 785); but here, *I come to be in a certain state* (LSJ II: 1347). • **ὦ** — a "marker of personal address" (BDAG: 1100). • **ἀπαίδευτος** → ἀπαίδευτος, ον, *uneducated, uninstructed.* • **ἀσύνετος** → ἀσύνετος, ον, *lacking understanding, senseless, foolish.* • **ἀλλὰ μᾶλλον** — *but even more* (BDAG, μᾶλλον 1: 613); here w. οὔτε following, *but even less.* • **μικρόν** → μικρός, ά, όν, *little.* • **καυχήσωμαι** → καυχάομαι, *I boast, brag.* • **ὑπερόπτης** → ὁ ὑπερόπτης, *one who distains/is contemptuous of.* • **θείων** → θεῖος, α, ον, *divine.* • **διατάξεων** → ἡ διάταξις, *arrangement; regulation.* • **καθάπερ** — *just as.* • **ἄρχον** — pres. act. ptc. → ἄρχω. • **οἷον** → οἷος, α, ον, *of what sort;* here neut. as an adv., *so to speak, as it were* (LSJ V2d: 1209). • **προκαθεζόμενον** → προκαθέζομαι, *I preside* (LSJ: 1483). • **οὕτω** → οὕτως. • **κἀν** — crasis for καὶ ἐν. • **διέταξεν** → διατάσσω, *I appoint.* • **ἰσότητος** → ἡ ἰσότης, *equality.* • **ἐχούσης** → ἔχω, here, *I involve, imply, include* (LSI AI9: 341; BDAG 8: 422). • **ἀξίαν** → ἄξιος, α, ον, *worthy, fit.* τὸ κατ' ἀξίαν, "that which is according to worthiness,"

ἄρχεσθαι, ὅσοις τοῦτο λυσιτελέστερον, καὶ λόγῳ καὶ ἔργῳ πρὸς τὸ δέον ἰθυνομένους· τοὺς δὲ εἶναι ποιμένας καὶ διδασκάλους, πρὸς τὸν καταρτισμὸν τῆς Ἐκκλησίας, ὅσοι τῶν πολλῶν εἰσιν ἀνωτέρω κατ' ἀρετὴν καὶ τὴν πρὸς τὸν Θεὸν οἰκείωσιν, λόγον ψυχῆς πρὸς σῶμα, ἢ νοῦ πρὸς ψυχὴν ἐπέχοντας· ἵν' ἀμφότερα συντεθέντα ἀλλήλοις καὶ συγκραθέντα, τό τε ὑστεροῦν καὶ τὸ πλεονάζον, ὥσπερ ἐν μέλεσι, καὶ τῇ ἁρμονίᾳ τοῦ πνεύματος συμβιβασθέντα καὶ συνδεθέντα ἓν ἄρτιον ἀποδειχθῇ σῶμα, καὶ αὐτοῦ Χριστοῦ τῆς κεφαλῆς ἡμῶν ὄντως ἄξιον.

Oration 2.21–22 The Pastor as Physician of the Heart

2.21 Ταῦτά ἐστιν, οἷς ἐγὼ τὴν καθ' ἡμᾶς ἰατρικὴν τῆς περὶ τὰ σώματα ἐργωδεστέραν τίθεμαι μακρῷ, καὶ διὰ τοῦτο τιμιωτέραν· καὶ ὅτι ἐκείνη

---

here, *the idea of worthiness.* • **ἢ καί** — "In this combination ἤ separates two ideas objectively, in point of fact, while καί denotes that, subjectively, both must be kept before the mind. Render often 'or again': but sometimes καί means 'also,' or marks a climax, 'even'" (Denn: 306). • **προνοίας** → ἡ πρόνοια, *providence.* • **συνέδησε** → συνδέω, *I bind together.* • **τοὺς μέν . . . τοὺς δέ** — *some . . . and others* (BDAG 1c: 630). • **ποιμαίνεσθαί** → ποιμαίνω, *I tend, shepherd.* • **ὅσοις** — dat. of advantage (Wal: 142; Smy: 1481). • **λυσιτελέστερον** → λυσιτελέστερος, α, ον, *more profitable/advantageous,* comparative of λυσιτελής, ές. Pred. compl. • **δέον** — pres. act. ptc. neut. acc. sg. → δέω. τὸ δέον, *that which is binding, proper, right.* • **ἰθυνομένους** → ἰθύνω, *I guide.* • **ποιμένας** → ὁ ποιμήν, *a shepherd.* • **καταρτισμόν** → ὁ καταρτισμός, *equipping.* • **πολλῶν** → πολύς, τῶν πολλῶν, *the majority* (LSJ II3: 658; BDAG 1bβℵ: 848). • **ἀνωτέρω** → ἀνώτερος, α, ον, *higher, above.* • **ἀρετήν** → ἡ ἀρετή, *goodness, virtue.* • **οἰκείωσιν** → ἡ οἰκείωσις, *appropriation; friendship, fellowship* (*PGL* 6c: 938). • **λόγον** — here, *relation, correspondence* (LSJ II: 1057). • **νοῦ** — gen. sg. → ὁ νοῦς, *mind, intellect.* • **ἐπέχοντας** → ἐπέχω, *I hold, occupy.* • **ἀμφότερα** → ἀμφότερος, α, ον, *both.* • **συντεθέντα** → συντίθημι, *I put together.* • **συγκραθέντα** → συγκεράννυμι, *I mix together, blend together.* • **ὑστεροῦν** → ὑστερέω, *I lack.* • **πλεονάζον** → πλεονάζω, *I am/have more than enough.* • **ὥσπερ** — adv., *just as.* • **μέλεσι** → τὸ μέλος, *member, limb.* • **ἁρμονίᾳ** → ἡ ἁρμονία, *harmony.* • **συμβιβασθέντα** → συμβιβάζω, *I bring together;* pass., *am joined/knit together.* • **συνδεθέντα** → συνδέω, *I bind together.* • **ἄρτιον** → ἄρτιος, α, ον, *complete, perfect.* • **ἀποδειχθῇ** — aor. pass. subjun. 3 sg. → ἀποδείκνυμι, *I make, produce.* • **ὄντως** — adv., *really, in reality.*

2.21 **οἷς** — dat. of cause (Wal: 167; Smy: 1517). ταῦτα ἐστιν, οἷς, "it is these things because of which," *for these reasons.* • **καθ'** — here used for a poss. w. a limiting force, "ours" in contrast to that of others (BDAG B7b: 513). καθ' ἡμᾶς, *our.* • **ἰατρικήν** → ἰατρικός, ή, όν, *pertaining to a physician,* fem. because of implied τέχνη (*craft, art, skill*), *the practice of medicine.* • **ἐργωδεστέραν** → ἐργωδέστερος, α, ον, *more difficult.* W. gen. of comparison (Wal: 110; Smy: 1069). • **τίθεμαι** — here mid., *I regard.* W. double acc. of obj. and compl. (Wal: 182; Smy: 1613). • **μακρῷ** → μακρός, ά, όν, *far.* Dat. used to strengthen a comparative (LSJ I5: 485), *by far.*

μὲν, ὀλίγα τῶν ἐν τῷ βάθει κατοπτευούσῃ, περὶ τὸ φαινόμενον ἡ πλείων τῆς πραγματείας· ἡμῖν δὲ περὶ τὸν κρυπτὸν τῆς καρδίας ἄνθρωπον ἡ πᾶσα θεραπεία τε καὶ σπουδή, καὶ πρὸς τὸν ἔνδοθεν ἡμῖν ἀντιπολεμοῦντα καὶ ἀντιπαλαίοντα ἡ μάχη, ὃς ἡμῖν αὐτοῖς ὅπλοις καθ' ἡμῶν χρώμενος, τὸ δεινότατον, τῷ τῆς ἁμαρτίας θανάτῳ δίδωσι. Πρὸς οὖν ταῦτα πολλῆς μὲν καὶ παντελοῦς τῆς πίστεως, μείζονος δὲ τῆς παρὰ Θεοῦ συνεργίας, οὐκ ὀλίγης δὲ τῆς ἡμετέρας ἀντιτεχνήσεως (ὥς γε ἐμαυτὸν πείθω), χρεία, τῆς καὶ λόγῳ καὶ ἔργῳ θεωρουμένης, εἰ δεῖ καλῶς ἡμῖν θεραπεύεσθαι καὶ ἀποκαθαίρεσθαι, καὶ ὡς πλείστου ἀξίας εἶναι, τὸ τιμιώτατον ὧν ἔχομεν, τὰς ψυχάς.

2.22 Τά γε μὴν ἀμφοτέρων τῶν θεραπειῶν τέλη, τοῦτο γὰρ ἡμῖν εἰς τὴν ἐξέτασιν ἔτι λείπεται, τῇ μὲν ὑγίειαν, ἢ εὐεξίαν σαρκός, ἢ οὖσαν φυλάξαι,

---

• **τιμιωτέραν** → τιμιώτερος, α, ον, *of more value/respect/honor.* • **ἐκείνῃ** — dat. of ref. (Wal: 144; Smy: 1496). • **μέν** — signals the comparison between the two forms of medicine, picked up by δέ below. • **ὀλίγα** → ὀλίγος, η, ον, *few.* Dir. obj. of κατοπτευούσῃ. • **τῶν ἐν τῷ βάθει** — partitive gen. (Wal: 84; Smy: 1306). • **βάθει** → τὸ βάθος, *depth.* • **κατοπτευούσῃ** → κατοπτεύω, *I investigate.* Attrib. ptc., mod. ἐκείνῃ. • **περί** — pred. compl. of an elided verb. • **φαινόμενον** → φαίνω, *I appear, am seen.* • **πραγματείας** → ἡ πραγματεία, *act, deed, activity; undertaking, task, occupation.* • **ἡμῖν** — dat. of ref. • **δέ** — picks up the comparison signaled by μέν above. • **περί** — pred. compl. of an elided verb. • **κρυπτόν** → κρυπτός, ή, όν, *hidden.* • **θεραπεία** → ἡ θεραπεία, *medical treatment.* • **σπουδή** → ἡ σπουδή, *zeal, exertion, effort.* • **πρός** — here, *against* (LSI CI4: 684; BDAG 3d: 874). • **ἔνδοθεν** — adv., *within.* • **ἡμῖν** — dir. obj. of both ptcs. • **ἀντιπολεμοῦντα** → ἀντιπολεμέω, *I war against,* w. dat. • **ἀντιπαλαίοντα** → ἀντιπαλαίω, *I wrestle against,* w. dat. • **μάχη** → ἡ μάχη, *fight, battle.* • **ἡμῖν** — dir. obj. of χρώμενος. • **ὅπλοις** → τὸ ὅπλον, *weapon.* Pred. nom., *as weapons* (Smy: 910, 1509). • **χρώμενος** → χράομαι, *I use.* W. double dat., *use* x *as* y (BDAG 1a: 1088, near the end of the art.). • **δεινότατον** → δεινότατος, η, ον, *most terrible, horrible, fearful,* superlative of δεινός. • **δίδωσι** — here the dir. obj. must be supplied, "us." • **πολλῆς** — the start of a long string of gen. mod. χρεία, several lines ahead. • **παντελοῦς** → παντελής, ές, *complete, absolute.* • **μείζονος** → μείζων, ον, *greater.* • **συνεργίας** → ἡ συνεργία, *cooperation; assistance, help* (*PGL* 2: 1323). • **ὀλίγης** → ὀλίγος, η, ον, *few, little.* • **ἡμετέρας** → ἡμέτερος, α, ον, *our.* Subj. gen. (Wal: 113; Smy: 1328). • **ἀντιτεχνήσεως** → ἡ ἀντιτέχνησις, *counter-maneuvering.* • **γε** — enclitic particle, *at least, indeed.* • **ἐμαυτόν** → ἐμαυτοῦ, *myself.* • **χρεία** → ἡ χρεία, *need.* • **θεωρουμένης** → θεωρέω, *I observe, perceive, notice.* Attrib. ptc., mod. ἀντιτεχνήσεως. • **εἰ** — here, *since* (BDAG 3: 278), though cf. Wal: 690. • **δεῖ** — here w. dat (ἡμῖν) and inf. (LSI I1: 175). • **καλῶς** — adv., *well, rightly, deservedly.* • **θεραπεύεσθαι** → θεραπεύω, *I heal.* • **ἀποκαθαίρεσθαι** → ἀποκαθαίρω, *I cleanse,* w. δεῖ. • **ὡς** — used w. a superlative for, *as . . . as possible* (Smy: 1086). • **πλείστου** → πλεῖστος, η, ον, *most.* Here used as the superlative w. ὡς. • **ἀξίας** → ἄξιος, α, ον, *worthy.* • **εἶναι** — w. δεῖ. • **τιμιώτατον** → τιμιώτατος, η, ον, *most valuable, most honorable.* Acc. of respect (Wal: 203; Smy: 1600).

2.22 **γε μήν** — This combination of particles often has the same use as ἀλλὰ μήν, which often moves the argument forward by introducing a new stage in the line of

ἢ ἀπελθοῦσαν ἀνακαλέσασθαι, ὧν οὔπω δῆλον, εἴ τι συνοίσει τοῖς κεκτημένοις· ἐπεὶ καὶ τὰ ἐναντία πολλάκις πλείω τοὺς ἔχοντας ὤνησεν, ὥσπερ πενίαι τε καὶ πλοῦτοι, δόξαι τε καὶ ἀδοξίαι, ταπεινότητες καὶ λαμπρότητες, καὶ ὅσα ἐν μέσῳ κείμενα κατὰ τὴν φύσιν, καὶ οὐδὲν μᾶλλον τῇδε ἢ τῇδε νεύοντα, τῇ χρήσει καὶ τῇ προαιρέσει τῶν κεκτημένων τὸ βέλτιον ἢ τὸ χεῖρον λαμβάνει· τῇ δὲ τὸ προκείμενον πτερῶσαι ψυχήν, ἁρπάσαι κόσμου, καὶ δοῦναι Θεῷ, καὶ τὸ κατ' εἰκόνα ἢ μένον τηρῆσαι, ἢ κινδυνεῦον

---

thought, *turning now to.* Cf. Denn: 344, 347. • **ἀμφοτέρων** → ἀμφότερος, α, ον, *both.* • **θεραπειῶν** → ἡ θεραπεία, *medical treatment.* • **τέλη** → τὸ τέλος, *goal, end.* • **ἐξέτασιν** → ἡ ἐξέτασις, *close examination.* • **λείπεται** → λείπω, *I leave;* pass., *am left, remain.* • **τῇ μέν** — dat. of ref., fem. due to the subject under discussion, θεραπεία. The two types of treatment are contrasted, first that of the flesh, and then that of the soul (see τῇ δέ later in the passage), *regarding the one form of treatment.* • **ὑγίειαν** → ἡ ὑγίεια, *health.* Dir. obj. of φυλάξαι. • **εὐεξίαν** → ἡ εὐεξία, *good condition.* ἢ indicates this is an alternate expression for ὑγίειαν. • **ἢ οὖσαν** — This ἢ goes w. the one following: "either . . . or." The ptc. is a conditional circ., "if it exists," and ref. to the comp. expression, "health or good condition of the flesh." • **φυλάξαι** — aor. act. inf. → φυλάσσω, *I guard, maintain.* The inf. states the goal of the first form of treatment. • **ἀπελθοῦσαν** — 2 aor. act. ptc. fem. acc. sg. → ἀπέρχομαι, *I depart.* Conditional circ. ptc. • **ἀνακαλέσασθαι** → ἀνακαλέω, *I summon;* mid., *call back, recall.* • **ὧν** — gen. of ref., *concerning which* (Wal: 127). • **οὔπω** — adv., *not yet; not at all.* • **δῆλον** → δηλόω, *I reveal, make clear.* The ptc. is used for, "it is clear." • **συνοίσει** — fut. act. indic. 3 sg. → συμφέρω, *I benefit,* w. dat. • **κεκτημένοις** — pf. pass. ptc. → κτάομαι, *I acquire;* pf., *possess.* • **ἐπεί** — *since.* • **ἐναντία** → ἐναντίος, α, ον, *opposite.* Here a ref. to ill health. • **πολλάκις** — adv., *often.* • **πλείω** — neut. acc. sg. → πλείων, an alternate form to πλείονα. Here as an adv. • **ὤνησεν** — aor. act. indic. 3 sg. → ὀνίνημι, *I profit, benefit.* • **ὥσπερ** — adv., *just as.* • **πενίαι** → ἡ πενία, *poverty.* The beginning of a long complex subj. w. λαμβάνει. • **πλοῦτοι** → ὁ πλοῦτος, *wealth.* • **δόξαι** → δόξα, here, *reputation, renown, honor.* The pl. may suggest experiences of these conditions. • **ἀδοξίαι** → ἡ ἀδοξία, *disgrace, obscurity.* • **ταπεινότητες** → ἡ ταπεινότης, *lowness, low estate, abasement.* • **λαμπρότητες** → ἡ λαμπρότης, *brilliancy, splendor, distinction.* • **μέσῳ** → μέσος, η, ον, *middle.* • **κείμενα** → κεῖμαι, *I lie, am situated.* • **φύσιν** → ἡ φύσις, *nature.* • **οὐδέν** → οὐδείς. Here the neut. acc. sg. is an adv., *not at all* (LSJ III: 1269). • **τῇδε** → ὅδε, ἥδε, τόδε, *this.* The fem. dat. sg. is used as an adv. of place and manner (LSJ IV1: 1198), *to this side than to that.* • **νεύοντα** → νεύω, *I bow, incline.* Attend. circ. • **χρήσει** → ἡ χρῆσις, *a use.* • **προαιρέσει** → ἡ προαίρεσις, *free choice, deliberate choice* (*PGL*: 1133–34). • **κεκτημένων** — here, *possess* in the sense of *experience* since poverty and wealth, etc., are in view. • **βέλτιον** → βελτίων, ον, *better.* Dir. obj. of λαμβάνει. • **χεῖρον** → χείρων, ον, *worse.* Dir. obj. of λαμβάνει. • **λαμβάνει** — here perhaps w. a noun as a periphrasis for a pass. (BDAG 10c: 584), τὸ βέλτιον ἢ τὸ χεῖρον λαμβάνει, *be improved or worsened.* The verb is sg. perhaps because the last item in the complex subj. is a neut. pl., though a complex subj. often takes a sg. verb (Wal: 401; Smy: 968). • **τῇ δέ** — picks up the τῇ μέν earlier in the section. • **προκείμενον** → πρόκειμαι, *I set before.* • **πτερῶσαι** → πτερόω, *I furnish with wings.* The inf. states the goal of the second form of treatment. • **ἁρπάσαι** — aor. act. inf. → ἁρπάζω, *I snatch away.* Supply the dir. obj.,

χειραγωγῆσαι, ἢ διαρρυὲν ἀνασώσασθαι, εἰσοικίσαι τε τὸν Χριστὸν ἐν ταῖς καρδίαις διὰ τοῦ Πνεύματος· καὶ τὸ κεφάλαιον, Θεὸν ποιῆσαι, καὶ τῆς ἄνω μακαριότητος, τὸν τῆς ἄνω συντάξεως.

Oration 2.35–36 The Pastor as Distributor of the Word

2.35 Αὐτὴν δὲ τὴν τοῦ λόγου διανομήν, ἵνα τελευταῖον εἴπω τὸ πρῶτον τῶν ἡμετέρων, τοῦ θείου λέγω καὶ ὑψηλοῦ, καὶ ὃν νῦν πάντες φιλοσοφοῦσιν, εἰ μέν τις ἄλλος θαρρεῖ, καὶ πάσης διανοίας ὑπολαμβάνει, θαυμάζω τοῦτον ἐγὼ τῆς συνέσεως, ἵνα μὴ λέγω τῆς εὐηθείας· ἐμοὶ δ' οὖν πρᾶγμα φαίνεται οὐ τῶν φαυλοτάτων, οὐδὲ ὀλίγου τοῦ πνεύματος, διδόναι κατὰ καιρὸν

"soul." • **κόσμου** — gen. of separation (Wal: 107; Smy: 1392). • **δοῦναι** — aor. act. inf. → δίδωμι. Supply the dir. obj., "soul." • **εἰκόνα** → ἡ εἰκών, *image.* • **ἢ** — beginning a series of alternatives. • **μένον** — pres. act. ptc. neut. acc. sg. → μένω. Conditional ptc. • **τηρῆσαι** → τηρέω, *I watch over, protect.* • **κινδυνεῦον** → κινδυνεύω, *I am in danger.* Conditional ptc. • **χειραγωγῆσαι** → χειραγωγέω, *I lead by the hand.* • **διαρρυέν** — aor. pass. ptc. neut. acc. sg. → διαρρέω, *I flow through; fall away like water, waste away.* Conditional ptc. • **ἀνασώσασθαι** → ἀνασῴζω, *I recover, restore* (*PGL:* 125). • **εἰσοικίσαι** → εἰσοικίζω, *I bring in as a dweller, inhabit* (*PGL:* 423–24). • **κεφάλαιον** → κεφάλαιος, α, ον, *of the head; chief/main point, the sum of the matter.* • **ποιῆσαι** — here w. double acc. of obj. and compl. (Wal: 182; Smy: 1613). • **ἄνω** — adv., *up, above, in heaven.* • **μακαριότητος** → ἡ μακαριότης, *happiness, bliss.* • **συντάξεως** → ἡ σύνταξις, *an order; company.*

2.35 **αὐτήν** — intensifies διανομήν by way of announcing the next topic, as the first part of the following ἵνα clause indicates, "Now regarding . . ." • **τοῦ λόγου** — ref. to the Scriptures or to the teaching in general. • **διανομήν** → ἡ διανομή, *distribution.* • **τελευταῖον** → τελευταῖος, α, ον, *at the end, last,* neut. acc. for adv. • **ἡμετέρων** → ἡμέτερος, α, ον, *our.* Supply something like, "of our responsibilities." • **θείου** → θεῖος, α, ον, *in honor of God, sacred, holy.* • **ὑψηλοῦ** → ὑψηλός, ή, όν, *high, lofty.* • **φιλοσοφοῦσιν** → φιλοσοφέω, *I discuss philosophically; treat/investigate philosophically; investigate, study.* • **μέν** — the view of these people will be contrasted soon with that of Gregory, ἐμοὶ δ' οὖν. • **θαρρεῖ** → θαρρέω, *I am of good courage, am confident; am overly confident,* a form of θαρσέω. • **διανοίας** → ἡ διανοία, *thought, mind, understanding.* • **ὑπολαμβάνει** → ὑπολαμβάνω, *I assume, suppose; take up, understand,* often of an "ill-grounded opinion" (LSJ III: 1886). πάσης διανοίας ὑπολαμβάνει could mean, "understands (the meaning) of every thought (in Scripture)," but the context supports the translation of Browne and Swallow in *NPNF*[2], "supposes it within the power of every man's intellect." • **θαυμάζω** → θαυμάζω, *I am amazed.* • **συνέσεως** → ἡ σύνεσις, *understanding, intelligence.* • **εὐηθείας** → ἡ εὐήθεια, *simplicity, honesty; silliness, folly.* • **πρᾶγμα** → τὸ πρᾶγμα, *deed, act; thing, matter.* • **φαίνεται** → φαίνω, *I make appear;* mid., *make known, reveal;* pass., *appear, am seen.* • **φαυλοτάτων** → φαυλότατος, η, ον, *easiest.* οὐ τῶν φαυλοτάτων, "not among the easiest." Partitive gen. (Wal: 84; Smy: 1306). • **ὀλίγου** → ὁ ὀλίγος, *little.* ὀλίγου

ἑκάστῳ τοῦ λόγου τὸ σιτομέτριον, καὶ οἰκονομεῖν ἐν κρίσει τὴν ἀλήθειαν τῶν ἡμετέρων δογμάτων· ὅσα περὶ κόσμων ἢ κόσμου πεφιλοσόφηται, περὶ ὕλης, περὶ ψυχῆς, περὶ νοῦ, καὶ τῶν νοερῶν φύσεων, βελτιόνων τε καὶ χειρόνων, περὶ τῆς τὰ πάντα συνδεούσης τε καὶ διεξαγούσης προνοίας, ὅσα τε κατὰ λόγον ἀπαντᾶν δοκεῖ, καὶ ὅσα παρὰ λόγον τὸν κάτω καὶ τὸν ἀνθρώπινον.

2.36 Ἔτι τε ὅσα περὶ τῆς πρώτης ἡμῶν συστάσεως, καὶ τῆς τελευταίας ἀναπλάσεως, τύπων τε καὶ ἀληθείας, καὶ διαθηκῶν, καὶ Χριστοῦ παρουσίας πρώτης τε καὶ δευτέρας, σαρκώσεώς τε καὶ παθημάτων, καὶ ἀναλύσεως, ὅσα τε περὶ ἀναστάσεως, περὶ τέλους, περὶ κρίσεως καὶ ἀνταποδόσεως, σκυθρωποτέρας τε καὶ ἐνδοξοτέρας· καὶ τὸ κεφάλαιον ὅσα περὶ τῆς ἀρχικῆς καὶ μακαρίας Τριάδος ὑποληπτέον· ὅσπερ δὴ καὶ κινδύνων μέγιστος τοῖς φωτίζειν πεπιστευμένοις, ὡς μήτε εἰς μίαν ὑπόστασιν συναιρεθέντα τὸν

τοῦ πνεύματος, "(requiring) little of the Spirit/spirit." • **διδόναι** — in appos. to πρᾶγμα, describing the matter Gregory is talking about, "namely, to give." • **σιτομέτριον** → τὸ σιτομέτριον, *measured portion.* • **οἰκονομεῖν** → οἰκονομέω, *I manage, regulate.* • **κρίσει** → ἡ κρίσις, *judgment.* • **δογμάτων** → τὸ δόγμα, *opinion; fixed belief, tenet.* • **ὅσα . . . πεφιλοσόφηται** — "all that has been investigated philosophically." Gregory now begins to list some of the topics to be taught. • **ὕλης** → ἡ ὕλη, *matter, stuff.* • **νοῦ** — fem. gen. sg. → ἡ νοῦς, *mind, intellect.* • **νοερῶν** → νοερός, ά, όν, *intellectual, rational; spiritual* (*PGL*: 915–16). • **φύσεων** → ἡ φύσις, *nature.* • **βελτιόνων** → βελτίων, ον, *better.* • **χειρόνων** → χείρων, ον, *worse.* • **συνδεούσης** → συνδέω, *I hold together.* • **διεξαγούσης** → διεξάγω, *I order, arrange.* • **προνοίας** → ἡ πρόνοια, *providence.* • **κατὰ λόγον**, "according to thought/reason" (LSI, λόγος B1: 477). • **ἀπαντᾶν** → ἀπαντάω, *I meet, encounter; happen.* • **δοκεῖ** → δοκέω, *I seem.* • **παρά** — here, *against* (LSI C4c: 593; BDAG C6 p. 758). • **κάτω** — *down, beneath, below.* • **ἀνθρώπινον** → ἀνθρώπινος, η, ον, *human.*

2.36 **ἔτι** — here, *furthermore, moreover* (LSI II1: 321; BDAG 2b: 400). • **συστάσεως** → ἡ σύστασις, *construction, structure, constitution.* • **τελευταίας** → τελευταῖος, α, ον, *last.* • **ἀναπλάσεως** → ἡ ἀνάπλασις, *remaking, renewal.* • **τύπων** → ὁ τύπος, *type.* • **διαθηκῶν** → ἡ διαθήκη, *testament, covenant.* • **παρουσίας** → ἡ παρουσία, *arrival, coming; presence.* • **δευτέρας** → δεύτερος, α, ον, *second.* • **σαρκώσεως** → ἡ σάρκωσις, *incarnation.* • **παθημάτων** → τὸ πάθημα, *suffering.* • **ἀναλύσεως** → ἡ ἀνάλυσις, *dissolving, dissolution; departure.* • **ἀναστάσεως** → ἡ ἀνάστασις, *resurrection.* • **τέλους** → τὸ τέλος, *end.* • **κρίσεως** → ἡ κρίσις, *judgment.* • **ἀνταποδόσεως** → ἡ ἀνταπόδοσις, *requital, retribution.* • **σκυθρωποτέρας** → σκυθρωπότερος, α, ον, *more gloomy/sad.* • **ἐνδοξοτέρας** → ἐνδοξότερος, α, ον, *more glorious/wonderful.* • **κεφάλαιον** → τὸ κεφάλαιον, *head, chief/main point/topic.* • **ἀρχικῆς** → ἀρχικός, ή, όν, *royal, sovereign, supreme; primal, original.* • **μακαρίας** → μακάριος, α, ον, *blessed.* • **Τριάδος** → ἡ Τριάς, *the Trinity.* • **ὑποληπτέον** — verbal adj. → ὑπολαμβάνω, *I must suppose/understand/regard.* καὶ τὸ κεφάλαιον ὅσα . . . ὑποληπτέον, "and the chief (topic), all that which . . . one must understand." • **ὅσπερ** → ὅσπερ, ἥπερ, ὅπερ, *the very one/thing who/which.* • **δή** — particle, *indeed, surely, really.* • **κινδύνων**

λόγον δέει πολυθεΐας, ψιλὰ καταλιπεῖν ἡμῖν τὰ ὀνόματα, τὸν αὐτὸν Πατέρα καὶ Υἱὸν καὶ ἅγιον Πνεῦμα ὑπολαμβάνουσι· μήτε εἰς τρεῖς, ἢ ἐκφύλους καὶ ἀλλοτρίας διαιρεθέντα, ἢ ἀτάκτους καὶ ἀνάρχους, καὶ οἷον εἰπεῖν, ἀντιθέους, πρὸς κακὸν ἴσον ἐκ τῶν ἐναντίων μεταπεσεῖν· ὥσπερ φυτοῦ διαστροφῆς ἐπὶ θάτερα πολὺ μετακλινομένης.

Oration 29.20 The Mystery of the Incarnation: A Scriptural Tapestry of Jesus as Man and God

29.20 Ἐβαπτίσθη μὲν ὡς ἄνθρωπος, ἀλλ' ἁμαρτίας ἔλυσεν ὡς θεός· οὐ καθαρσίων αὐτὸς δεόμενος, ἀλλ' ἵνα ἁγιάσῃ τὰ ὕδατα. ἐπειράσθη ὡς ἄνθρωπος, ἀλλ' ἐνίκησεν ὡς θεός· ἀλλὰ θαρρεῖν διακελεύεται, ὡς κόσμον νενικηκώς. ἐπείνησεν, ἀλλ' ἔθρεψε χιλιάδας, ἀλλ' ἄρτος ἐστὶ ζωτικὸς καὶ

→ ὁ κίνδυνος, *danger, risk, hazard.* • **μέγιστος** → μέγιστος, η, ον, *greatest.* • **φωτίζειν** → φωτίζω, *I illuminate, enlighten.* • **ὡς** — w. inf. for a result clause (LSJ BIII: 908; BDAG 4: 1105; Smy: 3000), *so that.* • **μήτε** — *and not.* μήτε . . . μήτε, *neither . . . nor.* • **ὑπόστασιν** → ἡ ὑπόστασις, *substance, Person (of the Trinity)* (*PGL* B: 1456). • **συναιρεθέντα** → συναιρέω, *I bring together, contract, reduce.* • **λόγον** — here, *teaching* (LSJ AVII: 477; BDAG 1aβ: 599). • **δέει** → τὸ δέος, *fear.* • **πολυθεΐας** → ἡ πολυθεΐα, *polytheism.* • **ψιλά** → ψιλός, ή, όν, *bare.* • **καταλιπεῖν** → καταλείπω, *I leave.* W. ὡς for a result clause. • **τὸν αὐτόν** — pred. compl. • **ὑπολαμβάνουσι** — pres. act. ptc. masc. dat. pl. → ὑπολαμβάνω, *I assume, suppose; take up; understand,* often of an "ill-grounded opinion" (LSJ III: 1886). Circ. ptc. for result (Wal: 637), mod. ἡμῖν, w. double acc. of obj. and compl. (Wal: 182; Smy: 1613). • **ἐκφύλους** → ἔκφυλος, ον, *alien, strange.* • **ἀλλοτρίας** → ἀλλότριος, α, ον, *foreign, strange.* • **διαιρεθέντα** → διαιρέω, *I divide.* • **ἀτάκτους** → ἄτακτος, ον, *disorderly.* • **ἀνάρχους** → ἄναρχος, ον, *without head/chief, anarchical.* • **οἷον** → οἷος, α, ον, *such as.* W. inf. to express fitness or ability (LSJ III: 549). οἷον εἰπεῖν, *one could say.* • **ἀντιθέους** → ὁ ἀντίθεος, *rival god.* • **ἴσον** → ἴσος, η, ον, *equal.* • **ἐναντίων** → ἐναντίος, α, ον, *opposite.* • **μεταπεσεῖν** → μεταπίπτω, *I fall (differently), change.* • **ὥσπερ** — *just as, as, as indeed, like.* • **φυτοῦ** → τὸ φυτόν, *plant, tree.* Subj. of gen. abs. • **διαστροφῆς** → ἡ διαστροφή, *distortion.* • **θάτερα** → θάτερος, α, ον, *other, different,* a form of ἕτερος, α, ον. ἐπὶ θάτερα, "to the one/other side" (LSJ, ἕτερος IV2a: 702). • **πολύ** — neut. for adv., *much, very, greatly.* • **μετακλινομένης** → μετακλίνω, *I shift to the other side, bend back.* Gen. abs. • ὥσπερ φυτοῦ διαστροφῆς ἐπὶ θάτερα πολὺ μετακλινομένης, *like a distorted plant/tree being bent far over to one side.*

29.20 **ἔλυσεν** → λύω, *I loosen, release; put an end to, destroy.* • **καθαρσίων** → καθάρσιος, ον, *cleansing;* subst., *purifying sacrifice/rite.* • **δεόμενος** → δέω, *I am in need of.* • **ἁγιάσῃ** → ἁγιάζω, *I sanctify.* • **ἐπειράσθη** → πειράζω, *I tempt.* • **ἐνίκησεν** → νικάω, *I conquer.* • **ἀλλά** — The second ἀλλά (which occurs several times in this chapter) is "rhetorically ascensive" (BDAG 4b: 45), extending the contrast further, *(not only this) but . . . even/also.* • **θαρρεῖν** → θαρρέω, *I am - confident/courageous.* • **διακελεύεται** → διακελεύομαι, *I exhort, encourage.* • **ὡς** — *since* (LSJ BIV: 908). • **ἐπείνησεν** → πεινάω, *I am hungry.* • **ἔθρεψε** — aor.

οὐράνιος. ἐδίψησεν, ἀλλ' ἐβόησεν· Ἐάν τις διψᾷ, ἐρχέσθω πρός με, καὶ πινέτω· ἀλλὰ καὶ πηγάζειν ὑπέσχετο τοὺς πιστεύοντας. ἐκοπίασεν, ἀλλὰ τῶν κοπιώντων καὶ πεφορτισμένων ἐστὶν ἀνάπαυσις. ἐβαρήθη μὲν ὕπνῳ, ἀλλ' ἐπὶ πελάγους κουφίζεται, ἀλλ' ἐπιτιμᾷ πνεύμασιν, ἀλλὰ Πέτρον κουφίζει βαπτιζόμενον. δίδωσι τέλος, ἀλλ' ἐξ ἰχθύος, ἀλλὰ βασιλεύει τῶν ἀπαιτούντων. Σαμαρείτης ἀκούει καὶ δαιμονῶν, πλὴν σώζει τὸν ἀπὸ Ἰερουσαλὴμ καταβαίνοντα καὶ λῃσταῖς περιπεσόντα, πλὴν ὑπὸ δαιμόνων ἐπιγινώσκεται, καὶ ἀπελαύνει δαίμονας, καὶ λεγεῶνα πνευμάτων βυθίζει, καὶ ὡς ἀστραπὴν ὁρᾷ πίπτοντα τὸν ἀρχηγὸν τῶν δαιμόνων. λιθάζεται, ἀλλ' οὐχ ἁλίσκεται. προσεύχεται, ἀλλ' ἐπακούει. δακρύει, ἀλλὰ παύει δάκρυον. ἐρωτᾷ ποῦ Λάζαρος, ἄνθρωπος γὰρ ἦν· ἀλλ' ἐγείρει Λάζαρον, θεὸς γὰρ ἦν. πωλεῖται, καὶ λίαν εὐώνως, τριάκοντα γὰρ ἀργυρίων, ἀλλ' ἐξαγοράζει κόσμον, καὶ μεγάλης τιμῆς, τοῦ ἰδίου γὰρ αἵματος. ὡς πρόβατον

act. indic. → τρέφω, *I feed.* • **χιλιάδας** → ἡ χιλιάς, *thousand.* • **ζωτικός** → ζωτικός, ή, όν, *living; life-giving* (*PGL*: 599). • **οὐράνιος** → οὐράνιος, α, ον, *heavenly, of/from heaven.* • **ἐδίψησεν** → διψάω, *I thirst.* • **ἐβόησεν** → βοάω, *I cry out, shout.* • **πηγάζειν** → πηγάζω, *I spring/gush forth.* Inf. for indir. disc., the content of what he promised (Wal: 603; Smy: 2016). • **ὑπέσχετο** — aor. mid. indic. → ὑπέχω, *I maintain;* mid., *promise.* Cf. LSJ: 1871 (at the end of the article) and p. 1873 on ὑπισχνέομαι. • **τοὺς πιστεύοντας** — subj. of inf. • **ἐκοπίασεν** → κοπιάω, *I am tired, grow weary.* • **πεφορτισμένων** → φορτίζω, *I load;* pass., *am heavy laden.* • **ἀνάπαυσις** → ἡ ἀνάπαυσις, *a rest.* • **ἐβαρήθη** → βαρέω, *I weigh down, am heavy.* • **ὕπνῳ** → ὁ ὕπνος, *a sleep.* • **πελάγους** → τὸ πέλαγος, *sea.* • **κουφίζεται** → κουφίζω, *I am light; make light;* pass., *am lifted up, soar.* • **ἐπιτιμᾷ** → ἐπιτιμάω, *I rebuke.* • **πνεύμασιν** → τὸ πνεῦμα — here, *wind.* • **βαπτιζόμενον** → βαπτίζω — here, *I sink.* • **τέλος** → τὸ τέλος, *an end; tax.* δίδωσι τέλος, *he pays tax.* • **ἰχθύος** → ὁ ἰχθῦς, *a fish.* • **βασιλεύει** → βασιλεύω, *I am king; rule.* • **ἀπαιτούντων** → ἀπαιτέω, *I demand.* • **Σαμαρείτης** → ὁ Σαμαρείτης (listed in BDAG under the alternate form Σαμαρίτης), *Samaritan.* • **ἀκούει** → ἀκούω, here w. a pass. sense, *I hear myself called* (LSI V: 29; LSJ III: 54). • **δαιμονῶν** → ὁ δαίμων, *demon.* Gen., "of demons," i.e., *one possessed by demons.* • **πλήν** — *but.* • **καταβαίνοντα** → καταβαίνω, *I go down.* • **λῃσταῖς** → ὁ λῃστής, *robber.* • **περιπεσόντα** → περιπίπτω, *I fall among.* • **πλήν** — Now πλήν is repeated instead of ἀλλά w. the same effect. • **ἐπιγινώσκεται** → ἐπιγινώσκω, *I know; recognize.* • **ἀπελαύνει** → ἀπελαύνω, *I drive away/out, expel.* • **λεγεῶνα** → ἡ λεγεών (listed in BDAG under the alternate form λεγιών), *legion.* Cf. Luke 8:33. • **βυθίζει** → βυθίζω, *I sink.* • **ἀστραπήν** → ἡ ἀστραπή, *lightning.* • **ἀρχηγόν** → ὁ ἀρχηγός, *ruler.* • **λιθάζεται** → λιθάζω, *I stone.* • **ἁλίσκεται** → ἁλίσκω, *I catch, conquer.* • **προσεύχεται** → προσεύχομαι, *I pray.* • **ἐπακούει** → ἐπακούω, *I listen to, hear,* i.e., he hears prayers. • **δακρύει** → δακρύω, *I weep.* • **παύει** → παύω, *I cause to cease, make stop.* • **δάκρυον** → τὸ δάκρυον, *a tear.* English idiom here uses the pl. • **ποῦ** — interrogative adv., *where.* After this word Barbel's text adds τέθειται (pf. pass. → τίθημι). • **Λάζαρος** → ὁ Λάζαρος, *Lazarus.* • **ἐγείρει** → ἐγείρω, *I raise.* • **πωλεῖται** → πωλέω, *I sell.* • **λίαν** — adv., *very.* • **εὐώνως** — adv., *cheaply.* • **τριάκοντα** → οἱ, αἱ, τά τριάκοντα, *thirty.* • **ἀργυρίων** → τὸ ἀργύριον, *a piece of silver, a silver coin.* Gen. of price/value (Wal: 122; Smy: 1336). Supply "it is." • **ἐξαγοράζει** →

ἐπὶ σφαγὴν ἄγεται, ἀλλὰ ποιμαίνει τὸν Ἰσραήλ, *νῦν δὲ* καὶ πᾶσαν τὴν οἰκουμένην. ὡς ἀμνὸς ἄφωνος, ἀλλὰ λόγος ἐστί, φωνῇ βοῶντος ἐν τῇ ἐρήμῳ καταγγελλόμενος. μεμαλάκισται, τετραυμάτισται, ἀλλὰ θεραπεύει πᾶσαν νόσον, καὶ πᾶσαν μαλακίαν. ἐπὶ τὸ ξύλον ἀνάγεται, προσπήγνυται, ἀλλὰ τῷ ξύλῳ τῆς ζωῆς ἀποκαθίστησιν, ἀλλὰ σώζει καὶ λῃστὴν συσταυρούμενον, ἀλλὰ σκοτίζει πᾶν τὸ ὁρώμενον. ὄξος ποτίζεται, χολὴν βρωματίζεται· τίς; ὁ τὸ ὕδωρ εἰς οἶνον μεταβαλών, ὁ τῆς πικρᾶς γεύσεως καταλυτής, ὁ γλυκασμὸς καὶ ὅλος ἐπιθυμία. παραδίδωσι τὴν ψυχήν, ἀλλ' ἐξουσίαν ἔχει πάλιν λαβεῖν αὐτήν, ἀλλὰ καταπέτασμα ῥήγνυται, τὰ γὰρ ἄνω παραδείκνυται, ἀλλὰ πέτραι σχίζονται, ἀλλὰ νεκροὶ προεγείρονται. ἀποθνήσκει, ζωοποιεῖ δέ, καὶ καταλύει τῷ θανάτῳ τὸν θάνατον. θάπτεται, ἀλλ' ἀνίσταται. εἰς ᾅδου κάτεισιν, ἀλλ' ἀνάγει ψυχάς, ἀλλ' εἰς οὐρανοὺς ἄνεισιν, ἀλλ' ἥξει κρῖναι ζῶντας καὶ νεκρούς, καὶ τοὺς τοιούτους βασανίσαι λόγους. εἰ ταῦτα ἐμποιεῖ σοι τῆς πλάνης τὴν ἀφορμήν, ἐκεῖνά σου λύει τὴν πλάνην.

ἐξαγοράζω, *I buy back, redeem.* • **τιμῆς** → ἡ τιμή, *honor; price.* • **αἵματος** — gen. of price/value (Wal: 122; Smy: 1336). Supply "it is." • **πρόβατον** → τὸ πρόβατον, *sheep.* • **σφαγήν** → ἡ σφαγή, *slaughter.* • **ποιμαίνει** → ποιναίνω, *I tend a flock, shepherd.* • **οἰκουμένην** → ἡ οἰκουμένη, *the inhabited world.* • **ἀμνός** → ὁ, ἡ ἀμνός, *lamb.* • **ἄφωνος** → ἄφωνος, ον, *voiceless, silent.* • **ἐρήμῳ** → ἐρῆμος, η, ον, *desolate;* subst., *desert.* • **καταγγελλόμενος** → καταγγέλλω, *I declare, proclaim.* • **μεμαλάκισται** → μαλακίζομαι, *I am/become weak; bear infirmity.* • **τετραυμάτισται** → τραυματίζω, *I wound.* • **θεραπεύει** → θεραπεύω, *I heal.* • **νόσον** → ἡ νόσος, *disease.* • **μαλακίαν** → ἡ μαλακία, *weakness, infirmity, sickness.* • **ξύλον** → τὸ ξύλον, *wood; tree; cross.* • **ἀνάγεται** → ἀνάγω, *I lead/bring up; lift up* (LSI I6: 54). • **προσπήγνυται** → προσπήγνυμι, *I fix to.* • **ἀποκαθίστησιν** → ἀποκαθίστημι, *I restore.* • **συσταυρούμενον** → συσταυρόω, *I crucify with.* • **σκοτίζει** → σκοτίζω, *I make dark.* • **ὄξος** → τὸ ὄξος, *cheap wine; vinegar.* • **ποτίζεται** → ποτίζω, *I give to drink.* • **χολήν** → ἡ χολή, *bile.* • **βρωματίζεται** → βρωματίζω, *I feed.* • **οἶνον** → ὁ οἶνος, *wine.* • **μεταβαλών** → μεταβάλλω, *I change.* • **πικρᾶς** → πικρός, ά, όν, *sharp, bitter.* • **γεύσεως** → ἡ γεῦσις, *a taste.* • **καταλύτης** → ὁ καταλυτής, *destroyer* (*PGL*: 711). • **γλυκασμός** → ὁ γλυκασμός, *sweetness.* • **ἐπιθυμία** → ἡ ἐπιθυμία, *a desire.* Here mod. by the masc. ὅλος, following Song 5:16. • **καταπέτασμα** → τὸ καταπέτασμα, *curtain, veil.* • **ῥήγνυται** → ῥήγνυμι, *I break, tear apart.* • **ἄνω** — adv., *above.* τὰ ἄνω, *what is above,* i.e., *heaven* (BDAG 1: 92). • **παραδείκνυται** → παραδείκνυμι, *I exhibit, bring forward.* • **πέτραι** → ἡ πέτρα, *rock.* • **σχίζονται** → σχίζω, *I split.* • **προεγείρονται** → προεγείρω, *I wake up before; rise before(hand).* Cf. Matt 27:52 (where ἠγέρθησαν is used). Barbel's text has ἐγείρονται. • **ζωοποιεῖ** → ζωοποιέω, *I make alive.* • **καταλύει** → καταλύω, *I destroy.* • **θάπτεται** → θάπτω, *I bury.* • **ᾅδου** → ὁ ᾅδης, *Hades.* • **κάτεισιν** → κάτειμι, *I go down,* from κατά and εἶμι (*I go*), not εἰμί (*I am*). • **ἄνεισιν** → ἄνειμι, *I go up,* from ἀνά and εἶμι (*I go*), not εἰμί (*I am*). • **ἥξει** → ἥκω, *I have come, am present; come.* • **κρῖναι** — aor. act. inf. → κρίνω. • **βασανίσαι** → βασανίζω, *I put to the test.* • **ἐμποιεῖ** → ἐμποιέω, *I introduce, produce, cause.* • **πλάνης** → ἡ πλάνη, *error.* • **ἀφορμήν** → ἡ ἀφορμή, *starting point.*

Oration 31.26 The Holy Spirit Was Revealed Gradually

31.26 Ἐκήρυσσε φανερῶς ἡ παλαιὰ τὸν πατέρα, τὸν υἱὸν ἀμυδρότερον. ἐφανέρωσεν ἡ καινὴ τὸν υἱόν, ὑπέδειξε τοῦ πνεύματος τὴν θεότητα. ἐμπολιτεύεται νῦν τὸ πνεῦμα, σαφεστέραν ἡμῖν παρέχον τὴν ἑαυτοῦ δήλωσιν. οὐ γὰρ ἦν ἀσφαλές, μήπω τῆς τοῦ πατρὸς θεότητος ὁμολογηθείσης, τὸν υἱὸν ἐκδήλως κηρύττεσθαι· μηδὲ τῆς τοῦ υἱοῦ παραδεχθείσης, τὸ πνεῦμα τὸ ἅγιον, ἵν' εἴπω τι καὶ τολμηρότερον, ἐπιφορτίζεσθαι· μὴ καθάπερ τροφῇ τῇ ὑπὲρ δύναμιν βαρηθέντες, καὶ ἡλιακῷ φωτὶ σαθροτέραν ἔτι προσβαλόντες τὴν ὄψιν, καὶ εἰς τὸ κατὰ δύναμιν κινδυνεύσωσι· ταῖς δὲ κατὰ μέρος προσθήκαις, καί, ὡς εἶπε Δαβίδ, ἀναβάσεσι, καὶ ἐκ δόξης εἰς δόξαν

31.26 **ἐκήρυσσε** → κηρύσσω, *I preach, proclaim.* • **φανερῶς** — adv., *openly, publicly.* • **παλαιά** → παλαιός, ά, όν, *old,* fem. because of the understood διαθήκη, Old Testament. • **ἀμυδρότερον** → ἀμυδρότερος, α, ον, *more dimly, obscurely, faintly,* comparative of ἀμυδρός, ά, όν. • **ἐφανέρωσεν** → φανερόω, *I manifest; make known.* • **καινή** → καινός, ή, όν, *new,* fem. because of the understood διαθήκη, New Testament. • **ὑπέδειξε** → ὑποδείκνυμι, *I show secretly, give a glimpse.* • **θεότητα** → ἡ θεότης, *divinity, divine nature.* • **ἐμπολιτεύεται** → ἐμπολιτεύομαι, *I dwell in* (*PGL* 2: 456). • **σαφεστέραν** → σαφέστερος, α, ον, *clearer, more distinct,* comparative of σαφής, ές. • **παρέχον** → παρέχω, *I provide.* • **δήλωσιν** → ἡ δήλωσις, *manifestation* • **ἀσφαλές** → ἀσφαλής, ές, *safe.* • **μήπω** — adv., *not yet.* • **ὁμολογηθείσης** → ὁμολογέω, *I allow, admit, confess, agree upon.* Gen. abs. • **ἐκδήλως** — adv., *plainly.* • **κηρύττεσθαι** → κηρύττω, an alternate form of κηρύσσω. Epex. inf. w. ἀσφαλές (Wal: 607; Smy: 2006). • **μηδέ** — neg. particle, *and not, nor.* • **τῆς τοῦ υἱοῦ** — τῆς goes w. an elided repetition of θεότητος. • **παραδεχθείσης** → παραδέχομαι, *I receive, admit, accept.* Gen. abs. • **τὸ πνεῦμα τὸ ἅγιον** — acc. of ref. (Wal: 203; Smy: 1600). • **ἵν'** — introduces an exclamation (Smy: 2685). ἵν' εἴπω τι καὶ τολμηρότερον, "that I may say something very audacious indeed," *to put it rather audaciously indeed!* • **τολμηρότερον** → τολμηρότερος, α, ον, *very/quite/rather daring/bold/audacious,* comparative of τολμηρός, ά, όν (BDAG: 1010). • **ἐπιφορτίζεσθαι** → ἐπιφορτίζω, *I load heavily, overload* (LSJ: 671). W. κηρύττεσθαι as an epexegetic inf. w. ἀσφαλές. • **μή** — here introducing a neg. purpose clause, *lest, so that . . . not* (BDAG 2b: 646), w. κινδυνεύσωσι. • **καθάπερ** — *just as, like.* • **τροφῇ** → ἡ τροφή, *food.* • **ὑπέρ** — here, *beyond* (LSI BII: 833; BDAG B: 1031). • **δύναμιν** — here, *power,* in the sense of *capacity, ability, capability* (LSI II: 213; BDAG 2: 263). • **βαρηθέντες** → βαρέω, *I weigh down.* • **ἡλιακῷ** → ἡλιακός, ή, όν, *of the sun.* • **σαθροτέραν** → σαθρότερος, α, ον, *more unsound/weak,* comparative of σαθρός, ά, όν, here in an intensive sense, *very unsound/weak* (Smy: 1067). • **προσβαλόντες** → προσβάλλω, *I strike; assault.* • **ὄψιν** → ἡ ὄψις, *vision, eyesight, the eyes.* • **καί** — ascensive, *even.* • **εἰς** — here, *with regard to, with reference to* (LSI IV: 231; BDAG 5: 291). εἰς τὸ κατὰ δύναμιν, *with regard to that which is in keeping with their ability.* • **κινδυνεύσωσι** → κινδυνεύω, *I take a risk; am in danger.* • **ταῖς δέ** — introduces the contrast. μή . . . ἐκλάμψῃ now gives the positive purpose, *but that.* • **μέρος** → τὸ μέρος, *part.* κατὰ μέρος, *part by part, one part at a time, gradually.* Distributive use of κατά (BDAG B3: 512; LSI II: 403). • **προσθήκαις** → ἡ προσθήκη, *an addition.* • **Δαβίδ** → Δαβιδ, alternate form of ὁ Δαυίδ, *David* (BDAG: 212). • **ἀναβάσεσι** → ἡ ἀνάβασις, *a going up, ascent.* • **προόδοις** →

προόδοις καὶ προκοπαῖς, τὸ τῆς Τριάδος φῶς ἐκλάμψῃ τοῖς λαμπροτέροις. διὰ ταύτην, οἶμαι, τὴν αἰτίαν καὶ τοῖς μαθηταῖς κατὰ μέρος ἐπιδημεῖ, τῇ τῶν δεχομένων δυνάμει παραμετρούμενον, ἐν ἀρχῇ τοῦ εὐαγγελίου, μετὰ τὸ πάθος, μετὰ τὴν ἄνοδον, τὰς δυνάμεις ἐπιτελοῦν, ἐκφυσώμενον, ἐν γλώσσαις πυρίναις φαινόμενον. καὶ ὑπὸ Ἰησοῦ κατ' ὀλίγον ἐκφαίνεται, ὡς ἐπιστήσεις καὶ αὐτὸς ἐντυγχάνων ἐπιμελέστερον· Ἐρωτήσω, φησί, τὸν πατέρα καὶ ἄλλον παράκλητον πέμψει ὑμῖν, τὸ πνεῦμα τῆς ἀληθείας· ἵνα μὴ ἀντίθεος εἶναι δόξῃ τις, καὶ ὡς ἀπ' ἄλλης τινὸς ἐξουσίας ποιεῖσθαι τοὺς λόγους. εἶτα, Πέμψει μέν, ἐν δὲ τῷ ὀνόματί μου. τὸ Ἐρωτήσω παρείς, τὸ Πέμψει τετήρηκεν. εἶτα, Πέμψω, τὸ οἰκεῖον ἀξίωμα· εἶτα, Ἥξει, ἡ τοῦ πνεύματος ἐξουσία.

Oration 45.28–29 The Effect of the Blood of Christ

45.28 Νῦν δὲ ἀναγκαῖον ἡμῖν οὕτω κεφαλαιῶσαι τὸν λόγον· Γεγόναμεν, ἵν' εὖ πάθωμεν· εὖ πεπόνθαμεν, ἐπειδὴ γεγόναμεν. Τὸν παράδεισον ἐπιστεύθημεν,

---

ἡ πρόοδος, *a going on, advance, progress.* • **προκοπαῖς** → ἡ προκοπή, *a progress, advance.* • **Τριάδος** → ἡ Τρίας, *triad; the Trinity.* • **ἐκλάμψῃ** → ἐκλάμπω, *I shine forth.* The subjun. continues w. κινδυνεύσωσι, now giving the positive side. • **λαμπροτέροις** → λαμπρότερος, α, ον, *brighter; more radiant,* comparative of λαμπρός, ά, όν. • **οἶμαι** → οἶμαι (an alternate form of οἴομαι), *I think, suppose.* • **αἰτίαν** → ἡ αἰτία, *a reason, cause.* • **ἐπιδημεῖ** → ἐπιδημέω, *I come to dwell in; come upon, visit, descend upon* (*PGL* B: 520 and F1: 521). • **παραμετρούμενον** → παραμετρέω, *I adjust to, adapt to* (*PGL* 1: 1021), neut. ptc. due to the assumed subj., τὸ πνεῦμα (so also for the following ptc). Note the mid., *adapting himself.* • **ἐν ἀρχῇ** — Three stages are now mentioned followed by three activities corresponding to the stages in the same order. • **πάθος** → τὸ πάθος, *suffering; the passion.* • **ἄνοδον** → ἡ ἄνοδος, *way up; the ascension.* • **ἐπιτελοῦν** → ἐπιτελέω, *I complete, accomplish, perform; perfect.* • **ἐκφυσώμενον** → ἐκφυσάω, *I breathe out.* • **πυρίναις** → πύρινος, η, ον, *of fire, fiery.* • **φαινόμενον** → φαίνω, *I make appear;* pass., *appear, am seen.* • **ὀλίγον** → ὀλίγος, η, ον, *few.* κατ' ὀλίγον, *little by little.* Distributive use of κατά. • **ἐκφαίνεται** → ἐκφαίνω, *I bring to light, reveal.* • **ἐπιστήσεις** → ἐφίστημι, *I perceive, observe* (*PGL* 3: 587). • **ἐντυγχάνων** → ἐντυγχάνω, *I meet with; read.* Conditional ptc. • **ἐπιμελέστερον** → ἐπιμελέστερος, α, ον, *more attentive/careful,* comparative of ἐπιμελής, ές; neut. acc. for adv., *more carefully/attentively.* • **παράκλητον** → ὁ παράκλητος, *the Paraclete.* • **ἀντίθεος** → ἀντίθεος, η, ον, *rival to God* (*PGL* 2c: 153). • **εἶναι** — inf. for indir. disc., the content of what one might think (Wal: 603; Smy: 2016). • **ποεῖσθαι** — another inf. continuing the indir. disc. w. δόξῃ; mid., "as periphrasis of a simple verbal idea" (BDAG 7a: 841; cf. LSI AII4: 651). ποεῖσθαι τοὺς λόγους, *he discourses.* • **λόγους** — here, *discourse* (LSI AIII: 477; BDAG 1aβ: 599). • **εἶτα** — adv., *then, next.* • **παρείς** — aor. act. ptc. masc. nom. sg. → παρίημι, *I leave out.* • **οἰκεῖον** → οἰκεῖος, α, ον, *personal.* • **ἀξίωμα** → τὸ ἀξίωμα, *dignity, high status* (*PGL* 3: 168). • **ἥξει** → ἥκω, *I have come; come.*

45.28 **ἀναγκαῖον** → ἀναγκαῖος, α, ον, *necessary.* Supply, "it is." • **οὕτω** — οὕτως. • **κεφαλαιῶσαι** → κεφαλαιόω, *I sum up.* • **λόγον** → λόγος, here, *discourse; the*

ἵνα τρυφήσωμεν. Ἐντολὴν ἐλάβομεν, ἵν' εὐδοκιμήσωμεν ταύτην φυλάξαντες· οὐκ ἀγνοοῦντος τοῦ Θεοῦ τὸ ἐσόμενον, ἀλλὰ νομοθετοῦντος τὸ αὐτεξούσιον. Ἠπατήθημεν, ἐπειδὴ ἐφθονήθημεν· ἐκπεπτώκαμεν, ἐπειδὴ παρέβημεν· ἐνηστεύσαμεν, ἐπειδὴ μὴ ἐνηστεύσαμεν, τοῦ ξύλου τῆς γνώσεως ὑποκρατηθέντες. Ἀρχαία γὰρ ἦν ἡ ἐντολή, καὶ ἡμῖν ὁμόχρονος ψυχῆς τις οὖσα παιδαγωγία, καὶ τρυφῆς σωφρόνισμα· ἣν ἐπετάχθημεν εἰκότως, ἵν' ὃ μὴ φυλάξαντες ἀποβεβλήκαμεν, φυλάξαντες ἀπολάβωμεν. Ἐδεήθημεν Θεοῦ σαρκουμένου καὶ νεκρουμένου, ἵνα ζήσωμεν· συνενεκρώθημεν, ἵνα καθαρῶμεν· συνανέστημεν, ἐπειδὴ συνενεκρώθημεν· συνεδοξάσθημεν, ἐπειδὴ συνανέστημεν.

45.29 Πολλὰ μὲν δὴ τοῦ τότε καιροῦ τὰ θαύματα· Θεὸς σταυρούμενος, ἥλιος σκοτιζόμενος, καὶ πάλιν ἀναφλεγόμενος (ἔδει γὰρ τῷ Κτίστῃ συμ-

---

matter/subject under discussion (LSI AIII: 477; BDAG 1aβ: 599). W. art. for possession (Wal: 215; Smy: 1121). • **γεγόναμεν** → γίνομαι, here, *I create.* Pf. for simple past tense (cf. Wal: 578). • **εὖ** — adv., *well.* • **πάθωμεν** — 2 aor. act. subjun. → πάσχω, *I experience.* εὖ πάσχω, *am well off.* • **πεπόνθαμεν** — pf. indic. act. → πάσχω. Pf. for simple past tense (cf. Wal: 578). • **ἐπειδή** — *when, because, since.* • **παράδεισον** → ὁ παράδεισος, *Paradise.* • **τρυφήσωμεν** → τρυφάω, *I live luxuriously.* • **εὐδοκιμήσωμεν** → εὐδοκιμέω, *I am held in honor/esteem.* • **φυλάξαντες** → φυλάσσω, *I keep, observe.* Circ. ptc. for means. • **ἀγνοοῦντος** → ἀγνοέω, *I do not know, am ignorant of.* Gen. abs. • **τὸ ἐσόμενον** — fut. ptc. → εἰμί, "that which shall be," *what would happen.* • **νομοθετοῦντος** → νομοθετέω, *I make law; ordain* something *by law,* w. acc. Continues the gen. abs. • **αὐτεξούσιον** → αὐτεξούσιος, ον, *in one's own power,* τὸ αὐτεξούσιον, *free-will* (*PGL*: 266–67). • **ἠπατήθημεν** → ἀπατάω, *I trick, deceive.* • **ἐφθονήθημεν** → φθονέω, *I envy.* • **ἐκπεπτώκαμεν** → ἐκπίπτω, *I am driven out.* • **παρέβημεν** — aor. act. indic. → παραβαίνω, *I transgress.* • **ἐνηστεύσαμεν** → νηστεύω, *I fast.* • **ξύλου** → τὸ ξύλον, *tree.* Gen. of means (Wal: 125). • **γνώσεως** → ἡ γνῶσις, *knowledge.* • **ὑποκρατηθέντες** → ὑποκρατέω, *I master, overpower.* • **ἀρχαία** → ἀρχαῖος, α, ον, *ancient.* • **ὁμόχρονος** → ὁμόχρονος, ον, *contemporaneous.* • **ψυχῆς** — mod. παιδαγωγία. • **παιδαγωγία** → ἡ παιδαγωγία, *education.* • **τρυφῆς** → ἡ τρυφή, *luxury.* Obj. gen. • **σωφρόνισμα** → τὸ σωφρόνισμα, *chastisement; lesson.* • **ἐπετάχθημεν** → ἐπιτάσσω, *I order to do.* • **εἰκότως** — adv., *fairly, reasonably.* • **ἀποβεβλήκαμεν** → ἀποβάλλω, *I throw away, lose.* • **ἀπολάβωμεν** → ἀπολαμβάνω, *I get back, regain.* • **ἐδεήθημεν** → δέω, *I lack, am in need of,* w. gen. This word is listed in LSI and LSJ as δέω (B) to distinguish it from δέω (A), *bind.* δέω (B) is not used in the New Testament. • **σαρκουμένου** → σαρκόω, *I make flesh.* • **νεκρουμένου** → νεκρόω, *I put to death.* • **συνενεκρώθημεν** → συννεκρόω, *I put to death with* (*PGL*: 1333). Supply the dir. obj. *him* for the verbs in this section. • **καθαρῶμεν** — aor. act. subjun. → καθαίρω, *I cleanse, purify.* This is an alternate form of the aor., common in later Greek (LSJ: 849). • **συνανέστημεν** → συνανίστημι, *I rise with.* • **συνεδοξάσθημεν** → συνδοξάζω; pass., *I glorify with.*

45.29 **μέν** — introduces the description of the miracles at the passion, which will be contrasted (δέ) near the end of the section w. the miracle of salvation. • **δή** — particle, *indeed.* • **τότε** — "of the time then," *at that time.* • **θαύματα** → τὸ θαῦμα,

παθεῖν καὶ τὰ κτίσματα)· καταπέτασμα σχιζόμενον, αἷμα καὶ ὕδωρ τῆς πλευρᾶς χεόμενον· τὸ μέν, ὡς ἀνθρώπου, τὸ δέ, ὡς ὑπὲρ ἄνθρωπον· γῆ σειομένη, πέτραι ὑπὲρ τῆς πέτρας ῥηγνύμεναι, νεκροὶ ἀνιστάμενοι εἰς πίστιν τῆς τελευταίας καὶ κοινῆς ἀναστάσεως· τὰ ἐπὶ τῷ τάφῳ σημεῖα, τὰ μετὰ τὸν τάφον, ἃ τίς ἂν ἀξίως ὑμνήσειεν; Οὐδὲν δὲ οἷον τὸ θαῦμα τῆς ἐμῆς σωτηρίας· ῥανίδες αἵματος ὀλίγαι κόσμον ὅλον ἀναπλάττουσαι, καὶ γίνονται καθάπερ ὀπὸς γάλακτι πᾶσιν ἀνθρώποις, εἰς ἓν ἡμᾶς συνδέουσαι καὶ συνάγουσαι.

---

a wonder. • **σταυρούμενος** → σταυρόω, *I crucify.* • **ἥλιος** → ὁ ἥλιος, *sun.* • **σκοτιζόμενος** → σκοτίζω, *I darken.* • **ἀναφλεγόμενος** → ἀναφλέγω, *I light up, rekindle.* • **ἔδει** — impf. of δεῖ, *it was necessary/fitting.* Imper. w. inf. and acc. • **κτίστῃ** → ὁ κτίστης, *creator.* • **συμπαθεῖν** — 2 aor. act. inf. → συμπάσχω, *I suffer with.* • **κτίσματα** → τὸ κτίσμα, *creature.* • **καταπέτασμα** → τὸ καταπέτασμα, *curtain, veil.* • **σχιζόμενον** → σχίζω, *I split, divide.* • **πλευρᾶς** → ἡ πλευρά, *side.* Art. for possession. • **χεόμενον** → χέω, *I pour.* • **τὸ μέν . . . τὸ δέ** — *the one . . . the other.* • **σειομένη** → σείω, *I shake.* • **πέτραι** → ἡ πέτρα, *a rock.* • **ῥηγνύμεναι** → ῥήγνυμι, *I break.* • **πίστιν** → πίστις, here, *assurance, pledge, guarantee* (LSJ II1: 641; BDAG 1c: 818). • **τελευταίας** → τελευταῖος, α, ον, *last, final.* • **κοινῆς** → κοινός, ή, όν, *common.* • **ἀναστάσεως** → ἡ ἀνάστασις, *resurrection.* • **τάφῳ** → ὁ τάφος, *grave, tomb.* • **ἃ** — acc. of ref. (Wal: 203; Smy: 1600). • **ἀξίως** — adv., *worthily.* • **ὑμνήσειεν** — aor. act. opt. 3 sg. → ὑμνέω, *I sing, celebrate, commemorate.* Potential opt. (Smy: 2662c). • **οἷον** → οἷος, η, ον, *such as.* οὐδὲν οἷον, *nothing such as this.* Pred. compl. • **σωτηρίας** → ἡ σωτηρία, *salvation.* • **ῥανίδες** → ἡ ῥανίς, *a drop.* • **ὀλίγαι** → ὀλίγος, η, ον, *few.* • **ἀναπλάττουσαι** → ἀναπλάττω (listed in lexicons under the alternate form ἀναπλάσσω), *I form anew, recreate.* Attend. circ. • **καθάπερ** — *just as, as, like.* • **ὀπός** → ὁ ὀπός, *juice.* Used especially of sap from fig trees that was used to coagulate milk and to produce cheese (cf. LSJ I: 1241), *rennin.* • **γάλακτι** — neut. dat. sg. → τὸ γάλα, *milk* • **συνδέουσαι** → συνδέω, *I bind together, unite.* • **συνάγουσαι** → συνάγω, *I bring together, gather together.*

Desert Fathers and Mothers

Apophthegmata Patrum

Introduction

The teaching of Paul did not come just through his sermons and writings. In many of his letters he referred to his own life as an example of discipleship, as when he instructed Timothy to remind the Corinthians of "my ways in Christ" (1 Cor 4:17). In a similar manner, the Desert Fathers and Mothers were counter-cultural believers whose engaging stories of the life of faith were passed on so that other Christians could benefit from their "ways in Christ."

The collection of stories about these early Christian hermits is known as the *Apophthegmata Patrum* (*Sayings of the Fathers*). Most of the stories are about monks living in Egypt from about 330 to 460, though a few stories are from Syria and Palestine as well. The stories originally circulated orally in Coptic and Greek and came to be collected and written down in Palestine, probably late in the fifth century.

The monastic ideal in early Christianity arose as an expression of the renunciation of the world, the flesh, and the devil, which had been elements of Christian discipleship from the beginning. During the years of persecution, such renunciation was exemplified especially in the martyrs. But as persecution ceased and Christianity became assimilated to the empire, the idea of removing oneself from the patterns of ordinary life in order to seek first the kingdom of God caught on with an increasing number of people. Anthony of Egypt (251–346) influenced many to move to the desert, and his life became a major model of the monastic ideal, especially after Athanasius wrote the *Life of Anthony.*

At first these individuals lived solitary lives on the outskirts of their villages, but then many moved to more isolated spots, some completely alone and others living a short distance away from other monks. Eventually, communities of monks developed in addition to the solitary hermits. The development of this communal form of monastic life is attributed to Pachomius (292–346), who, at his death, was overseeing about 3,000 monks in nine monasteries and two nunneries along the Nile. No wonder Athanasius could say, "the desert was made a city by monks" (*Life of Anthony* 14).

The stories of the *Apophthegmata Patrum* are about the solitary monks, mostly men but also a few women. Almost all of the stories are very brief and describe encounters with the monks. Often the stories begin with someone coming to a hermit to ask for a word of advice regarding discipleship. Rather than offering theological or spiritual discourses, the monks most often gave *apothegms* (from ἀπόφθεγμα), that is, short, pithy instructive sayings. These apothegms were meant for the particular person addressed, giving them what they needed at that particular time. The details of the instruction are often meant for those living this particular monastic lifestyle. Some of the stories describe extreme asceticism, while others advocate less severe renunciation, though they are still quite extreme by normal standards. Along with the distinctively ascetic stories, there are others that keep such practices in perspective, as illustrated in several of the selections included here.

While the teachings of the *Apophthegmata Patrum* are given to particular, usually monastic, individuals, these stories have, in fact, spoken to many people leading more ordinary Christian lives right down to the present day. Some of the recurring themes include humility, self-control, watchfulness, integrity, simplicity, self-denial, and mercy. They describe a life centered in God and free to love him and serve others. In an age when Christians were becoming comfortable, unfocused, and undisciplined, these hermits issued radical, sometimes uncomfortable calls to counter-cultural discipleship. No wonder their voice resonates with many today as well!

Editions used:
Abba Anthony the Great 13: *PG* 65, cols. 77, 80
Abba Gelasios 1: *PG* 65, cols. 145, 148
Amma Theodora 6: *PG* 65, col. 204
Abba Joseph of Panephysis 7: *PG* 65, col. 229
Abba Cassian 1: *PG* 65, col. 244
Abba Macarius the Great 19: *PG* 65, col. 269; 23: *PG* 65, col. 272
Abba Moses the Ethiopian 2: *PG* 65, cols. 281, 284
Abba Mios 3: *PG* 65, cols. 301, 304
Abba Poemen 184: *PG* 65, col. 368
Abba Sisoes 17: *PG* 65, col. 397

Level of difficulty: Easy to intermediate [1–3]

Abba Anthony the Great 13 The Hunter and His Bow

Ἦν δέ τις κατὰ τὴν ἔρημον θηρεύων ἄγρια ζῷα, καὶ εἶδε τὸν ἀββᾶν Ἀντώνιον χαριεντιζόμενον μετὰ τῶν ἀδελφῶν. Θέλων δὲ αὐτὸν πληροφορῆσαι ὁ γέρων, ὅτι χρὴ μίαν συγκαταβαίνειν τοῖς ἀδελφοῖς, λέγει αὐτῷ· Βάλε βέλος εἰς τὸ τόξον σου, καὶ τεῖνον· καὶ ἐποίησεν οὕτως. Λέγει αὐτῷ· Πάλιν τεῖνον· καὶ ἔτεινεν. Καὶ πάλιν φησί· Τεῖνον. Λέγει αὐτῷ ὁ θηρευτής· Ἐὰν ὑπὲρ τὸ μέτρον τείνω, κλᾶται τὸ τόξον. Λέγει αὐτῷ ὁ γέρων· Οὕτως καὶ εἰς τὸ ἔργον τοῦ Θεοῦ· ἐὰν πλεῖον τοῦ μέτρου τείνωμεν κατὰ τῶν ἀδελφῶν, ταχὺ προσρήσσουσι. Χρὴ οὖν μίαν μίαν συγκαταβαίνειν τοῖς ἀδελφοῖς. Ταῦτα ἀκούσας ὁ θηρευτὴς, κατενύγη, καὶ πολλὰ ὠφεληθεὶς παρὰ τοῦ γέροντος, ἀπῆλθε· καὶ οἱ ἀδελφοὶ στηριχθέντες ἀνεχώρησαν εἰς τὸν τόπον αὐτῶν.

Abba Gelasios 1 The Leather-bound Bible

Ἔλεγον περὶ τοῦ ἀββᾶ Γελασίου, ὅτι εἶχε βιβλίον ἐν δέρμασιν, ἄξιον δεκαοκτὼ νομισμάτων· εἶχε δὲ τὴν Παλαιὰν καὶ Καινὴν Διαθήκην γεγραμμένην

Abba Anthony the Great 13

κατά - here, *in* (BDAG B1a: 511). • **ἔρημον** → ἔρημος, ον, *isolated, deserted;* here as subst., *desert.* • **θηρεύων** → θηρεύω, *I hunt.* • **ἄγρια** → ἄγριος, α, ον, *wild.* • **ζῷα** → τὸ ζῷον, *animal.* • **ἀββᾶν** → ὁ ἀββᾶ, *a father.* • **Ἀντώνιον** → Ἀντώνιος, *Anthony.* • **χαριεντιζόμενον** → χαριεντίζομαι, *I am witty, jest.* • **πληροφορῆσαι** → πληροφορέω, *I fully satisfy, assure.* • **γέρων** → ὁ γέρων, *elder, old man.* • **χρή** → χρή, *it is necessary.* An imper. verb, often w. inf. • **μίαν** → εἷς, μία, ἕν. Adv. acc., *once (in a while), sometimes.* • **συγκαταβαίνειν** → συγκαταβαίνω, *I come down with; make allowances* (*PGL* 2: 1267). • **λέγει** — The historical present (Wal: 526; Smy: 1883) occurs frequently in these stories to introduce speech. • **βέλος** → τὸ βέλος, *arrow.* • **τόξον** → τὸ τόξον, *a bow.* • **τεῖνον** — aor. act. impv. 2 sg. → τείνω, *I stretch.* • **θηρευτής** → ὁ θηρευτής, *hunter.* • **μέτρον** → τὸ μέτρον, *a measure; proper measure.* • **κλᾶται** → κλάω, *I break.* Pres. for fut. (Wal: 535; Smy: 1879). • **κατά** — here, *regarding, concerning* (LSI AII5: 402). • **ταχύ** → ταχύς, εῖα, ύ, *quickly.* • **προσρήσσουσι** → προσρήσσω (listed in LSI under the alternate form, προσρήγνυμι), *I dash/beat against, burst;* intrans., *am dashed against; burst forth, launch an attack* (*PGL* 2: 1181). The comparison with the bow suggests the idea that the brothers will "break," but the word used suggests instead either that the brothers will be "dashed against," that is, assaulted, presumably by temptation, or that they will "burst forth," that is, rebel. • **μίαν μίαν** — here perhaps doubled for emphasis, *at least once in a while.* • **κατενύγη** — 2 aor. pass. → κατανύσσομαι, *I am pierced.* The Fathers often use this word for being moved to repentance (*PGL* 1b: 713). • **πολλά** — *very much, greatly* (LSI II4: 658; BDAG 3aβ: 849). • **ὠφεληθείς** → ὠφελέω, *I help.* • **στηριχθέντες** → στηρίζω, *I make fast, set up, establish, support;* pass., *am firmly set/established.* • **ἀνεχώρησαν** → ἀναχωρέω, *I return, go back.*

ὅλην· καὶ ἔκειτο ἐν τῇ ἐκκλησίᾳ, ἵνα ὁ θέλων τῶν ἀδελφῶν ἀναγνῷ. Ἐλθὼν δέ τις ἀδελφῶν ξένος παραβαλεῖν τῷ γέροντι, ὡς εἶδεν αὐτὸ, ἐπεθύμησεν αὐτοῦ, καὶ κλέψας ἐξῆλθεν. Ὁ δὲ γέρων οὐκ ἐδίωξεν ὀπίσω αὐτοῦ, ὥστε καταλαβεῖν αὐτὸν, καίπερ νοήσας. Ἀπελθὼν οὖν ἐκεῖνος εἰς τὴν πόλιν, ἐζήτει πωλῆσαι αὐτό· καὶ εὑρὼν τὸν θέλοντα ἀγοράσαι, ἀπῄτει τὴν τιμὴν νομίσματα δεκαέξ. Ὁ δὲ θέλων ἀγοράσαι, λέγει αὐτῷ· Δός μοι πρῶτον, δοκιμάσω αὐτὸ, καὶ οὕτω τὸ τίμημά σοι παρέχω. Δέδωκεν οὖν αὐτό. Ὁ δὲ λαβών, ἤνεγκε τῷ ἀββᾷ Γελασίῳ δοκιμάσαι αὐτό, εἰρηκὼς αὐτῷ τὴν ποσότητα ἣν καὶ ὁ πωλῶν εἶπε. Καὶ λέγει ὁ γέρων· Ἀγόρασον αὐτό, καλὸν γάρ ἐστι καὶ ἄξιον ἧς εἴρηκας τιμῆς. Καὶ ἐλθὼν ὁ ἄνθρωπος εἶπε τῷ πωλοῦντι ἄλλως, καὶ οὐ καθὼς εἶπεν ὁ γέρων, λέγων· Ἰδοὺ ἔδειξα αὐτὸ τῷ ἀββᾷ Γελασίῳ, καὶ εἶπέ μοι ὅτι πολλοῦ ἐστι, καὶ οὐκ ἔστιν ἄξιον ἧς εἴρηκας τιμῆς. Ἐκεῖνος ἀκούσας, λέγει αὐτῷ· Οὐδέν σοι ἄλλο εἶπεν ὁ γέρων; Λέγει αὐτῷ· Οὐχί. Τότε λέγει· Οὐκέτι θέλω πωλῆσαι αὐτό. Κατανυγεὶς δὲ ἦλθε πρὸς τὸν γέροντα μετανοῶν, καὶ παρακαλῶν αὐτὸν δέξασθαι αὐτό. Ὁ δὲ γέρων οὐκ ἤθελε λαβεῖν. Τότε λέγει αὐτῷ ὁ ἀδελφός, ὅτι Ἐὰν

Abba Gelasios 1

ἀββᾶ → ὁ ἀββᾶ, *a father.* • **Γελασίου** → Γελασίος, *Gelasios.* • **εἶχε** — impf. → ἔχω. • **βιβλίον** → τὸ βιβλίον, *book.* • **δέρμασιν** → τὸ δέρμα, *skin, leather.* • **ἄξιον** → ἄξιος, α, ον, *worth,* w. gen. of price/value (Wal: 122; Smy: 1372). • **δεκαοκτώ** — *eighteen.* • **νομισμάτων** → τὸ νόμισμα, *coin.* • **παλαιάν** → παλαιός, ά, όν, *old.* • **καινήν** → καινός, ή, όν, *new.* • **διαθήκην** → ἡ διαθήκη, *covenant.* • **ἔκειτο** → κεῖμαι, *I lie.* • **ἀδελφῶν** — partitive gen. (Wal: 84; Smy: 1306). • **ἀναγνῷ** — aor. subjun. → ἀναγινώσκω, *I read.* • **ξένος** → ξένος, η, ον, *strange, foreign;* here, *a foreigner among the brothers.* • **παραβαλεῖν** → παραβάλλω, *I visit* (*PGL* B3: 1007). • **γέροντι** → ὁ γέρων, *elder, old man.* • **ὡς** — here, *when* (LSI BV: 908; BDAG 8a: 1105). • **ἐπεθύμησεν** → ἐπιθυμέω, *I set my heart on, desire,* w. gen. • **κλέψας** → κλέπτω, *I steal.* • **ἐδίωξεν** → διώκω, *I pursue.* • **ὀπίσω** — *after, behind, following.* • **καταλαβεῖν** → καταλαμβάνω, *I seize, catch, overtake.* • **καίπερ** — *although.* • **νοήσας** → νοέω, *I observe, notice.* Attend. circ. • **πωλῆσαι** → πωλέω, *I sell.* • **ἀγοράσαι** → ἀγοράζω, *I buy.* • **ἀπῄτει** — impf. → ἀπαιτέω, *I ask.* • **τιμήν** → ἡ τιμή, *value, price.* • **νομίσματα** — in appos. to τιμήν. • **δεκαέξ** — *sixteen.* • **δός** — aor. impv. → δίδωμι. • **δοκιμάσω** — fut. → δοκιμάζω, *I test, examine.* • **οὕτω** — οὕτως. • **τίμημα** → τὸ τίμημα, *estimate, valuation.* • **παρέχω** → παρέχω, *I provide.* The context suggests the fut. use of the pres. (Wal: 536; Smy: 1879). τὸ τίμημά σοι παρέχω, "I will provide the valuation to you," *I will let you know what it is worth.* • **δέδωκεν** — pf. for aor. (Wal: 578). • **εἰρηκώς** — pf. ptc. → λέγω. • **ποσότητα** → ἡ ποσότης, *amount, sum of money.* • **ἄλλως** — *in another way, in a different way, otherwise, differently.* • **ἔδειξα** — aor. → δείκνυμι, *I show.* • **πολλοῦ** → πολύς, here, *of great value.* Gen. of price/value (Wal: 122; Smy: 1372). • **οὐχί** — intensive form of οὐ. • **οὐκέτι** — *no longer.* • **κατανυγείς** — aor. pass. ptc. → κατανύσσω, *I pierce, stab.* The Fathers often use this word for being moved to repentance (*PGL* 1b: 713). • **μετανοῶν** → μετανοέω, *I repent.* • **παρακαλῶν** → παρακαλέω, *I encourage, entreat.* • **ἤθελε** → θέλω, augmented in keeping w.

μὴ λάβῃς αὐτό, οὐκ ἔχω ἀνάπαυσιν. Λέγει αὐτῷ ὁ γέρων· Εἰ οὐκ ἀναπαύῃ, ἰδοὺ δέχομαι αὐτό. Καὶ ἔμεινεν ὁ ἀδελφὸς ἐκεῖνος ἕως τῆς τελευτῆς αὐτοῦ, ὠφεληθεὶς ἀπὸ τῆς ἐργασίας τοῦ γέροντος.

Amma Theodora 6 The Victory of Humility

Ἔλεγε πάλιν ἡ αὐτή, ὅτι οὐκ ἄσκησις, οὔτε ἀγρυπνία, οὔτε παντοῖος πόνος σώζει· εἰ μὴ γνησία ταπεινοφροσύνη. Ἦν γάρ τις ἀναχωρητὴς ἀπελαύνων δαίμονας· καὶ ἐξήταζεν αὐτούς· Ἐν τίνι ἐξέρχεσθε, ἐν νηστείᾳ; Καὶ ἔλεγον· Ἡμεῖς οὔτε ἐσθίομεν, οὔτε πίνομεν. Ἐν ἀγρυπνίᾳ; Καὶ ἔλεγον· Ἡμεῖς οὐ κοιμώμεθα. Ἐν ἀναχωρήσει; Ἡμεῖς εἰς τὰ ἐρήμους διάγομεν. Ἐν τίνι οὖν ἐξέρχεσθε; Καὶ ἔλεγον, ὅτι Οὐδὲν ἡμᾶς νικᾷ, εἰ μὴ ταπεινοφροσύνη. Ὁρᾷς ὅτι ἡ ταπεινοφροσύνη νικητήριόν ἐστι δαιμόνων;

Abba Joseph of Panephysis 7 Become Like Fire

Παρέβαλεν ὁ ἀββᾶς Λὼτ τῷ ἀββᾷ Ἰωσήφ, καὶ λέγει αὐτῷ· Ἀββᾶ κατὰ δύναμίν μου ποιῶ τὴν μικράν μου σύναξιν, καὶ τὴν μικρὰν νηστείαν μου,

---

its older form ἐθέλω. • **ἔχω . . . ἀναπαύῃ . . . δέχομαι** — further possible examples of the pres. for fut. (Wal: 536; Smy: 1879). • **ἀνάπαυσιν** → ἡ ἀνάπαυσις, *rest.* • **ἀναπαύῃ** — pres. pass. → ἀναπαύω, *I rest;* pass., *am at rest.* • **ἔμεινε** — aor. act. → μένω. • **τελευτῆς** → ἡ τελευτή, *end, death.* • **ὠφεληθείς** → ὠφελέω, *I help.* • **ἐργασίας** → ἡ ἐργασία, *work; way of life* (*PGL* 4: 545).

Amma Theodora 6

πάλιν — here, *also* (BDAG 3: 752) • **ἄσκησις** → ἡ ἄσκησις, *exercise, practice, training; asceticism.* • **ἀγρυπνία** → ἡ ἀγρυπνία, *sleeplessness, watching, keeping vigil.* • **παντοῖος** → παντοῖος, α, ον, *all kinds of.* • **πόνος** → ὁ πόνος, *hard work, toil.* • **εἰ μή** — *but, except.* • **γνησία** → γνήσιος, α, ον, *true, genuine.* • **ταπεινοφροσύνη** → ἡ ταπεινοφροσύνη, *humility.* • **ἀναχωρητής** → ὁ ἀναχωρητής, *one who has withdrawn from the world* (cf. ἀναχωρέω, *withdraw, retire*); *anchorite.* • **ἀπελαύνων** → ἀπελαύνω, *I drive away.* • **δαίμονας** → ὁ and ἡ δαίμων, *demon, evil spirit.* • **ἐξήταζεν** → ἐξετάζω, *I question closely.* • **νηστείᾳ** → ἡ νηστεία, *fasting.* • **κοιμώμεθα** → κοιμάω, *I put to sleep;* pass. *sleep.* • **ἀναχωρήσει** → ἡ ἀναχώρησις, *withdrawal, separation from the world.* • **ἐρήμους** → ἔρημος, ον, *desolate.* ἡ ἔρημος (χώρα), *desert.* • **διάγομεν** → διάγω, *I go through, live.* • **νικᾷ** → νικάω, *I conquer.* • **νικητήριον** → νικητήριος, α, ον, *belonging to a conqueror* or *to a victory, victorious;* subst., *victory* (*PGL* 2: 914). • **δαιμόνων** — obj. gen. (Wal: 116; Smy: 1328).

Abba Joseph of Panephysis 7

παρέβαλεν → παραβάλλω, *I visit* (*PGL* B3: 1007). • **ἀββᾶς** → ὁ ἀββᾶ, *a father.*

καὶ τὴν εὐχήν, καὶ τὴν μελέτην, καὶ τὴν ἡσυχίαν, καὶ τὸ κατὰ δύναμίν μου καθαρεύω τοῖς λογισμοῖς. Τί οὖν ἔχω ποιῆσαι λοιπόν; Ἀναστὰς οὖν ὁ γέρων, ἥπλωσε τὰς χεῖρας εἰς τὸν οὐρανόν· καὶ γεγόνασιν οἱ δάκτυλοι αὐτοῦ, ὡς δέκα λαμπάδες πυρός· καὶ λέγει αὐτῷ· Εἰ θέλεις, γενοῦ ὅλος ὡς πῦρ.

Abba Cassian 1 Hospitality over Fasting

Διηγήσατο ὁ ἀββᾶς Κασιανός, ὅτι Παρεβάλομεν ἐγώ τε καὶ ὁ ἅγιος Γερμανὸς εἰς Αἴγυπτον, πρός τινα γέροντα. Καὶ φιλοξενήσας ἡμᾶς ἠρωτήθη παρ' ἡμῶν· Τίνος ἕνεκεν ἐν τῷ καιρῷ τῆς ὑποδοχῆς τῶν ξένων ἀδελφῶν, τὸν κανόνα τῆς νηστείας ἡμῶν, ὡς ἐν Παλαιστίνῃ παρελάβομεν, οὐ φυλάττετε; Καὶ ἀπεκρίθη λέγων· Ἡ νηστεία πάντοτε μετ' ἐμοῦ ἐστιν· ὑμᾶς δὲ κατέχειν πάντοτε μεθ' ἑαυτοῦ οὐ δύναμαι· καὶ ἡ μὲν νηστεία καὶ χρήσιμόν ἐστι πρᾶγμα καὶ ἀναγκαῖον, τῆς ἡμετέρας δέ ἐστι προαιρέσεως·

• **Λώτ** → Λώτ, indecl., *Lot.* • **Ἰωσήφ** → Ἰωσήφ, indecl., *Joseph.* • **δύναμιν** → ἡ δύναμις, here, *strength.* • **μικράν** → μικρός, ά, όν, *little, small.* • **σύναξιν** → ἡ σύναξις, *gathering, assembly;* here, a "form of worship or prayer obligatory upon monks and nuns, perhaps sometimes ref. to eucharist, but also to an *office*" (*PGL* E: 1303). • **νηστείαν** → ἡ νηστεία, *a fast.* • **εὐχήν** → ἡ εὐχή, *prayer.* The art. w. this word and several that follow are good examples of the poss. art. (Wal: 215; Smy: 1121). • **μελέτην** → ἡ μελέτη, *care; exercise; study, meditation* (*PGL* 5: 841). • **ἡσυχίαν** → ἡ ἡσυχία, *stillness, silence.* • **τό** — here packaging the clause that follows as a further item in the list. • **καθαρεύω** → καθαρεύω, *I am clean/pure.* • **λογισμοῖς** → ὁ λογισμός, *thought, imagining.* • **γέρων** → ὁ γέρων, *elder, old man.* • **ἥπλωσε** → ἁπλόω, *I unfold, stretch out.* • **δάκτυλοι** → ὁ δάκτυλος, *finger.* • **δέκα** — *ten.* • **λαμπάδες** → ἡ λαμπάς, *torch, lamp.* • **γενοῦ** — 2 aor. impv. mid. (depon.) 2 sg. → γίνομαι. • **ὅλος** — perhaps a pred. nom., *I become whole;* or the masc. nom. as an adv., *wholly* (BDAG 2: 704).

Abba Cassian 1

διηγήσατο → διηγέομαι, *I tell, relate.* • **ἀββᾶς** → ὁ ἀββᾶ, *a father.* • **Κασιανός** → Κασιανός, *Cassian.* • **παρεβάλομεν** → παραβάλλω, *I visit* (*PGL* B3: 1007). • **Γερμανός** → Γερμανός, *Germanus.* • **Αἴγυπτον** → ὁ Αἴγυπτος, *Egypt.* • **πρός** — here, *with* (LSI CI5: 684; BDAG 3dβ: 874). • **γέροντα** → ὁ γέρων, *elder, old man.* • **φιλοξενήσας** → φιλοξενέω, *entertain hospitably.* Probably a causal circ. ptc. • **ἕνεκεν** (listed in lexicons under its alternate form ἕνεκα) — *because of.* τίνος ἕνεκεν, *because of what; why.* It usually follows the word that goes with it. • **ὑποδοχῆς** → ἡ ὑποδοχή, *reception, entertainment.* ἐν τῷ καιρῷ τῆς ὑποδοχῆς, "in the time of your reception," *when you receive.* • **ξένων** → ξένος, η, ον, *strange, foreign,* i.e., "visitors." • **κανόνα** → ὁ κανών, *a rule.* • **νηστείας** → ἡ νηστεία, *a fast.* • **Παλαιστίνῃ** → Παλαιστίνη, *Palestine.* • **παρελάβομεν** → παραλαμβάνω, *I receive.* When they visited in Palestine the monks did not break their fast. • **φυλάττετε** → φυλάττω (listed in lexicons under the alternate form φυλάσσω), *I keep.* • **πάντοτε** — *always.* Cf. John 12:8. • **κατέχειν** → κατέχω, *I*

τὴν δὲ τῆς ἀγάπης πλήρωσιν ἐξ ἀνάγκης ἀπαιτεῖ ὁ τοῦ Θεοῦ νόμος. Ἐν ὑμῖν οὖν δεχόμενος τὸν Χριστόν, χρεωστῶ μετὰ πάσης θεραπεῦσαι σπουδῆς. Ἐπὰν δὲ ὑμᾶς προπέμψω, τὸν κανόνα τῆς νηστείας δύναμαι ἀνακτήσασθαι. Οὐ δύνανται γὰρ οἱ υἱοὶ τοῦ νυμφῶνος νηστεύειν, ἐφ' ὅσον χρόνον ὁ νυμφίος μετ' αὐτῶν ἐστιν· ὅταν δὲ ἀρθῇ ὁ νυμφίος, τότε μετ' ἐξουσίας νηστεύσουσιν.

Abba Macarius the Great 19 Simplicity in Prayer

Ἠρώτησάν τινες τὸν ἀββᾶν Μακάριον, λέγοντες· Πῶς ὀφείλομεν προσεύχεσθαι; Λέγει αὐτοῖς ὁ γέρων· Οὐκ ἔστι χρεία βαττολογεῖν, ἀλλ' ἐκτείνειν τὰς χεῖρας, καὶ λέγειν· Κύριε, ὡς θέλεις καὶ ὡς οἶδας, ἐλέησον. Ἐὰν δὲ ἐπίκειται πόλεμος· Κύριε, βοήθει. Καὶ αὐτὸς οἶδε τὰ συμφέροντα, καὶ ποιεῖ μεθ' ἡμῶν ἔλεος.

Abba Macarius the Great 23 Dead to the World

Ἀδελφὸς παρέβαλε τῷ ἀββᾷ Μακαρίῳ τῷ Αἰγυπτίῳ, καὶ λέγει αὐτῷ· Ἀββᾶ, εἰπέ μοι ῥῆμα πῶς σωθῶ. Καὶ λέγει ὁ γέρων· Ὕπαγε εἰς τὸ μνημεῖον, καὶ

---

hold, have in possession, keep. • **χρήσιμον** → χρήσιμος, η, ον, *useful.* • **πρᾶγμα** → τὸ πρᾶγμα, *thing.* • **ἀναγκαῖον** → ἀναγκαῖος, α, ον, *necessary.* • **ἡμετέρας** → ἡμέτερος, α, ον, *our.* • **προαιρέσεως** → ἡ προαίρεσις, *choice, choosing.* Perhaps gen. of agency (Wal: 126) or source (Wal: 109; Smy: 1410). • **πλήρωσιν** → ἡ πλήρωσις, *filling, fulfilling.* • **ἀνάγκης** → ἡ ἀνάγκη, *necessity.* • **ἀπαιτεῖ** → ἀπαιτέω, *I demand.* • **χρεωστῶ** → χρεωστέω, *I am in debt, owe; ought* (*PGL*: 1527). • **θεραπεῦσαι** → θεραπεύω, *I serve, take care of, provide for.* • **σπουδῆς** → ἡ σπουδή, *haste, zeal.* • **ἐπάν** (→ ἐπεὶ ἄν) — *when.* • **προπέμψω** → προπέμπω, *I send forth.* • **ἀνακτήσασθαι** → ἀνακτάομαι, *I recover, get back.* • **νυμφῶνος** → ὁ νυμφών, *bridal chamber.* οἱ υἱοὶ τοῦ νυμφῶνος, *the bridegroom's attendants* (BDAG 2: 681). • **ἐφ' ὅσον χρόνον** — *as long as* (BDAG, ἐπί 18cβ: 367). • **νυμφίος** → ὁ νυμφίος, *bridegroom.* • **ἀρθῇ** — aor. pass. subjun. → αἴρω. • **μετ' ἐξουσίας** — this phrase is not included in the canonical forms of this quote.

Abba Macarius the Great 19

ἀββᾶν → ὁ ἀββᾶ, *a father.* • **Μακάριον** → Μακάριος, *Macarius.* • **ὀφείλομεν** → ὀφείλω, *I am obliged, ought.* • **γέρων** → ὁ γέρων, *elder, old man.* • **χρεία** → ἡ χρεία, *a need.* • **βαττολογεῖν** → βαττολογέω, *I stammer, say the same thing over and over.* Cf. Matt 6:7. • **ἐκτείνειν** → ἐκτείνω, *I stretch out.* • **ἐλέησον** → ἐλεέω, *I have mercy.* • **ἐπίκειται** → ἐπίκειμαι, *I press upon, am urgent.* • **πόλεμος** → ὁ πόλεμος, *war,* here most likely spiritual warfare. Cf. *PGL* 6: 1112. • **βοήθει** → βοηθέω, *I help, come to the rescue.* • **συμφέροντα** → συμφέρω, *I am useful/profitable.* • **ἔλεος** → ὁ or τὸ ἔλεος, *mercy.* ποιεῖ μεθ' ἡμῶν ἔλεος, "he does mercy with us," *he has mercy on us* (BDAG, ποιέω 2d: 839).

ὕβρισον τοὺς νεκρούς. Ἀπελθὼν οὖν ὁ ἀδελφός, ὕβρισε καὶ ἐλίθασε· καὶ ἐλθὼν ἀπήγγειλε τῷ γέροντι. Καὶ λέγει αὐτῷ· Οὐδέν σοι ἐλάλησαν; Ὁ δὲ ἔφη· Οὐχί. Λέγει αὐτῷ ὁ γέρων· Ὕπαγε πάλιν αὔριον, καὶ δόξασον αὐτούς. Ἀπελθὼν οὖν ὁ ἀδελφός, ἐδόξασεν αὐτούς, λέγων· Ἀπόστολοι, ἅγιοι, καὶ δίκαιοι. Καὶ ἦλθε πρὸς τὸν γέροντα, καὶ εἶπεν αὐτῷ· Ἐδόξασα. Καὶ λέγει αὐτῷ· Οὐδέν σοι ἀπεκρίθησαν; Ἔφη ὁ ἀδελφός· Οὐχί. Λέγει αὐτῷ ὁ γέρων· Οἶδας πόσα ἠτίμασας αὐτούς, καὶ οὐδέν σοι ἀπεκρίθησαν, καὶ πόσα ἐδόξασας αὐτούς, καὶ οὐδέν σοι ἐλάλησαν· οὕτως καὶ σύ, ἐὰν θέλῃς σωθῆναι, γενοῦ νεκρός· μήτε τὴν ἀδικίαν τῶν ἀνθρώπων, μήτε τὴν δόξαν αὐτῶν λογίσῃ, ὡς οἱ νεκροί· καὶ δύνασαι σωθῆναι.

Abba Moses the Ethiopian 2 The Basket of Sand

Ἀδελφός ποτε ἐσφάλη εἰς Σκῆτιν· καὶ γενομένου συνεδρίου, ἀπέστειλαν πρὸς τὸν ἀββᾶν Μωϋσῆν. Ὁ δὲ οὐκ ἤθελεν ἐλθεῖν. Ἀπέστειλεν οὖν πρὸς αὐτὸν ὁ πρεσβύτερος, λέγων· Ἐλθέ, ὅτι σε ὁ λαὸς περιμένει. Ὁ δὲ ἀναστὰς ἦλθε. Καὶ λαβὼν σπυρίδα τετρημμένην, καὶ γεμίσας ἄμμου, ἐβάστασεν. Οἱ δὲ ἐξελθόντες εἰς ἀπάντησιν αὐτοῦ, λέγουσιν αὐτῷ· Τί ἐστι τοῦτο, Πάτερ; Εἶπε δὲ αὐτοῖς ὁ γέρων· Αἱ ἁμαρτίαι μού εἰσιν ὀπίσω μου καταρρέουσαι, καὶ οὐ βλέπω αὐτάς· καὶ ἦλθον ἐγὼ σήμερον, ἁμαρτήματα ἀλλότρια

Abba Macarius the Great 23

παρέβαλε → παραβάλλω, *I visit* (*PGL* B3: 1007). • **ἀββᾷ** → ὁ ἀββᾶ, *a father.* • **Μακαρίῳ** → Μακάριος, *Macarius.* • **Αἰγυπτίῳ** → Αἰγύπτιος, α, ον, *Egyptian.* • **γέρων** → ὁ γέρων, *elder, old man.* • **μνημεῖον** → τὸ μνημεῖον, *tomb;* here, *cemetery.* • **ὕβρισον** → ὑβρίζω, *I mistreat, insult.* • **ἐλίθασε** → λιθάζω, *I throw stones/rocks.* • **ἀπήγγειλε** → ἀπαγγέλλω, *I report.* • **ἔφη** → φημί. • **οὐχί** — intensive form of οὐ. • **αὔριον** — *tomorrow.* • **ἀπόστολοι** — here a voc., as also ἅγιοι and δίκαιοι. • **πόσα** → πόσος, η, ον, *how much.* • **ἠτίμασας** → ἀτιμάζω, *I dishonor.* • **γενοῦ** → γίνομαι. • **μήτε** — *and not.* μήτε . . . , *neither . . . nor.* • **ἀδικίαν** → ἡ ἀδικία, *wrong, injury.* • **λογίσῃ** → λογίζομαι, *I take account of, reckon.* Cf. Rom 6:11; 8:18 for a somewhat similar use of this verb.

Abba Moses the Ethiopian 2

ποτε — *at some time or other, once.* • **ἐσφάλη** — 2 aor. pass. → σφάλλω, *I throw down;* pass., *am overthrown; err, go wrong.* The imagery of being thrown down is in the context of spiritual warfare. • **Σκῆτιν** → ἡ Σκῆτις, *Scetis.* • **συνεδρίου** → τὸ συνέδριον, *council.* Subj. of the gen. abs. • **ἀββᾶν** → ὁ ἀββᾶ, *a father.* • **Μωϋσῆν** → ὁ Μωϋσῆς, *Moses.* • **ἤθελεν** — aor. → θέλω. • **πρεσβύτερος** → ὁ πρεσβύτερος, *elder, presbyter;* here perhaps *priest,* though the word was used for both lay and ordained leaders at this time (*PGL:* 1129–31). • **λαός** — here perhaps *congregation* (*PGL* 5: 792; cf. Justin, *Apology* 65.3), but the ref. may be to a gathering of monks. • **περιμένει** → περιμένω, *I wait for.* • **σπυρίδα** → ἡ σπυρίς, *large basket.* • **τετρημμένην** — pf. pass. ptc. → τετραίνω, *I perforate, make holes in.* • **γεμίσας** → γεμίζω, *I fill full of,* w. gen. • **ἄμμου** → ἡ ἄμμος,

κρῖναι. Οἱ δὲ ἀκούσαντες, οὐδὲν ἐλάλησαν τῷ ἀδελφῷ· ἀλλὰ συνεχώρησαν αὐτῷ.

Abba Mios 3 God's Care

Ἠρωτήθη ὁ ἀββᾶς Μιὼς ὑπὸ στρατευομένου, εἰ ἄρα δέχεται μετάνοιαν ὁ Θεός. Ὁ δὲ μετὰ τὸ κατηχῆσαι αὐτὸν ἐν πολλοῖς λόγοις, λέγει πρὸς αὐτόν· Εἰπέ μοι, ἀγαπητέ· ἐὰν σχισθῇ σου τὸ χλανίδιον, βάλλεις τοῦτο ἔξω; Λέγει· Οὔ· ἀλλὰ ῥάπτω αὐτό, καὶ χρῶμαι αὐτῷ. Λέγει πρὸς αὐτὸν ὁ γέρων· Εἰ οὖν σὺ τοῦ ἱματίου φείδη, ὁ Θεὸς τοῦ ἰδίου πλάσματος οὐ φείσεται;

Abba Poemen 184 What to Kill

Παρέβαλεν ὁ ἀββᾶς Ἰσαὰκ τῷ ἀββᾷ Ποιμένι· καὶ ἰδὼν αὐτὸν βάλλοντα μικρὸν ὕδωρ εἰς τοὺς πόδας αὐτοῦ ὡς ἔχων πρὸς αὐτὸν παρρησίαν, εἶπεν αὐτῷ· Πῶς τινες ἐχρήσαντο τῇ ἀποτομίᾳ, σκληραγωγήσαντες τὸ σῶμα αὐτῶν; Καὶ λέγει αὐτῷ ὁ ἀββᾶς Ποιμήν· Ἡμεῖς οὐκ ἐδιδάχθημεν σωματοκτόνοι, ἀλλὰ παθοκτόνοι.

---

sand. • **ἐβάστασεν** → βαστάζω, *I bear, carry.* Dir. obj. to be supplied. • **ἀπάντησιν** → ἡ ἀπάντησις, *meeting;* "unto his meeting," *to meet him.* • **γέρων** → ὁ γέρων, *elder, old man.* • **ὀπίσω** — *back, behind, following.* • **καταρρέουσαι** — pres. act. ptc. → καταρρέω, *I flow/rush/stream down.* Periphrastic. • **σήμερον** — *today.* • **ἁμαρτήματα** → τὸ ἁμάρτημα, *sin.* • **ἀλλότρια** → ἀλλότριος, α, ον, *belonging to another.* • **συνεχώρησαν** → συγχωρέω, *I assent to; forgive* (*PGL* 5: 1277).

Abba Mios 3

ἀββᾶς → ὁ ἀββᾶ, *a father.* • **Μιώς** → Μιώς, *Mios.* • **στρατευομένου** → στρατεύω, *I serve as a soldier, do military service.* • **ἄρα** — "freq. in questions that draw an inference fr. what precedes; but oft. simply to enliven the question" (BDAG 1b: 127). • **μετάνοιαν** → ἡ μετάνοια, *repentance.* • **μετά** — w. art. inf. for a temp. clause, *after.* • **κατηχῆσαι** → κατηχέω, *I teach, instruct.* • **λόγοις** — here probably the *matters* covered in the instruction (LSI AVII: 477; BDAG 1bε: 600). • **ἀγαπητέ** → ἀγαπητός, ή, όν, *beloved, dear.* • **σχισθῇ** → σχίζω, *I split, torn in two.* • **χλανίδιον** → τὸ χλανίδιον, *a cloak.* • **ῥάπτω** → ῥάπτω, *I sew/stitch together.* • **χρῶμαι** → χράομαι, *I use.* • **γέρων** → ὁ γέρων, *elder, old man.* • **φείδη** → φείδομαι, *I spare,* w. gen. • **πλάσματος** → τὸ πλάσμα, *image.* • **φείσεται** — fut. mid. (depon.) indic. → φείδομαι.

Abba Poemen 184

παρέβαλεν → παραβάλλω, *I visit* (*PGL* B3: 1007). • **ἀββᾶς** → ὁ ἀββᾶ, *a father.* • **Ἰσαάκ** → ὁ Ἰσαάκ, *Isaac.* • **Ποιμένι** → Ποιμήν, *Poemen* (the word means *shepherd*). • **μικρόν** → μικρός, α, ον, *small, little.* • **ὡς** — here, *since* (LSI BIV: 908; BDAG 3aβ: 1104). • **παρρησίαν** → ἡ παρρησία, *freedom of speech, boldness.* • **ἐχρήσαντο** → χράομαι, *I use.* Perhaps a gnomic aor. (Wal: 562; Smy:

Abba Sisoes 17 How to Share from the Scriptures

Ἠρώτησεν ὁ ἀββᾶς Ἀμμῶν ὁ τῆς Ῥαϊθοῦ τὸν ἀββᾶν Σισόην· Ὅταν ἀναγινώσκω Γραφήν, θέλει ὁ λογισμός μου φιλοκαλῆσαι λόγον, ἵνα ἔχω εἰς ἐπερώτημα. Λέγει αὐτῷ ὁ γέρων· Οὐκ ἔστι χρεία· ἀλλὰ μᾶλλον ἐκ τῆς καθαρότητος τοῦ νοὸς κτῆσαι σεαυτῷ καὶ τὸ ἀμεριμνεῖν καὶ τὸ λέγειν.

1931). • **ἀποτομίᾳ** → ἡ ἀποτομία, *severity.* • **σκληραγωγήσαντες** → σκληραγωγέω, *I treat harshly.* • **σωματοκτόνοι** → ὁ σωματοκτόνος, *one who kills or mortifies the body.* • **παθοκτόνοι** → ὁ παθοκτόνος, *one who kills or mortifies the passions.*

Abba Sisoes 17

ἀββᾶς → ὁ ἀββᾶ, *a father.* • **Ἀμμών** → Ἀμμών, *Ammon.* • **Ῥαϊθοῦ** → Ῥαϊθοῦ, *Rhaithou.* • **Σισόην** → Σισόης, *Sisoes.* • **ἀναγινώσκω** → ἀναγινώσκω, *I read.* • **Γραφήν** → ἡ γραφή, *writing, Scripture.* • **λογισμός** → ὁ λογισμός, *thought, imagination, reason, mind.* • **φιλοκαλῆσαι** → φιλοκαλέω, *I prepare* (*PGL* 3: 1479). • **ἐπερώτημα** → τὸ ἐπερώτημα, *question.* • **γέρων** → ὁ γέρων, *elder, old*

John Chrysostom

Homiliae in Matthaeum

Introduction

John Chrysostom (ca. 347–409) was one of the greatest preachers in the ancient church. Indeed, the name *Chrysostom* ("golden mouth") is really a nickname given to him by admirers in the fifth or sixth century. Of his many writings that survive, the majority are sermons on biblical texts. In addition, there are a number of topical sermon series, along with several treatises, including the influential work *Priesthood* and 241 letters.

John was brought up in an upper class Christian home in Antioch, Syria, and was given an excellent education in both rhetoric and biblical interpretation. His rhetorical style was greatly admired for its clarity and power. In his biblical exposition he focused on the literal sense of the text, as was typical of exegetes in Antioch, in distinction from the more allegorical approach of those of the Alexandrian school.

John suffered from poor health for most of his life, which he attributed to overzealous asceticism in his youth, when, between the completion of his education and his ordination to the diaconate in 381, he had spent four years living in the mountains near Antioch under the guidance of a hermit. Following that, he had lived alone in a cave for two years, memorizing the entire Bible. Although he later returned from seclusion and took up active ministry, he continued to exemplify a radical approach to discipleship throughout his life.

John was ordained a priest in 386 and served for twelve years in several of the churches of Antioch. He saw preaching as the central feature of his ministry, and the sermons on Matthew, from which the selection here is drawn, come from this period of his ministry. His messages stressed practical application rather than theological speculation, though he did at times discuss matters of theological controversy. In his sermons on John's Gospel, for example, he dealt with misinterpretations of particular texts by the Arians, who denied the full divinity of Christ.

His fame as a preacher spread widely. In 398 he was tricked into going to Constantinople, where he was consecrated bishop of Constantinople against his will. Once consecrated, however, he threw himself into the work. His sermons were very well received, often being interrupted by applause. He introduced reforms to address the low standard of discipleship among the clergy, promoted care for the poor, and spoke out against the luxuriant lifestyle of the upper class, including the emperor's household. While such efforts, along with his preaching, won him a strong following of supporters, they also made him many enemies. His reserved personality, sometimes interpreted as arrogance, also contributed to this negative response. He approached conflicts by speaking the truth plainly, at times publicly condemning the misdoings of prominent people. John's troubles greatly increased when Eudoxia, the wife of the emperor, set herself against him. In response John began a sermon during the liturgy celebrating the feast of John the Baptist, "Again Herodias raves; again she is troubled; she dances again; and again desires to receive John's head in a charger" (Socrates, *Church History* 6.18, *NPNF*[2])! Obviously, John was a preacher, not a politician, so, not surprisingly, his tenure in the most influential clerical position of the day was short-lived.

John's enemies in both court and church succeeded in getting him exiled. The last exile, in 404, was to Cucusus, Armenia. After three years in that place, he was sent even further away to Pityus, an isolated village at the east end of the Black Sea. He died on September 14, 407, while on his way to Pityus, as he was forced to march, despite poor health, in difficult weather over harsh terrain.

The selection included here is part of John' sermon on Matthew 14:22–36. It illustrates his Greek style, which is grammatically correct, clear, and simple, without the pretentiousness of many of the other trained orators of his day. This selection also illustrates John's interpretation of Scripture, including his attention to the context of a passage and his concern for the implications of a text for theology and discipleship. We also see in this selection the way John uses particular details of a text as starting points to include practical applications he has on his heart. Two of John's favorite themes, the condemnation of the false use of wealth and the concern for the poor, also come through clearly, as does his eucharistic theology.

Edition used: *PG* 58, col. 507–9.

Level of difficulty: Easy to intermediate [1–3]

Καὶ ἐπιβάντων αὐτῶν τοῦ πλοίου, τότε ἐπαύσατο ὁ ἄνεμος. Πρὸ τούτου μὲν ἔλεγον· **Ποταπός ἐστιν ὁ ἄνθρωπος οὗτος, ὅτι καὶ οἱ ἄνεμοι καὶ ἡ θάλασσα ὑπακούουσιν αὐτῷ;** νυνὶ δὲ οὐχ οὕτως. **Οἱ γὰρ ἐν τῷ πλοίῳ,** φησίν, **ἐλθόντες προσεκύνησαν αὐτῷ, λέγοντες· Ἀληθῶς Θεοῦ Υἱὸς εἶ.** Ὁρᾷς πῶς κατὰ μικρὸν ἐπὶ τὸ ὑψηλότερον ἅπαντας ἦγε; Καὶ γὰρ ἀπὸ τοῦ βαδίσαι ἐν τῇ θαλάσσῃ, καὶ ἀπὸ τοῦ ἑτέρῳ κελεῦσαι τοῦτο ποιῆσαι, καὶ κινδυνεύοντα διασῶσαι, πολλὴ λοιπὸν ἡ πίστις ἦν. Τότε μὲν γὰρ ἐπετίμησε τῇ θαλάσσῃ, νυνὶ δὲ οὐκ ἐπιτιμᾷ, ἑτέρως τὴν δύναμιν αὐτοῦ δεικνὺς μειζόνως. Διὸ καὶ ἔλεγον· **Ἀληθῶς Θεοῦ Υἱὸς εἶ.** Τί οὖν; ἐπετίμησε τοῦτο εἰρηκόσι; Τοὐναντίον μὲν οὖν ἅπαν, καὶ ἐβεβαίωσε τὸ λεχθέν, μετὰ μείζονος ἐξουσίας θεραπεύων τοὺς προσιόντας, καὶ οὐχ ὡς ἔμπροσθεν. **Καὶ διαπεράσαντες,** φησίν, **ἦλθον εἰς τὴν γῆν Γεννησαρέτ. Καὶ ἐπιγνόντες αὐτὸν οἱ ἄνδρες τοῦ τόπου ἐκείνου, ἀπέστειλαν εἰς ὅλην τὴν περίχωρον ἐκείνην, καὶ προσήνεγκαν αὐτῷ πάντας τοὺς κακῶς ἔχοντας, καὶ παρεκάλουν**

Homiliae in Matthaeum

50.2 **ἐπιβάντων** — 2 aor. act. ptc. → ἐπιβαίνω, *I go up/onto, board.* Gen. abs. • **ἐπαύσατο** → παύω, *I stop;* mid., *cease.* • **ἄνεμος** → ὁ ἄνεμος, *a wind.* • **πρό** — *before.* • **ποταπός** → ποταπός, ή, όν, *of what sort/kind.* • **ὑπακούουσιν** → ὑπακούω, *I obey.* • **νυνί** — adv., *now,* emphatic form of νῦν. • **ἀληθῶς** — adv., *truly.* • **μικρόν** → μικρός, ά, όν, *small, little.* κατὰ μικρόν, *little by little.* Distributive use of κατά (LSI II: 403; BDAG 1d; 2c: 512). • **ἐπί** — here, *towards* (LSI C5: 287; BDAG 4: 364). • **ὑψηλότερον** → ὑψηλότερος, α, ον, *higher,* comparative of ὑψηλός. • **ἅπαντας** → ἅπας, ἅπασα, ἅπαν, *all, whole.* • **βαδίσαι** — aor. act. inf. → βαδίζω, *I walk.* • **κελεῦσαι** — aor. act. inf. → κελεύω, *I command, order.* • **κινδυνεύοντα** → κινδυνεύω, *I am in danger.* Attrib. ptc., dir. obj. of the inf.; or circ. ptc. • **διασῶσαι** — aor. act. inf. → διασῴζω, *I bring safely through, save, rescue.* • **πολλή** → πολύς, here, *great.* • **ἡ πίστις** — art. for possession (Wal: 215; Smy: 1121), *their faith.* • **ἐπετίμησε** → ἐπιτιμάω, *I rebuke,* w. dat. • **ἑτέρως** — adv., *differently, in a different way, otherwise.* • **δεικνύς** — pres. act. ptc. masc. nom. sg. → δεικνύμι, *I show, make known.* • **μειζόνως** — adv., *in a great way,* adv. of μείζων, comparative of μέγας. • **διό** — *therefore, for this reason.* • **εἰρηκόσι** — pf. act. ptc. masc. dat. pl. → εἶπον. Attrib. dir. obj. • **τοὐναντίον** → τὸ ἐναντίον, adv., *contrary, opposite, on the other hand.* On crasis see Smy: 62–69. • **μὲν οὖν** — Here this combination is used to correct a statement, *no rather* (LSI II4: 498). • **ἅπαν** → ἅπας, ασα, αν, neut. sg. for adv., *entirely.* • **ἐβεβαίωσε** → βεβαιόω, *I confirm, establish.* • **λεχθέν** — aor. pass. ptc. neut. acc. sg. → λέγω. • **μείζονος** → μείζων, ον, *greater,* comparative of μέγας. • **θεραπεύων** → θεραπεύω, *I heal.* • **προσιόντας** — pres. act. ptc. → πρόσειμι, *I approach.* • **ἔμπροσθεν** — *before.* • **διαπεράσαντες** → διαπεράω, *I cross over.* Cf. Matt 14:34–36. • **Γεννησαρέτ** → ἡ Γεννησαρέτ, indecl., *Gennesaret.* • **ἐπιγνόντες** — aor. act. ptc. → ἐπιγινώσκω, *I recognize, notice.* • **περίχωρον** → περίχωρος, ον,

ἵνα ἅψωνται τοῦ κρασπέδου τοῦ ἱματίου αὐτοῦ· καὶ ὅσοι ἥψαντο ἐσώθησαν. Οὐδὲ γὰρ ὁμοίως ὡς πρότερον προσῄεσαν, εἰς τὰς οἰκίας αὐτὸν ἕλκοντες, καὶ χειρὸς ἁφὴν ἐπιζητοῦντες, καὶ προστάγματα διὰ ῥημάτων· ἀλλ' ὑψηλότερον πολλῷ καὶ φιλοσοφώτερον, καὶ μετὰ πλείονος τῆς πίστεως τὴν θεραπείαν ἐπεσπῶντο. Ἡ γὰρ αἱμορροοῦσα ἅπαντας ἐδίδαξε φιλοσοφεῖν. Δεικνὺς δὲ ὁ εὐαγγελιστής, ὅτι καὶ διὰ πολλοῦ χρόνου τοῖς μέρεσιν ἐπέβη, φησίν, ὅτι **Ἐπιγνόντες οἱ ἄνδρες τοῦ τόπου ἀπέστειλαν εἰς τὴν περίχωρον, καὶ προσήνεγκαν αὐτῷ τοὺς κακῶς ἔχοντας.** Ἀλλ' ὅμως ὁ χρόνος οὐ μόνον οὐκ ἐξέλυσε τὴν πίστιν, ἀλλὰ καὶ μείζονα εἰργάσατο, καὶ ἀκμάζουσαν διετήρησεν. Ἁψώμεθα τοίνυν καὶ ἡμεῖς τοῦ κρασπέδου τοῦ ἱματίου αὐτοῦ· μᾶλλον δὲ, ἐὰν θέλωμεν, ὅλον αὐτὸν ἔχομεν. Καὶ γὰρ καὶ τὸ σῶμα αὐτοῦ πρόκειται νῦν ἡμῖν· οὐ τὸ ἱμάτιον μόνον, ἀλλὰ καὶ τὸ σῶμα· οὐχ ὥστε ἅψασθαι μόνον, ἀλλ' ὥστε καὶ φαγεῖν καὶ ἐμφορηθῆναι. Προσερχώμεθα τοίνυν μετὰ πίστεως, ἕκαστος ἀσθένειαν ἔχων. Εἰ γὰρ οἱ

---

neighboring; subst., *neighborhood, region around.* • **προσήνεγκαν** — aor. act. indic. 3 pl. → προσφέρω, *I bring.* • **κακῶς** — adv., *bad, badly.* κακῶς ἔχοντας, *am ill/sick* (BDAG 1: 502). • **παρεκάλουν** → παρακαλέω, *I request, implore, entreat.* • **ἅψωνται** — aor. mid. (depon.) subjun. → ἅπτομαι, *I touch.* • **κρασπέδου** → τὸ κράσπεδον, *hem.* • **ἐσώθησαν** — aor. pass. indic. → σῴζω, here, *I save/free from disease* (BDAG 1c: 982). • **ὁμοίως** — adv., *likewise, so, similarly, in the same way.* • **πρότερον** → πρότερος, α, ον, *earlier.* • **προσῄεσαν** — impf. act. indic. 3 pl. → πρόσειμι. • **ἕλκοντες** → ἕλκω, *I draw, drag.* • **ἁφήν** → ἡ ἁφή, *a touch.* • **ἐπιζητοῦντες** → ἐπιζητέω, *I seek.* • **προστάγματα** → τὸ πρόσταγμα, *a command, order.* • **πολλῷ** → πολύς. Dat. sg. for the "degree of difference" (BDAG 2aβb: 849, cf. LSI III1b: 658), *very much, far, by far.* • **φιλοσοφώτερον** → φιλοσοφώτερος, α, ον, *more philosophical,* neut. sg. for adv. See note on φιλοσοφεῖν below. • **θεραπείαν** → ἡ θεραπεία, *treatment; healing, cure.* • **ἐπεσπῶντο** → ἐπισπάω, *I draw;* mid., *draw to oneself, bring upon.* Here perhaps the conative (Wal: 550; Smy: 1895), *they were trying to bring upon themselves.* • **αἱμορροοῦσα** → αἱμορροέω, *I have a discharge of blood, bleed, suffer with hemorrhage.* • **φιλοσοφεῖν** → φιλοσοφέω, *I live like a philosopher.* In Christian texts this means to live, "rationally and virtuously, and esp. in accordance with Christian morality" (*PGL* B: 1481). • **εὐαγγελιστής** → ὁ εὐαγγελιστής, *evangelist.* Here ref. to the Gospel writer, Matthew. • **διὰ πολλοῦ χρόνου** — *at long intervals* (LSI AII2: 184). • **μέρεσιν** → τὸ μέρος, *part;* pl. ref. to geographical parts, *region, district* (BDAG 1bγ: 633). • **ἐπέβη** — 2 aor. act. indic. 3 sg. → ἐπιβαίνω, here meaning, *I set foot in, enter* (BDAG 2: 367; *PGL* C: 517). • **ὅμως** — adv., *equally, likewise; all the same, yet.* • **ἐξέλυσε** → ἐκλύω, *I set free, put an end to.* • **εἰργάσατο** — aor. mid. (depon.) indic. → ἐργάζομαι, *I make.* • **ἀκμάζουσαν** → ἀκμάζω, *I flourish.* Perhaps circ. ptc. of manner. • **διετήρησεν** → διατηρέω, *I maintain.* • **ἁψώμεθα** → ἅπτω, *I fasten;* mid., *touch.* Hortatory subjun. The translation in *NPNF*[2] begins 50.3 here; *PG* continues 50.2. • **τοίνυν** — *therefore.* • **μᾶλλον δέ** — *or rather* (BDAG 3d: 614, cf. LSI, μάλα II4: 485). • **καὶ γὰρ καί** — *for indeed.* The first καί strengthens the γάρ (cf. BDAG, καί 2i: 496) and the second καί is ascensive. • **πρόκειται** → πρόκειμαι, *I am set before,* w. dat. • **φαγεῖν** → ἐσθίω. • **ἐμφορηθῆναι** → ἐμφορέω, *I pour in;* pass., *take one's fill of.* • **ἀσθένειαν** →

τοῦ κρασπέδου τοῦ ἱματίου αὐτοῦ ἁψάμενοι τοσαύτην εἵλκυσαν δύναμιν, πόσῳ μᾶλλον οἱ ὅλον αὐτὸν κατέχοντες; Τὸ δὲ προσελθεῖν μετὰ πίστεως οὐ τὸ λαβεῖν ἐστι μόνον τὸ προκείμενον, ἀλλὰ καὶ τὸ μετὰ καθαρᾶς καρδίας ἅψασθαι, τὸ οὕτω διακεῖσθαι, ὡς αὐτῷ προσιόντας τῷ Χριστῷ. Τί γάρ, εἰ μὴ φωνῆς ἀκούεις; Ἀλλ' ὁρᾷς αὐτὸν κείμενον· μᾶλλον δὲ καὶ φωνῆς ἀκούεις, φθεγγομένου αὐτοῦ διὰ τῶν εὐαγγελιστῶν.

Homiliae in Matthaeum 50.3 Approaching God with a Pure Soul

Πιστεύσατε τοίνυν, ὅτι καὶ νῦν ἐκεῖνο τὸ δεῖπνόν ἐστιν, ἐν ᾧ καὶ αὐτὸς ἀνέκειτο. Οὐδὲν γὰρ ἐκεῖνο τούτου διενήνοχεν. Οὐδὲ γὰρ τοῦτο μὲν ἄνθρωπος ἐργάζεται, ἐκεῖνο δὲ αὐτός, ἀλλὰ καὶ τοῦτο κἀκεῖνο αὐτός. Ὅταν τοίνυν τὸν ἱερέα ἐπιδιδόντα σοι ἴδῃς, μὴ τὸν ἱερέα νόμιζε τὸν τοῦτο ποιοῦντα, ἀλλὰ τὴν τοῦ Χριστοῦ χεῖρα εἶναι τὴν ἐκτεινομένην. . . .

Βούλει τιμῆσαι τοῦ Χριστοῦ τὸ σῶμα; Μὴ περιίδῃς αὐτὸν γυμνόν· μηδὲ ἐνταῦθα μὲν αὐτὸν σηρικοῖς ἱματίοις τιμήσῃς, ἔξω δὲ ὑπὸ κρυμοῦ καὶ

ἡ ἀσθένεια, *sickness, disease, illness.* • **τοσαύτην** → τοσοῦτος, τοσαύτη, τοσοῦτον, *so great, so much.* • **εἵλκυσαν** — 2 aor. act. indic. → ἕλκω. • **πόσῳ μᾶλλον** — *how much more* (BDAG, μᾶλλον 2b: 614). • **κατέχοντες** → κατέχω, *I hold fast.* • **προσελθεῖν** → προσέρχομαι. • **καθαρᾶς** → καθαρός, ά, όν, *pure, clean.* • **οὕτω** — οὕτως. • **διακεῖσθαι** — pres. mid. (depon.) inf. → διάκειμαι, *I am in a certain state, am disposed.* • **προσιόντας** — pres. act. ptc. → πρόσειμι, *I approach,* w. dat. • **τί γάρ** — *what, then?; what does it matter?* (BDAG, τίς 1aβℶ: 1007), so a literal rendering gives an exact equivalent, *so what?* • **εἰ μή** — *except, unless, if not.* • **κείμενον** → κεῖμαι, *I lie.* • **φθεγγομένου** → φθέγγομαι, *I speak loud and clear.* Gen. abs.

50.3 **τοίνυν** — *therefore.* • **δεῖπνον** → τὸ δεῖπνον, *a meal.* • **ἀνέκειτο** → ἀνάκειμαι, *I lie, recline, dine.* • **οὐδέν** → οὐδείς, *in no respect, in no way* (LSI III1: 576; BDAG 2bγ: 735). • **διενήνοχεν** — pf. act. indic. 3 sg. → διαφέρω, *I differ, am different from,* w. gen. Intensive pf. (Wal: 574; Smy: 1946–7). • **ἐργάζεται** → ἐργάζομαι, *I work, make.* • **ἐκεῖνο δὲ αὐτός** — αὐτός, ref. to the Lord. • **κἀκεῖνο** → καὶ ἐκεῖνο. • **ὅταν** → ὅτε and ἄν, *whenever.* • **ἱερέα** → ὁ ἱερεύς, *priest.* • **ἐπιδιδόντα** → ἐπιδίδωμι, *I give, deliver.* • **ἴδῃς** — 2 aor. act. subjun. 2 sg. → εἶδον/ὁράω. • **νόμιζε** → νομίζω, *I acknowledge, consider as, think, believe.* • **ἐκτεινομένην** → ἐκτείνω, *I stretch out.* Due to constraints of space I have omitted the material that comes next. In it Chrysostom develops further the topic of God's gift in the Eucharist, and then turns to challenge his hearers, "Let no Judas then approach this table . . ." I pick up the text in the midst of this challenge. In *PG* this further material is still part of 50.3, but in *NPNF*[2] it is found in 50.4. • **βούλει** → βούλομαι, *I wish, will.* • **τιμῆσαι** → τιμάω, *I honor.* • **περιίδῃς** — 2 aor. act. subjun. 2 sg. → περιοράω, *I overlook.* • **γυμνόν** → γυμνός, ή, όν, *naked.* • **ἐνταῦθα** — adv., *here, there.* • **σηρικοῖς** → σηρικός, ή, όν, *silk(en).* • **ἔξω** —

γυμνότητος διαφθειρόμενον περιίδης. Ὁ γὰρ εἰπών, **Τοῦτό μού ἐστι τὸ σῶμα,** καὶ τῷ λόγῳ τὸ πρᾶγμα βεβαιώσας, οὗτος εἶπε· **Πεινῶντά με εἴδετε, καὶ οὐκ ἐθρέψατε·** καί, **Ἐφ' ὅσον οὐκ ἐποιήσατε ἑνὶ τούτων τῶν ἐλαχίστων, οὐδὲ ἐμοὶ ἐποιήσατε.** Τοῦτο μὲν γὰρ οὐ δεῖται ἐπιβλημάτων, ἀλλὰ ψυχῆς καθαρᾶς· ἐκεῖνο δὲ πολλῆς δεῖται ἐπιμελείας. Μάθωμεν τοίνυν φιλοσοφεῖν, καὶ τὸν Χριστὸν τιμᾷν ὡς αὐτὸς βούλεται· τῷ γὰρ τιμωμένῳ τιμὴ ἡδίστη, ἣν αὐτὸς θέλει, οὐχ ἣν ἡμεῖς νομίζομεν. Ἐπεὶ καὶ Πέτρος τιμᾷν αὐτὸν ᾤετο τῷ κωλῦσαι νίψαι τοὺς πόδας, ἀλλ' οὐκ ἦν τιμὴ τὸ γινόμενον, ἀλλὰ τοὐναντίον. Οὕτω καὶ σὺ ταύτην αὐτὸν τίμα τὴν τιμήν, ἣν αὐτὸς ἐνομοθέτησεν, εἰς πένητας ἀναλίσκων τὸν πλοῦτον. Οὐδὲ γὰρ σκευῶν χρείαν ἔχει χρυσῶν ὁ Θεός, ἀλλὰ ψυχῶν χρυσῶν.

Homiliae in Matthaeum 50.4 Showing Mercy to Those in Need

Καὶ ταῦτα λέγω, οὐ κωλύων ἀναθήματα κατασκευάζεσθαι τοιαῦτα· ἀξιῶν δὲ μετὰ τούτων, καὶ πρὸ τούτων, τὴν ἐλεημοσύνην ποιεῖν. Δέχεται μὲν γὰρ

---

adv., *outside.* • **κρυμοῦ** → ὁ κρυμός, *icy cold.* • **γυμνότητος** → ἡ γυμνότης, *nakedness.* • **διαφθειρόμενον** → διαφθείρω, *I destroy, kill.* • **τοῦτο** — Cf. Matt 26:26. • **πρᾶγμα** → τὸ πρᾶγμα, *deed, thing, occurrence, matter.* • **βεβαιώσας** → βεβαιόω, *I confirm, establish.* • **πεινῶντα** → πεινάω, *I hunger, am hungry.* Cf. Matt 25:42, 45. • **ἐθρέψατε** — aor. act. indic. → τρέφω, *I feed.* • **ἐφ' ὅσον** — *inasmuch, to the degree that, in so far as* (BDAG, ἐπί 13: 366). • **ἐλαχίστων** → ἐλάχιστος, η, ον, *least,* superlative of ἐλαχύς. • **δεῖται** → δέομαι, *I am in want/need of,* w. gen. • **ἐπιβλημάτων** → τὸ ἐπίβλημα, *a covering.* • **καθαρᾶς** → καθαρός, ά, όν, *pure, clean.* • **ἐπιμελείας** → ἡ ἐπιμελεία, *care, attention.* • **μάθωμεν** — 2 aor. act. subjun. → μανθάνω, *I learn.* Hortatory subjun. • **τοίνυν** — *therefore.* • **φιλοσοφεῖν** → φιλοσοφέω, *I live like a philosopher,* which in Christian texts means to live "rationally and virtuously, and esp. in accordance with Christian morality" (*PGL* B: 1481). • **τιμᾷν** — pres. act. inf. → τιμάω, *I honor.* • **τιμή** → ἡ τιμή, *honor.* • **ἡδίστη** → ἥδιστος, η, ον, *most pleasing,* superlative of ἡδύς. • **νομίζομεν** → νομίζω, *I acknowledge, consider as, think, believe.* • **ἐπεί** — *since, because, for.* • **Πέτρος** → ὁ Πέτρος, *Peter.* • **ᾤετο** — impf. mid. (depon.) indic. → οἴομαι, *I suppose, think.* • **κωλῦσαι** — aor. act. inf. → κωλύω, *I hinder, prevent.* • **νίψαι** → νίπτω, *I wash.* Supplemental inf. • **τοὐναντίον** → τὸ ἐναντίον, *contrary, opposite, on the other hand.* On crasis see Smy: 62–69. • **οὕτω** → οὕτως. • **ἐνομοθέτησεν** → νομοθετέω, *I make law, legislate, ordain.* • **πένητας** — acc. pl. → ὁ πένης, *a poor person.* • **ἀναλίσκων** → ἀναλίσκω, *I use up, spend, lavish.* • **πλοῦτον** → ὁ πλοῦτος, *wealth, riches.* • **σκευῶν** → τὸ σκεῦος, *vessel.* • **χρείαν** → ἡ χρεία, *use, need.* • **χρυσῶν** → χρυσός, ή, όν, *gold(en).*

50.4 **κωλύων** → κωλύω, *I hinder, prevent;* w. acc. and inf., *hinder/prevent* one *from* doing. Here, circ. ptc., purpose. • **ἀναθήματα** → τὸ ἀνάθημα, *offering.* • **κατασκευάζεσθαι** → κατασκευάζω, *I make, furnish.* • **ἀξιῶν** → ἀξιόω, *I expect, require, demand.* • **πρό** — *before,* w. gen. • **ἐλεημοσύνην** → ἡ ἐλεημοσύνη, *pity,*

καὶ ταῦτα, πολλῷ δὲ μᾶλλον ἐκεῖνα. Ἐνταῦθα μὲν γὰρ ὁ προσενεγκὼν ὠφελήθη μόνον, ἐκεῖ δὲ καὶ ὁ λαβών. Ἐνταῦθα δοκεῖ καὶ φιλοτιμίας ἀφορμὴ τὸ πρᾶγμα εἶναι· ἐκεῖ δὲ ἐλεημοσύνη καὶ φιλανθρωπία τὸ πᾶν ἐστι. Τί γὰρ ὄφελος, ὅταν ἡ τράπεζα αὐτῷ γέμῃ χρυσῶν ποτηρίων, αὐτὸς δὲ λιμῷ διαφθείρηται; Πρότερον αὐτὸν ἔμπλησον πεινῶντα, καὶ τότε ἐκ περιουσίας καὶ τὴν τράπεζαν αὐτοῦ κόσμησον. Ποτήριον χρυσοῦν ποιεῖς, καὶ ποτήριον ψυχροῦ οὐ δίδως; καὶ τί τὸ ὄφελος; Χρυσόπαστα ἐπιβλήματα κατασκευάζεις τῇ τραπέζῃ, αὐτῷ δὲ οὐδὲ τὴν ἀναγκαίαν παρέχεις σκέπην; καὶ τί τὸ κέρδος ἐκ τούτου; Εἰπὲ γάρ μοι· εἴ τινα ἰδὼν τῆς ἀναγκαίας ἀποροῦντα τροφῆς, ἀφεὶς αὐτῷ λῦσαι τὸν λιμὸν, τὴν τράπεζαν ἀργύρῳ περιέβαλες μόνον, ἆρα ἂν ἔγνω σοι χάριν, ἀλλ' οὐχὶ μᾶλλον ἠγανάκτησε; Τί δέ; εἰ ῥάκια περιβεβλημένον ὁρῶν, καὶ ὑπὸ κρυμοῦ πηγνύμενον, ἀφεὶς αὐτῷ δοῦναι ἱμάτιον, κίονας κατεσκεύαζες χρυσοῦς, λέγων εἰς ἐκείνου

---

alms. • **ποιεῖν** → ποιέω. Inf. for indir. disc., the content of the demand (Wal: 603; Smy: 2016), here w. ἐλεημοσύνην, *I give.* • **δέχεται** → δέχομαι, *I receive, accept.* • **πολλῷ δὲ μᾶλλον** — *but much/even more* (BDAG, μᾶλλον 1:613). • **ἐνταῦθα** — adv., *here, there.* • **προσενεγκών** — 2 aor. act. ptc. → προσφέρω, *I offer.* • **ὠφελήθη** → ὠφελέω, *I help, aid* • **δοκεῖ** → δοκέω, *I seem.* • **φιλοτιμίας** → ἡ φιλοτιμία, *ambition; generosity.* Either of these meanings work in this sentence, though with very different effect. • **ἀφορμή** → ἡ ἀφορμή, *base of operations, occasion.* • **πρᾶγμα** → τὸ πρᾶγμα, *deed, thing, occurrence, matter.* • **φιλανθρωπία** → ἡ φιλανθρωπία, *love towards humanity, benevolence.* • **ὄφελος** → τὸ ὄφελος, *advantage, help; use.* • **ὅταν** → ὅτε and ἄν, *when.* W. subjun. for indef. temp. clause. • **τράπεζα** → ἡ τράπεζα, *table.* • **γέμῃ** → γέμω, *I am full.* • **χρυσῶν** → χρυσός, ή, όν, *golden.* • **ποτηρίων** → τὸ ποτήριον, *drinking cup.* • **λιμῷ** → ὁ λιμός, *hunger, famine.* • **διαφθείρηται** → διαφθείρω, *I destroy utterly;* here, *waste away* (BDAG 1: 239). • **πρότερον** → πρότερος, α, ον, *before, first.* • **ἔμπλησον** — aor. act. impv. 2 sg. → ἐμπίμπλημι, *I fill.* • **πεινῶντα** → πεινάω, *I hunger, am hungry.* • **ἐκ** — for an adv., (LSI III7: 235; BDAG 6c: 298). ἐκ περιουσίας, *abundantly.* • **περιουσίας** → περιούσιος, ον, *more than enough, special.* • **κόσμησον** → κοσμέω, *I order; adorn, furnish, deck out.* • **ψυχροῦ** → ψυχρός, ά, όν, *cold.* • **δίδως** → δίδωμι. • **χρυσόπαστα** → χρυσόπαστος, ον, *sprinkled with gold, gold-spangled.* • **ἐπιβλήματα** → τὸ ἐπίβλημα, *a covering.* • **κατασκευάζεις** → κατασκευάζω, *I make, prepare.* • **ἀναγκαίαν** → ἀναγκαῖος, α, ον, *necessary.* • **παρέχεις** → παρέχω, *I furnish, provide, supply.* • **σκέπην** → ἡ σκέπη, *covering, shelter.* • **κέρδος** → τὸ κέρδος, *gain, profit, advantage.* • **ἰδών** → εἶδον. • **ἀποροῦντα** → ἀπορέω, *I am at a loss, am in want.* • **τροφῆς** → ἡ τροφή, *food.* • **ἀφείς** — aor. act. ptc. masc. nom. sg. → ἀφίημι, *I leave alone, neglect.* • **λῦσαι** → λύω, *I loosen, undo, do away with, put an end to.* • **ἀργύρῳ** → ὁ ἄργυρος, *silver.* • **περιέβαλες** — 2 aor. act. indic. → περιβάλλω, *I throw around, wrap, enclose;* here, *overlay.* • **ἆρα** — interrogative particle expecting a neg. answer. • **ἔγνω** → γίνωσκω. ἔγνω σοι χάριν, "would he acknowledge thanks to you," *would he feel grateful to you.* Cf. the similar expression in Classical Greek using οἶδα (LSJ, χάρις II2: 1979). • **ἠγανάκτησε** → ἀγανακτέω, *I feel irritation, am annoyed/angry/vexed.* • **ῥάκια** → τὸ ῥάκιον, *rag.* • **ὁρῶν** — here perhaps attend. circ. • **κρυμοῦ** → ὁ κρυμός, *icy cold.* • **πηγνύμενον** → πηγνύμι, *I make fast;* pass., *am solid/stiff.* • **δοῦναι** — aor. act. inf. → δίδωμι. • **κίονας** → ὁ κίων,

τιμὴν ποιεῖν, οὐκ ἄν σε καὶ εἰρωνεύεσθαι ἔφη, καὶ ὕβριν ἐνόμισε, καὶ ταύτην τὴν ἐσχάτην; Τοῦτο δὲ καὶ ἐπὶ τοῦ Χριστοῦ λογίζου, ὅταν ἀλήτης καὶ ξένος περιέρχηται, δεόμενος ὀροφῆς· σὺ δὲ αὐτὸν ἀφεὶς ὑποδέξασθαι, ἔδαφος καλλωπίζῃς καὶ τοίχους καὶ κιόνων κεφαλάς· καὶ ἀργυρᾶς ἁλύσεις διὰ λαμπάδων ἐξάπτῃς, αὐτὸν δὲ ἐν δεσμωτηρίῳ δεδεμένον μηδὲ ἰδεῖν ἐθέλῃς. Καὶ ταῦτα λέγω, οὐχὶ κωλύων ἐν τούτοις φιλοτιμεῖσθαι, ἀλλὰ ταῦτα μετ' ἐκείνων, μᾶλλον δὲ ταῦτα πρὸ ἐκείνων παραινῶν ποιεῖν. Ὑπὲρ μὲν γὰρ τοῦ ταῦτα μὴ ποιῆσαι οὐδεὶς ἐνεκλήθη ποτέ· ὑπὲρ δὲ ἐκείνων καὶ γέεννα ἠπείληται, καὶ πῦρ ἄσβεστον, καὶ ἡ μετὰ δαιμόνων τιμωρία. Μὴ τοίνυν τὸν οἶκον κοσμῶν, τὸν ἀδελφὸν θλιβόμενον περιόρα· οὗτος γὰρ ἐκείνου ναὸς κυριώτερος.

---

pillar, column. • **κατεσκεύαζες** — perhaps ingressive/inchoative (Wal: 544; Smy: 1900). • **ποιεῖν** — inf. for indir. disc., the content of what was said (Wal: 603; Smy: 2016). • **σε** — subj. of inf. • **εἰρωνεύεσθαι** → εἰρωνεύομαι, *I insult* (*PGL* 3: 421). Inf. for indir. disc. • **ὕβριν** → ἡ ὕβρις, *insolence.* • **ἐνόμισε** → νομίζω, *I consider as.* • **ἐσχάτην** → ἔσχατος, here in the sense, *uttermost, the most extreme, worst.* • **ἐπί** — here, *in regard to, concerning, about* (BDAG 8: 365). • **λογίζου** → λογίζομαι, *I reckon, evaluate, look upon as, consider, think about.* • **ἀλήτης** → ὁ ἀλήτης, *wanderer, vagabond.* • **ξένος** → ὁ ξένος, *stranger.* • **περιέρχηται** → περιέρχομαι, *I go about.* • **δεόμενος** → δέομαι, *I am in want, need, stand in need of.* • **ὀροφῆς** → ἡ ὀροφή, *roof.* • **ὑποδέξασθαι** → ὑποδέχομαι, *I receive, receive into one's house.* • **ἔδαφος** → τὸ ἔδοφος, *foundation, pavement.* • **καλλωπίζῃς** → καλλωπίζω, *I beautify, embellish.* • **τοίχους** → ὁ τοῖχος, *wall.* • **κεφαλάς** → κεφαλή, here the capital of a column. • **ἀργυρᾶς** → ἀργυροῦς, ᾶ, οῦν (listed in LSJ under the uncontracted form ἀργύρεος), *silver.* • **ἁλύσεις** → ἡ ἅλυσις, *chain.* • **λαμπάδων** → ἡ λαμπάς, *lamp.* • **ἐξάπτῃς** → ἐξάπτω, *I fasten.* • **δεσμωτηρίῳ** → τὸ δεσμωτήριον, *prison.* • **δεδεμένον** — pf. pass. ptc. → δέω, *I bind.* • **Καὶ ταῦτα** — *NPNF*[2] begins 50.5 here; *PG* continues 50.4. • **κωλύων** → κωλύω. Circ. ptc., purpose. • **φιλοτιμεῖσθαι** → φιλοτιμέομαι, *I am ambitious, strive eagerly.* • **παραινῶν** → παραινέω, *I exhort, recommend, advise.* Circ. ptc., purpose. • **ποιεῖν** — inf. for indir. disc., the content of the demand (Wal: 603; Smy: 2016). • **ἐνεκλήθη** → ἐγκαλέω, *I accuse.* • **ποτέ** — *ever.* • **γέεννα** → ἡ γέεννα, *Gehenna, hell.* • **ἠπείληται** — pf. pass. indic. → ἀπειλέω, *I threaten, warn.* Intensive pf. (Wal: 574; Smy: 1946–7). • **ἄσβεστον** → ἄσβεστος, ον, *unquenchable, inextinguishable.* • **δαιμόνων** → ὁ δαίμων, *demon, evil spirit.* • **τιμωρία** → ἡ τιμωρία, *punishment.* • **τοίνυν** — *therefore.* • **κοσμῶν** → κοσμέω. Attend. circ. • **θλιβόμενον** → θλίβω, *I oppress, afflict.* • **περιόρα** — pres. act. impv. → περιοράω, *I overlook.* • **ἐκείνου** — gen. of comparison (Wal: 110; Smy: 1069). • **ναός** → ὁ ναός, *temple.* • **κυριώτερος** → κυριώτερος, α, ον, *more properly/legitimately,* comparative of κύριος, α, ον.

Hesychios the Priest

On Watchfulness and Holiness

Introduction

In recent decades contemplative forms of prayer have become increasingly popular among Christians. As many people have turned toward the religions of the East, Christians in the West have begun to discover the rich resources for contemplation that were present in the ancient church and that have been practiced continuously in the Eastern church. Hesychios' *On Watchfulness and Holiness* is one of those resources.

In the past *On Watchfulness and Holiness* was thought to be by Hesychios of Jerusalem, a prolific writer of the fifth century. But actually the author is a different Hesychios, about whom very little is known apart from the fact that he was the abbot of the Monastery of the Mother of God of the Burning Bush, located on the Sinai peninsula.[1] Accordingly, he is sometimes known as Hesychios the Sinaite. Because he appears to be familiar with the *Ladder of Divine Ascent* by John Climacus (ca. 575–ca. 650), Hesychios is believed to have lived in the seventh or eighth century.

On Watchfulness and Holiness is included in a collection of various patristic spiritual writings known as the *Philokalia* (also spelled *Philocalia*). This collection of Greek texts from the fourth to the fifteenth centuries was compiled in the eighteenth century by Nikodimos Hagiorites (Nikodimos of the Holy Mountain) and Makarios of Corinth. It was published in Venice in 1782, and was soon translated into church Slavonic and published in 1793 by Paisij Velichkovskij. The present five volume Greek edition contains over 1,400 pages of text. Four of the five volumes are currently available in English.[2]

The *Philokalia* plays a fundamental role in Eastern Orthodoxy, and it is becoming more influential in the West as well, especially through the popularity of the Jesus Prayer, which is the invocation of Jesus using the prayer, "Lord Jesus Christ, Son of God, have mercy on me, a sinner," or some shorter version of these or similar words. Such simple, repeated prayer was a part of the spirituality of the Desert Fathers and Mothers, as well as

---

[1] C. Schmidt, "Hesychius, Abbot of the Monastery of the Burning Bush," in *Dictionary of Early Christian Literature* (ed. Siegmar Döpp and Wilhelm Geerlings; trans. Matthew O'Connell; New York: Crossroad Publishing, 2000), 279.

[2] St Nikodimos of the Holy Mountain and St Makarios of Corinth, compilers, *The Philokalia: The Complete Text* (trans. and eds. G. E. H. Palmer, Philip Sherrard and Kallistos Ware, with the assistance of the Holy Transfiguration Monastery [Brookline], Constantine Cavarnos, Basil Osborne, and Norman Russell; 4 vols.; London: Faber and Faber, 1979–1995).

others, from very early on, and plays a very important role in early Christian spirituality and throughout the history of Eastern Orthodox spirituality.

The spirituality of the *Philokalia* is called Hesychasm, from the Greek word ἡσυχία, meaning "stillness." This refers to "a state of inner tranquility or mental quietude and concentration which arises in conjunction with, and is deepened by, the practice of pure prayer and the guarding of the heart . . . and intellect. . . . Not simply silence, but an attitude of listening to God and of openness towards Him."[3] It is an intense form of practicing the presence of God, stepping back from all other thoughts and feelings except for an attentiveness to Jesus and a sense of love for him. It is not passivity, but rather vigilance, watching and listening in Christ, with Christ, and for Christ. Its goal is to experience, through union with Christ, a love for God and a sharing in God's love for people, and, indeed, a sharing in God's love for all that exists.

Most of the texts in the *Philokalia* were written for monastics and thus contain material that is not always directly applicable to non-monastics. Hesychios the Priest's *On Watchfulness and Holiness* is one of the more accessible writings. The brief selections presented here give an idea of the meaning of watchfulness, which is fundamental to hesychastic spirituality, and also provide a glimpse of the vision of life in Christ that these writings express.

There is no critical edition for this text. The text used here from *PG* differs in several places from the edition published by Astir (see the bibliography). Since the main English translation (Palmer, et al.) is based on the Astir edition, I have indicated in the notes those differences that might confuse a student consulting the English translation.

Editions used:	Sections 1–6: *PG* 93, cols. 1480, 1481, 1484 Sections 27–29: *PG* 93, cols. 1488, 1489 Sections 79–82: *PG* 93, cols. 1504, 1505
Level of difficulty:	Intermediate [2–4]

[3] Nikodimos and Makarios, *Philokalia*, 1:364.

On Watchfulness and Holiness 1–6 Invoking Jesus with a Still Heart

Section 1

Νῆψίς ἐστι μέθοδος πνευματική, ἐμπαθῶν νοημάτων καὶ λόγων καὶ πονηρῶν ἔργων πάμπαν τὸν ἄνθρωπον σὺν Θεῷ ἀπαλλάττουσα, χρονίζουσα, καὶ προθύμως ὁδευομένη· γνῶσίν τε ἀσφαλῆ Θεοῦ τοῦ ἀκαταλήπτου ὁδευομένη χαρίζεται, καθ' ὅσον ἐφικτόν, καὶ μυστηρίων θείων καὶ ἀποκρύφων ἀποκρύφως λύσιν· ὑπάρχει τε πάσης ἐντολῆς Θεοῦ Παλαιᾶς καὶ Νέας Διαθήκης ποιητική, καὶ παντὸς ἀγαθοῦ τοῦ μέλλοντος αἰῶνος παρεκτική. Αὕτη δὲ κυρίως ἐστίν, ἡ τῆς καρδίας καθαρότης· ἥτις διὰ τὸ μέγεθος καὶ τὴν καλλονὴν αὐτῆς, ἢ κυριωτέρως εἰπεῖν, διὰ τὴν ἀπροσεξίαν καὶ ἀμέλειαν ἡμῶν, σπανίζει σήμερον πάνυ ἐν μοναχοῖς· ἣν ὁ Χριστὸς μακαρίζει λέγων· **Μακάριοι οἱ καθαροὶ τῇ καρδίᾳ, ὅτι αὐτοὶ τὸν Θεὸν ὄψονται.**

Sections 1–6

1 **νῆψις** → ἡ νῆψις, *sobriety, sober-mindedness; alertness, watchfulness.* • **μέθοδος** → ἡ μέθοδος, *pursuit; investigation; method.* • **πνευματική** → πνευματικός, ή, όν, *spiritual.* • **ἐμπαθῶν** → ἐμπαθής, ές, *passionate, impassioned.* • **νοημάτων** → τὸ νόημα, *thought.* • **πάμπαν** — adv., *wholly, altogether.* • **ἀπαλλάττουσα** → ἀπαλλάττω (listed in lexicons under the alternate form ἀπαλλάσσω), *I set free, release, liberate;* w. acc. and gen., "someone from something." Attrib. ptc. • **χρονίζουσα** → χρονίζω, *I take time, spend time, last, continue.* Attrib. ptc. • **προθύμως** — adv., *eagerly, zealously, actively.* • **ὁδευομένη** → ὁδεύω, *I go, travel, journey, proceed.* While the ptc. ὁδευομένη can mean *highway, pathway* (LSJ: 1198), here it seems to be simply an attrib. ptc. In the rest of the sentence it is a circ. ptc. • **γνῶσιν** → ἡ γνῶσις, *knowledge.* • **ἀσφαλῆ** → ἀσφαλής, ές, *steadfast, firm, sure, certain.* • **ἀκαταλήπτου** → ἀκατάληπτος, ον, *what cannot be touched/grasped/understood.* • **χαρίζεται** → χαρίζομαι, *I give freely.* • **καθ' ὅσον** — *so far as, so much as* (LSI, ὅσος V: 573). • **ἐφικτόν** → ἐφικτός, ή, όν, *easy to reach, accessible.* • **μυστηρίων** → τὸ μυστήριον, *mystery.* • **θείων** → θεῖος, α, ον, *divine.* • **ἀποκρύφων** → ἀπόκρυφος, ον, *hidden.* • **ἀποκρύφως** — adv., *secretly.* Not in the Astir ed. • **λύσιν** → ἡ λύσις, *loosing; solution (to a problem), interpretation* (LSJ II4a: 1066; *PGL* 6: 815). • **Παλαιᾶς** → παλαιός, ά, όν, *old.* • **Νέας** → νέος, α, ον, *new.* • **Διαθήκης** → ἡ διαθήκη, *covenant, testament.* • **ποιητική** → ποιητικός, ή, όν, *able to make/create,* w. gen. (LSJ: 1429); here w. ἐντολῆς, *able to keep, fulfill.* • **παρεκτική** → παρεκτικός, ή, όν, *able to cause.* • **κυρίως** — adv., *properly, in the proper sense.* • **καθαρότης** → ἡ καθαρότης, *purity.* • **μέγεθος** → τὸ μέγεθος, *greatness.* • **καλλονήν** → ἡ καλλονή, *beauty.* • **κυριωτέρως** — adv., *more properly.* • **ἀπροσεξίαν** → ἡ ἀπροσεξία, *lack of attention.* Not in the Astir ed. • **ἀμέλειαν** → ἡ ἀμέλεια, *negligence.* • **σπανίζει** → σπανίζω, *I am rare, scarce.* • **σήμερον** — adv., *today.* • **πάνυ** — adv., *altogether, entirely, very, exceedingly.* • **μοναχοῖς** → μοναχός, ή, όν, *single, solitary;* subst., *monk.* • **μακαρίζει**

Τοιαύτη οὖν οὖσα, πολλοῦ ἀγοράζεται. Νῆψις ἐν ἀνθρώπῳ χρονίζουσα, ὀρθοῦ καὶ θεαρέστου βίου ὁδηγὸς γίνεται. Τούτου καὶ ἐπίβασις, θεωρίαν καὶ τὸ τριμερὲς τῆς ψυχῆς δικαίως κινεῖν ἡμᾶς ἐκδιδάσκει, τὰς αἰσθήσεις τε ἀσφαλῶς τηρεῖ, καὶ τὰς γενικὰς τέσσαρας ἀρετὰς ἐν τῷ μετόχῳ αὐτῆς καθ' ἡμέραν αὔξει.

Section 2

Ὁ μέγας νομοθέτης Μωσῆς, μᾶλλον δὲ τὸ Πνεῦμα τὸ ἅγιον, ὑποδεικνύων τὸ ἄμεμπτον καὶ καθαρόν, καὶ περιεκτικόν, καὶ ὑψοποιὸν τῆς τοιαύτης ἀρετῆς, καὶ διδάσκων ἡμᾶς, ὅπως ταύτης ἄρχεσθαι καὶ ἐκτελεῖν δεῖ, **Πρόσεχε σεαυτῷ,** φησί, **μὴ γένηται ῥῆμα κρυπτόν,** τὴν μονολόγιστον ἐμφάνειαν ὀνομάζων πράγματός τινος μισουμένου πονηροῦ ὑπὸ Θεοῦ· ἣν

→ μακαρίζω, *I bless.* • **μακάριοι** → μακάριος, α, ον, *blessed.* • **καθαροί** → καθαρός, ά, όν, *clean, pure.* • **ὄψονται** → ὁράω. • **πολλοῦ** — gen. of price, "for much," *at/for a great price* (Wal: 122; Smy: 1336). • **ἀγοράζεται** → ἀγοράζω, *I buy.* • **ὀρθοῦ** → ὀρθός, ή, όν, *straight, upright, true, correct.* • **θεαρέστου** → θεάρεστος, ον, *pleasing to God.* • **βίου** → ὁ βίος, *life.* • **ὁδηγός** → ὁ ὁδηγός, *a guide.* • **Τούτου** — the gender indicates the ref. is ὁδηγός. • **ἐπίβασις** → ἡ ἐπίβασις, *means of approach, access, entrance.* • **θεωρίαν** → ἡ θεωρία, *contemplation.* The Astir ed. reads τοῦτο καὶ ἐπίβασις θεωρίας, "This (guide) is also an entrance to con- templation." • **τριμερές** → τριμερής, ές, *three part, threefold, tripartite.* • **δικαίως** — adv., *rightly, correctly.* • **κινεῖν** → κινέω, *I set in motion, arouse.* • **ἐκδιδάσκει** → ἐκδιδάσκω, *I teach thoroughly.* • **αἰσθήσεις** → ἡ αἴσθησις, *perception, sense* (i.e., one of the senses). • **ἀσφαλῶς** — adv., *firmly, steadfastly, surely, certainly.* • **γενικάς** → γενικός, ή, όν, *principal* (LSJ 2: 344). • **τέσσαρας** → τέσσαρες, τέσσαρα, *four.* • **ἀρετάς** → ἡ ἀρετή, *virtue.* • **μετόχῳ** → μέτοχος, ον, *sharing/participating in.* • **αὐτῆς** — the gender indicates the ref. is νῆψις. Obj. gen. • **καθ' ἡμέραν** — *daily, day by day.* Distributive use of κατά (LSI BII2: 403; BDAG B2c: 512). • **αὔξει** → αὔξω (listed in lexicons under the alternate form αὐξάνω), *I cause to grow/increase.*

2 **νομοθέτης** → ὁ νομοθέτης, *lawgiver.* • **Μωσῆς** → ὁ Μωσῆς (listed in BDAG under the alternate form Μωϋσῆς), *Moses.* • **μᾶλλον δέ** — *or rather, much more* (LSI, μάλα II4: 485; BDAG, μᾶλλον 3d: 614). • **ὑποδεικνύων** → ὑποδείκνυμι, *I indicate, point out.* • **ἄμεμπτον** → ἄμεμπτος, ον, *blameless, faultless.* A noun such as *character* should be supplied for this string of adj. • **καθαρόν** → καθαρός, ά, όν, *clean, pure.* • **περιεκτικόν** → περιεκτικός, ή, όν, *comprehensive.* • **ὑψοποιόν** → ὑψοποιός, ή, όν, *exalting, elevating.* • **ἀρετῆς** → ἡ ἀρετή, *virtue.* • **ὅπως** — *how.* • **ταύτης** — fem. in agreement w. ἀρετή, gen. because ἄρχομαι takes a gen. • **ἐκτελεῖν** → ἐκτελέω, *I bring to an end, complete, accomplish, achieve.* • **πρόσεχε** → προσέχω, *I take care, give heed.* • **σεαυτῷ** → σεαυτοῦ, *yourself.* • **ῥῆμα** → τὸ ῥῆμα, *word; thing, matter.* • **κρυπτόν** → κρυπτός, ή, όν, *hidden.* The Astir ed. adds ἐν τῇ καρδίᾳ σου ἀνόμημα, "lest there be in your heart a hidden thing, an iniquity" (ἀνόμημα → τὸ ἀνόμημα, *lawless deed/action, iniquity.* In appos. to ῥῆμα). • **μονολόγιστον** → μονολόγιστος, ον, *of a single thought* (*PGL*: 882). • **ἐμφάνειαν** → ἡ ἐμφάνεια, *manifestation.* τὴν μονολόγιστον ἐμφάνειαν, "the single-thoughted manifestation," *manifestation of a single thought.* The Astir ed. has ἔμφασιν (→ ἡ ἔμφασις, *impression*). • **ὀνομάζων** → ὀνομάζω, *I*

δὴ καὶ προσβολὴν λέγουσιν οἱ Πατέρες, προσαγομένην τῇ καρδίᾳ σου παρὰ τοῦ διαβόλου, ᾗ ἐπακολουθοῦσιν οἱ ἡμῶν λογισμοί, εὐθὺς παραφανείσῃ τῷ νῷ, ἐμπαθῶς τε αὐτῇ προσδιαλέγονται.

Section 3

Νῆψίς ἐστιν ὁδὸς πάσης ἀρετῆς καὶ ἐντολῆς Θεοῦ, ἥτις καὶ καρδία καὶ ἡσυχία, καὶ ἀφάνταστος τελειωθεῖσα φυλακὴ νοὸς ἡ αὐτή.

Section 4

Οὐχ ὁρᾷ φῶς ἡλίου ὁ γεννηθεὶς τυφλός· οὕτως οὐδὲ ὁ μὴ νήψει ὁδεύων ὁρᾷ πλουσίως τὰς μαρμαρυγὰς τῆς ἄνωθεν χάριτος· οὔτε δὲ ἐλευθερωθήσεται ἐκ πονηρῶν καὶ μισητῶν Θεῷ ἔργων τε καὶ λόγων καὶ ἐννοιῶν, ὅς οὐκ ἐλευθερίῳ τρόπῳ ἐν τῇ ἐξόδῳ τοὺς ταρταρίους παρελεύσεται ἄρχοντας.

---

call, name, specify, speak specifically of. • **πράγματος** → τὸ πρᾶγμα, *deed, act, thing, matter.* • **μισουμένου** → μισέω, *I hate.* • **δή** — *indeed, in fact.* • **προσβολήν** → ἡ προσβολή, *attack, assault.* • **λέγουσιν** — here, *I call* (BDAG 4: 590). • **προσαγομένην** → προσάγω, *I bring to/upon.* Attrib. ptc. • **διαβόλου** → ὁ διάβολος, *slanderer, the devil.* • **ἐπακολουθοῦσιν** → ἐπακολουθέω, *I follow after, pursue, chase,* w. dat. • **λογισμοί** → ὁ λογισμός, *reasoning, thought.* • **εὐθύς** — here, *as soon as.* • **παραφανείσῃ** — aor. pass. ptc. fem. dat. sg. → παραφαίνω, *I show beside;* pass., *appear, disclose itself.* • **νῷ** → ὁ νοῦς, *mind.* • **ἐμπαθῶς** — adv., *passionately.* • **προσδιαλέγονται** → προσδιαλέγομαι, *I converse with,* w. dat. (LSJ 2: 1506).

3 **νῆψις** → ἡ νῆψις, *sobriety, sober-mindedness; alertness, watchfulness.* See note in the translation of section 1. • **ἀρετῆς** → ἡ ἀρετή, *virtue.* • **καρδία** — The Astir ed. has ἥτις καὶ καρδιακὴ ἡσυχία λέγεται, "which is also called stillness of the heart" (καρδιακή → καρδιακός, ή, όν, *of the heart*). • **ἡσυχία** → ἡ ἡσυχία, *stillness.* The Astir ed. adds after this word, λέγεται, here, *call* (BDAG 4: 590). • **ἀφάνταστος** → ἀφάνταστος, ον, *free from fancy/mental images.* Pred. nom. w. a pass. (Wal: 40). The Astir ed. has ἀφαντάστως (adv., *really, in reality, not imaginarily, PGL:* 273), "when it is, in reality, perfected." • **τελειωθεῖσα** — aor. pass. ptc. → τελειόω, *I make perfect, complete.* Temp. circ. ptc. • **φυλακή** → ἡ φυλακή, *watching, guarding.* • **νοός** — gen. → ὁ νοῦς, *mind.* See note in the translation of section 2.

4 **ἡλίου** → ὁ ἥλιος, *sun.* • **γεννηθείς** → γεννάω. • **οὕτως** — here, *likewise.* • **νήψει** → ἡ νῆψις, *sobriety, sober-mindedness; alertness, watchfulness.* See note in the translation of section 1. • **ὁδεύων** → ὁδεύω, *I go, travel, journey, proceed.* • **πλουσίως** — adv., *richly, abundantly.* Here the adv. does not fit well with the verb ὁρᾷ and so seems to function as an adj. (cf. Smy: 1097). • **μαρμαρυγάς** → ἡ μαρμαρυγή, *flashing, sparkling.* • **ἄνωθεν** — adv., *from above.* • **ἐλευθερωθήσεται** → ἐλευθερόω, *I set free, free;* pass., *am set free.* • **μισητῶν** → μισητός, ή, όν, *hateful.* • **ἐννοιῶν** → ἡ ἔννοια, *thought, notion.* • **ὅς** — here for a demonstrative pron. (LSI A: 572; BDAG 2: 727). • **ἐλευθερίῳ** → ἐλευθέριος, α, ον, *appropriate for a free person.* • **τρόπῳ** → ὁ τρόπος, *manner, way.* ἐλευθερίῳ τρόπῳ, "in a free manner," *freely.* • **ἐξόδῳ** → ἡ ἔξοδος, *departure,* here ref. to one's death. • **ταρταρίους** → ταρτάριος, α, ον (listed in LSI under the alternate

Section 5

Προσοχή ἐστι, καρδιακὴ ἀδιάλειπτος ἡσυχία ἀπὸ παντὸς λογισμοῦ, Χριστὸν Ἰησοῦν τὸν Υἱὸν τοῦ Θεοῦ καὶ Θεὸν ἀεὶ καὶ ἀεννάως καὶ ἀδιαλείπτως μόνον αὐτὸν ἀναπνέουσα, καὶ ἐπικαλουμένη, καὶ ἀνδρείως πρὸς τοὺς ἐχθροὺς συντασσομένη αὐτῷ, αὐτῷ τε ἐξομολογουμένη τῷ ἐξουσίαν ἔχοντι συγχωρεῖν ἁμαρτήματα. Περιπτυσσομένης γὰρ συνεχῶς Χριστῷ δι' ἐπικλήσεως κρυπτῶς μόνῳ τῷ τὰς καρδίας ἐξεταζομένῳ, τοὺς ἀνθρώπους τε πάντας παντοίως λαθεῖν πειρωμένης τῆς ψυχῆς τὴν γλυκύτητα αὐτῆς, καὶ τὸν ἔνδον ἀγῶνα, μήτε ὁ πονηρὸς λαθὼν εὐοδώσει κακίαν, καὶ ἀφανίσει καλλίστην ἐργασίαν.

---

form ταρτάρειος), *of/belonging to Tartarus/hell, hellish.* • **παρελεύσεται** → παρέρχομαι, *I go past.* • **ἄρχοντας** → ὁ ἄρχων, *ruler.*

5 **προσοχή** → ἡ προσοχή, *attention, attentiveness.* • **καρδιακή** → καρδιακός, ή, όν, *of the heart.* • **ἀδιάλειπτος** → ἀδιάλειπτος, ον, *unceasing, constant.* • **ἡσυχία** → ἡ ἡσυχία, *stillness.* See note in the translation of section 3 above. • **λογισμοῦ** → ὁ λογισμός, *reasoning, thought.* See note in the translation of section 2 above. • **ἀεί** — adv., *always, continually, constantly.* • **ἀεννάως** — adv. (listed in LSJ under the alternate form ἀενάως), *eternally, continually* (*PGL* 39). • **ἀδιαλείπτως** — adv., *unceasingly, constantly.* • **ἀναπνέουσα** → ἀναπνέω, *I breathe, breathe forth.* This ptc. and the next three describe προσοχή, i.e., what the heart does in its stillness. • **ἐπικαλουμένη** → ἐπικαλέω, *I call upon, invoke.* • **ἀνδρείως** — adv., *courageously.* • **πρός** — here, *against* (LSJ I4: 684; BDAG 3d: 874). • **ἐχθρούς** → ὁ ἐχθρός, *enemy.* • **συντασσομένη** → συντάσσω, *I put in order together;* pass., *am drawn up in battle order.* The Astir edition has σὺν αὐτῷ παρατασσομένη, which has a similar meaning. • **ἐξομολογουμένη** → ἐξομολογέομαι, *I confess,* w. dat, here a double dat. of obj. and compl. • **ἔχοντι** — The Astir edition adds μόνῳ, "who alone has." • **συγχωρεῖν** → συγχωρέω, *I forgive* (LSJ 5: 1669; *PGL* 5: 1277). Epex. inf. w. ἐξουσίαν (Wal: 607; Smy: 2006). • **ἁμαρτήματα** → τὸ ἁμάρτημα, *a sin.* • **περιπτυσσομένης** → περιπτύσσω, *I enfold, enwrap.* Gen. abs., attend. circ., w. ψυχῆς as subj. The Astir ed. has the nom. sg. form of the ptc. • **συνεχῶς** — adv., *continuously, continually, constantly.* • **ἐπικλήσεως** → ἡ ἐπίκλησις, *invocation, appeal.* • **κρυπτῶς** — adv., *hiddenly, secretly.* • **ἐξεταζομένῳ** → ἐξετάζω, *I examine closely.* The Astir ed. has ἐπισταμένῳ (→ ἐφίστημι, *I set over, establish;* mid. in trans. sense, *understand* [*PGL* C: 587]). • **παντοίως** — adv., *variously, in all kinds of ways.* • **λαθεῖν** — 2 aor. act. inf. → λανθάνω, *I escape notice of, am hidden from,* w. acc. • **πειρωμένης** → πειράομαι, *I attempt, endeavor, try.* Continues the gen. abs. The Astir ed. has the nom. sg. form of the ptc. • **ψυχῆς** — subj. of gen. abs. • **γλυκύτητα** → ἡ γλυκύτης, *sweetness.* Acc. of ref. (Wal: 203; Smy: 1600). • **ἔνδον** — adv., *in, within.* • **ἀγῶνα** → ὁ ἀγών, *a contest, struggle, battle.* Acc. of ref. (Wal: 203; Smy: 1600). • **μήτε** — *and not.* The Astir ed. has μήποτε (*lest, that at no time, that . . . not,* often w. subjun.). • **λαθών** — 2 aor. act. ptc. → λανθάνω. Attend. circ. • **εὐοδώσει** → εὐοδόω, *I prosper, succeed;* here, *successfully promote.* The Astir ed. has the aor. subjun. εὐοδώσῃ. • **κακίαν** → ἡ κακία, *wickedness, vice.* • **ἀφανίσει** → ἀφανίζω, *I make unseen; destroy utterly.* The Astir ed. has the aor. subjun. ἀφανίσῃ. • **καλλίστην** → κάλλιστος, η, ον, *most beautiful,* superlative of καλός. • **ἐργασίαν** → ἡ ἐργασία, *work.*

Section 6

Νῆψίς ἐστιν, ἔμμονος λογισμοῦ πῆξις, καὶ στάσις αὐτοῦ ἐν πύλῃ καρδίας, ἣ τοὺς ἐρχομένους λογισμοὺς λεπτῶς ὁρᾷ καὶ ἀκούει τί μὲν λέγουσι, τί δὲ ποιοῦσιν οἱ φόνιοι, καὶ τίς ἐστιν ἡ ἐγγλυφεῖσα καὶ στηλωθεῖσα μορφὴ παρὰ τῶν δαιμόνων, καὶ πειρωμένη δι' ἑαυτῆς φανταστικῶς καταλῦσαι τὸν νοῦν. Ταῦτα γὰρ φιλοπονούμενα τὴν πεῖραν τοῦ νοητοῦ πολέμου ἐπιστημόνως ἄγαν ἡμῖν, ἐὰν θέλωμεν, δεικνύουσι.

On Watchfulness and Holiness 27–29 The Example of the Spider

Section 27

Καρδιακῆς ἡσυχίας οὗτος τύπος καὶ τάξις· εἰ βούλει ἀθλεῖν, τὸ μικρὸν ζωΰφιον, ἡ ἀράχνη ἔστω σοι τοῦτο ὑπόδειγμα· εἰ δὲ μή, οὔπω ὡς δεῖ

---

6 **νῆψις** → ἡ νῆψις, *sobriety, sober-mindedness, alertness, watchfulness.* See note in the translation of section 1 above. • **ἔμμονος** → ἔμμονος, ον, *steadfast.* • **λογισμοῦ** → ὁ λογισμός, *reasoning, thought.* See note in the translation of section 2 above. • **πῆξις** → ἡ πῆξις, *fixing.* • **στάσις** → ἡ στάσις, *standing; halting, stoppage, cessation* (*PGL* 2: 1251). • **πύλῃ** → ἡ πύλη, *gate, door.* • **ἣ** — The Astir ed. has ὅς, which signals a shift from νῆψις to the one who practices it (cf. LSJ BI: 1259 for similar shifts). • **λεπτῶς** — adv., *subtly, with perceptive insight* (LSJ, λεπτός, ή, όν II: 1039). The Astir ed. has κλέπτας (→ ὁ κλέπτης, *thief*), which mod. τοὺς ἐρχομένους λογισμούς, "the thoughts that come as thieves." • **φόνιοι** → φόνιος, α, ον, *bloody, murderous, deadly.* • **ἐγγλυφεῖσα** — aor. pass. ptc. fem. nom. sg. → ἐγγλύφω, *I carve.* • **στηλωθεῖσα** — aor. pass. ptc. fem. nom. sg. → στηλόω, *I set up as a monument; inscribe on a monument.* • **μορφὴ** → ἡ μορφή, *form, shape.* • **δαιμόνων** → ὁ and ἡ δαίμων, *demon.* • **πειρωμένη** → πειράομαι, *I attempt, endeavor, try.* • **ἑαυτῆς** — The fem. shows the ref. is to μορφή, *through itself, through the form itself.* • **φανταστικῶς** — adv., *by means of mental images.* • **καταλῦσαι** — aor. act. inf. → καταλύω, *I destroy.* The Astir ed. has ἀπατῆσαι (aor. act. inf. → ἀπατάω, *I trick, deceive*). • **νοῦν** → ὁ νοῦς, *mind.* See note in the translation of section 2 above. • **φιλοπονούμενα** → φιλοπονέω, *I work hard.* Perhaps concessive circ. ptc. • **πεῖραν** → ἡ πεῖρα, *trial, attempt, experience.* • **νοητοῦ** → νοητός, ή, όν, *of the mind/thought; spiritual* (*PGL* II: 917). • **πολέμου** → ὁ πόλεμος, *battle, war.* • **ἐπιστημόνως** — adv., *with knowledge/understanding/skill/expertise.* • **ἄγαν** — adv., *very much;* here perhaps, *very clearly.* • **δεικνύουσι** → δεικνύω (listed in lexicons under the alternate form δείκνυμι), *I show.*

Sections 27–29

27 **καρδιακῆς** → καρδιακός, ή, όν, *of/belonging to the heart.* • **ἡσυχίας** → ἡ ἡσυχία, *stillness.* See note in the translation of section 3 above. • **οὗτος** — The Astir

ἡσύχασας νῷ. Κἀκείνη μὲν μυίας μικρὰς θηρεύει· σύ δὲ εἰ οὕτω καὶ ὡς αὐτὴ ἐν ψυχῇ πονῶν ἡσυχάζεις, οὐ παύσει κτείνων ἀεὶ νήπια Βαβυλώνια, καθ' ὃν φόνον μακαρίζῃ ὑπὸ τοῦ Πνεύματος τοῦ ἁγίου, διὰ Δαβίδ.

Section 28

Ὡς οὐ δυνατὸν τὴν Ἐρυθρὰν θάλασσαν ἐν τῷ στερεώματι ὀφθῆναι μέσον ἀστέρων· καὶ ὡς οὐκ ἔνι ἄνθρωπον ἐν γῇ περιπατοῦντα μὴ τὸν ἀέρα τοῦτον ἀναπνέειν· οὕτως ἀδύνατον καθαρίσαι τὴν ἡμῶν καρδίαν ἐξ ἐμπαθῶν

---

ed. has ὦ οὗτος w. οὗτος functioning as a voc., *you there.* This usage often includes contempt, *you poor fellow, you wretch* (LSI I6–7: 579; BDAG 1aα: 740). • **τύπος** → ὁ τύπος, *type, model, example.* Pred. nom. w. the verb elided. • **τάξις** → ἡ τάξις, *an order, rule* (*PGL*: 1372–73). Part of the comp. pred. nom. • **βούλει** — pres. mid. (depon.) indic. 2 sg. (alternate form for βούλῃ) → βούλομαι, *I will, wish, want, desire.* • **ἀθλεῖν** → ἀθλέω, *I engage in battle.* • **μικρόν** → μικρός, ά, όν, *small.* • **ζωύφιον** → τὸ ζωύφιον, *little animal, insect.* Subj. (*PGL*: 599). • **ἀράχνη** → ἡ ἀράχνη, *spider.* In appos. to τὸ ζωύφιον. • **τοῦτο** — Instead of this word, the Astir ed. has ἀεὶ τό (ἀεί — adv., *always, ever; constantly, continually*). • **ὑπόδειγμα** → τὸ ὑπόδειγμα, *a pattern, example.* • **εἰ δὲ μή** — *otherwise.* (LSI, εἰ AII3: 226; BDAG, εἰ 6d: 278). • **οὔπω** — adv., *not yet,* usually w. pres. or past, especially the pf. or an aor. in a pf. sense (LSJ: 1272). • **ἡσύχασας** — aor. act. indic. → ἡσυχάζω, *I am still, have stillness,* in a pf. sense w. οὔπω. The aor. ptc. would have a different accent, ἡσυχάσας, since the final α is long in this ending. • **νῷ** → ὁ νοῦς, *mind.* See note in the translation of section 2 above. • **κἀκείνη** → καὶ ἐκεῖνος, here simply, *that one* (BDAG 2b: 500). • **μυίας** → ἡ μυῖα, *fly.* • **θηρεύει** → θηρεύω, *I hunt.* • **οὕτω** — οὕτως. • **εἰ οὕτω καὶ ὡς αὐτή** — "if thus also as she," *if you follow the spider's example.* • **πονῶν** → πονέω, *I work hard.* Circ. ptc. for concession or means, *by working hard.* • **παύσει** → παύω, *I stop, cease.* • **κτείνων** → κτείνω, *I kill, slay.* • **ἀεί** — adv., *always, ever; constantly, continually* • **νήπια** → νήπιος, α, ον, *of a child.* Both masc. and neut. are used for the subst., *child, infant.* • **Βαβυλώνια** → Βαβυλώνιος, α, ον, *Babylonian.* • **καθ'** → κατά, here, *during* (LSI VII: 403; BDAG B2a: 512). • **φόνον** → ὁ φόνος, *slaughter.* • **μακαρίζῃ** — pres. pass. indic. 2 sg. → μακαρίζω, *I bless.* • **Δαβίδ** → ὁ Δαβίδ, indecl. (listed in BDAG under the alternate form Δαυίδ), *David.*

28 **δυνατόν** → δυνατός, ή, όν, *able, possible.* Supply, "it is." • **ἐρυθράν** → ἐρυθρός, ά, όν, *red.* • **θάλασσαν** — subj. of the inf. • **στερεώματι** → τὸ στερέωμα, *steadfastness; the firmament,* i.e., "the sky as a supporting structure" (BDAG 1: 943). Cf. Gen 1:6. ἐν τῷ στερεώματι mod. ἀστέρων. • **ὀφθῆναι** — aor. pass. inf. → ὁράω. Epex. (Wal: 607; Smy: 2006). The pass. can be used in an act. sense, *I appear, become visible* (BDAG A1d: 719), but this usage usually implies the idea of letting oneself be seen (LSI V: 565), making an appearance, as it were. So the simple pass. seems best in this context. • **μέσον** → μέσος, η, ον, *middle, in the middle/midst, among, amidst,* neut. sg. for adv. (BDAG 1c: 635). • **ἀστέρων** → ὁ ἀστήρ, *star.* • **ἔνι** — shortened form of ἔνεστι → ἔνειμι, *I am in; I am possible.* The imper. use is common, *it is possible.* • **ἄνθρωπον** — subj. of inf. • **περιπατοῦντα** → περιπατέω, *I walk.* • **ἀέρα** → ὁ and ἡ ἀήρ, *air.* • **ἀναπνέειν** → ἀναπνέω, *I breathe, draw breath.* • **ἀδύνατον** → ἀδύνατος, ον, *impossible.* Supply, "it is." • **καθαρίσαι** → καθαρίζω, *I cleanse, make clean.* • **ἐμπαθῶν** → ἐμπαθής, ές, *emotional,*

νοημάτων, καὶ ἀποδιῶξαι νοητοὺς ἐχθροὺς ἐξ αὐτῆς ἄνευ συχνῆς ἐπικλήσεως Ἰησοῦ.

Section 29

Ἐὰν μετὰ ταπεινώσεως φρονήματος καὶ μνήμης θανάτου, καὶ ἀπὸ μέμψεως, καὶ ἀντιρρήσεως, καὶ ἐπικλήσεως Ἰησοῦ Χριστοῦ τὰς διατριβὰς πάντοτε ποιεῖς ἐν τῇ σῇ καρδίᾳ· καὶ τὴν στενὴν μέν, ἀλλὰ χαροποιὸν καὶ τερπνὴν ὁδὸν τῆς διανοίας καθ' ἡμέραν, μετὰ τούτων τῶν ὅπλων ὁδεύεις νηφόντως, εἰς θεωρίας ἁγίας ἁγίων ἐλεύσῃ, καὶ φωτισθήσῃ μυστήρια βαθέα παρὰ Χριστοῦ. **Παρ' ᾧ οἱ θησαυροὶ τῆς σοφίας καὶ τῆς γνώσεως ἀπόκρυφοι·Ἐν ᾧ κατοικεῖ πᾶν τὸ πλήρωμα τῆς θεότητος σωματικῶς·** αἰσθηθήσῃ γὰρ πρὸς

---

impassioned, passionate. • **νοημάτων** → τὸ νόημα, *thought, perception.* • **ἀποδιῶξαι** → ἀποδιώκω, *I drive away, expel.* • **νοητούς** → νοητός, ή, όν, *intelligible, noetic,* i.e., belonging to the νοῦς. See note above, section 2, on νοῦς. • **ἐχθρούς** → ἐχθρός, ά, όν, *hated;* subst., *an enemy.* • **ἄνευ** — *without,* w. gen. • **συχνῆς** → συχνός, ή, όν, *long, many, frequent.* • **ἐπικλήσεως** → ἡ ἐπίκλησις, *a calling upon, invocation, appeal.*

29 **ταπεινώσεως** → ἡ ταπείνωσις, *lowliness, humility.* • **φρονήματος** → τὸ φρόνημα, *mind, thought.* • **μνήμης** → ἡ μνήμη, *remembrance* • **ἀπό** — here, *by* (LSI III6: 94; BDAG 5b: 106). • **μέμψεως** → ἡ μέμψις, *blame, censure, reproach.* The Astir ed. has αὐτομεμψίας (→ ἡ αὐτομεμψία, *self-reproach* [*PGL*: 271]). • **ἀντιρρήσεως** → ἡ ἀντίρρησις, *contradiction, rebuttal, refutation.* The ref. is probably to one's spiritual enemies, a major theme of this writing. • **ἐπικλήσεως** → ἡ ἐπίκλησις, *a calling upon, invocation, appeal.* • **διατριβάς** → ἡ διατριβή, *a way of spending time,* either in the sense of a *serious occupation/study* or of *amusement* (LSI: 196). Since ποιέω can be used w. a noun to form a periphrasis for a simple verbal idea (BDAG 2d: 839), here, *you spend your time.* • **πάντοτε** — adv., *always.* • **ποιεῖς** — The Astir ed. has ποιῇς. For the use of ἐάν w. indic. instead of the more common subjun., see BDAG 1b: 267. • **σῇ** → σός, ή, όν, *your* (sg.). • **στενήν** → στενός, ή, όν, *narrow.* • **χαροποιόν** → χαροποιός, όν, *bringing joy, gladdening.* • **τερπνήν** → τερπνός, ή, όν, *delightful.* • **διανοίας** → ἡ διάνοια, *mind, understanding.* • **καθ' ἡμέραν** — distributive use of κατά (LSI BII: 403; BDAG B2c, p.512), *day by day.* • **ὅπλων** → τὸ ὅπλον, *tool, weapon.* • **ὁδεύεις** → ὁδεύω, *I go, travel.* Continuing the conditional clause w. ἐάν. The Astir ed. has ὁδεύῃς. Cf. note on ποιεῖς above. • **νηφόντως** — , adv., *soberly, vigilantly, alertly.* • **θεωρίας** → ἡ θεωρία, *vision.* A major theme in this literature (cf. *PGL*: 648–49). • **φωτισθήσῃ** → φωτίζω, *I enlighten, illuminate.* • **μυστήρια** → τὸ μυστήριον, *mystery.* Acc. of ref. (Wal: 203; Smy: 1600). • **βαθέα** → βαθύς, εῖα, ύ, *deep.* • **θησαυροί** → ὁ θησαυρός, *treasure.* • **γνώσεως** → ἡ γνῶσις, *knowledge.* • **ἀπόκρυφοι** → ἀπόκρυφος, ον, *hidden.* Pred. position. • **κατοικεῖ** → κατοικέω, *I dwell.* • **πλήρωμα** → τὸ πλήρωμα, *fullness.* • **θεότητος** → ἡ θεότης, *divinity, divine nature, Godhead.* • **σωματικῶς** — adv., *bodily.* • **αἰσθηθήσῃ** — fut. mid. (depon.) indic. 2 sg. → αἰσθάνομαι, *I perceive, sense.* The Astir ed. has αἰσθανθήσῃ. Both forms are alternatives for αἰσθήσομαι (LSJ 42). In the Astir ed. a comma before ὅτι suggests that what is perceived is "that the Holy Spirit sprang upon your soul." The context, however, is focused on one's vision of Jesus, suggesting that it is Jesus

Ἰησοῦ· ὅτι Πνεῦμα ἅγιον ἐφήλατο τῇ σῇ ψυχῇ, παρ' οὗ νοῦς ἀνθρώπων δᾳδουχεῖται ὁρᾶν, ἀνακεκαλυμμένῳ προσώπῳ. **Οὐδείς**, φησί, **λέγει Κύριον Ἰησοῦν, εἰ μὴ ἐν Πνεύματι ἁγίῳ,** δηλαδὴ βεβαιῶν μυστικῶς τὸ ζητούμενον.

On Watchfulness and Holiness 79–82 Christlike Humility

Section 79

Ὁ Κύριος πᾶσαν ἐντολὴν ὀφειλομένην δεῖξαι θέλων, τὴν δὲ υἱοθεσίαν ἰδίῳ αἵματι τοῖς ἀνθρώποις δεδωρημένην, φησίν, **Ὅταν πάντα ποιήσητε τὰ προστεταγμένα ὑμῖν, εἴπατε, ὅτι Ἀχρεῖοι δοῦλοί ἐσμεν, καὶ ὃ ὠφείλομεν ποιῆσαι, πεποιήκαμεν.** Διὰ τοῦτο οὐκ ἔστι μισθὸς ἔργων ἡ βασιλεία τῶν οὐρανῶν, ἀλλὰ χάρις Δεσπότου πιστοῖς δούλοις ἡτοιμασμένη· οὐκ ἀπαιτεῖ δοῦλος ὡς μισθόν, τὴν ἐλευθερίαν, ἀλλ' εὐχαριστεῖ ὡς ὀφειλέτης, καὶ κατὰ χάριν ἐκδέχεται.

---

who is perceived. The punctuation in *PG* seems to imply this meaning and so is probably preferable. • **πρός** — here, *near, in the presence of* (LSI: 684). Ἰησοῦ in form could be either gen. or dat., but this sense is found w. both cases. If the punctuation in the Astir ed. is followed (see previous note), then the meaning would be, "you will perceive in the presence of Jesus that . . ." In *PG* the meaning seems to be, *you will perceive (yourself to be) in the presence of Jesus.* • **ἐφήλατο** — aor. mid. (depon.) indic. 3 sg. → ἐφάλλομαι, *I spring upon,* w. dat. This verb is used of the Spirit coming upon Saul and David (1 Sam 10:6; 11:6; 16:13). • **νοῦς** → ὁ νοῦς, *mind.* See note on νοῦς at section 2. • **δᾳδουχεῖται** → δᾳδουχέω, *I carry a torch; illuminate, illumine* (*PGL* 5: 327). • **ἀνακεκαλυμμένῳ** → ἀνακαλύπτω, *I uncover, unveil.* • **εἰ μή** — *except.* • **δηλαδή** — adv., *clearly, plainly.* • **βεβαιῶν** → βεβαιόω, *I confirm, establish, secure.* • **μυστικῶς** — adv., *mystically.*

Sections 79–82

79 Note that sections 79–82 are numbered differently in the Astir edition, as indicated by the numbers in parentheses. • **ὀφειλομένην** → ὀφείλω, *I owe, am bound, am obligated;* subst. • **δεῖξαι** — aor. act. inf. → δείκνυμι, *I show.* Here w. two sets of double acc. of obj. and compl. (Wal: 182; Smy: 1613). • **υἱοθεσίαν** → ἡ υἱοθεσία, *adoption.* • **δεδωρημένην** → δωρέω, *I give, present.* • **ποιήσητε** — aor. for pf. (Smy: 1940, cf. Wal: 559 note 12). • **προστεταγμένα** — pf. pass. ptc. → προστάσσω, *I command, order.* • **εἴπατε** → εἶπον. This 2 aor. often uses an α variable vowel like the 1 aor. • **ἀχρεῖοι** → ἀχρεῖος, ον, *useless, worthless, unworthy.* • **ὠφείλομεν** — impf. → ὀφείλω. • **διὰ τοῦτο** — *therefore* (BDAG B2b: 225). • **μισθός** → ὁ μισθός, *reward, wage, pay.* • **Δεσπότου** → ὁ δεσπότης, *lord, master.* • **πιστοῖς** → πιστός, ή, όν, *faithful.* • **ἡτοιμασμένη** — pf. pass. ptc. → ἑτοιμάζω, *I prepare.* • **ἀπαιτεῖ** → ἀπαιτέω, *I demand.* • **ἐλευθερίαν** → ἡ ἐλευθερία, *freedom.* • **εὐχαριστεῖ** → εὐχαριστέω, *I am thankful, give thanks.* • **ὀφειλέτης** → ὁ ὀφειλέτης, *debtor, one under obligation.* • **κατὰ χάριν** — *as a gracious gift* (cf. BDAG, χάρις 2a: 1079). Cf. Rom 4:4, 16. • **ἐκδέχεται** → ἐκδέχομαι, *I receive.*

Section 80 (80, 81)

Ὡς ἀπέθανεν ὑπὲρ τῶν ἁμαρτιῶν ἡμῶν κατὰ τὰς Γραφάς, καὶ τοῖς εὖ δουλεύουσιν αὐτῷ τὴν ἐλευθερίαν χαρίζεται· φησὶ γάρ· **Εὖ, δοῦλε ἀγαθὲ καὶ πιστέ, ἐπὶ ὀλίγα ἐγένου πιστός, ἐπὶ πολλῶν σε καταστήσω, εἴσελθε εἰς τὴν χαρὰν τοῦ Κυρίου σου.** Οὔπω δὲ δοῦλός ἐστι πιστός, ὁ ψιλῇ τῇ γνώσει ἐπερειδόμενος, ἀλλ' ὁ δι' ὑπακοῆς τῷ ἐντειλαμένῳ Χριστῷ πιστεύων, (81) τὸν Δεσπότην τιμῶν, ποιεῖ τὰ κελευόμενα· σφαλεὶς δὲ ἢ παρακούσας, ὑπομένει ὡς ἴδια τὰ ἐπερχόμενα. **Φιλομαθὴς** οὖν γίνου καὶ φιλόπονος· ἡ γὰρ ψιλὴ **γνῶσις φυσιοῖ** τὸν ἄνθρωπον.

Section 81 (82)

Οἱ ἀπροσδοκήτως ἡμῖν συμβαίνοντες πειρασμοί, οἰκονομικῶς ἡμᾶς φιλοπόνους διδάσκουσι γίνεσθαι.

Section 82 (83)

Ἴδιον μὲν ἀστέρος τὸ περὶ αὐτὸν φῶς, τοῦ δὲ θεοσεβοῦς καὶ Θεὸν φοβουμένου ἴδιον, εὐτέλεια καὶ ταπείνωσις· ἐπεὶ μηδ' ἄλλο τι γνωριστικὸν

---

80 **ὡς** — here as an exclamation that extends to the whole sentence (LSI D2: 908). The Astir ed. has Χριστός instead of ὡς, further aligning this clause w. 1 Cor 15:3. • **ἀπέθανεν** — 2 aor. act. indic. → ἀποθνῄσκω. • **εὖ** — adv., *well; well done!* • **δουλεύουσιν** → δουλεύω, *I serve.* • **ἐλευθερίαν** → ἡ ἐλευθερία, *freedom.* • **χαρίζεται** → χαρίζομαι, *I give (freely/graciously).* • **πιστέ** → πιστός, ή, όν, *faithful.* • **ὀλίγα** → ὀλίγος, η, ον, *few.* • **ἐγένου** — 2 aor. mid. (depon.) indic. 2 sg. → γίνομαι. • **καταστήσω** → καθίστημι, *I appoint.* • **εἴσελθε** → εἰσέρχομαι. • **οὔπω** — adv., *not yet.* • **ψιλῇ** → ψιλός, ή, όν, *bare.* • **γνώσει** → ἡ γνῶσις, *knowledge.* • **ἐπερειδόμενος** → ἐπερείδω, *I drive against;* mid., *rest in/on/upon,* w. dat. • **ὑπακοῆς** → ἡ ὑπακοή, *obedience.* • **ἐντειλαμένῳ** — aor. mid. ptc. → ἐντέλλω, often, as here, a mid. depon., *I command, order.* • **Δεσπότην** → ὁ δεσπότης, *lord, master.* The Astir ed. begins a new sentence and a new section at this point, Ὁ τὸν Δεσπότην. . . . • **τιμῶν** → τιμάω, *I honor.* • **κελευόμενα** → κελεύω, *I command, order.* • **σφαλείς** — 2 aor. pass. ptc. masc. nom. sg. → σφάλλω, *I slip, stumble.* • **παρακούσας** → παρακούω, *I disobey, refuse to listen.* • **ὑπομένει** → ὑπομένω, *I submit to, obey.* • **ὡς ἴδια** — *as his/her own.* • **ἐπερχόμενα** → ἐπέρχομαι, *I come upon.* • **φιλομαθής** → φιλομαθής, ές, *fond of learning, eager for knowledge.* • **γίνου** — pres. mid. (depon.) impv. → γίνομαι. • **φιλόπονος** → φιλόπονος, ον, *fond of work, eager for work, industrious, conscientious.* • **ψιλή** → ψιλός, ή, όν, *bare.* • **γνῶσις** → ἡ γνῶσις, *knowledge.* • **φυσιοῖ** → φυσιόω, *I puff up.*

81 **ἀπροσδοκήτως** — adv., *unexpectedly.* • **συμβαίνοντες** → συμβαίνω, *I happen.* • **πειρασμοί** → ὁ πειρασμός, *trial.* • **οἰκονομικῶς** — adv., *in a well-ordered manner* (LSJ, οἰκονομικός, ή, όν: 1204), *providentially, by divine dispensation* (*PGL* 5: 943). • **φιλοπόνους** → φιλόπονος, ον, *fond of work, industrious, conscientious.*

82 **ἴδιον** → ἴδιος, here, *a peculiarity, a peculiar/distinct/special property* (LSI II: 375; BDAG 6: 467). • **ἀστέρος** → ὁ ἀστήρ, *star.* • **θεοσεβοῦς** → θεοσεβής, ές,

πέφυκεν εἶναι, καὶ δηλότερον σημεῖον τῶν τοῦ Χριστοῦ μαθητῶν, ὡς ταπεινὸν φρόνημα καὶ εὐτελὲς σχῆμα. Καὶ τοῦτο πάντα βοῶσι τὰ τέσσαρα Εὐαγγέλια· ὁ δὲ μὴ οὕτως ταπεινῶς βιούς, τοῦ μέρους ἐκπίπτει τοῦ ἑαυτὸν ἑκουσίως **ταπεινώσαντος μέχρι σταυροῦ καὶ θανάτου,** τοῦ καὶ τῶν θείων Εὐαγγελίων πρακτικοῦ νομοθέτου.

God-fearing, devout. • **εὐτέλεια** → ἡ εὐτέλεια, *cheapness, thrift, frugality, simplicity; low-estate.* • **ταπείνωσις** → ἡ ταπείνωσις, *humility.* • **ἐπεί** — *because, since, for.* • **μηδ'** → μηδέ. μηδ' ἄλλο τι, "no other thing," *nothing else.* • **γνωριστικόν** → γνωριστικός, ή, όν, *making known, indicative of; characteristic, distinctive* (*PGL*: 318). • **πέφυκεν** → φύω, *I grow, arise.* Pf. w. inf., *I am by nature disposed to do/be* so and so. • **δηλότερον** → δηλότερος, α, ον, comparative of δῆλος, α, ον, *more manifest, clearer.* • **ταπεινόν** → ταπεινός, ή, όν, *humble.* • **φρόνημα** → τὸ φρόνημα, *mind, spirit.* • **εὐτελές** → εὐτελής, ές, *cheap; simple; lowly.* • **σχῆμα** → τὸ σχῆμα, *appearance, bearing, look, manner.* • **πάντα** — The Astir ed. has πάντῃ (adv., *in every way, on every side, altogether*). • **βοῶσι** → βοάω, *I shout.* • **τέσσαρα** → τέσσαρες, τέσσαρα, *four.* • **ταπεινῶς** — adv., *humbly, in a lowly/humble manner.* • **βιούς** — aor. act. ptc. masc. nom. sg. → βιόω, *I live.* • **μέρους** → τὸ μέρος, *part.* • **ἐκπίπτει** → ἐκπίπτω, *I fall; lose,* w. gen. • **ἑκουσίως** — adv., *voluntarily.* This word is not in the Astir ed. • **ταπεινώσαντος** → ταπεινόω, *I humble.* Attrib. ptc., partitive gen. w. μέρους (Wal: 84; Smy: 1306). • **μέχρι** — *as far as, to the point of,* w. gen. • **σταυροῦ** → ὁ σταυρός, *cross.* • **θείων** → θεῖος, α, ον, *divine.* • **πρακτικοῦ** → πρακτικός, ή, όν, *active, effective.* • **νομοθέτου** → ὁ νομοθέτης, *lawgiver.*

Symeon the New Theologian

Hymns

Introduction

Symeon the New Theologian (949–1022) was one of the greatest of the Byzantine mystics. In the Eastern Church two teachers are given the title "Theologian," the Apostle John and Gregory of Nazianzus. Symeon's title of "New Theologian" may originally have been given to him by his opponents as an "offensive nickname."[1] But it came to represent high regard for him as one who knew God and conveyed genuine insight regarding the mystery of God.[2]

Symeon was born in Galatia, a city in Paphlagonia (in modern north central Turkey). His parents were provincial nobility of the Byzantine Empire and well-to-do. Symeon began his education in Galatia, but moved to Constantinople when he was eleven, where he continued his education until he was fourteen. At that time Symeon came under the spiritual direction of the monk Symeon the Studite. Symeon wanted to enter the Stoudion Monastery to join the Studite, but Symeon the Studite counseled him to wait.

So Symeon remained under the Studite's direction while he worked in a patrician's household. While working in the world, he practiced a strenuous spiritual life and experienced a vision of the divine light of God for the first time when he was twenty (*Discourse* [*Disc.*] 22.2–4). Such direct experience of God is a central motif throughout Symeon's writings.

He was allowed to enter the monastery when he was twenty-seven. After only a few months at the Studion Monastery, he was sent to the Monastery of St. Mamas, also in Constantinople. By the time Symeon was thirty-one, he had become a monk, been ordained to the priesthood, and been established as the Abbot of his monastery. The spiritual level of St. Mamas was very low, and for twenty-five years Symeon worked to raise it. Symeon's *Discourses* represent a number of his teachings to these monks. This effort at reform was not easy, and the monks revolted against him at one point, for which they were sent into exile by the Patriarch.

Not all of the church's hierarchy, however, supported Symeon. In particular, Archbishop Stephen, chief theologian to the emperor, thought Symeon did not properly respect

---

[1] Hilarion Alfeyev, *St. Symeon the New Theologian and Orthodox Tradition* (Oxford Early Christian Studies; Oxford: Oxford University Press, 2000), 1.

[2] On the meaning of *theologian* in this context see further the introduction to Gregory of Nazianzus.

hierarchical authority. Symeon, for example, thought a spiritual director could absolve sins even if not ordained, as had been the practice of his own director, Symeon the Studite, a layman. Stephen also charged Symeon with heresy based on some of his teachings about God and the possibility of a conscious experience of God's grace. Stephen represented a more rational and philosophical approach to theology, while Symeon was less systematic in his teachings and emphasized the mystery of God that lies beyond all language. Furthermore, Stephen represented the formalism of much of Byzantine Christianity at that time and rejected Symeon's claims regarding the possibility of experiencing God. Symeon, for his part, said the real heresy is the teaching that it is impossible to experience what the saints of old experienced (e.g., *Disc.* 29.4). While Symeon's teaching is grounded in Scripture and the teachings of the church, nevertheless his language is often open to misunderstanding, some of his ascetical views are extreme, and the importance he places on the conscious experience of God seems to set personal experience against the authority of the church.

In 1009 Stephen was successful in getting Symeon exiled to Paloutikon, a small village on the Bosphorus. There Symeon rebuilt a ruined chapel and established a small monastery with a few monks who went into exile with him. The exile was later lifted, but Symeon chose not to return, remaining in Paloutikon for the rest of his life.

Many of Symeon's writings have survived. Along with his *Discourses* to the monks at St. Mamas Monastery, we have a number of essays on theology and discipleship, as well as fifty-eight hymns. Throughout his writings he emphasizes repentance, ascetical discipline, love, and the possibility of conscious encounter with God. *Hymn* 16 is included here as a brief sample of his description of such an encounter. *Hymn* 10 expresses Symeon's love for a friend who has died, confirming the transient nature of this life.

Edition used:	Athanasios Kambylis, ed., *Symeon Neos Theologos, Hymnen.* Supplementa Byzantina 3. Berlin: de Gruyter, 1976.
Level of difficulty:	Intermediate [3–4]

Hymn 10 Life's Fleeting Things

῞Οτι ὁ θάνατος τῇ λύπῃ καὶ τῶν στερροτέρων καθάπτεται.

Ἤκουσα πρᾶγμα ξένον καὶ πλῆρες θάμβους·
φύσιν ἄϋλον τὴν λίθου στερροτέραν
ἶσ' ἀδάμαντος καλουμένου παθοῦσαν,
ὃς μὴ μαλαχθεὶς ἢ πυρὶ ἢ σιδήρῳ
γέγονε κηρὸς ἐμπλεχθεὶς τῷ μολύβδῳ·
ἄρτ' ἐπίστευσα μικρὸν ὕδατος ῥεῦμα
πέτρας τὸ στερρὸν ἐγχρονίζον κοιλαίνειν·

Hymn 10

Title

ὅτι — here introduces the title, *that.* • **λύπῃ** → ἡ λύπη, *grief.* Dat. of means (Wal: 162; Smy: 1507). • **καί** — ascensive, *even.* • **στερροτέρων** → στερρότερος, α, ον, comparative → στερρός, ά, όν, *hard; solid, firm, steadfast.* Here it is an example of the comparative for the superlative (BDF: 60), *the most steadfast.* • **καθάπτεται** → καθάπτω, *I fasten;* mid., w. gen., *lay hold of, assail, attack.*

Lines 1–4

πρᾶγμα → τὸ πρᾶγμα, *a thing, something.* • **ξένον** → ξένος, η, ον, *strange.* • **πλῆρες** → πλήρης, ες, *full of, filled with.* • **θάμβους** → τὸ θάμβος, *astonishment, amazement.* • **φύσιν** → ἡ φύσις, *nature; substance* (LSJ Vb [sic.]: 1965). Appos. to πρᾶγμα. • **ἄϋλον** → ἄϋλος, ον, *immaterial.* • **λίθου** — gen. of comparison (Wal: 110; Smy: 1069). • **στερροτέραν** — now a proper comparative w. the sense, *harder.* The double meaning of this term is the foundational image to this hymn. • **ἀδάμαντος** → ὁ ἀδάμας, *adamant.* The word means "the untamed/unconquerable" and ref. to that which is the hardest, often ref. to steel or diamonds. • **παθοῦσαν** — 2 aor. act. ptc. fem. acc. sg. → πάσχω, *I suffer;* here in the word's root sense of "being acted upon," *receive an impression from* (LSI: 612; LSJ IV: 1347). Here it ref. to the resistance of the material, continuing the description of that which is τὴν λίθου στερροτέραν., "which receives an impression equal of that which is called adamant," *with a resistance equal to what is called adamant.* • **μαλαχθείς** — aor. pass. ptc. → μαλάσσω, *I soften.* Circ. ptc., concessive. • **σιδήρῳ** → ὁ σίδηρος, *iron, an iron tool.*

Lines 5–9

γέγονε — gnomic pf. for a generic occurrence (Wal: 580). • **κηρός** → ὁ κηρός, *wax.* • **ἐμπλεχθείς** — aor. pass. ptc. → ἐμπλέκω, *I entwine, form a connection with, join with/to.* • **μολύβδῳ** → ἡ μόλυβδος, *lead.* • **ἄρτ'** → ἄρτι, adv., *now;* w. aor., *just now* (LSI 2: 120). • **ἐπίστευσα** — w. ἄρτι perhaps ingressive, *I recently came to believe.* • **μικρόν** → μικρός, ά, όν, *small.* • **ῥεῦμα** → τὸ ῥεῦμα, *flow, stream.* Subj. of κοιλαίνειν. • **πέτρας** → ἡ πέτρα, *rock.* • **στερρόν** → στερρός, ά, όν, *firm, solid.* • **ἐγχρονίζον** → ἐγχρονίζω, *I am long about something, continue over a period of time.* • **κοιλαίνειν** → κοιλαίνω, *I make hollow, hollow out.*

καὶ ὄντως οὐδὲν ἄτρεπτον τῶν ἐν βίῳ·
μηδείς μ' ἐκ τοῦ νῦν ἀπατᾶν νομιζέτω·
φεῦ τῷ βλέποντι τὰ φεύγοντα τοῦ βίου
ὡς κρατούμενα καὶ τερπομένῳ τούτοις·
ταὐτὰ πείσεται ἅπερ κἀγὼ ὁ τάλας·
νύξ μ' ἐχώρισεν ἀδελφοῦ γλυκυτάτου
τὸ ἄτμητον φῶς τῆς ἀγάπης τεμοῦσα.

Hymn 16 God's Loving Caress

Ὅτι ποθεινόν τε καὶ ἐπιθυμητὸν κατὰ φύσιν μόνον τὸ θεῖον, οὗ ὁ μετέχων πάντων ἐν μετοχῇ γέγονε τῶν καλῶν.

Ὢ τί τὸ πρᾶγμα τὸ κρυπτὸν πάσῃ κτιστῇ οὐσίᾳ;
καὶ τί τὸ φῶς τὸ νοητόν, ὅ τινι οὐχ ὁρᾶται;

Inf. for indir. disc., the content of ἐπίστευσα (Wal: 603; Smy: 2016). • **ὄντως** — adv., *really, certainly, in truth.* • **ἄτρεπτον** → ἄτρεπτος, ον, *unchangeable.* • **βίῳ** → ὁ βίος, *life.* • **μ'** → με. • **ἀπατᾶν** → ἀπατάω, *I deceive.* • **νομιζέτω** → νομίζω, *I think.*

Lines 10–14

φεῦ — *woe!,* exclamation of grief or anger. This word can also express astonishment or admiration, *ah!, oh!* • **φεύγοντα** → φεύγω, *I flee.* τὰ φεύγοντα, *the fleeting things.* • **κρατούμενα** → κρατέω, *I seize, hold fast.* • **τερπομένῳ** → τέρπω, *I satisfy, delight.* • **ταὐτά** → τὰ αὐτά. • **πείσεται** — fut. mid. (depon.) indic. → πάσχω. • **ἅπερ** → ὅσπερ, ἥπερ, ὅπερ, *the very one who, the very thing which.* ἅπερ, *as* (LSI II: 573). • **κἀγώ** → καὶ ἐγώ. • **τάλας** → τάλας, α, αν, *suffering, wretched.* • **ἐχώρισεν** → χωρίζω, *I separate, divide.* • **γλυκυτάτου** → γλυκύτατος, η, ον, *sweet, dear,* superlative of γλυκύς, εῖα, ύ. Gen. of separation (Wal: 107; Smy: 1392). • **ἄτμητον** → ἄτμητος, ον, *undivided, indivisible.* • **τεμοῦσα** — 2 aor. act. ptc. → τέμνω, *I cut, divide, cut off, sever.*

Hymn 16

Title

ὅτι — here introduces the title, *that.* • **ποθεινόν** → ποθεινός, ή, όν, *longed for/desired.* Pred. compl. • **ἐπιθυμητόν** → ἐπιθυμητός, ή, όν, *precious, pleasant; to be desired.* Pred. compl. (*PGL*: 524). • **φύσιν** → ἡ φύσις, *nature.* κατὰ φύσιν, *by nature* (BDAG, φύσις 1: 1069). • **θεῖον** → θεῖος, α, ον, *divine.* τὸ θεῖον, *the Divine Being, the Divinity, Deity.* • **μετέχων** → μετέχω, *I partake of, share in,* w. gen. • **μετοχῇ** → ἡ μετοχή, *participation.* • **γέγονε** — γίνομαι with ἐν is used of a state of being, or entrance into a state of being (BDAG, γίνομαι 5c: 198). So ἐν μετοχῇ γέγονε, "has become in participation," i.e., *has participated in; has come into participation.* • **καλῶν** → καλός, ή, όν. This is a rich word that includes both beauty and goodness, here ref. to all that is worth desiring.

Lines 1–4

Ὢ — *O!,* exclamation of surprise, joy or pain. • **πρᾶγμα** → τὸ πρᾶγμα, *thing, matter.* • **κρυπτόν** → κρυπτός, ή, όν, *hidden.* • **κτιστῇ** → κτιστός, ή, όν, *cre-*

καὶ τίς ὁ πλοῦτος ὁ πολύς, ὃν οὐδεὶς ἐν τῷ κόσμῳ
εὑρεῖν ὅλως ἐξίσχυσεν ἢ κατασχεῖν εἰς ἅπαν;
ἔστι γὰρ πᾶσιν ἄληπτος, ἀχώρητος τῷ κόσμῳ,
ἔστι καὶ ποθεινότατος ὑπὲρ ἅπαντα κόσμον,
ἔστι καὶ ἐπιθυμητός, καθ' ὅσον ὑπερέχει
τῶν ὁρωμένων ὁ αὐτὰ θεὸς κατασκευάσας·
κατὰ τοῦτο τιτρώσκομαι τῇ ἀγάπῃ ἐκείνου,
καθ' ὅσον δ' οὐχ ὁρᾶταί μοι ἐκτήκομαι τὰς φρένας,
τὸν νοῦν καὶ τὴν καρδίαν μου φλεγόμενος καὶ στένων,
περιπατῶ καὶ καίομαι ζητῶν ὧδε κἀκεῖσε
καὶ οὐδαμοῦ τὸν ἐραστὴν εὑρίσκω τῆς ψυχῆς μου·
καὶ περιβλέπομαι συχνῶς ἰδεῖν τὸν ποθητόν μου,
κἀκεῖνος ὡς ἀόρατος οὐχ ὁρᾶταί μοι ὅλως·

---

ated (*PGL*: 784). • **οὐσίᾳ** → ἡ οὐσία, *being, essence,* here perhaps something like, *existent being* (cf. *PGL* I: 980–82). See *PLG* (980–85) for an overview of this rich word in the Fathers. Kambylis has a nom. here instead of the dat., but this makes little sense, so a dat. is read, following Koder. • **νοητόν** → νοητός, ή, όν, *intelligible, noetic,* i.e., belonging to the νοῦς. • **ὁρᾶται** → ὁράω. Could have a pass. sense, *I am seen,* but the pass. can also be used in an act. sense, *become visible, appear* (LSI V: 565; BDAG A1d: 719). • **πλοῦτος** → ὁ πλοῦτος, *wealth.* • **πολύς** — here, *great, abundant.* • **ὅλως** — adv., *completely, wholly; actually, in fact.* • **ἐξίσχυσεν** → ἐξισχύω, *I am strong enough, am able.* • **κατασχεῖν** — 2 aor. act. inf. → κατέχω, *I hold fast, possess.* Supplemental inf. • **ἅπαν** → ἅπας, ἅπασα, ἅπαν, *whole, all.* εἰς ἅπαν, *at all, in the least* (LSJ II: 181).

Lines 5–9

ἄληπτος → ἄληπτος, ον, *not to be grasped, not to be apprehended.* • **ἀχώρητος** → ἀχώρητος, ον, *not to be contained; incomprehensible.* • **ποθεινότατος** → ποθεινότατος, η, ον, *most desired,* superlative of ποθεινός. • **καθ' ὅσον** — *in as much as* (BDAG, κατά 5aα: 513). • **ὑπερέχει** → ὑπερέχω, *I surpass,* w. gen. • **ὁρωμένων** → ὁράω. • **αὐτά** — dir. obj. of κατασκευάσας. • **κατασκευάσας** → κατασκευάζω, *I prepare, build, create.* • **κατὰ τοῦτο** — *because of this* (BDAG, κατά 5aδ: 512). • **τιτρώσκομαι** → τιτρώσκω, *I wound.*

Lines 10–14

ἐκτήκομαι → ἐκτήκω, *I let melt away;* pass., *melt/pine/waste away.* • **φρένας** → ἡ φρήν, *heart, mind.* Acc. of ref. (Wal: 203; Smy: 1600). This word is almost always in the pl. and there is no difference between the sg. and pl. (LSJ: 1954, end of the art.). • **νοῦν** → ὁ νοῦς, *mind.* • **φλεγόμενος** → φλέγω, *I burn, burn up;* pass., *catch fire.* • **στένων** → στένω, *moan, sigh, groan.* • **περιπατῶ** → περιπατέω, *I walk, walk about.* • **καίομαι** → καίω, *I light, kindle;* pass., *burn.* • **κἀκεῖσε** → καί and ἐκεῖσε, *to that place, there.* • **οὐδαμοῦ** — adv., *nowhere.* • **ἐραστήν** → ὁ ἐραστής, *lover.* • **περιβλέπομαι** → περιβλέπω, *I look around (at), look for, hunt;* mid. for act. (BDAG: 799). • **συχνῶς** — adv., *often.* • **ἰδεῖν** → εἶδον. • **ποθητόν** → ποθητός, ή, όν, *longed for, beloved.*

Lines 15–19

κἀκεῖνος → καί and ἐκεῖνος. • **ὡς** — here perhaps, as an augment to the adj., *quite invisible* (LSI AIII2: 908). • **ἀόρατος** → ἀόρατος, ον, *unseen, invisible.*

ὅτε δὲ ἄρξομαι θρηνεῖν ὡς ἀπελπίσας, τότε
ὁρᾶταί μοι καὶ βλέπει με ὁ καθορῶν τὰ πάντα·
θαυμάζων καταπλήττομαι κάλλους τὴν εὐμορφίαν
καὶ πῶς ἀνοίξας οὐρανοὺς διέκυψεν ὁ κτίστης
καὶ δόξαν μοι παρέδειξε τὴν ἄφραστον καὶ ξένην·
καὶ τίς ἄρα ἐγγύτερον γενήσεται ἐκείνου
ἢ πῶς ἀνενεχθήσεται εἰς ἀμέτρητον ὕψος;
λογιζομένου μου αὐτὸς εὑρίσκεται ἐντός μου,
ἔνδον ἐν τῇ ταλαίνῃ μου καρδίᾳ ἀπαστράπτων,
πάντοθεν περιλάμπων με τῇ ἀθανάτῳ αἴγλῃ,
ἅπαντα δὲ τὰ μέλη μου ἀκτῖσι καταυγάζων,
ὅλος περιπλεκόμενος ὅλον καταφιλεῖ με
ὅλον τε δίδωσιν αὐτὸν ἐμοὶ τῷ ἀναξίῳ,
καὶ ἐμφοροῦμαι τῆς αὐτοῦ ἀγάπης καὶ τοῦ κάλλους,
καὶ ἡδονῆς καὶ γλυκασμοῦ ἐμπίπλαμαι τοῦ θείου·

• **θρηνεῖν** → θρηνέω, *I sing a dirge, wail.* • **ἀπελπίσας** — aor. act. ptc. → ἀπελπίζω, *I give up in despair, despair.* • **καθορῶν** → καθοράω, *I look down upon; perceive, notice.* • **θαυμάζων** → θαυμάζω, *I wonder, marvel, am astonished.* • **καταπλήττομαι** → καταπλήττω (listed in lexicons under the alternate form καταπλήσσω), *I strike with amazement, astound, terrify.* • **κάλλους** — gen. → τὸ κάλλος, *beauty.* • **εὐμορφίαν** → ἡ εὐμορφία, *beauty of form, elegance.* Acc. of ref. (Wal: 203; Smy: 1600). • **ἀνοίξας** → ἀνοίγω (listed in LSJ under ἀνοίγνυμι), *I open.* • **διέκυψεν** → διακύπτω, *I stoop to look in; look to, concern oneself with* (*PGL* 2b: 355). • **κτίστης** → ὁ κτίστης, *creator.*

Lines 20–24

παρέδειξε — aor. act. indic. → παραδείκνυμι, *I exhibit, bring forward.* • **ἄφραστον** → ἄφραστος, ον, *unutterable, inexpressible.* • **ξένην** → ξένος, η, ον, *strange.* • **ἄρα** — interrogative particle expecting a neg. answer. Other editions give, ἄρα, *then, so then,* which makes better sense. • **ἐγγύτερον** → ἐγγύτερος, α, ον, *nearer,* comparative of ἐγγύς. • **γενήσεται** → γίνομαι, here, *I move* (BDAG 6: 198). • **ἀνενεχθήσεται** — fut. pass. indic. → ἀναφέρω, *I take up, bring up.* • **ἀμέτρητον** → ἀμέτρητος, η, ον, *unmeasured, immeasurable.* • **ὕψος** → τὸ ὕψος, *height.* • **λογιζομένου** → λογίζομαι, *I consider.* Gen. abs. • **μου** — subj. of gen. abs. • **ἐντός** — adv., *within.* • **ἔνδον** — adv., *in, within.* • **ταλαίνῃ** → τάλας, τάλαινα, τάλαν, *suffering, wretched.* • **ἀπαστράπτων** → ἀπαστράπτω, *I flash forth.*

Lines 25–29

πάντοθεν — adv., *from every side.* • **περιλάμπων** → περιλάμπω, *I shine around.* • **ἀθανάτῳ** → ἀθάνατος, η, ον, *undying, immortal.* • **αἴγλῃ** → ἡ αἴγλη, *radiance.* • **ἅπαντα** → ἅπας, ἅπασα, ἅπαν, *all.* • **μέλη** → τὸ μέλος, *member, limb.* • **ἀκτῖσι** → ἡ ἀκτίς, *ray, beam.* • **καταυγάζων** → καταυγάζω, *I shine upon.* • **περιπλεκόμενος** → περιπλέκω, *I entwine, enfold.* • **καταφιλεῖ** → καταφιλέω, *I kiss, caress.* • **ἀναξίῳ** → ἀνάξιος, ον, *unworthy.* • **ἐμφοροῦμαι** → ἐμφορέω, *I pour in;* pass., *take one's fill of,* w. gen.

Lines 30–34

ἡδονῆς → ἡ ἡδονή, *delight, enjoyment, pleasure.* • **γλυκασμοῦ** → ὁ γλυκασμός,

μεταλαμβάνω τοῦ φωτός, μετέχω καὶ τῆς δόξης
καὶ λάμπει μου τὸ πρόσωπον ὡς καὶ τοῦ ποθητοῦ μου
καὶ ἅπαντα τὰ μέλη μου γίνονται φωτοφόρα·
ὡραίων ὡραιότερος τότε ἀποτελοῦμαι,
πλουσίων πλουσιώτερος καὶ δυνατῶν ἁπάντων
ὑπάρχω δυνατώτερος καὶ βασιλέων μείζων
καὶ τιμιώτερος πολὺ τῶν ὁρωμένων πάντων,
οὐχὶ τῆς γῆς καὶ τῶν τῆς γῆς, ἀλλὰ καὶ οὐρανοῦ δὲ
καὶ πάντων τῶν ἐν οὐρανῷ, τὸν πάντων ἔχων κτίστην,
ᾧ πρέπει δόξα καὶ τιμὴ νῦν καὶ εἰς τοὺς αἰῶνας·

ἀμήν.

---

sweetness. • **ἐμπίπλαμαι** — pres. pass. indic. → ἐμπίπλημι, *I fill very full,* w. gen. • **μεταλαμβάνω** → μεταλαμβάνω, *I have/get a share, share in, participate in.* • **μετέχω** → μετέχω, *I partake of, share in,* w. gen. • **λάμπει** → λάμπω, *I shine.* • **φωτοφόρα** → φωτοφόρος, α, ον, *light-bearing, brilliant.* • **ὡραίων** → ὡραῖος, α, ον, *seasonable, ripe, beautiful.* Gen. of comparison (Wal: 110; Smy: 1069). • **ὡραιότερος** → ὡραιότερος, α, ον, *more seasonable/ripe/beautiful,* comparative of ὡραῖος. • **ἀποτελοῦμαι** → ἀποτελέω, *I complete, perfect.*

Lines 35–40

πλουσίων → πλούσιος, α, ον, *rich, wealthy.* Gen. of comparison (Wal: 110; Smy: 1069). • **πλουσιώτερος** → πλουσιώτερος, α, ον, *more rich/wealthy,* comparative of πλούσιος. • **δυνατῶν** → δυνατός, ή, όν, *mighty.* • **δυνατώτερος** → δυνατώτερος, α, ον, *more mighty,* comparative of δυνατός. • **μείζων** → μείζων, ον, *greater,* comparative of μέγας. • **τιμιώτερος** → τιμιώτερος, α, ον, *more precious,* comparative of τίμιος. • **ὁρωμένων** → ὁράω. • **οὐχί** — a strengthened form of οὐ, *not;* w. ἀλλά, *not only . . . but also.* • **τῆς γῆς** — This string of gen. may be taken in appos. to τῶν ὁρωμένων πάντων. • **τῶν τῆς γῆς** — "Those of the earth" could ref. to the people of earth, or all the things of earth. • **οὐρανοῦ** — here probably the physical heavens since the focus is on things seen, and Symeon would not be more precious than those in heaven, in the sense of God's abode, who likewise share in the divine Glory. • **ἔχων** — circ. ptc., cause. **πρέπει** → πρέπω, *I am fitting.* πρέπει w. dat. is an imper. construction, *it is fitting for someone.* Comp. subj. w. sg. verb (Wal: 401; Smy: 968). • **τιμή** → ἡ τιμή, *honor.*

Translations of All Texts

The Didache

Didache 1–6 The Way of Life and the Way of Death

Teaching of the Lord through the twelve apostles to the nations

1.1 There are two ways, one of life and one of death, and great is the difference between the two ways. 1.2 So then, "the way of life"[1] is this: first, "you shall love the God" who made you; second, "your neighbor as yourself";[2] and "whatever you want not to happen to you, you also do not do to another."[3] 1.3 And the teaching of these matters is this: "Bless those who curse you and pray for your enemies," and fast "for those who persecute you. For what credit [is there for you] if you love those who love you? Do not even the Gentiles do the same thing? But you, love those who hate you,"[4] and you will not have an enemy. 1.4 Keep away from fleshly and bodily desires. "If someone gives you a blow on the right cheek, turn to him also the other,"[5] and you will be perfect. "If someone forces you [to go] one mile, go with him two." "If someone takes your cloak, give to him also your tunic." "If someone takes from you what is yours, do not ask [for it] back,"[6] for neither are you able [to do so]. 1.5 "Give to everyone who asks you and do not ask [for it] back,"[7] for the Father desires that [something] from his own gifts be given to everyone. Blessed is the one who gives in keeping with the commandment, for he is guiltless. Woe to the one who takes, for if indeed someone having a need takes, he will be guiltless, but the one who does not have need shall give a satisfactory account, [explaining] why he took [it] and for what purpose. And after arriving in prison, he will be questioned concerning the things he did, and "he will not come out from there until he pays back the last quadrans."[8] 1.6 Not only this, but also concerning this it has been said, "Your alms are to sweat in your hands until such time as you know to whom you are to give them."[9]

---

[1] Jer 21:8.

[2] Matt 22:37–39; Mark 12:30–31; Luke 10:27; Deut 6:5; Lev 19:18.

[3] Matt 7:12; Luke 6:31.

[4] Matt 5:44, 46–47; Luke 6:28, 32–33, 35.

[5] Matt 5:39.

[6] Matt 5:40–41; Luke 6:29–30.

[7] Matt 5:42; Luke 6:30.

[8] Matt 5:26. The quadrans was the smallest Roman coin. Luke 12:59 uses λεπτός, another small coin.

[9] The source of this quotation is unknown.

2.1 And the second commandment of the teaching [is]: 2.2 "You shall not murder; you shall not commit adultery";[10] you shall not commit sodomy; you shall not engage in illicit sex; "you shall not steal";[11] you shall not practice magic; you shall not make magic potions; you shall not murder a child by abortion, nor after children have been born shall you kill [them]; "you shall not desire things belonging to your neighbor."[12] 2.3 "You shall not swear falsely; you shall not give false testimony";[13] you shall not speak evil; you shall not bear a grudge; 2.4 you shall not be double-minded nor double-tongued, for duplicity is a deadly trap. 2.5 Your word shall not be false or empty, but fulfilled in action. 2.6 You shall not be a greedy person, nor a robber, nor a hypocrite, nor malicious, nor arrogant. You shall not devise an evil plan against your neighbor. 2.7 "You shall not hate" any person; "but rather, some you shall correct," others you shall pray for, and "others you shall love"[14] more than your own soul.

3.1 My child, flee from every evil and from everything resembling it. 3.2 Do not be quick-tempered, for anger leads to murder; nor [be] a jealous person, nor quarrelsome, nor hot-tempered, for acts of murder are born from all these things. 3.3 My child, do not be one who lusts, for lust leads to sexual sin; nor [be] a foul-mouthed person, nor one with immodest eye, for acts of adultery are born from all these things. 3.4 My child, "do not be an augur,"[15] since it leads to idolatry; nor [be] an enchanter, nor an astrologer, nor a magician, nor desire to see these things, for idolatry is born from all these things. 3.5 My child, do not be a liar, since falsehood leads to stealing; nor [be] fond of money, nor conceited, for acts of stealing are born from all these things. 3.6 My child, do not be a grumbler, since it leads to blasphemy; nor [be] self-willed, nor evil-minded, for blasphemies are born from all these things. 3.7 But rather be humble, since "the humble will inherit the earth."[16] 3.8 Be patient and merciful and innocent and "tranquil" and good and always "trembling at the words"[17] you heard. 3.9 You shall not exalt yourself, nor shall you allow your soul to be arrogant. Your soul shall not be joined with haughty ones, but you shall associate with righteous and lowly ones. 3.10 You shall welcome the experiences happening to you as good things, knowing that nothing happens apart from God.

4.1 My child, night and day "you shall remember the one who speaks the word of God to you,"[18] and you shall honor him as the Lord, for the place from which the Lord's nature is spoken, there the Lord is.[19] 4.2 And you shall seek out daily the faces of the saints, that you may find rest in their words. 4.3 You shall not cause a division, but you shall reconcile those quarreling. You shall judge righteously, and you shall not show partiality that you

---

[10] Exod 20:13–14.
[11] Exod 20:15.
[12] Exod 20:17.
[13] Exod 20:16; Matt 5:33.
[14] Lev 19:17–18.
[15] Lev 19:26.
[16] Matt 5:5; Ps 37:11.
[17] Isa 66:2.
[18] Heb 13:7.
[19] The point is that the Lord is present where his lordship is proclaimed. "There, in the mouth of the teacher and in his teaching, the *Kyrios* himself is present. Thus the teacher himself should be honored as if the *Kyrios* himself were standing before you" (Niederwimmer: 105). Cf. *Did.* 11.2.

may reprove offenses. 4.4 You shall not be double-minded, whether it shall be or not.[20] 4.5 "Do not be one who stretches out the hands when it comes to receiving, but who draws [them] together when it comes to giving."[21] 4.6 If you have [something] through [working with] your hands, you shall give [something as] a ransom for your sins.[22] 4.7 You shall not hesitate to give, nor, when you give, shall you grumble, for you shall recognize who is the good paymaster of the reward. 4.8 You shall not reject the one who is in need, but you shall share everything with your brother, and you shall not say that [anything] "is your own."[23] For if you are partners in what is immortal, how much more in mortal things? 4.9 You shall not take your hand away from your son or from your daughter, but from [their] youth you shall teach [them] the fear of God. 4.10 You shall not give orders in your bitterness to your male slave or your female slave, those who hope in the same God, lest they shall certainly not fear the God who is over both [of you], for he does not come to call [people] with partiality, but [he comes] upon those whom the Spirit prepared. 4.11 And you slaves shall be subject to your lords as to a type of God, in reverence and fear. 4.12 You shall hate every instance of hypocrisy and everything that [is] not pleasing to the Lord. 4.13 You shall certainly not forsake the commandments of the Lord, but you shall guard those things that you received, neither adding nor subtracting. 4.14 In church you shall confess your transgressions, and you shall not come to your prayer with an evil conscience. This is the way of life.

5.1 And this is the way of death: first of all, it is evil and full of curse—murders, acts of adultery, lusts, sexual sins, thefts, idolatries, acts of magic, sorceries, robberies, false testimonies, hypocrisies, duplicities, deceit, arrogance, wickedness, stubbornness, greediness, obscene talk, jealousy, arrogant boldness, pride, pretension; 5.2 [It is the way of those who are] persecutors of good people; those hating truth, loving falsehood, not knowing righteousness' reward, not "adhering to good"[24] nor to right judgment, not being alert to the good but to the evil, from whom gentleness and patience are far away, loving worthless things, pursuing rewards, not having compassion on the poor, not toiling for the one being oppressed, not knowing the one who made them, murderers of children, corrupters of what God has formed, rejecting the one who is in need, oppressing the one who is afflicted, defenders of the rich, lawless judges of the poor, utterly sinful people. May you be delivered, children, from all these!

6.1 See that no one leads you astray from this way of teaching, because [that person] teaches you apart from God. 6.2 For if you are able to bear the whole yoke of the Lord, you will be perfect. And if you are not able [to bear the whole yoke], what you are able [to bear], do this.

6.3 And concerning food, bear what you are able, but beware especially of food sacrificed to idols, for it is worship of dead gods.

---

[20] Niederwimmer (106) notes that this ackward expression is a *crux interpretum.* See my Greek note on this passage.

[21] Sir 4:31.

[22] For the redemptive power of almsgiving see Tob 12:9; Sir 3:30; Dan 4:27 LXX (4:24 in some editions); *2 Clem.* 16.4; Pol. *Phil.* 10.2; cf., possibly, 1 Pet 4:8 (quoting Prov 10:12, also quoted in *2 Clem.* 16.4).

[23] Acts 4:32.

[24] Rom 12:9.

Didache 7 Concerning Baptism

7.1 And concerning baptism, baptize thus: after having first explained all these things, baptize "in the name of the Father, and the Son, and the Holy Spirit,"[25] in flowing water. 7.2 And if you do not have flowing water, baptize in other water, and if you are not able [to baptize] in cool [water, then] in warm. 7.3 And if you do not have either, pour water on the head three times in the name of the Father and of the Son and of the Holy Spirit. 7.4 And before the baptism let the one baptizing and the one being baptized, and others if some are able, fast beforehand. And command that the one being baptized fast for one or two days before.

Didache 8 Concerning Fasting and Prayer

8.1 And your fasts are not to be with the hypocrites. For they fast on the second day of the week[26] and the fifth,[27] but you, fast on the fourth[28] and on Preparation.[29] 8.2 Do not pray "like the hypocrites,"[30] but as the Lord commanded in his gospel pray thus, "Our Father in heaven, your name be hallowed, your kingdom come, your will be done, as in heaven, also on earth; give us today our bread for life in the Kingdom,[31] and forgive us our debts as we also are forgiving our debtors; and do not lead us into temptation, but rescue us from the evil one; for yours is the power and the glory unto the ages."[32] 8.3 Pray thus three times a day.

Didache 9–10 Concerning the Eucharist

9.1 And concerning the Thanksgiving,[33] give thanks thus: 9.2 First, concerning the cup: "We thank you, our Father, for the holy vine of David your servant, which you made known to us through Jesus your servant; to you be the glory unto the ages." 9.3 And concerning the fragment [of bread]: "We thank you, our Father, for the life and knowledge you made known to us through Jesus your servant; to you be the glory unto the ages. 9.4 Just as this fragment had been scattered upon the mountains and, having been brought together, became one, so let your church be gathered from the ends of the earth into your kingdom; for yours is the glory and the power through Jesus Christ unto the ages." 9.5 And let no one eat or drink from your Thanksgiving, but those who have been baptized in the Lord's name. For indeed the Lord has spoken concerning this, "Do not give the holy thing to the dogs."[34]

10.1 And after being filled, give thanks thus: 10.2 "We thank you, holy Father, for your holy name, which you caused to dwell in our hearts, and for the knowledge and faith and immortality, which you made known to us through Jesus your servant; to you be the glory unto the ages. 10.3 You, almighty Master, created everything for the sake of your name;

---

25 Matt 28:19.

26 Monday.

27 Thursday.

28 Wednesday.

29 Friday, according to the Jewish usage, since Friday was the day of preparation for the Sabbath, which begins at sundown on Fridays.

30 Matt 6:16.

31 For this unusual translation, see the discussion in the Greek notes.

32 Matt 6:9–13; cf. Luke 11:2–4.

33 That is, the Eucharist.

34 Matt 7:6.

you gave food and drink to humans for enjoyment, that we might give thanks to you. And to us you graciously gave spiritual food and drink and eternal life through your servant. 10.4 Above all, we thank you because you are mighty; to you be the glory unto the ages. 10.5 Remember, Lord, your church to rescue her from all evil and to 'perfect' her 'in your love'[35] and 'gather' her 'from the four winds,'[36] that [church] which you have sanctified, into your kingdom which you prepared for her; for yours is the power and the glory unto the ages." 10.6 Let grace come and let this world pass away. Hosanna[37] to the God of David. If anyone is holy, let him come. If anyone is not [holy] let him repent. 'Maranatha.'[38] Amen." 10.7 Permit the prophets to give thanks as much as they want.

Didache 11–13 Concerning Teachers, Apostles, and Prophets

11.1 So, whoever comes and teaches you all these things that have just been explained, receive him. 11.2 But if the teacher himself turns and teaches another teaching to the destroying [of the true teaching], do not listen to him. But [if someone teaches a teaching] so that righteousness and knowledge of the Lord increase, receive him as the Lord. 11.3 And concerning the apostles and prophets, in keeping with the rule of the gospel do thus: 11.4 Every apostle coming to you is to be received as the Lord. 11.5 But he shall not remain except for one day, and if need be, also another. But if he remains three [days], he is a false prophet. 11.6 And the apostle, when he goes out, is to take nothing except bread until he finds lodging for the night. But if he asks for money, he is a false prophet. 11.7 And you shall not test nor judge any prophet speaking in the Spirit, for every sin will be forgiven, but this sin will not be forgiven. 11.8 But not everyone who speaks in the Spirit is a prophet, but [only] if he has the ways of the Lord. Therefore, by their ways the false prophet and the prophet shall be recognized. 11.9 And every prophet ordering in the Spirit a meal shall not eat from it; otherwise he is a false prophet.[39] 11.10 And every prophet teaching the truth, if he does not do what he teaches, he is a false prophet. 11.11 And every prophet having been proven to be genuine, if he does [something] for an earthly mystery of the church,[40] but does not teach [others] to do all that he himself does, shall not be judged by you, for he has his judgment with God. For the ancient prophets also did likewise. 11.12 And whoever might say in the Spirit, "Give me money or something

[35] 1 John 4:18.

[36] Matt 24:31.

[37] From an Aramaic expression meaning "help," "save, I pray" (cf. the related Hebrew word *hôšîʾâ* in Ps 118:25), which became a liturgical formula (cf. Matt 21:9, 15; Mark 11:9–10; John 12:13).

[38] From an Aramaic expression which means either "(our) Lord has come" (if spelled, μαρὰν ἀθά) or, more likely, "(our) Lord, come!" (if spelled, μαράνα θᾶ). It seems to have been a liturgical expression, familiar even to Gentile converts (cf. 1 Cor 16:22). Cf. BDAG: 616.

[39] Perhaps the reference is to the prophet ordering that a meal be organized for the needy in the community, similar to the action mentioned in 11.12 (cf. Niederwimmer: 179).

[40] It is not clear what the author is referring to. Many see a reference to "spiritual marriage," i.e., marriage without sexual intercourse; the prophet and his spouse thus supposedly symbolize the mystery of Christ and his church (cf. Eph 5:22–33). Some find this practice mentioned already in Paul's writings (1 Cor 7:36–38). See Niederwimmer: 179–82. See further the discussion in the Greek notes on this passage.

else," you shall not listen to him. But if he says to give for others who are in need, let no one judge him.

12.1 And everyone "coming in the name of the Lord"[41] is to be received; and then, having examined [him], you will know him, for you will have understanding of truth and falsehood.

12.2 If the one who comes is traveling through, help him as much as you are able. But he shall not remain with you except for two or three days, if it is necessary. 12.3 But if he wants to settle with you, if he is a skilled laborer, let him work and eat. 12.4 But if he does not have a trade, according to your knowledge take thought [for] how he shall live with you as a Christian, without being idle. 12.5 But if he does not want to do thus, he is one who trades on Christ. Beware of such people.

13.1 But every true prophet wanting to settle with you is "worthy of his food." 13.2 Likewise, a true teacher is also himself "worthy of his food,"[42] like the worker. 13.3 So, taking all the first fruit of that which is produced from the wine-press and the threshing floor, cattle and sheep, you shall give the first fruit to the prophets, for they themselves are your high priests. 13.4 But if you do not have a prophet, give to the poor. 13.5 If you make bread, take the first fruit and give according to the commandment. 13.6 Likewise, if you open a jar of wine or olive oil take the first fruit and give to the prophets. 13.7 And take the first fruit of money, and clothing, and every possession, as it seems [right] to you, and give according to the commandment.

Didache 14 Concerning the Lord's Day

14.1 And being gathered on each of the Lord's own days,[43] break bread and give thanks, confessing your offenses beforehand so that your sacrifice may be pure. 14.2 But no one having a quarrel with his companion is to join with you until they are reconciled, that your sacrifice may not be defiled. 14.3 For this is the sacrifice that was spoken of by the Lord, "In every place and time offer to me a pure sacrifice, for I am a great king, says the Lord, and my name is marvelous among the Gentiles."[44]

Didache 15 Some Gospel Admonitions

15.1 Therefore, appoint for yourselves bishops and deacons worthy of the Lord, men who are humble, not in love with money, true, and having been approved. For even they themselves perform for you the ministry of the prophets and teachers. 15.2 So do not disdain them, for they themselves are your honored ones, with the prophets and teachers.

15.3 And correct one another, not in anger but in peace, as you have [instruction] in the gospel. And no one is to talk to anyone who wrongs another, nor is he to hear [a word] from you, until he repent. 15.4 And do your prayers, and alms, and all your deeds thus, as you have [instruction] in the gospel of our Lord

---

[41] Ps 118:26 (LXX 117:26); Matt 21:9; Mark 11:9; Luke 19:38.
[42] Matt 10:10.
[43] That is, Sunday, so the idea is "Sunday by Sunday."
[44] Mal 1:11, 14.

Didache 16 Live in the Light of the Lord's Coming

16.1 "Watch"[45] over your life. "Do not let your lamps be quenched, and do not let your loins be weakened, but be ready, for you do not know the hour in which our Lord comes."[46] 16.2 And you shall gather together often, seeking the things related to your souls. For the whole time of your faith will not help you if you are not perfect in the last time. 16.3 For in the last days "the false prophets"[47] and corrupters will increase, and the sheep will be turned into wolves, and love will be turned into hate. 16.4 For, lawlessness having increased, "they will hate and persecute and betray one another. And then will appear" the deceiver of the world as a son of God "and will do signs and wonders,"[48] and the earth will be handed over into his hands, and he will do disgusting things that have never happened since the beginning. 16.5 Then the [part of] creation that consists of humans will come to the fiery test, and many will fall away and perish, but "those who have endured" in their faith "will be saved"[49] by the accursed one himself.[50] 16.6 "And then the signs" of the truth "will appear":[51] first a sign which is an opening in heaven, then a sign which is a trumpet's sound, and third the resurrection of the dead; 16.7 but not [the resurrection] of all, rather, as it has been said, "The Lord will come, and all his saints with him."[52] 16.8 Then the world will see the Lord "coming upon the clouds of heaven."[53]

---

[45] Matt 25:13.

[46] Luke 12:35, 40.

[47] Matt 24:11, 24.

[48] Matt 24:10, 30, 24 (this order of verses is that of the three quotations/allusions).

[49] Matt 24:13.

[50] This is probably a reference to Christ as cursed by his enemies (cf. Niederwimmer: 221–22).

[51] Matt 24:30.

[52] Zech 14:5; 1 Thess 3:13.

[53] Matt 24:30.

Clement of Rome

1 Clement

1 Clement 5–6 The Deaths of Peter and Paul

5.1 But that we might cease [giving] examples of the ancients, let us come to those who were athletes quite recently. Let us take our generation's noble examples. 5.2 Because of jealousy and envy, the greatest and most righteous pillars were persecuted and competed unto death. 5.3 Let us set before our eyes the good apostles. 5.4 Peter, who, because of unrighteous jealousy, endured not one or two but many afflictions, and having thus borne witness, he went to the place of glory, which he deserved. 5.5 Because of jealousy and strife Paul set forth the prize of endurance. 5.6 Having worn chains seven times, having been banished, having been stoned, having become a herald in the East and in the West, he received the genuine renown for his faith, 5.7 having taught the whole world righteousness, and having gone to the limit of the West; and having borne witness before the rulers, he thus was set free from the world and went to the holy place, having become a supreme example of patient endurance.

6.1 To these men who led their lives in a holy manner there was joined a great multitude of elect ones, who, having suffered by many tortures and torments because of jealousy, became an exquisite example among us. 6.2 Because of jealousy, women, "Danaids and Dirces,"[1] having been persecuted and having suffered terrible and unholy torments, securely reached the goal in the race of faith, and these women who were weak in body received a noble reward. 6.3 Jealousy estranged wives from husbands and changed that which was said by our father Adam, "This now is bone of my bones and flesh of my flesh."[2] 6.4 Jealousy and strife overturned great cities and uprooted great nations.

1 Clement 47–50 Love

47.1 Take up the letter of the blessed Paul the apostle. 47.2 What did he write to you earlier, at the beginning of the gospel? 47.3 In truth, he sent you a letter in a spiritual manner con-

[1] The Danaids were figures in Greek mythology, daughters of Danaus, who all suffered mistreatment. The reference might be to the public rape of Christian martyrs. Dirce was a woman in Greek myth, wife of Lycus, the king of Thebes, who was dragged to death by a wild bull. The obscurity of the allusion to the Danaids and Dirce has led some scholars to suggest emendations, though there are no variations in the manuscripts. See the notes in BDAG, Ehrman, Holmes, and Lightfoot, *Clement*, 2:32–34.

[2] Gen 2:23.

cerning himself and Cephas and Apollos, because even then you had engaged in partisan strife. 47.4 But that partisan strife brought upon you a lesser sin, for you were split into factions over apostles of good reputation and a man approved by them. 47.5 But now consider what sort of persons have perverted you and diminished respect for your famous brotherly love. 47.6 It is shameful, beloved, exceedingly shameful indeed, and unworthy of your conduct in Christ, that it be heard that the well-established and ancient church of the Corinthians is rebelling against its presbyters because of one or two persons. 47.7 And this report has reached not only to us, but also to those who differ from us, so that, in fact, blasphemies are brought upon the name of the Lord because of your senselessness, and they produce, in addition, danger for yourselves.

48.1 Therefore, let us remove this quickly and fall down before the Master and weep, beseeching him that he, being gracious, might be reconciled to us and restore us to the honorable, pure conduct of our brotherly love. 48.2 For this is a gate of righteousness standing open to life, just as it stands written, "Open to me gates of righteousness, so that, entering by them, I may praise the Lord. 48.3 This is the gate of the Lord; righteous ones will enter by it."[3] 48.4 Therefore, although many gates have opened, this is the one that is in righteousness, [even] the [gate] which is in Christ, by which all who enter are blessed and make straight their journey in holiness and righteousness, accomplishing everything without disturbance. 48.5 Let a person be faithful, let him be able to speak forth knowledge, let him be wise in distinguishing of words, let him be vigorous in deeds, let him be pure. 48.6 For the greater he seems to be, by as much more he ought to be humble and seek the common good of all, and not that which is his own.

49.1 The one who has love in Christ must do the precepts of Christ. 49.2 Who is able to explain the bond of God's love? 49.3 Who is adequate to declare the magnificence of his beauty? 49.4 The height unto which love leads up is indescribable. 49.5 Love binds us closely to God; "love covers a multitude of sins";[4] love endures all things, is patient in all things; [there is] nothing coarse in love, nothing haughty; love does not cause schism, love does not rebel, love does all things in harmony. In love all the elect of God were made perfect; without love nothing is well-pleasing to God. 49.6 In love the Master received us. Because of the love he had for us, Jesus Christ our Lord gave his blood for us by the will of God, and his flesh for our flesh, and his soul for our souls.

50.1 You see, beloved, how great and amazing love is; and there is no description of its perfection. 50.2 Who is fit to be found in it, except those whom God considers worthy? Therefore, let us plead and ask from his mercy, that we might be found in love without human partisan strife, blameless. 50.3 All the generations from Adam to this day passed away, but those who are perfected in love on the basis of the grace of God have a place among the godly, who will be revealed at the visitation of the kingdom of God. 50.4 For it is written, "Enter into your inner rooms for a very little while, until my wrath and anger pass away, and I will remember a good day and will raise you from your graves."[5] 50.5 We were blessed, beloved, if we were doing the commandments of God in the harmony of love, so

---

[3] Ps 118 (LXX 117):19–20.

[4] 1 Pet 4:8.

[5] Isa 26:20; Ezek 37:12.

that our sins may be forgiven us through love. 50.6 For it stands written, "Blessed are [those] whose lawless deeds were forgiven and whose sins were covered; blessed is the man whose sin the Lord will certainly not take into account, nor in whose mouth is there deceit."[6] 50.7 This blessing comes upon those who have been chosen by God through Jesus Christ our Lord, to whom be glory unto the ages of ages. Amen.

[6] Ps 32:1–2.

Ignatius of Antioch

To the Romans

To the Romans Salutation I Greet the Church in Rome

Ignatius, also called Theophorus, to the church that has been shown mercy in the majesty of the Father Most High and of Jesus Christ, his only son, [a church] beloved and enlightened by the will of the one who willed all things that exist, according to the faith and love of Jesus Christ our God; which [church] also presides in the place of the environs of Rome, worthy of God, worthy of honor, worthy of blessing, worthy of praise, worthy of success, worthy of sanctification, and which presides over love, keeping the law of Christ, bearing the name of the Father; which [church] I also greet in the name of Jesus Christ, the Father's Son; to those who have been united with respect to flesh and spirit to every commandment of his, to those who have been filled with God's grace without wavering and who have been filtered from every alien color, heartiest greetings blamelessly in Jesus Christ our God.

To the Romans 1–2 Do Not Try to Prevent My Martyrdom

1.1 Since by praying to God I obtained [my desire] to see your god-worthy faces, so that I have received more than I asked—for, having been bound [in chains] in Christ Jesus, I hope to greet you, if indeed it be [God's] will that I be considered worthy to reach the end. 1.2 For the beginning is well-ordered, if I reach the end, that I might receive my portion unhindered. For I fear your love, lest it wrong me. For it is easy for you to do what you want, but it is difficult for me to attain God,[1] if indeed you yourselves do not spare me.

2.1 For I do not want you to please people, but to please God, as indeed you are pleasing [him]. For I will never [again] have such an opportunity to attain God; nor can you, if you keep silent, be recorded with a better deed. For if you are silent and leave me alone, I [will be] a word of God. But if you desire my flesh I will again be a [mere] voice.[2] 2.2 But grant me nothing more than to be poured out as an offering to God while there is still an altar ready, so that, becoming a chorus in love, you may sing to the Father in Jesus Christ, because God has considered the bishop of Syria worthy to be found at the setting, having

---

[1] This expression, "attain God" (τοῦ θεοῦ ἐπιτυχεῖν), occurs eleven times in Ignatius's letters, including four times in this letter. It is a, "specif. Ignatian expr., meant to designate martyrdom as a direct way to God" (BDAG: 385). See Schoedel: 28–29. The related expression, "attain Jesus Christ" (ἐπιτυγχάνω Ἰησοῦ Χριστοῦ), is used twice in 5.3 below.

[2] Ignatius believes that his martyrdom, "will authenticate his claim to be a Christian and transform that claim from an empty sound to a meaningful word" (Schoedel: 171).

summoned him from the rising.[3] It is good to "set" from the world to God, that I may "rise" to him.

To the Romans 3 Pray for Me that I May Be a True Christian

3.1 You never envied anyone. You taught others. And I want those things you command when instructing disciples to be consistent.[4] 3.2 Only pray for power for me, both inward and outward, that I may not only speak, but also may will, so that I not only be called a Christian, but also be found [such]. For if I be found [to be a Christian], I am able also to be called [one], and then [I am able] to be faithful, when I am not visible to the world. 3.3 Nothing that is visible is good. For our God Jesus Christ, being in the Father, is visible now more than ever. The Work[5] is not [a matter] of persuasion, but Christianity is [a matter] of greatness when it is hated by the world.

To the Romans 4–5 May I Attain God through the Wild Beasts

4.1 I am writing to all the churches and am commanding them all, because I am dying willingly for God, if indeed you do not hinder [me]. I implore you that you not be an unseasonable kindness to me. Permit me to be possessed by wild beasts, through whom I can attain God. I am God's wheat, and I am ground by the beasts' teeth that I may be found Christ's pure bread. 4.2 Rather [than hinder me], entice the wild beasts that they may become a tomb for me and leave absolutely nothing of my body, so that when I fall asleep I do not become a burden to anyone. Then I truly will be a disciple of Jesus Christ, when the world will not even see my body. Petition the Lord for me, that through these instruments I be found a sacrifice to God. 4.3 I am not ordering you like Peter and Paul. They were apostles, I am one condemned; they were free, but I am a slave right up to now. But if I suffer I am Jesus Christ's freedman, and I will rise in him, free. In the meantime I am learning, by having been bound [in chains], to desire nothing.

5.1 From Syria as far as Rome I am fighting wild beasts, through land and sea, night and day, having been bound to ten leopards, which is a detachment of soldiers, who, in fact, become worse when treated well. But by their mistreatments I am becoming more a disciple, "but I have not been justified because of this."[6] 5.2 May I have the benefit of the wild beasts that have been prepared for me, which [beasts] I also pray be found ready for

---

[3] The double meaning of the words used (δύσις, setting/West and ἀνατολή, rising/East) enable Ignatius's play on words in speaking of his journey from Syria in the East to Rome in the West. He also uses the double meaning of δύσις in the next sentence to allude to the completion of his life.

[4] "Ignatius fears that the instructions given by the Romans to others about dying for the faith will not apply to him; he wants them to be consistent" (BDAG, βέβαιος 3:172).

[5] "Work" (τὸ ἔργον) here perhaps signifies Christianity. So also in Ign. *Eph.* 14.2. Lightfoot capitalized the word to catch this usage, and Holmes retained this translation. BDAG takes ἔργον as the thing/matter under discussion, "*not a matter of persuasion*" (BDAG 4:391).

[6] 1 Cor 4:4.

me, which [beasts], indeed, I will entice to devour me promptly, not as, indeed, with some whom they [the beasts] do not touch, being fearful. And if, in fact, they do not want [to do so] willingly, I will use force. 5.3 Indulge me. I know what is profitable for me. Now I am beginning to be a disciple. May nothing among things visible and invisible envy me, so that I may attain Jesus Christ. Fire and cross and encounters with wild beasts, mutilations, tearings apart, scatterings of bones, manglings of limbs, grindings of my whole body, evil tortures of the devil—let them come upon me, only that I may attain Jesus Christ.

To the Romans 6–8 I No Longer Desire the World, Only Christ

6.1 The ends of the earth profit me in no way, the kingdoms of this age [profit me] in no way. It is better for me to die because of Jesus Christ than to reign over the ends of the earth. I am seeking that one, the one who died on our behalf; I want that one, the one who rose on account of us. The childbearing is upon me.[7] 6.2 Agree with me, brothers. Do not hinder me from living. Do not want me to die. Do not give to the world the one who wants to be God's, nor entice [him] with material stuff. Permit me to receive pure light; arriving there I will be a human being. 6.3 Allow me to be an imitator of the suffering of my God. If anyone has him [God] in himself, let that person understand what I want and sympathize with me, knowing the things that are impelling me.

7.1 The ruler of this age wants to take me captive and to corrupt my intention regarding God. Therefore, let none among you who are present help him. Rather, be [a helper] to me, that is, God's [helper]. Do not talk about Jesus Christ and at the same time desire the world. 7.2 Envy must not dwell in you, not even if I, when I am present, exhort you, "Be persuaded by me"; but rather believe these things I am writing to you. For while living I am writing to you desiring to die. My desire has been crucified, and there is not in me a fire that loves material things; rather, [there is] water living and speaking in me, saying from within me, "Come to the Father." 7.3 I do not take pleasure in food of corruption nor in pleasures of this life. I want the bread of God, which is the flesh of Christ, [who is] the seed of David, and I want a drink, [namely,] his blood, which is love incorruptible.

8.1 I no longer want to live in conformity with humans. And this will take place if you want [it]. Want [it], that you yourselves also may be wanted. 8.2 Through a few letters I am asking you. Believe me. And Jesus Christ, the mouth that does not lie or deceive, in whom the Father spoke truly, will reveal these things to you, because I am speaking truly. 8.3 Pray for me that I may attain [God] by the Holy Spirit. I do not write to you according to the flesh, but according to the intention of God. If I suffer, you wanted it; if I am rejected, you hated [me].

---

[7] "What Ignatius hopes for is likened by him to the pangs of birth, apparently both because he will soon suffer like a woman in labor and because he will be born (that is, reborn) like a child" (Schoedel: 182).

To the Romans 9–10 My Concluding Greetings and Requests

9.1 Remember in your prayer the church in Syria, which resorts to God as shepherd instead of me. Jesus Christ alone will be her bishop, and [so will] your love. 9.2 But I am ashamed to be called one of them, for I am not worthy, being least of them and an untimely birth, but I was shown mercy, that I might be someone, if I attain God. 9.3 My spirit greets you, and [so does] the love of the churches that received me in the name of Jesus Christ, not as a passerby. For even churches that were not near me on my physical route were going before me from city to city.

10.1 I write these things to you from Smyrna through the Ephesians, who are most worthy of blessing. And there is also together with me, with many others, even Crocus, a name dearly beloved to me. 10.2 I believe that you have had information concerning those who preceded me from Syria to Rome to the glory of God, to whom also make clear that I am near. For they are all worthy of God and of you, whom it is fitting for you to refresh in every way. 10.3 And I am writing these things to you on the ninth day before the calends of September.[8] Be strengthened to the end by the patient endurance of Jesus Christ.

[8] August 24th.

The Epistle to Diognetus

Christians in the World

5.1 For Christians are differentiated from the rest of humanity neither by land, nor by language, nor by clothing. 5.2 For nowhere do they live in their own cities, nor use some peculiar language, nor practice an odd life. 5.3 Not, of course, by some thought and reflection of inquisitive people has such knowledge of theirs been found, nor have they cared for human doctrine, as [have] some. 5.4 Rather, dwelling in both Greek and non-Greek cities, as each one's lot was cast, and following the local customs in clothing, food, and the rest of life, they demonstrate the amazing and undeniably remarkable character of their citizenship. 5.5 They live in their own native countries, but as aliens; they participate in everything as citizens, and yet they endure everything as foreigners; every foreign [country] is their native country, and every native country is foreign. 5.6 They marry as all [do], they have children, but they do not expose their offspring. 5.7 They set a common table, but not a [common] bed. 5.8 They find themselves [to be] in the flesh, but they do not live according to the flesh. 5.9 They remain upon earth, but they have their citizenship in heaven. 5.10 They obey the set laws, and in their own lives they surpass the laws. 5.11 They love all, and yet are persecuted by all. 5.12 They are unknown and condemned; they are put to death, and yet they are brought to life. 5.13 They are poor, and yet they make many rich; they lack everything, and yet they abound in everything. 5.14 They are dishonored, and yet they are glorified in their dishonor; they are slandered, and yet they are vindicated. 5.15 They are reviled, and yet they bless; they are insulted, and yet they honor. 5.16 Although doing good, they are punished as evil; being punished, they rejoice as those who are being brought to life. 5.17 They are fought against as foreigners by Jews, and they are persecuted by Greeks, and those who hate [them] are not able to say the reason for their hostility.

6.1 In a word, that which, in fact, a soul is in a body, this Christians are in the world. 6.2 The soul is spread throughout all the members of the body, and Christians [are spread] throughout the cities of the world. 6.3 While a soul lives in the body, it is not of the body; and Christians live in the world, but they are not of the world. 6.4 Invisible, the soul is confined in the visible body; and Christians are known, since they are in the world, but their religion remains invisible. 6.5 The flesh hates the soul, and wages war against [it], although not being mistreated in anything, because it is forbidden to indulge its pleasures; and the world hates Christians, although not being mistreated in anything, because they set themselves against its pleasures. 6.6 The soul loves the flesh that hates [it], even the flesh's members; and Christians love those who hate [them]. 6.7 The soul has been enclosed in the body, but it itself sustains the body; and Christians are confined in the world as in a prison, but they themselves sustain the world. 6.8 Immortal, the soul lives in a mortal dwelling, and Christians live as strangers among perishable things, waiting for the imperishable in heaven. 6.9 When treated badly with regard to food and drink, the soul improves, and Christians, being punished daily, increase more. 6.10 God placed them in so great a position, which it is not right for them to refuse.

7.1 For, as I said, not as an earthly discovery was this handed down to them, nor are they considering a mortal idea worth guarding so carefully , nor have they been entrusted with administration of a human mystery. 7.2 Rather, in reality, the Almighty himself, even the Creator of the universe, and the invisible God himself, established from heaven among humans and fixed firmly in their hearts his Truth, even his holy and incomprehensible Word, not, as some person might suppose, sending some assistant, or an angel, or a ruler, or one of those who manage earthly things, or one of those having been entrusted with administrative duties in heaven; but rather [he sent] the Designer and Creator of the universe himself, by whom he created the heavens, by whom he enclosed the sea in its own boundaries, whose mysteries all the elements faithfully guard, from whom the sun has received the measures of the courses of the day to keep, whom the moon obeys when he commands [it] to shine at night, whom the stars obey, following the course of the moon,[1] by whom everything has been set in order and has been given limits and has been put into subjection—the heavens and things in the heavens, the earth and the things on the earth, the sea and the things in the sea, fire, air, depth, the things in the heights, the things in the depths, the things in between; this one he sent to them! 7.3 Well, then, as some human might suppose, [did he send him] for despotic rule and fear and terror? 7.4 Not at all. Rather, he sent [him] in gentleness and humility, as a king sending a son [who is] a king; he sent [him] as God; he sent [him] as a human to humans; he sent him as one who saves, as one who persuades, not as one who dominates, for violence is not an attribute of God. 7.5 He sent him as one who calls, not as one who persecutes; he sent him as one who loves, not as one who judges. 7.6 For he will send him as one who judges, and who will endure his coming? . . . [2] 7.7 Do you not see those who are being thrown to beasts, in order that they might deny their Lord, and yet they are not being conquered? 7.8 Do you not see that the more the majority are punished, the more others increase? 7.9 These things do not seem like the works of a human; these things are God's power; these things are proofs of his presence.

[1] Perhaps Gen 1:16 is in mind, since the stars would be associated with the night, over which the moon was to rule.

[2] The manuscript has a missing section at this point.

The Martyrdom of Polycarp

Polycarp's Arrest, Trial, and Martyrdom

8.1 And when at last he (Polycarp) finished his prayer, having remembered all those who had ever come into contact with him, both small and great, distinguished and obscure, and all the universal church throughout the inhabited world, the hour having come to depart, they seated him on a donkey and brought him into the city; it was a Great Sabbath. 8.2 And Herod, the chief of police, and his father, Nicetes, went to meet him, and having transferred him to their carriage, they were trying to persuade [him], sitting beside [him] and saying, "What harm is there to say, 'Caesar is Lord,' and to offer a sacrifice, and so forth, and to save yourself?" And at first he did not answer them, but since they persisted, he said, "I am not about to do what you are advising me." 8.3 And they, having failed to persuade him, began speaking fearful words, and started putting him down with haste, so that as he was getting down from the carriage he scraped his shin. And not turning, as if he had suffered nothing, he went eagerly with speed, being led into the stadium. The clamor was very great in the stadium, so that one was not even able to be heard.

9.1 Now when Polycarp entered the stadium there was a voice from heaven, "Be strong, Polycarp, and act like a man."[1] And no one saw the one who spoke, but those who were present from among our people heard the voice. And finally, after he was brought forward, there was a great clamor from those who heard that Polycarp had been apprehended. 9.2 So, after he was brought forward, the proconsul started asking him whether he were [the man]. And when he confessed [that he was], he [the proconsul] tried to persuade [him] to deny [it], saying, "Have regard for your age," and other such things, as [it is] a custom for them to say. "Swear by the Fortune of Caesar; repent; say, 'Take away the atheists.'" And Polycarp, with a serious face, looking at the whole crowd of lawless unbelievers in the stadium, and shaking his fist at them, and sighing, and looking up to heaven said, "Take away the atheists." 9.3 But when the proconsul was insisting and saying, "Swear, and I will release you; revile Christ," Polycarp said, "For eighty-six years I have been his servant, and he did me no wrong. And how am I able to blaspheme my king who saved me?"

10.1 But when he [the proconsul] continued again, and was saying, "Swear by the Fortune of Caesar," he [Polycarp] answered, "If you vainly imagine that I will swear by the Fortune of Caesar, as you say, and you pretend to be ignorant of who I am, hear plainly: I am a Chris-

[1] Josh 1:6 (LXX), cf. 1 Cor 16:13.

tian. And if you want to learn the message of Christianity, give a day and hear." 10.2 The proconsul said, "Persuade the crowd." But Polycarp said, "You, at least, I considered worthy of a word, for we have been taught to show an honor that does not harm us, as is fitting, to rulers and authorities put in place by God. But those people I do not regard as worthy that I should defend myself to them."

11.1 So the proconsul said, "I have wild animals. I will throw you to them unless you repent." And he said, "Call [them]. For repentance from the better to the worse is impossible for us; but it is good to change from things that are evil to those that are righteous." 11.2 Then he again [said] to him, "I will cause you to be consumed by fire, since you scorn the wild animals, unless you repent." And Polycarp [said], "You threaten a fire that burns for a short while, and after a little it is quenched, for you are ignorant of the fire of the coming judgment and eternal punishment, which is kept for the ungodly. But why do you delay? Bring on what you want."

12.1 And as he was saying these things and many others, he was filled with courage and joy, and his face was filled with grace, so that not only did he not collapse, being shaken by what was being said to him, but on the contrary, he astounded the proconsul, so that he [the proconsul] sent his own herald to proclaim three times in the midst of the stadium, "Polycarp confessed that he is a Christian." 12.2 This having been said by the herald, the whole crowd of both Gentiles and Jews dwelling in Smyrna[2] cried out loudly with uncontrollable rage and a loud voice, "This is the teacher of Asia,[3] the father of the Christians, the destroyer of our gods, he who is teaching many not to sacrifice nor to worship." Saying these things, they were crying out loudly, and asking Philip the Asiarch[4] that he might let a lion loose upon Polycarp. But he said that it was not permitted for him [to do so] since the animal hunts had finished. 12.3 Then it seemed best to them to cry out loudly together that he burn up Polycarp alive. For it was necessary that the vision that was revealed concerning his pillow be fulfilled, when, seeing it burning while he was praying, he said prophetically, turning to the faithful with him, "It is necessary for me to be burned alive."

13.1 These things then happened with such speed, more quickly than it is told, the crowd at once gathering wood and brushwood from the workshops and bathhouses, and the Jews assisting especially eagerly in these matters, as is their custom. 13.2 And when the funeral pyre was prepared, having taken off all his garments by himself and having untied his belt, he was trying also to take off his sandals himself, although not previously doing this because each of the faithful was always zealous [to do it], whoever might more quickly touch his skin. For he had been made beautiful in every way because of a good way of life, even before his old age. 13.3 Immediately then the incendiary materials that had been prepared for the pyre were placed around him. And as they were also about to nail [him], he said, "Leave me thus. For he who grants [me] to endure the fire will also grant [me] to remain in the fire unmoved, without your security from the nails."

---

[2] A city on the west coast of Asia Minor (modern Turkey). Cf. Rev 2:8–11.

[3] A Roman province of western Asia Minor.

[4] The head of the confederation of the main cities of Asia Minor, who also served as chief-priest for Asia, as *Mart. Pol.* 21 indicates. Cf. BDAG: 143.

14.1 And they did not nail him, but rather they bound him. And he, having put his hands behind him, and having been bound just like a splendid ram [chosen] from a great flock for a sacrifice, a whole burnt offering that has been prepared, acceptable to God, looking up to heaven, he said, "Lord God Almighty, Father of your beloved and blessed child Jesus Christ, through whom we have received knowledge about you, God of angels, and of powers, and of all creation, and of all the race of the righteous ones who live before you, 14.2 I bless you because you considered me worthy of this day and hour, so that I may receive a share among the number of the martyrs in the cup of your Christ, 'to resurrection of life'[5] eternal, both of soul and body, by the immortality of the Holy Spirit, among whom may I be received before you today, by a fat and acceptable sacrifice, just as you, the trustworthy and true God, prepared and revealed beforehand and fulfilled. 14.3 Because of this, and for everything, I praise you, I bless you, I glorify you through the eternal and heavenly High Priest, Jesus Christ, your beloved child, through whom to you, with him, and with the Holy Spirit, be glory both now and always and unto the coming ages. Amen."

15.1 And after he sent up the "Amen" and completed his prayer, the men in charge of the fire kindled the fire. And a great flame blazed up, and we saw a wonder, [we] to whom it was given to see, we who also were kept that we might report to the rest the things that happened. 15.2 For the fire, making the form of a vaulted room, just like a boat's sail filled by wind, surrounded with a wall around the body of the martyr. And he was in the middle, not like burning flesh, but like baking bread, or like gold and silver being burned in a furnace. For indeed we noticed such a strong aroma, like blowing incense or some other precious spice.

16.1 Then, finally, the lawless ones, seeing that his body was not able to be destroyed by the fire, ordered an executioner to go to him and plunge a short-sword into [him]. And having done this, a dove[6] and a large amount of blood came out, so that it put out the fire, and the whole crowd was amazed that there is so great a difference between the unbelievers and the elect. 16.2 One of those [the elect] was indeed this one, the most remarkable Polycarp, becoming in our times an apostolic and prophetic teacher, a bishop in Smyrna of the holy church. For every word that left his mouth was fulfilled and will be fulfilled.

17.1 But the one [who is] jealous and envious and evil, the adversary of the race of the righteous, seeing both the greatness of his martyrdom and his irreproachable way of life from the beginning, [and seeing him] both having been crowned with the crown of immortality and having won the incontestable prize, he [the adversary] took care that not even his [Polycarp's] poor body be taken by us, although many were desiring to do this and to have a share in his holy flesh.[7] 17.2 So he incited Nicetes, the father of Herod and brother of Alce, to appeal to the ruler that he not give [us] his body, "lest," he said, "leaving the one who has been crucified they begin to worship this one"; and they said these things because

---

[5] John 5:29.

[6] Eusebius does not include reference to a dove in his account (*Hist. eccl.* 4.15.39), and most scholars believe it was added later, perhaps as an expression of, "the connection in Greece and elsewhere between bird and soul" (Schoedel: 73).

[7] Perhaps this is a reference to having a part of the body for a relic (cf. BDAG 1bα: 552), though elsewhere BDAG translates this text, "to share some moments with his holy bit of flesh" (σαρκίον, BDAG: 914).

the Jews were instigating and insistently urging, who also kept watch when we were about to take him out of the fire, not knowing that we will never be able to abandon the Christ, who suffered for the salvation of the whole world of those being saved, the blameless one [suffering] on behalf of sinners, nor [will we ever be able] to worship some other one. 17.3 For while we worship this one who is God's Son, we love, in a suitable manner, the martyrs as disciples and imitators of the Lord, on account of the unexcelled affection [they have] for their own king and teacher. May we also become their partners and fellow-disciples.

18.1 Therefore, the centurion, seeing the contentiousness created by the Jews, put it [the body] in the middle, as is their custom, and burned [it]. 18.2 And so later, having taken away his bones, which are more costly than very expensive stones and more precious than gold, we deposited [them] where it was quite suitable. 18.3 There, gathering ourselves together, as we are able, in exultation and joy, the Lord will grant us to celebrate the birthday of his martyrdom, both for the memory of those who have competed in former times and [for] the training and preparation of those to come in the future.

First Apology 61 Baptism

61.1 And we will also recount the way in which we dedicated ourselves to God, having been made new through Christ, lest, if we omit this, we seem to act wickedly in our description. 61.2 All those who are persuaded and believe that these things that are being taught and spoken of by us are true, and who undertake to be able to live thus, are taught to pray and to request from God, while fasting, pardon for their previous sins, while we are praying and fasting with them. 61.3 Then they are led by us where there is water, and they are regenerated in the way of regeneration in which we ourselves also were regenerated. For then they wash in the water "in the name of" God, "the Father and Master of the universe, and [in the name] of our Savior Jesus Christ, and [in the name] of the Holy Spirit."[1] 61.4 For Christ also said, "If you are not regenerated, you most certainly will not enter the kingdom of heaven."[2] 61.5 Now, that it is in fact impossible for those who have once been born to enter into the wombs of those who bore [them] is evident to all. 61.6 And through Isaiah the prophet, as I wrote before, it is told in what way those who have sinned and who repent will flee their sins. 61.7 And it was said thus, "Wash yourselves, become clean, remove the wickednesses from your souls, learn to do good, see to it that justice is done for the orphan, show justice to the widow, and come and let us argue, says the Lord. Even if your sins be as crimson, I will make [you] white as white wool; and if they be as scarlet, I will make [you] white as snow. 61.8 And if you do not obey me, a sword will devour you, for the mouth of the Lord said these things."[3] 61.9 And as a reason for this,[4] we learned from the apostles this [which follows]. 61.10 Since we were ignorant during our first birth, and have been brought forth by force from moist seed by a mingling of our parents with one another, and have been engaging in base customs and wicked up-bringing—in order that we may not remain children of necessity or ignorance but [may be children] of choice and understanding, and [that] we may have pardon for sins we formerly committed, in the water is pronounced the name of God, the Father and Master of the universe, over the one who chooses to be regenerated and who repents of the sins that have been committed; the one

---

[1] Cf. Matt 28:19.

[2] John 3:5.

[3] Isa 1:16–20.

[4] The reference could be to the rite of baptism, or the need of regeneration, or the whole subject in general.

who leads to the washing of the one who shall be washed says over [him] only this very [name]. 61.11 For no one is able to speak the name of the ineffable God. And if someone dare to say that it is [possible], he is raving with a hopeless madness. 61.12 And this washing is called illumination, because those who are learning these things are being illumined in their mind. 61.13 And the one who is being illumined is washed also in the name of Jesus Christ, who was crucified in the time of Pontius Pilate, and in the name of the Holy Spirit, who through the prophets proclaimed in advance everything concerning Jesus.

First Apology 65–67 Eucharist and Sunday Worship

65.1 And after the one who has been persuaded [by the gospel] and consented [to be baptized] has thus washed, we lead [him] to those who are called brothers, where they are gathered together, in order to pray common prayers vigorously, both for themselves and for the one who has been illumined, and for all others everywhere, so that we may be considered worthy, having learned the things that are true, and through good works to be found [to be] good devotees and guardians of the things that have been commanded, so that we may be saved with an eternal salvation. 65.2 Having finished our prayers, we greet one another with a kiss. 65.3 Then bread and a cup of water and mixed wine are brought to the leader of the brothers, and taking [them] this one sends up praise and glory to the Father of the universe, through the name of the Son and of the Holy Spirit, and he gives thanks for a long time for being considered by him worthy of these things. After he has finished the prayers and the thanksgiving, all the people who are present shout assent, saying, "Amen!" 65.4 And "Amen" in the Hebrew language means, "May it be!" 65.5 And the leader having given thanks, and all the people having shouted assent, those who are called deacons by us give to each of those present a share of the bread and wine and water for which thanksgiving was made, and they carry [them] away to those not present.

66.1 And this food is called by us Thanksgiving, which no one else is allowed to share in except the one who believes that the things that have been taught by us are true, and who has allowed himself to be washed with the washing for the pardon of sins and for regeneration, and who lives thus as Christ delivered [to us]. 66.2 For we do not receive these as ordinary bread or ordinary drink. But in the same way as Jesus Christ our Savior, having been made flesh through God's word, had both flesh and blood for our salvation, so also we have been taught that the food for which thanks has been given through a word of prayer that is from him,[5] by which our blood and flesh are nourished in accordance with [its] change,[6] are the flesh and blood of that one who became flesh, Jesus. 66.3 For the apostles, in the memoirs that were produced by them, which are called Gospels, thus passed on that which had been commanded them—that, "Jesus, having taken bread and given thanks, said, 'Do this in remembrance of me, this is my body,'[7] and, likewise, having taken the cup and given thanks, that he said, 'This is my blood,'"[8] and that he shared with these alone. 66.4 Which also in

[5] Justin is referring to the dominical elements in the eucharistic prayer, which he goes on to give in the rest of this chapter.

[6] Justin is referring to a change in the bread and drink, since he has just noted that they are not ordinary bread and drink.

[7] Luke 22:19; 1 Cor 11:24.

[8] Matt 26:27–28; Mark 14:23–24.

the mysteries of Mithras[9] the evil demons, imitating, passed on that they [that is, such things] are to be done, for you either know or are able to learn that bread and a cup of water are placed with certain incantations in their mystic rites of one being initiated.

67.1 And finally, after these things, we always remind one another of these things. And those of us who have [resources] help all of those who are in want, and we are always with one another. 67.2 And for all that we have been given, we bless the Maker of all things through his Son Jesus Christ and through the Holy Spirit. 67.3 And on the day called Sun's[10] there is a meeting together of all who live in cities or country areas, and the memoirs of the apostles, or the writings of the prophets, are read as long as time permits. 67.4 Then, when the reading has stopped, the leader admonishes and challenges us in a message to imitate these good things. 67.5 Then we all rise together and we send prayers, and, as we said before, when we have stopped the prayer, bread and wine and water are brought, and the leader in the same way sends up prayers and thanksgivings according to his ability, and the people shout assent, saying, "Amen." And the distribution and the participation by each one in those things for which thanks has been given take place, and through the deacons it is sent to those who are absent. 67.6 And those who are well off and who are willing, each according to his own choice, give what they want, and that which is collected is put aside by the leader. And he himself helps the orphans and widows, and those who are in want because of sickness or for some other reason, and those who are in bonds, and the sojourning strangers, and, in a word, he is guardian for all who are in need. 67.7 We all gather together in common on Sunday because it is the first day, on which God, altering darkness and matter, made the world. And Jesus Christ our Savior rose from the dead on this same day. For they crucified him on the day before Saturn's,[11] and on the day after Saturn's, which is Sun's day, he appeared to his apostles and disciples, and taught these things, the very things we have offered also to you for consideration.

---

[9] The Persian sun god, the center of a very popular mystery religion at the time of Justin.
[10] Sunday.
[11] Saturday.

Melito of Sardis

On Pascha

On Pascha 1–45 The Mystery of the Pascha

1 The Scripture about the Hebrew exodus has been read,
and the events of the mystery have been made very clear,
how the sheep is sacrificed
and how the people are saved
and how Pharaoh is scourged through the mystery.
2 Therefore understand, O beloved ones,
how it is new and old,
eternal and temporary,
perishable and imperishable,
mortal and immortal, the mystery of the Pascha;
3 old with respect to the law,
but new with respect to the word;
temporary with respect to the type,
eternal because of the grace;
perishable because of the slaughter of the sheep,
imperishable because of the life of the Lord;
mortal because of the burial in the ground,
immortal because of the resurrection from the dead.
4 While the law is old,
the word is new;
the type is temporary,
but the grace is eternal;
the sheep is perishable,
the Lord is imperishable;
not having been broken as a lamb,
but having been raised as God.
For although, "he was led as a sheep to slaughter,"[1]
yet he was not a sheep;
although silent as a lamb,
yet he was not a lamb.

---

[1] Isa 53:7.

For the type was in existence,
but the reality was becoming able to be found.
5 For instead of the lamb there was a son
and instead of the sheep, a man;
and in the man, Christ who contains all things.
6 Therefore the slaughter of the sheep
and the display of the blood
and the writing of the law have reached towards Christ Jesus,
because of whom everything in the older law happened,
and still more in the new word.
7 For indeed the law became word,
and the old [became] new,
having gone out together from Zion and Jerusalem;
and the commandment [became] grace,
and the type, reality;
and the lamb, a son;
and the sheep, a man;
and the man, God.
8 For, having been born as a son,
and led as a lamb,
and slaughtered as a sheep,
and buried as a man,
he rose from the dead as God, by nature being God and man.
9 He is all things.
He is law, because of which he judges;
he is word, because of which he teaches;
he is grace, because of which he saves;
he is father, because of which he begets;
he is son, because of which he is begotten;
he is sheep, because of which he suffers;
he is man, because of which he is buried;
he is God, because of which he is raised.
10 This is Jesus the Christ,
"to whom be the glory unto the ages of ages. Amen."[2]
11 This is the mystery of the Pascha,
just as it has been written in the law,
as has been read a short time earlier.
And I will set out in detail the events of Scripture,
how God has commanded Moses in Egypt,
when he wanted, on the one hand, to bind Pharaoh under a lash,
and, on the other, to set Israel free from a lash through the hand of Moses.
12 "For behold," he says, "you shall take a lamb without spot and without blemish,
and toward evening you shall slaughter it with the sons of Israel;

[2] This is a common expression in the New Testament, e.g., Gal 1:5; 2 Tim 4:18; Heb 13:21; 1 Pet 5:11; 2 Pet 3:18.

and at night you shall eat it with haste;
and you shall not break a bone of it."[3]

13 "Thus," he says, "you shall do:
in one night you shall eat it by families and companies,
having girded your loins
and your staffs in your hands.
For this is the Pascha of the Lord,
an eternal memorial for the sons of Israel.

14 And taking the blood of the sheep,
anoint the front doors of your houses,
placing upon the doorposts of the entrance
the sign of the blood for the persuasion of the angel.
For behold, I am striking Egypt
and in one night she shall be made childless from beast to human."

15 Then Moses, after slaughtering the sheep,
and at night completing the mystery with the sons of Israel,
sealed the doors of their houses
for a guard for the people and for persuasion of the angel.

16 When the sheep is being slaughtered,
and the Pascha is being eaten,
and the mystery is being completed,
and the people are celebrating,
and Israel is being sealed,
then arrived the angel to strike Egypt,
[Egypt] uninitiated in the mystery,
without a share in the Pascha,
unsealed by the blood,
unguarded by the Spirit,
hostile,
unbelieving,
(17)[4] in one night he struck and made childless.

17 For the angel, after going around Israel
and seeing that he had been sealed with the blood of the sheep,
came upon Egypt,
and subdued the stiff-necked Pharaoh through grief,
clothing him not with a gray garment,
nor with a torn robe,
but with the whole of Egypt torn,
grieving for her firstborn.

18 For the whole of Egypt, having come to be in distress and wounds,
in tears and lamentations,

---

[3] Sections 12–14 are a loose retelling of the account of the Passover in Exod 12.

[4] Other editions, including Perler, begin section 17 at this point, which Hall indicates in the margin.

came to Pharaoh, a complete lamentation,
not only in appearance, but also in soul,
torn not only in her garments that were covering [her],
but also in her delicate breasts.
19 And it was a remarkable sight to see,
here [people] striking themselves, there wailing,
and in the middle a lamenting Pharaoh,
sitting on sackcloth and ashes,
palpable darkness thrown around him as a mourning garment,
clothed with all Egypt as a tunic of grief.
20 For Egypt was lying around Pharaoh
like a shrieking covering.
Such a tunic was woven for the tyrannical body,
such a garment the angel of righteousness
put on hard Pharaoh,
bitter grief and palpable darkness
and remarkable childlessness upon her firstborn.
21 For swift and insatiable was the death of the firstborn,
(21)[5] and it was a remarkable trophy, namely, to look
upon those who fell dead in one critical moment.
And the rout of those lying down
became death's food.
22 If you hear, marvel at this remarkable misfortune.
For these things encompassed the Egyptians:
long night,
and palpable darkness,
and death groping about,
and an angel squeezing hard,
and Hades gulping down their firstborn.
23 But you have to hear what is unprecedented and more dreadful:
In the palpable darkness untouchable death hid itself,
and, on the one hand, the unfortunate Egyptians were touching darkness,
while on the other, death was searching out and touching the Egyptians' firstborn,
as the angel was commanding.
24 So if anyone touched the darkness,
he was led away by death.
And a certain firstborn, clasping by hand a dark body,
was greatly frightened in his soul, and cried out piteously and terribly,
"On what does my right hand lay hold?
At what is my soul trembling?
Who is the dark one who has embraced me, my whole body?
If a father, help [me];
if a mother, sympathize with [me];

---

[5] Other editions, including Perler, begin section 21 at this point, which Hall indicates in the margin.

if a brother, talk to [me];
if a friend, stand by [me];
if an enemy, depart from [me], because I am a firstborn."
25 And before the firstborn became silent,
the long silence held him fast, saying to him,
"You are my firstborn,
I, the silence of death, am your destiny."
26 And another firstborn, noticing the capture of those who are firstborn,
began utterly denying himself, that he might not die bitterly.
"I am not a firstborn,
I have been begotten at third [place in the order of] offspring."
But the one who is not able to be deceived was laying hold of the firstborn,
and he fell face downwards, and was still.
At one critical moment the firstborn offspring of the Egyptians perished:
the first-begotten,
the firstborn,
the longed-for one,
the dandled one was dashed to the ground;
not only the [firstborn] of humans,
but also of brute beasts.
27 And a lowing was heard in the plains of the land,
beasts lamenting bitterly over their nurslings.
For indeed a young cow with a nursing calf under her,
and a horse with a foal under her,
and the rest of the beasts, having given birth and full to bursting [with milk],
were lamenting bitterly and piteously over their firstborn offspring.
28 And there was a loud wailing and mourning over the destruction among the people,
over the destruction of the dead firstborn.
For all Egypt began to stink in the presence of the unburied bodies.
29 And it was a fearful sight to behold,
mothers among the Egyptians with hair undone,
fathers with minds undone,
wailing aloud terribly in the Egyptian language,
"At one critical moment we unfortunate ones were made childless of our firstborn offspring."
And they were beating themselves upon [their] breasts,
striking instruments with [their] hands for the dance of the dead.
30 Such a misfortune encompassed Egypt,
and suddenly made her childless.
But Israel was being guarded by the slaughter of the sheep,
and indeed she was being illumined together by the shedding of blood,
and the death of the sheep was being found to be a wall for the people.
31 O mystery remarkable and indescribable!
The slaughter of the sheep was being found to be the salvation of Israel,
and the death of the sheep became life for the people,
and the blood persuaded the angel.

32 Tell me, O angel, why were you persuaded?
The slaughter of the sheep or the life of the Lord?
The death of the sheep or the type of the Lord?
The blood of the sheep or the Spirit of the Lord?
33 It is clear that you were persuaded
because you saw that the mystery of the Lord was taking place in the sheep,
the life of the Lord in the slaughter of the sheep,
the type of the Lord in the death of the sheep.
Because of this you did not strike Israel,
but only Egypt you made childless.
34 What is this remarkable mystery,
Egypt is struck unto destruction,
but Israel is guarded unto salvation?
Hear the meaning of the mystery.
35 There is nothing, beloved, which is spoken and produced
without an analogy and a preliminary pattern.
Everything whatsoever that is produced and that is spoken gets an analogy—
that which is spoken [gets] an analogy,
that which is produced [gets] a prototype;
so that, as that which is produced is explained through the prototype,
so also that which is spoken may be illumined through the analogy.
36 This indeed happens during preparation [for construction].
The work [itself] is not built,
but [something is built] because of that which will be seen through its typal image.
Because of this, a preliminary pattern of that which is to come is made,
whether of wax or clay or wood,
so that the thing that is about to be built,
taller in height,
and stronger in power,
and beautiful in appearance,
and rich in craftsmanship,
may be seen through a small and perishable preliminary pattern.
37 But when [that thing] is built regarding which [it is] the type,
that which once bore the image of the thing to come,
this [i.e., the type] is destroyed, since it has become useless,
yielding the image concerning it to that which is real by nature.
And that which was once precious becomes worthless,
since the thing that is precious by nature has been made manifest.
38 For to each its own time,
the type's own time,
the material's own time,
the reality's own time.
You make the type;
you desire this [type],
because you see in it the image of that which will come.

You bring forward the material for the type.
You desire this [material]
because of the thing that is about to be built by means of it.
You complete the work [itself],
this [work] alone you desire,
this [work] alone you love,
because you see in it alone the type and the material and the reality.
39 As, therefore, with the perishable models,
so indeed also with things imperishable,
as with things earthly,
so indeed also with things heavenly.
For indeed the salvation and truth of the Lord were prefigured in the people,
and the decrees of the gospel were proclaimed in advance by the law.
40 Therefore the people were a type for a preliminary pattern,
and the law was a writing for an analogy;
and the gospel is a statement and completion of the law,
and the church is a storehouse of the reality.
41 Therefore the type was precious before the reality,
and the analogy was marvelous before the interpretation;
that is, the people were precious before the church was raised,
and the law was marvelous before the gospel was brought to light.
42 But when the church was raised
and the gospel went forth,
the type was emptied, passing on its meaning to the reality,
and the law was fulfilled, passing on its meaning to the gospel.
43 Just as the type is emptied, passing on the image to that which is real by nature,
and the analogy is fulfilled, having been brought to light by the interpretation,
so indeed also the law was fulfilled, when the gospel had been brought to light,
and the people were emptied, when the church had been raised,
and the type was destroyed, when the Lord had been manifested,
and today the things once precious have become worthless,
because the things precious by nature have been made manifest.
44 For the slaughter of the sheep was once precious,
but now it is worthless because of the life of the Lord;
the death of the sheep was precious,
but now it is worthless because of the salvation of the Lord;
the blood of the sheep was precious,
but now it is worthless because of the Spirit of the Lord;
the voiceless lamb was precious,
but now it is worthless because of the unblemished Son;
the temple below was precious,
but now it is worthless because of the Christ above;
45 the Jerusalem below was precious,
but now it is worthless because of the Jerusalem above;
the narrow inheritance was precious,
but now it is worthless because of the broad grace.

For neither upon one place nor on a narrow piece of land
    is the glory of the Lord settled,
but upon all the ends of the inhabited world
    has his grace been poured out,
and there the Almighty God settled,
    through Christ Jesus,
    to whom be glory unto the ages. Amen.

Clement of Alexandria

Miscellanies

Miscellanies 1.5 Philosophy Was a Form of Preparation for the Gospel

Therefore, before the coming of the Lord philosophy was necessary for the Greeks for righteousness, but now it is useful for godliness, being a sort of preparatory training for those deriving profit from the faith through demonstration, since it says, "your foot will not stumble,"[1] ascribing the good things to divine providence, whether they be Greek or ours.[2] For God is the cause of all good things, but of some in a primary way, as with the Old Testament and the New, but of others consequentially, as with philosophy. And perhaps indeed it [philosophy] was given to the Greeks directly, in an earlier time before the Lord called the Greeks also. For, in fact, this [philosophy] used to "train" the Greek as "the law" [trained] the Hebrews "unto Christ."[3] Therefore, philosophy prepares beforehand, preparing the way before the one being perfected by Christ. Now Solomon says, "Surround wisdom with a stockade, and it will greatly exalt you, and it will protect you with a crown of delight."[4] For you also, because you have made it [wisdom] exceedingly firm with a wall through philosophy and right expense, you will keep [it] inaccessible to the sophists. Therefore, the path of truth is one, but into it, just as into an ever-flowing river, other streams flow forth from different places. So then it has been said by inspiration, "Listen, my son, and receive my words," he says, "that many paths of life may belong to you. For I teach you paths of wisdom, that the springs may not fail you,"[5] which gush out of the earth itself. Surely he tallied not only many saving paths of one righteous person, but he adds many other paths of many righteous persons, revealing somehow thus: "The paths of the righteous ones shine like light."[6] And both the commandments and the preparatory trainings would be paths and starting points of life.

---

[1] Prov 3:23.
[2] The Christians'.
[3] Gal 3:24.
[4] Prov 4:8–9.
[5] Prov 4:10–11, 21 (LXX).
[6] Prov 4:18 (LXX).

Miscellanies 1.20 While Philosophy Was an Aid towards the Truth, the Fullness of the Truth Is in Christ

Therefore the teaching that is in keeping with the Savior is complete in itself and without need of addition, being, "the power and wisdom of God."[7] And adding Greek philosophy does not make the truth more powerful, but, causing the sophistic attack against it to be powerless, and getting rid of the deceitful plots against the truth, it is said to be a proper "fence" and wall "of the vineyard."[8] And that which is necessary for life, like bread, is the truth that is in keeping with the faith, while the preparatory training is like a side dish and a dessert; and when dinner comes to an end, dessert is sweet, according to the Theban Pindar.[9]

Miscellanies 6.13 The Covenant of Salvation is One throughout Time

For, in reality, the saving covenant, which extends from the foundation of the world to us, is one, though thought of in different generations and times as different in regard to gift. For it is fitting that there is one unchangeable gift of salvation from one God, through one Lord, although providing help in many ways. For which reason the "dividing wall"[10] that separates the Greek from the Jew is taken away that [there may be] a special people. And thus both arrive to the unity of the faith, and the election of both is one.

Miscellanies 6.15 The Rule of the Truth Is the Harmony of the Old and New Testaments in Christ

So, in reality, the liars are not those who show indulgence because of the order of salvation,[11] nor those who are mistaken concerning some of the particular parts, but those who are going astray in the principle matters and denying the Lord as much as they can, withdrawing from the true teaching of the Lord, who are not speaking and handing down the Scriptures in a manner worthy of God and the Lord. For the insight and training of the God-fearing tradition, which is in keeping with the teaching of the Lord through his apostles, is the deposit rendered to God. "And what you hear in the ear," that is to say, in a hidden manner and in a mystery (for such things are said allegorically to be spoken in the ear), he says, "proclaim upon the housetops,"[12] receiving [them] with high thoughts and passing them on in lofty language, and interpreting the Scriptures clearly, in keeping

---

[7] 1 Cor 1:24.

[8] Matt 21:33; Isa 5:1–2.

[9] A lyric poet (518–438 BC) from Cynoscephalae in Boeotia in central Greece, about 130 miles northwest of Athens.

[10] Eph 2:14.

[11] Perhaps a reference to those who apply the commands of the gospel less strictly in particular instances for the sake of gospel work in certain people. Some Eastern Orthodox priests today say such pastoral application is for the sake of οἰκονομία, the word translated here, "order of salvation."

[12] Matt 10:27.

with the rule of the truth. For neither prophecy nor the Savior himself spoke so simply about the divine mysteries in plain language that they would be things easily caught by any people who happened [to hear them], but rather, he instructed in parables. At any rate, the apostles say concerning the Lord, "he spoke all things in parables and he was speaking nothing to them without a parable."[13] And if, "all things were made by him, and without him was made not one thing,"[14] then both the prophecy and the law were made by him and they were spoken by him in parables. But, "all things are straight in the presence of those who understand,"[15] says the Scripture, that is to say, as many as are receiving and preserving, in keeping with the ecclesiastical rule, the interpretation of the Scriptures that has been made clear by him [the Lord]. And the ecclesiastical rule is the concord and harmony of the law and the prophets in the covenant that is being handed on in keeping with the arrival of the Lord.

Miscellanies 7.16 Scripture Interprets Scripture, in Contrast to the Abuse of Scripture by the False Teachers

For we have the source of the teaching, the Lord, who introduces knowledge through the prophets and through the gospel and through the blessed apostles, "in many ways and in many parts,"[16] from beginning to the end. And regarding the source, if someone might suppose that another [source] is needed, then the source would no longer truly be maintained. Therefore, the one who of himself is faithful to the Lord's Scripture and voice, [his voice] which is effective through the Lord for the benefit of humans, would be rightly [considered] trustworthy. Certainly we use it [the Scripture/voice] as a criterion for the discovery of things. And everything that is being judged is not yet trusted before it is judged, so that the thing that is in need of judgment is not a first principle. Therefore, as is reasonable, by embracing in faith the indemonstrable first principle, and receiving out of the abundance of its store the very proofs from the first principle itself concerning the first principle, we are being trained by the voice of the Lord regarding the knowledge of the truth. For we would not give heed to people simply expressing opinions, for whom it is also equally possible to hold a contrary opinion. But if it is not enough only simply to state one's opinion, but one must prove what has been said, [then] we do not wait for testimony from humans, but rather we prove that which is being investigated by the voice of the Lord, which [is] more trustworthy than all proofs, or rather, which is the only proof, regarding which knowledge those who have only taken a taste of the Scriptures are faithful, while those who have advanced further are precise interpreters of the truth, the mature Christians,[17] since even in matters pertaining to life the skilled workers have something more than the ordinary people, and they model that which is better, beyond common thoughts. So then we also, by demonstrating fully from the Scriptures concerning the Scriptures themselves, we are persuaded from faith by demonstration. And even if those who are

[13] Matt 13:34.
[14] John 1:3.
[15] Prov 8:9.
[16] Heb 1:1.
[17] The term used here for mature Christians is γνωστικοί (*gnostikoi*), as noted in the introduction to Clement of Alexandria.

among the heretics also dare to use the prophetic Scriptures, first, not all of them [do they use]; next, not complete [do they use them]; nor [do they use them] as the body and web of prophecy prescribes; but, selecting things that are said ambiguously, they transfer [them] to their own opinions, plucking a few phrases here and there, not examining the meaning [that comes] from them, but being content with the bare saying itself. For in nearly all the passages that they use you would find that they attend to them as only expressions, altering their meanings, neither understanding [them], as they claim for themselves, nor using passages that they actually bring up in keeping with their true nature. But the truth is not found in changing meanings (for in this way they will overturn all true teaching), but rather in examining what fully belongs to and is appropriate to the Lord and to Almighty God, and in establishing each of the points being proven according to the Scriptures, in turn, from similar Scriptures themselves.

Eusebius Ecclesiastical History and Life of Constantine

Ecclesiastical History 3.24.1–5 On the Style of the Gospels

24.1 Come now, and let us indicate the undisputed writings of this apostle.[1] 24.2 Above all the Gospel according to him, which has been recognized by the churches under heaven, must be acknowledged first. Nevertheless, that with good reason it has been listed according to the ancients in the fourth place with reference to the other three, would be clear in this way [which follows]. 24.3 Those who were divine and most truly worthy of God, and I'm speaking of Christ's apostles, having been utterly purified in their life, and having been adorned in their souls with all virtue, being unskilled in speech, nevertheless having confidence in the divine and wonderworking power that had been given to them from the Savior, while they neither knew how, nor attempted, to represent the lessons of their teacher with subtle and artistic words, but using only the proof of the divine Spirit, who was working in them, and the miracle-working power of Christ that was being carried out through them, they were proclaiming the knowledge of the kingdom of heaven to all the inhabited world, caring little for attention to writing books. 24.4 And this they were doing, seeing that they were serving a greater, superhuman ministry. Certainly Paul, being the most able of all in the preparation of words, and most competent in understanding, has handed down in writing no more than the briefest letters, although, in fact, having countless and ineffable things to say, inasmuch as he attained the visions even to the third heaven, and was carried away to god-worthy Paradise itself, and was considered worthy to hear there words that are not to be spoken. 24.5 Now, indeed, the rest of the students of our Savior, the twelve apostles, the seventy disciples, and countless others in addition to these, also were not without experience of the same things. And yet, nevertheless, of all the Lord's disciples only Matthew and John have left behind for us records, who, in fact, came to writing by compulsion, word has it.

---

[1] John.

Life of Constantine 1.28–29 Constantine's Vision of the Cross

1.28 Certainly he[2] repeatedly invoked him[3] in prayers, entreating and crying aloud that he, whoever he might be, would reveal himself to him and would hold out his right [hand to offer help] regarding the things that were lying before [him]. And while the king was praying these things and beseeching earnestly, a certain most incredible sign from God appeared, which perhaps it would not be easy to accept if someone else were saying [it], but since the conqueror king himself reported the matter and confirmed [it] with oaths to us, who a long time later are setting out in detail the writing [of it], when we were considered worthy of his acquaintance and company, who would doubt to trust the account, especially when, indeed, the time after these things showed the testimony to the matter to be true? He said that, about noon, the sun's hour, the day already declining, they saw with their own eyes in the sky itself, lying above the sun, a trophy of a cross, consisting of light, and an inscription fastened to it that said, "By this conquer." Now, at the sight amazement might well seize both him and the whole army—which [army], indeed, while being dispatched on a journey to some place, both confirmed and was an eyewitness of the miracle.

1.29 And, in fact, he was saying that it was greatly perplexing to him, whatever the apparition might be. And while he was thinking deeply, and pondering for a long time, night came on and overtook [him]. Then, in fact, while he was sleeping, the Christ of God, with the sign that appeared in the sky, appeared and commanded [him] to copy the sign that appeared in heaven, and to use this as protection in his engagements with his enemies!

---

[2] Constantine.

[3] God.

On the Incarnation 3 Creation and Fall

3.1 These people[1] tell these myths.[2] But the divinely inspired teaching and the faith that is in accord with Christ reproves the foolish talk of these people as godlessness. For it [the teaching/faith] knows that [it was] not of its [the universe's] own accord [that God has brought the universe into existence through the Word], because there was not a lack of forethought, nor [was it] out of pre-existent matter, because God was not weak, but out of things that do not exist, indeed, not existing in any way whatsoever, that God has brought the universe into existence through the Word, as he says, first through Moses, "In the beginning God created the heaven and the earth";[3] and then through the most useful book of the Shepherd, "First of all believe that God is one, the one who created and prepared the universe and brought it into existence from what does not exist."[4] 3.2 Which indeed Paul also indicates and says, "By faith we understand that the ages have been made by the word of God, so that the things seen have not come into being from things that are visible."[5] 3.3 For God is good, or rather he is the fount of goodness, and in one who is good there would be jealousy concerning no one. Therefore, begrudging existence to no one, he has made the universe out of what does not exist, through his own Word, our Lord Jesus Christ. Among which [things he had created], above all those upon earth, he had mercy upon the race of humans, and, considering that it [the race of humans] would not be able to continue forever, in keeping with the limitation of its own origin, he graciously gave something more to them and did not merely create humans like all the irrational animals upon earth, but he made them in keeping with his own image, sharing with them even the power of his own Word, so that, having as it were certain reflections of the Word and becoming rational, they might be able to continue in blessedness, living the true and real life of the holy ones in Paradise. 3.4 And furthermore, knowing the faculty of people for free choice, which is able to incline towards either side, anticipating [this] he secured with a law

[1] Greek philosophers.

[2] Athanasius has been describing various views of how the universe came into existence, in particular those of the Epicureans, who deny providence, and of Plato who reduces God to a mere craftsman working with pre-existent matter.

[3] Gen 1:1.

[4] *Hermas, Mandate* 1.1. *The Shepherd of Hermas* is a second century document which Athanasius recommended for edification, but which he did not view as canonical (cf. *Festal Letter* 39.7).

[5] Heb 11:3.

and a place the grace given to them. For, having brought them into his own paradise, he gave them a law, so that, if they would guard the grace and remain good, they would have the life in paradise, free from sorrow, pain and care, in addition to them having also the promise of immortality in heaven. But if they transgressed and, turning around, became evil, they would know that they themselves were enduring the corruption in death in keeping with nature, and that no longer were they living in paradise, but that, having died, they would remain from now on outside it in death and corruption. 3.5 And this also the divine Scripture proclaims, saying from the presence of God, "From every tree that is in paradise you may indeed eat, but from the tree of knowing good and evil you shall not eat from it; and in whatever day you may eat, you shall indeed die."[6] And the "you shall indeed die"—what else might it be than not only to die, but also to remain in the corruption of death?

On the Incarnation 8–9 The Purpose of the Incarnation

8.1 For this reason,[7] then, the incorporeal, incorruptible and immaterial Word of God came into our realm , not being at all distant formerly. For no part of creation has been left empty of him, but he himself has filled all things through all things, while being with his own Father. But he comes, condescending in his benevolence and manifestation unto us. 8.2 And seeing the race that is endowed with reason perishing, and death exercising its reign against them through corruption; and seeing also the transgression's threat of punishment holding fast the corruption against us, and that it was absurd that the law was destroyed before it was fulfilled; and seeing also the impropriety in what had happened, that the things of which he himself was the maker, these were being done away with; and seeing also the exceeding evil of humans, that little by little and to an intolerable degree they increased it against themselves; and seeing also the liability of all people to death, having mercy on our race and having compassion upon our weakness, condescending to our corruption and not putting up with the power of death, lest that which had been brought into being should perish and the work of his Father towards humans should be without effect, he took to himself a body, and this [body] was not foreign to our own. 8.3 For he did not simply want to become embodied, nor did he want to merely appear. For if he merely wanted to appear he was able to bring about his divine manifestation through some other, better means. But he took our [body], and not only this, but [he did so] from an immaculate, undefiled virgin without experience of a man, pure and in reality unmixed with sexual intercourse with men. For he himself, being powerful and maker of all, prepared for himself in the Virgin a body as a temple, and appropriated it to himself as an instrument, becoming known in it and indwelling [it]. 8.4 And thus taking from our [bodies a body] like [them], because all were subject to the corruption of death, handing it over to death on behalf of all, he was offering [it] to the Father; and he did this in lovingkindness towards mankind, so that, for one thing, the law regarding the corruption of humans might be abolished, since all were dying in him (seeing that its [the law's] power was brought to an end in the Lord's body and it no longer applied against humans who were of like [nature to the Lord]); and [he took a body] so that, for another thing, he might turn again to

[6] Gen 2:16–17.

[7] In context Athanasius has just said, "For being Word of the Father, and above all, He alone of natural fitness was both able to recreate everything, and worthy to suffer on behalf of all and to be ambassador for all with the Father" (7.5, *NPNF*[2]).

incorruption the humans who had turned back to corruption and might make them alive from death by the appropriation to himself of the body and by the grace of the resurrection, removing death from them like straw from a fire.[8]

9.1 For the Word, seeing clearly that the corruption of humans would not be undone in any other way except, obviously, through dying; and, of course, in the case of the Word there was no dying, since he was immortal and the Father's Son—because of this he took to himself a body that is able to die, so that this [body], partaking of the Word who is above all, might be qualified for death on behalf of all, and, because of the indwelling Word, he might continue incorruptible, and from now on the corruption might cease from all by the grace of the resurrection. Therefore, as a sacrifice and offering free of all stain, he offered unto death the body he himself took to himself, and he immediately put away death from all those like [him], by the offering of that which corresponds [to them]. 9.2 For, being over all, the Word of God, by offering his own temple, even his bodily instrument, as a substitute for all, reasonably fulfilled by his death that which was owed, and thus, since the incorruptible Son of God was united with all through his like [body], he clothed everyone, reasonably, with incorruption by the promise concerning the resurrection. For indeed the corruption itself in death no longer applies against humans because of the Word who indwelt them through the one body. 9.3 And as when a great king enters some great city and dwells in one of the houses in it, obviously such a city is considered worthy of great honor and no longer does some enemy or robber come upon it and upset it, but rather it is considered worthy of all care because of the king who dwells in one of its houses. So also it has happened in the case of the King of all. 9.4 For, since he has come to our region and has dwelt in one body among those of like [body], henceforth the entire plot against humans by their enemies has been brought to an end, and the corruption of death, which formerly was powerful against them, has been put away. For the race of humans would have perished if the Master and Savior of all, God's Son, had not come to put an end to death.

On the Incarnation 13 The Renewal of the Image of God

13.1 So, therefore, after humans became devoid of reason, and thus the demonic error was overshadowing every place and hiding the knowledge concerning the true God, what was God supposed to do? [Was he supposed] to keep silent regarding so great a thing, and permit humans to be lead astray by demons, and for them [the humans] not to know God? 13.2 And what was the use, in fact, of the man having been made from the beginning according to the image of God? For he should have been made simply as a creature without reason, or, having been made a rational creature, [he should] live[9] the life of the irrational creatures. 13.3 And what use was it at all for him to receive ideas about God from the beginning? For if he is not now fit to receive [them], neither should [they] have been given to him at the beginning. 13.4 And also what is the profit to God who has made [the humans], or what sort of glory would it be to him, if the humans who have been made by him do not worship him, but think that others are the ones who have made them? For God is found

[8] The idea is not that straw is removed by fire, but that it has no place in a fire, any more than death has a rightful place in humans. See the further use of this imagery in ch. 44.

[9] Other editions, including Thomson and Kannengiesser, have, "not live."

having made these [humans] for others and not for himself. 13.5 Furthermore, a king, who is a human, does not allow the regions colonized by himself to be delivered over to serve others nor to flee to others; but he reminds them by letters, and often even sends [messages] to them through friends, and even if need be, he himself comes, further shaming them by his presence, only that they may not serve others, and his work be without effect. 13.6 Shall not God much more spare his own creatures in order that they not be lead astray from him and serve those who do not exist? Especially since such going astray was the cause of ruin and destruction for them, and it was not fitting for the creatures that had once shared the image of God to be destroyed. 13.7 So what was God supposed to do? Or what was supposed to happen, except to renew again that which was in keeping with the image, so that through it humans might again be able to know him? But how could this have happened, except by the coming of the very Image of God, our Savior Jesus Christ? For through humans it was not possible, since in fact they themselves have been created in keeping with the image; but neither through angels, for they themselves are certainly not images. From which fact the Word of God came in his own person, so that, as one who is the Image of the Father, he is able to create anew mankind that is in keeping with the image. 13.8 And again, it could not have happened in another way, except death and corruption were utterly destroyed. 13.9 From which fact, he took, reasonably, a mortal body, so that by it death indeed might be able to be utterly destroyed from then on, and the humans, who are in keeping with the image, might be renewed again. Accordingly, there was not someone else [sufficient] for this need, except the Image of the Father.

On the Incarnation 20 The Effects of the Cross

20.1 So we stated above, as it was possible, in part, and as we ourselves were able to understand [it], the reason for his bodily manifestation—that it did not belong to someone else to change corruption to incorruption, except the Savior himself, even the one who had made all things throughout the beginning from that which does not exist; and it did not belong to someone else to create anew again in humans that which is in keeping with the image, except the Image of the Father; and it did not belong to someone else to make the mortal immortal, except the Absolute Life, who is our Lord Jesus Christ; and it did not belong to someone else to teach about the Father and to bring down the worship of idols, except the Word, who sets in order all things and who alone is the Father's true, only-begotten Son. 20.2 And, since it was also necessary for that which was in fact owed from all still to be repaid—for, as I said above, it was owed for all to die—precisely because of which, in fact, he came to reside amongst [us]; [and] on account of which, after the proofs concerning his divinity from his works, now at last he also offered up the sacrifice for all, on behalf of all giving over his own temple to death, so that, on the one hand, he might make all to be without liability and free from the ancient transgression and, on the other, [that] he might show himself, in fact, better than death, displaying his own body as incorruptible, the first fruit of the resurrection of all. 20.3 And do not be surprised if we say the same things often concerning these same matters. For since we are speaking concerning the good pleasure of God, because of this we explain the same idea in many ways, lest perhaps we seem to leave out something, and there be a charge as against those who have spoken insufficiently. For, indeed, it is better to submit to blame for repetition than to leave out something of those things that ought to be written. 20.4 Therefore, his body, since it had also itself the being that is common to all—for it was a human body—even if it was formed from a virgin alone by an unprecedented miracle, nevertheless, it was mortal and died in conformity with those like it. But, by the entrance of the Word into it, no longer was it corrupt, in keeping with its own nature, but, because of the indwelling Word of God, it became free of corruption. 20.5 And it happened that two things occurred at the same time in a miraculous fashion—that the death of all was completed in the Lord's body, and that death and corruption were utterly destroyed because of the Word that was united [with the body]. For there was need for a death, and it was necessary that there be a death for all, so that it [the death] might be that which was owed by all. 20.6 From which fact, as I stated above, the Word, since it was not possible for him to die—for he was immortal—took to himself a body that was able to die, so that he might offer it as his own on behalf of all, and [so that], since he himself suffered for all because of his entrance to it [the body], "he might abolish the one who holds the power of death, that is, the devil, and set free those who through all their lifetime were subject to slavery through fear of death."[10]

On the Incarnation 44 The Necessity of the Incarnation

44.1 But perhaps they will be ashamed and will agree with these [points[11]], and will want to say that when God wanted to teach and save humans he should have done [so] with only a nod, and his Word should not have touched a body, just as, then, in fact, he had done long ago, when he constituted things out of what does not exist. 44.2 To this objection of theirs these things could reasonably be said—that long ago, when nothing, not one thing, was in existence, there was need of only a nod and a will for the creating of all; but when the human had been made and need demanded the healing not of things that do not exist but of things that had come into existence, it followed that the Healer and Savior come in/among those who had already come into existence, in order that he might heal those things that in fact exist. And he became a human because of this, and has used his body as a human instrument. 44.3 For if it should not have happened this way, how should the Word have come, since he wanted to use an instrument? Or from where should he take it, if not from things already in existence and needing his divinity through one like [themselves]? For things that do not exist were not needing salvation, so that, in fact, they would be satisfied with only a command; but mankind, which already existed, was being ruined and destroyed, for which reason, fairly and rightly, the Word has used a human instrument and revealed himself to all. 44.4 Then one must see this also, that the corruption that took place was not outside the body, but had attached itself to it, and it was a necessity that life should attach to it instead of corruption, so that, just as death has been in the body, so life also might be in it. 44.5 So if death was outside the body, life also should have been outside it. But if death was plaited together with the body and dominated it, since it [death] was joined with it [the body], [it was] necessary for life also to be plaited with the body, so that the body, having put on life instead, might throw off corruption. Otherwise, if in fact the Word had been outside the body and not in it, death would have been defeated by him most naturally, seeing that certainly death does not prevail against life, but nonetheless the

[10] Heb 2:14–15.

[11] In context Athanasius has been arguing that it is proper for the Word to be known through works of the body.

corruption that had attached itself would have remained in the body. 44.6 Because of this, reasonably, the Savior put on a body, so that, the body being plaited to life, it might no longer stay in death as mortal but, since it put on immortality, henceforth it might arise and remain immortal. For, once having put on corruption, it would not arise unless it put on life. And furthermore, death would not appear, in keeping with itself, unless in the body. Because of this he put on a body, so that he might find and wipe out death in the body. For how, in fact, would the Lord be shown to be life unless he made alive that which was mortal. 44.7 And just as straw naturally is destroyed by fire, if someone keeps the fire away from the straw, the straw is not burned, but, in turn, the straw remains in fact straw, looking apprehensively at the threat of fire, for by nature fire consumes it. But if someone cover the straw with a lot of asbestos, which indeed is said to be a remedy for fire, the straw no longer fears the fire, having the assurance of its incombustible covering. 44.8 In the same way, indeed, also with regard to both the body and death one might say that if death had been kept away by him with only a command, nonetheless, it [the body] was, in turn, mortal and corruptible in keeping with the essential disposition of bodies. But that this might not happen, it [the body] put on the incorporeal Word of God, and thus no longer fears either death or corruption, having life as a covering, and corruption having been utterly destroyed by it.

On the Incarnation 54 The Immeasurable Greatness of What the Incarnate Christ Achieved

54.1 Therefore, just as if someone wishes to see God, who is invisible by nature and not seen at all, he understands and knows him from his works, so let the one who does not see Christ with his mind at least learn well about him from the works of his [Christ's] body, and let him test whether they are human [works] or those of God. 54.2 And if they are human, let him scoff; but if he determine that they are not human but of God, let him not laugh at things that are not to be mocked, but rather let him marvel that through such lowly means things divine have been manifested to us, and that through death immortality reached to all, and that through the incarnation of the Word the providence that is over all was made known, as well as its Provider and Creator, the Word of God himself. 54.3 For he himself was made man that we might be made God. And he himself manifested himself through a body in order that we ourselves might receive an idea of the invisible Father. And he himself endured insolence from humans in order that we ourselves might inherit immortality. For while he himself was in no way injured, being impassible and incorruptible and the very Word and God, he was keeping and rescuing by his own impassibility the suffering humans, for whose sake he endured these things. 54.4 And, in a word, the achievements of the Savior that came about through his incarnation are of such a kind and so many, which, if one were to wish to describe [them], he would be like those who look at the vast expanse of the sea and want to count its waves. For as one is not able to take in with his eyes all the waves, since those [waves] that are coming on surpass the perception of the one making the attempt, so also for the one who wants to take in all the achievements of Christ in the body, [it is] impossible to receive them all, at least by counting, since those that surpass his consideration are greater than those which he himself thinks that he has taken in. 54.5 Therefore it is better not to aim at speaking regarding everything, concerning which one is not even able to declare a part, but to mention yet one [more thing], and [then] to leave everything for you to marvel at. For everything alike holds one's wonder and wherever one looks, from that place he is exceedingly amazed, seeing the divinity of the Word.

On the Incarnation 57 Prerequisites for Understanding the Things of God

57.1 But for the searching of the Scriptures and true knowledge [there is] need of a good life and a pure soul and the virtue that is in keeping with Christ, so that the mind, traveling via it [virtue] may be able to attain what it is aiming at and to grasp [it], to the degree that it is accessible to human nature to learn about the Word of God. 57.2 For without a pure mind and the imitation of the life in accordance with the saints, one would not be able to grasp the words of the saints. 57.3 For just as if one would want to see the light of the sun, certainly he would wipe clean his eye and make [it] bright, thoroughly cleansing himself nearly like that which is desired, so that the eye, thus becoming light, might see the light of the sun; or just as if someone would want to see a city or region, certainly he would arrive at the place for the sake of the sight. Thus he who wants to grasp the thought of those who speak of God must first wash and cleanse his soul by his life, and come to the saints themselves by the likeness of their deeds, so that, being with them in the conduct of a common life, he might understand the things, in fact, revealed to them by God, and henceforth, since united with them, he might escape the sinners' danger and their fire in the day of judgment, and he might receive the things laid up in store for the saints in the kingdom of heaven, "which eye has not seen, nor ear heard, nor has arisen in the heart of humans, all that has been prepared for those"[12] who live in keeping with virtue and who love God, even the Father, in Christ Jesus our Lord, through whom and with whom, to the Father himself with the Son himself in the Holy Spirit, be honor and power and glory unto the ages of ages. Amen.

[12] 1 Cor 2:9. Paul concludes the sentence, "who love him" (τοῖς ἀγαπῶσιν αὐτόν), so the word "love" (ἀγαπῶσιν) also could have been set off as part of the quotation in Athanasius's text.

Gregory of Nazianzus

Orations

Oration 1.3–5 The Christian's Experience of Pascha and a Call to Christlikeness

1.3 Yesterday the Lamb was slaughtered[1] and the doorposts were anointed, and Egypt sang a funeral dirge for her firstborn, and the destroyer passed over us, and the seal was fearful and awe-inspiring, and we were walled in by the precious blood. Today we cleanly fled Egypt and Pharaoh, the bitter despot, and the oppressive commanders; and we were liberated from the mud and the brick-making; and there is no one to hinder us from celebrating an exodus feast to the Lord our God and from celebrating, "not with old leaven of depravity and wickedness, but with unleavened bread of sincerity and truth,"[2] bringing nothing of Egyptian, godless dough.

1.4 Yesterday I was crucified with Christ,[3] today I am glorified with [him];[4] yesterday I was put to death with [him], today I am made alive with [him];[5] yesterday I was buried with [him],[6] today I am raised with [him].[7] But let us make an offering to the one who suffered and rose for us. Perhaps you think that I speak of gold or silver or woven robes or transparent and precious stones, earthly stuff that flows along and remains below, [things] of which those who are evil, slaves of this world below and of the world-ruler, always have the larger part. We are to offer our very selves, the possession most precious to God and most fitting; we are to give back to the Image that which is in keeping with the Image;[8] we are to acknowledge our dignity; we are to honor the archetype; we are to know the power of the mystery, even [that] for which Christ died.

1.5 Let us become like Christ, since Christ also [became] as we [are]. Let us become gods for his sake, since that one also [became] man for our sake. He took the worse that he

---

[1] The beginning of a series of allusions in this section to Exod 12.
[2] 1 Cor 5:8.
[3] Cf. Rom 6:6; Gal 2:19.
[4] Cf. Rom 8:17.
[5] Cf. Eph 2:5; Col 2:13.
[6] Cf. Rom 6:4.
[7] Cf. Eph 2:6.
[8] Cf. Matt 22:20–21; Mark 12:16–17; Luke 20:24–25.

might give the better; he was poor that by that one's poverty we might be rich;[9] he took a slave's form[10] that we might receive our freedom; he came down that we might be lifted up; he was tempted that we might conquer; he was dishonored that we might be honored; he died that he might save; he ascended that he might draw to himself those lying below in the fall of sin. One must give all, offer all, to the one who gave himself as a ransom for us and an exchange. And one will give nothing like oneself, understanding the mystery, and becoming for that one's sake all that that one [became] for our sake.

Oration 2.3 The Key Prerequisite for Pastors and Their Role in the Body of Christ

2.3 For I came to this [present situation],[11] people, not as one uneducated and senseless, but even less, that I may boast a little,[12] as one who distains divine laws and regulations.[13] For just as in the body there is something that rules and, as it were, presides, and something that is ruled and is led, so also in the churches, by a law of equality, which includes the idea of worthiness,[14] or again [by a law] of providence, by which he bound together all things, God appointed some to be shepherded and led (for as many as this is more profitable), [that is,] those who are guided both by word and deed to that which is proper; and [God appointed] others to be shepherds and teachers for the equipping of the church,[15] as many as are above the majority in virtue and fellowship with God, occupying a relation of soul to body, or mind to soul, so that, both of them being put together with one another and blended together (both that which lacks and that which has more than enough, just as among members [of a body]), and being joined together and bound together by the harmony of the Spirit, one complete body may be produced, and worthy, in reality, even of Christ himself, our head.

Oration 2.21–22 The Pastor as Physician of the Heart

2.21 For these reasons[16] I regard our practice of medicine to be more difficult by far than that which concerns bodies, and for this reason, worthy of more honor; also because, with respect to that [form of medicine] which investigates few things among those in the depth

[9] Cf. 2 Cor 8:9.

[10] Cf. Phil 2:7.

[11] Gregory is referring to his flight after his ordination, and the resulting disapproval of those whom he is now addressing.

[12] Cf. 2 Cor 11:16.

[13] He is countering the impression given by his flight as being in disobedience to the bishop's placement of him in Nazianzus.

[14] Gregory is developing the point that a candidate for ordination must be worthy. There is an equality among Christians, but some Christians are more virtuous than others and thus more fit for leadership, whose appointment is also connected with God's providential rule. Later (*Or.* 2.9) Gregory will cite his own sense of unworthiness as the main reason for his flight.

[15] Cf. Eph 4:11–12.

[16] In context Gregory has been speaking of the difficulties of diagnosing and treating human sins, the diseases of the soul.

[of a person], the majority of its activities [are] concerned with that which is seen. But for us, the whole medical treatment and effort is concerned with the hidden person of the heart,[17] and the battle is against that which is within, warring and wrestling against us, which, using our own selves as weapons against ourselves—the most terrible thing—it gives [us] to the death of sin. Therefore, against these [enemies there is] need of great and complete faith and greater assistance from God, and not a little counter-maneuvering on our part (as indeed I persuade myself)—which [counter-maneuvering] is observed in both word and deed, since it is necessary for us to be rightly healed and cleansed, and to be as worthy as possible with regard to that which is the most precious of those things which we have, our souls.

2.22 Turning now to the goals of both of the medical treatments—for this still remains for close examination by us—regarding the one form of treatment, [the goal is] to maintain, if it exists, the health or good condition of the flesh, or, if it has departed, to call it back; concerning which [that is, the health and good condition of the flesh] it is not at all clear whether a certain thing will benefit those who possess [them, that is, health and good condition of the flesh], since, in fact, their opposites often are of more benefit to those who have them, just as experiences of poverty and wealth, honor and disgrace, low estate and splendor, and all such things as lie in the middle according to nature and do not at all incline more to this side than to that, are improved or worsened by the use and free choice of those who experience [them]. Regarding the other [form of treatment] that is set before [us], [the goal is] to furnish the soul with wings, to snatch away [the soul] from the world, and to give [the soul] to God, and either to watch over that which is in keeping with the image, if [it] remains, or, if [it] is in danger, to lead [it] by the hand, or, if [it] is wasting away, to restore [it], to bring Christ in as a dweller in their hearts through the Spirit, and, the sum of the matter, to make the one who is of the heavenly company and the heavenly bliss to be a god.

Oration 2.35–36 The Pastor as Distributor of the Word

2.35 Now regarding the distribution of the word[18]—that I might speak last regarding the first of our [responsibilities]—I am talking of that which is sacred and lofty, and which everyone now discusses philosophically. If someone else is confident and supposes [the distribution of the word is within the power] of each person's understanding, I myself am amazed at this person of intelligence—lest I say, of folly. But then, the matter appears to me not among the easiest, nor [requiring] little of the Spirit, namely, to give in a timely fashion to each person his measured portion of the word, and to manage with judgment the truth of our tenets, [namely,] all that has been investigated concerning worlds or [the] world; concerning matter; concerning soul; concerning mind, and spiritual natures, both better and worse; concerning providence, which holds together and orders the universe, all that seems to happen according to reason and all that [seems to happen] against that reason which is below and belongs to humanity.

[17] Cf. 1 Pet 3:4.

[18] Since Gregory has just been developing the image of the pastor as physician, perhaps he continues that image by referring to preaching/teaching as "distribution."

2.36 And furthermore [the distribution of the word involves] all that concerns our first construction and our last remaking, both types; and truth; and covenants; and the coming of Christ, both first and second; both incarnation and sufferings; and dissolution;[19] and everything concerning resurrection; concerning [the] end; concerning judgment and retribution, both more gloomy and more glorious; and the chief topic, namely, all that which one must understand concerning the supreme and blessed Trinity, the very thing which indeed [involves] the greatest of dangers for those entrusted to enlighten [others], so that they neither leave us bare names by their teaching being contracted to one person of the Trinity through fear of polytheism, so that we suppose "Father" and "Son" and "Holy Spirit" are the same, nor fall from the opposite [errors] to an equal evil, like a distorted plant being bent far over to one side, by [the Trinity] being divided [in their teaching] into three, whether alien and strange [entities], or disorderly and anarchical [entities], even, one could say, rival gods.

Oration 29.20 The Mystery of the Incarnation: A Scriptural Tapestry of Jesus as Man and God

He was baptized[20] as man, but he destroyed sins[21] as God; he himself was not in need of purifying rites, but [he was baptized/he came] that he might sanctify the waters. He was tempted[22] as man, but he conquered as God; not only this but he even encouraged [us] to be courageous, since he had conquered the world.[23] He was hungry, but he fed thousands;[24] not only this but he is indeed life-giving and heavenly bread.[25] He was thirsty,[26] but he shouted, "If anyone thirst, let him come to me and drink";[27] not only this but he also promised that those who believe would gush forth [with water].[28] He was tired,[29] but for those who are tired and heavy laden he is rest.[30] He was heavy with sleep,[31] but he is light upon the sea; not only this but he even rebukes winds; not only this but he even makes Peter light when he is sinking.[32] He pays tax, but [he does so] from a fish;[33] not only this but he is even king of those demanding [the tax]. He hears himself called a Samaritan and demon-possessed,[34] but he saves the one who went down from Jerusalem and fell

---

[19] This is probably a reference to Christ's death. The word used here (ἀναλύσις) has this meaning elsewhere in Gregory's writings (*Or.* 7.21), and see 2 Tim 4:6.

[20] Matt 3:13.

[21] Matt 9:6.

[22] Matt 4:1.

[23] John 16:33.

[24] John 6:10.

[25] John 6:51.

[26] John 4:7; 19:28.

[27] John 7:37.

[28] John 7:38.

[29] John 4:6.

[30] Matt 11:28.

[31] Matt 8:24.

[32] Matt 14:25, 29; Matt 8:26.

[33] Matt 17:24–27.

[34] John 8:48.

among robbers;[35] not only this but he is even recognized by demons[36] and drives out demons,[37] and he sinks a legion of spirits[38] and sees the ruler of the demons falling like lightning.[39] He is stoned, but he is not caught.[40] He prays,[41] but he hears [prayers].[42] He weeps,[43] but he causes tears to cease. He asks where Lazarus [is laid],[44] for he was man, but he raises Lazarus,[45] for he was God. He is sold, and very cheaply, for [it was] for thirty silver coins,[46] but he buys back the world, and [it was] for a great price, for [it was] for his own blood.[47] He was led as a sheep to slaughter,[48] but he shepherds Israel, and now, indeed, the whole inhabited world.[49] [He is] silent like a lamb,[50] but he is the Word,[51] being proclaimed by a voice of one shouting in the desert.[52] He has been weakened, wounded, but he heals every disease and every infirmity.[53] He is lifted up upon the tree,[54] he is fixed [to it],[55] but he restores by the tree of life;[56] not only this but he saves even a robber crucified with [him];[57] not only this but he darkens everything that is seen.[58] He is given cheap wine to drink,[59] he is fed bile.[60] Who? The one who changed the water into wine,[61] the destroyer of the bitter taste,[62] the [one who is] sweetness and all desire.[63] He hands over his life, but he has authority to take it again;[64] not only this but the curtain is torn apart;[65] for the things above are exhibited;[66] not only this but rocks are split; not only this but dead are raised beforehand.[67] He dies, but he makes alive, and by death he destroys death. He is buried,

---

35 Luke 10:30.
36 Mark 1:24; Luke 4:34.
37 Matt 8:16.
38 Luke 8:33.
39 Luke 10:18.
40 John 8:59.
41 Matt 14:23; 26:36; Heb 5:7
42 Acts 7:59.
43 John 11:35.
44 John 11:34.
45 John 11:43.
46 Matt 26:15.
47 1 Pet 1:18–19.
48 Isa 53:7.
49 John 10:11.
50 Isa 53:7; Matt 26:63.
51 John 1:1.
52 John 1:23.
53 Isa 53:5.
54 John 12:32.
55 Acts 2:23.
56 John 6:51.
57 Luke 23:43.
58 Luke 23:44.
59 Luke 23:36.
60 Matt 27:34.
61 John 2:1–11.
62 Heb 2:9.
63 Song 5:16.
64 John 10:18.
65 Matt 27:51.
66 Cf. Rev 11:19; 15:5.
67 Matt 27:51–52.

but he rises. He goes down into Hades,[68] but he brings up souls; not only this but he goes up into heaven; not only this but he will come to judge the living and the dead, and to put to the test such words.[69] If these things produce a starting point of error for you, those things destroy your error.[70]

Oration 31.26 The Holy Spirit Was Revealed Gradually

31.26 The Old [Testament] proclaimed the Father openly, the Son more obscurely. The New [Testament] manifested the Son [and] gave a glimpse of the divinity of the Spirit. Now the Spirit dwells in [us], providing us a clearer manifestation of himself. For it was not safe while the divinity of the Father was not yet confessed for the Son to be proclaimed plainly, nor while [the divinity] of the Son was not received to be overloaded regarding the Holy Spirit—to put it rather audaciously indeed!—so that [people] not risk even that which is in keeping with their ability, like those weighed down with food that is beyond their capacity, and those who assault their eyesight, which is yet very weak, with the light of the sun—but [that] with additions one part at a time, and, as David said, with "ascents,"[71] and with advances and progresses "from glory to glory,"[72] the light of the Trinity might shine forth upon those who are more radiant. For this reason, I think, he came to dwell in the disciples gradually, adapting himself to the capacity of those receiving [him], at the beginning of the gospel,[73] after the passion,[74] after the ascension,[75] performing miracles, being breathed out [upon them],[76] appearing in fiery tongues.[77] And he was revealed by Jesus little by little, as you yourself also will observe if you read more carefully.[78] "I will ask," he says, "the Father and he will send to you another Paraclete, the Spirit of truth,"[79] that one might not think that he is a rival to God and that he discoursed as from some other authority. Then, [he says] "He will send," but "in my name."[80] Leaving out the, "I will ask" he has kept the, "He will send." Then, "I will send,"[81] [showing] his personal high status; then, "He will come,"[82] [showing] the authority of the Spirit.

---

[68] 1 Pet 3:18–19.

[69] God will put to the test words such as those used by the false teachers, whom Gregory is engaging.

[70] If the evidence in Scripture of Christ's humanity has caused the false teachers to err, the evidence for his divinity that Gregory has just recited should correct them.

[71] Ps 84:5 (LXX 83:6).

[72] Ps 84:7; 2 Cor 3:18.

[73] E.g., Luke 1:15, 35; 2:25–26.

[74] Matt 28:19.

[75] Acts 1:5.

[76] John 20:22.

[77] Acts 2:3–4.

[78] Gregory begins a careful gathering of scriptural details that reveal something of the relation of the Spirit to the Father and the Son.

[79] John 14:16–17.

[80] John 14:26.

[81] John 16:7, cf. 15:26.

[82] John 16:7–8.

Oration 45.28–29 The Effect of the Blood of Christ

45.28 And now it is necessary for us to sum up our discourse thus: We were created that we might be well off; we were well off when we were created. We were entrusted with paradise, that we might live luxuriously. We received a commandment, that we might be held in honor by keeping it, God not being ignorant of what would happen but ordaining freewill by law. We were deceived because we were envied. We were driven out because we transgressed. We fasted because we did not fast, having been overpowered by the tree of knowledge. For the commandment was ancient and contemporaneous with us, being a certain education for the soul and a lesson regarding luxury, which [commandment] we were reasonably ordered to do, that we might regain by keeping that which we had thrown away by not keeping [that is, the commandment]. We needed a God made flesh and put to death, so that we might live. We were put to death with [him] that we might be purified. We rose with [him] because we were put to death with [him]. We were glorified with [him] because we rose with [him].

45.29 Many indeed were the wonders at that time. God crucified; sun darkened and rekindled again (for it was fitting for the creatures to suffer also with their Creator); curtain split; blood and water pouring from his side, the one as of a man, the other as on behalf of man; earth shaken; rocks broken on behalf of the Rock; dead raised for a pledge of the final and common resurrection; the signs at the tomb; the [signs] after the tomb; concerning which [many wonders], who could worthily sing? But nothing such as this is the wonder of my salvation. A few drops of blood recreate the whole world, and become to all people like rennin to milk, binding and gathering us together into one.

Desert Fathers and Mothers

Apophthegmata Patrum

Abba Anthony the Great 13 The Hunter and His Bow

Now, there was someone hunting wild animals in the desert, and he saw Abba Anthony joking around with the brothers. And the old man, wanting to assure him that it was necessary once in a while to make allowances for the brothers, said to him, "Put an arrow in your bow and stretch [it]." And he did so. He said to him, "Stretch [it] again," and he stretched [it]. And again he said, "Stretch [it]." The hunter said to him, "If I stretch [it] beyond the proper measure the bow will be broken." The old man said to him, "So also in the work of God. If, with regard to the brothers, we stretch [them] beyond the proper measure they will quickly be dashed. Therefore, it is necessary to make allowances for the brothers at least once in a while." Hearing these things the hunter was pierced, and being greatly helped by the old man, he departed. And the brothers, being firmly established, went back to their own place.

Abba Gelasios 1 The Leather-bound Bible

They used to say about Abba Gelasios that he used to have a book in leather, worth eighteen coins. And it had the Old and New Testament written whole. And it used to lay in the church, so that the one among the brothers who wanted [to do so] could read [it]. Now a certain foreigner among the brothers,[1] coming to visit the old man, when he saw it he set his heart on it, and, stealing it, he went out. And the old man did not pursue after him that he might catch him, although he noticed [what had happened]. So that one, departing to the city, was trying to sell it. And having found one who wanted to buy [it], he was asking sixteen coins as the price. And the one who wanted to buy [it] said to him, "Give [it] to me first; I shall examine it, and in this way I will let you know what it is worth." So he gave it [to him]. And he took it and brought it to Abba Gelasios to examine it, having told him the amount which, in fact, the seller said. And the old man said, "Buy it, for it is beautiful and worth the price you have said." And the man went and spoke to the seller in a different way and not as the old man had said, saying, "Look, I showed it to Abba Gelasios and he told me that it is of great value, and it is not worth the price you have said."[2] And that one, hearing [this], said to him, "The old man said nothing else to you?" He said to him, "No." Then

---

[1] The reference is to a visiting monk unknown to the local brothers.

[2] We might expect the dealer to change Abba Gelasios's statement in the opposite direction, that is, to claim the book is not worth as much as the thief asked, which would enable the dealer to

he said, "I no longer want to sell it." And being pierced, he went to the old man, repenting and entreating him to take it. But the old man did not want to take [it]. Then the brother said to him, "If you do not take it I will not have rest." The old man said to him, "If you will have no rest, look, I will take it." And that brother remained until his death, being helped by the way of life of the old man.

Amma Theodora 6 The Victory of Humility

This woman also used to say that neither asceticism, nor keeping vigil, nor all sorts of hard work saves; [nothing] but genuine humility [saves]. For there was a certain anchorite driving away demons, and he questioned them closely. "By what are you coming out? By fasting?" And they were saying, "We neither eat nor drink." "By keeping vigil?" And they were saying, "We do not sleep." "By separation from the world?" "We live in the desolate places." "So, by what do you come out?" And they were saying, "Nothing conquers us except humility." You see that humility is victorious over demons.

Abba Joseph of Panephysis 7 Become Like Fire

Abba Lot visited Abba Joseph and said to him, "Abba, according to my strength I do my little office, and my little fasting, and my prayer, and my meditation, and my stillness,[3] and, according to my strength, I am pure in my thoughts. So what further have I to do?" So, the old man rose and stretched out his hands to heaven, and his fingers became like ten torches of fire, and he said to him, "If you want, become wholly like fire."

Abba Cassian 1 Hospitality Over Fasting

Abba Cassian related, "The holy Germanus and I visited with a certain old man in Egypt. And because he entertained us hospitably, he was asked by us, 'Why, when you receive foreign brothers, do you not keep the rule of our fast, as we received [it] in Palestine?' And he answered saying, 'The fast is always with me, but I am not able to keep you with me always. And the fast is indeed a useful thing and necessary, but it is by our choice; but the law of God demands the fulfilling of love [as something] of necessity. So, receiving Christ in you, I ought to serve [you] with all zeal. And when I will send you forth I am able to recover the rule of the fast. For the bridegroom's attendants are not able to fast as long as the bridegroom is with them, but when the bridegroom is taken away, then they will fast with power.' "[4]

---

buy it for less. The dealer's statement would allow the thief to make more money than he had hoped. The dealer's action is puzzling, but the book was worth more (eighteen vs. sixteen coins), underlining Abba Gelasios's non-possessiveness towards an item of great monetary value.

[3] This is a major theme in the Desert Fathers and Eastern Christianity in general. It includes solitude and, as here, stillness of soul: "a state of inner tranquility or mental quietude and concentration which arises in conjunction with, and is deepened by, the practice of pure prayer and the guarding of the heart and intellect. Not simply silence, but an attitude of listening to God and of openness towards Him" (Palmer: 364). See *PGL*: 609–610 for an outline of the uses of "stillness" (ἡσυχία).

[4] Cf. Matt 9:15; Mark 2:19–20; Luke 5:34–35.

Abba Macarius the Great 19 Simplicity In Prayer

Some people asked Abba Macarius, saying, "How ought we to pray?" The old man said to them, "The need is not to say the same thing over and over, but to stretch out your hands and to say, 'Lord, as you will and as you know, have mercy.' And if the war is pressing [say], 'Lord, help.' And he himself knows what is profitable, and he has mercy on us."

Abba Macarius the Great 23 Dead to the World

A brother visited Abba Macarius the Egyptian and said to him, "Abba, speak a word to me [about] how I may be saved." And the old man said to him, "Go to the cemetery and insult the dead." So, having departed, the brother insulted [them] and threw rocks [at them], and he came and reported to the old man. And he said to him, "They said nothing to you?" And he said, "No." The old man said to him, "Go again tomorrow and praise them." So, the brother departed and praised them, saying, "Apostles, saints, and righteous ones!" And he came to the old man and said to him, "I praised [them]." And he said to him, "They answered nothing to you?" The brother said, "No." The old man said to him, "You know how much you dishonored them and they answered nothing to you, and how much you praised them and they said nothing to you. So also you, if you want to be saved, become dead. Take account neither of injury from humans nor their praise, like the dead, and you can be saved."

Abba Moses the Ethiopian 2 The Basket of Sand

Once a brother in Scetis[5] was thrown down [by a sin], and a council having been [called], they sent to Abba Moses. But he did not want to go. So they sent the elder to him, saying, "Come, since the people are waiting for you." And he arose and went. And taking a large basket with holes in it, and filling it with sand, he carried [it]. And those who went out to meet him said to him, "What is this, Father?" And the old man said to them, "My sins are streaming out behind me, and I do not see them, and I came today to judge the sins of another." And those who heard said nothing to the brother, but forgave him.

Abba Mios 3 God's Care

Abba Mios was asked by one serving as a soldier if God in fact receives repentance. And after instructing him in many matters, he said to him, "Tell me, beloved, if your cloak is torn, do you throw it out?" He said, "No, rather I sew it and use it." The old man said to him, "So if you spare your garment, will not God spare his own image?"

Abba Poemen 184 What to Kill

Abba Isaac visited Abba Poemen, and seeing him throwing a little water on his feet, since he had boldness with him, he said to him, "How is it that people use severity, treating their body harshly?" And Abba Poemen said to him, "We are not taught [to be] body-killers but passion-killers."

---

[5]Scetis was a major monastic center in a remote area of the Egyptian desert, about seventy miles south of Alexandria.

Abba Sisoes 17 How to Share from the Scriptures

Abba Ammon of Rhaithou[6] asked Abba Sisoes, "When I read Scripture my thought wants to prepare a word, so that I might have [something] for a question." The old man said to him, "There is no need, but rather [you need] to gain [something] for yourself by the purity of your mind, and to be without anxiety, and [then] to speak."[7]

---

[6] Rhaithou is located on the coast of the Sinai Peninsula, about thirty-five miles southwest of Mt. Sinai.

[7] For this thought see the selection from Athanasius, *On the Incarnation*, ch. 57.

John Chrysostom

Homiliae in Matthaeum

Homiliae in Matthaeum 50.2 The Power of Jesus

"And after they boarded the boat, then the wind ceased."[1] Before this they were saying, "What sort of man is this, that even the winds and the sea obey him?"[2] But now it is not so. For, "those in the boat," it says, "came and worshipped him, saying, 'Truly you are God's Son.'"[3] Do you see how, little by little, he was leading them all towards that which is higher? For both from the walking on the sea, and from the command to another to do this [same thing], and [from] the rescuing [of him] when he was in danger, their faith was great from then on. For then he rebuked the sea, but now he does not rebuke it, showing his power in a different, greater way. Therefore they were also saying, "Truly you are God's Son." Then what? Did he rebuke those who had said this? No, rather entirely on the contrary, he indeed confirmed what was said, healing with greater authority those who were approaching [him], and not as before. "And crossing over," it says, "they came to the land of Gennesaret. And when the men of that place recognized him they sent into that whole region and they brought to him all who were sick, and they were imploring [him] that they might touch the hem of his garment; and as many as touched [it] were saved from their disease."[4] For they were not approaching him as before, dragging him into their houses and seeking a touch of [his] hand and orders [from him] through words; but in a far higher and more philosophical way and with greater faith were they trying to bring his treatment upon themselves. For the woman with the hemorrhage taught everyone to live like a philosopher. And the Evangelist, showing that he [Jesus] also entered the regions at long intervals, says, "When the men of the place recognized [him], they sent into the region and they brought to him those who were sick." But all the same, the interval not only did not put an end to their faith, but even made [it] greater and maintained [it] flourishing.

Therefore, let us also ourselves touch the hem of his garment, or rather, if we are willing—we have him whole. For indeed his body is set before us now—not his garment alone, but indeed his body; not with the result that we may only touch, but that we may both eat and take our fill. Therefore, let us approach with faith, each having an illness. For if those who touched the hem of his garment drew such power, how much more those who hold him

---

[1] Matt 14:32.
[2] Matt 8:27.
[3] Matt 14:33.
[4] Matt 14:34–36.

fast, whole. And to approach with faith is not only to receive that which is set before [us], but also to touch [it] with a pure heart, to be thus disposed, as approaching Christ himself. So what if you do not hear a voice? But you see him lying [there], or rather, indeed you do hear a voice, for he is speaking loud and clear through the Evangelists.

Homiliae in Matthaeum 50.3 Approaching God with a Pure Soul

Therefore, believe that even now [this is] that supper at which also he himself was reclining. For in no way is that [supper] different from this [one]. For [it is] not [that] a human being makes this, but he himself [made] that; but rather, indeed, he himself [makes] both this and that. Therefore, whenever you see the priest delivering [it] to you, do not think of it as the priest doing this, but [consider it] to be the hand of Christ stretched out.[5]

Do you want to honor the body of Christ? Do not overlook him naked; and do not honor him here [in church] with silk garments but outside overlook him being killed by icy cold and nakedness. For the one who said, "This is my body,"[6] and by his word established the matter, this one [also] said, "You saw me hungry and did not feed [me],"[7] and, "In so far as you did [it] not to one of these least, neither did you do [it] to me."[8] For this one does not need coverings but a pure soul; but that one needs much attention. Therefore, we must learn to live like a philosopher and to honor Christ as he himself wants; for to the one being honored an honor he himself wants is most pleasing, not [an honor] which we ourselves think [best]. For Peter also was thinking to honor him by hindering [him] from washing his feet, but what happened was not honor but the contrary. So also you, honor him with this honor he himself ordained, spending your wealth on the poor. For God does not have need of golden vessels, but of golden souls.

Homiliae in Matthaeum 50.4 Showing Mercy to Those in Need

And I'm saying these things not to prevent such offerings from being made but to demand that with these, even before these, [you] give alms. For he receives these things indeed, but how much more those. For here only the one who makes the offering is helped, but there also the one who receives. Here the deed seems indeed to be an occasion of generosity, but there the whole thing is pity and love towards humanity. For what is the use when the table is filled for him with golden drinking cups but he himself is wasting away with hunger? First fill him who hungers, and then also adorn his table abundantly. Do you make a golden drinking cup and do not give a cup of cold [water]? And what is the use? You pre-

---

[5] Due to constraints of space, I have omitted the material that comes next. In it Chrysostom develops further the topic of God's gift in the Eucharist, and then turns to challenge his hearers, "Let no Judas then approach this table . . ." I pick up the text in the midst of this challenge, which in *NPNF*[2] is found in 50.4.

[6] Matt 26:26.

[7] Matt 25:42.

[8] Matt 25:45.

pare a gold-spangled covering for his table but you do not provide him necessary covering? And what is the profit from this? For tell me, if you see someone in want of necessary food, and, neglecting to put an end to his hunger for him, you only overlaid his table with silver, he would not feel grateful to you, but would he not rather feel irritation? Then what? If you saw someone wrapped in rags and stiff from the icy cold, [and] neglecting to give him a garment, you began preparing gold columns, saying that you were doing honor to that one, would he not say that you were in fact insulting [him], and consider [it] insolence, indeed this the most extreme [insolence]? And also consider this concerning Christ: whenever he goes about as a wanderer and a stranger, needing a roof, and you yourself, neglecting to receive him, beautify pavement and walls and capitals of columns, and you fasten gold chains through lamps, but him, bound [with chains] in prison, you do not want to see.

And[9] I say these things not to prevent the eager striving in these things but to exhort you to do these things with those things, or rather, these things before those things. For no one was ever accused for not doing these things; but for [not doing] those things, hell is threatened, and unquenchable fire, and punishment with demons. Therefore, do not adorn his house and overlook his afflicted brother; for this one is more properly a temple than that one.

---

[9] *NPNF*[2] begins 50.5 here, while *PG* continues with 50.4.

Hesychios the Priest

On Watchfulness and Holiness

On Watchfulness and Holiness 1–6 Invoking Jesus with a Still Heart

Section 1

Watchfulness[1] is a spiritual pursuit, which, with God [helping], liberates a person completely from passionate thoughts and words and from evil deeds; and [it is a pursuit] that takes time and is traveled with zeal. When traveled, it freely gives, as much as is accessible, a sure knowledge of the God who cannot be grasped and an interpretation of the divine and secretly hidden mysteries. It is able to keep every commandment of God of the Old and of the New Testament and to cause every good of the coming age. And this is, in the proper sense, purity of heart, which, because of its greatness and beauty, or to speak more properly, because of our lack of attention and negligence, is exceedingly rare today among monks; which [purity of heart] Christ blesses, saying, "Blessed are the pure in heart, for they shall see God."[2] Therefore, being of such a nature, it is bought at a great price. Watchfulness, continuing for some time in a person, becomes a guide for a correct and God-pleasing life. The very entrance of this [guide] thoroughly teaches us contemplation and to set in motion correctly the three aspects of the soul,[3] and, by participation in it [watchfulness] daily, it steadfastly keeps the senses and causes the growth of the four principal virtues.[4]

Section 2

The great lawgiver Moses—or rather, the Holy Spirit—indicating the blameless and pure and comprehensive and exalting [character] of such a virtue, and, teaching us how it is necessary to begin and to complete it, says "Give heed to yourself, lest there be a hidden thing,"[5] speaking specifically of the manifestation of a single thought of some evil matter

---

[1] In Hesychios's spiritual tradition (Hesychasm, see note in section 3 below) this word, "signifies an attitude of attentiveness . . . whereby one keeps watch over one's inward thought and fantasies . . . maintaining guard over the heart and intellect . . . . It is closely linked with purity of heart and stillness . . . . The title of the *Philokalia* is 'the Philokalia of the niptic Fathers,' i.e., of the Fathers who practised and inculcated the virtue of watchfulness" (Palmer: 366–67).

[2] Matt 5:8.

[3] The desiring aspect (τὸ ἐπιθυμητικόν), the intelligent aspect (τὸ λογιστικόν), and passionate aspect (τὸ θυμικόν), especially as discussed by Plato.

[4] Wisdom (σοφία), self-control (σωφροσύνη), courage (ἀνδρεία), and justice (δικαιοσύνη), especially as discussed by Plato. Cf. their appearance in Wis 8:5–7.

[5] Deut 15:9.

that is hated by God; which also, in fact, the Fathers call an attack; which is brought upon your heart by the devil; [and] which our thoughts[6] chase after as soon as it discloses itself to our mind,[7] and they passionately converse with it.

Section 3

Watchfulness is a path of every virtue and commandment of God, which is also heart and stillness,[8] and, when it is perfected as free from mental images, the same is a guarding of the mind.

Section 4

A person born blind does not see the light of the sun, likewise the one who does not travel in watchfulness does not see the abundant flashings of the grace from above, nor will he be set free from works and words and thoughts that are evil and hateful to God; this person will not freely go past the rulers of hell at his death.[9]

Section 5

Attentiveness is the heart's unceasing stillness from every thought, breathing forth and invoking always and continually and constantly only him, Christ Jesus the Son of God, indeed God; and courageously being drawn up in battle order with him against the enemies; and confessing him to be the one who has authority to forgive sins. For the soul is continuously enfolded with Christ through invocation of him who alone hiddenly examines closely our hearts, trying in all kinds of ways to be hidden from all people with regard to its sweetness and its inner contest, and [in this condition] the evil one will not escape notice and successfully promote evil and utterly destroy a most beautiful work.

Section 6

Watchfulness is a steadfast fixing of thought and a halting of it at the door of the heart; which [watchfulness] sees with perceptive insight the thoughts that come, and hears what they say, and what the murderous ones are doing, and what is the carved and inscribed form [which comes] from the demons, which [form] is trying, through itself, to destroy the mind by means of mental images.[10] For these things, although being hard work, show us, if we want, very clearly and with insight the trial of spiritual battle.

---

[6] In the hesychastic literature this word (λογισμός), "generally signifies not thought in the ordinary sense, but thought provoked by the demons, and therefore often qualified in translation by the adjective 'evil' or 'demonic'. It can also signify divinely-inspired thought" (Palmer: 366).

[7] In such texts the mind (νοῦς), "understands divine truth by means of immediate experience, intuition or 'simple cognition'" (Palmer: 361), in distinction from the reason (διάνοια) which works through deductive reasoning and abstract concepts. Since God transcends all human thought, the rational mind cannot think its way to God. One needs a pure heart (καρδία) and a still νοῦς to know God and understand aright the revelation of God. No English word is satisfactory for νοῦς.

[8] The word (ἡσυχία), from which the hesychast tradition derives its name, refers to, "a state of inner tranquility or mental quietude and concentration which arises in conjunction with, and is deepened by, the practice of pure prayer and the guarding of the heart . . . and intellect. . . . Not simply silence, but an attitude of listening to God and of openness towards Him" (Palmer: 364).

[9] A reference to the idea, sometimes referred to as the Toll House Theory, that at death the soul passes through the region ruled by "the prince of the power of the air" (Eph 2:2), and evil spirits take the opportunity to accuse the soul of sin and to tempt it, seeking to drag it down to hell.

[10] Hesychios is describing the mental images sent by the demons as monuments that attract one's attention.

On Watchfulness and Holiness 27–29 The Example of the Spider

Section 27

This is a model and rule for stillness of heart. If you wish to engage in battle, let the little animal, the spider, be this example for you; otherwise you have not yet been still in mind as it is necessary [to be]. That one hunts small flies; but you, if you follow the spider's example, by working hard you have stillness in soul, [and] you will not cease constantly killing "Babylonian children,"[11] during which slaughter you are blessed by the Holy Spirit through David.[12]

Section 28

As it is not possible for the Red Sea to be seen in the firmament amidst the stars, and as it is not possible for a person walking on earth not to breathe this air, so it is impossible to cleanse our heart from impassioned thoughts and to drive away spiritual enemies from it without frequent invocation of Jesus.

Section 29

If, with humility of mind, and remembrance of death, and by reproach and refutation [of spiritual enemies], and invocation of Jesus Christ, you spend your time always in your heart, and [if] you travel the path of the mind with these weapons, vigilantly, day by day, [a path] which is narrow but also joy-producing and delightful, you will come to a vision of the Holy of Holies, and you will receive illumination from Christ regarding deep mysteries. "With whom the treasures of wisdom and knowledge are hidden. In whom dwells all the fullness of the Godhead bodily."[13] For you will perceive [yourself to be] in the presence of Jesus, because the Holy Spirit sprang upon your soul, from whom the mind of people is illumined to see "with unveiled face." It says, "No one says 'Lord Jesus' except by the Holy Spirit,"[14] clearly confirming that which is being sought mystically.

On Watchfulness and Holiness 79–82 Christlike Humility

Section 79

The Lord, wanting to show that every commandment is something which is owed, and that adoption is something that has been given to people by his own blood, says, "Whenever you have done all that which has been commanded you, say, 'We are useless slaves and what we were obligated to do we have done.'"[15] Therefore, the kingdom of heaven is not a reward for works, but rather the Master's gracious gift that has been prepared for faithful

---

[11] Cf. Ps 137:9. "Babylonian children" is an image of evil thoughts when they first appear to the mind. The psalm refers to the children being dashed against a rock, which the Fathers see as a type for killing the thoughts by the invocation of Jesus, the Rock.

[12] This is perhaps a reference to the comfort which one who is in the midst of the spiritual conflict receives from the Spirit through David's psalm just alluded to.

[13] Col 2:3, 9.

[14] 1 Cor 12:3.

[15] Luke 17:10.

slaves. A slave does not demand his freedom as a reward, but he gives thanks as one in debt and receives [it] as a gracious gift.

Section 80

How "he died on behalf of our sins, according to the Scriptures,"[16] and to those who serve him well he graciously gives freedom! For he says, "Well done, good and faithful slave. You were faithful over a few things, I will appoint you over many things. Enter into the joy of your Lord."[17] The one who rests on bare knowledge is not yet a faithful slave; rather, the one who, believing in Christ through obedience to what he commanded, and honoring the Master, does the things that are commanded. And when one stumbles or disobeys, one submits to what comes upon [one] as one's own.[18] Therefore be eager for knowledge and eager for work, for bare "knowledge puffs up"[19] a person.

Section 81 (82)

The trials that happen to us unexpectedly teach us, by divine providence, to become conscientious.

Section 82 (83)

While the distinct property of a star is the light around it, the distinct property of the devout person who fears God is simplicity and humility, because nothing else is disposed by nature to be a characteristic and clearer sign of the disciples of Christ like a humble mind and a simple manner. And all four of the Gospels shout this. And the one who [is] not like this, [that is, who is not] living in a humble manner, loses his part in the one who "humbled himself voluntarily to the point of a cross and death,"[20] the active Lawgiver, in fact, of the divine Gospels.

---

[16] 1 Cor 15:3.

[17] Matt 25:21.

[18] The person owns the punishment as proper to the behavior; as the action was their own, so are the consequences.

[19] 1 Cor 8:1.

[20] Phil 2:8.

Symeon the New Theologian

Hymns

Hymn 10 Life's Fleeting Things

That by grief death assails even the most steadfast.

I heard about a thing strange and full of astonishment,
an immaterial substance harder than stone,
with a resistance equal to what is called adamant,
which, although not being softened by fire or an iron tool,
becomes wax after being joined to lead.
Recently I came to believe that a small stream of water,
continuing over a period of time, hollows out solid rock.
And in truth nothing is unchangeable among the things in life.
Let no one think to deceive me from now on.
Woe to the one who sees the fleeting things of life
as things to be held fast, and is delighted in them.
He will suffer the same things as also I, the wretched one.
Night separated me from a most dear brother,
dividing the indivisible light of love.

Hymn 16 God's Loving Caress

That the Divine Being alone is by nature to be longed for and desired; the one who shares in it has come into participation in all that is good.

O what is the thing, which is hidden to every created existent being?
And what is the noetic[1] light, which is not seen by anyone?
And what is the great wealth, which no one in the world
has been able to actually find, or to hold fast in the least?
For it is not able to be grasped by anyone, incomprehensible to the world,
it is also that which is most desired beyond the whole world,
it is also precious, inasmuch as God surpasses

---

[1] Noetic (νοητός) is that which belongs to the mind (νοῦς). For the meaning of νοῦς in this context, see the footnote above, on section 2 of *On Watchfulness and Holiness* by Hesychios the Priest.

the things that are seen, having created them.
Because of this I am wounded by love of that one,
and inasmuch as he is not seen by me, I waste away in my heart,
my mind and my heart catching fire and moaning.
I walk about and burn, searching here and there,
and nowhere do I find the lover of my soul.
And I look around often to see my beloved,
and that one, quite invisible, is not seen by me at all.
And when I will begin to wail, as one despairing, then
he is seen by me, and the one who perceives all things looks at me.
Marveling, I am astounded at his elegance of beauty
and how, having opened heaven, the Creator stooped
and exhibited to me his inexpressible and strange glory.
And who, then, will move nearer that one,
or how will one be taken up into the immeasurable height?
As I am considering [this], he himself is found within me,
flashing forth within, in my wretched heart,
shining around me from every side with an immortal radiance,
and shining with rays upon all my members.
Entirely enfolded, he caresses me entirely,
and gives himself entirely to me, the unworthy one.
And I take my fill of his love and beauty,
and I am filled with divine delight and sweetness.
I participate in his light, I share indeed in his glory,
and my face shines even like my beloved's,
and all my members become light-bearing.
Then I am made complete, more beautiful than the beautiful ones,
more wealthy than the wealthy ones, and I am more powerful
than all the powerful ones, and greater than kings,
and much more precious than all that is seen,
not only [more precious] than the earth and those of the earth, but also even than heaven
and all those in heaven, since I have the Creator of all,
to whom glory and honor are fitting now and unto the ages.
Amen.

Appendix A
Vocabulary List

The Greek notes assume a knowledge of the words in the following list—words that occur fifty times or more in the New Testament. When a passage uses one of these words in a way not listed here, I either provide help in a note or, occasionally, if it is close to a meaning listed here, I use the alternative in the translation.

Ἀβραάμ, ὁ	Abraham
ἀγαθός, ή, όν	good
ἀγαπάω	I love
ἀγάπη, ης, ἡ	love
ἀγαπητός, ή, όν	beloved
ἄγγελος, ου, ὁ	messenger, angel
ἅγιος, α, ον	holy
ἄγω	I lead, bring
ἀδελφός, οῦ, ὁ	brother
αἷμα,-ματος, τό	blood
αἴρω	I raise, carry, take away
αἰτέω	I request
αἰών, αἰῶνος, ὁ	age, period
αἰώνιος, ον	eternal
ἀκολουθέω	I follow
ἀκούω	I hear
ἀλήθεια, ας, ἡ	truth
ἀλλά	but, except, yet, rather
ἀλλήλων	of one another
ἄλλος, η, ο	other, another
ἁμαρτία, ας, ἡ	sin
ἀμήν	amen, truly, surely, indeed
ἄν	particle indicating contingency
ἀναβαίνω	I go up, come up
ἀνήρ, ἀνδρός, ὁ	man, husband

ἄνθρωπος, ου, ὁ	man, human being
ἀνίστημι	I raise, set up; 2 aor. and mid. forms: rise; pf. can be either trans. or intrans.
ἀνοίγω	I open
ἀπέρχομαι	I go away, depart
ἀπό	w. gen.: from; because of; by
ἀποθνῄσκω	I die
ἀποκρίνομαι	I answer
ἀποκτείνω	I kill
ἀπόλλυμι	I destroy; lose; mid.: I perish
ἀπολύω	I release
ἀποστέλλω	I commission, send
ἀπόστολος, ου, ὁ	messenger, apostle
ἄρτος, ου, ὁ	bread, loaf
ἀρχή, ῆς, ἡ	beginning; ruler
ἀρχιερεύς, έως, ὁ	high priest
ἄρχω	I rule; mid.: I begin
ἀσπάζομαι	I greet
αὐτός, αὐτή, αὐτό	self; same; he, she, it
ἀφίημι	I let go, leave, permit, forgive
βάλλω	I throw, put
βαπτίζω	I baptize, dip
βασιλεία, ας, ἡ	kingdom
βασιλεύς, έως, ὁ	king
βλέπω	I see, look at
Γαλιλαία, ας, ἡ	Galilee
γάρ	for, because, since
γεννάω	I beget; pass.: be born
γῆ, ῆς, ἡ	earth, land, ground
γίνομαι	I become, come about, happen; be made/produced/created; I am
γινώσκω	I know, come to know
γλῶσσα, ης, ἡ	tongue, language
γραμματεύς, έως, ὁ	scribe
γραφή, ῆς, ἡ	writing, Scripture
γράφω	I write
γυνή, γυναικός, ἡ	woman, wife
δαιμόνιον, ου, τό	demon
Δαυίδ, ὁ	David
δέ	and, now, then; but, but rather
δεῖ (w. acc. and inf.)	it is necessary, one must
δεξιός, ά, όν	right (hand, side)
δέχομαι	I take; receive
διά	w. gen.: through, by; w. acc.: on account of
διδάσκαλος, ου, ὁ	teacher
διδάσκω	I teach

δίδωμι	I give
δίκαιος, α, ον	righteous, just
δικαιοσύνη, ης, ἡ	righteousness, justice
διό	therefore
δοκέω	I think, seem
δόξα, ης, ἡ	glory, fame
δοξάζω	I praise, honor, glorify
δοῦλος, ου, ὁ	slave
δύναμαι	I am able, I can, I am powerful
δύναμις, έως, ἡ	power, miracle
δύο	two
δώδεκα	twelve
ἐάν	if, when
ἑαυτοῦ	of himself, his own
ἐγείρω	I raise up; rouse, wake
ἐγώ	I
ἔθνος, ους, τό	race, people, nation; pl.: Gentiles
εἰ	if
εἶδον	I saw (aor. of ὁράω)
εἰμί	I am
εἶπον	I said (aor. of λέγω)
εἰρήνη, ης, ἡ	peace
εἰς	w. acc.: into, to, in, among, for, concerning
εἷς, μία, ἕν	one
εἰσέρχομαι	I come in, go in
εἴτε	if, whether
ἐκ, ἐξ	w. gen.: out of, from; by; because of
ἕκαστος, η, ον	each, every
ἐκβάλλω	I throw out, drive out
ἐκεῖ	there
ἐκεῖνος, η, ο	that
ἐκκλησία, ας, ἡ	assembly, church
ἐλπίς, ἐλπίδος, ἡ	hope
ἐμός, ή, όν	my, mine
ἐν	w. dat.: in, among, on; with; by; because of
ἐντολή, ῆς, ἡ	commandment
ἐνώπιον	w. gen.: in the presence of, before
ἐξέρχομαι	I come out, go out
ἐξουσία, ας, ἡ	authority, right; power
ἔξω	w. gen.: out of; adv.: outside
ἐπαγγελία, ας, ἡ	promise
ἐπερωτάω	I ask for; question
ἐπί	w. gen.: on, over; when; w. dat.: on the basis of; at; w. acc.: on, to, against
ἑπτά	seven
ἔργον, ου, τό	work, deed

ἔρχομαι	I come, go
ἐρωτάω	I ask
ἐσθίω	I eat
ἔσχατος, η, ον	last
ἕτερος, α, ον	other, another, different
ἔτι	still; even; yet
εὐαγγελίζω	I bring good news, preach
εὐαγγέλιον, ου, τό	good news, gospel
εὐθύς, εὐθεῖα, εὐθύ	immediately
εὑρίσκω	I find
ἔχω	I have, hold
ἕως	w. gen.: as far as; conj.: until
ζάω	I live, come to life
ζητέω	I seek, search
ζωή, ῆς, ἡ	life
ἤ	or, than; ἤ . . . ἤ: either . . . or
ἤδη	now, already
ἡμεῖς	we
ἡμέρα, ας, ἡ	day
θάλασσα, ης, ἡ	sea, lake
θάνατος, ου, ὁ	death
θέλημα,-ματος, τό	will
θέλω	I will, wish, want, desire
θεός, οῦ, ὁ	God
θεωρέω	I look at, behold, consider
θρόνος, ου, ὁ	throne
ἴδιος, α, ον	one's own
ἰδού	Look! Behold!
ἱερόν, οῦ, τό	temple
Ἱεροσόλυμα, τά and ἡ	Jerusalem
Ἰερουσαλήμ, ἡ	Jerusalem
Ἰησοῦς, οῦ, ὁ	Jesus
ἱμάτιον, ου, τό	garment, cloak
ἵνα	in order that, that
Ἰουδαίος, α, ον	Jewish, Jew; Judea, Judean
Ἰσραήλ, ὁ	Israel
ἵστημι	I make to stand, set up; stand
Ἰωάννης, ου, ὁ	John
κἀγώ	and I, but I
κάθημαι	I sit (down), I am seated; I stay
καθώς	just as
καί	and, also, even, indeed, and yet
καιρός, οῦ, ὁ	appointed time, season, opportunity
κακός, ή, όν	evil, bad
καλέω	I call, invite
καλός, ή, όν	beautiful, noble, good

καρδία, ας, ἡ	heart
καρπός, οῦ, ὁ	fruit
κατά	w. gen.: down, against; by; w. acc.: according to; at; throughout; with
καταβαίνω	I go down, come down
κεφαλή, ῆς, ἡ	head
κηρύσσω	I preach
κόσμος, ου, ὁ	world
κράζω	I cry out, call out
κρίνω	I judge, condemn
κύριος, ου, ὁ	Lord, master, lord
λαλέω	I speak, say
λαμβάνω	I take, receive
λαός, οῦ, ὁ	a people
λέγω	I say, speak
λίθος, ου, ὁ	stone
λόγος, ου, ὁ	word, message, matter
λοιπός, ή, όν	remaining; noun: the rest; adv.: henceforth, further, finally
μαθητής, οῦ, ὁ	student, disciple
μακάριος, α, ον	blessed
μᾶλλον	more, rather
μαρτυρέω	I witness, testify, give evidence
μέγας μεγάλη, μέγα	great, large
μέλλω	I am about to, I am destined to, intend to (w. inf.)
μέν	on the one hand, indeed
μένω	I remain, stay
μέσος, η, ον	middle, in the midst
μετά	w. gen.: with; w. acc.: after; among
μή	not, lest
μηδέ	but not, nor, not even
μηδείς, μηδεμία, μηδέν	no one, nothing
μήτηρ, μητρός, ἡ	mother
μόνος, η, ον	sole, only, alone; adv.: only, merely
Μωϋσῆς, έως, ὁ	Moses
νεκρός, ά, όν	dead; subst.: corpse
νόμος, ου, ὁ	law, principle
νῦν	now
νύξ, νυκτός, ἡ	night
ὁ, ἡ, τό	the
ὁδός, οῦ, ἡ	way, road, path, journey
οἶδα	I know, understand (pf. used as a pres.)
οἰκία, ας, ἡ	house, home
οἶκος, ου, ὁ	house, household
ὅλος, η, ον	whole, all; adv.: entirely
ὄνομα,-ματος, τό	name

ὅπου	where
ὅπως	how, that, in order that;
ὁράω	I see, notice
ὄρος, ους, τό	mountain
ὅς, ἥ, ὅ	who, whom, which
ὅσος, η, ον	how great, how much; as much as; all that
ὅστις, ἥτις, ὅτι	whoever; such as; who, which
ὅταν	when, whenever
ὅτε	when
ὅτι	because, since, for; that; used to introduce a quotation
οὐ, οὐκ, οὐχ	not
οὐδέ	and not, not even, neither, nor
οὐδείς, οὐδεμία, οὐδέν	no one, nothing
οὖν	therefore, then, accordingly
οὐρανός, οῦ, ὁ	heaven, sky
οὔτε	and not, neither, nor
οὗτος, αὕτη, τοῦτο	this; he, she, it
οὕτως	thus, so, like this
οὐχί	not
ὀφθαλμός, οῦ, ὁ	eye
ὄχλος, ου, ὁ	crowd
παιδίον, ου, τό	child, infant
πάλιν	again
παρά	w. gen.: from; w. dat.: with, beside; w. acc.: by, near; because of; than
παραβολή, ῆς, ἡ	parable
παραδίδωμι	I hand over, hand down
παρακαλέω	I exhort, urge; encourage
πᾶς, πᾶσα, πᾶν	all, each, every, the whole
πατήρ, πατρός, ὁ	father
Παῦλος, ου, ὁ	Paul
πείθω	I persuade; 2 pf.: trust; pass. and mid.: believe; listen to, obey
πέμπω	I send
περί	w. gen.: about; because; for; concerning; w. acc.: around, with
περιπατέω	I walk
Πέτρος, ου, ὁ	Peter
Πιλᾶτος, ου, ὁ	Pilate
πίνω	I drink
πίπτω	I fall
πιστεύω	I believe, entrust
πίστις, εως, ἡ	faith, belief, trust
πιστός, ή, όν	faithful, reliable
πλείων, πλεῖον	more, larger; much, many
πληρόω	I fill, fulfill, complete

πλοῖον, ου, τό	boat
πνεῦμα,-ματος, τό	spirit, the Spirit
ποιέω	I do, make
πόλις, εως, ἡ	city
πολύς, πολλή, πολύ	much, many; adv.: often
πονηρός, ή, όν	evil, bad
πορεύομαι	I go, travel
πούς, ποδός, ὁ	foot
πρεσβύτερος, α, ον	elder, presbyter
πρός	w. gen.: from; w. dat.: near, at, by; w. acc.: to, towards, with
προσέρχομαι	I come/go to/towards
προσεύχομαι	I pray
προσκυνέω	I worship
πρόσωπον, ου, τό	face, presence
προφήτης, ου, ὁ	prophet
πρῶτος, η, ον	first
πῦρ, πυρός, τό	fire
πῶς	how?
ῥῆμα,-ματος, τό	word, saying
σάββατον, ου, τό	Sabbath, week
σάρξ, σαρκός, ἡ	flesh
σημεῖον, ου, τό	sign
Σίμων, ος, ὁ	Simon
σοφία, ας, ἡ	wisdom
σπείρω	sow, plant
στόμα,-ματος, τό	mouth
σύ	you (sg.)
σύν	w. dat.: with
συνάγω	I gather together, invite
συναγωγή, ῆς, ἡ	synagogue, meeting
σῴζω	I save, rescue
σῶμα,-ματος, τό	body
τε	and
τέκνον, ου, τό	child
τηρέω	I keep
τίθημι	I put, place
τίς, τί	who?, what?, which?, why?
τις, τι	someone, something
τοιοῦτος, τοιαύτη, τοιοῦτον	such, of such a kind
τόπος, ου, ὁ	place
τότε	then
τρεῖς, τρία	three
τρίτος, η, ον	third
τυφλός, ή, όν	blind
ὕδωρ, ὕδατος, τό	water
υἱός, οῦ, ὁ	son

ὑμεῖς	you (pl.)
ὑπάγω	I depart, go
ὑπάρχω	I am, exist
ὑπέρ	w. gen.: for, on behalf of; because of; about; w. acc.: above, beyond
ὑπό	w. gen.: by; because of; w. acc.: under
Φαρισαῖος, ου, ὁ	Pharisee
φέρω	I carry, bear
φημί	I say
φοβέομαι	I fear
φωνή, ῆς, ἡ	sound, voice
φῶς, φωτός, τό	light
χαίρω	I rejoice
χαρά, ᾶς, ἡ	joy
χάρις, χάριτος, ἡ	grace, favor, kindness; gracious gift
χείρ, χειρός, ἡ	hand
Χριστός, οῦ, ὁ	Christ, Messiah, anointed one
χρόνος, ου, ὁ	time
ψυχή, ῆς, ἡ	soul, life, self
ὧδε	here
ὥρα, ας, ἡ	hour
ὡς	as, when, that, how, about, since
ὥστε	so that; and so; w. inf.: so as to

Appendix B
Principal Parts of Common Verbs

The following list contains the most irregular forms among the verbs used fifty times or more in the Greek New Testament. I have also included πιστεύω as an example of a regular verb and ἀγαπάω, τηρέω, and πληρόω as examples of the patterns of contract verbs. Some forms not occurring in the New Testament have been included to make the list more useful for reading outside the New Testament.

Verbs often have alternative forms. For example, the aor. form εἶπον also occurs with first aor. endings (εἶπα, εἶπας, etc.), and a number of verbs have both first and second aor. forms. With a couple of exceptions, I have not included alternate forms. The notes give help with such irregularities.

Pres.—Fut.—Aor. Act.—Perf. Act.—Perf. Mid./Pass.—Aor. Pass.

ἀγαπάω, ἀγαπήσω, ἠγάπησα, ἠγάπηκα, ἠγάπημαι, ἠγαπήθην

ἄγω, ἄξω, ἤγαγον, ἦχα, ἦγμαι, ἤχθην

αἴρω, ἀρῶ, ἦρα, ἦρκα, ἦρμαι, ἤρθην

ἀπόλλυμι, ἀπολέσω, ἀπώλεσα, ἀπόλωλα, —, —

ἀποστέλλω, ἀποστελῶ, ἀπέστειλα, ἀπέσταλκα, ἀπέσταλμαι, ἀπεστάλην

ἀφίημι, ἀφήσω, ἀφῆκα, ἀφεῖκα, ἀφεῖμαι, ἀφέθην

βαίνω, βήσομαι, ἔβην, βέβηκα, —, —

βάλλω, βαλῶ, ἔβαλον, βέβληκα, βέβλημαι, ἐβλήθην

γίνομαι, γενήσομαι, ἐγενόμην, γέγονα, γεγένημαι, ἐγενήθην

γινώσκω, γνώσομαι, ἔγνων, ἔγνωκα, ἔγνωσμαι, ἐγνώσθην

δίδωμι, δώσω, ἔδωκα, δέδωκα, δέδομαι, ἐδόθην

ἔρχομαι, ἐλεύσομαι, ἦλθον, ἐλήλυθα, —, —

ἐσθίω, ἔδομαι and φάγομαι, ἔφαγον, ἐδήδοκα, ἐδήδεσμαι, —

εὑρίσκω, εὑρήσω, εὗρον, εὕρηκα, εὕρημαι, εὑρέθην

ἔχω, ἕξω, ἔσχον, ἔσχηκα, —, ἐσχέθην

ἵστημι, στήσω, ἔστησα, ἕστηκα, ἕσταμαι, ἐστάθην

καλέω, καλῶ and καλέσω, ἐκάλεσα, κέκληκα, κέκλημαι, ἐκλήθην

κρίνω, κρινῶ, ἔκρινα, κέκρικα, κέκριμαι, ἐκρίθην

λαμβάνω, λήμψομαι, ἔλαβον, εἴληφα, εἴλημμαι, ἐλήμφθην

λέγω, ἐρῶ, εἶπον, εἴρηκα, εἴρημαι, ἐρρέθην

μένω, μενῶ, ἔμεινα, μεμένηκα, —, —

ὁράω, ὄψομαι, εἶδον, ἑώρακα, ἑόραμαι, ὤφθην

πάσχω, πείσομαι, ἔπαθον, πέπονθα, —, —

πείθω, πείσω, ἔπεισα, πέποιθα, πέπεισμαι, ἐπείσθην

πίνω, πίομαι, ἔπιον, πέπωκα, πέπομαι, ἐπόθην

πίπτω, πεσοῦμαι, ἔπεσον, πέπτωκα, —, —

πιστεύω, πιστεύσω, ἐπίστευσα, πεπίστευκα, πεπίστευμαι, ἐπιστεύθην

πληρόω, πληρώσω, ἐπλήρωσα, πεπλήρωκα, πεπλήρωμαι, ἐπληρώθην

σῴζω, σώσω, ἔσωσα, σέσωκα, σέσῳσμαι, ἐσώθην

τηρέω, τηρήσω, ἐτήρησα, τετήρηκα, τετήρημαι, ἐτηρήθην

τίθημι, θήσω, ἔθηκα, τέθεικα, τέθειμαι, ἐτέθην

φέρω, οἴσω, ἤνεγκα, ἐνήνοχα, ἐνήνεγμαι, ἠνέχθην

χαίρω, χαρήσομαι, ἐχάρησα, κεχάρηκα, κεχάρημαι, ἐχάρην

Appendix C
The Selections Arranged in Order of Difficulty

This list is a rough guide to the difficulty level of the Greek found in each selection. Most texts contain both easy sections and more difficult sections. I indicate the approximate range for each text on a scale of 1 to 5, with 1 as the easiest.

Easiest Texts

1 Clement [1–2]
Didache [1]
Gregory of Nazianzus, *Orations* 1 and 29 [1]
Ignatius of Antioch, *To the Romans* [1–2]
Martyrdom of Polycarp [1–2]

Intermediate Texts

Desert Fathers and Mothers, Selections from the *Apophthegmata Patrum* [1–3]
Epistle to Diognetus [2–3]
Gregory of Nazianzus, *Orations* 31 and 45 [1–3]
Hesychios the Priest, *On Watchfulness and Holiness* [2–4]
John Chrysostom, *Homiliae in Matthaeum* [1–3]
Melito of Sardis, *On Pascha* [1–4]
Symeon the New Theologian, *Hymns* [3–4]

Advanced Texts

Athanasius, *On the Incarnation* [3–5]
Clement of Alexandria, *Miscellanies* [3–5]
Eusebius, *Ecclesiastical History* [3–5]
Gregory of Nazianzus, *Oration* 2 [4–5]
Justin Martyr, *First Apology* [3–5]

Bibliography

Greek Resources Cited

BDF Blass, F. and A. Debrunner. *A Greek Grammar of the New Testament and Other Early Christian Literature.* Translated and revised by Robert W. Funk. Chicago: University of Chicago Press, 1961.

BDAG Danker, Frederick William, rev. and ed. *A Greek-English Lexicon of the New Testament and Other Early Christian Literature.* 3d ed. Chicago: University of Chicago Press, 2000.

Denn Denniston, J. D. *The Greek Particles.* Revised by K. J. Dover. 2d ed. Oxford: Oxford University Press, 1950.

PGL Lampe, G. W. H., ed. *A Patristic Greek Lexicon.* Oxford: Clarendon Press, 1961.

LSI Liddell, Henry George. *An Intermediate Greek-English Lexicon Founded Upon the Seventh Edition of Liddell and Scott's Greek-English Lexicon.* Oxford: Clarendon Press, 1889.

LSJ Liddell, Henry George and Robert Scott. *A Greek-English Lexicon.* Revised and augmented by Henry Stuart Jones, with the assistance of Roderick McKenzie. 9th ed. With a revised supplement, 1996. Oxford: Clarendon Press, 1940.

Nunn Nunn, H. P. V. *A Short Syntax of New Testament Greek.* 5th ed. Cambridge: Cambridge University Press, 1938.

Smy Smyth, Herbert Weir. *Greek Grammar.* Revised by Gordon M. Messing. Cambridge, Mass.: Harvard University Press, 1956.

TLG *Thesaurus linguae graecae.* Online: http://www.tlg.uci.edu/

Wal Wallace, Daniel B. *Greek Grammar Beyond the Basics.* Grand Rapids, Mich.: Zondervan, 1996.

Yng Young, Richard A. *Intermediate New Testament Greek Grammar: A Linguistic and Exegetical Approach.* Nashville, Tenn.: Broadman and Holman, 1994.

Resources for Individual Selections

ANF *The Ante-Nicene Fathers.* Edited by Alexander Roberts and James Donaldson. 1885–1887. 10 vols. Repr. Peabody, Mass.: Hendrickson, 1994.

NPNF[1] *The Nicene and Post-Nicene Fathers, First Series.* Edited by Philip Schaff. 1886–1889. 14 vols. Repr. Peabody, Mass.: Hendrickson, 1994.

NPNF[2] *The Nicene and Post-Nicene Fathers, Second Series.* Edited by Philip Schaff. 1890–1899. 14 vols. Repr. Peabody, Mass.: Hendrickson, 1994.

PG Migne, J.-P., ed. *Patrologiae cursus completus: Series graeca.* 162 vols. Paris: Migne, 1857–1886.

Didache

Text and Translation

Ehrman, Bart D., ed. and trans. *The Apostolic Fathers, Vol. 1.* Loeb Classical Library 24. Cambridge, Mass.: Harvard University Press, 2003.

Lightfoot, J. B. and J. R. Harmer, trans. *The Apostolic Fathers.* Edited and revised by Michael W. Holmes. 2d ed. Grand Rapids, Mich.: Baker, 1989.

Studies

Jefford, Clayton, N., ed. *The Didache in Context: Essays on Its Text, History and Transmission.* Supplements to Novum Testamentum 77. Leiden: E. J. Brill, 1995.

Jefford, Clayton N., Kenneth J. Harder, and Louis D. Amezaga Jr. *Reading the Apostolic Fathers: An Introduction.* Peabody, Mass.: Hendrickson, 1996.

Niederwimmer, Kurt. *The Didache.* Translated by Linda M. Maloney. Hermeneia. Philadelphia: Fortress, 1998.

1 Clement

Text and Translation

Ehrman, *The Apostolic Fathers, Vol. 1.*

Lightfoot and Harmer, *The Apostolic Fathers.*

Studies

Grant, Robert M. and Holt H. Graham. *The Apostolic Fathers: A New Translation and Commentary, Vol. 2: First and Second Clement.* Edited by Robert M. Grant. Camden, N.J.: Thomas Nelson, 1965.

Jefford, *Reading the Apostolic Fathers.*

Lightfoot, J. B., ed. and trans. *The Apostolic Fathers: Clement, Ignatius, and Polycarp, Part 1: Clement.* 2 vols. 2d ed. 1889. Repr., Grand Rapids, Mich.: Baker, 1981.

Ignatius of Antioch, *To the Romans*

Text and Translation

Ehrman, *The Apostolic Fathers, Vol. 1.*

Lightfoot and Harmer, *The Apostolic Fathers.*

Studies

Grant, Robert M. and Holt H. Graham. *The Apostolic Fathers: A New Translation and Commentary, Vol. 4: Ignatius of Antioch.* Edited by Robert M. Grant. Camden, N.J.: Thomas Nelson, 1966.

Jefford, *Reading the Apostolic Fathers.*

Lightfoot, J. B., ed. and trans. *The Apostolic Fathers: Clement, Ignatius, and Polycarp, Part 2: S. Ignatius, S. Polycarp.* 3 vols. 2d ed. 1889. Repr., Grand Rapids, Mich.: Baker, 1981.

Schoedel, William R. *Ignatius of Antioch: A Commentary on the Letters of Ignatius of Antioch.* Hermeneia. Philadelphia: Fortress, 1985.

Epistle to Diognetus

Text and Translation

Ehrman, Bart D., ed. and trans. *The Apostolic Fathers,* Vol. 2. Loeb Classical Library 25. Cambridge, Mass.: Harvard University Press, 2003.

Lightfoot and Harmer, *The Apostolic Fathers.*

Studies

Jefford, *Reading the Apostolic Fathers.*

Martyrdom of Polycarp

Text and Translation

Ehrman, *The Apostolic Fathers, Vol. 1.*

Lightfoot and Harmer, *The Apostolic Fathers.*

Studies

Jefford, *Reading the Apostolic Fathers.*

Lightfoot, J. B., ed. and trans. *The Apostolic Fathers: Clement, Ignatius, and Polycarp, Part 2: S. Ignatius, S. Polycarp.*

Schoedel, William. *The Apostolic Fathers: A New Translation and Commentary, Vol. 5: Polycarp, Martyrdom of Polycarp, Fragments of Papias.* Edited by Robert M. Grant. Camden, N.J.: Thomas Nelson, 1967.

Justin Martyr, *First Apology*

Text

Goodspeed, E. J. *Die ältesten Apologeten.* Göttingen: Vandenhoeck & Ruprecht, 1915.

Translation

Roberts, Alexander and James Donaldson, ed. and trans. *Justin Martyr* in *ANF* 1:159–87. Available online at http://www.ccel.org/.

Studies

Barnard, L. W. *Justin Martyr: His Life and Thought.* Cambridge: Cambridge University Press, 1967.

Campenhausen, Hans von. *The Fathers of the Church.* Translated and revised by L. A. Garrard. Peabody, Mass.: Hendrickson, 1998. Pages 5–15. Repr. of *The Fathers of the Greek Church.* London: A. and C. Black, 1963.

Chadwick, Henry. *Early Christian Thought and the Classical Tradition: Studies in Justin, Clement, and Origen.* Oxford: Clarendon Press, 1966, 1–30.

Osborn, Eric Francis. *Justin Martyr.* Beiträge zur historischen Theologie 47. Tübingen: J. C. B. Mohr (Paul Siebeck), 1973.

Melito of Sardis, *On Pascha*

Text and Translation

Melito of Sardis. *Melito of Sardis: On Pascha and Fragments.* Edited and translated by Stuart George Hall. Oxford Early Christian Texts. Oxford: Clarendon Press, 1979.

Perler, O., ed. and trans. Méliton de Sardes. Sur la Pâque et fragments. Sources chrétiennes 123. Paris: Cerf, 1966.

Translation

Melito of Sardis. *On Pascha, With the Fragments of Melito and Other Material Related to the Quartodecimans.* Translated and annotated by Alistair Stewart-Sykes. Popular Patristics Series. Crestwood, N.Y.: St. Vladimir's Seminary Press, 2001.

Studies

Cohick, Lynn H. *The Peri Pascha Attributed to Melito of Sardis: Setting, Purpose, and Sources.* Brown Judaic Studies 327. Providence, R.I.: Brown University Press, 2000.

Stewart-Sykes, Alistair. *The Lamb's High Feast: Melito, Peri Pascha and the Quartodeciman Paschal Liturgy at Sardis.* Supplements to Vigiliae Christianae 42. Leiden: Brill, 1998.

Clement of Alexandria, *Miscellanies*

Text

L. Früchtel, O. Stählin, and U. Treu, eds. *Clemens Alexandrinus, vols. 2 and 3.* Vol. 2, 3d ed.; vol. 3, 2d ed. Die griechischen christlichen Schriftsteller der ersten jahrhunderte 52 (15), 17. Berlin: Akademie Verlag, 2:1960; 3:1970.

Translation

Wilson, W., trans. *Clement of Alexandria* in *ANF* 2:299–568. Available online at http://www.ccel.org/.

Studies

Campenhausen, *The Fathers of the Church.* Pages 25–36.

Chadwick, *Early Christian Thought and the Classical Tradition.* Pages 31–65.

Osborn, Eric Francis. *Clement of Alexandria.* Cambridge: Cambridge University Press, 2005.

Osborn, Eric Francis. *The Philosophy of Clement of Alexandria.* Cambridge: Cambridge University Press, 1957.

Eusebius, *Ecclesiastical History* and *Life of Constantine*

Text

Bardy, G., ed. and trans. *Eusèbe de Césarée. Histoire ecclésiastique.* 3 vols. Sources chrétiennes 31, 41, 55. Paris: Cerf, 1:1952; 2:1955; 3:1958.

Lake, Kirsopp, ed. and trans. *Eusebius, Ecclesiastical History, Vol. 1.* Loeb Classical Library. Cambridge, Mass.: Harvard University Press, 1926.

Oulton, J. E. L. and H. J. Lawlor, ed. and trans. *Eusebius, Ecclesiastical History, Vol. 2.* Loeb Classical Library. Cambridge, Mass.: Harvard University Press, 1932.

Winkelmann, F., ed. *Eusebius Werke, Band 1.1: Über das Leben des Kaisers Konstantin.* Die griechischen christlichen Schriftsteller der ersten jahrhunderte. Berlin: Akademie Verlag, 1975.

Translation

Eusebius. *The History of the Church from Christ to Constantine.* Translated by G. A. Williamson. Revised and edited by Andrew Louth. London: Penguin, 1989.

McGiffert, Arthur Cushman, trans. *The Church History of Eusebius* in *NPNF*[2] 1:81–387. Available online at http://www.ccel.org/.

Richardson, Ernest Cushing, trans. *The Life of Constantine By Eusebius Together With the Oration of Constantine to the Assembly of the Saints and the Oration of Eusebius in Praise of Constantine* in *NPNF*[2] 1:481–559. Available online at http://www.ccel.org/.

Studies

Grant, Robert M. *Eusebius as Church Historian*. Oxford: Clarendon Press, 1980.

Athanasius, *On the Incarnation*

Text

Kannengiesser, Charles, ed. and trans. *Sur l'incarnation du verbe*. Sources chrétiennes 199. Paris: Cerf, 1973.

Thomson, Robert W., ed. and trans. *Athanasius:* Contra Gentes *and* De Incarnatione. Oxford Early Christian Texts. Oxford: Oxford University Press, 1971.

Translation

Robertson, Archibald, trans. *Select Writings and Letters of Athanasius, Bishop of Alexandria* in *NPNF*[2] 4:31–67. Available online at http://www.ccel.org/.

Studies

Anatolios, Khaled. *Athanasius: The Coherence of His Thought*. Routledge Early Church Monographs. London and New York: Routledge, 1998.

Campenhausen, *The Fathers of the Church*. Pages 69–83.

Pettersen, Alvyn. *Athanasius*. Ridgefield, Conn.: Morehouse, 1995.

Gregory of Nazianzus, *Orations*

Text

Barbel, J., ed. and trans. *Gregor von Nazianz. Die fünf theologischen Reden*. Düsseldorf: Patmos-Verlag, 1963.

PG, vols. 35–36.

Translation

Browne, Charles Gordon and James Edward Swallow, trans. *Select Orations of Saint Gregory Nazianzen* in *NPNF*[2] 7:185–434. Available online at http://www.ccel.org/.

Williams, Frederick and Lionel Wickham, trans. *On God and Christ: The Five Theological Orations and Two Letters to Cledonius*. Popular Patristics Series. Crestwood, N.Y.: St. Vladimir's Seminary Press, 2002.

Studies

Campenhausen, *The Fathers of the Church*. Pages 101–14.

Hall, Christopher A. *Learning Theology with the Church Fathers*. Downers Grove: InterVarsity, 2002. Pages 56–74 contain a helpful brief overview of the Five Theological Orations.

McGuckin, John. *Saint Gregory of Nazianzus: An Intellectual Biography*. Crestwood, N.Y.: St. Vladimir's Seminary Press, 2001.

Norris, Frederick W. *Faith Gives Fullness to Reasoning: The Five Theological Orations of Gregory of Nazianzen*. Supplements to Vigiliae Christianae 13. Leiden: E. J. Brill, 1991.

Desert Fathers and Mothers, *Apophthegmata Patrum*

Text

PG, vol. 65: col. 72–440.

Translation

Ward, Benedicta, trans. *The Sayings of the Desert Fathers: The Alphabetical Collection.* Cistercian Studies 59. Kalamazoo, Mich.: Cistercian Publications, 1975.

Studies

Chryssavgis, John. *In the Heart of the Desert: The Spirituality of the Desert Fathers and Mothers.* Forward by Benedicta Ward. Bloomington, Ind.: World Wisdom, 2003.

Harmless, William. *Desert Christians: An Introduction to the Literature of Early Monasticism.* New York: Oxford, 2004.

John Chrysostom, *Homiliae in Matthaeum*

Text

PG, vol. 57.

Translation

Prevost, George, trans. *The Homilies of St. John Chrysostom, Archbishop of Constantinople, on the Gospel of St. Matthew.* Revised with notes by M. B. Riddle in *NPNF*[2] 10. Available online at http://www.ccel.org/.

Studies

Campenhausen, *The Fathers of the Church.* Pages 140–57.

Kelly, J. N. D. *Golden Mouth: The Story of John Chrysostom, Ascetic, Preacher, Bishop.* Grand Rapids, Mich.: Baker, 1995.

Hesychios the Priest, *On Watchfulness and Holiness*

Text

PG, vol. 93: col. 1479–1544.

Philokalia of the Holy Neptics, Complied from Our Holy and God-bearing Fathers. 5 vols. 3d/4th ed. Athens: Astir, 1957–1963. 1:141–73.

Translation

St Nikodimos of the Holy Mountain and St Makarios of Corinth, compilers. *The Philokalia: The Complete Text.* Translated and edited by G. E. H. Palmer, Philip Sherrard, and Kallistos Ware, with the assistance of the Holy Transfiguration Monastery (Brookline), Constantine Cavarnos, Basil Osborne, and Norman Russell. 4 vols. London: Faber and Faber, 1979–1995. 1:162–98.

Studies

I know of no studies of St. Hesychios the Priest in English. See *The Philokalia: The Complete Text* (161) and Döpp (Siegmar Döpp and Wilhelm Geerlings, eds., *Dictionary of Early Christian Literature* [trans. Matthew O'Connell; New York: Crossroad Publishing, 2000], 279) for refs. to articles in other languages. The following works may serve as a brief introduction to key elements in his spiritual tradition, along with *Desert Christians* by William Harmless, listed above in the bibliography for the Desert Fathers and Mothers.

A Monk of the Eastern Church [Lev Gillet]. *The Jesus Prayer.* Crestwood, N.Y.: St. Vladimir's Seminary Press, 1987.

Louth, Andrew. "The Theology of the *Philokalia.*" Pages 351–61 in *Abba: The Tradition of Orthodoxy in the West: Festscrift for Bishop Kallistos (Ware) of Diokleia.* Edited by John Behr, Andrew Louth, and Dimitri Conomos. Crestwood, N.Y.: St. Vladimir's Seminary Press, 2003.

Ware, Bishop Kallistos. "Silence in Prayer: The Meaning of Hesychia." Pages 89–110 in *The Inner Kingdom: Volume 1 of the Collected Works.* Crestwood, N.Y.: St. Vladimir's Seminary Press, 2000.

Symeon the New Theologian, *Hymns*

Text

Kambylis, Athanasios, ed. *Symeon Neos Theologos, Hymnen.* Supplementa Byzantina 3. Berlin: de Gruyter, 1976.

Koder, Johannes, ed. *Hymnes [par] Syméon le nouveau théologien.* Translated by Joseph Paramelle. Sources chrétiennes 156. Paris: Cerf, 1969.

Translation

Maloney, George, trans. *Hymns of Divine Love by St. Symeon the New Theologian.* Denville, N.J.: Dimension Books, 1976.

Studies

Alfeyev, Hilarion. *St. Symeon the New Theologian and Orthodox Tradition.* Oxford Early Christian Studies. Oxford: Oxford University Press, 2000.

Krivocheine, Basil. *In the Light of Christ: Saint Symeon the New Theologian (949–1022): Life-Spirituality-Doctrine.* Translated by Anthony P. Gythiel. Crestwood, N.Y.: St. Vladimir's Seminary Press, 1986.

Maloney, George. *The Mystic of Fire and Light: St. Symeon the New Theologian.* Denville, N.J.: Dimension Books, 1975.